Comparative Law and Jurisprudence in Namibia

Comparative Law and Jurisprudence in Namibia

Functions, Methods and Perspectives from Selected Jurisdictions

Edited by

Samuel Kwesi Amoo

Tapiwa Victor Warikandwa

Kennedy Kariseb

UNAM PRESS

UNIVERSITY OF NAMIBIA

University of Namibia Press
www.unam.edu.na/unam-press
unampress@unam.na
Private Bag 13301
Windhoek
Namibia

First published:	2025
Cover design:	Jigsaw Graphic Design and Layout
Copy-editing:	John Linnegar, McGillivray Linnegar Associates
Typesetting:	MPS Limited

ISBN 9789994557233 (Print Paperback)
ISBN 9789994557240 (PDF)
ISBN 9789994557257 (ePub)

Set in Minion Pro

In loving memory of the work and life of
Professor Walter J Kamba
(1931–2007)

Professor Walter J Kamba was a brilliant academic, an engaging public intellectual, a passionate advocate of comparative law and a builder of community. He was the founding Dean of the University of Namibia's (UNAM) Faculty of Law. Professor Kamba had an intellectual brilliance, an energetic personality, a warmth and wit that made him a wonderful colleague and an outstanding teacher. Such was his commitment to comparative law that he wrote a cutting-edge article which is featured as a key chapter in this book. Professor Kamba was a rigorous advocate of making comparative law a compulsory module particularly in African law schools but also more generally in the rest of the world.

Many tributes have been paid to his life, but it is doubtful whether any can fully capture Professor Kamba's impact on African and global scholarship, and on the public discourse of comparative law; nor can they adequately describe the place he held in the hearts of so many at UNAM and around the world.

Contents

Foreword 1 xi
Justice Peter Sam Shivute, *Chief Justice of the Republic of Namibia*

Foreword 2 xiii
Professor Peter H Katjavivi, *Speaker of the National Assembly of Namibia*

Preface xv

Acknowledgements xvii

Abbreviations xix

1 Comparative law in the 21st century: an introduction 1
Tapiwa V Warikandwa, Samuel K Amoo and Kennedy Kariseb

2 Comparative law: a theoretical framework 39
Walter J Kamba (republished with permission)

3 Tracing the early origins of comparative law 77
George Mousourakis (republished with permission)

4 An overview of major legal systems of the world 101
Kenneth F Mundia and Rebbeca Haimbili

5 Methodologies and techniques of comparative law 119
Ndatega V Asheela-Shikalepo and Kenneth F Mundia

6 An overview of socialist law from the perspective of an African legal framework 139
Tapiwa V Warikandwa

7 Comparative law and the internationalisation of laws and legal systems 181
Kennedy Kariseb

8 Relevance of African jurisprudential theories in comparative legal processes 209
Samuel K Amoo, Clever Mapaure and Kennedy Kariseb

9 The court system in Namibia: judicial cross-fertilisation and the courts 229
Petrus T Damaseb

10 Liability in unjustified enrichment: a comparative overview of the Namibian, Continental European, English, Argentinean and Brazilian legal systems 251
Aimite Jorge

11 Comparative law in Africa: an appraisal of the role of legal comparativism in the development of African law 303
Tapiwa V Warikandwa, Eugene L Libebe and Denis U Zaire

12 Decolonial theory: a critical analysis of the ways in which legal transplant manifests coloniality – a comparative study study of southern African and southern Asian states 337
Pilisano Masake and Eugene L Libebe

13 Comparative law and the transformation of legal education in the 21st century: lessons for Namibia 367
Tapiwa V Warikandwa

14 African customary law and comparative law in contemporary Africa: a Namibian perspective 395
Eugene L Libebe and Samuel K Amoo

15 Comparing in the ascertainment of customary law: jurisprudential remarks 417
Manfred O Hinz

16 Comparative constitutional law: application of the Bill of Rights 455
Samuel K Amoo

17 Expropriation: a comparative study of the jurisprudence of Ghana, Namibia, South Africa and Zimbabwe 473
Samuel K Amoo

18 Bail jurisprudence of Ghana, Namibia, Zambia and South Africa 501
Samuel K Amoo

19 Jurisprudence of the right to trial within a reasonable time in Namibia and Zambia 531
Samuel K Amoo

20 Law on adultery: a comparative overview of seven jurisdictions 559
Eugene L Libebe, Tapiwa V Warikandwa and Samuel K Amoo

21 Secessionism or self-determination vs territorial sovereignty: a comparative analysis of legal arguments for secessionist movements in Namibia, Canada and Spain 585
Christian Harris

22 *Locus standi* in Namibia: a serious impediment to social justice 609
John Nakuta

About the editors ... 631
About the authors ... 633
Index ... 637

Foreword 1

Comparative law is the study of the differences and similarities between the laws and the legal systems of different countries. More specifically, it involves the study of the different legal 'systems' (or 'families') in existence in the world, such as the common law, civil law (the two most common) and those of socialist and religious groupings. Its importance has increased enormously in the present age of internationalism, populism, (economic) globalisation and democratisation. Despite the relevance and importance of comparative law, locally in Namibia we have not produced any academic literature in this area. *Comparative Law and Jurisprudence in Namibia: Functions, Methods and Perspectives from Selected Jurisdictions* therefore fills an important gap in the dearth of literature on this area of the law.

This book is a collection of essays on comparative law from a variety of perspectives. It focuses on the conceptual framework of comparative law. In doing so, it covers areas such as the conceptual framework of comparative law; the interaction between courts and comparative law and the praxis or practical application of comparative law. The purpose of this collection is to provide deeper knowledge of the theoretical framework of comparative law and different legal systems and also to contextualise the importance, relevance and application of comparative law in the Namibian context – particularly in its contributing to a unified legal system. The book also sets out to explore the role of comparative law in transforming legal education in Namibia. It cuts across all the spectra of comparativism and embraces a multidisciplinary approach to the discourse. It is anticipated that, collectively, the contributions will serve to bring about the necessary reform in the laws of Namibia to ensure that Namibia's legal framework aligns with the societal and/or constitutional imperatives in the 21st century.

I have no doubt that this publication will be useful to many, especially those with a keen interest in comparative law and jurisprudence. Lawyers, academics, judges and students reading law are the most immediate audience who will find great value in its contents. The foregoing notwithstanding, though, there is a strong probability that this publication will appeal to those outside the legal profession, including sociologists and anthropologists. Regardless of the field of expertise and interest, the publication is important and appealing as it provides a sound account of the epistemological origins of law, particularly in the common- and civil-law legal traditions.

The editors of this book are academics with vast and varied knowledge of and experience and skills in the subject of comparative law, having previously also taught in the fields of comparative law and jurisprudence at both undergraduate and postgraduate levels. Equally, the contributors to this volume appear also to have garnered vast expertise in this field. The perspectives offered in the book reflect the tenacity and experience of the editors and contributors alike.

I am aware that this publication is dedicated to Professor Walter J Kamba, a comparative lawyer and academic of note, who previously served as the founding Dean of the Faculty of Law (now School of Law) of the University of Namibia. I sincerely thank the editors and contributors of this book for acknowledging the work of Professor Kamba through such a detailed and comprehensive publication on a topic he championed. May his life and legacy continue to live on and inspire us.

Justice Peter Sam Shivute
Chief Justice of the Republic of Namibia

Foreword 2

This volume seeks to provide a general framework for the theoretical aspects, methods, application and uses of comparative law, with a particular focus on the Namibian legal system. Informed by years of scholarship, teaching, research and personal insights into this subject-matter, the editors, together with the contributors, have put together a compelling text for use by all persons with a keen interest in comparative law in particular and, more generally, in jurisprudence. From what I have gathered, the book has the potential to attract legal practitioners, judges, parliamentarians, academics and students alike who wish to improve their understanding of the different legal systems, of the comparative use of laws and practices, and generally of basic jurisprudential theories.

I find this book extremely valuable, given its relevance in an ever-globalising world of competing interests and perspectives. In the world of legal systems, comparative law – in particular the comparative engagement of law and the exchange of ideas, principles and legal practices – acts as a bridge that enables legal principles and ideas to flow between different legal jurisdictions. Undoubtedly, over the years, this has proved to enrich the fabric of law and legal practice, enabling a deeper understanding of the way legal systems evolve, interact and function.

The benefits of comparative law are varied. Comparative law and practice cultivate an environment of legal innovation, encouraging legal thinkers to constantly re-evaluate established norms and consider alternative approaches where need be. By juxtaposing different legal systems and practices, we unravel the tapestry of cultural, historical and social influences that shape our laws, in this way fostering a deeper comprehension of the contexts in which they operate. Moreover, comparative law nurtures a sense of global camaraderie, bridging gaps between legal professionals across nations and promoting cross-border collaboration. This is indeed much needed in today's world where globalisation and a New World Order loom large. Accordingly, as we delve into the pages of this book, we embark on a journey that not only unveils the nuances of different legal systems but also highlights the remarkable interplay of ideas and principles across legal jurisdictions. We are aptly introduced to the origins of comparative law and its theoretical framework; to the major legal systems of the world; to the methodologies and techniques of comparative law; to African jurisprudential theories and their place in comparative law; to the Namibian court system and the status of comparative law, decoloniality and comparative law, and to the internationalisation of comparative law and a diversity of essays that apply comparative approaches to different legal principles and concepts.

I commend the editors of this volume and its contributors not only for their remarkable work but the more so for dedicating this publication to the life and memory of the late Professor Walter Joseph Kamba. Professor Kamba was known to me. We first met in the 1970s in the United Kingdom during my tenure as the South West Africa People's Organisation (SWAPO) Representative to the United Kingdom and Western Europe. At the time he was a professor of law at the University of Dundee. Our paths crossed once more in Namibia when I became the founding Vice-Chancellor of the University of Namibia and he the Founding Dean of the (then) Faculty of Law (now School of Law). I have known him to be a composed and reputable scholar noted for his distinguished scholarship. His interest and pioneering work in the field of comparative law is evidence of his transnational and global outlook. His immense contributions to higher education in Africa, and in particular his native Zimbabwe and Namibia, are self-explanatory and well known by all and therefore need no further elaboration. It is my sincere hope that this book will provide incentives for further exploration inspired by the work of Professor Kamba and his research contributions in the field of comparative law.

Finally, allow me to express my deep gratitude to the editors and contributors of this book for the time, vision and dedication they have invested in and brought to it, more so on a subject such as comparative law that has to date not been set out so eloquently and conveniently from a Namibian perspective, as is the case with this publication.

Professor Peter H Katjavivi
Speaker of the National Assembly of Namibia

Preface

Comparative law has been a cornerstone of legal studies in Namibia and the rest of the world for decades. Contemporary law schools and faculties, legal practitioners, legal academics, international law experts, judges and members of legal institutions and bodies with diverse academic and professional qualifications integrate interdisciplinary approaches in their research. The fact that legal education often takes place in classes comprising students from close to two dozen different nationalities contributes further to a uniquely international setting for the study of comparative law in Namibia. The demands of an increasingly internationalising and globalising world further underscore the importance of comparativism. Moreover, and as part of contributing to autochthonous Namibian legal literature, this publication seeks to expand on the rather fragmented and limited scholarship on comparative law, in particular with reference to the Namibian context.

The value of comparative law is largely dependent upon its method and critical scholarship. In order to be practically useful and intellectually valuable, comparative law has to compare more than rules. Comparative law, especially in relation to public, private and commercial law, has to embrace the law and society, different regulatory mechanisms, self-reflections, traditions and legal cultures, politics, history, economics and intellectual roots.

The book interrogates multiple facets of comparative legal studies, with a specific focus on Namibia. In order to highlight the significance of comparative law to Namibia, the various authors of the individual chapters engage with discourses on the subject in Africa and the rest of the world. The book therefore highlights the role of comparative legal studies in Namibia, the rest of Africa and beyond. It emphasises that comparative law is the art of comparing legal systems with a view, among other aims, to investigating the historical and philosophical issues relating to law and establishing a better regime in international relations. The authors also discuss the methodologies to be used in legal comparativism. Accordingly, part of this book hinges on the role of courts in comparativism and the ways in hich comparative law has been an aid to deciding cases brought before such courts.

Many of the contributions to this publication discuss the relevant methodological approaches to comparative legal studies. Accordingly, these contributions interrogate the ways in which the comparative law apparatus and procedure are, and can be, employed in the analysis, differentiation and assessment of legal systems in legal practice and legal education. Discussions about the methodology of comparative law in the study of law in general are therefore included. Overall, the contributions in this publication emphasise that the process of legal comparison takes place in all facets of life and influences every form of human decision-making. For the purposes of this book, the methodological approach to comparative legal studies is considered to encompass the theoretical tools, models and processes that are employed in the study of, and enquiry into, different legal systems. In the context of Namibia and the rest of Africa, legal comparativism is taken to refer to the ways in which legal comparison is undertaken by the African countries in the study of their legal systems and in comparing them to those of other legal systems. The various contributions also highlight the advantages and disadvantages of legal comparativism. Although no two legal systems are identical and it is difficult to find a common methodology of comparative legal studies, there is much convergence in the approaches taken by African countries in the study of their laws, and these approaches may not be that different from those of other jurisdictions such as the United States, Continental Europe and Asia.

Finally, we dedicate this work to a legal giant of note, particularly in the field of comparative law: (the late) Professor Walter J Kamba.

Editors
Windhoek, 2024

Acknowledgements

We would fail profoundly were we not to express our appreciation for the assistance rendered to us to bring this book to fruition. The debts we owe are many and considerable, and we may err seriously by not fully acknowledging every individual who or institution that made an invaluable contribution in one way or another. Of course, a word of appreciation is too terse and fragile to encompass fully the contributions made by many. Accordingly, we wish to acknowledge a number of individuals and institutions.

First, our contributors whose work constituted the collective contribution and eventually ensured that we have arrived at a manuscript that can be published in the form of this book. It is their intellectual generosity, skill and tenacity, as evinced through their masterful respective contributions, that have made possible a publication of this magnitude and quality. If we as editors are to be credited for this book, then, in all humility, it is not we but rather the authorial collective who have earned the due salutations. It became obvious during our editing that the contributors have both heart and passion for the field of comparative law and for legal education generally. For your collegiality, patience and acumen we are enormously grateful.

Second, the University of Namibia (UNAM), our institution of work which in many respects has become our home, also deserves mention. We therefore express our sincere gratitude to the university and its management for providing a conducive work environment in which we could take up a project of this nature and make a meaningful contribution to the development of knowledge. In the process of finalising this book we have used university resources and our privileged positions as academics to mobilise, initiate and spearhead this project to its completion. This would not have been possible had we not been affiliated to the UNAM. In fact, the outcome of this book is due largely to the university's press, which since the initial stages of this publication has been receptive and supportive of the project. Accordingly, we also extend our appreciation to UNAM Press and its Editorial Board. In particular, mention should be made of Dr Jill Kinahan, Ms Naitsikile Iizyenda, Ms Annapaula Vakamuena and the other members of the UNAM Press team, who guided and worked closely with us in finalising this volume. We remain indebted to the UNAM Press team for their courtesy, professional rigour, decorum and, most importantly, their humanity and kindness. The same should be attributed to John Linnegar for his concise and high-quality copy-editing of the book

The *International and Comparative Law Quarterly* Editorial Board has graciously granted us permission to republish Professor Walter Joseph Kamba's 1974 leading article on the theoretical framework of comparative law (see chapter 2). Equally, Springer has been kind enough to permit us to republish one of Professor George Mousourakis' seminal works on the origins of comparative law (see chapter 3). We appreciate the academic generosity of these publishers and scholars.

We acknowledge that this book is inspired in many ways by those who have gone before us. As this book is dedicated to the late Professor Kamba, we also acknowledge his immense contributions to the field of comparative law and legal education in Africa. To his family, particularly his wife and children, we express our eternal gratitude for your kindness in sharing your husband and father with us.

Our students (and those of Professor Kamba), whom we have had the honour of teaching comparative law over the years at UNAM and elsewhere, also shaped our thinking about and our approach to this unique branch of the law. Had it not been for their curious and thought-provoking questions, and their engagement with the subject-matter, we would not have been motivated to put pen to paper in this enterprise. Although many of them had to endure a fragmented approach to the teaching of this subject, owing to the scattered nature of the material in this field, we are keen to acknowledge, despite those harsh circumstances, that their endurance over the years catalysed the necessary fire and vigour in us to produce this publication. We hope that future students of courses in comparative law will be able to access and refer to a comprehensive and contextualised collection such as this.

To our spouses and families, for your invaluable and selfless patience and indulgence throughout this tedious and prolonged writing process we cannot thank you adequately. We hope that the production of this publication has in one way or another made up for the amount of precious family time lost.

To God be the glory, always.

The editors
Windhoek, 2024

Abbreviations

ACDEG	African Charter on Democracy, Elections and Governance in Africa
ACHPR	African Charter on Human and Peoples' Rights
AD	Anno Domini
AfCFTA	African Continental Free Trade Area
A-G	Attorney-General
AI	artificial intelligence
AMFS	Asset Movement and Financial Services
AU	African Union
AUC	African Union Commission
BCE	Before the Christian Era
CC	Constitutional Court
CCCN	National Civil and Commercial Code
CCG	Caprivi Concerned Group
CE	Christian Era
CEO	chief executive officer
DCFR	Draft Common Frame of Reference
DSA	Democratic Socialists of America
DSOC	Democratic Socialists Organizing Committee
EAC	East African Community
ESC	Economic, Social and Cultural
EU	European Union
FGC	female genital circumcision
FTLRP	Fast Track Land Reform Programme
ICC	International Criminal Court
ICCPR	International Covenant on Civil and Political Rights
ICESCR	International Covenant on Economic, Social and Cultural Rights
ICJ	International Court of Justice

ILC	International Law Commission
IMF	International Monetary Fund
JSC	Judicial Service Commission
JTC	Justice Training Centre
LLB	Bachelor of Laws
LLD	Doctor of Laws
LLM	Master of Laws
LRDC	Law Reform and Development Commission
NAM	New American Movement
NGO	non-governmental organisation
NPO	non-profit organisation
OAU	Organisation of African Unity
OHADA	Organization pour l'Harmonisation du Droit des Affaires en Afrique
PhD	Doctor of Philosophy
SADC	Southern African Development Community
SCA	Supreme Court of Appeal
SDS	Students for a Democratic Society
SME	small and medium enterprise
USSR	Union of Soviet Socialist Republics
UDHR	Universal Declaration of Human Rights
UDP	United Democratic Party
UN	United Nations
UNAM	University of Namibia
UNCITRAL	United Nations Commission on International Trade Law
UNESCO	United Nations Educational, Scientific and Cultural Organization
UNIN	United Nations Institute for Namibia

1

Comparative law in the 21st century: an introduction

Tapiwa V Warikandwa, Samuel K Amoo and Kennedy Kariseb

1.1 INTRODUCTION

In covering fundamental legal and academic discourses and comparative law methodology, comparative law provides an in-depth and methodical basis for comparing legal systems for judges, legal practitioners, legal academics and students. It critiques both conventional and modern approaches to the field and employs examples from a variety of jurisdictions to provide the reader with a genuinely global perspective. The contextualised and multidisciplinary approach of comparative law relies on examples from politics, economics and social sciences to make an innovative contribution to comparative-law themes.[1] However, Örücü has previously stated that 'colleagues are not interested in foreign law; students are ethnocentric jerks; the bar consists of monolingual hicks; deans will not finance foreign travel, and nobody will take comparative law'.[2] But comparative law is genuinely becoming a more important topic in legal education and practice in Namibia,[3] and the rest of the world,[4] in the midst of current processes of

---

[1] G Bellantuono 'Introduction: Comparative law and interdisciplinary bridges' (2023) 12(1) *Comparative Law Review* 6–23.

[2] E Örücü *The Enigma of Comparative Law: Variations on a Theme for the Twenty-First Century* (Martinus Nijhoff, 2004) 215.

[3] N Ndeunyema 'The Namibian Constitution, international law and the courts: A critique' (2020) 9(2) *Global Journal of Comparative Law* 271–296.

[4] K Uwe & A Hammel (eds) 'Aims of comparative law' in *Comparative Law* (Oxford Academic online, 17 April 2019), https://doi.org/10.1093/oso/9780198791355.003.0002, accessed 16 June 2023.

borrowing, copying and imposing law in addition to increasing both desirable,[5] and undesirable,[6] global interconnection.

This book is characterised by the writings of legal academics, legal practitioners and a judge who consider the main purpose of comparative law as being ultimately a practical one. In this regard, legal practitioners, judges, academics and law students will be encouraged to learn about solutions found in other jurisdictions to problems that have arisen in different areas of law. Legislators will also be encouraged to focus on the 'common core' of private, public and commercial law with a view to seeking objectively to promote legal harmonisation in the African Union (AU) and the rest of the world. Such a development is significant if one considers developments in the new world order and the recent adoption of the African Continental Free Trade Area (AfCFTA) agreement, both of which will thrive if a common body of laws were to be adopted to remove the legal barriers emanating from the existence of different laws in multiple jurisdictions. It is therefore necessary to go beyond the traditional pursuits of the law and reach towards the holistic aspirations of comparative legal studies.[7] With comparative law appearing to be undertaught and hardly offered in law schools in Africa and the rest of the world, Husa once argued:

> as regards the future of the discipline, we seem to have many incompatible directions and goals instead of one. Professional comparative law and

---

[5] Legal Assistance Centre *What is International Law and Why does It matter to Namibia?* (nd), http://www.lac.org.na/news/probono/Probono_54-INTERNATIONAL_LAW.pdf, accessed 16 June 2023.

[6] Recently, the courts in Namibia have passed judgments that are not in step with the customary values, norms or creeds of Namibian society. Such judgments have been informed by developments in other jurisdictions, a development which brings about the Westernisation and acculturation of Namibians with the law being used as an instrument for social engineering: see, eg, the case of *Van Straten v Bekker* (6056 of 2014) [2016] NAHCMD 243 (25 August 2016) at paras 24–38, in which a controversial ruling was passed to abolish third-party claims on adultery on account of the fact that the judges were of the opinion that such a practice no longer conforms to contemporary Namibian society. In particular, preference was given to developments in the United States, the United Kingdom and South Africa as the foundation upon which the decision passed in this controversial case was premised. More recently, the Supreme Court of Namibia, in the highly contested case of *Digashu & Another v GRN & Others; Seiler-Lilles & Another v GRN & Others* (SA 6/2022; SA 7/2022) [2023] NASC 14 (16 May 2023), ruled that same-sex marriages involving foreign nationals married to Namibians would be recognised in Namibia. This is contrary to the legal convictions of Namibian society as decided in the case of *Immigration Selection Board v Frank* 2001 NR 107 (SC). Reference was made to the South African case of *Pretoria City Council v Levinson* 1949 (3) SA 305 (A). The majority court held that 'the opinions expressed under the heading "The issue of the respondents' lesbian relationship and the alleged breach of their fundamental rights" of the majority in *Frank* were not necessary for the decision, went "beyond the occasion" and sought to lay down rules which were entirely unnecessary for the purpose at hand. They constituted *obiter dicta* (statements made along the way) in an application of both the common law set out in *Levinson* and English law.'

[7] P Legrand & R Munday (eds) *Comparative Legal Studies: Traditions and Transitions* (Cambridge University Press, 2003) 1–520.

academic comparative law are living together in an uneasy relationship buried under the European integration debate.[8]

It is cliché to claim that comparative law is approaching maturity in the 21st century, despite the fact that it is undertaught and hardly offered in law schools in Africa and the rest of the globe.[9] Uwe and Hammel have argued that the best way for comparative law to ensure its future is to delve into other fields in addition to calling for comparative lawyers to reconsider their own field.[10] This argument is plausible because comparative law has a variety of goals, including:

- assisting in law reform and policy development;
- serving as a research tool for developing a universal theory of law;
- providing students with a critical viewpoint and aiding in the practice of international law;
- facilitating the international unification and harmonisation of laws;
- assisting courts in filling legal gaps, and
- even contributing to the advancement of world peace and tolerance.[11]

The objective of comparative law ensuring its future can also be achieved by grouping aspects about teaching the subject into practical, sociological, political and pedagogical thematic areas. Furthermore, concepts such as 'traditional comparative law', 'mainstream comparative law', 'conventional comparative law', 'critical comparative law' and 'post-modern comparative law' must be used more in comparative legal education.

In the context of this book, it will unequivocally be emphasised that there is an increasing interest in comparative law.[12]

It is now mandatory for all doctoral candidates, legal academics, judges and law-makers, among other professionals, to access foreign literature regularly. For a long time, it appeared that comparative law was a topic for academic research, something difficult and, without doubt, extremely fascinating and nice to know something about but not directly relevant to the day-to-day practice of the law.[13]

---

[8] J Husa 'Review article of E Örücü – *The Enigma of Comparative Law: Variations on a Theme for the Twenty-first Century*' (2005) 9(3) *Electronic Journal of Comparative Law* 1.

[9] CM Fombad 'Comparative research in contemporary African legal studies' (2019) 67(4) *Journal of Legal Education* 984–1004. See also CM Fombad 'Africanisation of legal education programmes: The need for comparative African legal studies' (2014) 49(4) *Journal of Asian and African Studies* 383–398.

[10] Uwe & Hammel (note 4) 87–200.

[11] WJ Kamba 'Comparative law: A theoretical framework' (1974) 23(3) *The International and Comparative Law Quarterly* 485–519.

[12] Fombad (note 9) 984.

[13] Ibid.

For the past five to ten years, the legal climate in Africa seems to have been changing. This evolution of the legal climate is being influenced by globalisation, legal transformation and, to a certain extent, the decolonisation of the legal systems on the continent. Furthermore, the process of regional integration championed by the AU and lately by the AfCFTA may also expand the place for comparative law in legal studies and practice. The fact that globalisation is forcing people in Africa and the rest of the world to live closer together in the so-called global village has also increased the space for the significance of comparative law in the legal classifications of the world. In addition, the autonomous process of lawyers' search for fresh perspectives when faced with new legal problems brought about by the advent of artificial intelligence (AI) in the digital age driven by the 4th and 5th Industrial Revolutions[14] makes comparative law the more important in contemporary legal education and practice.

Prior to the emergence of modern events and difficulties influencing comparative law, Gutteridge once noted that 'the essential problem is not: What is comparative law? The question of real importance is: What is its purpose?'[15] It is submitted that the majority of comparative-law publications begin by attempting to describe the topic before asking what constitutes comparative law. One circular, ambiguous and open-ended definition Zweigert and Kötz noted, for example, states that 'the words suggest an intellectual activity with law as its object and comparison as its process'.[16] The practice of juxtaposing, contrasting and comparing legal systems or portions of them with the goal of identifying parallels and contrasts is known as comparative law and is frequently referred to as an 'incomplete theme'.[17] However, comparative law as a concept could be far broader than that because it is a discipline of knowledge with its own distinct field. It is a discrete field that produces theoretical distillate.[18] It is possible to think of comparative law as the critical method of legal science.[19]

Therefore, the major goal of this book is to provide some guiding principles for legal professionals, judges, scholars and students who are approaching this crucial, intriguing, but challenging subject. To this purpose, the book includes discussions of

[14] H Ballell 'Legal challenges of artificial intelligence: Modelling the disruptive features of emerging technologies and assessing their possible legal impact' (2019) 24(2) *Uniform Law Review* 302–314; see also R Rodrigues 'Legal and human rights issues of AI: Gaps, challenges and vulnerabilities' (2020) 4 *Journal of Responsible Technology* 100005.

[15] HC Gutteridge 'The comparative aspects of legal terminology' (1938) 12 *Tulane Law Review* 401; see also HC Gutteridge *Comparative Law* 2 ed (Cambridge University Press, 1949; reprint Wiley & Sons, 1974) 5.

[16] K Zweigert & H Kötz *An Introduction to Comparative Law* 3 ed (trans T Weir)(Clarendon Press, 1998) 2.

[17] Örücü (note 2) 19–32.

[18] J Ellis 'General principles and comparative law' (2011) 22(4) *European Journal of International Law* 949–971.

[19] R Leckey 'Review of comparative law' (2017) 26(1) *Social & Legal Studies* 3–24.

theory and substantive topics, and notable legal and social thinkers in addition to top authorities in comparative law have contributed to it. The contributors raise a wide range of theoretical perspectives throughout their chapters, and this introduction refers to their discussions. We do not claim to have covered everything, and there is no alternative to reading the writers in their own words. Regarding substantive topics, we have been successful in covering traditional private-law, public-law and, to a certain extent, commercial-law topics. Comparative constitutionalism, and the increasingly important types of transnational legal process, such as international criminal law and human rights law, have also been alluded to. The book is divided into 22 chapters, each of them authored by different professionals from around the world. The aim of each chapter is to present an accessible, unique and critical overview of the current status of comparative law in its specific subject area, which will help to define the agenda in the coming years.

1.2 WHAT IS THE BASIS FOR COMPARING LAWS FROM DIFFERENT JURISDICTIONS?

Lawyers, judges and legal scholars are highly specialised professionals who frequently operate in silos. Their aim to be global is characterised by comparative law. The majority of them are almost exclusively trained and specialised in the law of their own country or jurisdiction of study.[20] As a result, once they leave their native country and jurisdiction of study, they may feel trapped in an alien world.[21]

Learning about comparative law is intended to deal with this issue. But where do you begin? What approach do you use? Is it even possible to study all of the world's laws? Comparative lawyers, judges and legal academics constantly debate the purposes of comparative law. Although they frequently use various classifications, it is most fair to divide between three primary categories: knowledge and understanding, domestic comparative-law usage and international comparative-law usage.[22] The belief that comparative law serves an inherent function emphasises

[20] C Hagenmeier, T Shumba & O Mireku 'The admission and enrolment of foreign legal practitioners in South Africa under the Legal Practice Act: International trade law and constitutional perspectives' (2017) 19 *Potchefstroom Electronic Law Journal* 1–27. See also BW Heineman Jr, WF Lee & DB Wilkins *Lawyers as Professionals and as Citizens: Key Roles and Responsibilities in the 21st Century* (Center of the Legal Profession at Harvard Law School, nd), https://www.belfercenter.org/sites/default/files/files/publication/Heinemen_Lawyers%20as%20Professionals.pdf, accessed 16 June 2023.

[21] M Seims 'Foreign-trained legal scholars in the UK: "Irritants" or "change agents"?' (2021) 41(3) *Legal Studies* 1–17; see also D Marrani 'An essay on ideology and legal education in micro jurisdictions: The example of Jersey' (2022) 14 *Journal Civil Law Studies* 60–89.

[22] Kamba (note 11) 485–519.

its importance in legal studies and teaching.[23] On the one hand, knowledge of foreign laws is useful when they are important to the domestic legal system, such as when the domestic law is of a plural legal nature.[24] Knowledge of other laws, on the other hand, might cause lawyers, judges or law students to reflect on their own laws.[25] And it might be surprising to realise that some of the characteristics of the law which we take for granted do not exist in other regions of the world.

But a lawyer or a legal student exposed to foreign experiences may gain a broader, and perhaps more critical, understanding of their own law and the decisions taken by its law-makers and courts. In this way, comparative law broadens one's awareness of how legal norms function in context, going beyond simply knowledge of foreign laws.[26] This is also something that happens fairly naturally. If a comparative researcher discovers surprising commonalities, they may wish to investigate whether there are any shared historical foundations or contemporary globalisation tendencies that they are unaware of. If there are unexpected discrepancies, the comparative researcher may wish to investigate the political, cultural and socio-economic causes behind them.[27] It is also possible that comprehending the embeddedness of legal principles could encourage tolerance of diverse communities and legal systems.[28] The aspirant comparatist may then proceed to develop a broader intrinsic interest in the world's legal systems. This could provide insight, for instance, into the fact that African customary law is not uncivilised and that the Western concept of law is not universal.[29] Comparative law also allows for a broader understanding of the diversity of legal standards throughout the world.[30] A comparatist may also come to see law as a generic phenomenon, with various legal systems being variants of

---

[23] Ibid.

[24] H Quane 'Legal pluralism and international human rights law: Inherently incompatible, mutually reinforcing or something in between?' (2013) 33(4) *Oxford Journal of Legal Studies* 675–702; see also G Swenson 'Legal pluralism in theory and practice' (2018) 20(3) *International Studies Review* 438–462.

[25] Fombad (note 9) 984.

[26] Kamba (note 11) 485–519.

[27] JC Reitz 'How to do comparative law' (1998) 46(4) *The American Journal of Comparative Law* 617–636.

[28] C Himonga, M Taylor & A Pope 'Reflections on judicial views of ubuntu' (2013) 16(5) *Potchefstroom Electronic Law Journal* 1–612.

[29] TV Warikandwa & SK Amoo 'African law in comparative law: A case of undermining African jurisprudence and promoting a new world order agenda?' in A Nhemachena, TV Warikandwa & SK Amoo (eds) *Social and Legal Theory in the Age of Decoloniality: (Re-)Evisioning Pan-African Jurisprudence in the 21st Century* (Langaa, 2018) 299–326; M Ndulo 'African customary law, customs, and women's rights' (2011) 18(1) *Indiana Journal of Global Legal Studies* article 5; L Salaymeh & R Michaels 'Decolonial comparative law: A conceptual beginning' (2022) 86 *Max Planck-Institute* 167.

[30] Kamba (note 11) 485–519; see also Fombad (note 9) 984.

the same subject.[31] For example, they may attempt to discover a common core of legal norms or to construct generic jurisprudence concepts that include ideas from many regions of the world.

At the domestic level, comparative law can also be used to achieve a variety of goals. A common proposal is that comparative law might be a valuable tool for legislators.[32] Foreign laws can serve as models for the way different sets of legal norms function in solving a certain problem or pursuing a specific agenda.[33] This approach may be motivated by the concept of regulatory competition, since legislators may be interested in luring enterprises and investors.[34] It may also be owing to a desire for legal modernisation in emerging and transitional economies, because any attempt at reform must also examine the constraints of transplanting foreign models, as is commonly argued in the legal and social policy literature.[35]

Comparative law is used by law-makers at the international or supranational level when considering whether and how legal unity may be accomplished.[36] If a decision is taken to unify a specific field of law, the negotiating states may wish to compare existing domestic laws in order to determine whether to choose the lowest common denominator, the most common approach, a compromise solution with a combination of legal rules, the 'best solution'– however this may be defined – or a general solution that incorporates the existing models. This answer can then serve as the foundation for an international convention, a supranational act or a type of 'soft law'. A comparative study may also result in a recommendation not to unify the law, for example, because separate legal cultures are irreconcilable or because the costs of unification outweigh the advantages.

1.3 TRADITIONAL COMPARATIVE LAW

Comparative law has a long history in international legal theory and practice. When looking for a precise origin, views range from Aristotle's comparison of constitutions in the 3rd century BCE to comparisons between Roman, canonical

[31] Kamba (note 11) 485; see also VV Palmer 'From Lerotholi to Lando: Some examples of comparative law methodology' (2005) 53(1) *The American Journal of Comparative Law* 261–290; Leckey (note 19) 3.

[32] J Basedow 'Comparative law and its clients' (2014) 62(4) *The American Journal of Comparative Law* 821–857.

[33] A Peters 'The refinement of international law: From fragmentation to regime interaction and politicization' (2017) 15(3) *International Journal of Constitutional Law* 671–704.

[34] RA Prentice 'Regulatory competition in securities law: A dream (that should be) deferred' (2005) 66(6) *Ohio State Law Journal* 1155–1230.

[35] JMR Faria 'Future directions of legal harmonisation and law reform: Stormy seas or prosperous voyage?' (2009) 14(1–2) *Uniform Law Review* 5–34.

[36] Fombad (note 9) 984.

and customary sources in the 16th century, to Montesquieu's comparison of political systems in the 18th century.[37] More specifically, the evolution of comparative law as an academic field is more obvious, with 1861, 1869 and 1900 proposed as plausible birth years.[38] The establishment of nation-states and the enactment of codes in 19th-century Europe created an initial demand for legislative comparative law and, later, the potential for comparisons between these new national laws.[39] As opposed to postmodern and critical methods, what is commonly referred to as 'conventional comparative law' began in the early 20th century and has remained relevant to this day.[40] The use of comparative law does not imply that there are no distinctions among classic comparative lawyers, judges and academics. Every comparative lawyer is formed by their background, such as the legal systems in which they were educated or the domestic law of their primary field of competence or expertise.[41] Nevertheless, there are a few key concepts that are commonly regarded as pertaining to the major substance of conventional comparative law. Michaels, for example, speaks of a focus on positive state law and a 'legal scientific approach to comparative law';[42] Banakar views its central ideas as the concept of legal families, the harmonisation of laws, and the relationship between law and the state;[43] and Legrand[44] associates its 'doxa' with Zweigert and Kötz's functional approach.[45]

Traditional scholarly works on comparative law frequently provide guidelines, if not a model, on how to perform a comparative legal analysis.[46] Most of these guidelines are fairly similar, though the precise number of suggested steps depends on how some of those are grouped together.[47] The following distinguishes between four steps. First, a comparative analysis starts with preliminary considerations,

---

[37] M Seims *Comparative Law* 2 ed (Cambridge University Press, 2018) 13.
[38] Ibid.
[39] Ibid.
[40] Ibid.
[41] Ibid.
[42] R Michaels 'The functional method of comparative law' in *The Oxford Handbook of Comparative Law* (Oxford University Press, 2006) 339–382.
[43] R Banakar & M Travers (eds) *Theory and Method in Socio-Legal Research* (Hart Publishing, 2005).
[44] P Legrand 'European legal systems are not converging' (1996) 45 *International and Comparative Law Quarterly* 52.
[45] Seims (note 37) 13; see also Zweigert & Kötz (note 16) 34.
[46] See M Siems *Comparative Law* 3 ed (Cambridge University Press, 2022) ch 2; see also PG Monateri (ed) *Methods of Comparative Law* (Edward Elgar, 2012); M Adams & J Bomhoff (eds) *Practice and Theory in Comparative Law* (Cambridge University Press, 2012); M Oderkerk 'The need for a methodological framework for comparative legal research: Sense and nonsense of "methodological pluralism" in comparative law' (2015) 79(3) *Rabels Zeitschrift für Ausländisches und Internationales Privatrecht/The Rabel Journal of Comparative and International Private Law* 589–623.
[47] Kamba (note 11) 485–519.

deciding on the research question and the choice of legal systems.[48] Second, the comparatist has to describe the laws of these countries.[49] Third, the comparatist has to compare them, in particular exploring the reasons for unexpected similarities and differences.[50] Fourth, the comparatist should critically evaluate their findings, possibly also making policy recommendations.[51] The following section briefly outlines the function of civil law and common law in comparative legal studies.

1.4 CIVIL LAW AND COMMON LAW

Civil law and common law are concepts that carry many changeable characterisations. They are intended to refer to designations given to groupings of legal systems regarding their similarities and differences. To this end, common-law nations have legal systems that are founded on English law, whereas civil-law nations are those that have been influenced by traditions from continental Europe. The phrase 'common law' refers to the case law of a common-law jurisdiction, as opposed to statute law, which has more contemporary origins.[52] Furthermore, the term 'common law' might simply refer to the law that a larger group of people share as opposed to local laws.[53] Within a legal system, 'civil law' refers to disciplines such as contract and tort or delict law as opposed to criminal and public law.[54] It is helpful to begin with the roots of both legal families in order to comprehend the civil–common law divide in the context of comparative law. This is not as simple as it may appear, though. The civil-law heritage is founded on Roman law, which used to follow a casuistic approach that is now more connected to common law.[55] The Eastern Roman Emperor, Justinian, commissioned a synthesis of Roman law in the early 6th century CE. With the resurgence of Roman law in Continental Europe

---

[48] PI Bhat 'Comparative method of legal research: Nature, process and potentiality' (2015) 57(2) *Journal of the Indian Law Institute* 147–173; see also Fombad (note 9) 984.

[49] Kamba (note 11) 485–519; see also Reitz (note 27) 617–636.

[50] Kamba (note 11) 485–519.

[51] O Brand 'Conceptual comparisons: Towards a coherent methodology of comparative legal studies' (2007) 32 *Brooklyn Journal of International Law* 407–466.

[52] J Dainow 'The civil law and the common law: Some points of comparison' (1966) 15(3) *The American Journal of Comparative Law* 419–435.

[53] Ibid.

[54] W Tetley *Mixed Jurisdictions: Common Law v Civil Law (Codified and Uncodified)* (2000), https://digitalcommons.law.lsu.edu/cgi/viewcontent.cgi?article=5822&context=lalrev, accessed 18 June 2023.

[55] CM Lawson 'The family affinities of common-law and civil-law legal systems' (1982) 6 *Hastings International and Comparative Law Review* 85–131.

(also known as its 'reception') in the 11th century, this *Corpus Juris Civilis* became important once more.[56]

Three key qualities of this resurgence deserve special attention. First, universities or academies aided in the acceptance of Roman law, which is why civil law is sometimes referred to as 'learned law'.[57] Second, the common law (*ius commune*) of the accepted Roman law (which replaced or at least supplemented local customary rules) transcended national boundaries.[58] Third, the state maintained rigorous control over judicial enforcement of the law in order to thwart corruption and ensure that the law was applied consistently.[59] With the rise of nation-states in the 17th and 19th centuries, this type of civil law evolved. States started to codify Roman law, sometimes combining it with regional laws to establish a single, unified national law.[60] The *Code civil des Français* (Code civil) of 1804, which is sometimes seen as a symbol of the contemporary civil-law tradition, was the most significant of these new laws. While attempting to be accessible to the general public, the Code civil is written in an abstract manner ('as simple as the Bible'; 'simple and plain like the rules of nature').[61] This is in contrast to the *Bürgerliches Gesetzbuch* (BGB or German Civil Code) of 1900, which is more philosophical and professorial in tone.[62] As a result of the codification process, the laws in Continental Europe diverged.[63] However, these developments also aided in the expansion of civil law throughout the world. This occurred in part as a result of European countries' having colonial empires. Furthermore, several countries, such as Japan and Turkey, freely adopted large civil-law regimes.[64]

The beginnings of common law seem to be more obvious. William the Conqueror was anointed king of England in 1066, following the Norman invasion of that country.[65] William and his successors centralised government and the law

---

[56] JW Head 'Justinian's *Corpus juris civilis* in comparative perspective: Illuminating key differences between the civil, common, and Chinese legal traditions' (2013) 21(2) *Mediterranean Studies* 91–121.

[57] D Lee 'Hobbes and the civil law: The use of Roman law in Hobbes's civil science' in D Dyzenhaus & T Poole (eds) *Hobbes and the Law* (Cambridge University Press, 2012) 210–235.

[58] Ibid.

[59] Ibid.

[60] C Jacobson 'Law and nationalism in nineteenth century Europe: The case of Catalonia in comparative perspective' (2002) 20(2) *Law and History Review* 307–347.

[61] C Banks & J Baker *Systems of Law: Common Law, Civil Law, Socialist Law, Islamic Law, Indigenous Law* (SAGE Publications Inc, 2016), https://doi.org/10.4135/9781071801277.

[62] Ibid.

[63] Ibid.

[64] R Urinboyev & S Eraliev 'Russian and Turkish migration regimes in a comparative perspective' in *The Political Economy of Non-Western Migration Regimes. International Political Economy Series* (Palgrave Macmillan, 2022), https://doi.org/10.1007/978-3-030-99256-9_2.

[65] B Pohl (ed) 'Cultural perspectives'in *The Cambridge Companion to the Age of William the Conqueror* (Cambridge University Press, 2022) 223–309.

by employing a feudal system of land ownership and a new court system.[66] The common law was founded on standardised forms of action, or 'writs', which served as the foundation for the legal system.[67] London served as the main courthouse, although travelling judges often presided over cases in other regions of the nation.[68] In court procedures, fact-finding was delegated to jurors to help the local populace accept the royal justice system.[69] The royal influence on the judicial system was at first substantial. However, when King James I sought to use his feudal privileges to claim possession of the entire country in the 17th century, parliament interfered, leading to a greater protection of property rights being introduced and a more independent judiciary being formed.[70] Gradually, courts issued increasingly comprehensive judgments, changing the procedural roots of the 'writs' into more substantive regulations; as a result, it has been famously stated that '[t]he modes of action we have buried, but they still rule us from their graves'.[71]

As with civil law, colonialism brought this legal approach to other regions of the world, including Australia, India and the United States. The next section briefly explores the classification of the world's legal systems for the purposes of comparative law.

1.5 WORLD'S LEGAL SYSTEMS CLASSIFIED

Many academic subjects use classifications. The Linnaean taxonomy of animals, plants and minerals, created by Linnaeus in 1735, is the most renowned example in the natural sciences.[72] This taxonomy is also credited with inspiring 'the comparative lawyer as a biologist' to categorise legal regimes. In substance, however, the numerous taxonomies of the social sciences are closer to comparative law since some of those categories reflect the legal families detailed in the next section.[73]

In linguistics, for example, different language families, such as Indo-European, Afro-Asian and Sino-Tibetan, have different children. Classifications of religions may begin with the broad groups of Abrahamic, Indian and East Asian faiths

---

[66] Ibid.

[67] C Law *The Common Law and Civil Law Traditions* (2017), https://www.law.berkeley.edu/wp-content/uploads/2017/11/CommonLawCivilLawTraditions.pdf, accessed 19 June 2023.

[68] Ibid.

[69] Ibid.

[70] CJ Reid Jr 'The seventeenth-century revolution in the English land law' (1995) 43 *Cleveland State Law Review* 221.

[71] FW Maitland 'Equity also, the forms of action at common law: Two courses of lectures' in AH Chaytor & WJ Whittaker *Equity* (Cambridge University Press, 1910).

[72] GM Reid 'Carolus Linnaeus (1707–1778): His life, philosophy and science and its relationship to modern biology and medicine' (2009) 58(1) *Taxon* 18–31.

[73] Ibid.

or they may be listed by the number of adherents to, say, Christianity, Islam, Hinduism, and so on.[74] Different categorisations of civilisations are conceivable, too. Huntington, for example, named eight civilisations: Western, Confucian, Japanese, Islamic, Hindu, Slavic-Orthodox, Latin American and African. Political and economic systems are also frequently classified.[75]

In the area of politics, the world's electoral systems can be categorised in more complex ways, although the basic divisions between presidential and parliamentary republics, constitutional monarchies and absolute monarchs can be made.[76] Before the conclusion of the Cold War, it was also popular to distinguish between the 'three worlds' of capitalist, communist and non-aligned nations; nowadays, one theory suggests that nations may be divided into eight worlds, taking economic policies and wealth into account.[77] Wallerstein's historical study, which contends that the 'global system' is made up of nations in the core, semi-periphery and periphery, is significant in this alternative classification, which is based on political power.[78] This results in a contrast between developed nations, transition economies (emerging economies, newly industrialised countries) and developing countries (less developed countries) that is frequently made in the development literature.

Because taxonomies appear to be viable in these disciplines, it is possible that 'so too the comparatist can categorise laws by limiting them to a restricted number of families'.[79] Such a 'just do it' approach may also draw parallels to more mundane activities: 'classifying legal systems is similar to reorganizing the books in our library, or the knives in our kitchen,' writes Vanderlinden.[80]

1.6 CONSIDERING OTHER METHODS OF COMPARATIVE LAW

It is typical to separate conventional comparative law from 'other forms of comparative law'. The other forms of comparative law are not a single school, but they all oppose the legalism and doctrinalism associated with traditionalists.[81]

[74] P Philomen 'Approaches to proto-Indo-European relative clauses' in *Early Greek Relative Clauses* (Oxford Academic, 2015).

[75] SP Huntington *The Clash of Civilisation and the Remaking of World Order* (Simon & Schuster, 1996).

[76] MH Hansen 'The mixed constitution versus the separation of powers: Monarchical and aristocratic aspects of modern democracy' (2010) 31(3) *History of Political Thought* 509–531.

[77] MT Berger 'The end of the "Third World"?' (1994) 15(2) *Third World Quarterly* 257–275.

[78] I Wallerstein *The Modern World System I: Capitalist Agriculture and the Origins of the European World-Economy in the Sixteenth Century* (Academic Press, 1974).

[79] J Husa 'Classification of legal families today. Is it mine for a memorial hymn?'(2004) 56(1) *Revue International de Droit Compare* 11–38.

[80] J Vanderlinden 'Religious laws as systems of law – a comparatist's view' in A Huxley *Religion, Law and Tradition: Comparative Studies in Religious Law* (Routledge, 2002) 165.

[81] Siems (note 46) ch 2.

Comparative law needs to be based on an understanding of the theories and values underlying legal orders.[82] Detailed and comprehensive comparative law, for instance, could highlight profound differences between existing legal systems. A rule-based comparative legal analysis does not consider the real-world sense in which rules operate in selected jurisdictions of study; therefore, socio-legal research would need to be conducted. Comparative law, and legal research in general, has traditionally not embraced the use of the quantitative tools prevalent in many other academic disciplines. But there is no reason why this should not be done. Therefore, for instance, comparatists may want to compare quantitatively how often courts in Namibia and any other selected jurisdiction make judgments which recognise, for example, same-sex marriages. In the next section we discuss the numerical comparative law as a technique for conducting comparative legal studies.

1.6.1 Numerical comparative law

In 1883, Lord Kelvin stated:

> When you can measure what you're talking about and express it in numbers, you know something about it; but when you can't measure it, when you cannot express it in numbers, your knowledge is meagre and unsatisfactory.[83]

Lord Kelvin was a natural scientist, yet many social scientists now think that quantitative approaches to science are essential. Legal scholars have come late to the party, but there is now a burgeoning area of empirical legal studies that applies statistical methodologies to legal concerns. 'Counting facts about law' refers to information that can be readily counted, such as how frequently one court cites another or how many laws exist in a certain country. These statistics can also be socio-legal in nature, such as the number of days it takes for a court to decide certain cases.

Coding the law has become commonplace in the modern day informed by artificial intelligence (AI).[84] The concept of 'coding law' is based on systems that convert the form or substance of legal regulations into numbers. Empirical researchers use the term 'qualitative' (or 'categorical') information that is converted into and represented as numbers and can construct a coding process that considers additional subtleties. The goal of the coding of the qualitative data is to enable data to resemble a quantitative 'interval variable', which is a variable whose different values include significant information.

[82] Kamba (note 11) 385.

[83] W Thomson 'Electrical units of measurement' (1883) 1(73) *Popular Lectures and Addresses*.

[84] P Sales 'Algorithms, artificial intelligence, and the law' (2021) 105(1) *Judicature* 22–35.

For this reason, the phrase 'conducting surveys about the law' might refer to many kinds of data. Surveys can pose socio-legal questions about the law in action, but they can also enquire about the impact of foreign case law, the nature of legal research or the perceived quality of a country's laws. It is therefore dependent on the type of data if, similarly to the preceding category, a process for converting survey replies into numerical values is required.

1.6.2 Postmodern comparative law

The classic method of comparative law normally divides a comparative study into three segments: a description of the laws, a comparative analysis and a critical policy judgment.[85] The analysis often commences with a functional problem-based research question and occasionally a functional approach also includes comparison and policy assessment. Despite its acknowledged shortcomings, a reluctance to reject this conventional strategy is evident in the comparative legal literature.[86] This can be characterised as a modern response: the suggestion is that the comparatist ought to show more awareness and rationally explain their choices, in particular their preference for traditional methods and the values on which their policy evaluation is based.[87] This assumes that modernity is associated with a belief in rationality. Owing to the increased amount of work required, it is possible that contemporary comparative law will remain with the traditional functional method since more innovative, workable alternatives might not yet exist.

Postmodern comparative law, in contrast, has a higher objective: it seeks to question both the conventional and the contemporary.[88] As a result, it is sceptical of both the conventional technique of comparative law and the belief in perfect reason and objectivity as the foundation of modernity. Following in the footsteps of postmodernists in other subjects, it emphasises distinctions, specifically that seemingly equivalent terms and concepts often have diverse meanings in various legal systems.[89] Therefore, the major goal of comparative law is to grasp the complexity of legal systems rather than to establish common denominators across them.

This is consistent with the notion that 'one cannot understand a place unless one sees how it differs from others'; but postmodern comparative law frequently goes

---

[85] GP Fletcher 'Comparative law as a subversive discipline' (1998) 46(4) *The American Journal of Comparative Law* 683–700.

[86] A Peters & H Schwenke 'Comparative law beyond post-modernism' (2000) 49(4) *The International and Comparative Law Quarterly* 800–834.

[87] E Vargas Weil 'Map and territory in comparative law and economics' (2022) 11(1) *Global Journal of Comparative Law* 1–35.

[88] C Browne 'Postmodernism, ideology and rationality' (2010) 251 *Revue Internationale de Philosophie* 79–99.

[89] Ibid.

further.[90] It emphasises that the researcher's identity and self-awareness are vital in determining the researcher's interpretation of foreign legislation and, therefore, the assessment of similarity or difference. Because there is no 'view from nowhere', the postmodernist is said to start 'from the premise that reasoning, language and judgement are determined by inescapable and incommensurable epistemic, linguistic, cultural, and moral frameworks'.[91] Given the known ambiguity of the word 'postmodernism', this should not be taken as a closed definition. For example, it is connected to cultural studies, the denial of functionalism, the prominence of local narratives and an emphasis on 'plurality, intersubjectivity, experience, situated knowledge, hermeneutics, [and] hybridity' – which refers to movements that began in the middle to the end of the 20th century.[92]

This book emphasises the importance of culture, heterogeneity and subjectivity in law and frequently rejects the functionalism of comparative law in favour of local uniqueness rather than generalisations. Therefore, it is pragmatically accepted that the term 'postmodern comparative law' refers to a variety of methods that not only question the conventional approach but also go beyond simply suggesting modern adaptations. It should be made clear that not all of the academics whose research is covered in this book identify themselves as 'postmodernists' in this context. Nevertheless, it is also significant to note that other terms, such as critical, sceptical or hermeneutical comparative law, would have been less inclusive overall.

1.6.3 Socio-legal comparative law

The expanding use of 'socio-legal comparative law' is a reaction to the failure of conventional comparative law to consider both the law in practice and the link between law and society.[93] It also reflects broader advances in legal scholarship because many nations have experienced a shift towards scholarship in socio-legal studies, law and society, and empirical legal studies using either qualitative or quantitative methodologies. Socio-legal comparative law is distinguished by two features: first, it substitutes a socio-legal interpretation of 'law' (sometimes referred to as 'legal culture') for the formal one associated with classical comparative law;[94] second, it considers whether, and in what way, there is a causal relationship between law and society.[95] In socio-legal comparative law, methodologies might be

[90] T Duve 'Legal traditions: A dialogue between comparative law and comparative legal history' (2018) 6(1) *Comparative Legal History*15–33.

[91] Ibid.

[92] NNJ Fischer 'Culture and cultural analysis as experimental systems' (2007) 22(1) *Cultural Anthropology* 1–65.

[93] Siems (note 46) ch 2.

[94] W Twining 'Social science and diffusion of law' (2005) 32(2) *Journal of Law and Society* 203–240.

[95] Ibid.

qualitative, quantitative or even hybrid.[96] The ambiguity of the word '(legal) culture' is criticised. Alternative terms such as (legal) mentalities, formants, traditions, philosophies or styles are not much more specific. It is also feasible to pinpoint a number of particular elements that make up legal culture.

To begin with, a study on legal culture considers 'law in action' in addition to 'law in books'. Compliance with the law is important to legal culture. It investigates the way people generally feel about the law. Cross-country surveys can therefore be useful for comparing legal systems in socio-legal comparative law. By gathering and contrasting statistics on the frequency of lawsuits, attempts have been made to determine the significance of law in society. 'External legal culture' is the term Friedman uses to describe various facets of societal attitudes and behaviours.[97] In contrast, 'internal legal culture' refers to those who create the law: the perspectives of law-makers, judges and lawyers in practice. It is crucial to consider the institutional framework and functioning of the legal system with regard to the latter group. This might, for instance, apply to the number of lawyers in a given nation, the organisation of courts, the selection of judges, the structure of legal education and training, and the readiness of the police and the prosecution to enforce the law. Finally, legal culture encompasses more than simply the formal institutions of law-making and law-enforcement. Other means of creating social order are frequently as vital as, if not more important than, formal legislation. As a result, one must also evaluate informal forms of social control and conflict resolution, in addition to the structure of these institutions and the habits and attitudes that sustain them.

1.7 COMPARATIVE LAW IN A GLOBAL CONTEXT

The phrase 'globalisation' is fraught with ambiguity. William Twining argues that it may produce 'exaggerated, false, meaningless, superficial, or ethnocentric generalisations'.[98] There is also the obvious risk of presuming that globalisation is a contemporary phenomenon, when in reality several 'globalisations' may be found throughout history. The term 'global' is used pragmatically in this text to explain a variety of interconnected subjects; therefore, globalisation as it is used here has a range of meanings. For instance, it encompasses a range of scales: although certain phenomena, such as the internet, may be really global in scope, others may be about trends that are concentrated in major economic hubs or specific geographical areas. Diversity is a possibility when considering the topic of globalisation. Usually,

[96] Ibid.

[97] LM Friedman 'The place of legal culture in the sociology of law' in M Freeman (ed) *Law and Sociology* (Oxford University Press, 2006); see also Siems (note 46) ch 2.

[98] Twining (note 94) 203.

concrete elements are mentioned, including the globalisation of commerce, finance, manufacturing and labour. However, it is also possible to assert that globalisation is mostly an intellectual construct, which highlights the influence of the concepts about globalisation. In addition, the nations and cultures that may be considered the primary forces behind globalisation are diverse. Whereas emphasis is typically placed on the Westernisation or even the Americanisation of other civilisations, there may also be Asian and Islamic versions of globalisation. Ideas have also been put forward for taxonomies that are more intricate.

De Sousa Santos divides globalisation into two sub-categories: hegemonic and counter-hegemonic.[99] Hegemonic globalisation can take the form of 'localized globalism', where local patterns change as a result of transnational imperatives (such as considering the influence of multinational corporations) or it can take the form of 'globalized localism', where specific local phenomena spread to other parts of the world. Cosmopolitanism and the shared human heritage, which relate to cross-border solidarity among excluded people, on the one hand, and global issues such as the conservation of the environment, on the other, are the two types of counter-hegemonic globalisation.

Comparative attorneys are inevitably interested in globalisation. Its different components will recur under four major themes in this section. In addition to analysing recent 'Westernisations' and 'Americanisations' of legal systems as examples of 'globalized localism', 'legal transplants' demonstrate that globalising trends are not just things that happened in the 20th century.[100] Convergence, regionalisation and internationalisation can be considered as observable effects of 'localised globalism'. Transnational and global law are becoming more popular. These laws call into question the significance of state law and may therefore be interpreted as evidence of a paradigm change brought about by globalisation. Comparative law and development demonstrates how we not only view 'law under globalisation', but also 'law as a result of globalisation'. For this reason, it will be analysed in the light of the way globalisation affects expectations of adherence to the rule of law. Some chapters in this book examine whether a counter-hegemonic kind of legal globalisation is viable.

1.7.1 Comparative law and development

The effects and ramifications of globalisation for various areas of law are likely to vary. It appears plausible, for instance, to anticipate the creation of transnational

[99] B de Sousa Santos *Toward a New Legal Common Sense* 2 ed (Butterworths, 2002); Siems (note 46) ch 2.

[100] Siems (note 46) ch 2.

legal tools in a very international topic such as trade law.[101] The necessity for such norms may be less obvious in other areas of private law, but legal transplants may result in some convergence of legal systems. Public law is not immune to such developments, although globalising trends may be viewed as weakening national sovereignty. Concerns about a 'race to the bottom' may arise in other sectors of law with a social component – for example, the globalisation of labour law.[102] The broad concept of 'progress' is a key component of the Enlightenment's optimism in shaping the path of history.[103] This can be considered as a forerunner of the belief that development frequently happens in phases. For example, in economic development discourse, the typical pattern is described as one in which agricultural civilisations are superseded in turn by pre-industrial, industrial and eventually information societies.

Sir Henry Maine's *Ancient Law* established a comparable evolutionary approach in legal studies that linked legal growth to the level of civilisation: 'primitive nations' were believed to have pre-customary law, which eventually became customary law and, finally, positive law in developed society.[104] Maine in particular notably proposed that communities shift from 'status' rights and responsibilities to 'contract' rights and obligations.[105] Similarly, but more clearly, Weber linked the economic success of the Western capitalist economies to their formal–rational legal systems supported by professional legal institutions – and contrasted those from non-Western forms of order.[106] Maine and Weber's beliefs, in their purest form, are now regarded as unsuitable and ethnocentric, assuming the supremacy of Western laws and institutions. Nonetheless, the demand for clear standards, professional institutions and effective contract enforcement remains an important component of modern approaches to law and development.

---

[101] K Nowrot 'Legal consequences of globalization: The status of non-governmental organizations under international law' (1999) 6(2) *Indiana Journal of Global Legal Studies* 579–645.

[102] TV Warikandwa & P Osode 'Human rights, core labour standards and the search for a legal basis for a trade–labour linkage in the multilateral trade regime of the World Trade Organisation' (2014) 18 *Law, Democracy & Development* 240–263; see also TV Warikandwa & P Osode 'Forging institutional cooperation to protect core labour standards in trade: Are a world trade organisation and an international labour organisation joint dispute settlement system practical?' (2014) 47(3) *Comparative Law and International Law Journal of Southern Africa* 490–508; A Singh & A Zammit 'Labour standards and the "race to the bottom": Rethinking globalization and workers' rights from developmental and solidaristic perspectives' (2004) 20(1) *Oxford Review of Economic Policy* 85–104.

[103] Siems (note 46) ch 2.

[104] R Redfield 'Maine's ancient law in the light of primitive societies' (1950) 3(4) *The Western Political Quarterly* 574–589; Siems (note 46) ch 2.

[105] Siems (note 46) ch 2.

[106] F Webber 'The Pinochet case: The struggle for the realization of human rights' (1999) 26 *Journal of Law and Society* 523.

Initiatives promoting the rule of law are considered to be favourably welcomed because they 'obtain wider acceptance across ideologies, religions, and political regimes'.[107] Some attempts have been made to give broad definitions, such as the rule of law dealing with the 'problem of arbitrary power' and aiming to establish 'collective control of power' as a kind of 'social equality'.[108] However, lists of criteria are more commonly used in the literature and practice; but there is considerable debate over whether specific aspects should be included. The distinction between procedural (or formal) and substantive criteria is a useful one. The contrast between a thin and a thick version is related in that a thin version is primarily procedural whereas a thick version incorporates substantive requirements. However, as will be demonstrated, the thickness of the rule of law is a topic of discussion for both procedural and substantive criteria. Starting with the procedural features, the 'rule of law' differs from the 'rule by law', the latter implying that the head of state simply exploits the law opportunistically to fulfil their goals.[109]

In contrast, the rule of law demands explicit, transparent, broad and prospective laws that apply to everyone (including the ruler). This criterion also suggests a preference for unified formal rules over pluralistic systems based on customary and other informal norms. Furthermore, institutions such as the courts, public prosecution, police and administrative agencies must implement these laws in a consistent and equitable manner:[110] these institutions, including their constituents, must not exceed their authority. This necessitates the prevention of corruption, which is commonly described as the abuse of public power for personal benefit. Corruption is thought to be especially serious in the developing countries because it is exacerbated by inequality and poverty.

1.7.2 Legal transplants

The legal transplant literature has reached a high level of complexity.[111] If the Government of the Republic of Namibia enacts a new Companies Act that allows shareholders to file a claim on behalf of a company against its directors ('derivative action'), based on the model of UK law, a number of questions may arise, including: Why did Namibia do this? Was the United Kingdom involved? Is this imported legal regulation effective in Namibia? Is this typical of the way legislative reform occurs? Is this way of enacting legislation a good or a terrible model for other countries? Through the conceptual discussion concerning legal transplants and their efficacy,

[107] Siems (note 46) ch 2.
[108] Ibid.
[109] Ibid.
[110] Ibid.
[111] Ibid.

comparative law has the opportunity to explore the answers to the concerns stated above. The notion of legal transplants is connected to classic comparative-law topics: traditional comparative-law policy recommendations may include the suggestion of legal transplants as 'applied comparative law'. Legal transplants have also played an important role in the formation of legal families in Europe and the diffusion of similar models to other regions of the world.

1.7.3 Convergence, regionalisation and internationalisation

The notion of 'convergence' might be inspired by extending the concept of 'the end of history' to disparities in legal systems. It is also vital to comprehend the specific definition of convergence and the dynamics driving it. In 1989, Fukuyama stated:

> What we may be witnessing is not just the end of the Cold War, or the passage of a specific period of postwar history, but the end of history as such: that is, the end point of mankind's ideological evolution and the universalization of Western liberal democracy as the final form of human government.[112]

Fukuyama claims in a follow-up statement 20 years later that there has been a continuing movement towards liberal democracy. Furthermore, he believes that cultural values have been influenced: in particular, Fukuyama points to human rights, the accountability of government authorities and the rule of law – all of which non-Western cultures have been pursuing.[113] In legal studies, Hansmann and Kraakman argue that historical variations in corporate law have vanished in favour of conformity to the US model.[114] Other scholars have voiced similar sentiments. Dalhuisen describes current laws as 'practical, technical, and problem-solving', noting that they do not differ substantially from one country to the next.[115] According to Friedman, it seems obvious that a French lawyer and an English lawyer would have an easier time comparing notes on, say, urban planning, income tax deductions or software copyright protection than they would discussing legal problems with a lawyer from the reigns of Henry VIII or Louis XIV.[116] Those two monarchs' legal domains are no longer in existence.[117]

---

[112] F Fukuyama 'The end of history?' (1989) 16 *The National Interest* 3–18.

[113] F Fukuyama 'What is governance?' CGD Working Paper 314 (Center for Global Development, 2013).

[114] Siems (note 46) ch 2.

[115] JH Dalhuisen *Dalhuisen on International Commercial, Finance and Trade Law* 2 ed (Hart Publishing, 2004) 117.

[116] Siems (note 46) ch 22.

[117] Ibid.

The expression 'convergence of laws' means that legal events have grown more comparable. As a result, it refers to a process rather than implying that they are or will become similar. This is an essential aspect to emphasise because some of the literature uses distinct but potentially misleading language. For example, while it is said that we may have 'hybridisation' but not convergence since there cannot be a 'single best model', the perspective is that we do experience convergence in such a scenario because such hybrids are certain to be less distinct from each other than pure units of comparison. Legal transplants may play a part in this convergence process. However, one can imagine a situation in which a transplant makes the world's legal systems more dissimilar: for example, if all countries except one have similar laws on a particular topic but half of the countries decide to transplant the law of the outlier, this will result in a global divergence of legal systems.

But convergence can also occur without the use of legal transplants. For example, countries may work together to tackle a societal problem and find a solution that no other country has found. Alternatively, the rising similarity in law may be the indirect effect of the dissemination of other ideas and social events rather than a legal transplant. Terminologically, the link between legal harmonisation and convergence is not totally evident. Some perceive harmonisation to be an intentional process whereas others believe that convergence occurs spontaneously. More generally, though, convergence is viewed as a broader concept and therefore multiple types of convergence are described, some based on a purposeful programme of legal unification ('harmonisation') as opposed to 'natural' or 'evolutionary' convergence.

In any case, non-deliberate types of unification are frequently more fascinating to investigate since, if proven, they may demonstrate that formal harmonisation is not necessarily required. A variety of more particular forms of convergence have also been proposed in the literature. Hay distinguishes multiple causal chains in the context of law-making in political science: input, paradigm, policy, legitimatory rhetoric, result and process convergence.[118] Similarly to this, formal, functional, contractual, hybrid, normative and institutional kinds of convergence have been recognised in the legal literature, particularly in the area of business law. According to Gilson, functional convergence in company law is more likely than formal convergence because, despite there being similar underlying issues, formal harmonisation is hindered by too many barriers.[119] Functional convergence is defined as the production of a comparable outcome, such as the dismissal of incompetent managers under various statutory frameworks. Gilson proposes

[118] H Colin 'Common trajectories, variable paces, divergent outcomes? Models of European capitalism under conditions of complex economic interdependence' (2004) 11 *Review of International Political Economy* 231–262; see also H Colin 'Globalization's impact on states' in John Ravenhill (ed) *Global Political Economy* 3 ed (Oxford University Press, 2011) 312–344.

[119] RJ Gilson 'Globalizing corporate governance: Convergence of form or function' (2001) 49 *The American Journal of Comparative Law* 329–357.

the possibility of contractual convergence in which the formal distinctions may be functionally significant but the same consequences might be achieved by contractual agreements.[120] Rose adds the idea of 'hybrid convergence' in which a company 'escapes' local law by relocating its registered seat to a different nation.[121] In this case, approximation occurs since companies from different nations are subject to the same laws.

1.7.4 Shift from transnational to global law

Traditional comparative law has a strong focus on comparing and contrasting legal systems across nations. Therefore, it may be claimed that the growth of transnational and global law offers a challenge to comparative law since the need to compare laws at the state level becomes increasingly irrelevant. It is also conceivable to argue for its continued applicability in the legal system of today. The state is nevertheless crucial to international and transnational law, as is explained in the paragraphs that follow. Husa argues that 'the flexibility of comparative methodology may be an asset in today's transnational legal world' rather than that 'changes in the legal configuration may not be harmful for comparative law'.[122]

But should the techniques and resources used in comparative law change? And what precisely are these new international and transnational legal frameworks? A person who has a permanent population, a defined territory, a government and the ability to interact with other nations is considered to be a state under international law. As this connectivity is also reflected in the differences and similarities across legal systems, it may be crucial to comparative law that the relationship between population and area is not just coincidental and that its inhabitants share the same culture and values. However, the truth is frequently different. Even some islands are separated into multiple states, therefore some state borders are determined by geography, but they are rarely permanent.

State borders have also been drawn arbitrarily in many regions of the world – particularly those caused by external divides by colonial powers – which has led to weak national identities. Because many states are not cohesive 'nation-states', state-based comparisons initially have to contend with this issue. This is not a new occurrence, but it has gained in prominence as today's cultures become increasingly varied owing to migration. The state itself, however, faces the greatest threat. A common argument is that the forces of globalisation have reduced the state's sovereignty, causing it to 'erode' (or 'retreat', 'decline', 'disaggregate' or 'hollow

[120] Ibid.
[121] Ibid.
[122] Ibid.

out').[123] Both the internal and the foreign aspects of this claim overlap, though. Regarding the domestic level, the state may be decomposing, given that today's state functions are frequently divided among a number of entities, including regulatory agencies, public–private partnerships, self-regulatory bodies and other non-state entities in addition to the government, the Legislature and the courts.[124] This is sometimes referred to as 'governance' (as opposed to 'government') and it denotes the use of cooperative and other novel forms of law-making as opposed to required and hierarchical legal standards.[125]

The idea that the state has a monopoly of governance authority and that there is a clear separation between the state and society is also called into question by the privatisation of law-making.[126] At the international level, it is also claimed that the state continues to disintegrate.[127] Not only do governments communicate with one another, they also do so with courts, regulatory agencies and other public entities, which is considered a symptom of a new 'transgovernmentalism'.[128] The interconnection of civilisations also puts national sovereignty under threat, forcing governments to cooperate through increasingly intricate intergovernmental systems of global governance in addition to traditional international treaties. This covers the usage of 'soft law', which may be used to describe all those legal standards that lack the formality of a source of law or all those legal norms that are unenforceable. Given the lack of a world government and the influence of multinational corporations, credit agencies, investment funds, audit firms and other private organisations, it is anticipated that market forces, private regulatory bodies, contracts and arbitration will probably replace existing forms of order in a 'borderless world'.[129]

1.8 COMPARATIVE LAW: AN INHERENTLY OPEN SUBJECT?

The comparative technique is a tool that may be used in all the social sciences. The following list summarises a number of similar issues dealt with by the majority of these comparative studies. This is not to imply that comparative methods are used uniformly in the social sciences; however, given Hirschl's statement that 'despite (or

123 Ibid.
124 Ibid.
125 Ibid.
126 PB Stephan 'Privatizing international law' (2011) 97(7) *Virginia Law Review* 1573–1664.
127 Ibid.
128 Ibid.
129 L Yadong & RL Tung 'International expansion of emerging market enterprises: A springboard perspective' (2007) 38(4) *Journal of International Business Studies* 481–498.

perhaps because of) bitter debates about approaches and methods', there is now a rich framework to conduct comparative research in the social sciences.[130]

A common starting point in comparative law is to establish the aims of comparative law. Other comparative social sciences have comparable discussions. On the one hand, comparative research is interested in specific units for their own sake, whereas, on the other hand, comparative information is used as a tool to identify relationships between variables. A comparatist may describe the background of a small number of examples, such as nations, societies or cultures, with an emphasis on learning about the unique characteristics of these units. In addition, they could attempt to categorise nations, monitor patterns (such as convergences and divergences) or pinpoint some occurrences as universal. Such a study that stems from an interest in the relevant units might overlap with area studies research, and its focus on understanding particulars is indicative of an approach that seeks to link the social sciences with the humanities.

In the case of legal studies, this approach is comparable to the cultural approaches to comparative law that are covered later in this book. Comparative analysis, in contrast, uses comparative instances to evaluate theory-driven research hypotheses. Similarly to experimental research in the natural sciences, this may offer proof of causal linkages in particular. This study aspires to make universal generalisations about social life since it has a high degree of external validity and is therefore valid on a worldwide scale. However, even with this goal, it might be intriguing to discover that some regularities are system-specific. In addition, these comparisons may be used to guide state policy decisions or other judgements involving any unit of comparison. At a simple level, this can only demonstrate the availability of various policy alternatives, but it can also include more detailed information regarding the effects of particular legislation and the limits that must be considered.

1.9 CHAPTER OUTLINES

In chapter 1, Warikandwa, Amoo and Kariseb set out the conceptual framework of the book. They point out that in covering fundamental legal and academic discourses and comparative-law methodology, comparative law provides an in-depth and methodical basis for comparing legal systems for judges, legal practitioners, legal academics and students. They point to the significant role of comparative law in critiquing both conventional and modern approaches to the field and its use of examples from a variety of jurisdictions to provide the reader

[130] R Hirschl *Comparative Matters: The Renaissance of Comparative Constitutional Law* (Oxford University Press, 2014).

with a genuinely global perspective. They emphasise that the contextualised and multidisciplinary approach of comparative law relies on examples from politics, economics, social sciences, among other disciplines, to make an innovative contribution to comparative-law themes. They also set out the chapter outline of the book and its relevance to the contemporary Namibia and global contexts.

In chapter 2, the late Walter Kamba's seminal article on comparative law explores what comparative law is. Kamba emphasises that at the outset one is faced with a difficulty which stems from the use of the term 'comparative law'. He points out that comparative law is often regarded as suggesting a distinct branch of national law such as family law, criminal law, contract and the like, which comparative law is not. This ambiguity has contributed to much of the controversy and misunderstanding that have plagued comparative legal studies and research for a long time. Kamba then emphasises that never before has a comparative legal study and research attracted the attention and energies of so many eminent lawyers, both from the profession and from the universities. He points out that the spate of books and articles on particular comparative topics during the past three decades bears testimony to this development. There is no doubt that the days are over when comparative law represented an academic pastime that was good only for adding a scholarly touch to footnotes in learned articles. Yet, in spite of this greatly increased and increasing interest, Kamba bemoans the fact that comparative law still lacks a clearly formulated and widely accepted theoretical framework within which specific comparative legal studies and research may be undertaken in a meaningful and effective manner – a framework which would also be valuable to the legal practitioner for recognising and handling legal problems that involve foreign law.

In chapter 3, Mousourakis emphasises that comparative law, as a method of legal science and as an academic discipline, is largely a product of modern Western thought. However, the author contends that this does not mean that legal comparison, as a form of cognition involving the study of foreign laws, had no place in earlier civilisations. He notes that from a very early period people observed that the legal norms of different societies were not identical. These diverse norms were sometimes taken into consideration when new legal rules and institutions were being developed. The rationale appears to be that the laws of states or communities which were particularly dominant or were perceived as being more advanced were deliberately imitated or adopted by other states or communities, and this process was probably repeated in various parts of the world. Mousourakis examines the role of legal comparatism in ancient, medieval and early modern European legal thought and practice with a view to tracing some key ideas that contributed to the rise of comparative law. He gives special attention to the development of the comparative approach to law in the Renaissance and Enlightenment eras – a period marked by the emergence of scientific rationalism and the rise of the modern nation-state and national legal systems.

In chapter 4, Mundia and Haimbili underscore the fact that comparative law is an academic study of separate legal systems, each one evaluated in its basic elements; the ways in which the elements differ in the different legal systems and how their elements combine into a system. They discuss the legal systems of the world and their distinct characteristics and qualities which set them apart from other legal systems. The discussion includes a list of countries that fall under the respective legal systems and the criteria used for classification. Mundia and Haimbili emphasise that comparative law may be defined as the systematic application of comparison to law. It involves a method of ascertaining differences and similarities between the things compared, of explaining the differences and similarities and then of applying them to achieve a particular purpose – be it law reform, the promulgation of legislation, the harmonisation or unification of laws, judicial process or the formulation of international legal norms and principles.

In chapter 5, Asheela-Shikalepo and Mundia point out that it is widely accepted that there are varying approaches to comparative law and yet there has been no consensus on the methodology a comparatist should follow. They proceed to surmise that perhaps the criticisms of the past decades of what was established in comparative legal research may account for this paradox. They seek to explain what comparative law entails. In this chapter, the authors discuss the methodologies and techniques of comparative law. They answer questions such as: What is it that the comparatist compares? What does the comparatist use in order to make a comparison? and Is there a universal method of comparison? In essence, they offer both a theoretical and a practical framework that embodies a range of comparative techniques within which both micro- and macro-comparisons may be tackled. They also explore the methodological approaches of comparative law in Africa.

In chapter 6, Warikandwa points out that socialist or Soviet law is defined as a generic type of legal system used in communist and previously communist governments such as the former Soviet Union. It is based on the civil-law system but contains substantial modifications and changes adopted from Marxist–Leninist philosophy. It is debatable whether socialist law has ever been considered a separate legal system. If this were the case, by the time the Cold War ended, communist law would have risen to become one of the most significant legal systems in the world. He proceeds to note that socialism's legal systems call for the majority of property to be owned by the state or by agricultural cooperatives and for having special courts and laws for state enterprises, in contrast to civil-law systems that traditionally go to great lengths to define the concept of private property and how it may be acquired, transferred or lost. Some legal academics have argued that communist law was not a distinct legal classification. Despite the fact that the communist nations' command economy approach meant that most categories of property could not be owned, the Soviet Union always had a civil code, courts that interpreted this civil code and a civil-law approach to legal reasoning (therefore, both legal process and legal reasoning were largely analogous to the French or German Civil Code system). More significantly, Warikandwa analyses the relevance of socialist law in Africa.

In chapter 7, Kariseb argues that globalisation is often thought of in terms of economics, politics, market integration, technology and the like, but hardly ever in the context of law and legal systems. Yet, he continues, this phenomenon has fundamental impacts on laws and legal systems the world over. It affects to a greater extent the ways in which different countries interact and engage with one another, including their legal systems and laws. According to him, the need therefore exists to analyse and appreciate law in terms of its international or, rather, its transnational character. This is what Kariseb deals with in this chapter. In doing so, he provides specific examples and refers to the Namibian legal system. He points out that, owing to the increasing transnationalisation of activities subject to legal regulation, legal questions that transcend borders and geographies arise more frequently. No mature legal system, whether in the Global North or South is spared this reality. It is therefore not surprising that national laws and domestic legal systems are increasingly being viewed and appreciated in terms of their internationalisation. He contends that in this context internationalisation means that the laws and legal systems are increasingly harmonising legal cultures, practices, laws and principles as a result of transnational legal engagements.

In chapter 8, Amoo, Mapaure and Kariseb concede to the understanding that the question of an African jurisprudence – that is, a unique African philosophical foundation of theoretical questions about the nature of law and legal systems in Africa – partially emerges from the grand discourse on the existence of African philosophy. They contend that Africans, since time immemorial, have philosophised about their societies and the global world in which they live, including about law. They point out that, to Africans' dismay, much of their philosophical discourse has been conveyed orally and for the most part it has been distorted. Moreover, following the decolonisation processes in Africa that swept over it from the late 1950s onwards, the indigenous thought processes and laws have been overwhelmed by state laws. Jurisprudence in Africa has therefore remained strained. Consequently, according to Amoo, Mapaure and Kariseb, it is not misplaced to argue that there has been a historical privileging of 'Global North' knowledge and worldviews with a concomitant undervaluation and marginalisation of thoughts from Africa in comparative legal processes on the continent and beyond. The Global North is often thought of as being the source and creator of theory, whereas the Global South simply applies what was developed in the First World to their context without question. They conclude that it is not surprising that much of the comparative legal process in Africa, including that in Namibia, has not been informed by African thoughts, particularly African philosophical discourses that are unique and homegrown. And if it has, it has undeniably been minimal.

In chapter 9, Damaseb JP presents the central arguments of his chapter in two parts, A and B. Part A interrogates the following broad themes: the court system in Namibia; comparative law as a source of law and its impact on Namibia's jurisprudence; the approach of Namibia's courts to foreign precedent; judicial review in Namibia, and a comparison with some other legal systems. In Part B, the author deals with law reform and the influence of comparative law on judicial decision-making. Here he demonstrates that judicial review in the common-law tradition is not the only model available in the world as a check on legislative and executive power. Damaseb JP then concludes that there are alternative models, such as the French Code civil that has been successfully adapted in African countries such as Mozambique and Senegal. Every civilised legal system laying claim to being a democracy recognises the separation of the functions of the Legislature, the Executive and the Judiciary in ordering national affairs.

In chapter 10, Jorge focuses on the law of obligations, an area somewhat neglected in research in the Namibian legal system. The chapter reflects on the liability in unjustified enrichment in selected jurisdictions: Namibia, Continental Europe, the United Kingdom and two South American countries, Argentina and Brazil. With the exception of Namibia, in all of the selected jurisdictions there have been some developments in this field of law during the past 20 years or attempts to streamline the field so that its principles may respond more adequately to contemporary issues. The author then contends that, because there is a futuristic idea of a European Civil Code and with the creation of a single market in the European Union, the need has arisen to harmonise certain rules, such as 'contract law', and for consumers at least to have a frame of reference in certain legal matters.

In chapter 11, Warikandwa, Libebe and Zaire demonstrate that adopting comparative law in Africa may achieve positive scientific outcomes. They emphasise that such an approach will help Africans to understand their own legal systems and other legal systems in use in their society. Furthermore, it will help African countries to understand how to interact legally with the greater global or regional contexts. Therefore, they emphasise that legal comparativism has value in Africa and can be used to expand the role of African law in comparative legal studies. This development will most likely help modern African countries to use legal comparativism as a means to an end. In this context, according to the authors, the goal is to revolutionise and decolonise legal education in Africa. The use of comparative law in African judicial systems should therefore not be considered controversial and should instead be encouraged. It is widely acknowledged that, given the colonial backgrounds of most African countries, it would be difficult, if not impossible, for them to function in the legal realm if they had not used comparative-law principles to synthesise their countries' own multifaceted post-colonial legal systems. Warikandwa, Libebe and Zaire contend that comparative law, which entails the comparative study of laws and their refining in order to improve and standardise them, is crucial to Africa. The importance of continuing legal education and legal comparativism research is therefore emphasised by the authors, who conclude by pointing out that legal comparativism is rapidly fading in Africa, particularly among jurists and/or comparative academics, and also in African law schools and/or faculty curricula.

In chapter 12, Masake and Libebe contend that legal transplant can be effected in various ways, that is, colonialism, globalism and internationalism, to mention a few. They argue further that the decolonial theory, among other theories, acknowledges that colonialism disrupted the precolonial legal philosophies, of which the African and Asian legal philosophies are not an exception. It is common cause, according to them, that Africa and Asia were subjected to colonial rule. The disruption of the organically created legal philosophies at the behest of colonialism led to the legal paradigm shift, namely, the introduction of colonial laws. This legal paradigm shift, among others, witnessed the transplanting of laws from the colonial masters into the colonies. The concept of *legal transplant* is compound: it comprises *legal* and *transplant*. The authors then emphasise that the concept of legal transplant raises issues related to its conceptual meaning. For example: What does the concept of *legal* that precedes *transplant* mean? Is there a distinction between *law* and *legal* – *legal* as understood in the context of *legal transplant*? And what is that which is transplanted? Is it the *law* or *legal*? They answer these questions in this chapter.

In chapter 13, Warikandwa argues that, although it is crucial that judges, legal scholars, practitioners and law students receive instruction that is specifically geared to dealing with the issues of the modern world, the unknown can be frightening and it may seem superfluous to devote time to comparative law. He questions how comparative law is to be accommodated in overloaded curricula where room is being sought for an ever-increasing number of new topics, such as e-commerce, law and technology, communications law and law on terrorism. When offered, comparative-law courses are rarely taken by many students at institutions that teach law, especially at the undergraduate level. Nonetheless, it is undeniably true that judges and other legal professionals are now more closely connected to international law, foreign attorneys and overseas clients. The author then notes that, as a result, the subject of teaching foreign law is becoming more crucial. The two methods of teaching comparative law used by comparative lawyers – normative enquiry and contextual or jurisprudential research – are reflected in the way that comparative law is taught. The two variant techniques used throughout this work and this sub-topic of the comparative-law theme match each other quite well.

In chapter 14, Libebe and Amoo contend that there is no African country that is free of African traditions or free of at leastsome elements that belong to Western modernity and the effects of colonisation. Africa's colonial experience often demands a distinction to be made between indigenous African law and African customary law. They proceed to point out that whereas indigenous laws are surviving precolonial norms which people still observe in their ancient forms, customary laws are adaptations of these ancient norms to legal, religious, economic and cultural changes. African customary law is usually used as a generic term to denote the various laws of the indigenous people of southern Africa. The authors then point out that writers on the jurisprudence and legal systems of traditional African societies acknowledge that, before the advent of colonialism, African communities had and still have their own laws and legal systems regulating the affairs and behaviours in society. They then conclude that African customary law extensively covers areas such as criminal and civil liability, marriage, inheritance, succession and land-tenure systems. These are often described in the contemporary literature as either customary law or indigenous law. Customary law is plural (since it is an aggregate of the laws of a particular tribal community), diverse and unwritten because its primary source is oral tradition.

In chapter 15, Hinz points out that the goal of the chapter is to submit arguments in support of the thesis that the employment of comparative jurisprudence in its rather recent manifestation, which one may call *postmodern comparative jurisprudence*, is a methodologically indispensable tool with which to ascertain customary law and accommodate it in plural legal orders. He underscores the fact that, jurisprudentially interpreted, *postmodern comparative jurisprudence* is essential to *legal anthropology* and its contribution to *anthropological jurisprudence*. In the chapter, Hinz further describes in part 15.2 the use of legal comparison in the development of legal and political anthropology from its early developments to where anthropological jurisprudence stands today. In part 15.3, the author, on the basis of the observations in part 15.2, considers the Namibian customary-law ascertainment project. In part 15.4, he illustrates the successful or missed employment of comparative jurisprudence in reaching solutions in law-making, law reform and court decisions. Finally, in part 15.5, Hinz points to comparative jurisprudence as a methodological tool with which to achieve the reasoned ascertainment of customary law and, with this, to support the above-stated thesis.

In chapter 16, Amoo stresses that a Bill of Rights, which in most written constitutions contains the fundamental rights and freedoms of a jurisdiction, evolved historically from the Magna Carta of 1215, the United States Bill of Rights of 1791, the Universal Declaration of Human Rights of 1948 and the writings of naturalists such as Grotius, Montesquieu and Locke in the 16th to the 18th centuries. The author proceeds to point out that in the context of constitutional law and human rights jurisprudence, a Bill of Rights is associated with the concept of constitutional government, which is premised on and articulated according to the principles of constitutionalism. Amoo concludes by pointing out that constitutionalism therefore goes beyond a government according to the terms of a constitution: it implies limited government. This limitation on government recognises both the provision and guaranteeing of individual rights and freedoms, which is a *sine qua non* for attaining constitutionalism.

In chapter 17, Amoo emphasises that under international law states have a sovereign right over their natural resources. Public international law also recognises an individual's right to property. The problem that could result from these potentially conflicting rights could be resolved by the application of the principle that the right of a community overrides the right of an individual. Based on this premise, he argues that the power of the state to extinguish the individual's right to property could be justified only on the ground of public utility; and where expropriation is justified on this ground, the individual must be compensated for the deprivation of their rights. The author is of the view that the demands of natural justice and equity enjoin the expropriating authority to comply with the principles of natural justice since in essence the right to expropriate is discretionary. Amoo advances his thesis by undertaking a comparative study of the jurisprudence of Ghana, Namibia, South Africa and Zimbabwe.

In chapter 18, Amoo argues that topics such as bail jurisprudence more often than not conjure up emotions of security concerns about the 'bad guy who must be kept off the streets'. He points out that most often we tend to forget about the cardinal principle of the presumption of innocence in criminal justice. Contemporary international policies and measures taken by some powers to combat international terrorism testify to the dangers of actual pre-trial punishment. The root cause of this, the author submits, is the concentration of excessive powers over security matters in the Executive. The refusal of the right to bail assumes a position that our criminal justice systems are perfect and that individuals detained for allegedly committing serious offences will be charged and tried in accordance with the precepts of the due process of the law. He concludes by noting that, empirically, evidence proves the contrary: there are cases in certain jurisdictions of torture in detention camps and the inability of the state to bring detained persons for trial within a reasonable time. In advancing the thesis of this chapter, Amoo undertakes a comparative study of the bail jurisprudence of Ghana, Namibia, Zambia and South Africa.

In chapter 19, Amoo argues that the issue of the alleged violation of the rights of individuals who are detained for a long time before trial has become phenomenal and has raised global concerns. In his arguments, he refers to the interns in the infamous Guantanamo Bay detention facility. He also refers to the Zambian case of the *People v John Chisimba* and the Caprivi Treason Trial in Namibia. The author also argues that bail applications have been denied by the courts because of the nature of the offences. In its report, Amnesty International refers to alleged violations of the accused's pre-trial rights and concludes that these alleged violations may seriously undermine their right to a fair hearing in accordance with international standards as articulated in the International Covenant on Civil and Political Rights and the African Charter on Peoples' Rights. Amoo then notes that concerns have been raised about the duration of trials. The Government of the Republic of Namibia, in its Report to the United Nations Secretary-General, has responded to these allegations; one obvious reason for the prolonged duration of a trial, it is claimed, is the complex nature of cases.

In chapter 20, Libebe, Warikandwa and Amoo undertake a comparative overview of the law on adultery in several jurisdictions: Namibia, South Africa, Zimbabwe, Nigeria, Botswana, the United States and Indonesia. They do so as a basis for suggesting a frame of reference that would inform comparative law in Africa. Here they refer to court cases in Namibia, Zimbabwe and South Africa in which it had to be decided whether third-party claims for adultery are still an acceptable legal norm in contemporary African societies. They contend that most African societies recognise third-party claims for adultery. This chapter begins by considering the law on third-party claims for adultery in general and it proceeds with an analysis of the Namibian and South African positions (which are somewhat similar) and contrasts them with differing court decisions in other jurisdictions such as Zimbabwe, Nigeria, the United States and Indonesia. The authors conclude by arguing that the African philosophy of ubuntu, living customary laws and lore must aid as frames of reference and inform comparative law in Africa.

In chapter 21, Harris observes that one of the most controversial topics in international law is the right to self-determination. He argues that the extent to which international law in practice recognises this right has long elicited contentious disputations in this field. Proponents of self-determination have used the notion of remedial secession as a pillar of their argument, whereas opponents of self-determination, in particular African states, have embraced the international-law concept of *uti possidetis* to assert their right to territorial sovereignty. The author proceeds to argue that, although it is acknowledged that there are dozens of political entities (eg secessionist movements) that are seeking independence from a mother state, for the purposes of this chapter special emphasis will be placed on the separatist movements in Namibia, Canada and Spain. The secessionist movements in the Third World countries have manifested themselves in a variety of ways. Harris makes specific reference to the Namibian secessionist movement: a secessionist movement calling itself the Caprivi Liberation Army attacked government installations at Katima Mulilo, the capital of the then Caprivi strip, now renamed Zambezi region. Harris also studied the Quebec secessionist movement in Canada. He has advanced various arguments for and against the right to self-determination in relation to the both Caprivi and the Quebec issues.

In chapter 22, Nakuta starts by alluding to the commonly stated view that Namibia is said to be one of the most unequal societies in the world. He then quickly emphasises that Namibia is burdened with the triple challenges of poverty, unemployment and inequality. For him, the scourge of housing poverty in the form of housing informality has, in particular, reached alarming proportions in the country. This begs the question: Could a bona-fide public-spirited member of the general public wishing to challenge the abhorrent living conditions of informal settlements institute legal proceedings to challenge the inadequacies of government actions and/or omissions in this regard? Such a person, in all probability, would be characterised as an interfering busybody, the author contends. A group of women residing under such abhorrent conditions who are wishing to institute a legal challenge to demand better service would most likely suffer the same fate. Neither of these potential litigants has the necessary *locus standi* to institute such legal proceedings. That, needless to say, is in accordance with the Namibian legal position governing *locus standi*. He notes that the situation would be totally different if these hypothetical cases were to be instituted, say, in India, Kenya, South Africa or Zimbabwe. This is so because these jurisdictions reformed and liberalised the traditional common-law rules on *locus standi* to which their legal systems were previously hackled. Namibia lags behind in this regard. In this chapter, Nakuta strongly advocates change in this area of law as a way of facilitating, attaining and advancing social justice for the underprivileged.

1.10 CONCLUSION

This book aims to provide legal professionals with the information they need to become familiar with the opportunities, difficulties and issues associated with comparative law in Namibia and elsewhere. No book in Namibia currently discusses the current arguments and methodological advancements in contemporary comparative law; this book responds to that need in undergraduate education and is intended to serve as a springboard for additional reading and debate among postgraduates. Furthermore, comparative law has frequently been criticised for being theoretically deficient, Eurocentric and focused on black-letter law and private law. The aim of this book is to introduce students to both classic and fresh material in addition to topical and contentious themes in comparative law and comparative legal studies.

As the editors, we chose certain issues that are pertinent to the current comparative legal debate. Traditional comparative-law themes have been treated, as have emergent discussions on the subject. This book contains publications by notable legal academics such as Professor Walter Kamba. It begins with a broad introduction to comparative law and comparative legal studies, followed by a critical overview with a thorough signalling system that binds the book together, before moving on to modern and emerging topics of comparative law. This approach will, we hope, enable readers to discuss relevant contemporary debates and issues such as convergence or non-convergence, law in context (culture), cultural distinctiveness, globalism versus localism, systems in transition, the use of comparative law by judges and the role of comparative law in law-reform activities and harmonisation, public-law comparisons in both constitutional and administrative law, and human rights.

REFERENCES

Adams, M & Bomhoff, J (eds) *Practice and Theory in Comparative Law* (Cambridge: Cambridge University Press, 2012).

Ballell, TRH 'Legal challenges of artificial intelligence: Modelling the disruptive features of emerging technologies and assessing their possible legal impact' (2019) 24(2) *Uniform Law Review* 302–311.

Banakar, R & Travers, M (eds) *Theory and Method in Socio-Legal Research* (Hart Publishing, 2005).

Banks, C & Baker, J *Systems of Law: Common Law, Civil Law, Socialist Law, Islamic Law, Indigenous Law* (SAGE Publications, Inc, 2016), https://doi.org/10.4135/9781071801277.

Basedow, J 'Comparative law and its clients' (2014) 62(4) *The American Journal of Comparative Law* 821–857.

Bellantuono, G 'Introduction: Comparative law and interdisciplinary bridges' (2023) 12(1) *Comparative Law Review* 6–23.

Berger, MT 'The end of the "Third World"?' (1994) 15(2) *Third World Quarterly* 257–275.

Bhat, PI 'Comparative method of legal research: Nature, process and potentiality' (2015) 57(2) *Journal of the Indian Law Institute* 147–173.

Brand, O 'Conceptual comparisons: Towards a coherent methodology of comparative legal studies' (2007) 32 *Brooklyn Journal of International Law* 407–466.

Browne, C 'Postmodernism, ideology and rationality' (2010) 251 *Revue Internationale de Philosophie* 79–99.

Colin, H 'Common trajectories, variable paces, divergent outcomes? Models of European capitalism under conditions of complex economic interdependence' (2004) 11 *Review of International Political Economy* 231–262.

Colin, H 'Globalization's impact on states'in J Ravenhill (ed) *Global Political Economy* 3 ed (Oxford University Press, 2011).

Dainow, J 'The civil law and the common law: Some points of comparison' (1966) 15(3) *The American Journal of Comparative Law* 419–435.

Dalhuisen, JH *Dalhuisen on International Commercial, Finance and Trade Law* 2 ed (Hart Publishing, 2004).

De Sousa Santos, B *Toward a New Legal Common Sense* 2 ed (Butterworths, 2002).

Duve, T 'Legal traditions: A dialogue between comparative law and comparative legal history' (2018) 6(1) *Comparative Legal History* 15–33.

Ellis, J 'General principles and comparative law' (2011) 22(4) *European Journal of International Law* 949–971.

Faria, JAE 'Future directions of legal harmonisation and land reform: Stormy seas or prosperous voyage?' (2009) 14(1–2) *Uniform Law Review* 5–34.

Fischer, MMJ 'Culture and cultural analysis as experimental systems' (2007) 22(1) *Cultural Anthropology* 1–65.

Fletcher, GP 'Comparative law as a subversive discipline' (1998) 46(4) *The American Journal of Comparative Law* 683–700.

Fombad, CM 'Africanisation of legal education programmes: The need for comparative African legal studies' (2014) 49(4) *Journal of Asian and African Studies* 383–398.

Fombad, CM 'Comparative research in contemporary African legal studies' (2018) 67(4) *Journal of Legal Education* 984–1004.

Friedman, LM 'The place of legal culture in the sociology of law' in M Freeman (ed) *Law and Sociology* (Oxford University Press, 2006).

Fukuyama, F 'The end of history?' (1989) 16 *The National Interest* 3–18.

Fukuyama, F 'What is governance?' CGD Working Paper 314 (Center for Global Development, 2013).

Gilson, RJ 'Globalizing corporate governance: Convergence of form or function' (2001) 49 *The American Journal of Comparative Law* 329–357.

Gutteridge, HC 'The comparative aspects of legal terminology' (1938) 12 *Tulane Law Review* 401.

Gutteridge, HC *Comparative Law* 2 ed (Cambridge University Press, 1949; John Wiley & Sons, 1974).

Hagenmeier, C, Shumba, T & Mireku, O 'The admission and enrolment of foreign legal practitioners in South Africa under the Legal Practice Act: International trade law and constitutional perspectives' (2017) 19 *Potchefstroom Electronic Law Journal* 1–27.

Hansen, MH 'The mixed constitution versus the separation of powers: Monarchical and aristocratic aspects of modern democracy' (2010) 31(3) *History of Political Thought* 509–531.

Head, JW 'Justinian's *Corpus juris civilis* in comparative perspective: Illuminating key differences between the civil, common, and Chinese legal traditions' (2013) 21(2) *Mediterranean Studies* 91–121.

Heineman, BW Jr, Lee, WF & Wilkins, DB *Lawyers as Professionals and as Citizens: Key Roles and Responsibilities in the 21st Century* (Center on the Legal Profession at Havard Law School, nd), https://www.belfercenter.org/sites/default/files/files/publication/Heinemen_Lawyers%20as%20Professionals.pdf, accessed 16 June 2023.

Himonga, C, Taylor, M & Pope A 'Reflections on judicial views of ubuntu' (2013) 16(5) *Potchefstroom Electronic Law Journal* 1–612.

Hirschl, R *Comparative Matters: The Renaissance of Comparative Constitutional Law* (Oxford University Press, 2014).

Huntington, SP *The Clash of Civilisation and the Remaking of World Order* (Simon & Schuster, 2012).

Husa, J 'Classification of legal families today. Is it mine for a memorial hymn?' (2004) 56(1) *Revue International de Droit Compare* 11–38.

Husa, J 'Review article of E Örücü, *The Enigma of Comparative Law*: Variations on a theme for the twenty-first century' (2005) 9.3 *Electronic Journal of Comparative Law* 1.

Jacobson, S 'Law and nationalism in nineteenth century Europe: The case of Catalonia in comparative perspective' (2002) 20(2) *Law and History Review* 307–347.

Kamba, WJ 'Comparative law: A theoretical framework' (1974) 23(3) *The International and Comparative Law Quarterly* 485–519.

Law, C *The Common Law and Civil Law Traditions* (2017), https://www.law.berkeley.edu/wpcontent/uploads/2017/11/CommonLawCivilLawTraditions.pdf, accessed 19 June 2023.

Lawson, CM 'The family affinities of common-law and civil-law legal systems' (1982) 6 *Hastings International and Comparative Law Review* 85–131.

Leckey, R 'Review of comparative law' (2017) 26(1) *Social & Legal Studies* 3–24.

Lee, D 'Hobbes and the civil law: The use of Roman law in Hobbes's civil science' in D Dyzenhaus & T Poole (eds) *Hobbes and the Law* (Cambridge University Press, 2012) 210–235.

Legal Assistance Centre *What is International Law and Why does It matter to Namibia?* (nd), http://www.lac.org.na/news/probono/Probono_54INTERNATIONAL_LAW.pdf, accessed 16 June 2023.

Legrand, P 'European legal systems are not converging' (1996) 45 *International and Comparative Law Quarterly* 52.

Legrand, P & Munday, R (eds) *Comparative Legal Studies: Traditions and Transitions* (Cambridge University Press, 2003).

Maitland, FW 'Equity also, the forms of action at common law: Two courses of lectures' in AH Chaytor & WJ Whittaker (eds) (Cambridge University Press, 1910).

Marrani, D 'An essay on ideology and legal education in micro jurisdictions: The example of Jersey' (2022) 14 *Journal Civil Law Studies* 60–89.

Michaels, R 'The functional method of comparative law' in *The Oxford Handbook of Comparative Law* (Oxford University Press, 2006) 339–382.

Monateri, PG (ed) *Methods of Comparative Law* (Edward Elgar, 2012).

Ndeunyema, N 'The Namibian Constitution, international law and the courts: A critique' (2020) 9(2) *Global Journal of Comparative Law* 271–296.

Ndulo, M 'African customary law, customs, and women's rights' (2011) 18(1) *Indiana Journal of Global Legal Studies article* 5.

Nowrot, K 'Legal consequences of globalization: The status of non-governmental organizations under international law' (1999) 6(2) *Indiana Journal of Global Legal Studies* 579–645.

Oderkerk, M 'The need for a methodological framework for comparative legal research: Sense and nonsense of "methodological pluralism" in comparative law' (2015) 79(3) *RabelsZeitschrift Für Ausländisches Und InternationalesPrivatrecht/The Rabel Journal of Comparative and International Private Law* 589–623.

Örücü, E *The Enigma of Comparative Law: Variations on a Theme for the Twenty-First Century* (Martinus Nijhoff, 2004).

Örücü, E *The Enigma of Comparative Law: Variations on a Theme for the Twenty-first Century* (Springer, 2013).

Palmer, VV 'From Lerotholi to Lando: Some examples of comparative law methodology' (2005) 53(1) *The American Journal of Comparative Law* 261–290.

Peters, A 'The refinement of international law: From fragmentation to regime interaction and politicization' (2017) 15(3) *International Journal of Constitutional Law* 671–704.

Peters, A & Schwenke, H 'Comparative law beyond post-modernism' (2000) 49(4) *The International and Comparative Law Quarterly* 800–834.
Philomen, P *Approaches to Proto-Indo-European Relative Clauses: Early Greek Relative Clauses* (Oxford Academic, 2015).
Prentice, RA 'Regulatory competition in securities law: A dream (that should be) deferred' (2005) 66(6) *Ohio State Law Journal* 1155–1230.
Quane, H 'Legal pluralism and international human rights law: Inherently incompatible, mutually reinforcing or something in between?' (2013) 33(4) *Oxford Journal of Legal Studies* 675–702.
Redfield, R 'Maine's ancient law in the light of primitive societies' (1950) 3(4) *The Western Political Quarterly* 574–589.
Reid, CJ Jr 'The seventeenth-century revolution in the English land law' (1995) 43 *Cleveland State Law Review* 221.
Reid, GM 'Carolus Linnaeus (1707–1778): His life, philosophy and science and its relationship to modern biology and medicine' (2009) 58(1) *Taxon* 18–31.
Reitz, JC 'How to do comparative law' (1998) 46(4) *The American Journal of Comparative Law* 617–636.
Rodrigues, R 'Legal and human rights issues of AI: Gaps, challenges and vulnerabilities' (2020) 4 *Journal of Responsible Technology* 100005.
Salaymeh, L & Michaels, R 'Decolonial comparative law: A conceptual beginning' (2022) 86 *Max Planck-Institute* 167.
Sales, P 'Algorithms, artificial intelligence, and the law' (2021) 105(1) *Judicature* 22–35.
Seims, M *Comparative Law* 2 ed (Cambridge University Press, 2018).
Seims, M 'Foreign-trained legal scholars in the UK: "irritants" or "change agents"?' (2021) 41(3) *Legal Studies* 1–17.
Siems, M *Comparative Law* 3 ed (Cambridge University Press, 2022).
Singh, A & Zammit, A 'Labour standards and the "race to the bottom": Rethinking globalization and workers' rights from developmental and solidaristic perspectives' (2004) 20(1) *Oxford Review of Economic Policy* 85–104.
Stephan, PB 'Privatizing international law' (2011) 97(7) *Virginia Law Review* 1573–1664.
Swenson, G 'Legal pluralism in theory and practice' (2018) 20(3) *International Studies Review* 438–462.
Tetley, W *Mixed Jurisdictions: Common Law v Civil Law (Codified and Uncodified)* (2000), https://digitalcommons.law.lsu.edu/cgi/viewcontent.cgi?article=5822&context=lalrev, accessed 18 June 2023.
Thomson, W 'Electrical units of measurement' (1883) 1(73) *Popular Lectures and Addresses.*
Twining, W 'Social science and diffusion of law' (2005) 32(2) *Journal of Law and Society* 203–240.
Urinboyev, R & Eraliev, S 'Russian and Turkish migration regimes in a comparative perspective' in *The Political Economy of Non-Western Migration Regimes. International Political Economy Series* (Palgrave Macmillan, 2022), https://doi.org/10.1007/978-3-030-99256-9_2.

Uwe, K & Hammel, A (eds) 'Aims of comparative law' (2019) *Comparative Law* (Oxford Academic online, 17 April 2019), https://doi.org/10.1093/oso/9780198791355.003.0002, accessed 16 June 2023.

Vanderlinden, J 'Religious laws as systems of law – a comparatist's view' in *A Huxley Religion, Law and Tradition: Comparative Studies in Religious Law* (Routledge, 2002).

Vargas Weil, E 'Map and territory in comparative law and economics' (2022) 119(1) *Global Journal of Comparative Law* 1–35.

Wallerstein, I *The Modern World System I: Capitalist Agriculture and the Origins of the European World-Economy in the Sixteenth Century* (Academic Press, 1974).

Warikandwa, TV & Amoo, SK 'African law in comparative law: A case of undermining African jurisprudence and promoting a new world order agenda?' in A Nhemachena, TV Warikandwa & SK Amoo (eds) *Social and Legal Theory in the Age of Decoloniality: (Re-) Envisioning Pan-African Jurisprudence in the 21st Century* (Langaa, 2018) 299–326.

Warikandwa, TV & Osode, P 'Forging institutional cooperation to protect core labour standards in trade: Are a world trade organisation and an international labour organisation joint dispute settlement system practical?' (2004) 47(3) *Comparative Law and International Law Journal of Southern Africa* 490–508.

Warikandwa, TV & Osode, P 'Human rights, core labour standards and the search for a legal basis for a trade-labour linkage in the multilateral trade regime of the World Trade Organisation' (2014) 18 *Law, Democracy & Development* 240–263.

Webber, F 'The Pinochet case: The struggle for the realization of human rights' (1999) 26 *Journal of Law and Society* 523.

Yadong, L & Tung, RL 'International expansion of emerging market enterprises: A springboard perspective' (2007) 38(4) *Journal of International Business Studies* 481–498.

Zweigert, K & Kötz, H *An Introduction to Comparative Law* 3 ed (trans T Weir) (Clarendon Press, 1998).

CASES

Digashu & Another v GRN & Others; Seiler-Lilles & Another v GRN & Others (SA 6/2022; SA 7/2022) [2023] NASC 14 (16 May 2023)

Immigration Selection Board v Frank 2001 NR 107 (SC)

Pretoria City Council v Levinson 1949 (3) SA 305 (A)

Van Straten v Bekker (6056 of 2014) [2016] NAHCMD 243 (25 August 2016)

LEGISLATION

Magna Carta of 1215

United States Bill of Rights of 1791

Universal Declaration of Human Rights of 1948

2

Comparative law: a theoretical framework

Walter J Kamba*

2.1 INTRODUCTION

The years since the end of the Second World War have witnessed a dramatic resurgence of interest and activity in comparative law. A cursory reading of the calendars and prospectuses of most universities that offer law degrees in the United Kingdom and in many other countries reveals that comparative law is now widely recognised as an important part of legal education. Apart from the universities various institutes or organisations exist that are devoted mainly or partly to comparative legal research. These universities and organisations sponsor an increasing number of conferences and colloquia and, between them, publish an impressive list of periodicals which are chiefly concerned with comparative law or which from time to time include articles of particular interest to legal comparatists.

Never before has comparative legal study and research attracted the attention and energies of so many eminent lawyers, from both the profession and the universities. The spate of books and articles on particular comparative topics published during the past three decades bears testimony to this development. There is no doubt that the days are over when comparative law represented an academic pastime good only to add a scholarly touch to footnotes in learned articles.[1]

Yet, in spite of this greatly increased and increasing interest, comparative law still lacks a clearly formulated and widely accepted theoretical framework within which

---

*First published as 'Comparative law: A theoretical framework' (1974) 23 *International & Comparative Law Quarterly* 485; reprinted with permission.

[1] See, for instance, J Hazard 'Comparative law in legal education' (1951) 18(2) *University of Chicago Law Review* 264–279.

specific comparative legal studies and research may be undertaken in a meaningful and effective manner – a framework which would also be valuable to the legal practitioner for recognising and handling legal problems involving foreign law.

This chapter is written in the hope that it may contribute something to stimulating discussion which may lead to the formulation of a useful theoretical framework. The problems may be posed by asking four questions:

(1) What does the term 'comparative law' mean?
(2) Why does or should one engage in comparative legal study or research? (ie, the functions of comparative law).
(3) What is it that the legal comparatist compares? (ie, the subject-matter of comparative law).
(4) How should meaningful and effective comparison be carried out? (ie, the process of comparison).

The answers to these questions would in effect provide a framework for specific studies.

2.2 MEANING OF COMPARATIVE LAW

What is comparative law? At the outset, one is faced with a difficulty which stems from the use of the term 'comparative law'. It suggests a distinct branch of national law such as family law, criminal law, contract and the like – which comparative law is not. The ambiguity has contributed to much of the controversy and misunderstanding that have plagued comparative legal studies and research for a long time. One consequence has been, as McDougal remarks, 'a literature that is voluminous, obsessively repetitious and sterile ....'[2] The method of comparison is an integral part of thinking and knowing. Consequently, it is employed, in varying degrees, in all areas of human endeavour. As Hall so aptly put it: 'To be sapiens is to be a comparatist.'[3] Throughout history the comparative technique has contributed to most breakthroughs and advances in all the natural and social sciences. Comparative law signifies the systematic application of the comparative technique to the field of law. It means the study of, and research into, law by the systematic comparison of two or more legal systems or of parts, branches or aspects of two or more legal systems.

[2] MS McDougal 'The comparative study of law for policy purposes: Value clarification as an instrument of democratic world order' (1952) 61 *Yale Law Journal* 29.
[3] J Hall *Comparative Law and Social Theory* (Louisiana State University Press, 1963) 9.

As has been intimated previously, comparative law does not constitute a distinct branch of national law, that is to say, a body of law comprising normative prescriptions for regulating human conduct and relationships. There are no rules or principles of comparative law. This is what Kahn-Freund meant when he said:

> The trouble is that the subject he (ie, a professor of comparative law) professes has by common consent the somewhat unusual characteristic that it does not exist.[4]

Nor does the systematic use of the comparative method result in legal norms which can be designated as comparative law. Neither does such comparison result in a common or unified type of knowledge which can be described as comparative law. But, as will be shown below, the knowledge and information gained by comparing legal systems or their components may aid the legislator or judge in fashioning rules or principles of positive law.

Convenience and historical accident seem to account for the choice and continued use of the somewhat misleading name 'comparative law'. Other names which would more accurately designate the subject have been suggested: 'the comparison of laws', 'the comparative study of law or laws', 'comparative legal study and research.'[5] Although the adoption of any of these expressions would help to eliminate one of the sources of misunderstanding and controversy, none has so far succeeded in displacing the term 'comparative law'. The term, as Gutteridge observed, 'has become so firmly established that it must be accepted, even if it is misleading ....'[6] However, in recent years, there has been an increasing use of the expressions 'comparative study of law' and 'comparative legal study and research'. These phrases and 'comparative law'are used interchangeably in this chapter.

It would seem that today the definition of comparative law given above would meet with the general approval of most comparative lawyers and scholars. But some distorting notions, the relics of past controversy, persist and their discussion will be necessary. In the past, particularly before the publication of Gutteridge's classic, *Comparative Law*, in 1946, many writers sought to define or rename comparative law by reference to what they considered to be its proper object or objects. Even the exponents of the view that comparative law is a type or body of legal knowledge – an autonomous branch of

[4] O Kahn-Freund 'Comparative law as an academic subject' (1966) 82 *Law Quarterly Review* 40, 41; H Gutteridge *Comparative Law* 2 ed (Cambridge University Press, 1949) 2 is to the same effect.

[5] See Gutteridge (note 4) ch 1 for a discussion and criticism of some of the names that have been suggested.

[6] Gutteridge (note 4) 1. This observation is supported in substantially the same words by R David & J Brierley *Major Legal Systems in the World Today: An Introduction to the Comparative Study of Law* (Stevens & Sons Ltd, 1968) 2.

legal science in particular and social science in general – supported, and still support, their claims by reference to the functions of comparative law.

This view was dominant at the First International Congress of Comparative Law held in Paris in 1900. Salleilles, one of the leading participants at the congress, maintained that comparative law is a 'science' whose object is the discovery of concepts and principles common to all 'civilised' systems of law, that is to say, universal concepts and principles which constitute what he called '*droit idéalrelatif*. Lambert, another eminent comparative lawyer and reporter of the proceedings of the congress, urged, after distinguishing between comparative law as a legal technique and as a legal science, that as a legal science it had a purely scientific object: 'the discovery ... of the causes which underlie the origin, development and extinction of legal institutions, or, in other words, comparative legal history.'[7] The identification of comparative law with the 'scientific method' displayed at the congress reflects the dominant influence in the formative stages of comparative law as a branch of legal scholarship. Hall points out that the minutes of the congress:

> contain illuminating evidence of the theoretical foundations of the new discipline and of the intellectual background of these comparatists. It is plain that they were under the influence of Comte's sociology and the progress of biology, especially the theory of evolution.[8]

Among those associated with the view that comparative law is a 'science' are such eminent legal comparatists as Levy-Ullman, Kohler, Arminjon, Nolde;Wolff, Rabel and Brutau on the Continent, and Yntema, Rheinstein and Hall in the United States. Rheinstein is perhaps the most ardent contemporary exponent of this view. He argues that comparative law belongs to the realm of the exact sciences 'when its cultivator tries to observe, describe, classify and investigate in their relations among themselves and to other phenomena, the phenomena law'.[9] He goes on to say:

> Comparative law in that sense is the observational and exactitude-seeking science of law in general ... it endeavours to collect, observe, analyse, and classify them and, like other sciences in the narrow sense of the word, it searches for typical collocations, coincidences, and sequences, or, in other words, for 'laws' – ... laws of the kind of Newton's laws of gravitation or

[7] Gutteridge (note 4) 5.
[8] Hall (note 3) 16.
[9] M Rheinstein 'Teaching tools in comparative law: A book survey' (1952) 1(2) *The American Journal of Comparative Law* 95, 98.

> Gresham's law in economics … laws … in which the word is understood in modern natural science ….[10]

Rheinstein here clearly treats comparative law as a 'scientific method'. He states that in his academic teaching of comparative law he includes comparative law in the sense of the sociology of law.[11]

Gutteridge cogently demonstrated the futility of defining comparative law by reference to its functions. Comparative law, as defined above, embraces any legal study or research by the systematic use of the comparative technique and this includes study and research aimed at the discovery of 'universal' concepts and principles or aimed at the discovery, formulation or verification of 'natural laws' regarding legal phenomena. But comparative legal study and research need not entail an exclusive commitment to such aims. As will be shown in this chapter, such functions are only some of several objects of comparative law. To define all comparative legal study and research as a "science" in this sense would be to confine it to such and similar objects to the exclusion of many other perfectly legitimate and widely accepted functions, as, for example, the promotion of legislation and law reform or the harmonisation or unification of laws.

It should be emphasised that comparative law is the systematic application of comparison to law. Casual reference to, say, German law in a course on the English law of contract is not comparative law. It is part of the objective of this chapter to determine what 'the systematic application of the comparative technique to law' entails.

2.3 FUNCTIONS OF COMPARATIVE LAW

One of the main factors that impeded progress in comparative legal studies was the absence of a systematic and comprehensive treatment and appreciation of the functions of comparative law. As long as comparative law was regarded as 'nothing more than an amusing puzzle'; as long as its study was undertaken primarily because it offered a 'chance to satisfy idle curiosity', it was unlikely to attract the attention of many lawyers and scholars or to make much headway as a discipline in legal studies curricula.

By 1942 Schmitthoff was able to declare: 'No lawyer would embark on a comparative legal study without intending that his endeavours should be utilised either by him or by others.'[12] The clarification of its functions is therefore necessary

---

[10] Rheinstein (note 9) 98–99.
[11] Rheinstein (note 9) 99.
[12] M Schmitthoff 'The science of comparative law' (1939) 7(1) *The Cambridge Law Journal* 94–99.

for an appreciation of its value and importance. Moreover, the main purpose for which a particular project of comparative study or research is undertaken will, to a large extent, dictate the choice of legal systems or topics to compare and the method of comparison.

Many discussions on the functions of comparative law have taken place. To Maine, generally regarded as the founder of comparative law, '[t]he chief function of comparative jurisprudence is to facilitate legislation and the practical improvement of the law.'[13] Maine's view of the chief function of the subject influenced the expositions of most legal comparatists after him. The first serious attempts to formulate the aims of comparative law made at the 1900 Paris International Congress can be seen to have foreshadowed this general tendency. As already indicated, legal comparatists, in their various attempts to define or rename comparative laws, emphasised what appeared to them to be its appropriate or only function or functions. It was Gutteridge who effectively made the important point that comparative law serves a wide variety of purposes: '[I]f the comparative process,' he said, 'is to meet with success, it is eminently desirable, if not essential, that its employment should not be hampered by confining it to specified categories ....'[14]

Recently the point was well made by a distinguished Professor of Comparative Law: 'Comparative law is not in bondage to, or even in the service of any one particular purpose, not even that of legislation, for which it is extremely useful.'[15] It is therefore important to recognise that there are several closely related academic and practical aims which may be served by the systematic application of the comparative technique to legal study and research. The existence of multiple objects also means that a comparative lawyer enjoys considerable freedom in deciding which of these purposes to pursue in any particular study.

For convenience' sake, these functions are considered here under six general headings – headings which should not be regarded as exhaustive or in any way watertight compartments:

(1) Academic studies
(2) Legislation and law reform
(3) Judicial process
(4) Unification and harmonisation
(5) International law
(6) International understanding.

[13] HS Maine *Village-Communities in the East and West. Six Lectures Delivered at Oxford* (J Murray, 1871; republished by Trieste Publishing, 2017) 4.
[14] Gutteridge (note 4) 26.
[15] CJ Hamson *The Law: Its Study and Comparison* (Cambridge University Press, 1955a) 2.

2.3.1 Academic studies

Two main aspects are involved: one relates to the *teaching and study of law* and the other to *legal research.*

(a) Teaching and study of law

In this respect the role of comparative law depends very much on our conception of the objective of legal education. A large proportion of students who read law at universities and similar institutions will enter the legal profession as barristers, solicitors, law teachers and, later, if they are able and fortunate, as judges; or they will pursue careers in which a legal training is necessary or valuable. As a result of enormous technological advances and rapid industrialisation during the past century or so, societies all over the world have, to varying degrees, undergone rapid and profound socio-economic changes – changes which have generated new and complex social and economic problems whose solution in turn has resulted in new and complex forms of legal control. The law – both legislative and judicial – has also become more intricate and requires more specialisation. Apart from having to respond to new needs, the law has in recent years increasingly become a vehicle for promoting and guiding social and economic change. In these circumstances it is not surprising that the job of the modern lawyer has also become complex. Legal education must fulfil at least the following three functions:

> Firstly, it must cultivate the attributes and skills which are needed by lawyers. These include: the ability to reason methodically, the capacity of independent thought and a questioning and critical attitude to almost everything that is presented to him as true, false, good, bad, right or wrong. Secondly, it must provide the student with a sound knowledge and proper understanding of the principles and techniques of national law. Thirdly, it must provide the student with a broad-based education. Law is about people, their conduct and relations in society. Its practice, administration, and improvement, therefore, call for a wide and deep knowledge of human nature and an understanding of modern society and life.

Comparative law is especially suited to promoting these objectives. When one is confined to the study of one's own law within one's own country and therefore within one's own cultural environment, there is a strong tendency to accept without questioning the various aspects (norms, concepts and institutions) of one's own legal system. One is inclined to think that the solutions in one's own legal order are the only possible alternatives. This leads to an idealisation of one's own legal institutions and to treating them as inherent in the general nature of law. In the words of Lepaulle:

> Where one is immersed in his own law, in his own country unable to see things from without, he has a psychologically unavoidable tendency to

> consider as natural, as necessary, as given by God things which are simply due to historical accident or temporary social situations.[16]

Not to travel outside the borders of one's own law therefore tends to foster the kind of legal isolation and parochialism which David and Brierley castigate in these terms: 'Judicial nationalism is provincialism and irreconcilable with a truly scientific spirit; it impoverishes and indeed is dangerous to the development and even application of national law.'[17]

A further unfortunate tendency which may result from looking at one's own legal order from within is that of treating the law as a self-contained system of legal norms in isolation of the social and economic context in which it operates. In fact, although the scene is fortunately changing, this accords with the orthodox method of teaching and studying law in many countries of Western Europe and North America, under which the underlying socio-cultural assumptions need not be, and as a general rule are not, articulated. They are taken for granted even when the reasons for making them have ceased to exist. This way of teaching and studying law creates an environment in which legal education becomes introverted and tends to produce mere technicians. As David and Brierly put it: 'The withdrawal by jurists into the exclusive study of their own law means that they may become mere technicians inept to guide, as is their mission, its development.'[18] Indeed, comparative law liberates one from the narrow confines of the individual systems. It is one of the most effective instruments for gaining a better knowledge and a deeper understanding of one's own legal system. '[T]he work of comparing laws and institutions is very necessary, for the only way to perceive any object clearly is to compare it with something else.'[19] Lepaulle is of the same opinion, admitting that 'I never completely understood the French law before coming to the US and studying another system.'[20] Comparative law makes the student aware of the fact that the institutions, the laws and the methods of their own legal system are not the only possible ones in the world; that there are diverse ways in which different legal systems respond to similar types of social and economic problem.

The discovery of other legal possibilities not only stimulates a student's curiosity and imagination, but also brings into question the solutions of their national law.

[16] P Lepaulle 'The function of comparative law with a critique of sociological jurisprudence' (1922) 7 *Harvard Law Review* 838–858.

[17] David & Brierley (note 6) 8.

[18] Ibid.

[19] W Howe *Course in Comparative Jurisprudence, Synopsis: Second Year Class, 1899–1900, School of Comparative Jurisprudence and Diplomacy, Columbian University* (Palala Press, 2016) 2–3; quoted by WJ Kamba 'Research in comparative law: Some theoretical considerations' in R Abraham (ed) *Essays in Jurisprudence in Honor of RoscoePound* (Bobbs-Merrill, 1962) 511–513.

[20] Lepaulle (note 16) 858.

The student is compelled to question the soundness of the solutions, norms and many other aspects of their own law, to enquire into the whys and wherefores of the institutions. They are prompted to question and investigate the inarticulate assumptions on which the institutions of their own law rest. All this must inevitably lead to reflection, to the development of a critical mind and to new insights into their own legal system.

In addition, comparative law will impress upon the student the fact that a legal system is closely connected to the social and economic environment in which it operates. Comparison, as a popular pastime, may be content with merely identifying differences and similarities between the things compared; but comparative law, being systematic, goes further and seeks to explain the differences and similarities. The reasons or causes of such divergencies and resemblances are often non-legal; they are often to be found in the socio-economic milieu. In other words, comparative law serves to emphasise the interdependence between law and other social phenomena. The line of enquiry that it impels one must increase one's understanding of the law, sharpen one's intellectual faculties and broaden one's outlook. It also enables one to evaluate one's own legal system. In the words of Professor Hamson:

> The dispassionate external, critical or appreciative study of a system of law, at which the comparative method aims, does enable us, lawyers and laymen alike, to form some estimate of the relative value of the various parts or principles of our law in its function as a social institution in our society.[21]

And again,

> It is a good deal easier to have a dispassionate and clear view of our own system of law, of its advantages as much as of its disadvantages, if we begin to see it in the contrasts which it presents to another system; if we look at it in the tell-tale mirror of that other system which may reject as strange or even barbarous our most established and unquestioned principles.[22]

Comparative law teaches one the value of modesty: it makes one aware of the fact that there is much to learn from the experiences of other legal systems. It therefore promotes the cross-fertilisation of ideas and experience:

> Whoever seeks rational solutions of perplexing social problems – remarks Schlesinger –sooner or later will recognise that there is much to be gained,

[21] CJ Hamson*The English Trial and Comparative Law* (Cambridge University Press, 1955b) 6.

[22] Hamson (note 21) 7–8.

> not only by learning from the success and failures of other systems, but also by a broader perspective which a comparative approach provides.[23]

Just as comparative law promotes greater insight into one's own legal system, it also contributes to the better understanding of the foreign system or system of law embraced in the study. This, as will be shown here, has important practical value in the day-to-day application of the law.

(b) Legal research

The preceding discussion was concerned with the role of comparative law in the teaching and study of law. But legal education is more than simply the transmission of existing legal knowledge. It also involves research, on the part of scholars, that is to say, 'the constant refinement and extension of our knowledge of law ....'[24] In fact, the whole process of legal education is incomplete without legal research. In this area comparative law has been closely associated, and sometimes identified, with jurisprudence or aspects of it. All schools of jurisprudence – the historical, the sociological, the philosophical, the analytical, etc – rely on comparative legal research as part of their particular endeavours. It is impossible to see how jurisprudence can exist without comparative law.[25]

Global systematic legal comparison is essential to arriving at an accurate definition of law as a social phenomenon and to understanding the nature of law and its function in society generally. Comparative law is indispensable to the legal theorist or legal philosopher:

(i) for the formulation of general theories of law: generalisation must proceed by way of bringing together a number of particular instances of law,ie, legal systems.
(ii) for the testing of these general theories, for instance, how universal is the Western idea of law – with its close association with specialised agencies for its making, interpretation, application, and enforcement? How far do the traits of Western legal systems represent the characteristics of legal orders in all societies? The answers to these questions can only be given satisfactorily by comparative legal research.

Comparative legal research is also a *sine qua non* for the legal scholar – be they a legal historian, legal sociologist or social scientist – seeking to discover and

---

[23] RB Schlesinger 'The role of the "basic course" in the teaching of foreign and comparative law' (1971) 19(4) *The American Journal of Comparative Law* 616, 618.
[24] HE Yntema 'Comparative legal research: Some remarks on looking out of the cave' (1956) 54(7) *Michigan Law Review* 899, 901.
[25] G Paton *A Textbook of Jurisprudence* (Oxford University Press, 1972) 41.

formulate scientific 'laws' of legal evolution and development or 'laws' about the correlation between the law and other social phenomena, that is, the construction of generalisations modelled after those of the natural sciences. This is what Maine attempted to do in his two classics.[26] He sought to determine the general process of legal evolution by comparing different legal systems and institutions. A variant of this type of comparative law is Lambert's *Comparative Legal History*, which has already been referred to and which aims at 'the discovery by means of a process of comparison of the causes which underlie the origin, development and extinction of legal institutions'. As indicated previously, comparative legal research in this sphere is identified with the 'scientific method': it is regarded as performing the same function that comparison performs in the natural sciences. In fact, Yntema confines legal research to the scientific study of law, which, he states:

> involves two things: the formulation of more or less general propositions about the subject matter under scrutiny and their verification by observation, the ultimate ends being increased accuracy and economy in the representation of experience. The principal techniques employed in this process of the formulation and verification of hypotheses to ascertain whether they are true, are controlled experimentation in which the possible variables are previously fixed, or comparison of relevant historical events, whether in time or in place or more typically both, serving to cancel out variables.[27]

Yntema then proceeds to equate legal research to comparative law: 'In this sense Comparative law is another name for legal science, an integral part of the more comprehensive universe of social or human science.'[28] Reference has already been made to the views of some of the contemporary comparative legal scholars – Rheinstein, Hall and Brutau – who have championed this function of comparative law. There is no doubt that it is an important objective. The error, as pointed out earlier, which some of these distinguished legal scholars have fallen into committing is to regard this as the sole aim of comparative law.

Mention should be made of another jurisprudential purpose of comparative legal research – a purpose mainly espoused by the analytical jurisprudents: namely, the discovery of elements, concepts, principles, institutions – common to all or certain (for example 'mature') systems of law. This was the subject-matter of Austin's 'General Jurisprudence'. It was emphasised by Salleilles at the Paris Conference; he regarded it as necessary for the construction of an international common law.

[26] Maine (note 13) and HJS Maine *Ancient Law* (Creates Pace Independent Publishing Platform, [1861] 2017) 1–237.

[27] Yntema (note 24) 902.

[28] Yntema (note 24) 903.

2.3.2 Legislation and law reform

Comparative law fulfils one of its most important practical assignments when it is employed as an aid to the legislative process and to law reform by legislation. Some comparatists have regarded this as the principal function of comparative law. Although Maine's primary contribution to comparative legal scholarship was not in regard to this object, he nonetheless declared: 'The chief function of comparative jurisprudence is to facilitate legislation and the practical improvement of the law.'[29] It was to emphasise this objective that the French and English societies were named respectively the 'Société Française de Legislation Comparée' (1869) and the Society of Comparative Legislation (1895). In fact, one of the major factors that have facilitated the general recognition of comparative law especially after the Second World War has been its increasing use in relation to legislation and law reform. Only evidence demonstrating its practical value could dispel the legal practitioner's distrust and sometimes their antagonism towards what was considered a theoretical and purely 'academic' exercise.

Legislation and law reform are closely bound up because the former has become the main instrument of creating and changing in addition to improving the law in modern states. (The limited amount of law-making and law reform which occurs through the judicial process is referred to later.) There are at least three main problems which render the use of comparative law highly desirable and beneficial in this area:

(a) In creating new rules and solutions or modifying or abolishing existing ones

Through the legislative process, new rules and solutions are devised to deal with new or existing problems or old rules or solutions are modified or abolished. Where existing rules or solutions are abolished, it may have been intended to do away with legal regulation altogether. The experience of other systems of law would be, and has in the past been shown to be, valuable not only in suggesting a foreign legal institution or solution as a model or guide, but also in showing what solution to avoid. As observed by Tallon:

> Assuredly, to resort to a foreign model is not an innovation … Its aim is not to find a foreign institution which could be easily copied, but to acquire ideas from a careful survey of similar foreign institutions and to make a reasonable transportation of those which may be retained, according to local conditions.[30]

[29] Maine (note 13) 4.

[30] D Tallon 'Comparative law: Expanding horizons' (1968) 10(3) *Journal of Society Public Teachers of Law, New Series* 265–266.

The extent to which foreign law may be used as a model ranges from the study and occasional adoption of foreign legal institutions and ideas, at the one extreme, to the wholesale reception of foreign legal institutions, at the other. Many countries of the 'Third World' provide one of the most striking examples in modern times of the use of foreign legal experience. In grappling with the problems of modernising their systems of law to meet the needs of a modern industrial state, they have relied heavily on foreign legal material and experience. They have adopted and adapted, to varying degrees, aspects of Western or Socialist laws. In undertakings of this nature there is always a danger that foreign legal institutions and ideas may be adopted without sufficient adjustment to local circumstances. Where this has happened, it has often been with disastrous effects. Comparative law has an invaluable contribution to make by preventing the uncritical copying of foreign law.

(b) The second problem area is in regard to the technique of drafting or formulating legislation

The second problem area which calls for the employment of comparative legal study and research in legislation and law reform is in *regard to the technique of drafting or formulating legislation*:

> [A]ny intelligent group of draftsmen, states Morrow, charged with a task of any importance, will consider similar legislation in other states, and perhaps in England, and will not confine their efforts necessarily to a restatement of what they conceive to be 'the law' of their jurisdiction.[31]

The application of comparative law here is more limited and tends to be confined to systems which are closely related and operate in countries which have similar socio-economic conditions – for example, legal systems of the 'older' countries of the British Commonwealth.

(c) The third problem area is concerned with the question of the practicability and enforceability of the proposed law.

Experience gained by one legal system regarding the effectiveness of some legal solutions may be most valuable to another. The US experience regarding 'prohibition' served as a strong warning to many countries that entertained the passing of similar legislation. In the United Kingdom for many years there has been hesitation to make collective agreements in industrial relations legally binding. The main problem was thought to be the difficulty of enforcing such agreements. Before the passing of the 1971 Industrial Relations Act, references

[31] C Morrow 'Comparative law in action' (1951) 3(3) *Journal of Legal Education* 403.

were made to experience in other countries – the difficulties encountered concerning enforcement, the sanctions relied upon to ensure observance, and so on. There is no doubt that arriving at a solution to such problems would be greatly eased by the use of comparative law.

In many countries, comparative legal enquiry is now accepted as an important preliminary to most legislation and law reform. In the United Kingdom, comparative legal investigations directed at this purpose have been, and to a substantial extent continue to be, conducted by individual jurists, unofficial bodies such as Justice, the UK Institute of International and Comparative Law and, at the official level, by *adhoc* Royal Commissions and (since the end of the Second World War) by the various Law Revision and Law Reform Committees. Since 1965, responsibility for most of this work has devolved upon the two Law Commissions (one for England and Wales and the other – the Scottish Law Commission – for Scotland) set up under the Law Commissions Act of 1965. The Act gave statutory recognition to the utility of comparative law by providing in s 3 that the Law Commissions are under a duty 'to obtain such information as to the legal systems of other countries as appears to the Commissioners likely to facilitate the performance of their functions'. A reading of many of the reports of the commissions shows how extensively this provision has been used.

In some Continental countries it has been, for the greater part of this century, the accepted practice to precede important legislation with a comparative survey of pertinent legislation in other countries. In France, the stamp of official recognition to the value of comparative law was first accorded as far back as 1876, when a committee attached to the French Ministry of Justice was created whose main purpose was to inform judges about foreign law. In Germany, the Government of the Federal German Republic relies on a number of well-equipped institutes – such as the Max-Planck Institutes – for comparative legal studies and research and for advice on matters relating to legislation and law reform.

In the United States, at the national level the American Law Institute established in 1923 undertakes a great deal of comparative legal studies and research aimed at law reform and general restatement of the law. The institute's purpose, as set out in its constitution, is

> to promote the clarification and simplification of the law and its better adaption to social needs, to secure the better administration of justice, and to encourage and carry on scholarly and scientific legal work.

At the states' level leading examples of agencies which make extensive use of comparative law for legislative and law reform purposes are the Louisiana Law Institute and the New York Revision Commission. The former was created by the Louisiana Legislature in 1938 as an 'official, advisory law revision commission, law reform agency and legal research agency of the State of Louisiana'. Its main purposes were stated to be:

> to promote and encourage the clarification and simplification of the law of Louisiana and its better adaption to present social needs; to secure the better administration of justice and to carry on scholarly legal research and scientific legal work.

With the world becoming more and more interdependent comparative legal activity in this field will continue to increase.

2.3.3 Judicial process

Comparative law has an important part to play in national judicial process. Courts are increasingly confronted with various types of problem which can be dealt with more efficiently by invoking the aid of comparative legal study and research.

(a) Cases of first impression

No system of law is so complete as to be without any gaps. In systems of the common law tradition lacunae occur in cases which are not plainly covered by legislation or binding judicial precedents. In systems of the civil-law tradition gaps are said to exist when there are no code provisions directly in point. It is the function of the courts to fill up gaps and in doing so comparative legal studies can be of great assistance. Acquaintance with the law and practice of foreign courts may not only suggest possible and preferable solutions, but also indicate possible but undesirable options. It may be said that at this point the judicial function converges with the legislative function, and extends to the court's important and implicit, though limited, power to mould and adapt the law to meet changing conditions, that is, the power to effect reforms by the judicial process. This so that the points made in the preceding pages apply *mutatis mutandis* to judicial law-making.

(b) In the elucidation in national law of concepts and principles which have a foreign origin

Many systems of law have to varying degrees imported or have had imposed upon them principles, concepts and institutions from other legal systems. The 'hybrid' or 'mixed' systems of Scotland, South Africa, Louisiana and Quebec offer fascinating examples of an admixture of civil- and common-law elements. Many countries of the Third World – for example, sub-Saharan Africa – provide a striking and even more fascinating mixture of elements of various Western systems and indigenous customary systems of law. Comparative lawis an invaluable tool for the elucidation, understanding and intelligent application in domestic courts of the institutions which originated in other systems of law. Schlesinger states:

> [T]he problem presents itself retrospectively to the lawyer or judge, who in applying existing law discovers that the pertinent rule is an imported one, and who thus may be compelled to trace its foreign antecedants.[32]

(c) In the application of foreign law in national courts under the conflict of laws
With the ever-expanding international trade and travel in a rapidly shrinking world, an ever-increasing number of transactions which cut across national boundaries are entered into. As a result, national courts are, to an extent greater than before, involved in the settling of disputes which contain elements of foreign law. In such cases, the court is aided by the internal rules of conflict of laws under which it has to determine, first, whether it is competent to deal with the dispute, that is, whether it has jurisdiction; and, second, if it is competent, what system of law governs such a dispute, that is, the choice of law. Under the choice of law rules a national court may be directed to apply foreign law or laws. Comparative law is invaluable in dealing with the choice of law problem and, where this is the case, in the application of foreign law.

In order to invoke the appropriate choice of law rule the court may have to characterise a rule or concept of foreign law. For instance, it may have to determine whether a rule of foreign law relates to the capacity to marry or to the formalities of marriage; or whether a rule is concerned with the procedural or substantive law. This process requires not simply an acquaintance with but an understanding of the foreign law involved. Even if one does not have a good working knowledge of the foreign system, comparative law would assist in indicating how to set about enquiring into such law. A comparative lawyer would know that it would be folly to dash to the nearest library and simply look up the relevant provision of, say, the French Civil Code for the solution. They would also know that it would be misleading to consider a rule of any legal system in the abstract and that the particular written provision of the French Civil Code is not all the law on the point.

Comparative law is essential where, for instance, the English conflict of law rule points to a foreign system as being the appropriate law to govern the matter in dispute. The court has to ascertain the nature and content of the foreign law and then apply it. Under English law and most common-law jurisdictions the relevant foreign law is treated as a matter of fact and, like other facts, must be proved by evidence – expert evidence, that is, the evidence of persons with a practical knowledge of the legal system in question. Comparative law will help judges and practitioners to ask proper questions of the expert and to understand and apply the

[32] S Kimball 'Schlesinger: Comparative law: Cases-text-materials' (1959) 58(1) *Michigan Law Review* 10.

foreign law. It is not suggested that the judge or practitioner themself be himself be an expert in foreign law. In this regard, Schlesinger points out:

> No lawyer, not even one who has devoted his whole life to comparative legal studies will truly master all the law of all countries. What distinguishes the 'Comparatist' is that his technique enables him intelligently to deal with a (practical or theoretical) legal problem arising in terms of a 'foreign' legal system, ie, of a legal system with the details of which he is not necessarily familiar.[33]

Comparative lawis also indispensable to the practitioner who is generally engaged in the negotiation and conclusion of transnational transactions. In order to communicate with their opposite numbers, in order to advise their clients well, the practitioner must not only have a knowledge of foreign law but must also understand it in relation to their own:

> It will never be true that many American practitioners will be really skilled in French law, or if I venture to say so, that very many French jurists will be at home in an American Courtroom. It is not necessary that this [state of affairs should change] ... When the occasion arises, however ... it is possible and desirable that the lawyer from each jurisdiction shall have that modicum of understanding and of familiarity with concept and language which will make it possible for him really to grasp an opinion of local counsel.[34]

2.3.4 Unification and harmonisation of laws

Comparative legal studies and research have a great contribution to make to the unification or harmonisation of laws. Unification signifies the process by which two or more different legal provisions or systems are supplanted by a single provision or system: it creates an identity of legal provisions or systems. In contrast, harmonisation is designed to effect an approximation or co-ordination of different legal provisions or systems by eliminating major differences and creating minimum requirements or standards. What has given rise to the problem of unification or harmonisation is, of course, the existence of a large number of diverse legal systems in the world. Each independent state has its own individual system of law and, quite frequently, several systems co-exist in the same state, whether such state is constituted as a federal or a unitary state. There are three levels at which the

---

[33] R Schlesinger *Comparative Law* (Foundation Press, 1959) 19.

[34] PC Jessup 'Foreword' in M Aglion *Dictionnaire Juridique Anglais-Francais [English-French Legal Dictionary]* (Librairie Dalloz, 1947) 14, quoted by Schlesinger (1959) 24n1.

unification or harmonisation of laws may occur: the international or worldwide level, the regional level and the national level.

(a) International or worldwide level

At the 1900 Paris International Congress of Comparative Law, Lambert urged that the practical function of comparative law is to provide material which would form the basis of a general unification of those national systems of law which have attained the same degree of development or 'civilisation' and their replacement by an international common law. The underlying assumption was the belief in the existence of basic elements – principles, concepts and institutions – common to all 'civilised' systems of law and that these could be ascertained by the use of comparative law. The idea of a worldwide law exerted a great deal of influence on the development of comparative legal studies and research and on the various movements for unification which flourished in Europe in the post-First World War years. But research and experience have demonstrated that it is a 'pious hope' which is neither attainable nor desirable under existing world political and social conditions. It is now readily conceded that unification at the international level is feasible and desirable only in more limited spheres of law such as: commercial law, maritime law, conflict of laws, and in new areas such as space law, broadcasting law and atomic law.

Harmonisation has better prospects because, while it serves to eliminate or minimise major extant legal obstacles, it allows for a certain amount of variation in matters of detail. It is therefore not surprising that since the beginning of this century it has been steadily coming to the fore.

(b) Regional level

Unification or harmonisation stands a greater chance of success at the regional level. States situated in the same geographical area may be highly conscious of their regional affinity because of their cultural homogeneity and similar historical background – as is the case with the Scandinavian countries. Alternatively, the states may be organised in a regional community for the pursuit of some common purpose or purposes – as is the case with European Economic Community or the European Union. Realising such regional consciousness or common purpose or purposes makes a regional legal order necessary in various respects and the need to unify or harmonise some aspects of the legal systems of the Member States. The need for unification or harmonisation is rendered more pressing by the close interrelations which develop among the regional states: because of a greater circulation of goods and services, and a freer movement of people, many transactions occur which involve regional law and the laws of the Member States.

A large measure of success at the regional level has been marked in the Scandinavian countries. About this Professor Malmström has said: '[I]t may be declared that no-where in the world have efforts for the unification of law, made on a regional scale, been so successful as in Scandinavia.'[35] The United States also bears some of the features of a regional community of states. The 50 member states enjoy a high degree of autonomy and there are 50 state legal systems plus the federal systems. But, being a federal union, not only are there cultural ties, but the constitutional bonds are much stronger and the common objectives have a much greater unifying effect than in the Scandinavian countries. Consequently, the need to unify or harmonise their laws is much more pressing. Canada is another example akin to the United States.

(c) National level

At the national level, the unifying or harmonising is confined to the diverse laws found in the unitary state. For example, the United Kingdom, in which five systems of law co-exist: the legal systems of England, Scotland, Northern Ireland, the Channel Islands and the Isle of Man. The states of sub-Saharan Africa present one of the most striking examples in modern times of internal or national legal diversity and efforts at unification and harmonisation. In these territories, legal dualism or pluralism has been a dominant characteristic since the colonial era. Two, and sometimes three, different types of law or legal tradition operate simultaneously in the same country. On the one hand, you have systems of indigenous customary law and, on the other, the imported Western law which may be an offshoot of the common-law or civil-law tradition. Added to this, in most of the West African and East African countries there exists yet another legal tradition – Islamic law. The new governments are now grappling with the problems of (1) adapting the indigenous customary law to the needs of the emerging industrial states and (2) forging a single system out of the different legal traditions. Quite often they have to be content with harmonisation, which some governments regard as only a temporary measure.

In all cases of unification or harmonisation, comparative law is an indispensable pre-requisite. A thorough understanding of the various systems sought to be unified or harmonised is essential. Comparative legal studies and research are necessary not only for the actual unification or harmonisation, but also for the purpose of determining whether it is feasible, desirable or useful. The creation of a

[35] M von Würtemberg 'Die gemeinsame nordische Gesetzgebung' (1936) 10 *Zeitschrift für ausländisches und internationales Privatrecht* 705–723; see also B Malmström 'Die Zusammenarbeit der nordischen Staaten auf dem Gebiet der Gesetzgebung. Ergebnisse und Erfahrungen' in R Zweigert (ed) *Zusammenarbeit* (Mohr Siebeck, 1962) 18–32; R David 'The international unification of private law' in R David (ed) *International Encyclopedia of Comparative Law* (Mohr Siebeck, 1971) 178–194.

uniform or harmonised law is not the end of the matter. To achieve its purpose, it is necessary to secure uniformity, as far as possible, of interpretation and application in the several jurisdictions adopting the law. For this, comparative law is necessary and, in fact, becomes self-perpetuating. This is particularly so at the international and regional levels.

2.3.5 International law

One of the important tasks of comparative law lies in the sphere of international law. Comparative law is useful not only as an aid to the ascertainment, but also to the creation, formulation and application of principles of international law. Article 38:1 of the Statute of the International Court of Justice (ICJ) provides that the International Court, whose function is to decide in accordance with international law such disputes as are submitted to it, must apply:

> (a) International conventions, whether general or particular, establishing rules expressly recognised by the contesting states;
> (b) ...
> (c) The general principles of law recognised by civilised nations;
> (d) ...

In regard to clause *(c)* Schlesinger has remarked:

> The phrase '*general principles of law recognised by civilised nations*' refers to principles which find expression in the *municipal laws* of various nations. These principles, therefore, can be ascertained only by the comparative method.[36]

Regarding clause *(a)*, international conventions and treaties at play in the international sphere, determine the role that legislation fulfils in national law. They have become an important means of creating new and of modifying or abolishing old principles of international law. Comparative law is essential to performing all these functions. It facilitates communication among the lawyers and parties involved in the negotiation, preparation and drafting of the conventions or treaties. To this must be added the fact that national courts are increasingly being called upon to interpret and apply international law. If this is to be done in an orderly and uniform fashion, the aid of comparative legal studies and research must be summoned.

---

[36] U Mattei *Schlesinger's Comparative Law: Cases, Text, Materials* (Foundation Press, 2009) 25.

2.3.6 International understanding

A more modest, but nonetheless valuable, function of comparative law is its assistance in reducing international tensions and promoting international understanding and peaceful relations. In his opening paragraph, Hall states:

> The differences among human beings often dissolve in the discovery of their basic similarities and, in any case, they become intelligible when viewed in the context of a known pattern. Limited as we are, we begin with self-knowledge and self-love, and when we discover ourselves in ever-widening dimensions of common experience, friendship, and affection increase. This is the underlying emotional basis of comparative study in law and social science ....[37]

Law is a critical facet of any society. Its study is an important, if not indispensable, key to the understanding of society and human nature. Comparative law being transnational, it is therefore an important means of understanding societies generally, of understanding the essential nature of man and the intimate and enduring bonds that unite mankind 'in the constant endeavour to maintain and advance the cause of justice'.[38]

This role of comparative law was recognised by the preparatory committee which met at the UNESCO Conference in March 1949 to form an International Committee for Comparative Law. In its final declaration it proclaimed:

> We are in agreement not only that the legal profession throughout the world owes a duty to the peoples from which it springs to unite in an effort to overcome such of the tensions and understandings dividing the world community as lie within its special spheres of competence.[39]

Other distinguished comparative legal scholars have expressed views which are in similar vein. Papale, for instance, states:

> The lawman who is called upon to solve our international problems must have knowledge of the political philosophy and of the legal systems of foreign nations. Such knowledge is vital to the maintenance of friendly relations with foreign countries and to the removal of tension areas.[40]

---

[37] Hall (note 3) 3.

[38] HE Yntema 'Research in inter-American law at the University of Michigan' (1944) 43(3) *Michigan Law Review* 549–558.

[39] For the text of the declaration see R Schlesinger *Comparative Law* (Columbia University Press, 1950) 30.

[40] A Papale 'Why comparative law' (1951) 3 *Journal of Legal Education* 384.

The same author again states:

> It is only lawmen who can fully appreciate the legal traditions and institutions of other nations and thereby fully understand their legal systems. Who then can more adequately represent our nation in the deliberations that will take place?[41]

Clearly, comparative law promotes understanding of each other's outlook, each other's point of view and respect for differences.

2.4 SUBJECT-MATTER OF COMPARATIVE LAW

In terms of the definition, the subject-matter of comparative law is *two or more legal systems*; *or parts, branches or aspects of two or more legal systems*, that is, if one may adopt Rheinstein's rather convenient terms, *macro-comparison* or *micro-comparison*. Macro-comparison is concerned with two or more entire legal systems, whereas micro-comparison is limited to aspects or topics of two or more legal systems. Studies which concentrate on a single foreign system of law or some aspects of it have sometimes been referred to as being an exercise in comparative law, but this extension of the meaning of comparative law is unjustified and should be discarded. Surely comparison implies the existence of two or more entities? An entity cannot be compared to itself; two or more systems of law must therefore be involved. This is the essence of comparison and comparative law. A suggestion by some legal scholars that the study of a foreign system may involve implicit comparison with one's own legal system does not take the matter any further. Systematic comparison should be confined to explicit comparison and for that at least two or more systems of law are essential. Nor should the study of two or more legal systems in the same book without any thread connecting them be brought within the purview of comparative law.

A legal system in the wide sense – and this is the sense which it bears in the definition of comparative law given – 'is not made of rules alone but is also characterised by its institutions, practices, standards, methods of research and even the mental habit of lawyers, judges, legislators and administrators'.[42] In its narrow sense, a legal system is often equated to legal norms or systems of legal norms. These two shades of meaning must be borne in mind in reading the literature on comparative law. As mentioned previously, there are an enormous number of legal systems in the world: each independent state has its own system of law and often

[41] Papale (note 40) 385.

[42] G Razi 'Around the world's legal system' (1960) 6(1) *Howard Law Journal* 11.

two or more legal systems may exist side by side in the same state. Consequently, the range of legal systems available for systematic comparison is without effective limit. Macro-comparison may range from two legal systems to the systems of the entire world. For example, the actual studies undertaken, from a work such as Buckland and McNair's *Roman Law and Common Law* to David and Brierly's *Major Legal Systems in the World Today*.

The range of topics for micro-comparison is infinite. The important questions that arise are these: What legal systems and what topics should be selected for comparative study or research? How should such systems and topics be selected? The immediate and obvious reply to both questions is that the selection depends largely on the comparatist's primary purpose in undertaking the study or research.

2.4.1 Choice of legal systems for both macro- and micro-comparison

When Pound wrote at the end of the 20th century, he limited the subject-matter of comparative law to what he then considered mature legal systems, meaning the civil-law and common-law systems, that is, systems within the Western cultural tradition.[43]In fact, for many years comparative lawyers focused on these systems and tended to treat non-Western systems of law as being outside their sphere of expertise and as more the concern of ethnologists and cultural anthropologists. This was the case particularly when those non-Western systems were at a different level of development. This attitude seems to have led some comparatists to maintain that the legal systems to be compared must be comparable in the sense that they have attained the same stage of legal development. According to Gutteridge,

> it is quite feasible, for instance, to compare the law of the ancient races of the East with modern European law, but, as Pollock observes, such comparison 'can lead to nothing but ludicrous if not dangerous misunderstanding'.[44]

He continues:

> Like must be compared with like; the concepts, rules or institutions under comparison must relate to the same stage of legal, political and economic development.[45]

Gutteridge was endorsing a view which Schmitthoff had expressed a few years earlier in these words: 'The strict observance of comparability implies … that

[43] R Pound 'The study of common law' (1896) 36(4) *Nebraska Legal News* 1; R Pound *The Spirit of Common Law* (Marshall Jones, 1921) 1–216.

[44] Gutteridge (note 4) 73.

[45] Ibid.

the comparison must extend to the same evolutionary stage of the different legal systems which are under comparison.'[46] This view, which has – either expressly or implicitly – been supported by some contemporary legal comparatists, is unnecessarily restrictive. Surely the question whether one selects (for comparison) systems of law which are or are not at the same stage of development is to a large extent determined by the principal aim or aims of the specific comparative study or research? For a teacher of English law at an English university seeking to use comparative law to illuminate their students' understanding of the English law of contract it would be imprudent and of little value to opt to compare a non-Western system of law in which the concept of status dominates and the idea of contract is underdeveloped. On the other hand, a law teacher in an African university who invokes comparative law as an aid to increasing their students' comprehension of the modern African law of matrimonial property, which is in many instances a fusion of elements of Western law and non-Western indigenous customary law, would find it essential to compare systems which are at different stages of development. For example, they could choose to compare English law and, say, Luo customary law. To take another example: the legal scholar seeking to determine the function of law in society generally or attempting to test the universality of the Western idea of law must surely compare systems of 'all times and climes'.[47] Even Pound in his later writings recognised this and modified his original rigid position when he conceded: 'We are concerned with undeveloped systems only because and to the extent that they help us understand and treat scientifically developed systems ....'[48] One more example will suffice: for African countries engaged in programmes of law reform and unification, comparative studies of Western systems and indigenous customary systems of law are inevitable. But where it is sought to reform, say, English commercial law or aspects of it, it would not be fruitful to compare English law with a system in which commercial law does not exist or is underdeveloped.

These examples are sufficient to indicate that the functions which a comparatist emphasises may render the selection of certain systems advantageous and preferable or even inescapable, whether or not such systems have reached the same degree of development. During the past two decades or so there has been a steady increase in comparative studies and research which embrace Western and non-Western systems of law. However, it must be conceded that for the most part comparative legal studies and research have been, and will continue to be, primarily concerned with systems of law which are at similar stages of development. The two 'families' of legal systems which dominate the comparative law scene are those of the common-law and the civil-law traditions. In recent years, a third major group – the Socialist

[46] Schmitthoff (note 12) 96.
[47] Rheinstein (note 9) 95, 98.
[48] R Pound 'Comparative law in space and time' (1955) 4 *The American Journal of Comparative Law* 70.

systems of law – has steadily been coming into the comparative law fold. It seems obvious that making an intelligent selection of legal systems demands on the part of the comparatist a good conspectus or panoramic view of the legal systems of the world. They must be grounded in the bases or criteria for their classification and must have a good knowledge of the characteristics of the major groups or families of systems. The classification of legal systems therefore constitutes an important aspect of comparative law, but space does not allow its discussion in this chapter.

(a) Choice of topics for micro-comparison

The range of topics for micro-comparison is infinitely greater than that system of law. Again, the main purpose for undertaking the comparative study or research to a large extent dictates the choice of topics to compare. The topics may be concerned with:

(a) the various characteristics of a legal system: the structure, the sources of law, judicial systems and the judiciary, the legal profession, and so on;
(b) the various branches of national law;
(c) institutions or concepts;
(d) the historical development of legal systems.

It is essential that the topics selected be comparable in the sense that they relate to equivalent institutions, concepts, and so on; for example, marriage in English law and its equivalent in, say, French law. It is not always easy to determine equivalence. Where the comparison is of closely related systems of law –for example, common-law systems such as the systems of most members of the British Commonwealth – there is little difficulty in identifying comparable or equivalent elements and for the most part the counterparts will even bear the same names. The greater the disparity between legal systems, the greater the difficulty of recognising comparable elements. The difficulty is therefore more acute where systems are at different levels of development or belong to entirely different socio-cultural backgrounds. The same or similar names may mean quite different things in such systems; or the systems may use different bases for classifying their legal norms. The search for equivalents should, therefore, not be confined to institutions with similar or identical names because terminology may offer no assistance at all. In such circumstances the functional approach, which is discussed in the next section, seems particularly useful, if not indispensable.

Implicit in the view that the purpose of comparison is the main determinant in the selection of legal systems and topics is the fact that there are other factors which to a lesser or greater degree influence such choice. Often, a very strong and important element of personal preference is involved. This is particularly so where emphasis is placed on the use of comparative law in academic studies. Because the range of choice of systems and topics is without effective limit, since comparative law does not possess the recognised traditions of most fields of legal study regarding subject-matter, a comparative lawyer, in contrast to their colleagues in other fields of law, enjoys what Kahn-Freund has referred to as one of the most dangerous gifts that the gods can bestow: the freedom to decide for themself the fields (ie, subject-matter) they wish to cultivate.[49] In fact, assertions by many comparative lawyers as to which legal systems or which topics to compare for academic purposes represent to a certain extent personal interest and preference. However, this freedom of choice is conditioned by various other factors, which include the *comparatist's past experience,* the *manageability of the subject-matter* and the *time factor,* the *student's interest,* the *accessibility of source materials,* and *language.*

That the comparatist's own knowledge and past experience will influence their choice of subject-matter would seem so obvious as to require no elaboration. In exercising their freedom, though, the comparatist would be well advised to keep their choice within manageable limits. They'may and probably should limit [their] field of research and teaching both in the geographical sense and as regards subject-matter,'[50] if this can be done without defeating the main purpose of the comparison. In the teaching of law, with more and more courses competing for inclusion in the law studies curricula and with less and less time being made available for the teaching of those that gain acceptance, the choice of what to compare must be that which can properly be accommodated in the time available. In exercising their choice, the comparative law teacher must also broadly bear in mind the possible interests of their students. They may also find their selection limited by the availability (or non-availability) of source materials and textbooks. This factor is closely associated with the question of language. The more languages the comparatist can read and write, the greater their choice. For the English-speaker the position is increasingly being eased by the availability of material written in English on Continental systems, particularly French law and to a lesser extent German, Italian and Scandinavian legal systems. Over the past two decades, a great deal of material has accumulated on Socialist systems of law.

It is worth repeating here the advice given by Kahn-Freund and Lawson that the comparative-law teacher must remain flexible – more flexible than any other academic lawyer.[51]

2.5 PROCESS OF COMPARISON

Having decided on the purpose or purposes for undertaking a specific comparative project, and having selected the legal systems and topics, the next problem is that of

---

[49] Kahn-Freund (note 4) 40–61.

[50] Kahn-Freund (note 4) 42.

[51] Ibid; F Lawson 'The field of comparative law' (1949) 61(1) *Juridical Review* 16–36.

methodology: How should one carry out the comparison in a systematic manner? The application of a proper method is generally a prerequisite for success in any area of study. In comparative law it is of paramount importance because on it will depend, first, whether the specific comparative enquiry effectively serves the function or functions which the comparatist has decided to emphasise and, second, the accuracy and the value of the results secured and the validity of the conclusions drawn.

The process of comparison is perhaps the most difficult aspect of comparative law to clarify and there is little assistance to be derived from the extant comparative-law literature. This can partly be ascribed to a certain amount of confusion that continues to prevail in discussions on the functions and subject-matter of comparative law and the process of comparison and partly because of the virtual impossibility of devising a single comprehensive and standard technique that can be applied to all comparative studies and research. The technique employed must, for instance, necessarily vary to a considerable extent according to the degree of disparity or similarity in the socio-cultural foundations of the legal orders being compared. Therefore one technique may be well suited to what may be called *intra-cultural comparison* – that is, the comparison of legal systems rooted in similar cultural traditions and operating in similar socio-economic conditions (eg, English law and French law or, closer still, English law and Australian law). But this technique would be inappropriate for *cross-cultural* comparison –that is, the comparison of legal systems with totally different cultural and socio-economic backgrounds (eg, English or French law, on the one hand, and an African system of customary law, on the other). An important result of this is that a comparative lawyer must, to a considerable extent, rely on their individual judgment when deciding how to go about the comparison. The position is often exacerbated by the fact that many comparative lawyers do not themselves apply in practice what they recommend in theory as the appropriate technique. However, it is important to recognise that it is not possible, nor would it be prudent, to attempt to prescribe specific comparative procedures to be followed. The most that one can do is to suggest some broad pointers towards a meaningful technique or techniques.

It was stated previously that systematic comparison entails not merely ascertaining divergencies and resemblances between the legal systems compared, but also explaining such divergences and resemblances. There are, therefore, three main operations or stages involved in comparative law. The first may be called the *descriptive phase*. This may take the form of describing the norms, concepts and institutions of the systems concerned or it may consist of examining the socio-economic problems and the legal solutions provided by the systems in question. The second stage may, for the sake of convenience, be described as the *identification phase* and it is concerned with identifying or discerning differences and similarities between the systems under comparative consideration. The third stage is the *explanatory phase*, when the divergencies and the resemblances are accounted for.

These phases are not always distinctly separated from each other nor are they always dealt with in a particular order. They may all be intermingled in the same discussion. But all three are essential to any legal study which claims to be comparative law. Consequently, as pointed out above, the description of two or more legal orders or parts of such legal orders without making an effort to relate them to each other would not be comparative law. This includes the essentially tabular type of description of two or more legal orders or part(s) of such legal order without any effort to relate them to each other: such an approach would not be comparative law. This approach would include the essentially tabular type of description in which the author may collect or catalogue the norms or institutions of two or more systems of law and merely juxtapose them, leaving it to the reader to do what they like with the material provided. Gutteridge's 'Descriptive Comparative Law' would cover this; its aim, as he states it, is that of furnishing information.[52] Such studies should not be regarded as comparative law because the *identification* and the *explanatory* phases are omitted completely. Similarly, comparison which stops at the second phase – that of pointing out differences and similarities – would be incomplete, because it misses out the third, important phase. The ultimate test for evaluating the technique or techniques employed is encapsulated in these questions: Does the technique of comparison employed adequately or effectively fulfil the object or objects which the comparatist has decided on? Does it, for example, promote the better understanding of one's own law, the formulation of reliable theories of law and/or the promotion of law reform or unification? Can the results obtained be safely depended on as being accurate?

If the answer to any of these questions is in the negative, this would be an indication that the technique is inadequate and unsystematic. The position is otherwise if the replies are in the affirmative. The proper execution of the three phases of comparison is greatly influenced by three main factors: the first may, for convenience' sake, be called the comparatist's *Jurisprudential Outlook*; the second is the *Social Context* of the legal systems under comparison, and the third is the *Legal Context* of the legal topics under study in the case of micro-comparison.

2.5.1 Jurisprudential outlook

This is the comparatist's general attitude to law. 'An individual's jurisprudential outlook,' remarks Schlesinger, 'is bound to have a strong influence on the direction and intensity of his interest in Comparative law.'[53] For instance, an adherent of the sociologically or historically oriented view of law will naturally be more

[52] Gutteridge (note 4) 8.

[53] R Schlesinger 'The past and future of comparative law' (1995) 43(3) *The American Journal of Comparative Law* 39 or Mattei (note 36) 49.

favourably disposed towards a sociological or historical approach in comparative law. Concentration on textual material may reflect yet another jurisprudential orientation. Comparatists seldom articulate their jurisprudential perspective; this is often implied and has to be gathered from the particular comparative legal study or research and sometimes from the comparatist's other writings.

It should be added that one's practical legal experience is an important contributor to one's general attitude to law. Contact with or living under two or more legal systems may serve to emphasise that you cannot understand the law unless you penetrate the 'social forces and changes that promote or stunt the growth of the law'.[54] Practising in two or more systems of law which are at different stages of development renders one more receptive to a concept of law which is much wider than that which almost exclusively associates law with specialised machinery for law-creation, interpretation and application, and enforcement.

2.5.2 Social context

One's jurisprudential outlook aside, it is a fact that a legal system is an integral part of a society and is closely connected with all the elements of that society's social life. The law both profoundly affects and is affected by the socio-cultural conditions that surround it. Although it may be difficult to determine the precise correlation between the law and its socio-economic environment, there is no doubt that there is a significant relationship between legal development and socio-economic changes. Diverse socio-economic and cultural conditions produce, to varying degrees, differences in legal systems. Consequently, for an understanding and an accurate description of legal systems or their aspects, for the accurate identification of differences and similarities between them and for the explanation of such differences and similarities, that is, for carrying out all three phases of comparison – the legal systems under comparative study must be viewed in the socio-cultural context in which they thrive. Comparison which concentrates on the textual or formal rules of law – statutes, decided cases, codes – to the exclusion of the socio-economic context is likely to render an incomplete and distorted picture of the systems compared. Formal rules do not tell the whole story; they represent only a fraction of the law. As McDougal points out in his criticism of comparative studies which focus on formal rules:

> Comparison cannot relevantly and usefully be confined to rules alone … because rules are not the only variables that affect decision ….[55] It is the textual type of comparative study that has been critically characterised by

[54] O Kahn-Freund 'On uses and misuses of comparative law' (1974) 37(2) *Modern Law Review* 43.
[55] McDougal, (note 2) 30.

> some comparatists as the 'glib, overtly general and painfully superficial treatment which has so often passed current as comparative law[56] "the barren dissection of verbal texts"'.[57]

Most contemporary legal comparatists avow the importance of the social context. In praise of Montesquieu's contribution to comparative law, Gutteridge wrote:

> Montesquieu, in particular, has a claim to be considered as the founder of comparative law since it was he who first realised that a rule of law should not be treated as an abstraction, but must be regarded against a background of its history and of the environment in which it is called upon to function.[58]

Gutteridge himself states:

> The laws must be examined in the light of their political, social or economic purpose, and regard must be paid to their dynamic rather than to their static or doctrinal aspects.[59]

More recently, Kahn-Freund expressed a view to the same effect:

> The comparative lawyer's investigation cannot stop at what in his own or in any other legal order happen to be the frontiers of the law. To compare law and non-law, or, if you like, positive law and positive morality in the Austinian sense may be one of his principal tasks. If he fails to do so he may see the law in a distorting mirror.[60]

The views just cited have been endorsed and emphasised by many other comparatists. The statements suggest that the social context which should be taken into account is the whole socio-cultural environment in which the systems operate and not merely segments of it. In the words of Stone:

---

[56] A von Mehren 'The judicial process in the United States and in France: A comparative study' (1952) 22(1) *Revista Juridica de la Universidad de Puerto Rico; Harvard Law Review* 532–534; W Hug 'The history of comparative law' (1931) 45 *Harvard Law Review* 534; cf P Lepaulle 'Function of comparative law' (1921) 35(2) *Harvard Law Review* 534.

[57] JH Wigmore 'More jottings on comparative legal ideas and legal institutions' (1931b) 6 *Tulane Law Review* 244–263; see also JH Wigmore 'Jottings on comparative legal ideas and institutions' (1931a) 6 *Tulane Law Review* 48.

[58] Gutteridge (note 4) 12.

[59] Gutteridge (note 4) 174.

[60] Kahn-Freund (note 54) 43.

> We must study the history, the politics, the economics, the cultural background in literature and the arts, the religions, beliefs and practices, the philosophies, if we are to reach sound conclusions as to what is and what is not common.[61]

In other words, the good if not the 'perfect' comparatist is one who is fully conversant with the socio-cultural totality of the legal systems he examines comparatively. Clearly, the standard of scholarship demanded of comparative lawyers is extremely high – one well-nigh impossible to attain. It is difficult enough to gain mastery of the socio-economic environment of one's own legal system, much less than of two or more systems. However, as Wagner points out, 'the realities of life and the limitations of legal scholars engaging in comparative research must make it clear to us that the ideal and the real are far apart.'[62] In another passage he states:

> If perfection is the only thing which counts, the conclusion could be reached that there is hardly any hope to achieve this goal; that it is appropriate not to make any comparative research unless all the stringent pre-requisites are complied with.[63]

Although comparative legal scholarship demands a vast amount of knowledge of the socio-economic and cultural conditions that relate to the systems under comparative study, in practice the extent of the social context that is articulated is largely influenced, first, by whether the comparison is intra- or cross-cultural and, second, by the main purpose of the comparison.

(a) Intra- and cross-cultural comparison

Studies by sociologists, anthropologists, historians and some legal scholars provide some useful and meaningful classifications of types of society whose characteristic features they describe and to which different systems of law may be related – the Western industrial capitalist societies of Eastern Europe, the pre-industrial or traditional societies of Africa and Asia. Systems of law within the same general socio-cultural type tend to show fewer fundamental differences than those in different and contrasting socio-cultural types. The comparative study of systems of law within the same societal type – for example, Western systems – would constitute intra-cultural comparison. In such a case the social context articulated need not include the basic elements of social organisation of the Western societies – it need not be detailed and comprehensive. It would

[61] F Stone 'End to be served by comparative law' (1950) 25(1) *Tulane Law* Review 325.

[62] G Wagner 'Tort liability and insurance: Comparative report and final conclusions' in G Wagner (ed) *Tort Law and Liability Insurance* (Springer, 2005) 309–352.

[63] Wagner (note 62) 330.

be sufficient – and this is in fact what happens in practice – for the comparative lawyer to discuss the socio-economic variables which are of immediate relevance and application to their descriptive, identification and explanatory phases. The closer the socio-cultural context, the less detail of the general social context is required. For instance, less detail of social context is necessary in a comparative study of English and Australian law, than in a comparative study of English and French or German law. Social context in intra-cultural comparative studies may therefore be interpreted to mean the immediately relevant aspects of the social and economic environment. In a study of English and French law, one of the immediately relevant social variables is the historical development of the two systems and this accounts for many of the differences in the structure, concepts and other features of the two systems.

As comparative studies move further away from the cultural common denominators, more detailed background information must be given regarding socio-economic factors. In *cross-cultural* comparative studies – that is, comparative studies of legal systems that belong to distinct societies (eg, English law and Luo customary law) – a detailed discussion of the social structure and organisation of each is essential if the comparative study is to be meaningful. One of the main distinguishing features between Western industrial societies and pre-industrial or traditional societies is that in the former there is a high degree of social differentiation and the legal institutions are substantially separable from other social phenomena. It is therefore possible to make some sense out of comparative studies which exclude the social context to a considerable degree. But because traditional societies exhibit a low degree of social differentiation and the law is embedded in, and inseparable from, what people actually do (it is part of the usages and customs of the people), a comparative study of English law and Luo customary law that does not provide detailed social context would be highly distorted and misleading. This applies generally to any other cross-cultural study – for example, a comparative study of US and Soviet law.

(b) Purposes of comparison and social context

It seems clear that where the comparatist is seeking to determine the relationship between the law and society, a great deal of the general social context must be provided. But a comparatist seeking to use comparative law for the reform of company law may be content with only that socio-economic information which is immediately pertinent to company law.

2.5.3 Legal context in micro-comparison

In addition to the jurisprudential outlook and the social context, the third factor which affects the process of comparison is the legal context. Where one is engaged in micro-comparison, the topic under comparative study must be placed in the context of the entire legal system. In the words of the Schmitthoff:

> The quality of a legal institution may differ according to the structure of the legal system of which it forms part. The same institution may hold a key position in the legal system of one country and may be of subordinate character in another system where the corresponding needs are satisfied by other legal institutions.[64]

2.6 PROCESS OF COMPARISON AND COMPARABILITY

One of the main problems relating to the technique of comparison is that of expressing legal systems, their institutions and concepts in comparable terms and categories. An aspect of this has been discussed briefly under subject-matter regarding comparable topics. An examination of the formal or textual legal norms, institutions and concepts in one system may not disclose corresponding categories in another system. This is particularly so where systems are rooted in completely different social types. In such an instance seemingly identical terms in two or more systems of law may in fact have different meanings or seemingly different terms may have the same meaning. The fact that the classification and names of legal rules and institutions is far from conclusive in determining equivalence has led to increasing emphasis being placed on the functional and problem-solving approaches in comparative law.

The essence of the functional approaches is this: What legal norms, concepts or institutions in one system perform the equivalent functions performed by certain legal norms, concepts or institutions of another system? The comparatist seeks the institutions that fulfil the same role. This approach is indispensable in cross-cultural comparison where the determination of comparability is enormously difficult. It does not render superfluous any of the other approaches which are generally used – the analytical and historical. In fact, the multi-approach in comparative law is highly desirable and likely to yield better results.

Comparative lawyers are also increasingly relying on the problem-solving approach which takes a specific problem or specific problems – be they social, economic, legal or a mixture of these – in order to discover how these problems are solved in the various legal systems and why they are solved in a particular way. The pertinent questions in such a case are these: What is the social, economic or legal problem? What is the legal solution or control of such problem in the legal systems selected for comparison?

[64] Schmitthoff (note 12) 97–98.

It seems plain from what has been said that systematic comparison consists of a combination of a number of techniques or approaches which leave considerable room for individual judgement. What is indicated here are some of the important general and minimum aspects which can and should continually be examined and refined in the light of particular comparative legal studies and research and of developments in other social science disciplines.

2.7 CONCLUSION

In this chapter, an attempt has been made to provide a theoretical framework for comparative law. This framework, together with the classification of legal systems, constitutes what Graveson has called 'the indispensable generalities of Comparative Law'.[65] A theoretical framework is a necessary guide to action and impinges upon and constitutes the foundation of all specific comparative legal studies and research. It is this framework which gives unity to what appears to be discrete particular projects of comparative law. It is this theoretical aspect around which a common tradition can be derived – and around which a stock of knowledge capable of transmission and refinement can accumulate. What distinguishes a comparative lawyer from an ordinary lawyer is that the former has had a good grounding in comparative theory, which the latter has not.

Such a theoretical framework can be both learned and taught. In fact, this is what is meant by 'teaching comparative law' and is what justifies the inclusion of a basic comparative law course in law studies curricula. There are two main viewpoints which have been espoused by comparatists in the teaching of comparative law – views which, unfortunately, have sometimes been presented as if they are in opposition to each other. The one is *(a) the comparative teaching of law*, that is, that the majority of law courses should be taught comparatively; the other is *(b) the teaching of comparative law*, that is, providing a basic course in comparative law. These are distinguished in what follows.

(a) Comparative teaching of law

There is a substantial body of opinion among law teachers and comparative lawyers that the majority of or the main courses in law should be taught comparatively and that if this were done, it would be unnecessary to provide a basic course in comparative law. It seems clear from what has been discussed in this chapter that for this to be done properly and meaningfully, the students must at least have been

[65] RH Graveson 'Philosophy and function in comparative law' (1958) 7(4) *The International and Comparative Law Quarterly* 649.

exposed to the general theory of comparative law and to the classification and general characteristics of legal systems. As Schlesinger points out:

> Even where the foreign materials are in fact discussed in a bread-and-butter course, they may mislead rather than enlighten a student who has never had the benefit of a basic introduction to Comparative Law.[66]

As things are at present, most students are never exposed to comparative-law theory. A basic course in comparative law – either *eonomine* or as part of another course such as jurisprudence – would be necessary to remedy this deficiency.

Although it may be sufficient for the student to be exposed to the theoretical aspects of comparative law, it is of vital importance that the teacher be well grounded in such aspects if their teaching is to be effective and beneficial. One of the main obstacles to the teaching of law courses comparatively is that most law teachers do not possess the necessary training in comparative law, and this is likely to remain the case for quite a long time to come. Even in faculties where there are a number of comparative lawyers, limitations of time make it very difficult to teach more than a few courses comparatively. A basic course would therefore also be necessary to provide the future law teacher with the basic equipment that would enable them to pursue comparative studies in much greater depth later.

(b) Teaching comparative law – basic course

It is suggested that a basic course in comparative law comprise two main parts:

(i) A general introduction to comparative law which serves to provide the students with the theoretical framework plus the classification and characteristics of legal systems.

(ii) A specific comparative study which may entail either macro-comparison or micro-comparison. This would provide the students with an opportunity to apply the theory they have learnt to a particular study. At the same time, it would serve the academic functions elaborated upon in this chapter.

REFERENCES

David, R 'The international unification of private law' in R David (ed) *International Encyclopedia of Comparative Law* (Springer, 1971).

David, R & Brierley, J*Major Legal Systems in the World Today: An Introduction to the Comparative Study of Law* (Stevens, 1968).

[66] Schlesinger (note 23) 616–623.

Graveson, RH 'Philosophy and function in comparative law' (1958) 7(4) *The International and Comparative Law Quarterly* 649.

Gutteridge, H *Comparative Law* 2 ed (Cambridge University Press, 1949).

Hall, J *Comparative Law and Social Theory* (Louisiana State University Press, 1963).

Hamson CJ *The English Trial and Comparative Law* (Cambridge University Press, 1955a).

Hamson, CJ *The Law: Its Study and Comparison* (Cambridge University Press, 1955b).

Hazard, J 'Comparative law in legal education' (1951) 18(2) *University of Chicago Law Review* 264.

Howe, W *Course in Comparative Jurisprudence, Synopsis: Second Year Class, 1899–1900, School of Comparative Jurisprudence and Diplomacy, Columbian University* (Palala Press, 2016) 2–3.

Hug, W 'The history of comparative law' (1931) 45(6) *Harvard Law Review* 1027–1070.

Jessup, PC 'Foreword' in *M Aglion Dictionnaire Juridique Anglais–Francais [English–French Legal Dictionary]* (Librairie Dalloz, 1947).

Kahn-Freund, O 'Comparative law as an academic subject' (1966) 82 *Law Quarterly Review* 40.

Kahn-Freund, O 'On uses and misuses of comparative law' (1974) 37(2) *Modern Law Review* 1.

Kamba, WJ 'Research in comparative law: Some theoretical considerations' in R Abraham (ed) *Essays in Jurisprudence in Honor of Roscoe Pound* (Bobbs-Merrill, 1962) 511–513.

Kimball, S 'Schlesinger: Comparative law: cases-text-materials' (1959) 58(1) *Michigan Law Review* 151.

Lawson, F 'The field of comparative law' (1949) 61(1) *Juridical Review* 16.

Lepaulle, P 'Function of comparative law' (1921) 35(2) *Harvard Law Review* 340.

Lepaulle, P 'The function of comparative law with a critique of sociological jurisprudence' (1922) 35(7) *Harvard Law Review* 838.

Maine, HJS *Village Communities in the East and West. Six Lectures Delivered at Oxford* (J Murray, 1871; republished by Trieste Publishing, 2017) 4.

Malmström, B 'Die Zusammenarbeit der nordischen Staaten auf dem Gebiet der Gesetzgebung. Ergebnisse und Erfahrungen' in R Zweigert (ed) *Zusammenarbeit* (Paul Siebeck, 1962) 18–32.

Mattei, U *Schlesinger's Comparative Law: Cases, Text, Materials* (Foundation Press/ Thomson Reuters, 2009).

McDougal, MS 'The comparative study of law for policy purposes: Value clarification as an instrument of democratic world order' (1952) 61 *Yale Law Journal* 24.

Morrow, C 'Comparative law in action' (1951) 3(3) *Journal of Legal Education* 403.

Papale, A 'Why comparative law' (1951) 3 *Journal of Legal Education* 384.

Paton, G *A Textbook of Jurisprudence* (Oxford University Press, 1972).

Pound, R 'The study of common law' (1896) 36(4) *Nebraska Legal News.*

Pound, R *The Spirit of Common Law* (Marshall Jones, 1921).

Pound, R 'Comparative law in space and time' (1955) 4 *The American Journal of Comparative Law* 70.
Razi, G 'Around the world's legal system (II)' (1960) 6(1) *Howard Law Journal* 1.
Rheinstein, M 'Teaching tools in comparative law: A book survey' (1952) 1(2) *The American Journal of Comparative Law* 95.
Schlesinger, R *Comparative Law* (Columbia University Press, 1950).
Schlesinger, R *Comparative Law* 2 ed (Foundation Press, 1959).
Schlesinger, R 'The role of the "basic course" in the teaching of foreign and comparative law' (1971) 19(4) *The American Journal of Comparative Law* 616.
Schlesinger, R 'The past and future of comparative law' (1995) 43(3) *The American journal of Comparative law* 477.
Schmitthoff, M 'The science of comparative law' (1939) 7(1) *The Cambridge Law Journal* 94.
Stone, F 'End to be served by comparative law' (1950) 25(3) *Tulane Law Review* 325–335.
Tallon, D 'Comparative law: Expanding horizons' (1968) 10(3) *Journal of Society of Public Teachers of Law, New Series* 265.
Von Mehren, A 'The judicial process in the United States and in France – a comparative study' *Revista Juridica de la Universidad de Puerto Rico* (1952) 22(1) *Harvard Law Review* 532.
Von Würtemberg, M 'Die gemeinsame nordische Gesetzgebung' (1936) 10 *Zeitschrift für ausländisches und internationales Privatrecht* 705.
Wagner, G 'Tort liability and insurance: Comparative report and final conclusions' in G Wagner (ed) *Tort Law and Liability Insurance* (Springer, 2005).
Wigmore, JH 'Jottings on comparative legal ideas and institutions' (1931a) 6 *Tulane Law Review* 48.
Wigmore, JH 'More jottings on comparative legal ideas and legal institutions' (1931b) 6(1) *Tulane Law Review* 48.
Yntema, HE 'Research in the inter-American law at the University of Michigan' (1944) 43(3) *Michigan Law Review* 549.
Yntema, HE 'Comparative legal research: Some remarks on looking out of the cave' (1956) 54(7) *Michigan Law Review* 899.
Zweigert, R (ed) *Zusammenarbeit* (Mohr Siebeck, 1962) 18–32.

3

Tracing the early origins of comparative law

George Mousourakis*

3.1 INTRODUCTION

Comparative law, as a method of legal science and as an academic discipline, is largely a product of modern Western thought. This does not mean, however, that legal comparison as a form of cognition involving the study of foreign laws had no place in earlier civilisations. From a very early period, people observed that the legal norms of different societies were not identical. These diverse norms were sometimes taken into consideration when new legal rules and institutions were being developed.[1] The rationale appears to be that the laws of states or communities that were particularly dominant or perceived as being more advanced were deliberately imitated or adopted by other states or communities, and this process was probably repeated in various parts of the world. This chapter examines the role of legal comparatism in ancient, medieval and early modern European legal thought and practice with a view to tracing some key ideas that have contributed to the rise of comparative law. Special attention is given to the development of the comparative approach to law during the Renaissance and Enlightenment eras – a period marked by the emergence of scientific rationalism and the rise of the modern nation-state and national legal systems.

---

*G Mousourakis 'Tracing the early origins of comparative law' in *Comparative Law and Legal Traditions* (Springer, 2019a), https://doi.org/10.1007/978-3-030-28281-3_3, accessed 28 August 2023. (Re-published with permission.)

[1] M Siems *Comparative Law* 2 ed (Cambridge University Press, 2018) 13.

3.2 LEGAL COMPARATISM IN CLASSICAL ANTIQUITY

3.2.1 Ancient Greece

In ancient Greece the comparison of different systems of law was a source of inspiration for both law-makers and philosophers. In the domain of legislative practice, many examples point to the frequent adoption of legal norms by one Greek city-state from another. These include the so-called 'homicide laws' of Attica, which were initiated by a number of Greek cities; the legislation of Charondas, a celebrated law-giver of Catania in Sicily, which was adopted by several Greek colonies in Sicily and southern Italy; the legislation of Solon in Athens, elements of which were incorporated into the civil law of Alexandria, and a fragment of the assembly proceedings of Antinoopolis in Egypt, which demonstrates the application in that city of the marriage laws from the city of Naucratis.

References to legal comparison can also be found in the works of philosophers. For instance, in his *Laws*, Plato (429–348 BCE) discussed the laws of several Greek and other states in formulating the basic political structure and laws of an ideal city named Magnesia.[2] Similarly, in his *Politics*, Aristotle (384–322 BCE) considered the constitutions of 158 Greek city states[3] before settling on his three preferred forms of government (monarchy, aristocracy and constitutional government or 'polity') and their corrupt versions (tyranny, oligarchy and democracy).

Although it is unclear whether the conclusions of this work were based on extensive study of factual material or were the product of largely speculative thinking informed by a more casual empirical knowledge, there is little doubt that Aristotle's general approach was empirical, rooted in observations of the ways in which people actually governed themselves. Furthermore, scholars agree that Aristotle adopted the comparative method and that what he and his students were doing should be regarded as a form of comparative constitutional law.

In this connection, reference should also be made to Theophrastus (372–287 BCE), a student of Aristotle, who composed a work containing an exposition of the laws of Athens as compared to those of other city-states. From the fragment of this work handed down to us it appears that Theophrastus' approach was in a sense quite modern, since it involved an attempt to bring to light the broad principles

---

[2] The third book of the *Laws* discusses the origins and evolution of political systems and attempts to draw lessons for the legislator from the histories of several actual states, including Athens, Sparta, Argos, Crete and Persia.

[3] As stated in his work: 'Our purpose is to consider what form of political community is best of all for those who are most able to realize their ideal life. We must therefore examine not only this but other Constitutions, both such as actually exist in well-governed states, and any theoretical forms which are held in esteem, in order to ascertain which features of them are good and useful' Aristotle *Politics* Bk 2, 1.

underpinning the various laws and then to draw attention to particular rules that conflicted with them.[4]

The notion that comparative material may provide a basis for the justification of positive law was embraced by Greek philosophers such as Plato and Aristotle in the face of the legal particularism which prevailed in the Greek world at that time. The fact that every city-state (*polis*) had a legal system of its own led some thinkers, notably the Sophists, to draw the conclusion that law is a voluntary creation of individuals depending entirely on the public opinion in each particular *polis* community. There is no question here of law being grounded in a divine natural order: all law is positive law, a product of popular opinion in a particular time and place.[5] Aristotle's view of law represents a combination of sophistical legal thinking with its concomitant voluntarism and Platonic natural law, which enabled a philosophical phenomenon: all law is law of the *polis*.[6] But the comparative study of laws reveals certain common features. The Law of the Twelve Tables (see below) indicate that the influence of the Greek civilisation on Roman culture is undeniable and has features in different legal orders. These features are not incidental; they

[4] K Zweigert & H Kötz *An Introduction to Comparative Law* 3 ed (Oxford University Press, 1998) 49.

[5] This approach drew support from the doctrine of the Sophist philosopher Protagoras that 'man is the measure of all things'. This is understood to mean that all knowledge is relative to the person seeking it. What *seems* to each person *is*, as far as he is concerned. Reality exists only in relation to one's own feelings and convictions. The Sophists pointed out that customs and standards of behaviour earlier accepted as universal and absolute, and of divine creation, were in fact local and relative. It was against this view that Plato's work was directed. What Plato objected to was the general tendency of the Sophists' thinking to make relative the very norms that should possess absolute binding force. For him, law and the laws are an object of free philosophical speculation and they can be derived only from reason and the idea of the good. Every right law is merely an approximation of the external truths – an imperfect reproduction of the idea of law and justice. From this notion (associated with Plato's famous theory of forms) the strand of natural-law thinking is derived that regards values as having an eternal existence and an eternal veracity.

[6] Greek thinkers believed that the concept of a state (*polis*) is inconceivable unless the concept of law (*nomos*) is simultaneously thought of (see, eg, Plato *Laws* I 644d). The meaning of this is that the state is identified with a particular type of legal order and is also identified by reference to its laws. This is evident in the close connection between the laws and the 'community of citizens', the '*universitas civium*', the latter being endowed with a common will expressed through the legal order. The law is connected to the state because it makes it an object of knowledge. It may be described as the mould which bestows regularity and normality on the life of a given society. In this respect, the origin of law cannot be separated from the development of the community as a whole. This implies that legal development is basically a social one. At the same time, the development of the community is eminently rational, since the community may be grasped essentially through its legal order. This account perfectly agrees with the analysis of the origin and development of the law in Plato's *Laws* III.

point to the fact that in similar circumstances it would be rational to enact laws of a particular kind.[7]

In the Hellenistic and Roman periods, the notion that juridical life was restricted to the *polis* was gradually abandoned under the influence of the Stoic philosophy. The Stoics contemplated a *cosmopolis*: an all-embracing universal community permeated by a divine rational principle (*Logos*) in which all men are equal and equally capable of achieving the perfect moral life. According to them, natural law, as founded on divine reason, is universally valid and immutable and has the force of law per se, that is, independently of human positivisation. Compliance with its rules is a prerequisite for attaining justice as the essence of law in a broad sense. In this respect, one might say that the universal recognition of a legal principle among nations (as revealed by the comparative study of laws) may be taken to constitute prima facie (although not conclusive) evidence that such principle emanates from natural law.[8]

3.2.2 Ancient Rome

A well-known example of an alleged foreign influence on the drafting of legislation from the early Roman period concerns the Law of the Twelve Tables, the oldest compilation of Roman law enacted in the middle of the 5th century BCE. Both the writings of the orator and philosopher Cicero (106–43 BCE) and those of the jurist Gaius (2nd century CE) appear to suggest that they believed the apparent legend that, before work on the law code commenced, a three-member commission was sent to Greece to learn from the laws of the famous Athenian law-giver, Solon, and those of other Greek city-states. Contemporary historians now accept that it is unlikely that a delegation was sent to Greece. This view draws support from the fact that the preserved fragments of the Law of the Twelve Tables reveal very little that can be traced directly to a Greek influence, although certain parallels with the laws of other early societies are observed.[9]

---

[7] As Aristotle elaborates in Bk 5 of the *Nichomachean Ethics*: 'There are two kinds of political justice, one natural and the other legal. The natural is that which has the same validity everywhere and does not depend upon acceptance; the legal is that which in the first place can take one form or another indifferently, but which once laid down, is decisive … [L]aws that are not natural but man-made are the same everywhere, because forms of government, namely that which is best.' Although Aristotle seems to have accepted that there is a natural and universal right or wrong, apart from any human ordinance or convention, he fell short of developing a natural-law theory.

[8] CJ Friedrich *The Philosophy of Law in Historical Perspective* (University of Chicago Press, 1963) 32. Friedrich argued that '[t]he most that can be admitted is that there is a presumption in favour of the contention that a legal institution found in diverse *civitates* is part of the law of nature'.

[9] The Law of the Twelve Tables does have some elements in common with Athenian law, but these are not of the kind that could suggest a direct influence. The relevant provisions that, according to Cicero, were extracted from the laws of Solon pertain mainly to the settling of disputes

However, the story of the laws of the tendency that prevailed among the Roman jurists was to focus exclusively on the domestic law of Rome.[10] They sought to preserve this law while also developing it by devising new ways for the practical use of its doctrine and institutions in a satisfactory manner. But they did not consider that their tasks should encompass an analysis of law from ethical, historical or other more general viewpoints; nor were they directly interested in the laws and customs of other nations. They maintained a conservative attitude and demonstrated an almost total lack of interest in legal concepts and norms originating externally or divergent from the roman legal system as they understood it. Nevertheless, comparative enquiries into the laws and customs of different peoples play a part in the formation of the so-called 'law of nations' (*ius gentium*), the body of Roman law that regulated economic relations between Roman citizens and foreigners.

From an early period, the Romans realised that certain institutions of their own domestic law (*ius civile*) also existed in the legal systems of other nations. Because contracts of sale, service and loan, for example, were recognised by many systems, it was assumed that the principles governing these were enforced in the same way everywhere. The Romans considered that those institutions which Roman law had in common with other legal systems belonged to the law of nations (*ius gentium*) in a broad sense. But this understanding of the *ius gentium* was of little practical value to the Roman lawyer, because the specific rules governing the operation of such generally recognised institutions differed from one legal system to another. When the Romans began trading with foreigners, they must have realised that their own domestic law was an impossible basis for developing trading relations. Foreigner traders, too, had little inclination to conform to the tedious formalities of the Roman *ius civile*. Some common ground had to be discovered as the basis for a common court, which might adjudicate on claims of private international law, and this common ground was found in the *ius gentium* in a narrow, practical sense. Therefore, in contrast to the *ius civile* as the law that applied exclusively to Roman citizens, the term *ius gentium*, in a narrow practical sense, came to signify that part of Roman law which governed relations between citizens and foreigners and between foreigners belonging to different states. This body of law was constructed from the edicts of the *praetor peregrinus*, the special magistrate dealing with legal disputes involving foreigners and, to a lesser extent, from the edicts of provincial governors. Attending to disputes involving people of diverse

between neighbours, the right of forming associations (*collegia*) and restrictions on displays at funerals. See Cicero *de leg* 2.23.59, 2.25.64.

[10] Like other ancient peoples, the Romans observed the personality of the laws principle by which each person lived by the law of their community. Therefore, the Roman *ius civile* (the civil law of the Roman state) was the law that applied exclusively to Roman citizens and the term *ius civitatis* denoted the legal rights to which only Roman citizens were entitled.

national backgrounds would have been difficult without employing rules based on common sense, expediency and fairness that were confirmed by general and prevalent usage among many communities. In contrast to the *ius civile*, the *ius gentium* was therefore characterised by its simplicity, adaptability and emphasis on substance rather than form. For this reason, not only foreigners, but also Roman citizens often relied on it as a means of resolving legal disputes. Moreover, elements of the *ius gentium* entered the edict of the *praetor urbanus* (the magistrate in charge of the administration of the *ius civile*) and in this way the domain of the domestic Roman law. However, it was only during the classical period of Roman law (the imperial period) that the further development of the *ius gentium* was influenced by comparative enquiries, and therefore was denationalised and turned into a form of 'universal law'. This was accompanied by a combination of comparative jurisprudence and rational speculation.[11] It was now claimed that the Roman *ius gentium* was binding on all inhabitants of the empire because it was also natural law based on natural reason. This was justified by reference to its universal validity (ie, in the Roman *Orbis terrarum*).

The second-century CE jurist, Gaius, declared that Roman law was based in part on the law of nations (*ius gentium*), which he defined as 'the law that natural reason establishes among all mankind [and] is observed by all people alike'.[12] 'Therefore,' he continues, 'the Roman people observe partly their own particular law [and] partly which is common to all peoples.'[13] Although he does not provide a detailed schema by which one can discern which legal institution belongs to the former and which to the latter category, he gives us sufficient markers so that we can have a reasonably good idea of what he regarded as domestic Roman law (*ius proprium Romanorum*) and what was *ius gentium (ius commune)*. For instance, acquiring title by delivery (*traditio*) from the owner was an institution of *ius gentium* (which he identified with *iusnaturale*), whereas acquiring title by mancipation (*mancipatio*) was an institution of domestic Roman law (*ius civile*).[14] Furthermore, the partnership (*societas*) that was contracted by simple agreement (*consensus*) among the parties was an institution of the *ius gentium*, whereas the partnership among heirs that in early times prevailed in Rome pertained only to Roman citizens.[15] One may discern

---

[11] T Mommsen *Romisches Staatsrecht* (S Herzel, 1887) 606.

[12] Gaius *Institutes* 1.1.

[13] Ibid. Consider also the *Digest of Justinian* 41.1 pr 9.3 (Gaius).

[14] Gaius (note 13) 2.65. The *mancipatio* was a highly formal procedure that was employed when ownership over certain types of property, referred to as *res mancipi*, was transferred. *Res mancipi* included land and buildings situated in Italy, slaves, and draft animals such as oxen and horses. All other objects were *res necmancipi*. The ownership of *res necmancipi* could be passed on informally by simple delivery (*tradition*).

[15] Gaius (note 13) 3.154–154a.

behind Gaius' and other jurists' remarks a comparative effort. Unfortunately, however, the process by which the comparison was carried out was not committed to writing or, if it was, it has not survived. In all probability, that process had occurred prior to Gaius' time and he merely reports some of the conclusions.

A curious comparative work, dating from later imperial age, is the *Lex Dei quam praecipitad Moysen* ('The Divine Law which the Lord commanded unto Moses'), also known as *Collatio Legum Mosaicarum et Romanarum* ('A Comparison between Moisac and Roman Laws'). The exact date of this work is unclear, but the main body of the text appears to have been compiled in the first half of the 4th century CE.[16] The work is divided into titles, each of which starts with a quotation from the first five books of the Old Testament (especially the maxims of Moses) followed by extracts from the works of the classical Roman jurists Paulus, Ulpianus, Papinianus, Modestinus and Gaius, and imperial constitutions from the Gregorian and Hermogenian codes. Ostensibly, the purpose of this work was to compare some selected Roman norms, mainly of a penal character, to related norms of Mosaic law to demonstrate that Roman law, in its basic principles, was consistent with Mosaic law and that in some sense it implemented the latter law.[17]

3.3 LEGAL COMPARITISM IN THE MIDDLE AGES

After the demise of the Roman Empire in the West, the once universal system of Roman law was replaced by a plurality of legal systems. The Germanic tribes that settled in the lands of the former Roman Empire lived according to their own laws and customs, whereas the Roman population and the clergy remained governed by

[16] The *Collatio legum mosaicarum et romanarum* was first edited in the 16th century but more materials were added later based on two manuscripts discovered in the 19th century. The standard modern edition is that of Mommsen, included in *Collectio Librorum Iurisante Iustiniani* (Weidenfeld and Nicolson, 1980) III; see also A Baviera 'Civil law – Part Three' (1968) 43(38) *Philippine Law Journal* 543–589; B Kübler & E Seckel *Iusprudentiae ante Iustinian ae Reliquias in usum Maxime Academicum Compisitas a PE Huschke* 6 ed (Harvard University Press, 1927). For commentrary consider E Volterra *Collatio Legum Mosaicarum et Romanaru, Memorie della R Accademia Nazionale dei Lincei: Classe di Scienze Moralii, Storiche e Filologiche* (Bardi, 1930) 6.3.1; G Barone-Adesi 'L'etàdella lex dei. Pubblicazioni dell'Istituto di diritto romano e deidirittidell' Oriente meditteraneo' [*Publications of the Institute of Roman Law and the Rights of the Eastern Mediterranean*] (Jovelene, 1992) 71.

[17] The author of this work remains unknown, although the attempted comparison of Roman and Mosaic law suggests that he was probably of Jewish origin. For a closer look at the role of legal comparatism in Greek and Roman antiquity consider C Donahue 'Comparative law before the Code Napoléon' in M Reimann & R Zimmermann (eds) *The Oxford Handbook of Comparative Law* 2 ed (Oxford Handbooks, 2019) 3–7.

Roman law. This entitled a return to the ancient principle of the personality of law: the law applicable to a person was determined not by the territory they happened to live in but by the people or ethnic group to which they belonged.[18] To facilitate the administration of the law in territories, some Germanic kings ordered the compilation of legal codes containing the personal Roman law that regulated the lives of many subjects. Among the most important compilations of Roman law that appeared during this period were the *Lex Romana Visigothorum* (506 CE), the *EdictumTheoderici* (late 5th century CE) and the *Lex Romana Burgundionum* (517 CE).

The co-existence of Roman and Germanic laws in the same territory gave rise to an awareness of the differences between these systems and also the opportunity for comparison. That some form of legal comparison was carried out is reflected in the influence that Roman law exercised on the various codes of Germanic law which appeared in the West during this period. Most of these codes embraced the *Codex Euricianus*, enacted in about 480 CE by Euric the Visigoth king and drafted with the help of Roman jurists; the Salic Code (*Pactus Legis Salicae*) of the Franks, composed in the early 6th century CE; the *Lex Ribuaria*, promulgated in the late 6th century for the Franks of the lower and middle Rhine region, and the *Lex Burgundionum*, issued in the early 6th century for the inhabitants of the Burgundian kingdom. Of these codes, the Visigothic and Burgundian reflect a stronger Roman influence than the Salic and Ripuarian codes. In the course of time, as the fusion of the Roman and Germanic elements of the population progressed, the division of people according to their ethnic origin tended to break down. The system of personal laws was gradually superseded by the conception of law as entwined with a particular territory; a common body of customary norms (a mixture of debased Roman and Germanic law) now governed all persons living in a particular territory. In this way, the diversity of laws no longer persisted as an intermixture of personal laws but as a variety of local customs. Nevertheless, awareness of different sources of law and occasional attempts at laying such sources side by side appear to have continued throughout the Early Middle Ages.[19]

From the early 11th century, the growth of trade, commerce and industry and the return of a measure of order to Europe precipitated a revival of interest in the

---

[18] When Justinian reincorporated Italy into the Empire (553 CE), legislation was introduced to this realm. However, its validity suggests that it was sustained for only a brief period as most of the Byzantine territories in Italy fell to the Lombards in 568 CE. After that time, Justinian's legislation applied only in those parts of Italy that remained under Byzantine control. The rest of Italy displayed a similar pattern to that of Gaul and Spain because Roman law continued to exist through the application of the personality of the laws principle.

[19] In this connection reference should be made to the so-called 'code' of the Anglo-Saxon King, Alfred (849–899 CE). See P Wormald *The Making of English Law: King Alfred to the Twelfth Century* (Blackwell, 1999) 265–285.

study of law. Although the legal revival tended at first to concentrate on the study of the systematic exposition of native Germanic (especially Lombard) law,[20] it also embraced feudal law[21] and canon law, which were already part of the legal scene in Western Europe, and aspects of pre-Justinianic Roman law. However, by the end of the 11th century, the *antique* – the jurists concerned with the study of Germanic law – were suspended by the *moderni*, whose interest lay primarily in Roman law.

From the 11th to the 13th century, the systematic analysis and interpretation of the Roman law of Justinian was the exclusive preoccupation of the jurists from the famous law school of Bologna, known as the school of the Glossators. The jurists' work of interpretation was closely aligned

> with their methods of teaching and it was executed by means of notes (*glossae*) that elucidated difficult terms of phrases in a text, and provided the necessary cross-references and reconciliations that rendered the texts usable.[22]

The missing element in the Glossators' approach was the historical dimension; they attached little importance to the facts that Justinian's codification was compiled more than five hundred years before their own time and was mainly composed of extracts derived from an even earlier date. Instead, they perceived it as being an authoritative statement of the law that was complete in itself, as demonstrated by their rational methods of interpretation. They devoted little attention to the fact that the law actually in force was very different from the system embodied in it. Indeed, the Glossators rarely mention the existence of bodies of law different from those they were expounding on. Nevertheless, their new insight into the ancient texts galvanised the development of a true science of law that had a lasting influence on the legal thinking and practice of succeeding centuries.[23]

---

[20] After the annexation of the Lombard Kingdom by the Frankish Empire during the reign of Charles the Great (742–814 CE), Lombard law continued to apply in northern Italy. At Pavia, the centre of Lombard Italy, a school of Lombard law was established probably as early as the 9th century. The study of Lombard law was based primarily upon the *Liber Papiensis*, a work composed probably in the early years of the 11th century (this compilation contained materials dating from the Edict of Rothari, the basic statement of Lombard law, published in 643 CE). Reference should also be made here to the *Lombarda or Lex Langobarda* and the *Expositio ad Librum Papiensem* that combined materials drawn from Lombard and Roman sources with special reference to the *Institutes*, the Code and the Novels of Justinian.

[21] During this period, a sourcebook of feudal law, referred to as *Libri feudorum*, was used for study in northern Italy, although it is unclear exactly where.

[22] This method was by no means new – it had been relied upon by earlier medieval scholars and was similar to that used by the jurists in the law schools of Constantinople and Beirut during the later imperial era.

[23] G Mousourakis *Roman Law, Medieval Legal Science and the Rise of the Civil Law Tradition* (Springer, 2019b) 197–249.

During the same period, the law of the church, or canon law, also became the object of systematic study. The task of the canonical collections was to amalgamate and harmonise the mass of canons contained in earlier canonical collections, and this involved eliminating contradictions and updating matters as necessary. Their ultimate aim was to develop, expand and systemise cannon law as an independent body of law and not merely as a set of rules for ecclesiastics. The work that succeeded in transforming canon law into a complete system was the *Decretum* or *Concordia discordantium canonum*, composed by Gratian (a Bolognese monk) around the middle of the 12th century. The *Decretum Gratiani*, as this work came to be known, was both a code and a treatise of canon law. It presented in a systematic way and without inconsistencies and contradictions the rules governing priesthood, ecclesiastical jurisdiction, church property, marriage, and the sacraments and services of the church. Gratian's method of arranging the materials was similar to that followed by the drafters of Justinian's *Institutes*.[24] Although it was published as an unofficial private work, Gratian's *Decretum* was soon recognised as an authoritative statement of the canon law as it stood in his era. Like the codification of Justinian, it became the object of systematic study in the universities. Students could obtain their degree in either civil law or canon law, or they could qualify as bachelors of both civil and canon law. In carrying out their work, the canonists relied heavily on Roman law, especially in areas with respect to which the basic canonical sources were deficient. As the church was held to live by Roman law, it is unsurprising that whole branches of Roman law were incorporated into the canonical system. A particularly noteworthy development of this period was the creation of a system of Romano-canonical procedure, the result of a combined effort of canonist and civilian jurists, which provided the basis of the procedural system that continues to prevail in civil-law systems today.[25]

By the end of 13th century, jurists had shifted their attention from the purely dialectical analysis of Justinian's texts to the need to develop contemporary law. This development is associated with the emergence of a new breed of jurists in Italy, the so-called Post-Glossators or Commentators. Their primary interest lay in adapting the Roman law of Justinian, as explained by the Glossators, to the new social system and the Roman law, the customary law of Germanic or feudal origin, the statute law of the Holy Roman Empire of the German nation (established in the 10th century CE) and the self-governing municipalities, and canon law. The integration of these bodies of law into a unitary system was the concern of the Commentators. The result was the creation of a system of law in which the non-Roman element was, so to speak,

---

[24] J Goering '*The Making of Gratian's Decretum*, by Anders Winroth' (2002) 37(3) *Canadian Journal of History* 512–514.

[25] RC Van Caenegem 'History of European civil procedure' in RC Van Caenegem & M Cappelletti (ed) *International Encyclopedia of Comparative Law XVI* (Mohr Siebeck Publishing, 1973) 16.

Romanised. In carrying out their work, the commentators examined the statutes and customs of diverse states, and when they found it impossible to reconcile them with their learning, they simply recognised that they were different. But the Commentators did not rest content with merely acknowledging the different existence of bodies of law; they also sought to explain why there might be such differences and, on this basis, develop a system to deal with conflicts of laws.[26]

In general, medieval (and later) jurists regarded contemporary legal particularism as an evil, one they tried to remove by adopting Roman law as a common basis of European legal science. Their method involved both *auctoritas* and *ratio*, although *ratio* here does not refer to natural reason but to Aristotelian logical inference. As true medieval men, they construed Justinian's texts in the same way as theologians construed the Bible or contemporary philosophers construed the works of Aristotle. Just as Aristotle was regarded as infallible and his statements as applicable to all circumstances, so the texts of Justinian were also regarded by the Jurists as sacred and as the repository of all wisdom.[27] The law developed by the Glossators and the Commentators, as the product of a synthesis between non-Roman elements and the glossed Roman law, achieved universal validity as *ratio scripta* and it was received in nearly all European countries; therefore, it became the 'common law' (*ius commune*) of Continental Europe. Like the Latin language and the Universal Church, the *ius commune* was an aspect of the unity of the West at a time when there were no strong centralised political administrations and no unified legal systems, but rather a perpetual contest between the competing and often overlapping jurisdictions of local, feudal, ecclesiastical, mercantile and royal authorities.[28]

3.4 PIONEERS OF COMPARATIVE LAW DURING THE RENAISSANCE AND ENLIGHTENMENT ERAS

In medieval and even later times, there was no clear distinction between the state and the legal order. Therefore, a state could accommodate the existence of several

[26] The new school, with its main centres at the universities of Pavia, Perugia, Padua and Pisa, reached its peak in the 14th century and prevailed in the 15th and 16th centuries. The most influential of the Commentators embraced Bartolus de Saxoferrato (1314–1354) and his pupil Baldus de Ubaldis (1327–1400). Bartolus' commentary on the whole of Justinian's codification was acknowledged as a work of authority and was used extensively by legal practitioners and jurists throughout Western Europe.

[27] In the realm of philosophy, this period corresponded to the full flowering of medieval scholasticism. The scholastic method, as applied to law, sought to expose the general principles of the law so as to create a comprehensive theory of law.

[28] Donahue (note 17) 3–7.

legal orders within the same territory. The federal constellations, a characteristic feature of feudalism, were not based on the idea of national interest: their role was only instrumental. In contrast, the interests of commerce and agriculture were more stable as expressing relatively permanent structural elements of society. In relation to them, national frontiers were immediately relevant. From the 16th century onwards, the feudal nobility was defeated by a central power, which also represented the interests of the growing urban middle class and the lower gentry. As a result, the idea of legislation as a means of centripetal policy gained ground. And the idea of a national social consensus – the notion that the members of a nation had common interests – became a basic assumption.

In the 16th century, the homologation of customary law in France[29] prompted jurists to employ the comparative method in the study of law. This method had already been common among the French humanists, who are also credited with the invention of the modern historical method.[30] In this connection, reference may be made to Coquille's work *Institution au droit Francois*, published in 1607. Coquille (1523–1603) studied humanities in Paris and law in Padua and Orleans and practised law in the customary courts of Nivernais, where he worked as an advocate for the local *Parlement*.[31] In his works he sought to explore the laws and customs of France in a comprehensive and comparative manner. His *Institution* begins with titles of the homologated custom of Nivernais, stating the rules of that custom relating to each title and also comparing them with relevant rules prevailing in other regions. For instance, in the title on marital property, he notes that the rule applying in Nivernais is that a married woman must obtain her husband's consent

[29] In order to reduce the confusion caused by the multiplicity of customs, King Charles VII ordered the compilation of the customs of all regions of France in his Ordinance of Montils-les-Tours in 1453. Although the direction proved largely ineffectual, it was repeated by subsequent monarchs and, as a result, most of the customary law had been committed to writing by the end of the 16th century. Although the publication of the customs removed much of the confusion caused by local differences, legal unity was certainly not achieved. In addition to the differences between northern and southern France, considerable regional diversity persisted even within each of the main territorial divisions.

[30] The chief aim of the humanist scholars was to rediscover the Roman law that existed in Roman times by applying the historical method instead of the scholastic method of the medieval Commentators. The humanists' approach to Roman law as a historical phenomenon inspired the appreciation in the jurists of the differences between Roman law and the law of their own era. By drawing attention to the historical and cultural circumstances in which law develops, the humanists prepared the ground for the eventual displacement of the Roman *ius commune* and the emergence of national systems of law.

[31] The *parlements* were regional judicial and legislative bodies in France under the Valois and Bourbon dynasties from the 15th century to the time of the French Revolution in the late 18th century. There were 12 *parlements*, the largest of them being based in Paris and the remainder in the provinces. The relevant offices could be transferred by inheritance or acquired by purchase.

in order to make a testament (a will). He then proceeds to say that the same rule applies in the territory of Burgundy, while in Rheims, Auxerre, Berry and Poitou the rule is to the contrary. Once the conflict has been identified, Coquille (like other jurists of his era) proceeds to ask: What is the 'true rule' that should be applying is such cases? His answer to this question is that the correct rule is that a testament cannot depend on the will of another person, for this is the nature of a testament. He seeks to justify this view by reference to certain passages in the Digest of Justinian. Although this is not taken to render the custom of Nivernais or Burgundy invalid, it limits the scope of the relevant rule: if the custom is abolished, then the rule has no force because the *ius commune* provides otherwise. Furthermore, a rule that departs from the *ius commune* is regarded as introducing a kind of privilege, exercisable only by those persons to whom it has been given. In other words, Coquille does not deny that customs contrary to the *ius commune* exist, but regards such customs as applicable only in those (exceptional) situations to which they clearly pertain. A similar approach was followed by the Italian jurists of the 15th century when they were faced with statutes that were contrary to the *ius commune*: such statutes were narrowly construed. Occasionally, Coquille adopts the view that customary rule is flat-out wrong, either because it goes against higher principles or because it does not correspond to social reality (this argument is usually only hinted at).

Italian Jurists of the 15th century, in contrast, hardly ever employed arguments of the latter type. But Coquille and other French jurists of this period went beyond the earlier Italian jurists in another respect: they sought to find common principles that underpinned the divergent French customs when no reference to the *ius commune* could be made. Furthermore, they used principles and methods of the *ius commune* in analysing a customary system of law that, unlike the statutory enactments of the Italian city-states, was not regarded as being founded on the *ius commune.*

During the 17th and 18th centuries, as national systems of law began to burgeon, European jurists focused their attention on the study and mastery of their own domestic law. Despite the absence of a systematic practice of comparative law, a number of scholars stressed the importance to lawyers of the need to look outside their own systems of law in order to make a true assessment of their worth. The English philosopher Bacon (1561–1626), for example, proposed the development of a system of universal justice by means of which one might assess and seek to improve the legal system of one's own country.[32] However, although he asserted that the propositions of this system should be based, at least to some extent, on a study of diverse systems of law, he set them down without buttressing them with foreign

[32] See F Bacon *De Dignitate et Augmentis Scientiarum* (1623) Bk viii, c3; F Bacon *Francisci Baconi Baronis de Verulamio de Dignitate et Augmentis Scientiarum 2* (Kessinger Publishing LLC, 2010) 1–384.

legal material. The German philosopher, Von Leibniz (1646–1716), proposed a plan for the creation of a 'legal theatre' (*theatrum legale*), where the legal systems of all nations at different times could be portrayed and compared – although this idea was never realised.

Grotius (1538–1645), a leading representative of the School of Natural Law,[33] employed the comparative method to place the ideas of natural law on an empirical footing. Believing that one of the universal propositions of natural law could be proved, not only by mere deduction from reason but also by the fact that certain legal rules and institutions were recognised in all legal systems, he used legal material from diverse countries and ages to illustrate and support his system of natural law. Other members of the School of Natural Law's school of thought who used this method include John Selden (1584–1654), Samuel von Pufendorf (1632–1694) and Christian von Wolff (1679–1754). Selden, a celebrated lawyer and a man whose legal opinions ranked high among his contemporaries, stressed the importance of the comparative study of laws which, he believed, should be based on a profound understanding and knowledge of the history of legal institutions in different countries and ages.[34] In this respect, his work is viewed as marking the beginning of comparative legal history. Pufendorf was the first modern legal philosopher to elaborate a comprehensive system of natural law comprising all the branches of law.[35] His work exercised an influence on the structure of later codifications of law, in particular on the 'general part' that is commonly found at the beginning of codes and in which the basic principles of law are laid down.

Drawing on the work of Leibniz and Pufendorf, Von Wolff proposed a system of natural law that he claimed made law a rigorously deductive science. His system exercised considerable influence on the 18th- and 19th-century German codifiers and jurists, and also on legal education in German universities. Although their methods differed, both Pufendorf and Wolff sought to base their theories partly on deduction and partly on the observation of facts. And whereas their approach is

---

[33] G Mousourakis 'Roman law, medieval legal science and the rise of the civil law tradition' in *Comparative Law and Legal Traditions* (Springer Nature, 2019) 198–248.

[34] Selden explored the influence of Roman law on the common law of England and applied the comparative method in the *History of Tithes*, one of his best-known works, and in his treatises on Eastern legal systems.

[35] Pufendorf is best known for his book *De Jure Naturae et Gentium [On the Law of Nature and Nations]* (1672). His earlier work, *Elementa Jurisprudencetiae Universalis [Elements of a Universal Jurisprudence]* (1660) led to his being appointed to a chair in the Law of Nature and Nations especially created for him at the University of Heidelberg. As Wolf remarks in his work: 'Pufendorf combines the attitude of a rationalist who describes and systematizes the law in the geometrical manner with that of the historian who rummages through the archives and who explores historical facts and personalities' (E Wolf *Grosse Rechtsdenker der deutschen Giestesgeschichte* (Mohr, 1944) 298).

different from that employed by modern comparatists, some aspects of their work can be described as comparative in the sense that they occasionally rely on examples drawn from diverse systems of law to support the premises on which they worked. Elements of the comparative method can also be detected among Enlightenment thinkers who were only partially members of the School of Natural Law such as Robert-Joseph Pothier (1699–1772) in addition to authors who did not belong to this school, such as Giovanni Battista Vico (1668–1744) and, in particular, Charles-Louis de Secodat, Baron de la Brède et de Montesquieu (1689–1755).

3.4.1 Pothier

Pothier was born and studied in Orleans, where he served as a judge and, from 1749, as a university professor. His first major work, *La coutume d'Orleans avec des observations nouvelles,* published in 1740,[36] was concerned with the customary law of his home town. His next important work was a comprehensive treatise on Roman private law, titled *Pandectae Justineaneae in Novum Ordinem Digestae cum Legibus Codicis et Novellae* (1748–1752). This was followed by a series of works on a diversity of legal institutions.[37] In his writings, Pothier sought to overcome the problems for legal practice caused by the fragmentation of the law in France by means of a systematic restatement of fundamental legal concepts and principles.[38] In this way he contributed a great deal to the process of unification of private law in France. His work is regarded as the last expression of the doctrine concerning the law of France before the Revolution and, for that reason alone, apart from the high esteem in which it was held, it was bound to influence the compilers of the French Civil Code.[39]

---

[36] D Deroussin 'La coutume d'Orléans avec des observations nouvelles' in G Cazals & F Garnier (eds) *Decision Makers and Custom* (Toulouse Capitole University Press, 2017) 413–447.

[37] These include his *Traitè des Obligations I et II* (1761–1764); *Traitè du Contract de Vente* (1762); *Traitè des Retraits* (1762); *Traitè du Contrat de Constitution de Rente* (1763); *Traitè de Contrat de Louage;* (1764); *Traitè du Contrat de Societe* (1764); *Traitè de Cheptels* (1765); *Traitè du Contrat de Pret de Consomption* (1766); *Traite du Contrat de Depot et de Mandat* (1766); *Traitè du Contrat de Natissement* (1767): *Traitè du Contrat de Marriage I et II* (1766); *Traitè du Droit de Domoine de Propriete* (1772); and *Traitè de la Possession et de la Prescription* (1772). Pothier's works were widely used by jurists and lawyers throughout the 18th and 19th centuries. An important collection of these works in 11 volumes was published by Dupin in 1824–1825.

[38] For example, in his treatise on the institution of ownership Pothier shows how, in a feudal system that encompasses several forms of property and related entitlements, the fundamental Roman-law concept of property could be employed to overcome, in theory at least, many of the discrepancies in the current system.

[39] The Civil Code adopted many of the legal solutions proposed by Pothier, especially in the field of the law of obligations. The drafters of the code also adopted the systematic structure preferred

Although Pothier was not a particularly original thinker, he possessed immense knowledge and showed himself thoroughly familiar with the writings of Commentators such as Bartolus, humanists such as Cujas and natural lawyers such as Pufendorf. He devoted his enormous energy and organising ability to gaining a profound understanding of French law as it was in the period preceding the Revolution, going beyond mere description to give new proportions to French law, especially in the fields of the law of property and the law of obligations. In these fields it is unsurprising that the superior method of Roman law, with which he was so thoroughly acquainted, came to dominate the largely disorganised and fragmented customary law. This, however, does not mean that he neglected the latter law. Although he holds a central place in the mainstream of the civilian tradition, he adopted a great deal from the customary law. Like medieval jurists, Pothier cites and accurately reports rules and principles derived from many different legal systems: divine law, natural law, Roman law, Salic law and the customary law of France. Nevertheless, he was not concerned with exploring and explaining the differences and similarities between these systems into one coherent whole. Therefore, in contrast to other thinkers of this period, it is difficult to discern a connection between Pothier and modern comparatists.

3.4.2 Vico

Vico was born Naples, Italy, and spent most of his professional life as a professor of rhetoric at the University of Naples. He was trained in jurisprudence, but read widely in classics, philology and philosophy, all of which informed his highly original views on history, historiography and culture. His thinking is more fully expressed in his mature work, the *Scienza Nuova [New Science]*, first published in 1724. Although he initially adopted the methods of Grotius and Descartes, he subsequently departed from them and developed his own theory of *Scienza* (science or knowledge). Against Cartesian philosophy, with its emphasis on clear and distinct ideas, the simplest elements of thought from which all knowledge could be derived *a priori* by way of deductive rules, Vico argued that full knowledge of anything involves discovering *how* it came to be what it is as a product of human action. For him, the main drawback of Descartes's hypothetico-deductive method is that it renders phenomena that cannot be expressed logically or mathematically as mere illusions. The reduction of all facts to the ostensibly paradigmatic form of mathematical knowledge is a form of 'conceit', which arises from the fact that 'man

---

by Pothier, which goes back to the classical Roman jurist, Gaius, and was followed by Emperor Justinian: persons; things (including obligations and succession), and actions.

makes himself the measure of all things' and that 'whenever men can form no idea of distant and unknown things, they judge them by what is familiar and at hand'.

In view of this limitation, Vico maintains, one is obliged to recognise that phenomena can be known only via their origins or causes. In his *New Science,* he seeks to develop a conception of science that would allow one to understand the facts of the human world without either reducing them to mere contingency or explaining them by way of speculative ideas of the kind generated by traditional metaphysics. To this end, he introduces a distinction between 'the true' (*il vero*) and 'the certain' (*il certo*): the former, as being eternal and universal, is the object of knowledge (*Scienza*), whereas the latter, as being connected to human consciousness (*Coscienza*), is particular and individuated. From this perspective, he argues that philosophy contemplates reason, whence comes knowledge of the true, while history in a broad sense observes the empirical phenomena of the world arising from human choice: the languages, customs and actions of people that make up a civil society. When combined, philosophy and history can yield a full knowledge of both the universally true and the individually certain.

In his work Vico attempted to develop a science that, drawing on the history of the ideas, customs and deeds of mankind, would disclose the universal principles governing human nature. This requires tracing human society back to its origins with a view to revealing the common human nature and a universal pattern through which all nations progress. Nations need not develop at the same pace, but they all pass through certain distinct stages and evolve through a constant and uninterrupted order of cause and effects. Vico emphasises the cyclical feature of historical development: society progresses towards perfection, but without reaching it (therefore history is 'ideal'), interrupted as it is by a break or return to a relatively more primitive condition.[40] From this reversal, history begins its course anew, albeit from the irreversibly higher point which it has already reached. Furthermore, he observes that nations adopt, independently of one another, largely identical norms based on the common sense of mankind (*senso commune del géneroumano*). This observation is based on an anthropological theory according to which under certain circumstances people tend to act in a similar manner.[41] In many respects, Vico's approach is similar to that of modern comparatists, who do not confine themselves to the mere comparison of legal rules and institutions but also examine the broader historical and socio-cultural context in which such rules

[40] I Berlin *Three Critics of the Enlightenment: Vico, Hamann, Herder* (Pimlico, 2000) 47.

[41] E Jayme 'Rechtsvergleichung und Fortschrittsidee in Rechtsvergleichung' in *Ideengeschichte und Grundlagen von Emerico Amari zur Postmoderne* (Miller, 2000) 20. I translated it into English: 'Comparative law and the idea of progress in comparative law' in *Intellectual History and Foundations from Emerico Amari to Postmodernism* (Miller, 2000) 20.

and institutions are born and evolve.[42] For him the historical and comparative study of diverse cultures and nations is crucial to understanding the processes through which civilisations emerge, develop and decline.[43]

3.4.3 Montesquieu

Montesquieu studied law at the University of Bordeaux and, from 1716, held the office of Prèsident á Mortier in the Parlement of Bordeaux, which was at the time a mainly judicial and administrative body. In 1748 he published his famous work *On the Spirit of the Laws (de l'spirit des lois)*, in which he sought to explain the nature of laws and legal institutions.[44] According to Montesquieu, positive law is oriented towards the idea of justice. But since positive law constitutes only an approximation (rather than a realisation) of justice, this question presents itself: Upon what basis can such an approximation be envisaged? In responding this question, Montesquieu departs from the natural-law tradition which sought to provide a universal answer and proposes that every people must formulate its laws in accordance with its own particular spirit, as shaped by the historical, sociological, political and economic conditions in which it develops. From this perspective, the key to understanding different legal systems is to recognise that they should be adapted to the people for whom they are framed, to the nature and principle of each government, to the climate of each country, to the quality of its soil, to its situation and extent,

> to the principal occupation of the natives … [Laws] should have relation to the degree of liberty the constitution will bear, to the religion of the inhabitants, to their inclinations, riches, numbers, commerce, manners, and customs … [Laws] should have relation to each other, as also to their origin, to the intent of the legislator, and to the order of things on which they are established; in all of which different lights they ought to be considered.[45]

---

[42] J le Moigne *Les Epistimologies Constructivistes* 2 ed (Presses Universitaires de France, 1999) 49.

[43] In his conception of history Vico employs what may be described as an early version of the so-called 'reification theory', a form of 'alienation' (*Entfremdung*), according to which for long periods of time people are dominated by entrenched beliefs (especially religious beliefs), laws and institutions which, although created by human beings, derive their authority from their illusion that they are objective, eternal and universal, just like the laws of nature. According to him, the 'common mind' or collective consciousness of each people or nation regulates social life in a way that reflects the prevailing beliefs. See on this Berlin (note 40) 135–136.

[44] Montesquieu's work represents an early attempt to construct a theory of positive law and a veritable science of legal history. See M Rabello 'Montesquieu et la codification du droit privé (le Code Napoléon)' (2000) 52(1) *Revue Internationale de Droit Comparé* 147–156.

[45] *De l'Espirit des Lois*, Bk 1, ch 3. As Gutteridge has remarked, it was Montesquieu 'who first realised that a rule of law should not be treated as an abstraction but must be regarded against

In addition, Montesquieu asserts that laws are relative and that there are no 'good' or 'bad' laws in the abstract. Each law must be considered in relation to its framework, then it may be regarded as a good law. Montesquieu's approach is, then, similar to that of modern empirical social science, although this does not mean that his account is value-free.

Montesquieu's relativistic approach to laws and legal systems had its origins in the 16th century, when French Hueguenot thinkers called into question the universal authority of Roman law and the universal power of the Roman Catholic Church.[46] The same period is marked by the conflict between traditional Catholics who opposed the French monarchy and those moderate Catholics who, while remaining faithful to the king, sought to strike a compromise between Catholics and Protestants by limiting the power of the Catholic Church. One might say that three key elements of Montesquieu's work are marked by the great increase in the cultural and geographical range of the examples used – a product, without doubt, of the greater knowledge that was reaching Europe about countries such as China, Japan and India.[47] Therefore, less attention is given to examples from antiquity, although these are certainly not lacking.

Behind Montesquieu's realistic perspective lies a consistent and general principle pertaining to the distinction between three forms of government: republic, monarchy and despotism. These are in turn grouped according to whether they are founded in law or not: republic and monarchy are taken to rest on law, whereas despotism does not. What this implies is that law, and especially constitutional law, is particularly important. Therefore, whether the doctrine of the separation of powers, as devised by Montesquieu, operates in a monarchical or in a republican context, it is imperative that the powers are clearly separated by the basic law and are fixed with respect to their respective functions and provinces. Only when these conditions are met can political freedom be warranted.

---

a background of its history and the environment in which it is called upon to function' (H Gutteridge *Comparative Law: An Introduction to the Comparative Method of Legal Study and Research* (Cambridge, 1949) 6). It should also be noted here that, according to contemporary scholars, Montesquieu's work set the foundations of modern sociology. As Pospisil has remarked: 'With his ideas of the relativity of law in space as well as in time, and with his emphasis on specificity and empiricism, [Montesquieu] can be regarded as the founder of the modern sociology of law in general and of the field of legal dynamics in particular' (L Pospisil *Anthropology of Law: A Comparative Theory* (Harper & Row, 1971) 138); consider also R Launay 'Montesquieu: The spectre of despotism and the origins of comparative law' in A Riles (ed) *Rethinking the Masters of Comparative Law* (Hart Publishers, 2001) 22.

[46] The Huguenots were French Protestants who, owing to religious persecution, were forced to flee France to other countries in the 16th and 17th centuries.

[47] Launay (note 45) 22.

It would appear that Montesquieu himself was undecided about the choice between monarchy and republic, but the evidence suggests that, in the final analysis, he preferred constitutional monarchy as it existed in England. Besides the separation of powers, a further element is particularly important to this form of government: the existence of intermediary powers. Montesquieu particularly draws attention to the role of courts such as the French *parlements*, estates and other local corporations. Indeed, one might declare that his criticism of absolute monarchy as it emerges from his *The Spirit of Laws*[48] has its roots in the implicit conflict between the French *parlements* and the monarchy.[49] Montesquieu sought to defend the *parlements* and the interests of the aristocracy that they represented by drawing a comparison between France and Western Europe in general and other societies and forms of government that existed in Europe in the past or prevailed in other parts of the world. His chief concern was to demonstrate the supremacy of European political systems, especially constitutional monarchy, over Asian absolutism and other 'primitive' systems,[50] without, however, supporting European territorial ambitions because, according to him, such ambitions were the hallmark of absolutism.[51]

In his work Montesquieu combines a rational principle, namely, that of the constitutional state, with various laws of nature in order to construe the legal system of each society as an expression of its 'spirit'. The 'spirit' is not elevated to the status of an absolute principle (as in Hegel), but remains relative and, in the final analysis, subject to the abstract measuring rod of rational justice.[52] It is important to note, however, that Montesquieu seeks to detach laws from the fetters of rationalism[53]

---

[48] Launay (note 45) 25–26.

[49] The great majority of the members of these bodies belonged to the French aristocracy and tended to react with hostility whenever the monarchy introduced measures to undermine their own privileges.

[50] It should be noted here that not all of Montesquieu's contemporaries subscribed to his notion of 'Asian despotism', and this may be explained by reference to the political differences that prevailed among different classes in society. For instance, Voltaire, who opposed the privileges of the aristocracy and steadfastly supported the monarchy against the power of the *parlements*, spoke very highly of Chinese and other Asian systems of government. Consider on this Launay (note 45) 22, 37.

[51] It is therefore unsurprising that Montesquieu regarded the conquest of America by the Spanish as disastrous for both Spain and the peoples of that continent and opposed similar actions by the Europeans in Asia and Africa.

[52] Montesquieu's notion of the spirit of a nation bears a certain resemblance to Rousseau's concept of the general will and to some extent corresponds to the modern notion of a system of values or beliefs. According to him, one should not attempt to change the habits and customs of a people by means of laws, for such laws would appear to be too tyrannical. See Montesquieu *The Spirit of Laws, XIXX* (trans T Nuget) (Nourse & Vaillant, 1758) 14.

[53] The notion is that one can arrive at substantial knowledge about the nature of the world by pure reasoning alone and without appeal to any empirical premises.

and to explain them by reference to the nature of things on the ground and in terms of their functions. He identifies nine different kinds of law:

- the law of nature;
- divine law;
- ecclesiastical law;
- international law;
- general constitutional law;
- special constitutional law;
- the law of conquest;
- civil law; and
- family law.

These forms of law are taken to constitute disparate legal orders whose principles must clearly be kept apart if one wishes to create sound legal rules. From this general assumption Montesquieu proceeds to develop a series of important distinctions between diverse fields of law. The basis of these distinctions appears to be the legislative power that establishes constitutions or basic law. However, these distinctions are not rigid, for particular social institutions may feature in more than one legal sphere depending on the possibility of their possessing different legally relevant aspects.

At the beginning of Book XXIX of *The Spirit of Laws*, titled 'On the manner of composing laws', Montesquieu draws attention to the virtue of moderation as a prerequisite of good legislation. This notion holds a central place in constitutional legal philosophy that rests on the principle of separation of powers. In the same book, the importance to legislators of the comparative study of the laws of diverse nations is also emphasised. Montesquieu declares that 'to determine which of the systems [under comparison] is most agreeable to reason, we must take them each as a whole and compare them in their entirety'.[54] He adds that

> as the civil laws depend in the political institutions, because they are made for the same society, whenever there is a design of adopting the civil law of another nation, it would be proper to examine beforehand whether both [nations] have the same institutions and the same political law.[55]

Montesquieu's ideas found genuine resonance among later philosophers both in France and abroad. A prominent case in point is Hegel who, in his *Outlines of the Philosophy of Right*, pays tribute to the French thinker in many ways, while at the

[54] Montesquieu (note 52) 11.
[55] Montesquieu (note 52) 13.

same time bending the latter's views in the direction of his own absolute idealism. Therefore, in his discussion of the character of law and its relation to the 'nature of things', Hegel declares that 'natural law or law from the philosophical point of view is distinct from positive law, but to pervert them into an opposition and contradiction would be a gross misunderstanding'.[56] He then proceeds to add that on this point

> Montesquieu proclaimed the true historical view and the genuinely philosophical position, namely, that legislation both in general and in its particular provisions is to be treated not as something isolated and abstract but rather as a subordinate moment in a whole, interconnected with all the other features which make up the character of a nation and an epoch.[57]

It is only when viewed in this connectedness that laws acquire 'their true meaning and hence their justification'. At a later point in the section on constitutional law, Hegel reiterates his praise when he states that it was 'Montesquieu above all' who drew attention to both the 'connectedness of laws' and the 'philosophical principles of always treating the part in its relation to the whole'.[58]

REFERENCES

Aristotle *Politics* Bk 2 (Clarendon Press, 1916).

Aristotle *Nichomeclean Ethics* (G Bell, 1895).

Bacon, F *De Dignitate et Augmentis Scientiarum, Bk viii,* c3 (1623).

Bacon, F *Francisci Baconi Baronis de Verulamio de Dignitate et Augmentis Scientiarum* 2 (Kessinger Publishing LLC, [1623] 2010) 1–384.

Barone-Adesi, G 'L'etàdella Lex Dei, Pubblicazionidell'Istituto di diritto romano e deidiritti dell' Oriente meditteraneo' *[Publications of the Institute of Roman Law and the Rights of the Eastern Mediterranean]* (Jovelene, 1992).

Baviera, A 'Civil law – Part Three' (1968) 43(38) *Philippine Law Journal* 543–589.

[56] Hegel *Outlines of the Philosophy of Right* (Oxford University Press, 2008) 16

[57] Hegel *Outlines of the Philosophy of Right* (Oxford University Press, 2008) 16

[58] The praise extends also to the notion of a 'general spirit' animating political regimes. 'We must recognize, 'Hegel remarks, 'the depth of Montesquieu's insight in his famous treatment of animating principles of forms of government.' This insight is particularly obvious in the discussion of democracy, where 'virtue' is extolled as the governing principle 'and rightly so, because that constitution rests in point on moral sentiment seen as the purely substantial form in which the rationality of absolute will appears in democracy'. See Hegel (2008) Introduction paras 3, 261, 273. On the role of legal comparatism in the 17th- and 18th-century European legal thought see Donahue (note 17) 3, 19ff.

Berlin, I *Three Critics of the Enlightenment: Vico, Hamann, Herder* (Pimlico 2000).

Caenegem, RC Van 'History of European civil procedure' in RC van Caenegem & M Cappelletti (eds) *International Encyclopedia Comparative Law XVI* (Mohr Siebeck Publishing, 1973).

Cicero *De Legibus* (Presumably Titus Pomponius Atticus, 1949).

Deroussin, D 'La coutume d'Orléans avec des observations nouvelles' in G Cazals & F Garnier (eds) *Decision Makers and Custom* (Toulouse Capitole University Press, 2017).

Donahue, C 'Comparative law before the Code Napoléon' in M Reimann & R Zimmermann (eds) *The Oxford Handbook of Comparative Law* 2 ed (Oxford Handbooks, 2019).

Friedrich, CJ *The Philosophy of Law in Historical Perspective* (University of Chicago Press, 1963).

Gutteridge, HC *Comparative Law. An Introduction to the Comparative Method of Legal Study and Research* (Cambridge University Press, 1949).

Hegel, GWF *Outlines of the Philosophy of Right* (Oxford University Press, 2008).

Hyamson, M *Collatiolegum Mosaicarum et Romanarum* (Oxford University Press, 1913).

Jayme, E 'Rechtsvergleichung und Fortschrittsidee in Rechtsvergleichung' in *Ideengeschichte und Grundlagen von Emerico Amari zur Postmoderne* (Miller, 2000).

Kübler, B & Seckel, E 'Iusprudentiae ante iustinianae reliquias in usum maxime academicum compisitastrans' in *Iurisprudentiae ante Justinianae quae super sunt 6 ed (trans PE Huscke)* (BG Teubner Publisher, 1886).

Launay, R 'Montesquieu: The specter of despotism and the origins of comparative law' in A Riles (ed) *Rethinking the Masters of Comparative Law* (Hart Publishers, 2001).

Le Moigne, J *Les Epistimologies Constructivistes* 2 ed (Presses Universitaires de France, 1999).

Mommsen, T *Romisches Staatsrecht* (S Herzel, 1887).

Mommsen, T *Collectio Librorum iuris ante Justiniani* (Apud Weidmannos,1980), III.

Montesquieu, CLS *The Spirit of Laws Bk XXIX, Vol 1* (trans T Nuget) (Nourse & Vaillant, 1758).

Mousourakis, G 'Tracing the early origins of comparative law' in *Comparative Law and Legal Traditions* (Springer, 2019a), https://doi.org/10.1007/978-3-030-28281-3_3, accessed 28 August 2023.

Mousourakis, G 'Roman law, medieval legal science and the rise of the civil law tradition' in *Comparative Law and Legal Traditions* (Springer Nature, 2019b).

Plato, D *Laws I, III* (Harvard University Press, 1967 & 1968).

Pospisil, L *Anthropology of Law: A Comparative Theory* (Harper & Row, 1971).

Poste, E *The Institutes of Gaius Book* (Oxford, 1904).

Rabello, M 'Montesquieu et la codification du droit privé (le Code Napoléon)' (2000) 52(1) *RevueInternationale de DroitComparé* 147–156.

Siems, M *Comparative Law* 2 ed (Cambridge University Press, 2018).

Van Caenegem, RC 'History of European civil procedure'in M Cappelletti (ed) *International Encyclopedia of Comparative Law, Vol XVI* (JCB Mohr 1973).

Volterra, E *Collatio Legum Mosaicarum et Romanaru, Memorie della R Accademia Nazionale dei Lincei: Classe di Scienze Moralii, Storiche e Filologiche* (Bardi, 1930).
Winroth, A *The Making of Gratian's Decretum* (Cambridge University Press, 2000).
Wolf, E *Grosse Rechtsdenker der deutschen Giestesgeschichte* (Mohr, 1944).
Wormald, P *The Making of English Law: King Alfred to the Twelfth Century* (Blackwell, 1999).
Zweigert, K & Kötz, H *An Introduction to Comparative Law* 3 ed (Clarendon Press, 1998).

4

An overview of major legal systems of the world

Kenneth F Mundia and Rebbeca Haimbili

4.1 INTRODUCTION

Comparative law is an academic study of separate legal systems, each of them evaluated on its basic elements, how they differ in the different legal systems and the ways in which their elements combine into a system. This chapter discusses the legal systems of the world and their distinct characteristics and qualities which set them apart from other legal systems. The discussion includes a list of countries that fall under the respective legal systems and the criteria used for the classification. We saw in chapter 1 that comparative law may be defined as the systematic application of comparison to law. It involves a method of ascertaining the differences and similarities between the things compared, explaining the differences and similarities and applying them to achieve a particular purpose – be it law reform, the promulgation of legislation, the harmonisation or unification of laws, judicial process or the formulation of international legal norms and principles.

More specifically, comparative law involves the study of the different legal systems in existence in the world, including the common, civil, socialist and hybrid systems of law. It includes the description and analysis of foreign legal systems, even where no explicit comparison is undertaken, and it also involves the analysis of the constitutive elements of a legal system and the differences between different legal systems.

The importance of comparative law has increased enormously in the present age of internationalism, economic globalisation and democratisation.[1] Consequently, it has become customary as part of the initial topic of comparative law to classify

[1] R Cocks *Sir Henry Manie: A Study in Victorian Jurisprudence* (Cambridge University Press, 2004) 34.

the legal systems of the world into various categories by using criteria universally accepted by authorities.

Before we proceed to discuss the major legal systems of the world, it is important to draw a distinction between a legal system and a legal tradition. As De Cruz correctly avers, a legal system is an operating set of legal institutions, procedures and rules.[2] Dainow equates a legal system to a living organism that breathes, grows and evolves; he contends that a legal system is part of the people for whom it functions.[3] De Cruz defines a legal tradition, on the other hand,

> as a set of deeply rooted historically conditioned attitudes about the nature of law, the role of the law in the society and the political ideology, the organisation and operation of a legal system.[4]

He submits that a legal tradition puts a legal system into cultural perspective.[5] Similarly, Merryman[6] makes a distinction between a legal tradition and a legal system. He defines a legal tradition as a set of deeply rooted historical conditioned attitudes about the nature of law and the rule of law in society and the political ideology, the organisation and the operation of a legal system, on the one hand. On the other hand, for Merryman, a legal system amounts to an operating set of legal institutions, procedures and rules. And a legal tradition puts the legal system into cultural perspective.[7] He concludes that, despite the legal and academic dialectic on terminology, as a broad generalisation, it may be said that most legal systems in the world today possess characteristics which are predominantly identified with one or more of their major legal traditions or parent families. A clear distinction is drawn between legal tradition and legal system so as to ensure that there is no confusion between the two in the way they are used in this chapter.

4.2 GROUPING OF LEGAL SYSTEMS

It may perhaps be pertinent, even before considering any legal classification, first and foremost, to pose these questions: Why is it important to classify legal systems into legal families? Does it serve any purpose and, if so, what is the rationale

---

[2] P De Cruz *Comparative Law in a Changing World* 2 ed (Cavendish Publishing Limited, 1999) 33.

[3] J Dainow 'The civil law and the common law: Some points for comparison' (1966) 15(3) *The American Journal of Comparative Law* 420.

[4] De Cruz (note 2) 33.

[5] Ibid.

[6] See, generally, JH Merryman *The Civil Law Tradition: An Introduction to the Legal Systems of Western Europe and Latin America* 2 ed (Stanford University Press, 1983).

[7] Ibid.

behind it? For Hertel, classifying legal systems is important because it allows for a summarised description of legal orders in different countries that share distinctive common features. He considers it tedious to attempt to list legal systems country by country. His argument is that there is, strictly speaking, no correct or universally recognised classification into legal families.[8] As many authors have done, Hertel proposes a classification of legal families into seven categories:

(1) the common-law legal family;
(2) the Napoleonic Code (civil law);
(3) the German (the German-speaking legal family);
(4) the former or existing communist government states;
(5) other legal orders belonging to the Romano-Germanic legal family (East Asia);
(6) the Nordic legal family, and
(7) the Islamic legal family.[9]

With his classification, mixed systems fall under the legal systems with which they share the most features.[10]

De Cruz broadly states that most legal systems in the world today have characteristics which are primarily identified with one or more of the three major legal traditions or legal systems: civil, common and the socialist law.[11] As a result, it is possible to divide or group legal systems into classes because of the common characteristics they possess. He submits further that it has become a common practice to classify the legal systems of the world into these three main categories of family.[12] David and Brierly refer to these three legal systems as 'eponymous models'.[13]

Accordingly, the grouping of legal systems has seen its application further across continents such as Africa. However, the evolution of the legal systems in Africa has been different from developments in other parts of the world, especially those in Europe. This can be attributed to the intervention of colonialism, which brought

[8] C Hertel 'Comparative law. Legal systems of the world: An overview' (2009) 1(2) *Notarius International* 128.

[9] In this regard, he agrees with K Zweigert & H Kötz *An Introduction to Comparative Law* (Clarendon Press, 1998), who classified legal systems into either more or the same categories. Zweigert and Kötz distinguished six legal families, namely: the Roman, the German, the Anglo-American, the Nordic legal family, the law in the Far East and Religious Laws (Islam and Hindu).

[10] Ibid.

[11] De Cruz (note 2) 34.

[12] J Husa 'Classification of legal families today: Is it time for memorial hymn?' (2004) 56(1) *Revue Internationale de Droit Comparé* 14. Husa notes that in most orthodox or non-orthodox classifications of legal systems, the traditional systems – the civil, the common-law and the socialist – have dominated; see also De Cruz (note 2) 34.

[13] R David & J Brierly *Major Legal Systems in the World Today: An Introduction to the Comparative Study of Law* 3 ed (Stevens and Sons, 1985); De Cruz (note 2) 33.

with it the sudden imposition of foreign legal systems on African societies that had their own indigenous legal systems. This is why, even after colonialism ended, the foundation of the legal systems that remained dominant in these African states was the inherited ideas, statutes and practices from the former colonial powers. For example, the French Napoleonic Code was used as a foundation for the imposition of European legal systems on certain African societies, especially those in Francophone Africa.

Consequently, the legal systems in many African states to date still resemble those inherited from their colonial masters. Typical examples of African countries which inherited and retained the common-law tradition from their colonisers include Nigeria, Kenya, Uganda, Botswana and Zambia (all countries formerly under British rule). Civil law has largely been maintained by former French and Portuguese colonies such as Angola, the Central African Republic, Cameroon and the Democratic Republic of the Congo. Socialist influence has been relatively minimal in African legal systems, with a few exceptions, such as Tanzania.

Outside Africa, the three main legal systems have been widespread. For example, countries that fall under the common-law jurisdiction include, inter alia, England, Wales, the United States, Canada, Australia, New Zealand, Singapore, Malaysia and Hong Kong. Jurisdictions under the civil-law tradition can be classified into three distinct categories: French Civil Law, German Civil Law and Scandinavian Civil Law. Jurisdictions belonging to the French Civil Law comprise France, Italy, Spain and the former colonies of these countries.[14] German Civil Law jurisdictions include Germany, Austria, Croatia, Switzerland, Greece, Portugal, Turkey, Japan and South Korea.[15] The Scandinavian Civil Law tradition pertains in countries such as Denmark, Norway, Sweden, Finland and Iceland. Socialist countries with a strong socialist influence in their legal regimes include the Russian Federation, Yugoslavia, Cuba, Bangladesh, China, Guyana, India, Laos, Nepal, North Korea, Portugal, Sri Lanka, Tanzania and Vietnam.[16] In addition to these classifications, there are certain countries with relatively mixed legal traditions, adopting to a considerable extent both common law and to a lesser extent civil principles and traditions. Notable among these hybrid or mixed jurisdictions are countries such as Seychelles, South Africa, Namibia, Botswana, Zimbabwe, Guyana, Louisiana, the Philippines, Puerto Rico, Quebec, Cyprus, Scotland and Saint Lucia.[17]

[14] Monateri contends that, in the interpretation of codes, the French Civil Law appears much more centralised on the official organisation of courts. See PG Monateri 'Methods in comparative law: An intellectual overview' in PG Monateri (ed) *Methods of Comparative Law: Research Handbook in Comparative Law* (Edward Elgar Publishing Ltd, 2012) 19.

[15] Ibid. Monateri asserts that, in the German Model, legal scholars have played a central role in structuring legislation and paving the way for judicial decisions.

[16] Monateri (note 14) 19.

[17] Ibid.

4.3 CRITERIA USED TO CLASSIFY LEGAL SYSTEMS

Husa is of the view that classifying legal systems is a feature of macro-comparative law. This, he reasons, is because macro-comparison is focused on analysing and categorising legal systems according to their distinct macro-characteristics.[18] Accordingly, legal systems are classified according to some given criteria. The criteria suggested as a means of determining the classification of a particular system range from race and language, culture, substance (substantive content of laws), ideology, philosophy, conceptions of justice and legal technique to historical origins and juristic style.[19] De Cruz outlines the criteria for classifying a legal system as follows:[20]

1. the historical context and development of the system;
2. its distinctive manner of understanding;
3. its typical institutions;
4. the types of legal source it acknowledges, and
5. its ideology.

The above criteria employed to classify legal systems have been subjected to severe criticism by Husa. He charges that 'classifications are living systematisations and they are not generally meant to be everlasting'. He argues that the classification of legal systems is influenced by: different basic theoretical assumptions among comparatists, the point in time when the sketch of a legal family is constructed and the criteria used in classification. In summary, Husa identifies several criticisable groups for the classification of legal systems. The first is that legal classifications of legal systems lack neutrality and are based on Western views of adaptation leading to the comparatists' favouring Western legal thinking. Second, Husa argues that the classification criteria are rigid and there has been no change to the applicable methods. In fact, as Husa posits, not even the collapse of the socialist law was adequate to warrant a change in the classification criteria. This could be attributed to the historical background criterion discussed above. Various rules and principles have been grounded and cemented since historical times and accordingly they have been accepted as the status quo. This explains the rigidity we encounter today in the classification criteria.

Despite its possible shortcomings, the proposed classification system may offer a neat chronology from which to distinguish the major legal systems of the world. Accordingly, and using the above criteria, the eponymous models, the common law, civil law and socialist legal systems are discussed briefly.

---

[18] Husa (note 12) 14.
[19] De Cruz (note 2) 34.
[20] Ibid.

4.4 HISTORICAL DEVELOPMENT

Common law embodies a large aggregate of rules grounded in unformulated customary law which unfolded and developed throughout the centuries after the Norman Conquest in 1066. Common law bears the following characteristics: realism, strong sovereigns, an unwritten constitution and unified courts. De Cruz contends that it is this distinct development which warrants its separate classification:[21] common law was formulated in and by the courts, giving judge-made law substantial weight.[22] Its development was significantly contingent on the contenders bringing their cases to court. Over the years, the common law became a body of principles of law developed by the Superior Courts of England and the common-law system was spread by the British Empire to its historical colonies, many of which retain the common-law system today.[23] The common-law principles appear for the most part in reported judgments, usually of the higher courts, in relation to specific facts in situations arising in disputes which courts have adjudicated.[24] Common-law systems also rely on statutes passed by a Legislature, but may make less of a systematic attempt to codify their laws in a 'civil law' system. Furthermore, under common law, there is no legislative tradition to reform or redress laws through law reform.

Civil law is a legal system that originated in Europe primarily as a result of the codification of Roman law.[25] Civil law was formulated, compiled and refined in universities. It was later codified and given statutory force by a Legislature.[26] It is generally accepted that the civil law was greatly influenced by the *Corpus Juris Civilis* of Justinian or the Code of Justinian, and the codification of the principles by the universities in Europe.[27]

Socialist law denotes a general type of legal system which has been used in communist and formerly communist states. It is based on the civil-law system, with major

[21] De Cruz (note 2) 36.

[22] The courts referred to here are the courts of the English kings (*Curia Legis*) in the centuries following the Norman Conquest in 1066.

[23] De Cruz (note 2).

[24] Ibid.

[25] For De Cruz, civil law has strong roots in Roman law, the French Civil Code and the Germanic Code. See De Cruz (note 2) 36.

[26] Ibid.

[27] The *Corpus Iuris Civilis* (Body of Civil Law) is the modern name for a collection of fundamental works of jurisprudence, issued from 529 to 534 CE by order of Justinian I, the Eastern Roman Emperor. It has three parts: the Code, the Digest and the Institutes. All three parts were given the force of law. They were intended to be, together, the sole sources of law; reference to any other source, including the original texts from which the Code and the Digest had been taken, was forbidden.

modifications and additions from Marxist–Leninist ideology.[28] It is described as a legal system grounded primarily in Marxist command-style economics or Marxist–Leninist ideas.[29] Socialist law is most commonly understood as being a system of law linked to an economic aspect that envisioned public ownership of the means of production and which disappeared in the 1980s.[30] It is identified by this distinct economic factor, which is evidenced by ideas of national economic planning as the central core of economic development.[31] According to Partlet and Ip, the historical understanding of the socialist legal system is completely missing from its existing descriptions and this might be attributed to the fact that it has been neglected by scholars.[32]

4.5 MANNER OF LEGAL THINKING[33]

Typical of common law is its concrete court-based approach, one seeking realistic answers to issues before a court. Common law proceeds from case to case; unlike civil law, which proceeds from general principle to general principle.[34] The primary source of common law is case law. The common-law lawyer is trained to think in terms of the parties and their particular legal relationships. Common law is punctuated by the tendency to improvise, examining cases for possible precedents, which may or may not be binding on the court currently hearing a case.[35] The decision to legislate becomes necessary only if a particular area of law happens to be confused or obscure, or a gap in the law is revealed.[36] Case law is an important tool of interpretation: when a statute is enacted, it is generally a confirmation or consolidation of the existing case law and its function is to build on or improve case law; and common law makes use of the adversarial method of fact-finding.[37]

---

[28] De Cruz (note 2) 38.

[29] Some scholars argue that socialist law was not a separate legal system. Legal systems in all socialist states preserved formal criteria of the Romano-Germanic civil law. For this reason, law theorists in post-socialist states usually consider the socialist law as a particular case of the Romano-Germanic civil law.

[30] W Partlet & CE Ip 'Is socialist law really dead?' (2016) 48(1) *New York University Journal of International Law and Politics* 465.

[31] Ibid.

[32] Partlet & Ip (note 30) 469.

[33] De Cruz (note 2) 38.

[34] WK Dam 'Legal institutions, legal origins &governance' *Working Paper No 303, 2nd Series* (University of Chicago Law and Economics, 2006) 3 emphasises that the practice of precedents 'required judges to reason from case to case, distinguishing cases that could be said to be conflicting precedents, in order to find the controlling principles for new fact situations'.

[35] Ibid.

[36] Ibid.

[37] Ibid.

Civil-law lawyers tend to think in abstract, conceptual and symmetrical terms.[38] Because it is rule-based, civil law is always looking for solutions to a problem before court. Its lawyers have a tendency to think in terms of its institutions and its existing enacted rules (codified or statutory), which may be applied to a given situation.[39] Statutes and codified law are the primary sources of civil law. Civil law proceeds from general principles to general principles, unlike common law, which proceeds from case to case.[40] The system is characterised by lawyers with a propensity for planning, systematising and regulating issues as intelligibly as possible. Finally, the system of fact-finding in the civil-law legal system is an adversarial one.[41]

Socialist law has its roots in Marxist–Leninist ideas.[42] For this reason, it has relied on codification from early times and on statutory rules to the exclusion of case law and without any doctrine of precedent.[43] Socialist law employs a civil-law legal mode and civil-law groupings and formulations.[44] The distinct feature of socialist law is that it regards law as an instrument or tool of state policy or as a vehicle for carrying out Marxist–Leninist ideas whose sole purpose is to implement the state plan in accordance with Marxist philosophy.[45] Socialist law is at variance with both common- and civil-law systems in that it is regarded as a creature of a state and therefore subordinate to the state.[46]

4.6 DISTINCT LEGAL INSTITUTIONS[47]

The legal institutions typical of the common-law legal system include these: the trust, tort principles, agency, consideration, estoppel.[48] Civil-law jurisdictions are more inclined towards formalism and rules guarding the moral and economic integrity of the legitimate family as opposed to outsiders. There is direct action, oblique action and abuse of rights. The Germanic family has institutions such

---

[38] Dam (note 34) 6. Dam adds here that the 'abstract reasoning which characterized the Civil Code emphasised on generality and understandability which required one to take into consideration a variety of provisions in order to determine the legal rules covering a given set of facts'. See also De Cruz (note 2) 38.

[39] Dam (note 34) 6.

[40] Ibid.

[41] Ibid.

[42] De Cruz (note 2) 38.

[43] One can argue here that socialist law then has strong similarities to the civil law, more so than it does with the common law.

[44] De Cruz (note 2) 38.

[45] Ibid.

[46] De Cruz (note 2) 39.

[47] De Cruz (note 2) 38–39.

[48] Ibid.

as the abstract real contract, the concept of a legal act and the notion of unjust enrichment.[49] Legal institutions found under socialist jurisdictions include different types of ownership, the duty of rescue and unique notions of the role and status of contract in a planned economy.[50]

4.7 CHOICE OF SOURCES OF LAW

This criterion has lost importance in the context of legal families because, currently, all the systems use both statutes and case law as sources. This has rendered this criterion irrelevant to classification.[51] However, the following must be noted: while both common law and civil law use both cases and statutes as sources of law, what is different is their respective approaches to these sources, their methods and techniques of abstraction (which differ so profoundly as to warrant a distinction being made between them).

4.8 IDEOLOGY OF A LEGAL SYSTEM

Ideology refers to political or economic doctrines or religious beliefs.[52] An argument has been advanced that it is much simpler to classify systems with a distinct known ideology – for example, communism for socialist states or religious legal systems (Hindu or Muslim) – than it is to classify legal families of the West, owing to the fact that they have similar ideologies.[53] De Cruz agrees and submits that to classify legal systems based on the other criteria mentioned above, such as historical background, mode of legal thinking and distinctions, might suffice.

4.9 RELIGIOUS LEGAL SYSTEMS

Religious legal systems do not fit into the main three categories of legal system discussed above, that is, the common law, civil law and socialist law.[54] For this reason, they are studied separately or in groups of religious laws in relation to their legal abstractions. In this section we briefly discuss four religious legal systems:

[49] De Cruz (note 2) 38.
[50] De Cruz (note 2) 39.
[51] De Cruz (note 2) 40.
[52] Ibid.
[53] Ibid.
[54] Hertel (note 8) 139.

canon law, Hindu law, Jewish law and Islamic law. This is ultimately a summary of their general background, sources of law and objectives, where necessary.

4.9.1 Canon Law

Laschuk defines canon law as the rules and ordinances governing the Christian community. Regulations that are recognised today as early forms of canons began in the church and by the 2nd century manuals of conduct appeared, one of which is the Didache (ca 100 CE).[55] The Didache makes provision for liturgical practices and certain basic elements of church governance.[56] In 313 CE, Constantine legalised Christianity with the Edict of Milan. Following this legalisation, the Christian communities found it imperative to organise themselves in a more formalised manner.[57]

The most basic source of canon law is the New Testament. It provides a plethora of clear instructions regarding the various aspects of Christian life, such as baptism and the Eucharist; marriage; payment of clergy; the church's judicial authority, and relations with the state.[58] Guidelines for the Christian community are also provided for through the writings of Saint Paul. He gave instructions concerning the payment of the clergy; the requirements for ordination; how to handle accusations directed at the clergy, and how Christians are to relate with non-Christians.[59]

Following the legalisation of Christianity by Constantine and after the first three centuries of the Christian church, the Roman emperors started holding ecumenical councils at which bishops from different local churches and representing the entire church were present. These bishops used these opportunities to issue legislation, or canons, to respond to a variety of issues confronting the church. These canons, commonly referred to as the Sacred Canons, are the common canonical foundation of the church in both the East and the West. This tradition was taken up into the civil law of the Roman Empire and for centuries it was a standard part of civil law.[60]

According to Laschuk, in the West, the canons of ecumenical councils were taken up into a number of collections and then distilled via the writings of the Roman pontiffs. This made up a genre of sources referred to as decretals, which were codified by the Holy See into a single volume in the 20th century and known as the Code of Canon Law. A process of codification and reformation of canon law followed, resulting in three codifications of canon law in the 20th century: the 1917 *Codex iuriscanonici*, a revised 1983 *Codex iuriscanonici*, and the 1990 Code

---

[55] A Laschuk *The Role of Canon Law in the Catholic Tradition and the Question of Church and the State* (Cardus Religious Freedom Institute, 2018) 4.
[56] Ibid.
[57] Ibid.
[58] Ibid.
[59] Laschuk (note 55) 5.
[60] Ibid.

of Canons for the Eastern churches. These canonical collections are considered as universal, exclusive and authentic collections of law.[61] In the Catholic tradition, canon law has four main functions:

(a) it makes visible the hierarchical and organic structure of the church. It does not only define the way the church should operate, but also provides good order for the church;
(b) it guarantees the appropriate exercise of the sanctifying function of the church. This is about the salvation of humanity as its principal purpose;
(c) it makes provision for rights, obligations and ways of resolving conflicts in the church. It clearly articulates the rights of both physical and juridical members of the church and makes provision for a system of trials and recourse to see to it that these rights and obligations are properly exercised, and
(d) it attempts to provide structures for directing and sustaining the common initiatives of the church.[62]

Having discussed the salient details of canon law, we now briefly outline how different or similar canon law is to civil law. Whereas civil law concentrates on temporal happiness, canon law focuses on eternal happiness: it has as its supreme law and end the salvation of souls.[63] However, there are also notable similarities. Both systems are types of positive law formed by a legislator; they receive their ultimate governing authority from God; they regulate the relationships of members within an organisation, and they try to make provision for the requisite structures of governance to ensure a society that functions well.[64]

4.9.2 Hindu law

The history and origin of Hindu law is discussed by Rautenbach and Goolam, who explain that Hindu law is rooted in customary law.[65] However, it has gone through extensive transformation and continues to evolve. In short, Hindu law is private law which is reformed by custom and legislation. In India, it is applied to three categories of person: Hindus, Jains, Sikhs or Buddhists by religion; descendants of the persons above, and any person who does not follow the Islamic, Christian, Jewish or Parsi religion and who is not regulated by any other law.[66]

---

[61] Laschuk (note 55) 6.
[62] Laschuk (note 55) 7.
[63] Ibid.
[64] Laschuk (note 55) 8.
[65] C Rautenbach & NMI Goolam *Introduction to Legal Pluralism in South Africa, Part II: Religious Legal Systems* (Butterworths, 2002) 3.
[66] Ibid.

Owing to the development that Hindu law has undergone, a distinction is drawn between its ancient and its modern sources. We discuss the ancient sources first. Rautenbach and Goolam list the following ancient sources of Hindu law:[67]

i *Vedas* (believed to be the most important scriptures and seen as the essence of Hindu civilisation).
ii *Brahmanas* (outlines the different religious rites and rituals to be executed by Hindus and how to affect them).
iii *Upanishads* (philosophical exposition of the Vedas, structured in a dialogue format).
iv *Smritis* (explanation of the Vedas by the scholars; formulated at different intervals of time and rulers, they are regarded as peremptory statements of law). They are split up into *Dharmasutras* (earlier *Smritis*) and *Dharmashastras* (later *Smritis*).[68]
v *Commentaries and digests* (Nibhandas) – they augmented rules in the *Smritis,* utilising their particular reasoning and integrating applicable customs. Commentaries and digests have played a role where the *Smritis* did not cover every aspect of the law; where the *Smritis* did not give adequate detail on particular aspects of the law; and where the *Smritis* contained discordant opinions.
vi *Customs* (its formal shape is attributable to *Vedas*, *Smritis*, commentaries and digests. Customs are split up into three groups, namely: that of the community (binds all community members), that which is local or territorial (binds all persons within the particular geographical area) and that of families (must be proved first before they can become enforceable).[69]
For validity, a Hindu custom must observe the following specifications, that is, it should: be ancient or well-established; be definite; be rational; not be immoral; not contend with law; and not be against public policy.[70]
vii Other Hindu scriptures such as *Puranas*, the *EPICS*, and the *Bhagavad Gita*.

The modern sources of Hindu law include equity and justice, precedent and legislation.[71] In addition, the predominant principles of Hindu law have been consolidated in case law.

---

[67] Rautenbach & Goolam (note 65) 3.
[68] Rautenbach & Goolam (note 65) 4.
[69] Rautenbach & Goolam (note 65) 5.
[70] Ibid.
[71] Rautenbach & Goolam (note 65) 6.

There are two schools of thought under Hindu law. This is a result of distinct approaches to and methods of interpretation of the commentaries and digest. The two schools are:

i the orthodox *Mitakshara*; and
ii the heterodox *Dayabhaga*(Bengal) law schools.

In summary, the way of thinking under Hindu law incorporates morality and religion. It is not surprising, then, that ethics, religion and law are intrinsically linked, to the extent that if a rule of law is contrary to ethical principles, it will not be given effect. Concepts of justice and reason articulated in Hindu law show the moral aspect of law. This means that in making decisions regard is had not only to the black letter of the law, but also to the concepts of justice and reason. Justice triumphs if there is discord between law and justice. Sacred law is viewed as being sovereign; however, customs are equally important and there is room for sacred law to be subordinated to custom in the face of new developments and local needs.[72]

4.9.3 Jewish law

Judaism is the religion of the Jewish people. It is regarded as the source of all the world's moral religious cultivation such as Christianity and Islam; it is also the *fons et origo* of the belief in a single God.

Bernhard defines judaism as a collection of beliefs and principles combined with a legal system that applies those beliefs and principles to all circumstances.[73] Jewish law brings into play judaic faith, bestowing a method for living that corresponds to its ideas and principles and for helping to achieve its objectives.[74] Its ideas contribute to the well-being of society in general because all its laws, rules and customs are regarded as pedagogic devices for the building up of a person's nature and personality in the ethical image.[75]

Judaism is therefore broadly defined as a way of life rather than a mere religion. This, Bernhard observes, is because it consists of a set of guidelines to regulate behaviours for all facets and sections of life, resulting in a wide array of laws covering all sorts of areas which are not usually covered in most religious systems.[76]

Bernhard asserts that there is what is called the Beth Din or the Rabbinal Court in Jewish law, a court which adjudicates on matters of Jewish law and arbitrates

[72] Rautenbach & Goolam (note 65) 9.
[73] NM Bernhard 'Jewish law' in C Rautenbach & NMI Goolam (eds) *Introduction to Legal Pluralism in South Africa, Part II: Religious Legal Systems* (Butterworths, 2002) 9.
[74] Ibid.
[75] Ibid.
[76] Ibid.

disputes in line with Jewish law (*Halacha*). This court also deals with mediation and settles compromises. In addition to that, the court is tasked with the administration of matters of personal status, including marriage, divorce and dietary matters.[77]

Similarly to the civil-law legal system, many religious legal systems have codified law. The Jewish legal system is no exception. There are 613 commandments, of which 248 are 'dos' while the other 365 are 'do nots' or prohibitions. These 613 commandments are divided into two groups or categories: those between humankind and God, and those between fellow human beings.[78]

The belief of the Jewish people is that the commandments given by God are rooted in justice coupled with kindness and mercy. They regard justice as including the following: distributive justice (equitable doings between human beings); public justice (this includes the community's role in determining and enforcing duties and guarding the rights of individuals and groups; and the integrity of individualised character.[79] In addition to this, there are 39 legislated principles regulating the Sabbath day to ensure it is not just a day off but a day of rest.[80]

Jewish people enjoy various freedoms, one of which is freedom of choice. It is left to each person to determine the moral quality of their life. This means that each person is then responsible for the consequences of exercising their freedom of choice. In this case, punishment must be meted out. Some of the mitigating factors of culpability present in Jewish law are these: a genuine lack of choice due either to incapacity or coercion.[81]

There are two main sources of Jewish law:[82]

1. The Bible (the five books of Moses, plus 19 books of the Jewish Holy Scriptures (old Testament)); and
2. the *Talmund*, *Midrash* and successive updated codifications of Jewish law.[83] These are the *Mishna* (which was the first codification of the written and oral laws given to Moses; it has been carefully scrutinised and expanded on by sages over the years. It is a highly concise compendium that contains case-law disputes, legal traditions, customs, definitions, usages, enactments and decrees); the *Gemara* (a well-organised discussion and addendum of the *Mishna* that pinpoints the fundamental concept and perspectives in its contention and often making a decision between them), and the *Talmund*, which is made up of both the *Mishna* and the *Gemara* and embodies the philosophical and theological

[77] Bernhard (note 73) 10.
[78] Ibid.
[79] Bernhard (note 73) 11.
[80] Bernhard (note 73) 12.
[81] Ibid.
[82] Bernhard (note 73) 13–14.
[83] Ibid.

beliefs and the historical traditions, moral perspectives and rules of life of Judaism.

4.9.4 Islamic law

Goolam defines Islam as a 'comprehensive system' regulating all sectors of human life at both the spiritual and the materialistic level.[84] He asserts that Islam consists of rationales of religion, the principles of ethics, the postulation of the law and the foundation of other disciplines. His view is that Islamic law regulates human belief and understanding.[85]

Sources of Islamic law are divided into two distinct categories: primary and secondary sources. It is important to note here that, just as with the other religious legal systems discussed above, Islamic law is codified – a characteristic of the civil-law legal system, even though Islamic law does not belong to the civil-law legal family.

Both the Qur'an and the Sunnah fall under the primary category of sources. The Qur'an is regarded as the main source of Islamic law. It is the most prominent because of the belief that it is the final word of God. It has not been altered and it is unalterable. Regarded as the higher law, it triumphs over the law of nations, constitutions and entrenched provisions in legislation.[86]

The Sunnah consists of the teachings and the sayings of the prophet Muhammad. Goolam explains it as the 'manner of acting, a rule of acting/conduct or way of life'.[87] The Sunnah passes its decisions in three different ways: it may restate or confirm a decision which comes from the Qur'an; elucidate or expound on the Qur'an, or pronounce on a matter on which the Qur'an is silent.[88] This allows for the further development of Islamic law.

Secondary sources of Islamic law entail *Ijma* (consensus) and *Qiyâs*. The *Ijma* comes into play when the primary sources do not deal with a matter.[89] Goolam asserts that its authority is derived from a 'distrust of individual opinion' and the tradition that 'my followers will not agree unanimously in error'. However, it must not contend with the primary sources. Its usefulness lies in the fact that it allows for the advancement of the law to fulfil the needs of a transforming world.[90] *Qiyâs* comes into play when the above three sources of law fail. It entails in-depth cogitation and scrutiny by scholars to come up with a suitable rule through analytical deduction.[91]

[84] Bernhard (note 73) 14.
[85] Ibid.
[86] Bernhard (note 73) 16.
[87] Ibid.
[88] Ibid.
[89] Ibid.
[90] Ibid.
[91] Ibid.

Supplementary sources include custom, juristic writings and decisions, and judicial contributions.

There are two schools of Islam law: those of (1) the *Shi'as* and (2) the *Sunnis.* The former is divided into three sub-schools;[92] the latter is divided into four sub-schools.[93]

4.10 CONCLUSION

The world's major legal systems have advanced over time. In a globalised world premised on a new world order, it should not be surprising that new legal systems might emerge or that the existing systems may become highly plural, if they are not already so.

Traditionally, and as shown in this chapter, three main legal systems are recognised: the common law, civil law and socialist. These three have now overwhelmingly and increasingly been referred to as the eponymous models. Unique in their respective manners, the eponymous legal traditions are distinguishable by reference to their historical context and development, distinctive manner of understanding, institutions, legal sources and ideological print and thought process.

Given that the politic being of the universe is either religious or informed by some religious connotations, religious systems have also been recognised as informing legal systems. Therefore, in some states, especially in the Islamic world, religion forms an important point of reference in the legal and judicial processes of those systems. Some of the most notable religious legal systems still extant and visible in the world today include religious Christian systems based on canon law, Hindu law, Islamic law and Jewish law.

This chapter has provided a brief outline of the major legal and religious systems of the world. It must be acknowledged that it has covered introductory aspects which outline the most basic features and characteristics of these systems. Therefore, further reading and studies would be necessary to comprehend fully the generic nature and scope of each of these sources. A further caution must be tendered as far as this chapter is concerned, and that has to do with the question of hierarchy. It must be noted that there is no hierarchy as far as these legal systems are concerned, despite what some would want to propose. Each has its own fair share of advantages and disadvantages which are recognised, appreciated and legitimised by its audience and a particular climate in which it applies.

---

[92] Ibid. They are: *Zaydis; Ithna Asharis* and *Ismailiyya.*
[93] Ibid. They are: *Hanafi, Maliki, Shafi'i* and *Hanbali.*

REFERENCES

Bernhard, NM 'Jewish law' in C Rautenbach & NMI Goolam (eds) *Introduction to Legal Pluralism in South Africa, Part II: Religious Legal Systems* (Butterworths, 2002).

Cocks, R *Sir Henry Manie: A Study in Victorian Jurisprudence* (Cambridge University Press, 2004).

Dainow, J 'The civil law and the common law: Some points for comparison' (1966) 15(3) *The American Journal of Comparative Law* 419–435.

Dam, WK 'Legal institutions, legal origins & governance' *Working Paper No 303, 2 series* (University of Chicago Law and Economics, 2006).

David, R & Brierly J *Major Legal Systems in the World Today: An Introduction to the Comparative Study of Law* 3 ed (Stevens and Sons, 1985).

De Cruz, P *Comparative Law in a Changing World* 2 ed (Cavendish Publishing Limited, 1999).

Hertel, C 'Comparative law. Legal systems of the world: An overview' (2009) 1(2) *Notarius International* 128–139.

Husa, J 'Classification of legal families today – Is it time for memorial hymn?' (2004) 56(1) *Revue Internationale de Droit Comparé* 11–38.

Laschuk, A *The Role of Canon Law in the Catholic Tradition and the Question of Church and the State* (Cardus Religious Freedom Institute, 2018).

Merryman, JH *The Civil Law Tradition: An Introduction to the Legal Systems of Western Europe and Latin America* 2 ed (Stanford University Press, 1983).

Monateri, PG 'Methods in comparative law: An intellectual overview' in PG Monateri (ed) *Methods of Comparative Law: Research Handbook in Comparative Law* (Edward Elgar Publishing, 2012).

Partlet, W & Ip, CE 'Is socialist law really dead?' (2016) 48(1) *New York University Journal of International Law and Politics* 463–511.

Rautenbach, C & Goolam, NMI (eds) *Introduction to Legal Pluralism in South Africa, Part II: Religious Legal Systems* (Butterworths, 2002).

Zweigert, K & Kötz, H *An Introduction to Comparative Law* 3 ed (Clarendon Press, 1998).

5

Methodologies and techniques of comparative law

Ndatega V Asheela-Shikalepo and Kenneth F Mundia

5.1 INTRODUCTION

It is widely accepted that there are varying approaches to comparative law, and yet there has been no consensus on the methodology a comparatist should follow. Perhaps the criticisms of the past several decades of what was established in comparative legal research may account for this paradox. So the question remains: What is comparative law? In this chapter, we discuss the methodologies and techniques of comparative law. Questions such as these are answered in the text that follows: What is it that the comparatist compares? What does the comparatist use in order to make a comparison? and Is there a universal method of comparison? In essence, we offer both a theoretical and a practical framework embodying a range of comparative techniques within which both micro- and macro-comparisons may be tackled. We also explore the methodological approaches of comparative law in Africa.

Before venturing into this chapter, though, it is imperative that our readers familiarise themselves with the following pitfalls, highlighted by De Cruz,[1] which await a comparatist in their quest to discover the truth about a legal phenomenon:

- problems with semantics and phraseology;
- ethnic differences;
- the question of arbitrariness in choosing the objects of study;
- challenges in attaining 'comparability' in comparisons;
- the inclination to detect a common legal style in legal systems;

[1] P de Cruz *Comparative Law in a Changing World* 3 ed (Routledge, 2007) 213.

- the propensity to force one's own (native) legal abstractions and presuppositions on the systems being compared, and
- the risk of leaving out extra-legal rules.

In short, in making a comparison, one must be aware of the challenges associated with language, culture and ethnic differences between legal systems over and above the dangers of omitting some extra-legal rules, among other challenges. It is worth noting at the outset that there is no one prescribed or universal method or approach to comparison. As many scholars would agree, in order for a legal researcher to decide on the method to use, they should be informed by their research questions and the goal they want to achieve.[2] This means that it is mostly the research questions and the goals of the researcher that determine which method of comparison would be plausible.

5.2 SUBJECT-MATTER OF COMPARATIVE LAW AND METHODS OF COMPARISON

Comparative law is not primarily concerned with the comparison of national law but rather with the legal systems of different jurisdictions. This is because comparative law is not a body of rules regulating human conduct and relationships. According to Kamba,[3] the subject-matter of comparative law is two or more legal systems or the parts, branches or aspects of two or more legal systems or, expressed differently, macro-comparison and micro-comparison.[4] De Cruz[5] defines a legal system as the legal rules and institutions of a country. In this, De Cruz agrees with Kamba, who adds that a legal system is made up of more than just rules: its institutions, practices, standards, methods of research and the mental habit of lawyers, judges, legislators and administrators give it character.[6]

The method of comparison is a fundamental part of any legal system and of the subject of comparative law itself. In fact, comparison is an essential aspect of human thinking and growing. As we have seen in the introduction to this chapter, comparative law signifies the systematic application of the comparative technique to the field of law. And although comparative law has been portrayed as voluminous

---

[2] See MV van Hoecke 'Methodology of comparative legal research' (2015) 12 *Law and Method Magazine* 41.

[3] WJ Kamba 'Comparative law: A theoretical framework' 1974 *International and Comparative Law Quarterly* 499.

[4] K Zweigert & H Kötz *An Introduction to Comparative Law* 3 ed (trans T Weir) (Clarendon Press, 1998) 4. The authors state that comparisons of the legal systems of different nations can be made either on a large scale (macro-comparison) or on a smaller scale (micro-comparison).

[5] De Cruz (note 1) 3.

[6] Kamba (note 3) 499.

and repetitive, the method of comparison is an essential part both for thinking and for knowing. Glanert[7] defines 'method' as the search for a certain form of truth. Etymologically, the word 'method' originates from the Middle French '*méthode*', which refers to a rational procedure. Glanert submits that in modern language it carries two principal meanings. First, it appoints a procedure for achieving a certain purpose – it outlines a way of doing something in a manner corresponding to a defined programme. According to Glanert,[8] the term elicits a special procedure or a typical set of procedures used in an academic discipline as a means of examination and enquiry. Second, it connotes the quality of being methodical and structured in thought or action. It denotes the orderly arrangement of ideas and topics in thinking or writing.

In this regard, the comparative method should be perceived as a tool with which to achieve breakthroughs and improvements across diverse legal spheres. Although there are no legal principles regulating the way a lawyer should compare distinct legal systems and the process requires experience, there are generally two scales upon which a comparison can be made: macro-comparison and micro-comparison.

Macro-comparison, on the one hand, generally refers to the method of thought and procedures used to compare the spirit and style of different legal systems. It may range from two specific legal systems to the systems of the entire world.[9] The focus in macro-comparison is not on individual concrete problems and their solutions but, instead, on researching methods of handling legal materials, procedures for resolving and deciding disputes and the roles of those engaged in the law. *Micro-comparison*, on the other hand, has to do with specific legal institutions or problems, that is, with the rules used to solve actual problems or particular conflicts of interest. It is a study of single institutes – for example, contract, marriage, penalty, value-added tax and electoral laws.

The question that is often raised, therefore, is this: What is the dividing line between micro- and macro-comparison? The answer to this broad question is not a straightforward one. Zweigert and Kötz,[10] for instance, admit that the line between these two is quite flexible and that one must do both at the same time; and, in many instances, micro-comparison makes sense only if one takes due account of the general institutional context in which the rules of the foreign systems under comparison are developed and applied.

While the macro–micro dichotomy offers a useful framework as a 'method' of comparison, such methods have not been free of criticism. Glanert[11] criticises the

---

[7] S Glanert 'Methods?' in PG Monateri (ed) *Methods of Comparative Law. Research Handbooks in Comparative Law* (Edward Elgar Publishing Ltd, 2012) 65.
[8] Ibid.
[9] Kamba (note 3) 499.
[10] Zweigert & Kötz (note 4) 5.
[11] Glanert (note 7) 65.

concept of method in comparative law on *four* grounds. Her first criticism is that method is not pan-disciplinary. On this ground, Glanert avers that it is impossible to find a method that would be valid and therefore be applicable to every domain. She contends further that inside each disciplinary formation there are an infinite number of methods that can be recognised. Her view is that method is threatened by pluralism. This is because new methods are always springing up, which a comparatist would regard as the better one, even replacing previous methods.[12] Second, Glanert argues that a method is not absolute. This is seen in how, among the variety of possible methods, there would always be proponents of a certain method claiming that their method should be pre-eminent. Her point of view is that, because of the sliding scale of methods, what should determine the right approach to comparison should be the particular objectives of the research, the instinctive abilities of a researcher and the costs involved.[13] And, third, Glanert opines that a method is not objective. This, she argues, is the case because the mere fact that any method is developed by human beings who are situated in time and space derails its objectivity. This means that time and space would have an influence on the type of method formulated.[14] Finally, her argument is that a method is speculative. In support of this criticism Glanert suggests that methods are composed and written in a given language and set in a singular discourse, rendering them inherently speculative.[15] In the light of the above, it is reiterated here that there is no prescribed method of comparison and that what will influence a researcher in finding the appropriate method for their analysis would be their research question and their objectives.

5.2.1 Choice of legal systems for both macro- and micro-comparison and process of comparison

There is a general attitude that one must choose to compare only those legal systems which are comparable in the first place. In other words, they must have attained the same level of legal development.[16] As Pollock has expressed it:[17]

> like must be compared with like; the concepts, rules or institutions under comparison must relate to the same stage of legal, political and economic development.

---

[12] Glanert (note 7) 65–66.
[13] Glanert (note 7) 66–67.
[14] Glanert (note 7) 67.
[15] Glanert (note 7) 70.
[16] Kamba (note 3) 499.
[17] F Pollock 'The history of comparative jurisprudence' (1903) 5(1) *Journal of the Society of Comparative Legislation* 74–89.

However, Kamba disagrees. His view is that

> the question whether one selects for comparison systems of law which are or are not at the same stage of development is highly determined by the principal aim(s) of the specific comparative study or research.[18]

Be that as it may, Kamba agrees that comparative legal studies and research have been and will continue to be concerned with comparing legal systems which are comparable (at similar levels of development). In this regard, the common- and civil-law traditions dominate the comparative law scene.[19] Accordingly, Kamba suggests that what is demanded of the comparatist in this regard is a good overview of the legal systems of the world, a grounding in the criteria for their classification and a sound knowledge of the characteristics of the major groups or families of systems.[20]

Kamba remarks that for micro-comparison the variety of topics from which the comparatist can choose is boundlessly greater than that system of law. One can choose topics concerning the following characteristics of a legal system: the structure; the sources of law; the judicial system and the judiciary; the legal profession, and so on. Then there are also the various branches of national law; institutions or concepts; and the historical development of legal systems.[21] In the next section, we elaborate on these dimensions, including offering a practical discussion of the process of comparison itself.

Often the question is raised: What does a comparatist compare? According to Michaels,[22] various themes of comparative law can be compared. He provides three:

(a) the actual comparison of legal systems – the discovery, explanation and evaluation of similarities and differences;
(b) the influence between legal systems, and
(c) the development of a general theory of law.[23]

Eberle[24] adds that the essence of comparison is looking at one mass of legal data in relation to another and then evaluating how the two lumps of legal data are alike and how they are distinct. His approach to the act of comparison is scientific in

---

[18] Ibid.
[19] Kamba (note 3) 500.
[20] Kamba (note 3) 501.
[21] Ibid.
[22] R Michaels 'Comparative law' in S Basedow, KJ Hopt & R Zimmermann (eds) *Oxford Handbook of European Private Law* (Oxford University Press, 2011) 1.
[23] On this point Eberle agrees. He states that the focus must be placed attentively on the similarities and differences between the data points derived from the different legal systems.
[24] EJ Eberle 'The methodology of comparative law' (2008) 16(51) *Roger Williams University Law Review* 52.

nature. He proposes that the comparatist must first of all discard their personal cultural bias in order to be able to look at law objectively.[25] The importance of a proper method of comparison cannot be over-emphasised. This is supported by Kamba's argument that to apply the proper method is imperative in determining whether the specific comparative enquiry effectively serves the function or functions which the comparatist has decided to emphasise. And, furthermore, on that determination will depend the accuracy and the value of the results arrived at and the validity of the conclusions drawn.[26]

Similarly to the difficulty in deciding what to compare, the technique or techniques to be employed can also prove to be equally challenging. While authors such as Eberle[27] suggest a scientific approach to the act of comparison, Kamba leaves it to the comparatist to rely, to a considerable extent, on their individual judgement in deciding which method they are going to use in their comparison. However, Kamba does suggest broad pointers towards a purposeful technique or techniques by outlining three main operations or stages involved in comparative law:

(a) The descriptive stage, where descriptions of the norms, concepts and institutions of the system concerned are set out. Such a description may also include socio-economic problems and the legal solutions provided by the systems under review.
(b) The identification phase has to do with pointing out or discovering differences and similarities between the systems under comparative consideration.
(c) The explanatory phase involves accounting for the similarities and differences.[28]

It should, however, be borne in mind that these three stages are not always distinctly separate from one another, nor do they apply in a particular chronological order; but they all remain imperative to any meaningful comparative study.

Kamba outlines the paramount test in evaluating the correctness of the technique or techniques used in making the comparison and asserts that the test calls for the following questions to be posed:[29]

- Does the technique of comparison employed adequately or effectively fulfil the object or objects which the comparatist has decided on?
- Does it, for example, promote the better understanding of one's own law, the formulation of reliable theories of law, the promotion of law reform or unification?
- Can the results obtained be safely depended on as accurate?

[25] Ibid.
[26] Kamba (note 3) 501.
[27] Eberle (note 24) 52.
[28] Kamba (note 3) 502.
[29] Ibid.

He argues further that if the answer to any of these questions is in the negative, this would be proof that the technique is meagre and unmethodical. The position is otherwise if the replies are in the affirmative.[30]

When one examines Eberle's approach, it becomes clear that he agrees to a certain degree with Kamba's three stages set out above. Eberle offers step-by-step guidelines to the ways in which a comparatist must carry out a comparison. In this regard, his approach is enlightening to someone who is new to the concept of legal comparison. To this end, Eberle proposes four rules for comparative methodology – which he hopes, when applied cautiously, neutrally and eagerly – will help to fulfil the mission of comparative law as a critical legal science. The steps are these:[31]

1. *Rule 1 – Acquiring the skills of a comparatist in order to evaluate law clearly, neutrally and in an objective manner.* Critical reasoning skills are imperative in understanding the legal rules and patterns driving a society. Therefore, this rule requires the comparatist to shed built-in cognitive lock-in (confinement to one's own laws) in order to allow room for objectivity. The comparatist must partake in cultural immersion into the political, historical, economic and linguistic context informing the legal system he/she wants to compare.
2. *Rule 2 – Evaluating external law as written or stated.* Here the comparatist must attentively look at the legal data under review and must evaluate and understand the content and meaning. This involves taking a careful evaluation of the legal data points; comparing and contrasting the similarities and differences between the legal points under study; and investigating and exploring those similarities and differences and then evaluating their significance within their legal culture.
3. *Rule 3 – Evaluating internal law.* The comparatist goes beyond the written law to discover a deeper dimension of law informed by internal forces like custom, geography, language, philosophy, religion, interpretation, etcetera. This is important if one has to understand how law actually functions in a society.
4. *Rule 4 – Assembling results of the investigation.* Under this rule the results of comparative observation can be a window into the world of the foreign culture which at the same time sheds light onto the comparatist's own legal culture. This entails asking the following questions: What is the significance of the data? What has been learnt? Has the investigation shed light into the operation and meaning of the foreign legal system? Can one understand the foreign legal system better?

Another approach worth considering in this discussion on the process of comparison is Cruz's proposed blueprint,[32] within which the comparative technique

[30] Kamba (note 3) 503.
[31] Eberle (note 24) 57.
[32] De Cruz (note 1) 235.

may be applied. He offers it as a plan of action and cautions against regarding it as being exhaustive. It is but a guide that a comparatist can make use of. Eight useful steps are underlined, as set out briefly below in summarised form. With that in mind, one must be careful not to confuse them with the preceding steps in this chapter. The difference lies in this explanation: Kamba lays down the three stages of the comparing method; Eberle offers a scientific approach or guide to comparison which is similar in some ways to what De Cruz hopes to attain by setting out these eight steps, which may be understood in the context of Kamba's three phases:

Step 1

- Formulate the specific issue and determine how long it will take you to complete it. Ascertain whether or not the topic is too wide or too narrow?
- Look for a second opinion, if it is possible, otherwise commence with initial research.

Step 2

- Identify the jurisdictions you are comparing according to their legal families.
- To do this, make use of the usual criteria for the classification stipulated above.

Step 3

- Decide which primary sources or materials you are going to make use of, depending on their availability.

Step 4

- Put together the materials which are appropriate to the jurisdictions being examined. This should include bibliographies from current periodicals, encyclopaedias, written constitutions, law reports, journals and legal periodicals.

Step 5

- Arrange the materials by headings to show the legal philosophy and ideology of the legal system being examined.[33] Under this step, Cruz suggests a working outline which includes (i) the working title, subtitle and subtexts; (ii) the main sources of law of the systems under comparison; (iii) the hierarchy of sources; and (iv) background or socio-cultural material.[34]

Step 6

- Prepare the possible answers to the problem by meticulously comparing the distinct approaches.

---

[33] This accords profoundly with the descriptive phase suggested by Kamba.
[34] De Cruz (note 1) 238.

- Keep in mind the hidden dimensions of the law, such as cultural differences, socio-economic factors as well as any other non-legal factors.
- These two questions should be asked throughout the enquiry: How does the rule or institution really operate in practice? And, why?

Step 7

- Analyse the legal principles in terms of their innate meaning rather than according to any Western or other standards.
- Double-check the correctness of the translations you might have had to scrutinise.

Step 8

- This is where you layout your conclusions within a comparative framework. If it is necessary, you must do so with caution and with critical commentary, wherever appropriate, and link it to the original objective of the enquiry.
- If you considered the nature of the systems under study, their parent legal family or their historical or socio-economic developments as well as the effects of those socio-economic developments on the legal development of a particular area of law, indicate that.
- Finally, you can explain your conclusions, justifying them, so that other researchers in the future would be able to decipher the approach you took and why.

5.3 METHODOLOGICAL APPROACHES TO COMPARATIVE LAW IN AFRICA

Comparative legal studies has received relatively scant attention in Africa. Simply put, Africa has been precluded from the scheme of studies. An exception to this is South Africa, which was fortunate enough to enjoy some attention.[35] Okeke argues that comparitivism in Africa has been made challenging by the fact that African law comprises distinct legal systems ranging from the common- and civil-law systems to customary-law systems. [36] In order for a comparatist to make a comparison, it is imperative that they become acquainted with the ways in which the systems they want to compare operate. Once a person gains a broader perspective and is able to handle compound legal issues, then they understand how the other legal system operates.[37] Without this general grasp, the comparator's task becomes difficult. Okeke believes that the objectives of comparative law are interlinked. He states that

[35] C Okeke *Comparative Law in Africa: Methodologies and Concepts* (Juta & Co, 2015) 36, http://digitalcommons.law.ggu.edu/book_chapters/26.

[36] Okeke (note 35) 36.

[37] Okeke (note 35) 37–38.

it is only when we comprehend how a legal system operates that we can comprehend whether it can serve as a model of law reform for any other legal system.[38]

Okeke posits that in order to understand a legal system or how it operates, it is necessary to 'lay bare the whole apparatus upon which it thrives', in other words, to remove its skin and see its bones. In this exercise, one must take cognisance of any foreign and municipal changes in law.[39] In this regard, Okeke argues that understanding the distinct legal systems in Africa would help African people to tackle the various challenges confronting them; and it would empower and guide respective governments in developing better policies.[40] Accordingly, and specifically in the case of Africa, Okeke argues that there are some challenges in and obstacles to the study of comparative law in mixed legal systems in Africa. These include the fact that, due to the colonial law that was imposed on these countries, they are susceptible to experiencing political and cultural tensions. Another outcome of such an imposition is that the indigenous law has lost its purity.[41]

Legal reform operates through the concept of legal borrowing, by means of which a legal system looks at the experiences of another and draws from those experiences in order either to implement similar laws or to be a guide to identifying what to avoid.[42] Okeke asserts that the comparison of laws is an indispensable instrument for legal borrowing. In this regard, he poses two important questions when taking a decision to reform the law: What elements should enlighten the decision to reform or ameliorate an existing law or legal regime? and Who should make that decision?[43]

To impose upon a people an agenda of law reform that is solely in the interests of the agent suggests it is revolting. Okeke argues that for the comparative-law objective of law reform to be realised in Africa, such reform must be premised on sound and well-thought-out policies; it must be an outcome of comparative research, and it must not merely emerge from the narrow-minded concerns of the leaders.[44]

Another positive inroad comparativism can make for Africans is the international harmonisation and unification of their systems. Again, on this point, Okeke argues that this function of comparative law is an imperative if uniformity and certainty are to be brought to legal systems. He proposes that Africa needs to form a united front to resolve problems such as poverty, human rights violations, and corrupt governments and leaderships. He believes that the best way to take

[38] Ibid.
[39] Okeke (note 35) 37.
[40] Ibid.
[41] Okeke (note 35) 42.
[42] Ibid.
[43] Ibid.
[44] Okeke (note 35) 38–39.

on these challenges is for African countries to be united and harmonised.[45] In this regard, he suggests that we look at Europe and how it has maintained the unification of its states through, for instance, the European Union. However, he advises that this must be done cautiously because unification in Europe is not without its problems.[46] One of the leading challenges with unification, particularly in Europe, is the fact there is a limit to the extent to which comparative law can be used to attain unification because it is impossible to have a truly unified legal system. Moreover, there is also the challenge that the process of unification calls for a balancing of interests exercised by those countries which are striving towards harmonisation.[47]

5.4 METHODOLOGY OF COMPARATIVE LAW IN AFRICA

Okeke defines 'methodology' as the 'set or system of methods, principles, and rules for regulating a given discipline'.[48] He explains that methodology refers to the theoretical examination of the methods suitable to a field of study or to the body of methods and principles specific to a branch of knowledge. In the context of comparative law, he argues that its methods are complemented by its many functions and purposes.

The process of comparison is not an easy task. It requires a comparatist to have a set of skills if they are to carry out a successful comparative study or analysis. Okeke lays down three steps which a comparatist must consider taking in order to determine the right methodology:[49]

1. Possession of the skills of objectivity and neutrality and the knowledge of how to effectively scrutinise the law by taking a broader approach to ascertain the underlying factors of the law;
2. The capacity to analyse the law as it is given, regardless of whether it is written or not; and
3. Societal immersion in a given society in order to inspect how the law functions therein.

Previously in this chapter we discussed the methods of comparative law, its methodologies and concepts. We also noted that the methodologies advanced by those comparatists are not exhaustive. At this juncture, we discuss additional

[45] Ibid.
[46] Ibid.
[47] Ibid.
[48] Okeke (note 35) 22.
[49] Okeke (note 35) 43.

comparative-law methods as advanced by Okeke and why they are significant to the African context. Okeke outlines the eight comparative-law methods:

(1) historical;
(2) functional;
(3) legal harmonisation and unification;
(4) reviewing customary or natural law;
(5) economic analysis;
(6) law and cultural;
(7) critical approach, and
(8) the convergence and the non-convergence approaches.

These methods are briefly set out below.

5.4.1 Historical method

A historical background study of the laws under comparison is imperative in order to gain insights into how a legal system works, how its laws operate and why its laws work for it. This is particularly important when legal borrowing is the objective, because what works for one country may not necessarily work for a different country.[50] In the African context, the need for a historical approach to comparison may be necessary in order to ensure that forgotten useful African cultural ideas can be re-acquired and to examine the ways in which a legal measure has had on impact on conduct or practice. It is also an efficient way of making sense of and finding solutions through the lens of the study of past and foreign concepts.

5.4.2 Functional method[51]

This method is premised on the view that the process of comparison involves not only the evaluation of laws, but that it goes deeper than that to cover the kinds of problem those rules solve. In other words, their potential to provide solutions to legal problems is also analysed. There are several justifications for the functional method approach:

- it is focused on getting results and it is employed for ample social purposes;
- its problem-solving abilities are not limited to a geographical entity;
- it is highly endorsed and accepted as the primary methodology of comparative legal studies;

[50] Okeke (note 35) 44.
[51] Okeke (note 35) 44–45.

- it is advanced on the presupposition that although dissimilar societies exist, they tend to have homogenous problems which can be resolved using different methods, but the outcomes would be similar to the advantage of all, and
- it is preferred because its emphasis is not on what the legal rules stipulate but on what they can in reality do.

5.4.3 Legal harmonisation and unification[52]

Unification and harmonisation are not simply a function of comparative law, but also serve as a methodological approach. As Okeke aptly puts it, harmonisation and unification are realised through the negotiation of both bilateral and multilateral treaties. This is done in order to minimise discrepancies in the same legal fields with a view to producing homogenous laws in particular areas among the countries in consensus.

5.4.4 Reviewing customary or natural law

As discussed above, Africa is a largely diverse continent with a plethora of uncodified customary laws in each of its 54 countries. Some of these countries treat and regard customary law as a question of fact which needs to be ratified by evidence, whereas other countries treat it as a question of law. Okeke suggests that in order to harmonise and unify customary law, all countries must adopt a similar approach to the treatment of customary law as a question of fact.[53]

5.4.5 Economic analysis method[54]

This is an approach that surfaced as a result of discontentment with the functional approach; it therefore has a link to the functional approach. Its primary aim is to generate a standard for determining an appropriate legal solution. The standard it identifies is efficiency. It is based on the view that in order to analyse legal rules appropriately, it is necessary to apply economic concepts. By applying economic concepts to the analysis of the law, the result will be an efficient legal system which will be recognised as one that contains subsidiary waste, curtails transaction costs and improves resource allocation. This has the potential to provide substantial freedom for individuals to interact. In the context of Africa, Okeke argues that this approach would be more helpful to countries which are engaged in developing a uniform economic law to regulate their affairs.

---

[52] Okeke (note 35) 45.
[53] Okeke (note 35) 46.
[54] Ibid.

5.4.6 Law and cultural method or approach[55]

This approach can be differentiated from the functional approach in that it attributes uniqueness to every culture. It focuses on discrepancies in legal systems and is premised on the ground that culture forms an indispensable part of law. Law therefore cannot be totally divorced from culture since law is in essence an expression of culture. Therefore, when engaging in comparative exercises, one must have regard to the cultural context. This requires the comparatist to use a technique of cultural immersion in which they consider the invisible dimensions of the law (the historical, political, economic and linguistic context) which moulded the legal system.

5.4.7 Critical approach[56]

This approach is geared towards dismantling comparative law's Eurocentric robe. In order to strip comparative law of this Eurocentric attire, Okeke suggests three processes which must be followed: the first step is to detach the many-sided literal speculations from the social context and place them in a legal set-up; second, it needs one to analyse the process of decision-making to bring to the fore any political interests intrinsic to this process, and, finally, the cultural context must be restored to the legal set-up from which it had been removed earlier.

5.4.8 Convergence approach and non-convergence approach[57]

With this approach, the way legal systems are viewed is that they exist in distinct forms but they share common characteristics. The argument today is that legal studies should focus on the homogeneity, not on the differences, among legal systems.

5.5 CREATING AFRICAN LAW

It has been suggested that a need exists to create and develop African law as a distinct legal system. This requires African states to unite into cohesive groups. In this regard, Okeke states that African countries will triumph if they begin to understand one another and grasp how they can assist one another socially, economically and legally.[58] Proponents of this idea believe that only Africa can solve many of Africa's

---

[55] Okeke (note 35) 47.
[56] Ibid.
[57] Okeke (note 35) 48.
[58] Okeke (note 35) 7.

problems.[59] This is supported by the view that African problems are highly peculiar to Africa. Therefore, transplanting Western laws into African states in an attempt to solve local problems may not produce the expected results. Instead, it is suggested that Africa should use the experiences of its own countries as the basis for forging mundane legal solutions.[60]

Mancuso argues that African law should go beyond the ineffective discussion of the main legal systems of the world because it possesses its distinctive characteristics. In addition, he contends that African law should be juxtaposed with the cardinal features of each system and by introducing those Western ideas and attributes which are also found in African traditions.[61] However, as Okeke notes, classifying Africa as a unitary legal system is a challenge. This is because African boundaries have been drawn by colonial powers who had no regard for cultural and tribal locations: the way most Africans identify themselves is first by their tribe or region and the state in which they are resident; however, many state borders cut through the middle of villages or tribes and the colonial powers disregarded this prior to drawing the boundary lines. As a result, within each African state there is a complex system of tribal laws which are as functional as any legal system of any state.[62]

How, then, would a distinct African legal system be created? Mancuso argues that African law can be realised through legal pluralism. As Mancuso argues, in order for this African juridical revolution to become a success, the vehicle that must be used is African legal pluralism.[63]According to Swenson,[64] legal pluralism 'whereby two or more legal systems co-exist in the same social field' is the presiding characteristic found in most legal orders globally. An example of countries which included pluralism in their constitutions are South Africa and Namibia. An investigation into the general core of African law should therefore be undertaken to ascertain the common characteristics from the distinct African traditions. In this regard, the jurists should adopt a pluralist approach, accompanied by an interdisciplinary analysis informed by the view of specialists from the sociology, anthropology, economics, history and linguistics fields.

In the quest to architect African law we should be wary of the challenges facing African law. First, African law is unwritten. Mancuso argues that attempts to codify customary laws in many African countries have proven futile. In addition to this, he observes that in many African countries people choose to live by their customary laws instead of the enacted law. This means that they prefer their customs to regulate

[59] Okeke (note 35) 6.
[60] Okeke (note 35) 10.
[61] S Mancuso 'New African law: Beyond the difference between common law and civil law' (2008) 14(1) *Annual Survey of International & Comparative Law* 39–58.
[62] Okeke (note 35) 7.
[63] Mancuso (note 61) 59.
[64] G Swenson 'Legal pluralism in theory and practice' (2018) 20(3) *International Studies Review* 1.

their affairs instead of legislation.[65] Besides Africa's vastly unwritten law and the need for codification, there is also the misleading perception that African law is problematic or difficult to decipher. Mancuso asserts that, apart from the famously known legal systems, through comparative studies a classical African legal system has been identified with its own particular features and differences.[66] As alluded to earlier, African law has largely been ignored or brushed aside by Westerners, who have failed to grasp its diversity – in most cases, the response has been to completely deny its existence. However, as it has become apparent in recent years, Africa, although highly diverse, in fact has its own laws. The idea that African law is too complex and difficult is harboured only by a jurist from the West who cannot and does not attempt to understand its core. This might be a consequence of not being taught law from an anthropological perspective. In this case, the jurist may attempt, without consideration, to make the Africans believe that it is either a vain or a useless pursuit.[67]

5.6 CONCLUSION

Comparativism in Africa does indeed have worth. As discussed in this chapter, Africa would benefit from comparative legal studies in many areas, including law reform and unification. The idea of a modified legal education tailored to African needs suggested by Kibwani[68] is plausible and must be endorsed. By using the correct methodology for comparative law, a number of goals can be realised. Even though the creation of African law as a distinct legal system might be easier said than done, we have an important tool with which to achieve this, and that is through legal pluralism.

REFERENCES

Bekker, JC, Rautenbach, C & Goolam, NMI *Introduction to Legal Pluralism in South Africa* 2 ed (LexisNexis, Butterworths, 2006).

Bennett, TW *A Sourcebook of African Customary Law for Southern Africa* (Juta & Co, 1991).

[65] Ibid.

[66] Mancuso (note 61).

[67] Mancuso (note 61) 56.

[68] K Kibwana *Enhancing Co-operation among African Law Schools: Comparative Law Studies within the African Context* (Centre for Human Rights, University of Pretoria, 1993).

Bennett, TW 'The meeting of comparative law and legal anthropology in Africa' in S Mancuso & CM Fombad (eds) *Comparative Law in Africa: Methodologies and Concepts* (Juta & Co, 2015).

Bennett, TW 'Comparative law and African customary law' in M Reimann & R Zimmermann (eds) *The Oxford Handbook of Comparative Law* 2 ed (Oxford Handbooks, 2019).

Bohannan, P (ed) *Law and Warfare: Studies in the Anthropology of Conflict* (The Natural History Press, 1977).

Brand, O 'Conceptual comparisons: Towards a coherent methodology of comparative legal studies' (2007) 32 *Brooklyn Journal of International Law* 405.

Curran, VG 'Cultural immersion, difference and categories in US comparative law' (1998) 46 *The American Journal of Comparative Law* 43.

De Cruz, P *Comparative Law in a Changing World* 3 ed (Routledge, 2007).

Diala, AC 'Curriculum decolonisation and revisionist pedagogy of African customary law' (2019) 22 *PER/PELJ* 1.

Diala, A *Understanding the Relevance of African Customary Law in Modern Times* (2020), https://theconversation.com/understanding-the-relevance-of-african-customary-law-in-modern-times-150762, accessed 20 August 2023.

Diala, A & Kangwa, B 'Rethinking the interface between customary law and constitutionalism in sub-Saharan Africa' 2019 *De Jure* 189.

Eberle, EJ 'The methodology of comparative law' (2008) 16(51) *Roger Williams University Law Review* 51.

Eberle, EJ 'The method and role of comparative law' (2009) 8 *Washington University Global Studies Law Review* 451.

Elechi, O, Morris SVC & Schauer, EI 'Restoring justice (ubuntu): An African perspective' 2010 *International Justice Review* 20.

Fenrich, J, Galizzi, P & Higgins, TE (eds) *The Future of African Customary Law* (Cambridge University Press, 2011).

Glanert, S 'Methods?' in PG Monateri (ed) *Methods of Comparative Law. Research Handbooks in Comparative Law* (Edward Elgar Publishing Ltd, 2012).

Gluckman, M 'Legal aspects of development in Africa' *[Les Aspects Juridiques du Developpement Economique] Legal Aspects of Economic Development* 59 (Association Internationale des Sciences Juridiques/International Association of Legal Sciences, 1966).

Himonga, C & Bosch, C 'The application of African customary law under the Constitution of South Africa: Problems solved or just beginning?' (2000) 117 *South African Law Journal* 306.

Himonga, C & Nhlapo, T (eds) *African Customary Law in South Africa: Post-apartheid and Living Law Perspectives* (Oxford University Press, 2015).

Hinz, M. 'Traditional governance and African customary law: Comparative observations from a Namibian perspective' in N Horn & A Bosl (eds) *Human Rights and the Rule of Law in Namibia* (Macmillan, 2008).

Hinz, MO & Gairiseb, A (eds) *Customary Law Ascertained, 2: The Customary Law of the Bakgalagari, Batswana ba Namibia and Damara Communities of Namibia* (UNAM Press, 2014).

Hinz, MO & Gairiseb, A (eds) *Customary Law Ascertained, 3: The Customary Law of the Nama, Ovaherero, Ovambanderu, and San Communities of Namibia* (UNAM Press, 2016).

Hinz, MO & Namwoonde, NE (eds) *Customary Law Ascertained, 1: The Customary Law of the Owambo, Kavango and Caprivi Communities* (Namibia Scientific Society, 2010).

Kamba, J 'Comparative law: A theoretical framework' (2008) 23(3) *International and Comparative Law Quarterly* 485–519.

Kane, M, Oloka-Onyango, J Tejan-Cole, A & Leone, S *Reassessing Customary Law Systems as a Vehicle for Providing Equitable Access to Justice for the Poor*. New Frontiers of Social Policy, Arusha Conference, 2005, http://landwise-production.s3.amazonaws.com/2022/03/Kane_Reassessing-customary-law-systems-as-a-vehicle-for-providing-equitable-access-to-justice-for-the-poor_2005-1.pdf, accessed 20 August 2023.

Kibwana, K *Enhancing Co-operation among African Law Schools: Comparative Law Studies within the African Context* (Centre for Human Rights, University of Pretoria, 1993).

Kuruk, P 'The role of customary law under *sui generis* frameworks of intellectual property rights in traditional and indigenous knowledge' (2007) 17(1) *Indiana International and Comparative Law Review* 67–118.

Mancuso, S 'New African law: Beyond the difference between common law and civil law' (2008) 14(1) *Annual Survey of International & Comparative Law* 39–60.

Mancuso, S 'Comparative law in the African context' in S Mancuso & CM Fombad (eds) *Comparative Law in Africa, Methodologies and Concepts* (Juta & Co, 2015).

Mapaure, C 'Reinvigorating African values for SADC' (2011) 1 *SADC Law Journal* 148–152.

Melissaris, E 'The more the merrier? A new take on legal pluralism' (2004) 13(4) *Social and Legal Studies* 57–79.

Menski, W *Comparative Law in a Global Context: The Legal Systems of Asia and Africa* (Cambridge University Press, 2006).

Michaels, R 'Comparative law' in S Basedow, KJ Hopt & R Zimmermann (eds) *Oxford Handbook of European Private Law* (Oxford University Press, 2011).

Mluleki, M 'The African concept of ubuntu/*Botho* and its socio-moral significance' (2005) 3 *Black Theology* 215–237.

Monateri, PG (ed) *Methods of Comparative Law: Research Handbooks in Comparative Law* (Edward Elgar Publishing Ltd, 2012).

Ndeunyema, N *Re-invigorating Ubuntu through Water: A Human Right to Water under the Namibian Constitution* (Pretoria University Law Press, 2021).

Okeke, C 'African law in comparative law: Does comparativism have worth?' (2011) 16(1) *Roger Williams University Law Review* 1–50.

Okeke, CN 'Methodological approaches to comparative legal studies in Africa' in S Mancuso & CM Fombad (eds) *Comparative Law in Africa: Methodologies and Concepts* (Juta & Co, 2015).

Okupa, E 'Is African customary law just?' in MO Hinz (ed) *In Search of Justice and Peace: Traditional and Informal Justice Systems in Africa* (Namibia Scientific Society, 2010).

Ongyango, P *African Customary Law: An Introduction* (African Books Collective, 2013).

Owino, L 'Application of African customary law: Tracing its degradation and analysing the challenges it confronts' (2016) 1(1) *Strathmore Law Review* 145.

Pollock, F 'The history of comparative jurisprudence' (1903) 5(1) *Journal of the Society of Comparative Legislation* 74–89.

Swenson, G 'Legal pluralism in theory and practice' (2018) 20(3) *International Studies Review* 438–462.

Van Hoecke, MV 'Methodology of comparative legal research' (2015) 12 *Law and Method Magazine* 41.

Verhelst, T 'Safeguarding African customary law: Judicial and legislative processes for its adaptation and integration' Occasional Paper No 7 (African Studies Centre, University of California, 1968).

World Intellectual Property Organization (WIPO) *Customary Law, Traditional Knowledge and Intellectual Property: An Outline of the Issues*, https://www.wipo.int/export/sites/www/tk/en/resources/pdf/overview_customary_law.pdf, accessed 20 August 2023.

Zweigert, K & Kötz, H *An Introduction to Comparative Law* 3 ed (Clarendon Press, 1998).

6

An overview of socialist law from the perspective of an African legal framework

Tapiwa V Warikandwa

6.1 INTRODUCTION

Socialist or Soviet law is defined as a generic type of legal system used by communist and previously communist governments in states such as the former Soviet Union.[1] It is based on the civil-law system but contains substantial modifications and changes derived from Marxist–Leninist philosophy.[2] It is debatable whether socialist law has ever been considered a separate legal system. If this were the case, by the time the Cold War ended, communist law would have risen to become one of the most significant legal systems in the world.[3] Socialism's legal systems call for the majority of property to be owned by the state or by agricultural cooperatives and

[1] From 30 December 1922 to 26 December 1991 the Soviet Union, also known as the Union of Soviet Socialist Republics (USSR), was a transcontinental state that ruled a significant portion of Eurasia. It was a role-model communist state that pretended to be a federal union of 15 national republics, but in reality both its economy and its government were highly centralised until its latter years. This one-party state was administered by the Communist Party of the Soviet Union, with Moscow serving as both the capital and the seat of government for its largest and most populous republic, the Russian SFSR. Other notable cities included Alma-Ata (Kazakh SSR), Novosibirsk, Kiev (Ukrainian SSR), Tashkent (Uzbek SSR), Minsk (Byelorussian SSR) and Leningrad (Russian SFSR). It was the largest nation in the world, covering more than 22 402 200 square kilometres (8 649 500 square miles) and 11 time zones.

[2] K Marx *Introduction to a Contribution to the Critique of Hegel's Philosophy of Right* (1843), available on the Marxist Internet Archive.

[3] U Mattei 'The Cold War and comparative law: A reflection on the politics of intellectual discipline' (2017) 65(3) *The American Journal of Comparative Law* 567–607.

having special courts and laws for state enterprises, in contrast to civil-law systems that traditionally go to great lengths to define the concept of private property and how it may be acquired, transferred or lost.[4] Some legal academics have argued that communist law was not a distinct legal classification.[5] Despite the fact that the communist nations' command-economy approach meant that most categories of property could not be owned, the Soviet Union always had a civil code, courts that interpreted this civil code and a civil-law approach to legal reasoning (therefore, both legal process and legal reasoning were largely analogous to the French or German civil code system).[6]

Legal scholars in post-socialist states often view socialist law as a particular example of Romano-Germanic civil law because the legal systems in all socialist regimes preserved formal aspects of the Romano-Germanic civil law.[7] There are no recorded instances of common law becoming socialist law, because the essential ideas of common law and socialism law are irreconcilable (common law presumes the influential rule-making role of courts, whereas courts in socialist states play a dependent role). Furthermore, African socialism has incorporated socialist law within the African legal framework.[8] African socialism has been criticised as being a doctrine that lacks an ethical foundation;[9] however, it incorporates an African natural-law concept and an associated African legality principle.

Some contemporary academics have maintained that the idea of African legality is compatible with the rule of law. However, in the contemporary decolonial era, which advocates the existence of an African jurisprudence, this perspective may be seen as contestable. African jurisprudence is a school of thought that stresses the importance, essence, characteristics and goals of African law and culture. There is much doubt whether or not African legality has been informed by an African legal philosophy. Decolonial legal thought in Africa submits that the legal past that produced our current legal reality and framework was not always kind to the African indigenes. African legality has not always been formulated in a transparent

---

[4] K Verdery *Property in Socialism: Collectivization, Administrative Rights, and the Circulation of Goods. The Vanishing Hectare: Property and Value in Post-socialist Transylvania* (Cornell University Press, 2003) 40–76, https://doi.org/10.7591/9781501717253-006.

[5] B Leiter 'Marx, law, ideology, legal positivism' (2015) 101(4) *Virginia Law Review* 1179–1196.

[6] SI Olympiad 'Law and economy in the USSR' (1982) 95(7) *Harvard Law Review* 1591–1625; see also V Gsovski 'The Soviet concept of law' (1938) 7(1) *Fordham Law Review*.

[7] E Kamenka & AES Tay 'Beyond the French Revolution: Communist socialism and the concept of law' (1971) 21(2) *The University of Toronto Law Journal* 109–140.

[8] Fr Simon I Sanga & R Pagnucco 'Julius Nyerere's understanding of African socialism, human rights and equality' (2020) 4(2) *The Journal of Social Encounters* 15–33; see also JN Hazard 'Negritude, socialism and the law' (1965) 65(5) *Columbia Law Review* 778–809.

[9] S Metz 'In lieu of orthodoxy: The socialist theories of Nkrumah and Nyerere' (1982) 20(3) *The Journal of Modern African Studies* 377–392.

manner. Instead, it has been crafted in a manner that appears to perpetuate colonial injustices, disparities, extreme poverty, labour exploitation, environmental degradation, torture, oppression, physical damage to lives and livelihoods, and sudden or gradual death, among other forms of injustice.

The law must simultaneously be a social reality, an official norm and an ethical guideline.[10] In contemporary African society as a whole, this ought to be the unquestionable triple manifestation of the law. The focus of the law has been the value element, which has grown in significance for the independent African governments. Understanding the value or ideal aspect of law was a key objective of the newly independent African countries' developmental trajectory.[11] The governments of these sovereign African countries are still dealing with nation-building and national development after independence. African nationalist leaders who led their individual countries to freedom envisioned establishing unified governments when they adopted socialism. The fact that the effects of colonial control still remain after independence has brought the far more difficult task of state politico-cultural integration to the forefront, along with the need to confront the significance of socialism in Africa's legal framework.[12] It should be noted at this point that colonial borders were frequently defined with little respect for pre-existing political and cultural differences. However, the collapse of colonial control removed a critical force holding artificial units together, at the same time raising the urgent question of the foundation on which the post-independence unification of African states would be based.

The late Kwame Nkrumah once argued that the African people's political, economic and social situations, and their desires for change, should be legally characterised in the law.[13] All laws in Africa, according to Nkrumah, must be written with African indigenes' needs and aspirations in mind.[14] Nkrumah's remarks were later echoed by Zambia's late former president, Kaunda, who stressed that, without the rule of law, society as a whole would collapse, particularly in cases where society lacked public respect for the law.[15] It therefore becomes critical to ascertain how

---

[10] W van der Burg & FWA Brom 'Legislation on ethical issues: Towards an interactive paradigm' (2000) 3(1) *Ethical Theory and Moral Practice* 57–75.

[11] T Mkandawire 'Thinking about developmental states in Africa' (2001) 25(3) *Cambridge Journal of Economics* 289–313.

[12] K Wiebke *Colonialism, National-Socialism and the Holocaust: On Modern Ways of Dealing with Deviance. Gauging and Engaging Deviance (1600–2000)* (2014), 978-93-82381-31-0.01091133; H Haferkamp & NJ Smelser (eds) *Social Change and Modernity* (University of California Press, c1992).

[13] E Sprinzak 'African traditional socialism: A semantic analysis of political ideology' (1973) 11(4) *The Journal of Modern African Studies* 629–647.

[14] Ibid.

[15] L Schler 'Dilemmas of post-colonial diplomacy: Zambia, Kenneth Kaunda, and the Middle East crisis, 1964–73' (2018) 59(1) *The Journal of African History* 97–119.

African societies in the 21st century will restore respect for excessively Westernised laws.

The law must be acknowledged by Africans as their law, reflecting their needs and aspirations. A radical mass ideology with roots in the society's own past yet living in the present and aiming for a new future is required. African leaders were sure that this could be accomplished after independence. This conviction culminated in the development of the idea of African socialism. The spontaneous rise of African socialism in various parts of Africa after independence was notable. In contemporary African society, it can only add impetus to the credibility of calls to decolonise Africa's legal system and the African continent at large. As a result, this chapter investigates why socialism appealed to African leaders in certain phases of post-independence Africa. It also discusses Soviet socialism, African socialism, scientific socialism, and other forms of socialism. The difficulties that socialism presents in Africa are also discussed in this chapter.

6.2 SOCIALIST OR SOVIET LAW: A CONTEXTUAL BACKGROUND

Several distinctive features of Soviet law emerged from the socialist nature of the Soviet state and reflected Marxist–Leninist philosophy.[16] Lenin embraced the Marxist theory of the law and the state as instruments of coercion in the hands of the capitalists and proposed the construction of popular informal tribunals to administer revolutionary justice.[17] During the early stages of the creation of socialist law, Stučka emerged as a prominent theorist of Soviet socialist legality. At the same time, Pashukanis created the concept of 'proletarian justice', which contributed to the formation of a dictatorial trend that advocated the use of law and legal institutions to suppress all dissent aimed at the ruling government.[18] This trend peaked under Stalin's reign, with the rise of Vyshinsky, when the administration of justice was mostly carried out by the security police in special tribunals.[19] During the de-Stalinisation of the Khrushchev era, a new movement emerged based on socialist legality, emphasising the necessity to safeguard citizens' procedural and

---

[16] VV Aspaturian 'The contemporary doctrine of the Soviet state and its philosophical foundations' (1954) 48(4) *The American Political Science Review* 1031–1057.

[17] T Smith 'Beyond hero worship: A Marxist critique of Bolshevik terror and its indebtedness to Jacobinism' (1996) 10(1) *Socialism and Democracy* 47–82.

[18] JM Campbell 'Is there a case for socialist jurisprudence?' PhD thesis (University of Glasgow, 1997), https://theses.gla.ac.uk/4247/1/1997CampbellPhD.pdf.

[19] R Dowling *Brezhnev's War on Crime: The Criminal in Soviet Society, 1963–1984* (2017), https://escholarship.org/content/qt44n3x1m7/qt44n3x1m7.pdf.

statutory rights yet requiring loyalty to the state.[20] New legal codes were adopted in 1960 as part of an effort to establish legal norms in the administration of laws.[21]

Despite the fact that socialist legality remained in force after 1960, authoritarian and utopian trends continued to affect the legal process.[22] The persecution of political and religious dissenters persisted, but there was a trend to decriminalise minor infractions by referring them to people's tribunals and administrative agencies and dealing with them through education rather than incarceration. Around the end of 1986, the Gorbachev administration emphasised the value of individual rights in relation to the state once more and criticised those who had violated procedural law when enforcing Soviet justice.[23] This indicated that socialist legality would once again be the dominant trend. However, it should be recalled that communist legality itself lacked several of the characteristics of Western jurisprudence.

6.3 CHARACTERISTICS OF SOCIALIST LAW

Regarding characteristics, socialist law has been considered as being similar to common law or civil law.[24] However, it has a much larger public-law and a much smaller private-law component. It also included partial or total expulsion of the former ruling classes from public life at the early stages of existence of each socialist state; however, in all socialist states this policy gradually changed into the policy of 'one socialist nation without classes'.[25] The diversity of political views was directly discouraged. The ruling Communist Party was eventually subjected to prosecution through party committees in the first place.[26] The abolition of private property was considered as a primary goal of socialism, if not its defining characteristic, which translated into the near-total collectivisation and nationalisation of the means of production; The Judiciary was subordinate to the Communist Party.[27] Respect for

---

20 B Nathans 'The dictatorship of reason: Aleksandr Vol'Pin and the idea of rights under "Developed Socialism"' (2007) 66(4) *Slavic Review* 630–663.

21 Ibid.

22 TH Bui 'Deconstructing the "Socialist" rule of law in Vietnam: The changing discourse on human rights in Vietnam's constitutional reform process' (2014) 36(1) *Contemporary Southeast Asia* 77–100.

23 FA Copeland '"Perestroika" and human rights: Steps in the right direction' (1991) 15(2) *The Fletcher Forum of World Affairs* 101–119.

24 L Lustgarten 'Socialism and the rule of law' (1988) 15(1) *Journal of Law and Society* 25–41.

25 JN Hazard 'Socialist law and the international encyclopedia' (1965) 79(2) *Harvard Law Review* 278–302.

26 Ibid.

27 K Marx & F Engels 'Manifesto of the Communist Party' in Karl Marx & Friedrich Engels *Collected Works*, 6 (International Publishers, 1976) 498.

privacy was low, the party exercising extensive control over private life; intellectual property (IP) was little respected because knowledge and culture were considered a right of humankind and not a privilege, as was the case in the free-market economies.[28] There were also extensive social warrants of the state in return for a high degree of social mobilisation.[29] The public prosecution was regarded as the provider of justice and the legal system lacked an adversarial nature. A specific institution characteristic of socialist law was the so-called bur law court, which decided on minor offences.

6.4 DIFFERENT FORMS OF SOCIALIST LAW

Socialism has been adopted by different countries to inform their legal systems.[30] This section discusses the different forms of socialist law and their characteristics. It begins with a discussion of the Chinese socialist law.

6.4.1 Chinese socialist law

The People's Republic of China is among the remaining notable communist governments in the world.[31] China adopted the socialist law and added extensive modifications to its legal systems. This was a result of its market-oriented economic changes. However, some communist influence can still be seen. For example, in Chinese real-estate law there is no unified concept of real property:[32] the state owns all the land but often not the structures that sit on that land. A rather complex ad hoc system of use rights to land property has developed, and these use rights are the things that are being officially traded (rather than the property itself). In some

---

[28] E Stacy-Ann 'Paying for privacy and the personal data economy' (2017) 117(6) *Columbia Law Review*, https://columbialawreview.org/content/paying-for-privacy-and-the-personal-data-economy/, accessed 7 March 2023.

[29] JI Dominguez 'Political participation and the social mobilization hypothesis: Chile, Mexico, Venezuela, and Cuba, 1800–1825' (1974) 5(2) *The Journal of Interdisciplinary History* 237–266.

[30] L Lustgarten 'Socialism and the rule of law' (1988) 15(1) *Journal of Law and Society* 25–41.

[31] See Art 1 of the Constitution of the Republic of China. It provides as follows: 'The People's Republic of China is a socialist state governed by a people's democratic dictatorship that is led by the working class and based on an alliance of workers and peasants. The socialist system is the fundamental system of the People's Republic of China. Leadership by the Communist Party of China is the defining feature of socialism with Chinese characteristics. It is prohibited for any organization or individual to damage the socialist system.'

[32] J Alsen 'An introduction to Chinese property law' (1996) 20(1) *Maryland Journal of International Law* 1–60.

cases (eg, in the case of urban residential property), the system results in something that resembles real property transactions in other legal systems.[33]

In other cases, the Chinese system results in something quite different. For example, it is a common misconception that reforms under Xiaoping resulted in the privatisation of agricultural land and the creation of a land-tenure system similar to those found in Western countries.[34] In actual fact, a village committee owns the land and contracts the right to use this land to individual farmers, who may use the land to make money from agriculture. Therefore, the rights that are normally unified in Western economies are split between an individual farmer and a village committee.[35]

This has a number of consequences. One of them is that, because the farmer does not have an absolute right to transfer the land, they cannot borrow against their use rights. But there is some insurance against risk in the system in that the farmer can return their land to the village committee if they wish to stop farming and start some other kind of business. Then, if this business does not work, they can get a new contract with the village committee and return to farming. The fact that the land is redistributable by the village committee also ensures that no one is left landless; this creates a form of social welfare.

There have been a number of proposals to reform this system and they have tended to be in the direction of fully privatising rural land for the alleged purpose of increasing efficiency. These proposals have usually not received any significant support, largely because of the popularity of the current system among the farmers themselves. There is little risk that a village committee will attempt to impose a bad contract on the farmers, since this would reduce the amount of money the village committee receives. At the same time, the farmer has some flexibility to decide to leave farming for other ventures and to return at a later time.

6.4.2 Christian socialism

Christian socialism refers to a movement of the mid-19th century that attempted to apply the social principles of Christianity to modern industrial life.[36] The term was generally associated with the demands of Christian activists for a social programme of political and economic action on behalf of all individuals, impoverished or wealthy, and the term was used in contradistinction to laissez-faire individualism.[37]

---

[33] Ibid.

[34] Z Xu 'Chinese agrarian change in world-historical context' (2014) 78(2) *Science & Society* 181–206.

[35] Ibid.

[36] RT Handy 'Christianity and socialism in America, 1900–1920' (1952) 21(1) *Church History* 39–54.

[37] Ibid.

Later, Christian socialism came to be applied in a general sense to any movement that attempted to combine the fundamental aims of socialism with the religious and ethical convictions of Christianity.[38]

Early in the 19th century, the French philosopher De Saint-Simon expounded a 'new Christianity' primarily concerned with the plight of the poor.[39] The Saint-Simonians believed that the keynote of social development would be a spirit of association, with religion as the dominating force, that would gradually supplant the prevailing spirit of egotism and antagonism in society.[40] They advocated (among other things) that inheritance rights be abolished so that capital could leave the hands of self-seeking capitalists and be placed at society's disposal.[41] The Saint-Simonians imagined that this and other related actions would effectively end the exploitation of the poor.[42]

The term 'Christian socialism' was first appropriated by a group of British men who included Frederick Denison Maurice, novelist Charles Kingsley, John Malcolm Ludlow and others, who founded a movement that took shape in England immediately after the failure of the Chartist agitation of 1848.[43] Their general purpose was to vindicate for 'the Kingdom of Christ' its 'true authority over the realms of industry and trade' and 'for socialism its true character as the great Christian revolution of the 19th century'.[44] Four years after Marx characterised religion as 'the opiate for the people', Kingsley (probably unaware of Marx's phrase) asserted that the Bible had been wrongly used as 'an opium-dose for keeping beasts of burden patient while they were being overloaded' and as a 'mere book to keep the poor in order' (in *Politics for the People*, 1848).[45]

Inspired principally by the writings of Buchez, a disciple of Saint-Simon, and by the emergence of cooperative societies in France, Ludlow – who had been reared and educated in France – enlisted other churchmen in an effort to promote the application of Christian principles in industrial organisations.[46] Stirred by the

---

[38] Ibid.

[39] Editors of *Encyclopedia Britannica* 'Barthélemy-Prosper Enfantin' *Encyclopedia Britannica*, 4 February 2023, https://www.britannica.com/biography/Barthelemy-Prosper-Enfantin, accessed 7 March 2023.

[40] Editors of *Encyclopedia Britannica* 'Christian Socialism' *Encyclopedia Britannica*, 28 May 2013, https://www.britannica.com/topic/Christian-Socialism, accessed 7 March 2023.

[41] Ibid.

[42] Ibid.

[43] JP Betts 'John Stuart Mill, Victorian liberalism, and the failure of co-operative production' (2016) 59(1) *The Historical Journal* 153–174.

[44] Ibid.

[45] Editors of *Encyclopedia Britannica* (note 40); see also J Horn '1848 and the language of politics' (2000) 25 *Saothar* 67–76, http://www.jstor.org/stable/23198964.

[46] Editors of *Encyclopedia Britannica* (note 40).

sufferings of the poor and by factory and workshop conditions, Ludlow's group vigorously criticised socially conservative Christianity and laissez-faire attitudes in the industrial sector.[47] Urging, among other measures, that cooperation replace competition, they joined forces with the cooperativist movement and financed several small cooperative societies that favoured co-partnership and profit-sharing in industry.[48] They created the Council for Promoting Working Men's Associations and in 1854 they founded the Working Men's College in London.[49] The movement itself dissolved in the late 1850s;[50] some members of the movement continued working for cooperativism, however, and numerous Christian socialist organisations were formed in the 1880s and 1890s in England.[51]

In addition to the French Roman Catholic social movement long in existence, movements similar to Ludlow's took shape among French Protestants in the latter half of the 19th century.[52] The Protestant Association for the Practical Study of Social Questions, founded in 1888, opposed bourgeois Protestantism while rejecting a strict, egalitarian socialism.[53] In Germany, the movement for Christian social action in the late 19th century became associated with violent anti-semitic agitation.[54] Stoecker, a court preacher and a founder of the Christian Social Workers' Party, took a leading role in the anti-semitic drive.[55] In the United States, James Sr, the father of novelist Henry James and philosopher William James, argued that the identity of the aims of socialism and Christianity was established as early as 1849.[56] The Society of Christian Socialists was organised in 1889.[57] The first years

[47] Ibid.

[48] Ibid.

[49] H Solly *Working Men's Social Clubs and Educational Institutes* rev ed by BT Hall (Simpkin, Marshall, Hamilton, Kent and Co, [1867]1904).

[50] Ibid.

[51] Ibid.

[52] Editors of *Encyclopedia Britannica* 'Albert, Count de Mun' *Encyclopedia Britannica*, 24 February 2023, https://www.britannica.com/biography/Adrien-Albert-Marie-comte-de-Mun, accessed 7 March 2023.

[53] S Berger 'Difficult (re-)alignments – comparative perspectives on social democracy and religion from late-nineteenth-century to interwar Germany and Britain' (2018) 53(3) *Journal of Contemporary History* 574–596.

[54] SAJ Telman 'Adolf Stoecker: Anti-semite with a Christian mission' (1995) 9(2) *Jewish History* 93–112; see also J Retallack 'Anti-semitism, conservative propaganda, and regional politics in late nineteenth century Germany' (1988) 11(3) *German Studies Review* 377–403.

[55] JD Klier 'German antisemitism and Russian judeophobia in the 1880s: Brothers and strangers' (1989) 37(4) *Jahrbücher für Geschichte Osteuropas* 524–540.

[56] Editors of *Encyclopedia Britannica* 'William DP Bliss' *Encyclopedia Britannica*, 4 October 2022, https://www.britannica.com/biography/William-D-P-Bliss, accessed 7 March 2023.

[57] PD Jones *Christian Socialist Revival, 1877–1914* (Princeton University Press, 1968).

of the 20th century witnessed the rise of the Social Gospel movement, which was an outgrowth of Christian socialism that stressed the social aspect of salvation.[58]

6.4.3 Democratic socialism

Democratic socialism refers to a political ideology that supports the establishment of a democratically run and decentralised form of socialist economy.[59] Modern democratic socialists vary widely in their views on the way in which a proper socialist economy should function, but all of them share the goal of abolishing capitalism rather than improving it through state regulation (as preferred by social democrats).[60] They also prioritise democracy as an end over democracy as a means, and some democratic socialists consider revolution as an acceptable method of achieving the democracy they desire.[61]

Democratic socialists reject Marxism–Leninism (ie, communism) as a legitimate form of socialism, arguing that command economies effectively belong to a small bureaucracy that treats the means of production as its own private property.[62] Democratic socialists also disagree with social democrats' attempts to harness capitalism to a strong welfare state, since such mixed economies still leave many businesses' ownership under private (and therefore undemocratic) control.[63] Instead, all employees should enjoy either democratic control or self-management in the workplace. Some democratic socialists believe that markets have a place in a socialist economy, so long as the competing businesses are publicly, cooperatively or otherwise socially owned.[64] Like social democrats, many democratic socialists advocate the enactment of state regulation and state welfare programmes, both as temporary means of ameliorating the harm of capitalism and as methods of transforming the system piecemeal.[65]

---

[58] M Bowman 'Sin, spirituality, and primitivism: The theologies of the American social gospel' 1885–1917' (2007) 17(1) *Religion and American Culture: A Journal of Interpretation* 95–126.

[59] L Peng 'Carsun Chang on democratic socialism: Liberalism, social democracy, and German idealism' (2019) 26(2) *American Journal of Chinese Studies* 107–127.

[60] M Makovi *The Impossibility of Democratic Socialism: Two Conceptions of Democracy* (2016), https://mpra.ub.uni-muenchen.de/70172/1/MPRA_paper_70172.pdf, accessed 7 March 2023; see also JH Kautsky 'Centralization in the Marxist and in the Leninist tradition' (1997) 30(4) *Communist and Post-Communist Studies* 379–400.

[61] F Cunningham 'The socialist retrieval of liberal democracy' (1990) 11(1) *International Political Science Review/Revue Internationale de Science Politique* 99–110.

[62] A Volle 'Democratic socialism' *Encyclopedia Britannica*, 6 October 2022.

[63] Ibid.

[64] D Miller 'Socialism and the market' (1977) 5(4) *Political Theory* 473–490.

[65] Ibid.

For decades, the meaning of the terms 'social democrat' and 'democratic socialist' were reversed, a fact that might cause confusion for the 21st-century reader of 20th-century socialist thought. In all cases, a completely socialist economy was the objective.[66] But those who called themselves 'social democrats' might have supported either revolution or reform, whereas democratic socialists were incrementalists.[67] The conceptual union of democratic and socialist thought began early in the latter's development. Marx hinted at an openness to democratic government in *The Civil War in France* (1871), his fawning account of the short-lived Paris Commune of 1871.[68] Marx, whose sketch of that aborted government includes a pyramid-like structure of elected delegates, continued to refer to the Paris Commune in later works as a model for socialism. Two decades later, Marx's partner, Engels, seemingly made Marx's suggestion explicit, writing that the democratic republic is 'the specific form for the dictatorship of the proletariat'. And Engels's own successor, Kautsky, established a clear continuity of thought on the matter by declaring socialism to be industry's ownership by the democratic state.[69]

A thread of insistence on democratic decision-making in government continued to be woven through socialist discourse in the West through the first half of the 20th century.[70] But democratic socialism as it is now defined, with its emphasis on decentralised decision-making, did not arise as a discrete political current until after 1956, when Khrushchev's 'secret speech' on Stalin's abuses resulted in widespread disenchantment with communism among leftists in the Western world.[71] Some members of other socialist groups – such as anarchists, disaffected communists and issue-based activists in the United States and Europe – subsequently rechristened themselves as members of the 'New Left' to distance themselves from the social democratic establishments in both the Soviet Union and Europe.[72] Many of the disparate groups that emerged under this banner, such as the emblematic Students for a Democratic Society (SDS) with its dedication to participatory democracy, either called themselves 'democratic socialists' or met the criteria by which future

[66] I Katznelson 'Considerations on social democracy in the United States' (1978) 11(1) *Comparative Politics* 77–99.
[67] Volle (note 62).
[68] Ibid.
[69] Ibid.
[70] D Sassoon 'The rise and fall of West European communism 1939–48' (1992) 1(2) *Contemporary European History* 139–169.
[71] S Pons & SA Smith (eds) *The Cambridge History of Communism* (Cambridge University Press, 2017) 277–636; see also Volle (note 62).
[72] Volle (note 62); see also R Balfour et al *Divide and Obstruct: Populist Parties and EU Foreign Policy* (German Marshall Fund of the United States, 2109), http://www.jstor.org/stable/resrep21237, accessed 7 March 2023.

democratic socialists would be known.[73] They never coalesced into a lasting political party (and many did not want to), yet the overlap in their concerns and their tactics – mass protests, strikes and civil disobedience, among other actions, made them a powerful movement into the 1970s.[74]

Cross-pollination among New Left groups led to the broadening of democratic socialist concerns to include social disparities that were previously ignored and accommodating such issues as gay rights, anti-colonialism and environmentalism.[75] Democratic socialist organisations that followed, such as the Democratic Socialists Organizing Committee (DSOC) and the New American Movement (NAM) in the United States, inherited this interest in multiple causes – a stance later described as multi-tendency or intersectional. As interest in social democracy declined from the 1980s to the 2010s in favour of neoliberalism, the membership of democratic socialist organisations also dwindled.[76] However, the recession of 2007–2009 reignited interest in left-wing economics, resulting in unexpected success for self-described socialists at the ballot box. In the United States, democratic socialist Sanders won more than two-fifths of the total votes cast in the 2016 Democratic primary elections and more than one-fourth in the more crowded 2020 primary elections.[77] Membership of the Democratic Socialists of America (DSA) correspondingly ballooned from 6 500 members in 2014 to nearly 100 000 by 2020. Democratic socialists have parlayed these new numbers into electoral victories, winning both state and federal offices on the Democratic ticket.[78]

6.4.4 Utopian socialism

Utopian socialism is a political and social idea of the mid-19th century.[79] Adapted from such reformers as Owen and Fourier, utopian socialism drew on early communist and socialist ideas.[80] Advocates included Blanc, noted for his theory of worker-controlled 'social workshops', and Noyes, founder of the Oneida Community in the United States. Utopian settlements were also attempted by religious groups such as the Mennonites, Shakers and Mormons.[81]

---

[73] Volle (note 62).
[74] Ibid.
[75] Ibid.
[76] Ibid.
[77] Ibid.
[78] Ibid.
[79] DW Lovell 'Socialism, utopianism and the "utopian socialists"' (1992) 14(2) *History of European Ideas* 185–201.
[80] R Paden 'Marx's critique of the utopian socialists' (2002) 13(2) *Utopian Studies* 67–91.
[81] J Vidalenc 'Louis Blanc' *Encyclopedia Britannica*, 2 December 2022, https://www.britannica.com/biography/Louis-Blanc, accessed 7 March 2023.

At independence, African countries had to decide which type of state to put in place, and between 1950 and the mid-1980s, 35 of Africa's countries adopted socialism at some point.[82] The leaders of these countries believed that socialism offered them their best chance to overcome the many obstacles these new states faced at independence. Initially, African leaders created new hybrid versions of socialism, known as 'African socialism', but by the 1970s, several states turned to the more orthodox notion of socialism, known as 'scientific socialism'.[83] But what was the appeal of socialism in Africa and what made African socialism different from scientific socialism?

The ideology of socialism is explicitly anti-imperial. Whereas the USSR (which was the face of socialism in the 1950s) was arguably an empire itself, its leading founder, Lenin, wrote one of the most famous anti-imperial texts of the 20th century: *Imperialism: The Highest Stage of Capitalism.*[84] In this work, Lenin not only criticised colonialism but also argued that the profits from imperialism would 'buy out' the industrial workers of Europe.[85] The workers' revolution, he concluded, would have to come from the unindustrialised and underdeveloped countries of the world.[86] This opposition of socialism to imperialism and the promise of revolution coming to underdeveloped countries made it appealing to anti-colonial nationalists around the world in the 20th century.[87] To be truly independent, African states needed to be not only politically but also economically independent. But most were trapped in the trading relations established under colonialism. European empires had used African colonies for natural resources and therefore when those states achieved independence, they lacked industries.[88] The major companies in Africa, such as the mining corporation Union Minière du Haut-Katanga, were European-based and European-owned.[89] By embracing socialist principles and working with socialist trading partners, African leaders hoped to escape the neo-colonial markets that colonialism had left them in.[90]

---

[82] MA Pitcher & KM Askew 'African socialisms and postsocialisms' (2006) 76(1) *Africa Journal of the International African Institute* 1–14.

[83] A Thompsell *Socialism in Africa and African Socialism* (2019), https://www.thoughtco.com/socialism-in-africa-and-african-socialism-4031311.

[84] D Sassoon 'The rise and fall of West European communism 1939–48' (1992) 1(2) *Contemporary European History* 139–169.

[85] Ibid.

[86] Ibid.

[87] Ibid.

[88] M wa Muiu '"Civilization" on trial: The colonial and post-colonial state in Africa' (2008) 25(1) *Journal of Third World Studies* 73–93.

[89] B Fetter 'The mines of southern and central Africa: An ecological framework' (1992) 2 *Health Transition Review* 125–135.

[90] H Campbell 'Socialism in Tanzania: A case study' (1975) 6(8) *The Black Scholar* 41–51.

When the USSR was formed in 1917 during the Russian Revolution, it was an agrarian state with little industry.[91] It was known as a backward country, but less than 30 years later the USSR had become one of two superpowers in the world.[92] To escape their cycle of dependency, African states needed to industrialise and modernise their infrastructures very quickly, and African leaders hoped that by planning and controlling their national economies using socialism they could create economically competitive modern states within a few decades.[93] Socialism seemed to many to be a more natural fit with African cultural and social norms than the individualist capitalism of the West. Many African societies place great emphasis on reciprocity and community. The philosophy of ubuntu, which stresses the connected nature of people and encourages hospitality or giving, is often contrasted with the individualism of the West, and many African leaders argued that the ubuntu values made socialism a better fit for African societies than capitalism.[94] One-party socialist states promised unity. At independence, many African states were struggling to establish a sense of nationalism among the different groups that made up their population. Socialism offered a rationale for limiting political opposition, which leaders – even previously liberal ones – came to see as a threat to national unity and progress.

6.4.5 African socialism

In the decades before decolonisation, a few African intellectuals, such as Senghor, were drawn to socialism in the decades before independence. Senghor read many of the iconic socialist works but was already proposing an African version of socialism, which would become known as 'African socialism' in the early 1950s.[95] Several other nationalists, such as the future President of Guinee, Sékou Touré, were heavily involved in trade unions and demands for workers' rights.[96] These nationalists were often far less educated than men such as Senghor, though, and few had the leisure to read, write and debate socialist theory.[97] Their struggle for living

[91] J Keep 'The agrarian revolution of 1917–1918 in Soviet historiography' (1977) 36(4) *The Russian Review* 405–423.

[92] Ibid.

[93] T Mkandawire 'Thinking about developmental states in Africa' (2001) 25(3) *Cambridge Journal of Economics* 289–313.

[94] SS Olusegun 'Ubuntu and the problem of belonging' 2023 *Ethics, Policy & Environment*, DOI: 10.1080/21550085.2023.2179818.

[95] MA Pitcher & MK Askew 'African socialisms and post-socialisms' (2006) 76(1) *Africa: Journal of the International African Institute*.

[96] M Tinsley 'Proclaiming independence: Language and national identity in Sékou Touré's Guinea' (2015) 18(3) *Postcolonial Studies* 237–256.

[97] E Schmidt 'Top down or bottom up? Nationalist mobilization reconsidered, with special reference to Guinea (French West Africa)' (2005) 110(4) *The American Historical Review* 975–1014.

wages and basic protections from employers made socialism attractive to them, particularly the type of modified socialism that men such as Senghor proposed.[98]

Epistemologically, law represents official norms, social facts and ethical values.[99] Accordingly, jurisprudence or the theory of law recognises three distinct though complementary approaches: the formalistic, the functional and the ethical.[100] Formalistic jurisprudence concerns itself with 'positive law' or the law as one finds it in official sources; functional or sociological jurisprudence is rather more interested in the 'living law', or positive law – as it is applied. Ethical jurisprudence operates on the 'natural law' or 'ought' level.[101] It is with the 'ought' modality of jurisprudence that I am concerned in this chapter, for the principle of African legality as espoused by the ideology of African socialism and the rule of law concept as hitherto formulated in the Western world are both politico-legal precepts.

In respect of Africa, ethical jurisprudence gained prominence for the first time during the anti-slavery campaign at the end of the 18th and the beginning of the 19th centuries.[102] It surfaced again at the conclusion of the First World War, when it resulted in the international mandate system. After the Second World War, it played an important role in the anticolonial and anti-apartheid struggle. Incidentally, it was during the era between the abolition of slavery and the First World War that colonialism in Africa reached its peak and the European scramble for Africa took place.[103] Was it coincidence that during this very same period formalistic jurisprudence, or 'legal positivism', as it is also known, reigned supreme in Europe, to the virtual neglect of ethical legal thinking? Be that as it may, the critical need for ethical reasoning in respect of Africa has not disappeared with the achievement of political independence. There remain the extremely delicate objectives of nation-building and national development. After all, it was colonies, not traditional political units, which became independent. Colonial frontiers in Africa were often drawn along arbitrary lines of latitude and longitude, which resulted in a new political map showing some 50-odd territories instead of the far

---

[98] Ibid.

[99] K Toh 'An argument against the social fact thesis (and some additional preliminary steps towards a new conception of legal positivism)' (2008) 27(5) *Law and Philosophy* 445–504.

[100] R Gavison 'Natural law, positivism and the limits of jurisprudence: A modern round (review of *The Authority of Law: Essays in Law and Morality; Natural Law and Natural Rights*, by J Raz & J Finnis)' (1982) 91(6) *The Yale Law Journal* 1250–1285.

[101] D Coffey et al 'Custom and living law' (2012) 3(1) *Jurisprudence* 71–210.

[102] A Sanders 'On African socialism and the rule of law' (1982) 15(3) *The Comparative and International Law Journal of Southern Africa* 299–305.

[103] JH Clarke 'Pan-Africanism: A brief history of an idea in the African world' (1988) 145 *Présence Africaine* 26–56.

greater number of traditional political societies.[104] It has been left to today's leaders to turn the artificial colonial units, which during colonial times were governed on a divide-and-rule basis, into nation-state and to give effect to popular demands for rapid Africanisation and economic and social development.

In response to these challenges, political leaders such as Nkrumah, Nyerere, Senghor, Sékou Touré, Mboya, Kaunda, Cabral and Mugabe have advocated an ideology which has come to be known as 'African socialism'.[105] In South Africa, African socialist ideology is very much alive. Black liberation movements subscribe to it, in some form or another, and for many a black youngster African socialism supplies the answers to their dreams of political, economic and social emancipation. For most whites and the ever-obliging 'system blacks', on the other hand, African socialism is a taboo. They see it as a form of communism, a movement of revolutionary blacks, the inevitable evil best forgotten for the moment. African socialism may be inevitable but it is certainly not communist, revolutionary or necessarily restricted to blacks.

The differences between African socialism and communism are fundamental: although both ideologies aim at social solidarity, African socialism does not visualise an ideal society where there will be no more state and no more law. African socialism does not view the state, the law or religion as instruments of oppression. On the contrary, it considers them to be indispensable elements of an ideal society which, like traditional African society, will again be characterised by religious feeling, a communal spirit and a belief in democracy based on government by popular discussion and consensus. In African socialist ideology, the society to be created takes the form of a unitary, non-racial one-party welfare state. As far as law is concerned, African socialism assigns it a permanent role. Elsewhere, I have pointed out that African socialism in fact contains a definite principle of legality.

According to the principle of African legality, behaviour on the part of the rulers and subjects alike should be in accordance with the concept of social solidarity as implied in the values of African tradition previously mentioned: religious feeling, a communal spirit and democratic government by popular discussion and consensus. African socialism also differs from communism in that it rejects the doctrine of the economic class struggle and the inevitability of revolution. While recognising social differences, African socialists deny, at least for their societies, the existence of fundamental social divisions and propagate peaceful national unification. Colonial

[104] J Herbst 'The creation and maintenance of national boundaries in Africa' (1989) 43(4) *International Organization* 673–692; see also Lord Salisbury, quoted in JC Anene 'The international boundaries of Nigeria, 1885–1960' in *The Framework of an Emergent African Nation* (Longman Press, 1970) 3.

[105] CR Stephens *The People Mobilized: The Mozambican Liberation Movement and American Activism (1960–1975)* (2011), https://scholarshare.temple.edu/bitstream/handle/20.500.12613/2461/Stephens_temple_0225E_10882.pdf?sequence=1, accessed 7 March 2023.

rule, not economic class struggle, was their defining experience, and the main impact of colonial rule was cultural, with its major features being racial discrimination and the denial of traditional institutions and values.[106] African socialism included socialist doctrines adopted by several African leaders at the close of French and British colonial rule during the 1950s and 1960s.[107]

As African countries gained independence, anticolonial nationalism could no longer play the unifying and mobilising role that it had in the early 1950s.[108] Instead, African socialism became a mobilising slogan to unite Africans around the challenge of economic development in their postcolonial societies.[109] The communal basis of most African precolonial societies and the absence of a tradition of private property appeared to justify the existence of an indigenous African path to socialism, one that seemingly offered a third way between Western capitalism and Soviet communism.[110]

Unlike Marxism, a historical–materialist method based on a well-established body of theoretical literature, African socialism emerged rapidly as an eclectic and pragmatic approach to development.[111] Its best-known proponents included Senghor and Dia of Senegal, Sékure Touré of Guinea, Nkrumah of Ghana, Mboya of Kenya and Nyerere of Tanzania.[112] Yet the Colloquium on Policies of Development and African Approaches to Socialism, a conference of African leaders held in Dakar, Senegal, in 1962, failed to produce a clear definition or a unified vision of African socialism.[113] The diverse participants interpreted African socialism to reflect the varied needs of their respective countries.[114] They generally agreed, however, that precolonial Africa's communal values and the relative absence of classes and class struggle should form the basis of an African path of development. Three main themes were emphasised: African identity, economic development, and class formation and social control.[115]

Senghor, probably the first to use the term 'African socialism', argued that Western and Soviet materialism should be replaced with values rooted in the continent's

---

[106] JA McCain 'Ideology in Africa: Some perceptual types' (1975) 18(1) *African Studies Review* 61–87.

[107] Ibid.

[108] S Salem 'Radical regionalism: Feminism, sovereignty and the pan-African project' (2022) 47(1) *Africa Development/Afrique et Développement* 159–191.

[109] Ibid.

[110] AJ Klinghoffer 'The Soviet view of African socialism' (1968) 67(268) *African Affairs* 197–208.

[111] K Nkrumah *African Socialism Revisited*, speech given at the Africa Seminar, Cairo, 1967, transcribed by Dominic Tweedie, available on the Marxist Internet Archive.

[112] A Drew 'African socialism' *Encyclopedia Britannica*, 27 October 2017, https://www.britannica.com/topic/African-socialism, accessed 7 March 2023.

[113] Ibid.

[114] Ibid.

[115] F Cooper 'Africa and the world economy' (1981) 24(2–3) *African Studies Review* 1–86.

precolonial collective tradition.[116] African socialism should draw on *negritude*, the celebration of black culture and the African personality.[117] Dia saw African socialism as a synthesis of individualist and socialist values, producing a humanist outlook that would accord with Christian and Muslim beliefs and allow Africa to follow its own trajectory independently of the West and the Soviet bloc.[118] For the Pan-Africanist, Padmore, African socialism was part of a threefold revolutionary movement encompassing national self-determination, social revolution and continental unity. African socialism should begin with communal land ownership and cooperative agriculture, along with joint state and private initiatives to build the economy.[119] The leadership's task was to unite all sections of society behind those development goals.

Despite the belief that African socialism was rooted in the continent's precolonial tradition, the approach was applied to societies that had been markedly transformed by the colonial experience in varied ways, making the implementation of a single doctrine problematic.[120] Ghana, for example, became a beacon for Pan-African unity and African socialism upon gaining its independence in 1957.[121] However, unlike most proponents of African socialism, who gave primacy to rural development, Nkrumah stressed the large-scale development of energy resources as a means of rapid industrialisation.[122] Ghana quickly became heavily indebted and Nkrumah became increasingly intolerant of criticism. In 1964 he declared himself to be president for life and banned opposition parties. He was overthrown in 1966.[123]

Guinea became independent in far more difficult conditions. Once it accepted France's offer of independence in 1958, it faced the complete withdrawal of the French colonial apparatus and civil service.[124] Guinea's African socialism was premised on the development of state-run mechanised farms and market controls, but the country lacked the educated personnel for state-led development: at independence it had fewer than 50 university graduates, a legacy of colonial policy.[125]

[116] B Jewsiewicki 'African historical studies academic knowledge as "usable past" and radical scholarship' (1989) 32(3) *African Studies Review* 1–76.
[117] JN Hazard 'Negritude, socialism and the law' (1965) 65(5) *Columbia Law Review* 778–809.
[118] Drew (note 112).
[119] Ibid.
[120] J McCain 'Perceptions of socialism in post-socialist Ghana: An experimental analysis' (1979) 22(3) *African Studies Review* 45–63.
[121] Ibid.
[122] Ibid.
[123] Ibid.
[124] M Thomas 'France accused: French North Africa before the United Nations, 1952–1962' (2001) 10(1) *Contemporary European History* 91–121.
[125] G Arrighi & JS Saul 'Socialism and economic development in tropical Africa' (1968) 6(2) *The Journal of Modern African Studies* 141–169.

Its state farms foundered and price controls alienated peasants and traders, who smuggled produce into neighbouring countries to obtain higher prices for their goods. As social discontent mounted, Touré's rule became increasingly centralised and authoritarian.[126] He remained in power until his death in 1984.[127]

In contrast to Nkrumah's emphasis on state-led development projects, Nyerere, the doctrine's best-known East African advocate, stressed village-level development.[128] But Nyerere shared Nkrumah's belief in a one-party state, arguing that class divisions were foreign to Africa, that their development should be suppressed and that social differences could be reconciled in a single party.[129] Capitalism was premised on exploitation and Marxism on class conflict, Nyerere contended. Socialist and democratic values were part of Africa's precolonial history, reflecting a time when all members of society contributed to production and wealth was distributed equitably.[130]

As the leader of Tanzania (formed in 1964 through the union of Tanganyika and Zanzibar), Nyerere promoted the idea of *ujamaa* (Swahili for 'familyhood') in which the extended family was the building block of African development.[131] Nyerere's 1967 Arusha Declaration stressed *ujamaa*, self-reliance and austerity as the key planks of African socialism. Nyerere launched a programme of villagisation – the forced relocation of rural people into collective and cooperative villages – as the basis of economic development.[132] But the initiative proved politically unpopular and economically non-viable. Once again, the peasants resisted the state's external interventions.

Babu, an influential critic of Nyerere, was imprisoned by Nyerere between 1972 and 1978.[133] In prison he wrote a significant appraisal of African socialism that was smuggled out of the country and later published as *African Socialism or Socialist Africa?* Babu contended that African socialists, like other African leaders, had pursued export-oriented strategies that perpetuated Africa's dependency on foreign investment and foreign aid.[134] He called for working-class organisation and

---

[126] ML Kilson 'Authoritarian and single-party tendencies in African politics' (1963) 15(2) *World Politics* 262–294.
[127] Ibid.
[128] B Ibhawoh & JI Dibua 'Deconstructing *ujamaa*: The legacy of Julius Nyerere in the quest for social and economic development in Africa' (2003) 8(1) *African Journal of Political Science* 59–83.
[129] JO Adesina 'Variations in postcolonial imagination: Reflection on Senghor, Nyerere and Nkrumah' (2022) 47(1) *Africa Development/Afrique et Développement* 31–58.
[130] D Allison 'African socialism' *Encyclopedia Britannica* (2017), https://www.britannica.com/topic/African-socialism, accessed 7 March 2023.
[131] JM Weiskopf 'Socialism on safari: Wildlife and nation-building in postcolonial Tanzania, 1961–77' (2015) 56(3) *The Journal of African History* 429–447.
[132] Allison (note 130).
[133] Taylor & Francis 'A tribute to AM Babu' (1996) 23(69) *Review of African Political Economy* 321–348.
[134] Allison (note 130).

for the development of Africa's productive forces.[135] Babu's criticism signalled the intellectual demise of African socialism, but the practical end of the doctrine was already evident in its failed economic projects and the repressive one-party regimes wielding power in its name.[136] Once in authority, African socialists proved no more democratic than their conservative counterparts.

The African socialist notion of state and society also offends the consociational thinking of which we hear so much in South Africa nowadays.[137] For the consociationalists, South Africa is a typical example of a 'deeply divided society', in respect of which it is felt that a coalition of the political leaders from each group is the only realistic possibility and that without such a 'grand coalition' there will be no democracy but rather violence and disruption.[138] Instead of simple majority rule, 'consociationalism' – a tongue rather than a heart-breaker for the African socialist – advocates government by group leadership consensus, mutual group veto, group proportionality and as much group autonomy as possible.[139] Simple majority rule and its winner-take-all character are also anathema to African socialism; but African socialism favours popular consensus, not group leadership consensus.[140] African socialism is also strongly committed to the idea of an overriding 'national kinship', and to that end it has advanced the concept of the one-party democracy. The one-party democracy is intended as a modern projection of traditional government – geared at a *Gesellschaft* (society) rather than a *Gemeinschaft* (community or association) (Tonrues) and at 'organic solidarity' rather than 'mechanical solidarity' (Durkheim) – but always embodying the traditional values of equal and free discussion, popular consensus and popularly controlled leadership.[141]

6.5 AFRICAN SOCIALISM AND DEMOCRACY

The African socialist conception of democracy is clearly a popular one, not a sectarian or segmental one; the new nation is seen as a new kinship or family grouping.[142] Even South Africa, after years of apartheid, is not seen by blacks, including those

---

[135] Ibid.

[136] Ibid.

[137] AJGM Sanders *International Jurisprudence in African Context* (Butterworths, 1979) 57–91.

[138] SG Simonsen 'Addressing ethnic divisions in post-conflict institution-building: Lessons from recent cases' (2005) 36(3) *Security Dialogue* 297–318.

[139] ID Duchacek 'Dyadic federations and confederations' (1988) 18(2) *Publius* 5–31.

[140] A Sanders 'On African socialism and the rule of law' (1982) 15(3) *The Comparative and International Law Journal of Southern Africa* 299–305.

[141] AJGM Sanders *On African Socialism and the Rule of Law* (nd), https://docplayer.net/212396028-5-on-african-socialism-and-the-rule-of-law.html, accessed 7 March 2023.

[142] A Thomson *Introduction to African Politics* (Routledge, 2000).

directly affected by the apartheid regime, as a society so deeply divided that it calls for institutionalised group accommodation. African socialism rejects any assumption, whether communist or consociationalist, about South African society consisting inherently of antagonistic groups.[143] It is indeed remarkable that whereas consociationalism has caught the imagination of white politicians, in opposition and government circles there has been a stony silence in black quarters. only broken by Chief G Buthelezi who in respect of his own 'commission of enquiry into the requirements for stability and development in KwaZulu and Natal', which forms the subject-matter of this seminar,[144] had to admit that

> many aspects of the findings are painful departures from black aspirations. The most obvious is the move away from the undiluted commitment of blacks to the principle of one-man-one-vote in a unitary state.

Having outlined what African socialism stands for and what it rejects, I shall now say a few words about the rule of law before I consider the questions of whether the principles of African legality and the rule of law are reconcilable and, if so, how.

The rule of law, just as with the principle of African legality, is a politico-legal concept by which positive law can be judged and guided in the light of a certain ideal.[145] Regarding the principle of African legality, the ideal situation is social solidarity; in the case of the rule of law it is the highest possible protection of the individual's fundamental human rights. Whereas the principle of African legality, with its emphasis on social solidarity, by its very nature applies to the governors and the governed alike, the rule of law is directed at the government only.[146] To put the rule of law concept in a nutshell: it is that politico-legal code for a government's conduct which is best suited to securing for the individual the highest possible enjoyment of those of their public claims which a particular political society regards as fundamental, due regard being had to competing individual interests, the necessities of government and the available national resources.[147]

---

[143] RJ Southall 'Post-apartheid South Africa: Constraints on socialism' (1987) 25(2) *The Journal of Modern African Studies* 345–374.

[144] LJ Boulle 'The Buthelezi Commission recommendations in the light of current constitutional trends' (1982) 15(3) *The Comparative and International Law Journal of Southern Africa* 262.

[145] C Murphy 'Lon Fuller and the moral value of the rule of law' (2005) 24(3) *Law and Philosophy* 239–262.

[146] M Ndulo 'African customary law, customs, and women's rights' (2011) 18(1) *Indiana Journal of Global Legal Studies* 87–120.

[147] A Sanders 'On African socialism and the rule of law' (1982) 15(3) *The Comparative and International Law Journal of Southern Africa* 299–305.

The rule of law obviously refers to a higher form of legality as embodied in 'natural law' but not necessarily embodied in 'positive law'.[148] The rule of law has its origins in Europe in the 17th- and 18th-century writings of people such as Locke, Rousseau and Montesquieu.[149] Their theories would lead to practical steps being taken aimed at advancing and safeguarding fundamental human rights.

In the United Kingdom, Dicey, writing towards the end of the 19th century, stressed the importance to the rule of law of legal certainty, equality before the law, the limitation of governmental powers and effective legal remedies for the protection of human rights in contradistinction to mere declarations of human rights.[150] He proudly equated the rule of law to 'the security given under the English Constitution to the rights of the individual'.[151] Yet the British type of constitution, because of its principle of the legislative sovereignty of parliament, contains no guarantee that human rights will be respected. In fact, it can be an ideal prescription for despotism. And it was the fate of Britain's colonies to discover this. The American colonies were among the earliest victims and also the first to throw off the colonial yoke. Their experience under the British constitution told them to adopt a written, inflexible constitution which would provide for separate and limited government powers. An entrenched Bill of Rights was included and Chief Justice Marshall's decision in *Marbury v Madison* 5 US (1 Cranch) affirming the courts' power of judicial review of legislation rounded off the US contribution to the rule of law as constitutionalism.

The contribution of the European continent to the rule of law lies in the sphere of the welfare state. Above all, it relates to the principle of the formal and material legality of administrative action and the introduction of judicial review of administrative action by specialised administrative courts. As a result, a sophisticated body of administrative-law rules developed which has proved particularly effective in protecting human rights.

Second, there is the well-known institution of the ombudsman which originated in Scandinavia.[152] Interestingly, the various national contributions to the rule-of-law concept have acquired a multi-national character. Consequently, constitutionalism has become a feature of many a Western and Third World constitution. Administrative courts have made their appearance in common-law

---

[148] J Dickinson 'The law behind law: II' (1929) 29(3) *Columbia Law Review* 285–319.

[149] L Claus 'Montesquieu's mistakes and the true meaning of separation' (2005) 25(3) *Oxford Journal of Legal Studies* 419–451.

[150] MI Principe 'Albert Venn Dicey and the principles of the rule of law: Is justice blind? A comparative analysis of the United States and Great Britain' (2000) 22 *The Loyola of Los Angeles International and Comparative Law Review* 357.

[151] Ibid.

[152] LB Orfield 'The Scandinavian ombudsman' (1966) 19(1) *Administrative Law Review* 7–74.

countries and the institution of the ombudsman has been adopted by countries far beyond Scandinavia, including some African states, notably Tanzania and Zambia – both one-party states.[153] The International Commission of Jurists has accordingly been able to characterise the rule of law as a dynamic supernational concept.[154] The commission, a private international organisation with headquarters in Geneva, has its origin in an international congress which was held in West Berlin in the summer of 1952 to discuss violations of the rule of law in East Germany and other Eastern European countries.[155]

The commission's membership is confined to a limited number of eminent jurists with an international reputation. Through its national sections, the commission is in contact with lawyers from all parts of the world, except the communist world, and through its conferences and publications it makes its influence felt on lawyers and their governments. It is an important achievement of the commission that it was able to list and secure wide international agreement with regard to the principles, institutions, techniques and procedures which together form the content of the modern rule of law. These are:

(1) respect by all branches of government for fundamental human rights;
(2) both formal and material equality of all people before the law;
(3) legal certainty;
(4) minimum standards of justice in the administration of the law;
(5) limitation of governmental powers, which implies a democratic form of government and the separation of powers;
(6) an independent and properly qualified Judiciary, and
(7) an independent and properly qualified legal profession.[156]

Finally, provision is made for cases of public emergency – which need, however, not be considered for the purposes of this chapter.

This leaves us with the question: To what extent, if at all, is the rule of law compatible with the principle of African legality and the African socialist concept of the state and society? There is no gainsaying that in African socialist ideology the state assumes a rather authoritarian position, for not only does African socialism aspire to a unitary welfare state – which of necessity implies strong government – it

[153] A Sanders 'On African socialism and the rule of law' (1982) 15(3) *The Comparative and International Law Journal of Southern Africa* 299–305.
[154] Ibid.
[155] Ibid.
[156] Ibid.

also demands that popular consensus be followed by discipline.[157] The latter implies that the civil service, the Judiciary, the armed forces, the police, the parastatals, the press, the trade unions and other professional bodies are expected to function in the spirit of the one-party democracy, ultimately in accordance with the principle of African legality.[158] Traditionally, African legality emphasises communalism and is wary of individualism and a glorification of human rights at the expense of society and effective government.[159]

This does not mean, however, that the idea of protecting human rights is foreign to African tradition or the modern concept of African legality. 'The Rule of Law is a part of socialism; until it prevails socialism does not prevail,' President Nyerere once said.[160] It is true that African socialists cannot uncritically accept Eurocentric formulations of human rights and theories for their protection.[161] This, however, does not detract from their commitment to the dignity of man. Theirs, too, is a campaign for human dignity. As President Kaunda has pointed out, 'our socialism is humanism.'[162] In fact, socialism and one-party democracy are regarded as preconditions for human dignity, whereas capitalism and apartheid are seen as assurances of its massive denial. The problem that faces African socialism is not that of recognising the dignity of man but of devising effective structures for its protection. In a unitary one-party welfare state, how does one protect people from the abuse of power? How does one ensure that interference with the individual's rights is no more than is necessary to achieve or preserve the greater good of social solidarity, and that the danger of the abuse of human rights is minimised? These and similar questions were considered at an international seminar on 'human rights, their protection and the Rule of Law in a one-party state' which was held in Dar es Salaam, from 23 to 28 September 1976 under the auspices of the International Commission of Jurists.[163] The seminar found that the one-party system was fully consistent with the rule of law and formulated a number of principles with which a one-party state ought to comply. The report and the conclusions of the seminar are

---

[157] DMC Ude 'Kwasi Wiredu's critique of Marxism: Its philosophical application to the "African socialism" via Nkrumah, Nyerere and Touré' (2018) 12(5) *Journal of Pan African Studies* 181.

[158] Ibid.

[159] Sanders (note 153) 299–305; see also MT Bradley '"The other": Precursory African conceptions of democracy' (2005) 7(3) *International Studies Review* 407–431.

[160] I Shivji *The Rule of Law and Ujamaa in the Ideological Formation of Tanzania* (nd), https://www.academia.edu/5028000/The_Rule_of_Law_and_Ujamaa_in_the_Ideological_Formation_of_Tanzania_, accessed 7 March 2023.

[161] Fr Sanga, S Innocent & R Pagnucco 'Julius Nyerere's understanding of African socialism, human rights and equality' (2020) 4(2) *The Journal of Social Encounters* 15–33.

[162] Sanders (note 153) 299–305.

[163] V Karel *International Dimensions of Human Rights* (nd), https://unesdoc.unesco.org/ark:/48223/pf0000056230, accessed 7 July 2023.

contained in the International Commission of Jurists' publication *Human Rights in a One-party State* (1978).[164] The seminar and its conclusions were the subject of a lively discussion at the 25th anniversary meeting of the commission held in Vienna in April 1977.[165] The commission, in an official finding, expressed the view that there were dangers of the abuse of power inherent in one-party systems which were less likely to arise if an effective multi-party system existed.

The commission realised, however, that human rights could be endangered by ineffective attempts to duplicate multi-party systems without due regard to cultural traditions and the historical development of particular countries. The commission finally pointed out that the rule of law would be facilitated in a one-party state if the following principles propounded at the seminar in Dar es Salaam were actually observed:

1. Electoral freedom of choice is essential to any democratic form of society. The party should guarantee genuine popular choice among alternative candidates.
2. Everyone should be free to join the party or to abstain from party membership or membership in any other organisation without penalty or deprivation of their civil rights.
3. The party must maintain effective channels of popular criticism, review and consultation. The party must be responsive to the people and make it clear to them that this is party policy.
4. In a one-party state it is particularly important that:
   (a) the policy-forming bodies of the party use all sources of information and advice, and
   (b) that within the party members should be completely free to discuss all aspects of party policy.
5. The independence of the judiciary in the exercise of its judicial functions and its security of tenure is essential to any society which has a respect for the rule of law. Members of the Judiciary at all levels should be free to dispense impartial justice, without fear, in conformity with the rule of law.
6. The independence of the legal profession being essential to the administration of justice, the duty of lawyers to be ready to represent fearlessly any client, however unpopular, should be understood and guaranteed. They should enjoy complete immunity of actions taken within the law in defence of their clients.
7. Facilities for speedy legal redress of grievances against administrative action in both party and government should be readily available to the individual.

[164] H Hannum 'The Butare Colloquium on Human Rights and Economic Development in Francophone Africa: A summary and analysis' (1979) 1(2) *Universal Human Rights* 63–87.

[165] Sanders (note 153).

8. The absence of an opposition makes it essential to provide mechanisms for continuous, impartial, and independent review and investigation of administrative activities and procedures. In this respect such institutions as the ombudsman and minister with powers to initiate action can be usefully adopted.
9. In a one-party state, criticism and freedom of access to information should be permitted and encouraged.
10. The right to organise special interest associations such as trade unions, professional, social, religious or other organisations, should be encouraged and protected. Such organisations should be free to affiliate or not with established political parties.
11. All members of the society must be made aware of their human rights to ensure their effective exercise, and for that reason education in human rights at all levels should be a matter of high priority. In particular, officials of the party and government should be made to understand the limits on the exercise of power which derives from the recognition of fundamental human rights and the rule of law.[166]

In part 6.3 of this chapter, different forms of socialism were described and the conceptual aspects and misconceptions of socialism were engaged with. Unfortunately, the more prominent South African adherents of this ideology have officially been silenced. This severely detracts from the value of the constitutional debate currently carrying on in South Africa and it has virtually limited the debate to white-dominated enquiries into various forms of consent at group leadership level only. One would have hoped that developments to the north of the country, most recently in Zimbabwe, would by now have convinced white South Africans in leadership positions to acknowledge African socialist ideology, which, deeply embedded as it is in the African mind, is bound to exercise considerable influence on future constitution-making in South Africa.

6.6 SOCIALISM AND LAW

One may anticipate that the function of law would be different in a socialist society. This change would reflect the change in social relationships. Throughout history, a main function of law has been to uphold and regulate property relationships. In protecting and enforcing property rights, it follows that in all eras of propertied society the various systems of law have favoured the dominant economic class. In socialism this historic function of law will end. In a society based on common ownership and voluntary cooperation the sole object of law would be to serve the

[166] Ibid.

needs of individuals and the interests of the entire community. Such law would provide a framework of freedom, enabling individuals to live out their chosen lives. Law in socialism would express the values of equality and democracy.

Even in the age of Pericles, Athenian democracy was practised exclusively by male citizens on a foundation of slavery that was sanctified by law.[167] Similarly, throughout Europe, under feudal law, the serf and his family were bound for life to the lord of the manor.[168] Runaway serfs were flogged, branded or worse. In capitalism, in contrast, wage slaves are free to change their employers but still remain locked into a life of making company profits. This is the modern form of economic bondage, the routine of debt and wage working to get the money to pay the mortgage, the rates, gas, electricity and the many other bills, all of them regulated by law.

The relationship of worker to employer is based on great differences in property ownership which again are upheld and enforced by law. This is not just in the corporate ownership of the means of life – natural resources, mining, industry, manufacturing and transport – it is also in the ownership of land. In viewing these vastly unequal property relationships and the part played by law in their development throughout history, some schools of political thought assert that a society based on equality and cooperation would abolish all law. In particular, this is an argument often put forward by anarchists. It is also true that such 19th-century socialist visionaries as Morris and even Engels held this view.[169] However, the idea that all law would be abolished should now be relegated to the irrelevant spheres of anarchist utopianism. The reason for this is that the abolition of all law is problematical to the point of being not just wholly impractical, but it would also be in direct opposition to the principles of socialist organisation. For example, the abolition of the law against paedophilia or rape would disregard the safety and well-being of children and others; this would be unacceptable in any circumstances. To raise a very different example, it would be impossible to run a modern democratic society without constitutional law being in place.

This brings us to the question that the subject of socialism and law is part of the wider question of social democracy. A basic working tool of democratic practice is making majority decisions. However, the very mention of a majority assumes a minority of people who did not agree and probably voted against a matter. Democracy means that minorities also have their rights, not just the right to vote

---

[167] TD Curran 'Politics in Classical Greece: The nature of the *polis* and the origins of the rule of law' (1989) 9(2) *Sacred Heart University Review* article 4.

[168] Ibid.

[169] F Boos & W Boos 'The utopian communism of William Morris' (1986) 7(3) *History of Political Thought* 489–510.

against but the freedom to persuade and bring a majority over to their view.[170] In a society based on voluntary cooperation, any who disagree with a decision would be free to abstain from any action that might flow from a decision.

However, it is as well to remember that minorities are not a particular human type who are always in the minority.[171] On other issues they may well be part of the majority and in these circumstances they would not take kindly to dissenters' acting to prevent the wishes of the majority from being carried out. So, it would be a condition of democratic practice that no individual or group may act against a majority decision, except within the bounds of democratic conduct. In socialism, this basic principle of democratic organisation would be applied in practical ways within a framework of democratic law.

Beyond the article of faith that in a socialist society absolute social accord will be absolutely guaranteed, without law and solely as a result of self-regulation, what we would have in practice is the absolute right of the individual to do what they want.[172] This would not only be the opposite of democracy; it would be the negation of freedom itself. This is not to dismiss self-regulation. Even now, and certainly in socialism, it will remain a most important way of achieving decent human relations. But we should not adopt this as dogma, saying that self-regulation will be the only way to achieve a safe, stable and democratic society. It can, of course, be argued that such cases as crimes against persons, which may be more difficult to relate directly to property relationships, are in fact at the end of a sequence of causes and effects that begin with the psychologically destructive pressures of life under the capitalist system. There can be little doubt that the emotions of stress, anxiety, insecurity and frustration, which are inherent in the system and which blight the lives of many people, can distort patterns of reasonable social conduct.[173]

The well-proven link between crime and economics adds great force to the argument that the conditions of life in socialist communities would greatly reduce crime. The welfare of all citizens would be the first objective of social organisation and this would be achieved through cooperation, and would provide a secure standard of living for every person. Its relationships would reduce psychological damage and would be more conducive to a healthier pattern of personal conduct. In place of economic individualism, exploitation, competition and social exclusion – all of which contribute to the conditions in which crime thrives – there would be social integration and equal standing among all members of a community. Seen in

---

[170] B Saunders 'Democracy, political equality, and majority rule' (2010) 121(1) *Ethics* 148–177.

[171] M Song 'Rethinking minority status and "visibility"' (2020) 8 *Comparative Migration Studies* 5.

[172] LL Fuller 'Positivism and fidelity to law: A reply to Professor Hart' (1958) 71(4) *Harvard Law Review* 630–672.

[173] NC Crawford 'The passion of world politics: Propositions on emotion and emotional relationships' (2000) 24(4) *International Security* 116–156.

this light, we may assume that not only would crime be greatly reduced but, with it, the machinery and administration of law.

This is not to wander too far onto the ground of economic determinism. People will always have choices, but under the pressure of psychological compulsion the proper choices are not always easy to make. Also, there seems to be no direct evidence to support the claim that capitalist productive relationships cause people to commit the crimes of child abuse, rape, child murder or domestic violence. There is no evidence to support the assertion that all people in a socialist system will at all times be models of democratic virtue. On the contrary, the evidence from this life is that socialists are capable of behaving badly and can even engage in child abuse.[174] It is also apparent that some socialists are just as likely to behave in an undemocratic manner as anyone else. So, from crimes of the utmost seriousness that threaten life and limb to lesser kinds of anti-social behaviour, the unfair treatment of individuals, democratic accountability or the abuse of positions of civic responsibility – all of these matters could be administered in an orderly, predictable and democratic manner in a socialist society only through legal procedures endorsed by an entire community.

The method of applying practical socialism to this question is in principle the same as the method for selecting any useful feature of present society that would be continued in socialism.[175] The criteria we apply to useful production, useful decision-making bodies and useful means of administration apply equally to law. In the case of law, it is a question of identifying the existing features of law that could continue to play a useful part in civic organisation together with the useful institutions that administer such law. Socially useful law should be distinguished from law that is concerned solely with upholding, regulating and enforcing the economic relationships of the capitalist system.

It follows from the retention of useful law that the institutions for administering it would also need to be retained. The administration of law in socialism would continue to respect the right of any person accused of an offence to defend themself.[176] This means being able to call witnesses, to question evidence and to put a defence before a body independently of those bringing the charges. Such a person should also be entitled to a right of appeal. This means that, subject to perhaps modification along more democratic lines, the present court system would also be retained. The use of law in socialism will be a means of safeguarding individuals and communities against

---

[174] RE Lane 'Waiting for lefty: The capitalist genesis of socialist man' (1978) 6(1) *Theory and Society* 1–28.

[175] K Korsch, F Denton & D Kellner 'What is socialization? A program of practical socialism' (1975) 6 *New German Critique* 60–81.

[176] L Lustgarten 'Socialism and the rule of law' (1988) 15(1) *Journal of Law and Society* 25–41.

dangerous or other anti-social behaviour.[177] It would be humanely administered with the sole object of solving problems without any kind of punishment. The vile prisons as we know them would be abolished. On the assumption that it would still be necessary to hold some persons in places of secure confinement, these would allow occupants to lead dignified lives in pleasant conditions. But the use of law in socialism would not only be concerned with avoiding dangerous or anti-social behaviour; it would also be practised to regulate democratic administration and would provide procedures for ensuring accountability.

In making a distinction between socially useful law that would be continued and law that could have no function in a socialist society, we begin with the fact that much of our present law exists to uphold and enforce property rights, to regulate the wage labour–capital relationship and to mediate between contesting parties over monetary or other property disputes.[178] However, over the past two centuries, legal systems have expanded enormously, partly into socially useful areas which are not directly to do with the protection of property rights. For example, laws regulating foetal experiments, abortion and the age of sexual consent, whatever we may think of them, arise from moral or ethical questions. This kind of law has changed over time within states and varies enormously between states in ways that have little bearing on economic relationships. Similarly, we have laws on drunk driving; professional qualifications; licences for drivers, airline pilots and ships' captains; laws on assault, murder, rape, child abuse and public nuisance; laws on planning and constitutional law – all of which define the boundaries of decision-making in public bodies. All of these examples arise from the organisation of civil society and would continue to be necessary.

Company law and income tax law would be redundant, together with civil law, in processing disputes over contracts, money transactions and property. Criminal law deals with theft, fraud and assault, etc, and so before the courts there is a sad parade of burglars, muggers, bank and building society robbers, car thieves, credit card fraudsters and drug offenders. But courts also deal with many cases which are less directly connected to present economic relationships. Here the law deals with drunk driving, speeding and other traffic offences such as unlicensed or dangerous driving. And when eventually that paedophile is arrested, the courts deal with the individual who moves from district to district, using different names, posing as that 'nice man' who helps out at the youth centre. They deal with the rapist, the violent schizophrenic, the psychopath, domestic violence and – occasionally but with

[177] See *Practical Socialism – Its Principles and Methods* (2006), quoted in A Buick *Socialism and Law* (2016), https://www.marxists.org/archive/lawrence/2006/6socialism_law.htm, accessed 7 March 2023.

[178] A Stone 'The place of law in the Marxian structure–superstructure archetype' (1985) 19(1) *Law & Society Review* 39–67.

predictable regularity, as we have noted – they deal with the child killer. Planning law would continue to regulate housing, the use of buildings and industrial or manufacturing development in accordance with social policy. And as is the case at present, neither individuals or nor any public body would be free to develop a site without following the procedures of planning consent.

Family law would continue. Just as night follows day, it is certain that couples will continue to fall in love and have families. Sadly, though, it is equally certain that some will fall out of love. Family courts would not need to decide matters such as monetary maintenance, but this still leaves plenty of scope for disputes in which courts would need to arbitrate. It is unlikely that any society, however conducive it is to reasonable behaviour, will succeed in removing the emotions of jealousy and bitterness that are inherent in family fallouts. This would be where couples cannot agree on questions such as who should leave or stay in the family home, the custody of children and the hours to be spent with one or the other parent. There is always a point at which a relationship is over; despite this, it is sometimes the case that one of the couples refuses to accept that it is 'over' and becomes a persistent nuisance, with a risk of violence. Here again is a situation in which the community, through the use of appropriate law, would need to intervene to protect a victim.

6.7 CONSTITUTIONAL LAW IN SOCIALISM

Constitutional law in socialism would regulate procedures for the election and running of public bodies such as parish, district, county and metropolitan councils and parliament.[179] This would define the freedoms and the boundaries of decision-making and action both in and between these various spheres of public organisation. Constitutional law would also provide rules for the running of public services such as hospitals and schools and also the democratic structure and management of units responsible for the production and distribution of goods.

It is prudent to anticipate a possible violent reaction to the capture of political control by a majority of socialists and the enactment of common ownership of all resources and means of production.[180] This would be action by a recalcitrant minority. The history of great social change does not bode well for a peaceful transition. From this record we should assume that at least some sections of society with a great interest in things staying as they are would be unlikely to respond with calm acceptance, even in the face of a popular and democratically organised movement.

---

[179] See *Practical Socialism* (note 177).

[180] Ibid.

Nor would such a recalcitrant minority have any difficulty in finding justification for any violent reaction. In the tradition of contriving moral authority for upholding sectional interests, and perhaps borrowing from some dubious 18th-century philosophy, it could be argued that the private ownership of land, natural resources and means of production is a natural human right that is integral to a democratic society. It would follow from this that the dispossession of an owning minority would be an undemocratic action against the natural rights of a social minority by a tyrannical majority. In these circumstances, it could be argued that violent reaction would be justified.

There would, of course, be not the slightest prospect of reversing a decision by a majority of people to commence the organisation of a socialist system.[181] The barriers to the establishment of socialism exist in the minds of most people who do not yet accept the ideas of socialism. With the growth of the socialist movement to the point where a majority exists, the consequence will be the capture of political control and, with it, the entire machinery of government. The conversion to common ownership will be legislated as a legal enactment and from this point on the entire framework of law will be adapted, enabling the formal enactment of common ownership to be applied as an action throughout society.

To reverse the process, the majority of people would have to be reconverted to supporting the capitalist system by means of propaganda.[182] The ruling groups would already have lost the battle of ideas and their social influence would have been eliminated together with their monopoly of the means of life. To suggest that at some point individuals will be able to take over socially owned property and force members of the community to work for wages and the profits of companies is a complete abandonment of logical reasoning. To argue that the same result could be obtained by violent minority action is equally absurd. This is not to suggest that a recalcitrant violent minority could not fight a desperate rear-guard action while being blindly unaware of the futility of their actions. The irrationality of such actions is possible, but this could not be described as a serious attempt to destroy socialism and restore the capitalist system. Socialism could not be forcibly overthrown.

Acts of violence, sabotage or any other form of anti-social activity could be carried out only by renegade groups acting outside the law. This would not be tolerated at any stage. If the hypothesis includes a residue of people 'at war with society' who make mindless attacks endangering the well-being and lives of other people, then the means of dealing with them would exist and would be used as necessary.[183] Such situations already exist under capitalism, but with this difference: that while

[181] Ibid.

[182] Ibid.

[183] Ibid.

capitalism has no solution because capitalist conditions create the problem, for socialist society the problem would be a passing phase of short duration.

On the assumption that we are speculating about acts of violence mainly during the post-change-over period, obviously force would be used if argument and reason failed. With the capture of political control, the machinery of government, including every section of the armed forces, would come under the control of the new democratic administration. Implicit in this is the recognition that, during the period of change-over, control of the armed forces would be continued for as long as necessary in the light of the conditions then existing. In view of the possibility of a violent reaction by a minority, it could not be guaranteed that, simultaneously with gaining control, the armed forces would at once be wholly dismantled.

This does not mean that armed forces would have to be used. The control of the armed forces by parliament would prevent their use by any renegade group and would act as an effective deterrent without these forces necessarily having to be used. The conditions for the success of the change-over from capitalism to socialism will already have been completed before the winning of a majority in parliament through the ballot box.

Achieving a socialist majority would mean that socialists will be in the majority throughout every section of production, distribution, services, administration and government departments.[184] From this basis, cooperation to run society directly to meet specific needs would be commenced. It is inconceivable that the police or the armed forces would remain outside these developments or would act against the tide of democratic events. It is against this background that the hypothesis of possible violent obstruction by an undemocratic minority has to be considered.

Not all of the hypothetical minority working to restore capitalism would be prepared to take violent action for that purpose.[185] This would present no problem to socialism. It is likely that diverse political groups would be active in trying to influence social policy. In line with democratic practice, a group wishing to return to the capitalist system would be free to propagate their views and to organise democratically to win over the majority. They would, of course, operate against the tremendous disadvantage of advocating a return to an outdated system of exploitation, economic chaos, waste, destruction and war.

6.8 ADMINISTRATION OF LAW IN SOCIALISM

The practical ways in which the structure of law and its administration could be adapted to serve the needs of communities in socialism is far beyond the competence

[184] Ibid.

[185] Ibid.

and scope of this chapter. Indeed, the subject is so extensive that it could not be attempted in any single chapter. In addition to its complexity, law has also evolved with great local and regional variations and no doubt this would continue: a single unified system would be neither possible nor desirable.

However, we have been able to suggest the general methods that we should apply to the question. In principle, the reasons for adapting law in socialism would be no different from the way in which law, throughout history, has had to adapt to new situations in line with evolving society. As in all societies, law in socialism would have the job of upholding the general aims of the new society and of setting out the procedures through which it could achieve those aims.

A socialist system is defined as one based on common ownership, voluntary cooperation, production solely for common needs, and democratic organisation.[186] Having been enacted as legislation, the relationships of common ownership would have the force of law and this would be the legal basis on which all means of production and all resources would pass into the common property of the whole community. From this point on, people performing socially useful jobs would carry on doing them as voluntary cooperation in production units under democratic management by workers themselves.

It is in these important fields of production and distribution where many of the existing functions of law would become redundant – for example, company law and the law regulating the wage labour–capital relationship.[187] It is also here where new law would be required to coordinate working relationships between public decision-making bodies and the actions of production units in implementing policy decisions. Together with new law, a great deal of existing law would be continued. The test to be applied is whether or not any existing law is able to continue to serve the needs of individuals or the wider community.

The administration of law would be humanised. The present hierarchical authoritarian procedures which govern the structure of the legal system would need to be democratised. The present use of juries and lay magistrates, drawn from a wide social background and acting under legal advice from qualified legal officers, offers an acceptable basis which could be extended. However, such anachronistic procedures by which judges are appointed by a Lord Chancellor and in some cases by a monarch on the recommendation of a prime minister, would hardly be compatible with the principles of democratic organisation.[188] Perhaps, after nomination, persons making judgments could be elected by a ballot of all barristers and solicitors. Rotating offices would also be a healthy practice. For the same general reasons that apply at present,

186 Ibid.
187 Ibid.
188 Ibid.

including the practice of democratic accountability, it would be important that the entire practice of law, though not beyond public criticism, should continue to remain independent of all other public bodies.

Finally, it should be emphasised that a fully democratic society, in which all citizens would be able to cooperate on equal terms around a common interest, would achieve a vast reduction in crime.[189] This would be both a moral and a material basis for decent human conduct. We also have every reason to trust that all public bodies would work conscientiously within their terms of reference according to the rules set by constitutional law. This being the case, we may anticipate that, overwhelmingly, in every sphere of life the conduct of people will be self-regulating, without a need for society to intervene in the use of law.

6.9 CONCLUSION

In general, socialism in Africa did not outlive the collapse of the USSR in 1989. The loss of a financial supporter and ally in the form of the USSR was certainly a part of this, but so, too, was the need many African states had for loans from the International Monetary Fund (IMF) and the World Bank. By the 1980s, these institutions required states to release state monopolies over production and distribution and privatise industry before they would agree to loans. The rhetoric of socialism was also falling out of favour, with populations pushing for multi-party states. With the changing tide, most African states that had embraced socialism in one form or another embraced the wave of multi-party democracy that swept across Africa in the 1990s. Development is associated now with foreign trade and investment rather than state-controlled economies, but many are still waiting for the social infrastructures, such as public education, funded healthcare and developed transportation systems, that both socialism and development promised.

REFERENCES

Adesina, JO 'Variations in postcolonial imagination: Reflection on Senghor, Nyerere and Nkrumah' (2022) 47(1) *Africa Development/Afrique et Développement* 31–58.

Allison, D 'African socialism' *Encyclopedia Britannica* (2017), https://www.britannica.com/topic/African-socialism, accessed 7 March 2023.

Alsen, J 'An introduction to Chinese property law' (1996) 20(1) *Maryland Journal of International Law* 1–60.

[189] Ibid.

Anene, JC 'The international boundaries of Nigeria, 1885–1960' in *The Framework of an Emergent African Nation* (Longman Press, 1970).

Arrighi, G & Saul, JS 'Socialism and economic development in tropical Africa' (1968) 6(2) *The Journal of Modern African Studies* 141–169.

Aspaturian, VV 'The contemporary doctrine of the Soviet state and its philosophical foundations' (1954) 48(4) *The American Political Science Review* 1031–1057.

Balfour, R, Basagni, L, Flotho-liersch, A, Fusaro, P, Gelhaus, L, Groenendaal, L, Hegedus, D, Von Homeyer, H, Kausch, K, Kutschka, T, Matrakova, M, Rempala, J & Tani, K *Divide and Obstruct: Populist Parties and EU Foreign Policy* (German Marshall Fund of the United States, 2019), http://www.jstor.org/stable/resrep21237, *accessed* 7 March 2023.

Berger, S 'Difficult (re-)alignments – comparative perspectives on social democracy and religion from late-nineteenth-century to interwar Germany and Britain' (2018) 53(3) *Journal of Contemporary History* 574–596.

Betts, JP 'John Stuart Mill, Victorian liberalism, and the failure of co-operative production' (2016) 59(1) *The Historical Journal* 153–174.

Boos, F & Boos, W 'The utopian communism of William Morris' (1986) 7(3) *History of Political Thought* 489–510.

Bowman, M 'Sin, spirituality, and primitivism: The theologies of the American social gospel, 1885–1917' (2007) 17(1) *Religion and American Culture: A Journal of Interpretation* 95–126.

Bradley, MT '"The other": Precursory African conceptions of democracy' (2005) 7(3) *International Studies Review* 407–431.

Bui, TH 'Deconstructing the "socialist" rule of law in Vietnam: The changing discourse on human rights in Vietnam's constitutional reform process' (2014) 36(1) *Contemporary Southeast Asia* 77–100.

Campbell, H 'Socialism in Tanzania: A case study' (1975) 6(8) *The Black Scholar* 41–51.

Campbell, JM 'Is there a case for socialist jurisprudence?' PhD thesis (University of Glasgow, 1997), https://theses.gla.ac.uk/4247/1/1997CampbellPhD.pdf, accessed 7 March 2023.

Clarke, JH 'Pan-Africanism: A brief history of an idea in the African world' (1988) 145 *Présence Africaine* 26–56.

Claus, L 'Montesquieu's mistakes and the true meaning of separation' (2005) 25(3) *Oxford Journal of Legal Studies* 419–451.

Coffey, D, Brady, P, Doyle, O, Hertogh, M, Barden, G & Murphy, T 'Custom and living law' (2012) 3(1) *Jurisprudence* 71–210.

Cooper, F 'Africa and the world economy' (1981) 24(2/3) *African Studies Review* 1–86.

Copeland, EA 'Perestroika and human rights: Steps in the right direction' (1991) 15(2) *The Fletcher Forum of World Affairs* 101–119.

Crawford, NC 'The passion of world politics: Propositions on emotion and emotional relationships' (2000) 24(4) *International Security* 116–156.

Cunningham, F 'The socialist retrieval of liberal democracy' (1990) 11(1) *International Political Science Review/Revue Internationale de Science Politique* 99–110.

Curran, TD 'Politics in classical Greece: The nature of the polis and the origins of the rule of law' (1989) 9(2) *Sacred Heart University Review article* 4.

Dickinson, J 'The law behind law: II' (1929) 29(3) *Columbia Law Review* 285–319.

Dominguez, JI 'Political participation and the social mobilization hypothesis: Chile, Mexico, Venezuela, and Cuba, 1800–1825' (1974) 5(2) *The Journal of Interdisciplinary History* 237–266.

Dowling, R *Brezhnev's War on Crime: The Criminal in Soviet Society, 1963–1984* (2017), https://escholarship.org/content/qt44n3x1m7/qt44n3x1m7.pdf, accessed 7 March 2023.

Drew, A 'African socialism' *Encyclopedia Britannica*, 27 October 2017, https://www.britannica.com/topic/African-socialism, accessed 7 March 2023.

Duchacek, ID 'Dyadic federations and confederations' (1988) 18(2) *Publius* 5–31.

Editors of *Encyclopedia Britannica* 'Albert, Count de Mun' *Encyclopedia Britannica*, 24 February 2023, https://www.britannica.com/biography/Adrien-Albert-Marie-comte-de-Mun, accessed 7 March 2023.

Editors of *Encyclopedia Britannica* 'Barthélemy-Prosper Enfantin' *Encyclopedia Britannica*, 4 February 2023, https://www.britannica.com/biography/Barthelemy-Prosper-Enfantin, accessed 7 March 2023.

Editors of *Encyclopedia Britannica* 'Christian Socialism' *Encyclopedia Britannica*, 28 May 2013, https://www.britannica.com/topic/Christian-Socialism, accessed 7 March 2023.

Editors of *Encyclopedia Britannica* 'William DP Bliss' *Encyclopedia Britannica*, 4 October 2022, https://www.britannica.com/biography/William-D-P-Bliss, accessed 7 March 2023.

Fetter, B 'The mines of southern and central Africa: An ecological framework' (1992) 2 *Health Transition Review* 125–135.

Fuller, LL 'Positivism and fidelity to law: A reply to Professor Hart' (1958) 71(4) *Harvard Law Review* 630–672.

Gavison, R 'Natural law, positivism, and the limits of jurisprudence: A modern round (review of *The Authority of Law: Essays in Law and Morality; Natural Law and Natural Rights*, by J Raz & J Finnis)' (1982) 91(6) *The Yale Law Journal* 1250–1285.

Gsovski, V 'The Soviet concept of law' (1938) 7(1) *Fordham Law Review.*

Haferkamp, Hans & Smelser, Neil J (eds) *Social Change and Modernity* (University of California Press, c1992).

Handy, RT 'Christianity and socialism in America, 1900–1920' (1952) 21(1) *Church History* 39–54.

Hannum, H 'The Butare colloquium on human rights and economic development in Francophone Africa: A summary and analysis' (1979) 1(2) *Universal Human Rights* 63–87.

Hazard, JN 'Negritude, socialism and the law' (1965) 65(5) *Columbia Law Review* 778–809.

Hazard, JN 'Socialist law and the international encyclopedia' (1965) 79(2) *Harvard Law Review* 278–302.

Herbst, J 'The creation and maintenance of national boundaries in Africa' (1989) 43(4) *International Organization* 673–692.

Horne, J '1848 and the language of politics' (2000) 25 *Saothar* 67–76, http://www.jstor.org/stable/23198964, accessed 7 March 2023.

Ibhawoh, B & Dibua, JI 'Deconstructing *ujamaa*: The legacy of Julius Nyerere in the quest for social and economic development in Africa' (2003) 8(1) *African Journal of Political Science* 59–83.

Jewsiewicki, B 'African historical studies academic knowledge as "usable past" and radical scholarship' (1989) 32(3) *African Studies Review* 1–76.

Jones, PD *Christian Socialist Revival*, 1877–1914 (Princeton University Press, 1968).

Kamenka, E & Tay, AES 'Beyond the French Revolution: Communist socialism and the concept of law' (1971) 21(2) *The University of Toronto Law Journal* 109–140.

Karel, V *International Dimensions of Human Rights (nd)*, https://unesdoc.unesco.org/ark:/48223/pf0000056230, accessed 7 July 2023.

Katznelson, I 'Considerations on social democracy in the United States' (1978) 11(1) *Comparative Politics* 77–99.

Kautsky, JH 'Centralization in the Marxist and in the Leninist tradition' (1997) 30(4) *Communist and Post-Communist Studies* 379–400.

Keep, J 'The agrarian revolution of 1917–1918 in Soviet historiography' (1977) 36(4) *The Russian Review* 405–423.

Kilson, ML 'Authoritarian and single-party tendencies in African politics' (1963) 15(2) *World Politics* 262–294.

Klier, JD 'German antisemitism and Russian judeophobia in the 1880s: Brothers and strangers' (1989) 37(4) *Jahrbücher für Geschichte Osteuropas* 524–540.

Klinghoffer, AJ 'The Soviet view of African socialism' (1968) 67(268) *African Affairs* 197–208.

Korsch, K, Denton, F & Kellner, D 'What is socialization? A program of practical socialism' (1975) 6 *New German Critique* 60–81.

Lane, RE 'Waiting for lefty: The capitalist genesis of socialist man' (1978) 6(1) *Theory and Society* 1–28.

Leiter, B 'Marx, law, ideology, legal positivism' (2015) 101(4) *Virginia Law Review* 1179–1196.

Lovell, DW 'Socialism, utopianism and the "utopian socialists"' (1992) 14(2) *History of European Ideas* 185–201.

Lustgarten, L 'Socialism and the rule of law' (1988) 15(1) *Journal of Law and Society* 25–41.

Makovi, M *The Impossibility of Democratic Socialism: Two Conceptions of Democracy* (2016), https://mpra.ub.uni-muenchen.de/70172/1/MPRA_paper_70172.pdf, accessed 7 March 2023.

Marx, K *Introduction to a Contribution to the Critique of Hegel's Philosophy of Right* (1843), available on the Marxist Internet Archive.

Marx, K & Engels, F 'Manifesto of the Communist Party' in *Karl Marx & Friedrich Engels Collected Works* (International Publishers, 1976).

Mattei, U 'The Cold War and comparative law: A reflection on the politics of intellectual discipline' (2017) 65(3) *The American Journal of Comparative Law* 567–607.
McCain, J 'Perceptions of socialism in post-socialist Ghana: An experimental analysis' (1979) 22(3) *African Studies Review* 45–63.
McCain, JA 'Ideology in Africa: Some perceptual types' (1975) 18(1) *African Studies Review* 61–87.
Metz, S 'In lieu of orthodoxy: The socialist theories of Nkrumah and Nyerere' (1982) 20(3) *The Journal of Modern African Studies* 377–392.
Miller, D 'Socialism and the market' (1977) 5(4) *Political Theory* 473–490.
Mkandawire, T 'Thinking about developmental states in Africa' (2001) 25(3) *Cambridge Journal of Economics* 289–313.
Murphy, C 'Lon Fuller and the moral value of the rule of law' (2005) 24(3) *Law and Philosophy* 239–262.
Nathans, B 'The dictatorship of reason: Aleksandr Vol'Pin and the idea of rights under "developed socialism"' (2007) 66(4) *Slavic Review* 630–663.
Ndulo, M 'African customary law, customs, and women's rights' (2011) 18(1) *Indiana Journal of Global Legal Studies* 87–120.
Nkrumah, Kwame *African Socialism Revisited*, speech given at the Africa Seminar, Cairo, transcribed by Dominic Tweedie (1967), available on the Marxist Internet Archive.
Olusegun, SS 'Ubuntu and the problem of belonging' *Ethics, Policy & Environment* (2023), DOI: 10.1080/21550085.2023.2179818.
Olympiad, SI 'Law and economy in the USSR' (1982) 95(7) *Harvard Law Review* 1591–1625.
Orfield, LB 'The Scandinavian ombudsman' (1966) 19(1) *Administrative Law Review* 7–74.
Paden, R 'Marx's critique of the utopian socialists' (2002) 13(2) *Utopian Studies* 67–91.
Peng, L 'Carsun Chang on democratic socialism: Liberalism, social democracy, and German idealism' (2019) 26(2) *American Journal of Chinese Studies* 107–127.
Pitcher, MA & Askew, KM 'African socialisms and postsocialisms' (2006) 76(1) *Africa Journal of the International African Institute* 1–14.
Pons, S & Smith, SA (eds) *The Cambridge History of Communism* (Cambridge University Press, 2017).
Principe, ML 'Albert Venn Dicey and the principles of the rule of law: Is justice blind? A comparative analysis of the United States and Great Britain' (2000) 22 *The Loyola of Los Angeles International and Comparative Law Review* 357.
Retallack, J 'Anti-semitism, conservative propaganda, and regional politics in late nineteenth century Germany' (1988) 11(3) *German Studies Review* 377–403.
Salem, S 'Radical regionalism: Feminism, sovereignty and the pan-African project' (2022) 47(1) *Africa Development/Afrique et Développement* 159–191.
Sanders, A 'On African socialism and the rule of law' (1982) 15(3) *The Comparative and International Law Journal of Southern Africa* 299–305.
Sanders, AJGM *International Jurisprudence in African Context* (Butterworths, 1979).

Sanders, AJGM *On African Socialism and the Rule of Law* (nd), https://docplayer.net/212396028-5-on-african-socialism-and-the-rule-of-law.html, accessed 7 March 2023.

Sanga, Innocent S Fr & Pagnucco, R 'Julius Nyerere's understanding of African socialism, human rights and equality' (2020) 4(2) *The Journal of Social Encounters* 15–33.

Sassoon, D 'The rise and fall of West European communism 1939–1948' (1992) 1(2) *Contemporary European History* 139–169.

Saunders, B 'Democracy, political equality, and majority rule' (2010) 121(1) *Ethics* 148–177.

Schler, L 'Dilemmas of post-colonial diplomacy: Zambia, Kenneth Kaunda, and the Middle East crisis, 1964–73' (2018) 59(1) *The Journal of African History* 97–119.

Schmidt, E 'Top down or bottom up? Nationalist mobilization reconsidered, with special reference to Guinea (French West Africa)' (2005) 110(4) *The American Historical Review* 975–1014.

Shivji, I *The Rule of Law and Ujamaa in the Ideological Formation of Tanzania* (nd), https://www.academia.edu/5028000/The_Rule_of_Law_and_Ujamaa_in_the_Ideological_Formation_of_Tanzania_, accessed 7 March 2023.

Simonsen, SG 'Addressing ethnic divisions in post-conflict institution-building: Lessons from recent cases' (2005) 36(3) *Security Dialogue* 297–318.

Smith, T 'Beyond hero worship: A Marxist critique of Bolshevik terror and its indebtedness to Jacobinism' (1996) 10(1) *Socialism and Democracy* 47–82.

Socialist Party of Great Britain Practical Socialism – Its Principles and Methods (Marxists Internet Archive, 2006), quoted in A Buick Socialism and Law (2016), https://www.marxists.org/archive/lawrence/2006/6socialism_law.htm, accessed 7 March 2023.

Solly H *Working Men's Social Clubs and Educational Institutes rev* ed by BT Hall (Simpkin, Marshall, Hamilton, Kent and Co, 1904).

Song, M 'Rethinking minority status and "visibility"' (2020) 8 *Comparative Migration Studies* 5.

Southall, RJ 'Post-apartheid South Africa: Constraints on socialism' (1987) 25(2) *The Journal of Modern African Studies* 345–374.

Sprinzak, E 'African traditional socialism – a semantic analysis of political ideology' (1973) 11(4) *The Journal of Modern African Studies* 629–647.

Stacy-Ann, E 'Paying for privacy and the personal data economy' (2017) 117(6) *Columbia Law Review*, https://columbialawreview.org/content/paying-for-privacy-and-the-personal-data-economy/, accessed 7 March 2023.

Stephens, CR *The People Mobilized: The Mozambican Liberation Movement and American Activism (1960–1975)* (2011), https://scholarshare.temple.edu/bitstream/handle/20.500.12613/2461/Stephens_temple_0225E_10882.pdf?sequence=1, accessed 7 March 2023.

Stone, A 'The place of law in the Marxian structure–superstructure archetype' (1985) 19(1) *Law & Society Review* 39–67.

Taylor & Francis 'A tribute to AM Babu' (1996) 23(69) *Review of African Political Economy* 321–348.

Telman, DAJ 'Adolf Stoecker: Anti-semite with a Christian mission' (1995) 9(2) *Jewish History* 93–112.

Thomas, M 'France accused: French North Africa before the United Nations, 1952–1962' (2001) 10(1) *Contemporary European History* 91–121.

Thompsell, A *Socialism in Africa and African Socialism* (2019), https://www.thoughtco.com/socialism-in-africa-and-african-socialism-4031311.

Thomson, A *Introduction to African Politics* (Routledge, 2000).

Tinsley, M 'Proclaiming independence: Language and national identity in Sékou Touré's Guinea' (2015) 18(3) *Postcolonial Studies* 237–256.

Toh, K 'An argument against the social fact thesis (and some additional preliminary steps towards a new conception of legal positivism)' (2018) 27(5) *Law and Philosophy* 445–504.

Ude, DMC 'Kwasi Wiredu's critique of Marxism: Its philosophical application to the "African Socialism" via Nkrumah, Nyerere and Toure' (2018) 12(5) *Journal of Pan African Studies* 181.

Van Der Burg, W & Brom, FWA 'Legislation on ethical issues: Towards an interactive paradigm' (2000) 3(1) *Ethical Theory and Moral Practice* 57–75.

Verdery, K *Property in Socialism: Collectivization, Administrative Rights, and the Circulation of Goods. The Vanishing Hectare: Property and Value in Post-socialist Transylvania* (Cornell University Press, 2003), https://doi.org/10.7591/9781501717253-006

Vidalenc, J 'Louis Blanc' *Encyclopedia Britannica*, 2 December 2022, https://www.britannica.com/biography/Louis-Blanc, accessed 7 March 2023.

Volle, A *'Democratic socialism' Encyclopedia Britannica*, 6 October 2022.

wa Muiu, M 'Civilization on trial: The colonial and post-colonial state in Africa' (2008) 25(1) *Journal of Third World Studies* 73–93.

Weiskopf, JM 'Socialism on safari: Wildlife and nation-building in postcolonial Tanzania, 1961–77' (2015) 56(3) *The Journal of African History* 429–447.

Wiebke K *Colonialism, National-Socialism and the Holocaust: On Modern Ways of Dealing with Deviance. Gauging and Engaging Deviance, 1600–2000* (2014), 978-93-82381-31-0.01091133.

Xu, Z 'Chinese agrarian change in world-historical context' (2014) 78(2) *Science & Society* 181–206.

LEGISLATION

Constitution of the People's Republic of China, 4 December 1982

7

Comparative law and the internationalisation of laws and legal systems

Kennedy Kariseb

7.1 INTRODUCTION

Globalisation is often thought of in terms of economics, politics, market integration, technology and the like, but hardly ever in the context of law and legal systems.[1] Yet this phenomenon has fundamental impacts on laws and legal systems the world over.[2] It affects to a greater extent the way different countries interact and engage with one another, including their legal systems and laws. A need therefore exists to analyse and appreciate law in terms of its international or, rather, its transnational character. This is the purpose of this chapter. In doing so, specific examples and references are made to the Namibian legal system.

Owing to the increasing transnationalisation of activities that are subject to legal regulation, legal questions that transcend borders and geographies are arising more frequently. No mature legal system, whether in the Global North or South, is spared this reality. It is therefore not surprising that national laws and domestic legal systems are increasingly being viewed and appreciated in terms of their internationalisation. By internationalisation in this context is meant that the laws and legal systems are increasingly having to harmonise with legal cultures, practices, laws and principles as a result of transnational legal engagements.

The internationalisation of law, and by extension legal systems, is also evident in Namibia; in fact, it is even more compelling and relatable to Namibia. Often characterised as a 'child of the international community', by some others as

---

[1] See, generally, A Slaughter *A New World Order* (Princeton University Press, 2004) 66–67.

[2] E Benvenisti 'The conception of international law as a legal system' (2008) 50(1) *German Yearbook of International Law* 393; G Capaldo *The Pillars of Global Law XVI* (Routledge, 2008) 1–3.

'international law-friendly', Namibia's remains one of the few presidential systems that embraces a monist approach as far as the use and application of international law is concerned.[3] Moreover, it is also relatively accepting of comparative law, both in theory and in practice. This renders the consideration of the ever-internationalising nature of Namibian law and its legal system worthy of academic consideration.

This chapter concerns itself with the role of comparative law in the internationalisation of laws and legal systems generally, with a particular focus on Namibia. It argues that comparative law, both as a technique and as an academic discipline of law, plays an important role in internationalising laws and legal systems. This is because comparative law, when viewed from an epistemological perspective, does three things. First, it aims to harmonise and unify laws and legal systems. Second, it contributes to the development of international law, the law most approximate to states. And, as a consequence, it establishes certain common core principles that cut across nation-states. Third, comparative law serves as a determinant of judicial cross-fertilisation, particularly in common-law jurisdictions, again contributing to the common alignment of jurisprudence, the standardisation of principles between different systems and the eventual evolution towards a 'global justice' system. These three determinants form the basis of the analysis in this chapter.

7.2 STATE SOVEREIGNTY AND THE PARADIGM OF INTERNATIONALISATION OF LAWS AND LEGAL SYSTEMS

An immediate consequence of any attempt to internationalise laws and legal systems is the gradual piercing of state sovereignty. This is an inherent aspect of any internationalisation process involving laws and legal systems. Therefore, as a precursor, it may be necessary to reflect on state sovereignty, particularly its conception, evolution and gradual contemporary appreciation and actual and potential impact on the internationalisation of laws and legal systems the world over.

One of the fundamental bases of international law has been the inviolability of state sovereignty.[4] The core basis of state sovereignty in international law is aptly captured by Perrez in one of his treatises, where he argues:

[3] See generally, O Tshosa 'The status of international law in Namibia: A critical appraisal of the constitutional strategy' (2010) 2(1) *Namibia Law Journal* 3–28; N Ndeunyema 'The Namibian Constitution, international law and the courts: A critique' (2020) 9(1) *Global Journal of Comparative Law* 271–296.

[4] For example, the UN Charter in Art 2(1) provides for the sovereign equality of all Members States (in the UN).

> [s]overeignty is the most important if not the only structural principle of international law that shapes the content of nearly all rules of international law, that the international legal order is merely an expression of the uniform principle of external sovereignty, that sovereignty is the criterion for membership in the international society, and that sovereignty in sum is the 'cornerstone of international law' and the 'controlling principle of world order'.[5]

Since states form the soul of international law, their sovereignty forms an essential element of their existence and their interaction in the international system. Without such sovereignty, states are said to be 'failed'. To this end, international law has developed on the understanding that states are equal in their exercise of rights and duties, and that they enjoy absolute supremacy over their territories. Despite this relatively common appreciation, state sovereignty as a concept has been afforded diverse meanings or, at the very least, has attracted a wide range of interpretations. In practice, the concept has a long history pre-dating the post-Second World War period.[6] Its interpretation has long also been influenced by political developments over the centuries.[7] What is clear, however, is that there has been a reorientation of state sovereignty in the theory and practice of the international legal system, which, as Kofi Annan once held, has been brought about 'not least by the forces of globalization and international co-operation'.[8] Therefore, today, state sovereignty cannot be curtailed in a neat definition but rather as broadly as a reference to the wide rights and privileges a state enjoys over its territory and population. Accordingly, Cassese writes that state sovereignty includes more or less the following sweeping powers and rights:

- the power to exercise authority over all the people living in a particular territory;
- the power to freely use and dispose of the territory under the state's jurisdiction and to perform all activities deemed necessary or to the benefit of the population living there;
- the right that no state intrudes in the state's territory;
- the right to immunity from the jurisdiction of foreign courts for acts or actions performed by the state in its sovereign capacity and for execution measures

[5] F Perrez *Cooperative Sovereignty from Independence to Interdependence in the Structure of International Environmental Law* (Springer, 2000) 13.

[6] See, generally, on the genealogy of the concept of state sovereignty, F Hinsley *Sovereignty* (Cambridge University Press, 1986); J Bartelson *A Genealogy of Sovereignty* (Cambridge University Press, 1995); a more recent work is R Jackson *Sovereignty: Evolution of an Idea* (Polity Press, 2007).

[7] R Jennings 'Sovereignty and international law' in G Kreijen (ed) *State, Sovereignty and International Governance* (Oxford University Press, 2002) 29.

[8] K Annan 'Two concepts of sovereignty' *The Economist*, 18 September 1999, 352, https://www.economist.com/international/1999/09/16/two-concepts-of-sovereignty, accessed 1 June 2019.

taken against the use or planned use of public property or assets for the discharge of public functions;

- the right to immunity of state representatives who act in their official capacity, and
- the right to respect for the State's nationals and its officials abroad. [9]

Although it is a feasible reflection of the wide powers and rights of a state, Cassesse's assertion is surely not exhaustive and may over time even be expanded as globalisation takes its toll the world over.

The epistemological parameters of what we know today as state sovereignty have drastically altered over the years. Fundamentally, state sovereignty was understood in absolutist terms. Jennings' narration of the work of Bodin as depicted in his *De Republica* treatise published in 1576 is illustrative of how, given the realities in Continental Europe at the time, states opted for an absolutist appreciation of state sovereignty that was premised on the idea that absolute power was placed in the hands of a sovereign who had the power to make laws and was themself not bound by the laws they made.[10] According to Bodin's jurisprudence, the sovereign was a reference to the state and its supreme ruler imbued with authority to make uncontestable laws that were not binding on them. According to Bodin, the concept of sovereignty primarily also entails the absolute and sole competence of law-making within the territorial boundaries of a state and that the state would not tolerate any other law-creating agent above it. He maintains that sovereignty, as the supreme power within a state, cannot be restricted except by the laws of God and by natural law.[11] Moreover no constitution can limit sovereignty and therefore a sovereign is regarded as being above the (positive) law.[12] Similarly, Bodley argued that

> [s]overeignty is the most extensive form of jurisdiction under international law. In general terms, it denotes full and unchallengeable power over a piece of territory and all the persons from time to time therein.[13]

This narration of state sovereignty affirms 'international legal sovereignty', which is concerned with establishing the status of a political entity in the international system.[14]

---

[9] A Cassese *International Law* (Oxford University Press, 2005) 49–52.

[10] Jennings (note 7) 29.

[11] See J Bodin *Les Six Livres de République* (Chez Jacques du Puys, 1577) Bk I ch 8. For an English translation see Jean Bodin on *Sovereignty: Four Chapters from the Six Books of the Commonwealth* (trans Julian Franklin) (Cambridge University Press, 1992) 1–45.

[12] Ibid.

[13] A Bodley 'Weakening the principle of sovereignty in international law: The international tribunal for the former Yugoslavia' (1998) 31(1) *New York University Journal of International Law and Politics* 419.

[14] S Krasner *Sovereignty: Organized Hypocrisy* (Princeton University Press, 1999) 127–157.

In the 19th century, however, concepts regarding state sovereignty were overhauled, a process that recognised the imminent power of the citizenry. In terms of this reconceptualisation, sovereignty was viewed as a power emanating from people who commune to form a state. The state therefore became an essential element of sovereignty and a fundamental actor in the international legal order that followed. The 1648 Peace of Westphalia consensus, which marked the end of political tensions in most of Continental Europe, also bought into being the idea of state-based sovereignty.

An important element of this conception of sovereignty was the principle of 'non-interference in matters falling within the territorial jurisdiction of a State'. Modern international law, although building on these earlier conceptions of state sovereignty, slowly began to dilute it in that it recognised the equality of nation-states and, more importantly, called for a new international legal order premised on hegemonic stability. This approach became more appropriate, especially after the end of the Second World War with the emergence of super powers which wielded more political command in the international legal regime. It was compelled by the political developments of the time. At the time the United Nations (UN) was instituted in 1945, most of sub-Saharan Africa was still under colonial rule. This in practice meant that those nations which were under colonial rule and which were for all practical considerations placed under the trusteeship system of the UN could not exercise sovereignty. This reality prompted a rethinking in international law that questioned state sovereignty because in practice some states did not enjoy sovereignty contrary to the ideals of the UN Charter. As a result, state sovereignty evolved from its formative roots, which were premised on individual anarchic sovereignty to state sovereignty, to more contemporary understandings that relegate and subject sovereignty to certain limitations under international law. In other words, the understanding nowadays, among other considerations, is that states are sovereign entities, first by virtue of being subjects of international law and therefore only subject to it and not to the domestic whims of any other state. This shows that state sovereignty is therefore in one of its contemporary facets – a reference to a state's legal independence from other states.[15]

Within the African regional system there is also a growing trend, in both practice and theory, that supports the dilution of absolute sovereignty – a somewhat surprising development. This is because the formation of the Organisation of African Unity (OAU) was deeply rooted in state sovereignty and in practice the OAU adopted an 'inflexible stance on sovereignty'.[16] That state sovereignty remained

[15] A Ansong 'The concept of sovereign equality of states in international law' (2016) 2(1) *Ghana Institute of Management and Public Administration Law Review* 23.

[16] J Warner 'The African Union and article 4*(h)*: Understanding changing norms of sovereignty and intervention in Africa through an integrated levels-of-analysis approach' in E Sahle (ed)

a core determinant in the identity and practice of the OAU is not surprising, given its political history at the time. The hard-won flag independence against colonial imperialism and racial segregation, among other factors, could be appraised only because it gave these states leverage with its former colonial masters.

The post-2002 reformation in the OAU, however, came with new paradigm shifts; one of these was to do away with an absolutist orientation of state sovereignty. Perhaps given the atrocities that permeated the African continent for the larger part since the early 1980s, the newly formed African Union (AU) ushered in a more relaxed stance on state sovereignty. One of the most overt illustrations of the relaxation of state sovereignty within the AU framework is visible in Art 4*(h)* of the AU Constitutive Act, which provides for

> the right of the Union to intervene in a Member State pursuant to a decision of the Assembly in respect to grave circumstances, namely: war crimes, genocide, and crimes against humanity.

The primary impact of Art 4*(h)* of the AU Constitutive Act, as explained in its wording, is that it empowers the AU with an unprecedented right of (military) intervention in a Member State in cases of war crimes, genocide and crimes against humanity. An acute problem with this provision, however, is the question whether prior UN Security Council authorisation is required.[17] The answer is not a settled one; however, the 2003 amendments to the AU Constitutive Act may serve as a hint of the possible interpretation that should be given. In terms of these amendments, the AU extended the right of intervention to what it termed

> a serious threat to a legitimate order to restore peace and stability to the Member State of the Union upon the recommendation of the Peace and Security Council,[18]

clearly ousting UN Security Council authorisation. Furthermore, states may, on the basis of this provision, interfere in the domestic policies and laws of other states where there is an imminent threat to the collective security of the AU Member States or gross violations of the fundamental human and peoples' rights of its citizens.

Democracy, Constitutionalism, and Politics in Africa: Historical Context, Developments, and Dilemmas (Palgrave Macmillan, 2017) 168.

[17] See, generally, G Amvane 'Intervention pursuant to article 4*(h)* of the Constitutive Act of the African Union without United Nations Security Council authorization' (2005) 15(2) *African Human Rights Law Journal* 282–298.

[18] African Union 'Protocol on Amendments to the Constitutive Act of the African Union' 11 July 2003, para 4*(h)*.

Another development within the African regional human rights system that can serve as an indicator of the pliable character of state sovereignty in Africa is the common position taken by the AU concerning unconstitutional changes to governments. In early 2007, the AU Assembly of Heads of States and Government adopted the African Charter on Democracy, Elections and Governance in Africa (ACDEG). The primary objective of the ACDEG is to 'promote adherence, by each state party, to the universal values and principles of democracy and respect for human rights'.[19] Viewed in this light, the ACDEG is a forerunner of the AU legal instruments, with a direct and immediate mandate aimed at remedying democratic deficits in AU Member States.

One of the pressing provisions of the African Charter on Democracy, Elections and Governance in Africa is located in Art 23, which deals with sanctions in cases of unconstitutional changes of government.[20] Described in the Lomé Declaration as an 'unacceptable and anachronistic act', the AU has introduced a firm policy position aimed at condemning and prohibiting illegitimate transitions of state authority. Accordingly, once the situation of an unconstitutional transition of government in any AU Member State occurs, the AU has through its policy undertaken to embark on one or more of the following actions:[21]

(a) a public condemnation by either the chairperson of the African Union Commission (AUC) or the chairperson of the AU Assembly of Heads of State and Government and a plea for the return of constitutional order in the state concerned;
(b) convening of an urgent meeting by the Peace and Security Council of the AU to discuss and strategise about the illegitimate transition;

[19] Article 2(1) of the African Charter on Democracy, Elections and Governance in Africa.

[20] The provision states that States Party agree that the use of, inter alia, the following illegal means of accessing or maintaining power constitutes an unconstitutional change ofgovernment and shall draw appropriate sanctions by the Union:

1. Any putsch or coup d'état against a democratically elected government.
2. Any intervention by mercenaries to replace a democratically elected government.
3. Any replacement of a democratically elected government by armed dissidents or rebels.
4. Any refusal by an incumbent government to relinquish power to the winning party or candidate after free, fair and regular elections, or
5. Any amendment or revision of the constitution or legal instruments, which is an infringement on the principles of democratic change of government.

[21] See, generally, for a detailed discussion on these policy considerations, I Souaré 'The AU and the challenge of unconstitutional changes of government in Africa' (Institute for Security Studies Policy Paper No 197, 2009), 1–16; M Vunyingah *Unconstitutional Changes of Government in Africa: An Assessment of the Relevance of the Constitutive Act of the African Union* (Africa Institute of South Africa Policy Brief No 44, 2011) 1–8.

(c) immediate suspension (preliminary for a period of six months) of the affected state (and consequently its representatives) from all policy organs of the AU, and
(d) after a period of six-months of suspension, and depending on the political climate in the affected state, introduce a range of limited yet targeted sanctions against any regime that refuses to restore constitutional order.

The policy position of the AU clearly referred to above is not only a form of international delegation but equally a manifestation of the changing attitudes towards the exercise of absolute state sovereignty in African states. The mere fact that the AU can institute targeted sanctions against its Member States is an indication of the advanced authoritative role the continental body has assumed and the delineation of state power on the part of African states. The intrusion on state sovereignty is discernable from the fact that the AU can undertake practical action against one of its Member States based on a violation of a treaty obligation.

As is evident from the above analysis, state sovereignty is not what it used to be, whether it is understood from a theoretical or a practical position. What is clear instead is that in the new millennium the international community no longer recognises the absolutist sovereignty of a political ruler or state. Instead, as a result of the repositioning of the international order caused primarily by determinants such as globalisation and changes in political, legal and economic value systems, states cannot evade their duties, both to their citizens and to the international community, solely on account of the exercise of their sovereignty. New millennium developments require costs or compromises where necessary and where applicable in the interests of sovereignty. This is more so in cases of gross human rights violations and the demands of a state's international-law obligations.

As stated above in this section, state sovereignty has not only changed as a concept over the years but this change can potentially affect what states recognise as law and as part of their respective legal systems. As part of internationalisation, states can easily be required to surrender some of their recognised and settled practices, laws, policy positions and even legal systems. This is because internationalisation, especially when viewed in the light of the processes of harmonisation and/or unification of laws, requires, among other requirements, that states adopt common legal positions on issues, whether such issues are of a domestic or transnational character.

In Namibia, state sovereignty remains deeply entrenched, which raises questions about the pace and feasibility of this jurisdiction in internationalising its legal system. A case example may be worth highlighting to illustrate how the stern insistence on sovereignty may possibly still leave Namibia as a relatively conservative, if not positivist, jurisdiction that places insistence and emphasis on its laws over, say, international laws or policy positions in some key areas. The adverse positions in *Minister of Home Affairs and Immigration v Chairperson of the*

Immigration Selection Board & Others[22] taken on the interpretation of s 22(2)*(b)* of the Immigration Control Act, 1992, which provides that

> … no person shall have a domicile in Namibia, unless such person resided in Namibia only by virtue of a right obtained in terms of a provisional permit issued under section 11 or an employment permit issued under section 27 or a student's permit issued under section 28 or a visitor's entry permit issued under section 29,

may give an indication of the current Namibian jurisprudence relating to the sovereign right of the Namibian state to regulate its own affairs, even if such affairs do not necessarily align with the policy positions in sister jurisdictions.

By way of background, two immigrant persons entered Namibia on valid work permits issued in terms of s 27 of the Immigration Control Act 7 of 1993 and resided lawfully in the country for more than two years. Their entrance into Namibia was with the intent to reside for an indefinite period of time. The Immigration Selection Board sought to deport them from Namibia under the coercive machinery (arrest, detention and removal of prohibited immigrants) of Part VI of the Immigration Control Act 1993 on the basis that their work permits had expired and they were unlawfully in the country.

The duo challenged their intended removals on the ground that, having severed their ties to their homelands (South Africa and Germany respectively) and having formed the intent to make Namibia their new home and making financial investments here, they had acquired domicile in Namibia in terms of s 22(1)*(d)* of the Immigration Control Act 1993. When the matter first came before the High Court, the court agreed with their arguments and granted them declarations to that effect. The decision was appealed to the Supreme Court guided by the argument that the High Court in its finding misdirected itself in holding that s 22(1)*(d)* of the Immigration Control Act, 1993 had not changed the common-law definition of domicile of choice which was acquired by proving: (a) lawful physical presence and *(b)* the intent to reside in Namibia indefinitely. The respondents relied on s 22(2) of the Immigration Control Act, 1993, which provides that domicile will not arise where the person relying on it resided in Namibia 'only by virtue of a work permit'.

On appeal to the Supreme Court, the respondents succeeded. Among the reasoning advanced by the Supreme Court was that s 22(1)*(d)* read with s 22(2) of the Immigration Control Act, 1993 had indeed changed the common law such that if an immigrant resides in Namibia 'only' on the strength of a work permit, they could not acquire domicile in Namibia; and further that the adverb 'only' in

---

[22] *Minister of Home Affairs and Immigration v Chairperson of the Immigration Selection Board & Others* (SA 2017/76) [2020] NASC 1 (19 March 2020).

s 22(2)*(b)* could not be interpreted in a way that extinguished the sovereign state's prerogative to control immigrants' entry into and residence in the country. In the premise, the Supreme Court argued that the conclusion reached by the High Court had that effect but also undermined the purpose and regulatory scheme of the Immigration Control Act, 1993.

Perhaps a more important consideration for the Supreme Court in this decision, and one of importance to our discussion here, was the court's position on sovereignty. As part of its reasoning, the Supreme Court contended that the High Court overlooked the principle of state sovereignty when considering what importance to assign to the adverb 'only' in s 22(1)*(d)* of Immigration Control Act. In other words, the court of appeal found that the High Court had misdirected itself by interpreting the Immigration Control Act and its relevant provisions in a way that 'extinguished the sovereign power of the Namibian state to regulate immigration policy and to protect the vital national interest through the machinery of the Immigration Control Act'.[23] The basis of this reasoning was that the High Court, in coming to its conclusion, had failed to take into account the important consideration that

> a State has the unfettered right and discretion to admit into its borders such persons, not being citizens of that State, as it chooses and to make such entry and presence subject to conditions. [24]

Therefore, such a finding, especially in the context of the interpretation of the adverb 'only', 'leaves no freedom of action on the part of the sovereign State of Namibia'. Instead, it removes from the state the internationally recognised discretion to choose the conditions under which immigrants settle in the country.[25]

The position of the Supreme Court in this decision clearly underlies the significance and standing the courts place on sovereignty as contemplated in Art 1(1) of the Namibian Constitution. Therefore, it is not a misplaced argument to suggest that Namibia's move towards internationalising its system and aligning its laws and legal positions on some key issues remains relatively modest. Surely, 'sovereignty' still plays a major role in the slow progress made towards internationalisation and alignment with some policy positions adopted in the liberalised predominantly Western states. Whether these policy positions are ideal for all states is surely a matter of interpretation. But as this volume illustrates, internationalisation should not necessarily be guided by geopolitics but rather by the prevailing common practices equally approved and accepted by nation-states over time.

---

[23] Paragraph 53.
[24] Paragraph 47.
[25] Paragraph 47.

7.3 COMPARATIVE INTERNATIONAL LAW AND THE INTERNATIONALISATION OF LAWS AND LEGAL SYSTEMS

7.3.1 International law

International law is a law of ages. Its precise theoretical genesis is not settled, but many trace its birth to the eminent writings of the late 16th-, 17th- and 18th-century jurists. Some others, most notably the Italian jurist and public international law expert, Antonio Cassese, label its formal origins as four distinct stages: beginning with the Peace of Westphalia (1648) to the First World War, followed by the period between the First and Second World Wars to the Cold War era and, finally, the post-Cold War period.[26] While these diverse narratives on the origin of international law are true and widely accepted, its *formalisation* and *institutionalization* are a rather modest advancement which began with the establishment of the United Nations in 1945 and then with the institutionalisation of the International Law Commission (ILC) two years later in 1947. Far-reaching developments in politics, law and economy all expounded by globalisation also inhibited the growth of international law over the years. The ever-increasing regional intergovernmental organisations, international treaties and multilateral agreements, advances in trade and economy and furthermore the establishment of international courts and tribunals also gave rise and prominence to international law. At times referred to as the 'law of nations' by some scholars, international law, has undergone so much transition over the years that it is almost impossible for states to interact with each other without reference of some sort to it.

While there is no doubt that international law has come a long way, an opaque question that one can ask is this: What role, if any, does international law play in an ever-globalising world order? This question remains important and is worth pondering, regard being had to the strengths and shortcomings of international law generally. In the first place, international law lacks the required enforcement machinery nor does it have a permanent security force that can compel domestic state compliance with international norms and practices. Even though it has embarked on sanctions as a means to flex its 'moral authority' over states, sanctions remain problematic as they either entirely fail or do not always achieve the anticipated outcomes. Moreover, international law, its institutions and processes are seen as remote and secluded from domestic systems, so much so that some regard it as weak and useless. Owing largely to this disconsolate state, some natural-law scholars have questioned whether international law is 'law' indeed.[27] Surely, in this day and age, such propositions that question the legitimacy and cogency of international law have become redundant and perhaps do not warrant interrogation,

[26] See, generally, Cassese (note 9) 271.
[27] HH Koh 'Why do nations obey international law?' (1997) 106 *Yale Law Journal* 2610–2611.

save for the fact that such criticisms require of us to genuinely reflect on the nature of international law and how best it can be mounted to meet contemporary challenges and aspirations. International law remains important because states, for some reason, keep obeying it. The reasons for this are mottled. One such reason could be founded on the fact that international law is based on and governed by the principle of *pacta sunt servanda*; that is, the idea that agreements freely entered must be obeyed. In fact, it is based and formulated on the basis of states' consensus. States do not easily flout international law, for quite obvious reasons. The motivations for states' obedience of international law are compounded and we need not look any further than to Koh's pioneering work titled 'Why do Nations obey International Law?', at least as starters for answers.[28]

Tracing international law from its philosophical foundations, Koh submits that states obey international law for hybrid reasons ranging from moral, normative and legal reasons and that these determinants are conjoined in the concept of *obedience* itself.[29] Dugard proposes, among other reasons, states' political interests; their urge for good standing, both at home and overseas; anticipated reciprocal treatment, and fear of sanctions as some of the facilitating factors for states obedience of international law.[30] Because states fear isolation and condemnation from other nation-states, they, although not always, do not lightly divert from international laws nor do they take them for granted.

Any attempt at comprehending the relevance of international law in any particular instance will most surely have to begin with self-introspection about international law itself. What better way can such solipsism be made other than by asking the simple question: What is international law? This is somewhat of a straightforward question, as international law means different things to different people. As can be expected, the answer to the question of what international law is has always birthed extreme views, though all of them of equal importance. Scholars have diverted along different lines of nuances.[31] Some, particularly the orthodox scholars, conceptualised international law through the prism of natural law, others through positivist perceptions, yet again some others are informed by critical legal analysis.

At a subminimum, international law, is the basic principles and rules, whether general or particular, that regulate states *inter se*.[32] This narrow definitional framework is particularly prominent in old standard scripts concerning

[28] Koh (note 27) 2599–2659.

[29] Koh (note 27) 2659.

[30] J Dugard *International Law: A South African Perspective* 4 ed (Juta & Co, 2012) 8–9.

[31] For a thorough analysis of the different schools of thought and basic history and the background to international law see, generally, M Akerhurst *A Modern Introduction to International Law* 5 ed (George Allen & Unwin Publishers, 1984) 12–22.

[32] See, generally, Dugard (note 30) 1.

international law but remains a dismally weak framework with which to capture the true province of what international law is or what it has at least become over the generations. A serious and obvious weakness of this definitional blueprint is not only its simplicity but equally its emphasis on the state as the epicentre of international law to the *exclusion* of all 'others'. Even if we have to accept that states are 'still at the heart of the international legal system',[33] as the former President of the ICJ, Higgins J once stated, international law has undergone what one may call a period of transitional repentance. This transformation is so drastic a reformation that a narration which views international law only as a system solely engulfing of rules governing relations between states is entirely misleading and should accordingly be rejected. Beginning with the 1949 advisory opinion of the ICJ on the *Reparation for Injuries suffered in the Service of the United Nations*,[34] it became clearer that states, together with other non-state subjects, form part of the fabric of international law. Furthermore, international tribunals and courts (both global and regional) and their binding decisions, fledgling jurisprudence, quasi-judicial entities within (regional) human rights systems and, furthermore, the increasing growth of intergovernmental organisations and agencies, all contribute to the substantive rules of international law. International treaties, be they within the scope of human rights law, environmental law, international criminal law or humanitarian law, have also extended the scope of international law to individuals.

A restrictive comprehension of international law focusing on only states (relations) fails to capture the ever evolving and mutilating character of international law. It excludes at worse all relevant stakeholders of the international-law process, fails to view international law as an entrenched system comprising multiple stakeholders and undervalues its processes. There is therefore the need for an expansive conceptual framework. To this end, the British barrister and professor, JG Starke's depiction of international law offers – although not flawlessly – a more modest understanding of contemporary international law. According to Starke, international law:

> [m]ay be defined as that body of law which is composed for its greater part of the principles and rules of conduct which states feel themselves bound to observe, and therefore, do commonly observe in their relations with each other, and which includes also (a) the rules of law relating to the functioning of international institutions or organisations, their relations with each other, and their relations with States and individuals; and (b) certain rules of law

---

[33] R Higgins *Problems and Process: International Law and How We use It* (Oxford University Press, 1993) 39.

[34] See, generally, 'Advisory Opinion on theReparation for Injuries Suffered in the Service of the United Nations' (1949) ICJ Report, 174.

> relating to individuals and non-state entities so far as the rights of duties of such individuals and non-State entities are the concern of the international community.[35]

Many contemporary scholars in the field of international law (and even international relations) have long taken note of the captivity of Starke's definition and have expanded the definition of international law by considering the role of private individuals and other non-state subjects as far as they are of importance to the international community and international law more closely. This has inescapably provoked teachers and scholars of this branch of law to begin to question what ought to be regarded as international law. Among those who have contested the more basic notion of international law are Boyle and Chinkin, who in their longitudinal study on the making of international law view international law as premised on and 'fundamental to a globalised world'.[36] They make the crude point that international law and its law-making process have moved away from a state-centric basis to a more broad-based process inclusive of other non-state actors and that these actors too are to be regarded as worthy actors and creators of the rules of international law. Simma and Paulus made similar arguments earlier when they held that 'other actors than States are assuming importance [in international law]: intergovernmental organisations, as well as nongovernmental organisations, global economic players and the global media'.[37] A credible contribution of these contemporary demystifications of international law is that it has not only extended the meaning of international law to be more reflective of its real stature, but also has the effect of harmonising the substantive component of international law with that of its processes, including all its relevant stakeholders and agencies. The advances Boyle, Chinkin, Simma and Paulus make divert from those made, for instance, by Delupis in 1987[38] and are supported by others such as Dugard, who believe that *only* states and intergovernmental organisations bear international personality and are the principal creators of the rules of international law.[39]

The comparative advantages of international law remain widespread, though. Since international law is principally the foremost branch of law that engages nation-states and regulates their relations with one another and towards the international community, it is the most approximate law within which states undertake to protect their citizens, whether individually or jointly. It offers, as Meyersfeld once

[35] JG Starke *Introduction to International Law* 9 ed (Butterworths, 1984) 3.

[36] A Boyle & C Chinkin *The Making of International Law* (Oxford University Press, 2007) 19.

[37] B Simma & A Paulus 'The responsibility of individuals for human rights abuses in internal conflicts: A positivist view' (1999) 93 *Australian Journal of International Law* 306.

[38] I Detter Delupis *The Concept of International Law* (Cambridge University Press, 1987) 130.

[39] Dugard (note 30) 2.

articulated, 'a legal structure, which regulates State behaviour, albeit through non-traditional mechanisms and by non-traditional agents'.[40] By undertaking international agreements, states not only demonstrate their willingness, at least in theory, to protect and promote the rights of its citizens and to maintain international peace and order, but more so a parallel duty to be held accountable in instances of failure of compliance with those norms and instruments.[41]

The international human rights systems, whether at the universal, regional or sub-regional level, offer far-reaching regimes and mechanisms of control. These include, among other mechanisms, complaints procedures, flexible special-procedure investigations and missions, observer and peacekeeping missions, non-governmental organisation (NGO) forums and periodic state peer reviews. Most of these mechanisms, although in most instances geographically dislocated, often come at no cost compared to the financially draining domestic legal processes. And while it is true that the decisions of the international system are merely persuasive, in principle they hold far greater moral inducement because of the 'naming and shaming' that comes with such adjudication.

The United Nations, for example, has an important political organ – its Security Council – which, in a way, determines the political agenda of states. So, too, does the African Union have its peace and security architecture which enforces international law in a variety of ways. The powers granted the Security Council in terms of Chapter VII of the UN Charter and those of the AU peace and security architecture are wide and can be coercive towards states. Changes can easily be introduced domestically if the Security Council or the AU peace and security architecture enforces these powers. Furthermore, international law has the potential to act as a catalyst for states to act in their municipal systems.

As stated in earlier chapters of this book,[42] comparative law has a central role to play both in the discovery, evolution and development of international law and in the internationalisation of laws and legal systems. Although not always manifest through the steady harmonisation and unification of laws throughout the world aimed at establishing 'common core' legal rules and principles that can be used and applied in various legal systems on the same terms, comparative law has had an influence in the internationalisation of laws, legal systems and practices in many jurisdictions.

---

[40] B Meyersfeld *Domestic Violence and International Law* (Hart Publishing, 2010) 254.

[41] J Jones 'The importance of international law and institutions' in R Manjoo & J Jones (eds) *The Legal Protection of Women from Violence: Normative Gaps in International Law* (Routledge, 2018) 2; see also A Clark 'The normative context of human rights criticism: Treaty ratification and UN mechanisms' in K Sikkink, Stephen C, Ropp, Steve C Ropp & T Risse (eds) *The Persistent Power of Human Rights* (Cambridge University Press, 2013) 127.

[42] See, generally, chapter 1 of this book.

7.3.2 Harmonisation and unification of laws

Traditionally, the main function of comparative law was seen to be the 'unification' or, less comprehensively, the 'harmonisation' of laws. In the past, these two aims were viewed as applying primarily to private law, especially to international transactions and trade. But the situation has changed drastically and today the scope of these processes has also penetrated aspects of public law.

Although there are no neat definitions of what constitutes the harmonisation or unification of laws, Zaphiriou argues that unification means the 'adoption of an agreed set of rules, standards or guidelines for the application to transnational transactions' whereas harmonisation 'does not lead to a settled set of agreed rules. It directs a change of rules, standards or processes in order to avoid conflicts and bring about equivalence.'[43] Similarly, Kamba states that

> unification signifies the process whereby two or more different legal provisions or systems are supplanted by a single provision, whereas harmonization is designed to effect an approximation or co-ordination of different legal provisions or systems by eliminating major differences and creating minimum requirements or standards.[44]

From this conceptual framework one can deduce that in the context of law, harmonisation can be defined as the process of creating common legal standards and norms across different legal systems. The aim of harmonisation is to create consistency of law between or among different states. This is often the case when the aim is to eliminate the likelihood of one state obtaining an (economic) advantage over others as a result of different legal rules. It is also intended to reduce compliance and regulatory burdens for transnational commercial purposes such as free trade.

It is vital, therefore, that at all material times a distinction be made between unification and harmonisation. This is not to suggest that conflation does not occur between the two. On the contrary, as far as the objective of both is concerned, which is the attainment of a unified or integrated legal system, the two can be said to be related. That is to say, both processes are concerned with approximating several legal systems as far as possible. Both are also oriented towards some level of legal integration. However, there are several distinguishable differences that are worth appreciating. First and foremost, unification aims at complete unity in substance and detail whereas harmonisation avoids complete uniformity. In the case of the unification of laws, therefore, a new law is brought in that completely

[43] G Zaphiriou 'Unification and harmonization of law relating to global and regional trading' (1994) 14 *Northern Illinois University Law Review* 407.

[44] WJ Kamba 'Comparative law: A theoretical framework' (1974) 23 *International and Comparative Law Quarterly* 501.

replaces national laws that existed before it. Unification focuses on substituting or combining two or more legal systems and replacing them with a single new legal regime. In contrast, harmonisation seeks to coordinate different legal systems by eliminating major differences and creating minimum requirements or standards. Overall, harmonisation can be said to be a gradual step towards unification.

The unification of laws has mostly been achieved in the sphere of private law, more especially in international economic law. To this end, international unification has penetrated areas such as negotiable instruments, the international sale of goods and the carriage of goods by sea. The League of Nations Geneva Conventions No 3313 and 3314 of 7 June 1930, Unified Rules of Substance and Conflict of Laws relating to bills of exchange and promissory notes, which was later replaced by the United Nations Convention on the International Bills of Exchange and International Promissory Notes, is an example of a unified instrument. The Convention on the Carriage of Goods by Sea of 1978 (known as the 'Hamburg Rules') is another illustrious example of unification. The Hamburg Rules strengthen the rights of cargo owners and reflects the interests of developing countries in the carriage of goods by sea.

The most overt manifestation of the harmonisation of laws can be traced to the European Union (EU): Art 100 of the European Economic Community Treaty, now Art 100*(a)*(1) of the EEC Treaty as amended by the Single European Act of 1987, enables the European Council to adopt measures by a qualified majority vote and in cooperation with the European Parliament to harmonise the approximation of the legislation of Member States. Such measures include the use of regulations that have direct effects in the Member States or a directive which leaves the method of legislative reform to each state. The EU's standard decision-making procedure is known as 'Ordinary Legislative Procedure' (ie 'codecision'). The directly elected European Parliament has to approve EU legislation together with the European Council (the governments of the 27 EU countries). Until now the European Council used directives in the harmonisation process: each directive contains a deadline by which EU countries must incorporate its provisions into their national legislation and inform the European Commission to that effect.

In the AU harmonisation seems far less attainable since there is no single law that empowers supranational law to be domesticated into national law. However, the momentum is gradually changing and it is believed that in the near future the AU will transform into a more integrated legal regime. The proposed reforms of the Pan-African Parliament including the possibility of introducing model laws would be an important reform that would serve as a trigger for harmonising African state laws. Already we see such a trend in the Southern African Development Community (SADC), which has produced several model laws that its Member States can incorporate into and develop further in their own domestic laws. These include the SADC Model Law on HIV in Southern Africa, the SADC Model Law on Gender Based Violence, the SADC Model Law on Public Financial Management and the SADC Model Law on Eradicating Child Marriage and Protecting Children Already in Marriage.

There are several problems with both the unification and the harmonisation of laws. Since different legal systems operate in different juridical climates, the differences in systems can hammer harmonisation and unification processes because they can lead to protracted processes of negotiation and adoption. During such processes, every state wants to defend its foreign policy, common regional position and interests and ensure that it is adequately covered during the negotiation process. This can lead to a protracted process of negotiation and drafting and cause incompatibilities during either the harmonisation or the unification of laws.

The second problem relates to the decision of a state to become bound by an instrument (either harmonising or unifying). States can easily halt harmonisation efforts by refusing to be bound by instruments. In deciding whether to be bound or not, states may consider, among other factors, the existence of other priorities other than those covered by the instrument, the costs of implementing and domesticating the instrument in its system and their preference for or their incompatibility with domestic law, etc.

7.3.3 Common core among nation-states

The ideals of the harmonisation and unification of laws are steadily gaining ground. Here one may make only brief reference to the increasing regional economic groupings and common marks, which have potential impacts on legal systems and practices, as indicators of the gradual shift towards harmonisation and unification. This is readily achieved by recognising that in order to trade and engage with each other or one another, states are bound by some common core legal norms that know no jurisdictional boundaries. Therefore, deeply engrained in the internationalisation of comparative law is the idea that legal systems across the world have some 'common core' legal rules that cut across legal systems and traditions. These legal rules are for the most part derived from international law, particularly treaties, conventions, customary international law and the general principles of law recognised and practised by most states. Comparative law has been instrumental in the identification of such legal rules that are common to all states. In fact, one may argue that the discovery of legal rules which are common – if not, at the very least, widespread among most legal systems – is one of the main functions of (applied) comparative law. This is often called the discovery of a new *ius naturale* or *ius commune*. Comparative law forms an essential part of this 'search' for common principles of law that can lead to a more harmonised legal system globally. The aim is to determine whether there are, in fact, any basic 'core' legal principles of law, whether private or public, that are generally recognised by nation-states. The idea of a common core of legal systems gives meaning to the principle of the sovereign equality of nations articulated in Art 2(1) of the UN Charter.[45] By relying on common principles of law, no legal system can be held to be superior, advanced or more civilised (for the lack of a better term) than another. This is because through a common core all legal norms are equal in status regardless of the manner in which they are practised in any legal system.

This notwithstanding, however, the reality is that, until fairly recently, the search for common legal rules among nations yielded little more than the mere discovery that vague principles and axioms such as *sic utere tuo ut alienam non laedas* (behave in such a manner that you do not cause harm to others) and the like underlie the majority of legal systems of the world. Therefore the existence of a common core among all nation-states of the world cannot be denied. When one has regard to the sources of international law as practised in international courts and tribunals and also the widely accepted norms of the international legal order, it is common cause that there are certain legal norms or principles of law that conflate and cut across all legal systems.

The enquiry for a common core in legal systems can be said as drawing its legal basis from Art 38(1)*(c)* of the Statute of the International Court of Justice (ICJ), which provides that the court may as a source of law draw on '... the general principles of law recognized by civilised nations'. In a sense these principles as articulated in Art 38(1)*(c)* can be accepted as some of the fundamentals to most, if not, all legal systems. To this end, international courts and tribunals and even municipal systems turn to these principles in so far as they are capable of application to relations between nation-states in order to settle disputes or fill the gaps in (international) law. Although sparse use is made of general principles in settling disputes, international tribunals have in the past invoked some of these principles: unjust enrichment,[46] reparation for breach of contract,[47] *res judicata*,[48] estoppel,[49] and *nemo judex in re sua*.[50] Other notable principles, which also find codification in treaties, include the principle of non-refoulement, freedom of the high seas, the precautionary principle (in environmental cases), the due diligence principle, the principle of the flagship, and state responsibility for international wrongful acts.

Moreover, through the practice of international law, certain peremptory norms have evolved which for all material purposes are regarded as binding and common to all legal systems. These norms and obligations, either from which no derogation

[45] See also Art 4*(a)* of the AU Constitutive Act, 2002.

[46] *Lena Goldfields Arbitration* (1930) 5 AD 3.

[47] *Chorzow Factory (Merits)* (1928) PCIJ, Series A, No 17 at 29.

[48] *Application of the Convention on Genocide (Bosnia and Herzegovina v Serbia and Montenegro)* 2007 ICJ Reports 43 at 89–102.

[49] *Temple of Preah Vihear* 1962 ICJ Reports 6 at 23 and 32.

[50] *Mosul Boundary* (1925) PCIJ, Series B, No 12 at 32.

is permitted (*jus cogens*) and/or which a state owes to the international community and in the enforcement of which all states have an interest (*erga omnes*), form an essential element of legal practice to nation-states.[51] In them are found some of the binding principles of law common to, and communally applied to, all nations. Therefore, the support for the view that acts such as slavery, genocide, racial discrimination and torture are peremptory and therefore prohibited under all legal systems speaks to the reality of the existence of a common core among nation-states.

A central difference between the 'unification' or 'harmonisation' function of comparative law and that of establishing a 'common core between legal systems' is that the former predominantly concerns itself with the formulation of new rules possibly acceptable to the various legal systems, whereas the latter focuses on exploring the existence of common legal rules already in force in the various civilised nations and of mapping out areas of actual agreement or disagreement among the various legal systems.

It must, however, be added that the notion that a key function of comparative law is the aspiration of a common core among the legal systems remains severely criticised. Critics argue, among other things, that the establishment of a common core among different nationalities can be viewed as an erosion of the sovereignty of nation-states – a principle deeply entrenched in international law.[52] This is because it detracts from states' sovereignty to govern matters that are essentially within their domestic jurisdiction. Unlike, for instance, in the case of treaties, common core principles do not have a consensual basis nor are they so widespread as to conflate all legal systems. Another challenge is that principles such as *jus cogens* and *erga omnes*, which are common to all legal systems, are often difficult to determine as being peremptory. For instance, a principle such as non-discrimination, especially as it related to women or other vulnerable groups, may be widespread and settled, but in practice it may be altered in a domestic legal system. Therefore, the principle may be acceptable and evenly applied in a liberalised system such as the United States or Continental Europe but fraught with exceptions in a conservative Islamic state such as Turkey. Despite these shortcomings, common core principles can be useful in diverse ways. They could, for instance:

- be the basis for the study of comparative law;
- facilitate, and indeed stimulate, the application of Art 38(1)*(c)* of the Statute of the ICJ;
- be extremely paramount to any process of drafting international treaties and standards, whether 'hard' or 'soft' law;
- be used in international contracts and investment agreements to obviate the use of one particular legal system;

[51] See, for instance, the decision in *South West Africa* 1966 ICJ Reports 6.

[52] See, for instance, Art 2(7) of the UN Charter and Art 4*(g)* of the AU Constitutive Act, 2002.

- be useful in adjudicing international disputes or conflict-of-law matters where the parties to such dispute come from different legal jurisdictions and legal cultures.

7.4 COMPARATIVE USE OF LAW AND THE INTERNATIONALISATION OF LEGAL SYSTEMS

As indicated in this chapter, one of the determinants or rather the manifestations in which the internationalisation of laws and legal systems is taking shape is through the use of comparative law by domestic courts. An influence of comparative law on national courts is noticeable in almost every legal system, despite the varied differences that exist between these systems.[53] By engaging in each other's jurisprudence, courts are increasingly contributing to the standardisation of laws among legal systems. Therefore, when a court gives judicial notice to a decision of another country, it accepts the jurisprudential value of such foreign law and accordingly incorporates such law into its system, as a result aligning itself with the law so received. Such alignment has the long-term effect that the mutual recognition of case law and other legal sources of each state can saturate into acceptable principles of law that cut across different jurisdictions.

The use of comparative law by courts as an aid that can internationalise laws and legal systems has its fair share of advantages. Perhaps the most obvious advantage of such cross-border use of each other's jurisprudence by municipal courts is its aiding role; that is, it can guide courts in dealing with matters they were not previously confronted with. Courts the world over are increasingly confronted with legal disputes that are of first impression to them. To contextualise: a few decades ago, no one would have considered the possibility of sexual minority rights having to be adjudicated by courts. But today certainly, sexual minority rights are increasingly being questioned in courts of law, both domestically and internationally. Courts have therefore begun to seek aid by drawing on the settled practices, laws and cases of allied legal systems. This is because, as the comparative-law jurist, Schlesinger, once argued,

> whoever seeks rational solutions of perplexing social problems must recognise that there is much to be gained, not only by learning from the successes and failures of other systems, but also by a broader perspective which a comparative approach provides.[54]

---

[53] G Mousouraki *Comparative Law and Legal Traditions: Historical and Contemporary Perspectives* (Springer, 2019) 27.

[54] RB Schlenger 'The role of the "basic course" in the teaching of foreign and comparative law' (1971) 19(4) *American Journal of Comparative Law* 618.

Similarly, Kamba argues:[55]

> [w]hen one is confined to the study of one's own law within one's own country and, thus within one's own cultural environment, there is a strong tendency to accept without question the various aspects (norms, concepts, and institutions) of one's own legal system. One is inclined to think that the solutions of one's own legal order are the only possible ones. This leads to an idealization of one's own legal institutions and to treating them as inherent in the general nature of law.

In common-law countries, lacunae occur in instances where there is no legislation or binding judicial precedent to solve matters before such courts that have not previously been dealt with. Similarly, in civil-law jurisdictions courts may be confronted with questions of law that are not covered under any established code.[56] In such instances, the courts are duty bound to fill the gaps left by these omissions and in doing so comparative engagements with allied legal systems and their laws may be apparent. Furthermore, the idea of judicial cross-fertilisation may also be useful in the elucidation in national legal systems of concepts, norms and principles which have a foreign origin. This transpires specifically in conflict-of-law cases,[57] where courts must make a choice of law between two or more legal systems.

The Namibian courts have often resorted to international law through the use of comparative techniques to deal with domestic legal issues. One classic example worth highlighting is the Namibian Supreme Court's decision in *Sibonga v Chacka & Another*.[58] In this decision, the court had to express itself on the question whether the delictual action of adultery is sustainable in law, more so in the context of the institution of marriage. This question arose after the plaintiff in this action instituted a divorce action against the first defendant in early 2011, after having committed adultery with the plaintiff's wife. The action was defended. On or around September 2012 the plaintiff amended his claim to join the second defendant and introduced a claim against him of having committed adultery with his wife. In his particulars of claim, the plaintiff claimed damages against the second defendant. It was broken down as N$50 000 claimed for *contumelia* and N$50 000 for loss of 'consortium, society and services' of the first defendant.

In its determination of whether the act of adultery is wrongful for the purposes of a delictual claim, the court was guided by two primary foreign sources of law:

[55] Kamba (note 44) 491.

[56] D Schneiderman 'Comparative constitutional law in an age of economic globalisation' in V Jackson & M Tushnet (eds) *Defining the Field of Comparative Constitutional Law* (Praeger, 2002) 37.

[57] See *Sperling v Sperling* 1975 (3) SA 707 (A) and *Herbst v Suriti* 1991 (2) SA 75 (Zm).

[58] SA 77/2014 [2006] NASC 16 (19 August 2016).

the first being the South African Supreme Court of Appeal (SCA) decision in *RH v DE*[59] and the second being the Constitutional Court of South Africa decision in *DE v RH*.[60] The court began its analysis from the common-law premise that the determination of a delictual action would have to be determined by reference to its wrongfulness, which by necessary implications would also require an enquiry into questions of the legal convictions of the community and public policy. These, in the view of the court, are, since Independence, informed by constitutional values and the changing nature of the prevailing norms of society. According to the court, an examination of the origin of the action of adultery and its development reveals that it is fundamentally inconsistent with our constitutional values of equality in marriage, human dignity and privacy; and that examination also demonstrates that the action has also lost its social and moral substratum and is no longer sustainable.

As stated earlier, in reaching this conclusion the court relied with ease on comparative foreign jurisprudence of both the Supreme Court of Appeal and the Constitutional Court in *RH v DE* and in *DE v RH*, which referred to the changing societal attitude to adultery and children born of adulterous relationships in both South Africa and elsewhere.[61] In addition, the courts in those decisions also referred to a comparative analysis of the jurisprudential positions in common-law jurisdictions such as New Zealand, Australia, Scotland, most provinces of Canada and in most states of the United States.

The court's decision, though commendable, raises more questions than answers, some of which have partly been settled by the court in its judgment. These are, among other matters, the value – depreciating or expanding – that should be attached to the institution of the family and the impact of this decision on the possible condonation, if not approval, of adultery in institutions of marriage. These are important questions which, when viewed broadly, manifest the growing changes and orders in marriage, the institution of the family in society and generally questions of morality and the law.

Marriage is an essential fabric of any society, including Namibia. In the case of Namibia, such importance can be traced to Art 14(3) of the Namibian Constitution, which provides that '[t]he family is the natural and fundamental group unit of society and is entitled to protection by society and the State'. Notwithstanding this firm constitutional provision, the Supreme Court seems to suggest in its decision that delictual actions based on adultery do not strengthen the institution of marriage. In fact, in the court's view, the maintenance and cementing of the institution of marriage is dependent on the moral convictions and practices of the parties to such a marriage. In support of this proposition, the court advanced

---

59 *RH v DE* 2014 (6) SA 436 (SCA).

60 *DE v RH* 2015 (5) SA 83 (CC).

61 *RH v DE* (note 59) paras 27–28; *DE v RH* (note 60) paras 23–44.

four primary arguments by approving and showing reliance on the South African Supreme Court of Appeal jurisprudence in *RH v DE*:

(a) First of all, as was pointed out by the German *Bundesgericht* in the passage from the judgment (*JZ* 1973, 668) from which I have quoted earlier, although marriage is a human institution which is regulated by law and protected by the Constitution and which, in turn, creates genuine legal duties. Its essence … consists in the readiness, founded in morals, of the parties to the marriage to create and to maintain it. If the parties to the marriage have lost that moral commitment, the marriage will fail, and punishment meted out to a third party is unlikely to change that.

(b) Grave doubts are expressed by many about the deterrent effect of the action. In most other countries it was concluded that the action (no longer) has any deterrent effect and I have no reason to think that the position in our society is all that different. Perhaps one reason is that adultery occurs in different circumstances. Every so often it happens without any premeditation, when deterrence hardly plays a role. At the other end of the scale, the adultery is sometimes carefully planned and the participants are confident that it will not be discovered. Moreover, romantic involvement between one of the spouses and a third party can be as devastating to the marital relationship as (or even more so than) sexual intercourse.

(c) If deterrence is the main purpose, one would have thought that this could better be achieved by retaining the imposition of criminal sanctions or by the grant of an interdict in favour of the innocent spouse against both the guilty spouse and the third party to prevent future acts of adultery. But, as we know, the crime of adultery had become abrogated through disuse exactly 100 years ago while an interdict against adultery has never been granted by our courts (see, for example, *Wassenaar v Jameson supra* at 352H–353H). Some of the reasons given in *Wassenaar* as to why an interdict would not be appropriate are quite enlightening and would apply equally to the appropriateness of a claim for damages. These include, firstly, that an interdict against the guilty spouse is not possible because he or she commits no delict. Secondly, that as against a third party –

> it interferes with, and restricts the rights and freedom that the third party ordinarily has of using and disposing of his body as he chooses; … it also affects the relationship of the third party with the claimant's spouse, who is and cannot be a party to the interdict, and therefore indirectly interferes with, and restricts her rights and freedom of, using and disposing of her body as she chooses' [at 353E].

(d) In addition, the deterrence argument seems to depart from the assumption that adultery is the cause of the breakdown of a marriage, while it is now widely recognised that causes for the breakdown in marriages are far more complex. Quite frequently adultery is found to be the result and not the cause of an unhappy marital relationship. Conversely stated, a marriage in which the spouses are living in harmony is hardly likely to be broken up by a third party.

In the light of the above, the court opined that in the particular circumstances of Namibia the delictual action of adultery is unsustainable in law more so because of its uneven (gendered) effects on the institution of marriage and its patriarchal origins. The *Chaka* decision is an illustration of the standardisation of laws among legal systems. Having relied on the South African Supreme Court and Constitutional Court decisions, the Namibian Supreme Court has mirrored its jurisprudential position with that of South Africa, giving rise to the reality that the law on the claim for adultery is the same in both countries. This is the internationalisation of the law because legal practitioners, given that the legal positions are the same in both countries, can rely not only on each other's decisions but develop the common law on similar areas of the law to a point where the unification or at the least harmonisation of laws has been achieved.

The question that remains to be considered is why domestic courts are increasingly engaging in each other's jurisprudence and therefore contributing to the internationalisation of laws and legal practice. The explanations that can be advanced are many, but worth mentioning is the fact that, inherently, courts can no longer solely rely on their own jurisprudence for the development of laws and legal systems. For instance, areas such as private international law necessitate the comparative use of law. In the context of Namibia, our courts often rely on sources from other jurisdictions, although cautiously,[62] given the historical linkages of its legal system to comparable jurisdictions, particularly in southern Africa; the influences of foreign legal training; the influence of international law, particularly in areas of human rights and constitutional law, and the use of expatriate judges.

7.5 CONCLUSION

As stated above in this chapter, state sovereignty has not only changed as a concept over the years, but this change can potentially affect what states recognise as law and as part of their respective legal systems. As part of internationalisation, states can easily be required to surrender some of their recognised and settled practices, laws,

[62] See, generally, Rule 19 of the Supreme Court Rules, 2017 and Rule 130 of the High Court Rules, 2014, which places limitations on the use of foreign case law and material.

policy positions and even legal systems. This is because internationalisation, especially when viewed in the light of the processes of harmonisation and/or unification of law, requires, among other matters, that states adopt common legal positions on issues, whether such issues are of a domestic or a transnational character.

In the state of Namibia, sovereignty remains deeply entrenched, raising questions about the pace and feasibility of this jurisdiction in internationalising its legal system. This is even corroborated more when one has regard to the fact that the African Union, of which Namibia is a part, has not advanced sufficiently in establishing a unifying legal regime, something that is now settled in the EU. Although we are not advanced in internationalising our system, there are clear signs of progress. The courts' use of comparative law is encouraging in this regard.

The use of comparative law by courts as an aid continues to contribute gradually not only to the harmonisation of our laws and legal system but also gradually towards internationalisation. The gradual discovery, recognition and use of legal rules and principles which are common to, if not, at the very least, widespread among most legal systems – the so-called *ius commune* – is a step in the right direction in shaping our legal system towards a global justice regime. That comparative law forms an essential part of this 'search' for common principles of law, for a more harmonised legal system globally, is not only undeniable but equally inevitable.

REFERENCES

Akerhurst, M *A Modern Introduction to International Law* 5 ed (George Allen & Unwin Publishers, 1984).

Amvane, G 'Intervention pursuant to Article 4(h) of the Constitutive Act of the African Union without United Nations Security Council authorization' (2005) 15(2) *African Human Rights Law Journal* 282–298.

Annan, K 'Two concepts of sovereignty' *The Economist*, 18 September 1999, https://www.economist.com/international/1999/09/16/two-concepts-of-sovereignty, accessed 1 June 2019.

Ansong, A 'The concept of sovereign equality of states in international law' (2016) 2(1) *Ghana Institute of Management and Public Administration Law Review* 23.

Bartelson, J *A Genealogy of Sovereignty* (Cambridge University Press, 1995).

Benvenisti, E 'The conception of international law as a legal system' (2008) 50(1) *German Yearbook of International Law* 393.

Bodin, J *Les Six Livres de République*, Book I Ch 8 (Chez Jacques du Puys, 1577).

Bodin, J *Sovereignty: Four Chapters from the Six Books of the Commonwealth* (trans J Franklin) (Cambridge University Press).

Bodley, A 'Weakening the principle of sovereignty in international law: The international tribunal for the former Yugoslavia' (1998) 31(1) *New York University Journal of International Law and Politics* 419.

Boyle, A & Chinkin, C *The Making of International Law* (Oxford University Press, 2007).

Capaldo, G *The Pillars of Global Law, XVI* (Routledge, 2008).

Cassese, A *International Law* (Oxford University Press, 2005).

Clark, A 'The normative context of human rights criticism: Treaty ratification and UN mechanisms' in K Sikkink et al (eds) *The Persistent Power of Human Rights* (Cambridge University Press, 2013).

Detter Delupis, I *The Concept of International Law* (Cambridge University Press, 1987).

Dugard, J *International Law: A South African Perspective* 4 ed (Juta & Co, 2012).

Higgins, R *Problems and Process: International Law and How We use It* (Oxford University Press, 1993).

Hinsley, F *Sovereignty* (Cambridge University Press, 1986).

Jackson, R *Sovereignty: Evolution of an Idea* (Polity Press, 2007).

Jennings, R 'Sovereignty and international law' in G Kreijen (ed) *State, Sovereignty and International Governance* (Oxford University Press, 2002).

Jones, J 'The importance of international law and institutions' in R Manjoo &J Jones (eds) *The Legal Protection of Women from Violence: Normative Gaps in International Law* (Routledge, 2018).

Kamba, WJ 'Comparative law: A theoretical framework' (1974) 23 *International and Comparative law Quarterly* 501.

Koh, HH 'Why do nations obey international law?' (1997) 106 *Yale Law Journal* 2610–2611.

Krasner, S *Sovereignty: Organized Hypocrisy* (Princeton University Press, 1999).

Meyersfeld, B *Domestic Violence and International Law* (Hart Publishing, 2010).

Mousouraki, G *Comparative Law and Legal Traditions: Historical and Contemporary Perspectives* (Springer, 2019).

Ndeunyema, N 'The Namibian Constitution, international law and the courts: A critique' (2020) 9(1) *Global Journal of Comparative Law* 271–296.

Perrez, F *Cooperative Sovereignty from Independence to Interdependence in the Structure of International Environmental Law* (Springer, 2000).

Sahle, E (ed) *Democracy, Constitutionalism, and Politics in Africa: Historical Context, Developments, and Dilemmas* (Palgrave Macmillan, 2017).

Schlesinger, RB 'The role of the "basic course" in the teaching of foreign and comparative law' (1971) 19(4) *American Journal of Comparative Law* 618.

Schneiderman, D 'Comparative constitutional law in an age of economic globalisation' in V Jackson & M Tushnet (eds) *Defining the field of Comparative Constitutional Law* (Praeger, 2002).

Simma, B & Paulus, A 'The responsibility of individuals for human rights abuses in internal conflicts: A positivist view' (1999) 93 *Australian Journal of International Law* 306.

Slaughter, A *A New World Order* (Princeton University Press, 2004).

Souaré, I 'The AU and the challenge of unconstitutional changes of government in Africa' *in Institute for Security Studies Policy Paper* (2009) No197, 1–16.

Starke, JG *Introduction to International Law* 9 ed (Butterworths, 1984).

Tshosa, O 'The status of international law in Namibia: A critical appraisal of the Constitutional Strategy' (2010) 2(1) *Namibia Law Journal* 3–28.

Vunyingah, M *Unconstitutional Changes of Government in Africa: An Assessment of the Relevance of the Constitutive Act of the African Union* (Africa Institute of South Africa Policy Brief No 44, 2011), 1–8.

Warner, J 'The African Union and article 4*(h)*: Understanding changing norms of sovereignty and intervention in Africa through an integrated levels-of-analysis approach' in E Sahle (ed) *Democracy, Constitutionalism, and Politics in Africa: Historical context, Developments, and Dilemmas* (Palgrave Macmillan, 2017).

Zaphiriou, G 'Unification and harmonization of law relating to global and regional trading' (1994) 14 *Northern Illinois University Law Review* 407.

CASES

Application of the Convention on Genocide (Bosnia and Herzegovina v Serbia and Montenegro) 2007 ICJ Reports 43

Chorzow Factory (Merits) (1928) PCIJ, Series A, No 17

DE v RH 2015 (5) SA 83 (CC)

Herbst v Suriti 1991 (2) SA 75 (Zm)

Lena Goldfields Arbitration (1930) 5 AD 3

Minister of Home Affairs and Immigration v Chairperson of the Immigration Selection Board & Others (SA2017/76) [2020] NASC 1 (19 March 2020)

Mosul Boundary (1925) PCIJ, Series B, No 12

RH v DE 2014 (6) SA 436 (SCA)

Sibonga v Chaka & Another SA 77/2014 [2006] NASC 16 (19 August 2016)

South West Africa case 1966 ICJ Reports 6

Sperling v Sperling 1975 (3) SA 707 (A)

Temple of Preah Vihear 1962 ICJ Reports 6

LEGISLATION

Advisory Opinion on the Reparation for Injuries Suffered in the Service of the United Nations (1949) ICJ Report

African Union, African Charter on Democracy, Elections and Governance, 30 January 2007

African Union (AU) Constitutive Act, 2002

African Union 'Protocol on Amendments to the Constitutive Act of the African Union' 11 July 2003

United Nations, Charter of the United Nations, 24 October 1945, 1 UNTS XVI

8

Relevance of African jurisprudential theories in comparative legal processes

Samuel K Amoo, Clever Mapaure and Kennedy Kariseb

8.1 INTRODUCTION

It may be conceded that the question of an African jurisprudence - that is, a unique African philosophical foundation of theoretical questions about the nature of law and legal systems in Africa - partially protrudes from the grand discourse on the existence of African philosophy.[1] Since time immemorial, Africans have philosophised about their societies and the global world in which they live, including about the law. To their dismay, much of their philosophical discourse has been made orally[2] and has been distorted for the most part. Moreover, following the decolonisation processes in Africa that swept the continent from the late 1950s onwards, the indigenous thought processes and indigenous laws have been overwhelmed by state laws. Jurisprudence in Africa has therefore remained strained. Consequently, it is not misplaced to advance the argument that there has been a historical privileging of 'Global North' knowledge and worldviews with a concomitant undervaluation and marginalisation of thoughts from Africa in comparative legal processes on the continent and beyond. The Global North is often thought of as being the source and creator of theory, while the Global South simply applies what has been developed in the First World to their context without question. It is therefore not surprising that much of the comparative legal process in Africa, including in Namibia, has not been informed by African thought,

[1] L Komolafe 'African jurisprudence as historical co-existence of diffused legal theories' (2002) 8(1) *Thought and Practice: A Journal of the Philosophical Association of Kenya* 53.

[2] See, generally, T Elias *The Nature of African Customary Law* (Manchester University Press, 1956).

particularly African philosophical discourse, that is unique and homegrown. If it has, it has undeniably been minimal.

The colonial context in Africa exacerbated the heavy reliance on discourses, principles and thoughts from elsewhere, which resulted in the marginalisation of African philosophical thoughts and theories. One of the immediate consequences of the colonisation of the African continent has been that local ways of interpreting the world around us, including law, have been replaced with colonial modalities of thought, which often claim universality.[3] Some have even questioned the existence of homegrown African theories of thought. As is shown in this chapter, Africa can pride itself on thoughts and theories that are homegrown and uniquely developed by Africans for Africa. In this premise, the universal claim of thought processes from the Global North has increasingly begun to be challenged as repeated attempts are being made by scholars to reinvigorate African values, theories and thoughts in mainstream legal processes.[4] It is our contention in this chapter that Africa, despite its vast and diverse nature, has its own jurisprudential discourses that can inform and guide its legal processes. This is not to suggest that Africa is homogenous and accustomed to one jurisprudential thought. Rather, the argument is that 'jurisprudence in Africa' is coterminous with various legal theories in other legal systems and therefore can be and in fact should be regarded as worthy of judicial notice in comparative legal processes.

This chapter is divided into three parts following this introduction. As a precursor to the overall analysis of African theories, Part 9.2 outlines the Namibian legal system and the relevance of comparative jurisprudence, including that of jurisprudence in the comparative legal processes. Part 9.3 sets out the various homegrown African legal theories, their content and potential in comparative legal processes in Africa (and beyond). Part 9.4 briefly concludes the chapter.

8.2 NAMIBIAN LEGAL SYSTEM AND RELEVANCE OF JURISPRUDENCE IN COMPARATIVE LEGAL PROCESSES

The discussion that follows establishes that comparative legal research is a *sine qua non* for the legal fraternity, more especially the Judiciary. Courts are increasingly confronted with various types of problem which can be dealt with more efficiently

[3] D Bilchits, T Metz & O Oyowe *Jurisprudence in an African Context* (Oxford University Press, 2021) 4.

[4] See, generally, C Mapaure 'Reinvigorating African values for SADC: The relevance of traditional African philosophical thought on law in a globalised world of competing perspectives' (2011) 1(1) *SADC Law Journal* 149–173; W Idowu 'Against the skeptical argument and the absence thesis: African jurisprudence and the challenge of positivist historiography' (2006) 6(1) *The Journal of Philosophy, Science & Law* 34–49.

by invoking the aid of comparative legal study and research. In the context of judicial process in Namibia, comparative law has played an important part in the national judicial process. For example, the jurisprudence that has developed from the decisions of the Namibian courts since independence has established a discernible epistemological paradigm that has been informed and influenced by the comparative jurisprudence from foreign jurisdictions and international law and conventions. This is especially so in the areas of the interpretation of the provisions of the Bill of Rights. These cases include interpreting the constitutionality of legislative provisions or practices relating to corporal punishment,[5] the restraining of prisoners by chaining them to each other by means of metal chains,[6] homosexual relationships,[7] property rights, fair trial, including trial within a reasonable time, the admissibility of illegally obtained evidence and corporal punishment.

It has been stated that comparative law fulfils one of its main practical undertakings when it is employed as an aid to the legislative process and to law reform by legislation. The Oxford professor, Henry James Sumner Maine,[8] stated that the chief function of comparative jurisprudence is to facilitate legislation and the practical improvement of the law. In the area of legislation in Namibia, various pieces of legislation, such as the Companies Act, the Environmental Management Act, the Water Act and the Human Tissue Act, were promulgated after extensive research in other jurisdictions. This was especially the case in the Southern African Development Community (SADC) region. One objective of this comparative enterprise is to achieve the harmonisation of the laws in the region in pursuit of some common purpose. A fundamental principle underpinning the functions of the Namibia Law Reform and Development Commission in the discharge of its statutory functions is, for example, the incorporation of best practices in its recommendations to parliament. This objective, however, cannot be achieved by reference only to internal institutions. The search for best practices is best achieved by investigating comparative law and the norms and practices from outside jurisdictions, that is, by undertaking a comparative study of laws in foreign jurisdictions in order to ensure compliance with best practices and recognised international norms and conventions. Consequently, the commission undertakes a great number of comparative legal studies and research aimed at law reform and a general restatement of the law.

---

[5] See *Ex parte Attorney-General, Namibia: in re Corporal Punishment* 1991 (3) SA 76 (NmS).

[6] See *Namunjepo & Others v Commanding Officer, Windhoek Prison & Another* 2000 (6) BCLR 671 (NmS).

[7] See *The Chairperson of the Immigration Selection Board v Erna Elizabeth Frank & Another*, Supreme Court of Namibia Case No SA 8/99.

[8] HS Maine *Village Communities* (Oxford University Lectures, 1987) 4.

The genesis of this subliminal attention to the relevance of legal theories in the legal process may be traced to the methodology and the anticipated learning outcomes of jurisprudence as a course of study in the curricula of law faculties. Conclusions to be drawn from experience tend to indicate that the teaching of jurisprudence, especially at the undergraduate level, has to a large extent been a restatement of theories which students are expected to agree or disagree with in lectures and tutorials. A similar approach has been adopted by the earlier writers of publications on jurisprudence, but one must concede that this trend has changed. Twining and Miers, in *How to do Things with Rules*,[9] depart from this traditional approach. Freeman, in his advocacy of the holistic approach to the study of jurisprudence under the title 'The relevance of jurisprudence', states as follows:

> Jurisprudence involves the study of general theoretical questions about the nature of laws and legal systems, about the relationship of law to justice and morality and about the social nature of law. A proper discussion of questions such as these involves understanding and use of philosophical and sociological theories and findings in their application to law. A study of jurisprudence should encourage the student to question assumptions and to develop a wider understanding of the nature and working of law. Questions of theory constantly spring up in legal practice, though they may not be given very sophisticated answers.[10]

Jurisprudential theories on the nature and function of law almost invariably deal with the relationship between theories of law and the legal process. In other words, hypotheses on law are meant to be used as tools with which to analyse law in pursuit of arriving at a better understanding of the law and the legal system. The task of unravelling and understanding the nature of law is an enterprise that encompasses applying legal theories to the entire legal process, including the promulgation of the law. In order to achieve this objective, the teaching of jurisprudence must be purposively oriented, and this is achievable. It is not difficult for one to identify theories of law as being the underlying principles of both the decisions of courts and legislation.

There is ample evidence in both the legislative and the judicial processes of the application of the principle advanced by the proponents of natural law that the validity of law must be measured against some moral, ethical and formal requirements or imperatives. Not all judgments on principles of legality are value-neutral, though. This is manifested in the judgments of superior courts in cases

---

[9] W Twining & D Miers *How to do Things with Rules* (Weidenfeld & Nicolson, 1986).

[10] MDA Freeman *Introduction to Jurisprudence* (Sweet & Maxwell, 2001) 2–5.

on, for example, inheritance, the defence of necessity, and sexual orientation. The question of the relationship between law and principles of morality or ethics and the moral criteria for evaluating positive law and the implications of their application constitute the core postulates of naturalists. It can certainly be argued that Lord Devlin[11] was an exponent of value judgements and advanced the position that law, especially criminal law, can be used to enforce principles of morality because the state has a claim to legislate on matters of morals. In the famous English case of *Shaw v DPP*,[12] the concept of the courts of law as possessing an inherent jurisdiction over the community's morals was discussed at length by the House of Lords. Shaw was convicted on charges that included publishing an obscene libel (a booklet in which prostitutes advertised their services) and conspiring to corrupt public morals. On appeal to the House of Lords, the question arose whether the courts possessed moral jurisdiction. Lord Simonds stated as follows:

> When Lord Mansfield … said (*R v Delaval* (1763)) that the Court of King's Bench was the *custos morum* (guardian of morals) of the people and had the superintendence of offences *contra bonos mores*) against good behaviour, he was asserting, as I now assert, that there is in that court a residual power, where no statute has yet intervened to supersede the common law, to superintend those offences which are prejudicial to the public welfare. Such occasions will be rare, for Parliament has not been slow to legislate when attention has been thoroughly aroused. But gaps remain and always will remain, since no man can foresee every way in which the wickedness of man may disrupt the order of society.

In *In re Sigsworth. Bedford v Bedford*,[13] the court had to pronounce itself on the propriety or validity of the claim of an adjudged murderer to inherit the property of his victim. The reasoning of the court was grounded on the well-established principles of morality that public policy precludes a sane murderer from taking a benefit under their victim's will. In arriving at this decision, the court stated that the principle was to be extended in its application in the construction of Acts of Parliament that general words which might include cases obnoxious to the principle must be read and construed as subject to it. Therefore, it was held that the principle of public policy which precludes a murderer from claiming a benefit conferred on them by their victim precludes them also from claiming a benefit conferred on them, in case of their victim's intestacy, by statute.

---

[11] P Devlin *The Enforcement of Morals* (Oxford University Press, 1965) 1–25.
[12] *Shaw v DPP* [1962] AC 220; [1961] 2 WLR 897 (HL).
[13] *In re Sigsworth. Bedford v Bedford* [1934] All ER Rep 113.

In *Riggs v Palmer*,[14] the facts of which are similar to those in *In re Sigsworth*, the court approached the issue on moral grounds and used the rationality or absurdity principle to deny the claim to the property. The principle of law applied by the court in interpreting the statutes that regulate the making, proof and effect of wills and the devolution of property was that if any absurd consequences arise that are manifestly contradictory to common reason, they are void. This means that judges are at liberty to expound on a statute by equity and only *quo ad hoc* disregard it. The court held that all laws and all contracts may be controlled in their operation and effect by general fundamental maxims of the law based on principles of morality. One such maxim was that no one shall be permitted to profit by their own fraud, to take advantage of their own wrong, to found any claim upon their own iniquity or to acquire property by their own crime. It was held that one cannot vest oneself with title by crime and consequently one ought to be deprived of any interest in an estate deemed to have been acquired under such circumstances.

In *Dudley v Stephens*,[15] two prisoners who had wilfully murdered a young boy on the high seas upon the chance of preserving their own lives by feeding upon his flesh and blood after he was killed, in their defence sought to rely on the defence of necessity. The court rejected the plea of necessity. The principle applied was that there is no absolute and unqualified necessity to preserve one's life, so that the killing of an innocent, unoffending and unresisting boy is murder unless the killing can be justified by some well-recognised excuse by law. In view of that principle, the court opined that although law and morality are not the same and though many things may be immoral which are not necessarily illegal, yet the absolute divorce of law from morality would be of fatal consequence and such divorce would follow if the temptation to murder in this case were to be held by law to be an absolute defence of it. It is not so. Consequently, the court found that there was no legal justification for the homicide and the prisoners were declared guilty of murder.

In *Port Elizabeth Municipality v Peoples Dialogue on Land and Shelter & Others*,[16] the respondents had unlawfully occupied land owned by the applicant and earmarked by it for housing. Upon refusal by the respondents to vacate the land so that the applicant could proceed with its development, the applicant applied for their eviction.

In dealing with this matter, the court was forced to balance two diametrically opposed fundamental principles emanating from the implementation of the Prevention of Illegal Eviction from and Unlawful Occupation of Land Act 19 of 1998 to bring about a 'just and equitable' decision. On the one hand, there was the

[14] *Riggs v Palmer* 115 NY 506.

[15] *Dudley v Stephens* [1881–5] All ER Rep 61.

[16] *Port Elizabeth Municipality v Peoples Dialogue on Land and Shelter & Others* 2000 (2) SA 1074 (SE).

traditional real right inherent in ownership reserving exclusive use and protection of his property to the landowner. On the other hand, there was the genuine despair of people in dire need of adequate accommodation. The court took the position that the interpretation and application of what constitutes 'just and equitable' in relation to both competing interests obliged the court to 'break away from a purely legalistic approach and have regard to extraneous factors such as morality, fairness, social values and implications and circumstances which would necessitate bringing out an equitably principled judgment'. That is, rationality had to be employed to temper the rigours of analytical positivism.

Common-law principles are grounded in rationality and reasonableness. Students of jurisprudence are well aware of the central position of rationality or reason in natural law. Lord Simonds, in *Shaw v DPP*,[17] alluded to the residual power of the courts, or judicial activism and advanced the reason for this. In the context of the interpretation of statutes this may arise in the interpretation of the penumbral, gray or nondescript areas of the law. Courts have often used the concept of reasonableness, public policy and what Justice Holmes termed the 'inarticulate major premise' as the basis of their decisions. Are these variables not related to theories of law such as natural law? Pound's jural postulates. And are they not related to the assertion by the realists that the law is what the judges declare to be the law? What is the role of jurisprudence in all this? Teachers of jurisprudence must be able to provoke students through appropriate pedagogic methodology to be able to trace the relationship between legal theories and the exercise of this jurisdiction by the courts. Several reasons are advanced for the courts to exercise this residual jurisdiction.

The oppressive or tyrannical use of positive law by a variety of political regimes has its jurisprudential dimensions or has its relevance in jurisprudence. It is not far-fetched, for example, for law students in Namibia and South Africa to discuss the constitutional developments of the two countries in the context and perspectives of legal theories.

In the context of the Namibian constitutional development, one can discuss the jurisprudence evolving from the decisions of the Namibian courts during the pre- and post-apartheid eras in the context and perspectives of, for example, natural law and analytical positivism. In the context of legal theories, analytical positivism can certainly be discussed as the underlying principle of the literal rule of interpretation where the courts treat fidelity to legislative enactment as the overriding value. It has also been pointed out that the South African legal system was constrained before the promulgation of that country's new Constitution by the jurisprudence and

[17] *Shaw v DPP* [1962] AC 220.

principles of legislative supremacy and analytical positivism.[18] Dugard asserts that an empirical study of the legal process in South Africa leads to the conclusion that 'judges adopt(ed) a neutral, non-activist position in their approach to human rights issues and that a form of positivism may account for this phenomenon'.[19]

8.3 HOMEGROWN AFRICAN LEGAL THEORIES AND COMPARATIVE LEGAL PROCESS

During colonial times, African laws existed as a hotchpotch of colonial compromises acceded to by expansionist figures consolidating their conquests. Central to this was the perception that Africa lacked a theory of jurisprudence. The belief in the non-existence of what qualifies as law was split into two schools of thought: the absence thesis and the sceptical argument. The absence thesis posits that there is no African jurisprudence.[20] The non-existence of an African philosophy of law is premised on the non-existence of written records about the law. Is this tenable? In all societies, a people's philosophy constitutes their system of thought and it has always served as the basis of their attitudes to life. In this light, to deny the existence of African law is to deny the premise of African life and the values that underpin it. Philosophy exists not only in written form but also in substance. A system of thought does not have to be written in order for a philosophy to exist. It is therefore disingenuous to suggest that because there are no written records in Africa regarding any jurisprudence there is no African jurisprudence. In fact, the problem of 'writtenness' is a defect common to almost all legal philosophy, whether in the West, Africa or the Far East.[21] The Africans saw no need to write as they viewed the verbal word as more effective than the written mode. Face-to-face storytelling is captivating and personal. Literacy was rare. The written word was therefore hard to come by and 'cool', distant and impersonal in comparison. Elders in oral societies passed down their wisdom in poetry and song. When those cultures disappeared, however, their ideas – and whole civilisations, in effect – were lost to us.[22]

Closely aligned to the absence thesis is the sceptical argument: it also rests on the premise that there is nothing called 'African jurisprudence'. The reason is not

[18] J Dugard 'Some realism about the judicial process and positivism – a reply' (1981) 98 *South African Law Journal* 372–387.

[19] Ibid.

[20] I William 'Against the skeptical argument and the absence thesis: African jurisprudence and the challenge of positivist historiography' (2006) 6(2) *The Journal of Philosophy, Science & Law* 9–24.

[21] W Durant *Our Oriental Heritage* (Simon and Schuster, 1954) 556–561.

[22] RC Solomon & MK Higgins *A Short History of Philosophy* (Oxford University Press, 1996).

that it is not written but that there is simply no philosophy of law with the label 'African'. Some ordered political systems in African communities are accepted, but they do not have a philosophy of law. This is basically scepticism, which has different variants among authors. Driberg denies that Africans have a clear conception of law and therefore, he argues, 'symbols of legal authority … are completely absent, and in the circumstances would be otiose.'[23] Holleman contends that an African jurisprudential frame is missing from an African system of rules and as a result there is nothing like an African jurisprudence.[24] M'Baye similarly argues that the rules governing social behaviour in traditional African societies are the very negation of law.[25] In the same vein, Smith postulated that African peoples know only of customs instead of law.[26] The thrust of the theory, therefore, is that even if Africans had indigenous systems of social control, they substantially lacked any trace of legality, legal concepts and legal elements.

The attack on the notion of African jurisprudence has been reduced to the idea that African rules of societal control and norms could not be distinguished from the rules of polite behaviour. The basis for this assertion and the denial of African jurisprudence, perceptually, can be explained by means of three reasons: first, the absence of a legislative system, including the existence of a formal court system and legal officials; second, owing to the absence of a recognised system of sanctions, and, third, the presence on a large scale of authoritarianism which is not subject to or controlled by law. Interestingly, the import of these attacks consists in the view that African jurisprudence is at best queasy.[27]

In order to appreciate African jurisprudential claims, it is important to put on one's Afrocentric goggles. Sustainable African peace and educational development should be informed by flexible Afrocentrism. Afrocentrism is a worldview that considers African peoples, their cultures, histories, collective struggles, needs and aspirations, to be central to the interpretation and use of data. Afrocentrists commonly contend that approaching knowledge from a Eurocentric perspective, in addition to certain mainstream assumptions in the application of information in the West, has led to injustices and inadequacies in meeting the needs of African peoples – meaning indigenous, black Africans and the peoples of the African Diaspora. As a result, the

[23] JG Driberg 'The African conception of law' (1934) 16 *Journal of Comparative Legislation and International Law* 237–238.

[24] JF Holleman *Issues in African Law* (Mouton, 1974) 12.

[25] K M'Baye 'The African conception of law' in R David (ed) *The Legal Systems of the World and Their Common Comparison and Unification, II* (International Association of Legal Science, 1975) 56.

[26] MG Smith 'The sociological framework of law' in H Kuper & L Kuper (eds) *African Law: Adaptation and Development* (Berkeley, 1965) 32.

[27] W Idowu 'African jurisprudence and the reconciliatory theory of law' (2006) 37(1) *The Cambrian Law Review* 1–16.

Afrocentrist paradigm is one that seeks to discover and also to reinterpret information through African eyes, using it in ways that inure to the benefit of Africans.

Contrary to Western scepticism about the existence of African jurisprudence, some of the first generation of African leaders – Nkrumah (Nkrumaism and Consciencism), Senghor (Negritude), Nyerere (Ujamaa), Kaunda (Humanism) and, more recently, Mbeki (African Renaissance) – have attempted to articulate philosophies that relate to the nature and soul of the African personality. These theories were regarded with a great deal of scepticism by academics, who regarded them as political ideologies rather than philosophical principles worthy of analysis and support by academia. Such has been the extent of this scepticism that these theories or philosophies have virtually vanished with the demise of these leaders from political office. These ideas about African jurisprudence are dealt with in more detail below.

8.3.1 Ubuntu and *ubuntuism:* African human rights?

If we take the celebrated concept of *unhu* (Shona) or ubuntu (isiZulu), for example, we see that there we have a typical African human rights jurisprudential concept. Ubuntu is in itself a revitalisation of African values and moral principles; it owes so much to African traditional law. This concept was born and bred and is developing in Africa. The book *African Philosophy through Ubuntu*, which Ramose published in Zimbabwe in 1999,[28] is in several respects a remarkable and refreshing contribution to African legal philosophy. It is clear in this book that African societies have suffered greatly in the process of law-making and in trying to identify themselves legally, but their lasting value orientation through *unhu* or ubuntu holds up an alternative in the sense that it advocates a renewed concern for the human person.

Ubuntu as a form of African philosophy therefore blends in with other potential, imagined or actual gifts of Africa to the wider world: African music and dance, orality and orature, kingship, healing rituals in which trance and divination play major roles, a specific appreciation of time, being and personhood – all of them cultural achievements from which especially the North Atlantic could learn a great deal and (to judge by the latter's dominant forms of popular music and dance throughout the 20th century) is increasingly prepared to learn. And it is doing so in a bid to compensate for such spiritual and corporeal limitations and frustrations as may be suspected to hide beneath the North Atlantic's economic, technological, political and military complacency.[29]

---

[28] MB Ramose *African Philosophy through Ubuntu* (Mond Books, 1999) 1–08.

[29] WMJ van Binsbergen 'Ubuntu and the globalisation of southern African thought and society' in WMJ van Binsbergen (ed) *Intercultural Encounters: African and Anthropological Lessons towards a Philosophy of Interculturality* (LIT, 2001) 6.

Viewed as a moral and political exhortation and an expression of hope for a better future, ubuntu – just like humanism discussed below – creates a moral community, admission to which is not necessarily limited by biological ancestry, nationality or actual place of residence.[30] To participate in this moral community, therefore, is not a matter of birthright in the narrower, parochial sense. If birthright applies at all, it is the birthright of any member of the human species to express concern about the conditions under which our fellow-human beings must live and to act in accordance with those conditions.[31] This moral community consists of people sharing a concern for the present and future of a particular local or regional society, seeking to add to the latter's resources, redressing its ills and searching its conceptual and spiritual repertoire for inspiration, blueprints, models and encouragement in the process. Therefore, ubuntu cannot exist in a society driven by purely positivistic principles. Ubuntu in Africa will be successful only if the principles of African natural law are maintained. In fact, the concept in itself embodies African traditional-law principles which have to be enforced from an Afrocentric perspective if societies divided by colonialism and apartheid are to be integrated. In South Africa this is referred to as the programme of the African Renaissance.[32]

Ubuntu has to be aided by the central concept of Afrocentricity, a concept which seeks to protect African values, creating such a moral community for revitalising African morals and values. This means cultivating concepts such as ubuntu, focusing not on a particular locality or region but on the African continent as a whole.[33] The people implicated in this way may be expected to identify with one another and to be solidly in pursuit of their concern.[34] Whoever sets out to publicly deconstruct and even debunk the available conceptual and spiritual repertoire dissociates themselves from this moral community, rents its fabric and jeopardises its project and the project of African integration.

8.3.2 Humanism: African Christianity?

During his presidency of Zambia, Kaunda promoted what he called 'Christian Humanism'. This was a philosophy with an African flavour heavily laden with natural-law principles. In this philosophical concept he stressed the importance of

[30] Van Binsbergen (note 29) 8.

[31] Incidentally, the inclusive principle identified is part of the African societal normative systems at the village level where, for instance, every adult has the obligation but also the right to guard the interests of all children, regardless of the specific genealogical ties between adult and child.

[32] Van Binsbergen (note 29) 8.

[33] Van Binsbergen (note 29) 10.

[34] See MK Asante *The Afrocentric Idea* (Temple University Press, 1987) 24.

the centrality of humanity while embracing a progressive conception of Christianity in an African context that incorporated principles of African culture. Kaunda believed that education which respects African values and cultural norms is the vehicle for uplifting an African people and for broadcasting humanist thought. On the humanitarian front, Kaunda believed that with humanism as a moral and truly African concept Zambia would become a leader in the fight against apartheid.[35]

In 1986 Kaunda lost a son to AIDS and, influenced by his humanism, he discussed the ordeal publicly. Driven by the same philosophy, he became and has since remained an outspoken activist opposing the disease and promoting the use of condoms in preventing its expansion. Bill Jones makes the point that black humanists reflect upon their own circumstances when developing their worldview. He writes:

> black Humanism emerges as part of a debate that is internal to black life and thought. It is not a spin-off of the enlightenment, the scientific revolution or, as Deotis Roberts has suggested, a borrowing from Comte. Rather, as Benjamin Mays, an eminent representative of black Christian theism, has correctly perceived, black incredulity about the divine, as well as agnosticism and atheism
>
> > do not develop as the results of modem science, nor from the observations that nature is cruel and indifferent; but primarily because in the social situation, [the black American] finds himself hampered and restricted ... Heretical ideas of God develop because in the social situation the 'breaks' seem to be against the Negro and the black thinkers are unable to harmonize this fact with the God pictured by Christianity.[36]

From the foregoing it is easy to see that Zambian humanism and ubuntu are not in the first place factual descriptions. Van Binsbergen comments that these concepts primarily express the speaker's dreams about norms and practices that allegedly once prevailed in what are now to be considered peripheral places,[37] while the speaker themself is situated at or near the national or global centre. Van Binsbergen goes on to postulate that such dreams about the past and the periphery are articulated not because the speaker proposes to retire there personally or wishes to exhort other people to take up effective residence there, but because of their inspiring modelling power with regard to central national and even global issues. In other words, it is

[35] Van Binsbergen (note 29) 11.

[36] See Bill Jones as quoted in BE Mays *The Negro's God as Reflected in His Literature* (New York, Atheneum, 1938) 281–282.

[37] Notably within the intimacy of allegedly closely knit villages, urban wards and kin groups.

because of these dreams' alleged persuasive or perlocutionary nature outside the peripheral domain in which they are claimed to originate and to which they refer back. Therefore, one commentator has said:

> If, thirty years later, I have much less difficulty in identifying, in my capacity as a social actor in a concrete Southern African setting, with Zambian humanism, and with ubuntu, it is because I have enjoyed, for these many years, the (part-time) membership of the kind of local communities by distant reference to these two ideologies have been constructed in the first place.[38]

Throughout the 1970s and 1980s Africa learnt that Zambian humanism was not so much a value system spelt out explicitly but expressed more implicitly as a diffuse value orientation informing the lives of people. It was according to this very value orientation that African people were allowed to share their lives, despite frequent transgressions both on the part of colonisers and the colonised and on the part of apartheid enforcers and the oppressed. This admission on both sides of the communities has been one of the greatest sources of pride and joy that underline both humanism and ubuntu alike.

Some philosophers have asked questions about whether large numbers of Africans accept a humanist life stance? That remains to be seen. However, there is no good reason why humanism cannot have great influence in Africa. We have already seen some of the precedents. With enough aid from the West, humanist organisations in Africa could make a number of positive contributions to the continent. Why should the 21st century not be the century of humanism if African traditional-law principles as embodied in humanism itself are not eroded or diluted? In the words of humanist philosopher Paul Kurtz:[39]

Is it not the turn of the Eupraxophers [ie, humanists] to set forth to draw wisdom, not based upon philosophy alone, but upon the sciences, and concerned not simply with the love, but the practice, of wisdom? We need men and women of good intentions and moral empathy and compassion, who drink deeply at the well of Sofia, and attempt to apply with reason and understanding the best knowledge of the day. They are unwilling to abandon ethical means to achieve ideal ends (as the Utopian purveyors of ideals of past generations did with tragic results), but will attempt to help develop the highest potentialities, for the fullness of life.

From this, there is no doubt that the success of humanism can be realised only if principles of traditional law in an African context have been revitalised and embraced.

---

[38] Van Binsbergen (note 29) 10.

[39] P Kurtz *In Defense of Secular Humanism* (Prometheus Books, 1983).

8.3.3 *Negritude*: flavour of blackness and Africanness

In 1990, Senghor, the former Senegalese president, was elected to the International Academy of Humanism. The academy is composed of humanists who are committed to free enquiry, the scientific methods of investigation and the furthering of 'humanist ethical values and principles'. Senghor was largely responsible for popularising the term '*negritude*', a way of identifying with 'Blackness' without having to draw upon culture, language or nationality.[40] He is therefore best known for championing *negritude* on a grand scale: as interpreted by Senghor, it encompasses 'the whole of the values of civilization – cultural, economic, social, and political – which characterize the ... Negro African World'.[41] Senghor admitted that *negritude* was spirit-centred and marked by a characteristic rhythm and symbolism when he said '[t]there is a certain flavor, a certain odor, a certain accent, a certain black tone inexpressible in European ... [languages]'.[42]

Inspired by African values and elements of African traditional law in a world of competing perspectives on law, Senghor's particular brand of *negritude* was largely a neo-African cultural challenge in which he equated cultural by-products such as art as a marker of civility.[43] This connects clearly to Okafor's assertion that African jurisprudence can be understood only in the context of African ontology. Once this happens, we are apt to have labels that indicate ubuntu, humanism or *negritude* is racism. This is what happened to Senghor. Because *negritude* surfaced partly from French colonial rejection, Mphahlele, in criticising it, claimed that '*negritude* is an inferiority complex'; however, Senghor retorted that negritude is neither self-hate nor racialism. Yet, considering Senghor's *negritude* against the Western notion of a universal civilisation, it becomes clear that Senghor's quest 'to assimilate, not be assimilated' indicates a more inclusive civilisation rather than sheer mimicry of Western concepts.

Senghor's cultural policies in Senegal reflect *negritude* schemata, fully aware of the potential power of African people to create and define their own images.[44] For example, in implementing the *Ecole de Dakar*, a school of art in Senegal, it was clear that he wanted Africa to have 'a certain active presence in the world,

[40] G Wilder *The French Imperial Nation-state: Negritude & Colonial Humanism between the Two World Wars* (University of Chicago Press, 2005) 1–352.

[41] LG Colvin *Historical Dictionary of Senegal* (The Scarecrow Press Inc, 1981) 229.

[42] JG Vaillant 'Perspectives on Leopold Senghor and changing the face of negritude' (1976) 2 *ASA Review of Books* 154–162.

[43] L Sidney & RDG Kelly (eds) *Imagining Home: Class, Culture, and Nationalism in the African Diaspora* (Verso, 1994) 87.

[44] CZ Campbell 'Sculpting a pan-African culture in the art of negritude: A model for African artist' (2006) 6 *The Journal of Pan African Studies* 33.

or better, in the universe'.[45] This indicates the spiritual and cosmological link between African values and African identity and culture. In this light, Senghor called African art a constructive 'spiritual food' parallel to the aim of being, while Skurnik argued that Senghor's artistic vision propelled African people from being mere consumers or recipients to being creators or producers in a civilised world.[46] Showing the foundation of *negritude* to be African natural law, Senghor illustrates that African art held opportunities for dignity, necessity and sustenance in the future via *negritude*,[47] his stance on African culture catalysing a national Senegalese identity within African nationalism and African socialism.[48] Therefore, African socialism can be regarded as an offshoot of African traditional law – an interesting relationship which needs deeper analysis.

8.3.4 *Consciencism*: principle of African liberty

The book *Consciencism: Philosophy and Ideology for De-colonization with Particular Reference to the African Revolution*[49] is pre-eminently a work in socio-political philosophy, but it remains helpful in exhuming some important concepts of African traditional legal thought in a world of competing perspectives. In this book, Nkrumah's conception of African particularity does not warrant the presumption that African and European cultural differences are mutually exclusive. But as Oruka insightfully observes,

> one remarkable characteristic of this [African professional] philosophy is that it employs techniques commonly associated with European or Western philosophy. Yet, contrary to the general claim, such techniques are not unique to the West.[50]

Consciencism formed the foundation of African nationalism: accordingly, the underlying principle is that of human liberty.

---

[45] LS Senghor '*Negritude*: A humanism of the 20th century' (1966) 16(1) *Optima* 1–8.

[46] WAE Skurnik 'Leopold Sedar Senghor and African socialism' (1965) 3(3) *The Journal of Modern African Studies* 349–369.

[47] Campbell (note 44) 34.

[48] Skurnik (note 46) 367.

[49] K Nkrumah *Consciencism: Philosophy and Ideology for De-Colonization with Particular Reference to the African Revolution* (Monthly Review Press, 1970) 1–122.

[50] HO Oruka 'Sagacity in African philosophy' (1983) 23(4) *International Philosophical Quarterly* 383–393; H McClendon 'Nkrumah's *Consciencism* as philosophical text: Matters of confusion' (2003) 3 *African Philosophy* 48.

Oruka[51] is clear on this point, stating that, although African professional philosophy shares certain commonalities – for example, definitive techniques – with European or Western philosophy, these techniques are not unique to Western legal or political philosophy. Nkrumah's philosophical practice, based on an ethnophilosophical assessment, approximates the Western prototype more, even though it assumes the character of an African Marxist philosophical text and therefore stands in opposition to bourgeois academic philosophy.[52] His professional philosophical outlook has a dialectical connection to ethnophilosophy. Indicating the influence of African natural-law principles, McClendon comments correctly that 'Nkrumah's adoption of the Marxist philosophical problematic over and against African metaphysical exclusivism was the *tour de force* that sustained his particular professional mode of discourse'.[53] McClendon continues:

> Nonetheless, when particularity is conflated with African exclusivism, we discern that texts in African philosophy assume the determinate character of ethnophilosophy. For instance, WE Abraham's *The Mind of Africa* and/or Julius Nyerere's *Ujamaa* are closer to ethnophilosophy. Nkrumah departed from this philosophical tradition and its idealist ontological foundation. Those readers who identify a philosophy of particularity with ethnophilosophy are bound to be lost when approaching his text. For in Consciencism, rather than describe how the Akan conceptualizes the nature of being as pivotal to philosophical practice, Nkrumah instead scrutinized and inquired into such philosophical problems as the contradiction between materialism and idealism and the dialectical process of categorial conversion.[54]

It is clear from this that for the African possessed of the colonial syndrome we find that the intrinsic value of African moral and value systems is uppermost. Their clarion call, 'Philosophy for the sake of philosophy', means that African philosophical and legal thought should not be lowered from the cultural clouds of speculation into the contaminated terrain of material practice.[55] Nkrumah himself writes repeatedly that philosophy is a purely cultural product not to be used as a means to any other ends; moreover, it is a product of a specific cultural heritage.[56]

---

[51] McClendon (note 50) 48.
[52] Oruka (note 50) 3.
[53] Ibid.
[54] Oruka (note 50) 4.
[55] Ibid.
[56] Nkrumah (note 49) 5, 55 and 63.

Given that some philosophers philosophise about African philosophy from the outside, Nkrumah states that such philosophies are bereft of African social and political conditions. He adds that such conceptions of philosophy can assume only an alienated form, an exclusivist approach which will not help revitalise African values and moral systems in a world of competing perspectives.[57]

Consciencism, for Nkrumah, is a Marxist text in an African context inspired by African values and black identity. It is therefore employed in the interests of the ideological struggle against African metaphysical exclusivism and African Socialism. It is a text that affirms scientific socialism (Marxism) in the particular circumstances of African reality by accentuating the need to affirm materialism as the ontological foundation of scientific socialism. Furthermore, these perspectives on philosophy fall short of the humanist values that are so vital and foundational to African traditional society and which constitute what Nkrumah defined as 'the African Personality'.[58] Therefore Nkrumah and Kaunda, as the Fathers of Africa, get their theories and ideologies married here – a clear reflection of the value of African ontology and the principles of African value systems and traditional law in contemporary African jurisprudence.

Cultural and national identity underpin the concepts of ubuntu, humanism, *negritude* and *conscienscism*. These four concepts have much in common; they are typical African ideologies which identify themselves with the values of the African race. They are underpinned by dignity, liberty and unity among people. These concepts advocate an Africanism that is founded on humanity, humanness, liberty and conscience as African identity. They cannot be divorced from African ontology and value systems; therefore, they were and remain generally acceptable across the continent. General acceptability indicates the universality of the principles of law that underpin the ontology and value systems – a typical characteristic of African traditional law in a globalised world of competing perspectives on law. Those universally acceptable and appreciable principles which underpin these broad ideologies are normative and derived from African cultural and moral precepts that can be revitalised for the purposes of sustainable continental development.

8.4 CONCLUSION

Jurisprudence is indeed a valuable source in legal processes. But while this is a widely accepted general truism, it is discouraging that African legal discourses and thoughts have not been optimally applied in comparative legal processes

[57] Ibid.

[58] Nkrumah (note 49) 79.

in Africa or more widely. There is ample evidence in the case law from various jurisdictions that demonstrates the relevance of jurisprudence generally in the judicial process, especially in comparative analysis. The purpose of this chapter was to highlight this primary fact and to establish that, in fact, Africa has jurisprudential discourses that can be employed in comparative legal processes. In addition, it attempted to establish that home-grown African theories and thoughts such as ubuntu, *negritude*, humanism, *consciencism*, and many others not discussed here, not only exist but also have the potential to solve legal problems in Africa in a manner that is responsive to African societies and their realities.

It is common cause that there cannot be regional or continental integration without a consideration of law or without a common theory of law. From a legal perspective, regional and/or continental integration requires a coherent and consistent value system which originates from the people who or the societies which are integrating. Africa's continental aspirations, such as the Agenda 2063 and its socio-economic integration, depend on Africans' values and thought processes. Moreover, in the quest to unify and harmonise laws and legal systems, African theories have much to offer. It is therefore up to the continent's legal jurists to take on the great task of engaging its local jurisprudential theories and thoughts in its legal processes in a manner that is responsive to the continent's needs and conditions in an ever-competitive and globalising world environment.

REFERENCES

Asante, MK *The Afrocentric Idea* (Temple University Press, 1987).

Bilchits, D, Metz, T & Oyowe, O *Jurisprudence in an African Context* (Oxford University Press, 2021).

Campbell, CZ 'Sculpting a pan-African culture in the art of *negritude*: A model for African artist' (2006) 6 *The Journal of Pan African Studies* 33.

Colvin, LG *Historical Dictionary of Senegal* (The Scarecrow Press Inc, 1981).

Devlin, P *The Enforcement of Morals* (Oxford University Press, 1965).

Driberg, JG 'The African conception of law' (1934) 16 *Journal of Comparative Legislation and International Law* 237–238.

Dugard, J 'Some realism about the judicial process and positivism – a reply' (1981) 98 *South African Law Journal* 372–387.

Durant, W *Our Oriental Heritage* (Simon and Schuster, 1954).

Elias, T *The Nature of African Customary Law* (Manchester University Press, 1956).

Freeman, MDA *Introduction to Jurisprudence* (Sweet & Maxwell, 2001).

Holleman, JF *Issues in African Law* (Mouton, 1974).

Idowu, W 'African jurisprudence and the reconciliatory theory of law' (2006) 37(1) *The Cambrian Law Review* 1–16.

Idowu, W 'Against the skeptical argument and the absence thesis: African jurisprudence and the challenge of positivist historiography' (2006) 6(1) *The Journal of Philosophy, Science & Law* 34–49.

Komolafe, L 'African jurisprudence as historical co-existence of diffused legal theories' (2002) 8(1) *Thought and Practice: A Journal of the Philosophical Association of Kenya* 53.

Kurtz, P *In Defense of Secular Humanism* (Prometheus Books, 1983).

M'Baye, K 'The African conception of law' in R David (ed) *The Legal Systems of the World and Their Common Comparison and Unification, II* (International Association of Legal Science, 1975).

Maine, HS *Village Communities* (Oxford University Lectures, 1987).

Mapaure, C 'Reinvogorating African values for SADC: The relevance of traditional African philosophical thought of law in a globalized world of competing perspectives' (2011) 1(1) *SADC Law Journal* 149–173.

Mays, BE *The Negro's God as Reflected in His Literature* (New York, Atheneum, 1938).

McClendon, JH 'Nkrumah's *Consciencism* as philosophical text: Matters of confusion' (2003) 3 *African Philosophy* 48.

Nkrumah, K *Consciencism: Philosophy and Ideology for De-colonization with Particular Reference to the African Revolution* (Monthly Review Press, 1970).

Oruka, HO 'Sagacity in African philosophy' (1983) 23(4) *International Philosophical Quarterly* 383–393.

Ramose, MB *African Philosophy through Ubuntu* (Mond Books, 1999).

Senghor, LS '*Negritude*: A humanism of the 20th century' (1966) 16(1) *Optima* 1–8.

Sidney, L & Kelly, RDG (eds) *Imagining Home: Class, Culture, and Nationalism in the African Diaspora* (Verso, 1994).

Skurnik, WAE 'Leopold Sedar Senghor and African socialism' (1965) 3(3) *The Journal of Modern African Studies* 349–369.

Smith, MG 'The sociological framework of law' in H Kuper & L Kuper (eds) *African Law: Adaptation and Development* (Berkeley, 1965).

Solomon, RC & Higgins, MK *A Short History of Philosophy* (Oxford University Press, 1996).

Twining, W & Miers, D *How to do Things with Rules* (Weidenfeld & Nicolson, 1986).

Vaillant, JG 'Perspectives on Leopold Senghor and changing the face of negritude' (1976) 2 *ASA Review of Books* 154–162.

Van Binsbergen, WMJ 'Ubuntu and the globalisation of southern African thought and society' in WMJ van Binsbergen (ed) *Intercultural Encounters: African and Anthropological Lessons towards a Philosophy of Interculturality* (LIT, 2001).

Wilder, G *The French Imperial Nation-state: Negritude & Colonial Humanism between the Two World Wars* (University of Chicago Press, 2005).

William, I 'Against the skeptical argument and the absence thesis: African jurisprudence and the challenge of positivist historiography' (2006) 6(2) *The Journal of Philosophy, Science & Law* 9–24.

CASES

The Chairperson of the Immigration Selection Board v Erna Elizabeth Frank & Another, Supreme Court of Namibia Case No SA 8/99

Dudley v Stephens [1881–5] All ER Rep 61

Ex parte Attorney-General, Namibia: in re Corporal Punishment 1991 (3) SA 76 (NmS)

In re Sigsworth. Bedford v Bedford [1934] All ER Rep 113

Namunjepo & Others v Commanding Officer, Windhoek Prison & Another 2000 (6) BCLR 671 (NmS)

Port Elizabeth Municipality v Peoples Dialogue on Land and Shelter & Others 2000 (2) SA 1074 (SE)

Riggs v Palmer 115 NY 506

Shaw v DPP [1962] AC 220; [1961] 2WLR 897 HL

9

The court system in Namibia: judicial cross-fertilisation and the courts

Petrus T Damaseb

9.1 INTRODUCTION

This chapter is divided into two parts, A and B. Part A interrogates the following broad themes: the court system in Namibia; comparative law as a source of law and its impact on Namibia's jurisprudence; the approach of Namibia's courts to foreign precedent; judicial review in Namibia and a comparison with some other legal systems. Part B deals with law reform and the influence of comparative law on judicial decision-making.

Part A

Two of the six functions of comparative law[1] identified by Professor Kamba in his seminal article on comparative law find resonance with the second and third broad themes identified above – these being *law reform* and the *influence on judicial decision-making*.

A1 Court system in Namibia[2]

The Namibian Constitution[3] provides for a three-tiered court system: the Supreme Court at the apex, below it the High Court and at the base the lower courts. The last of these are also known as magistrate's courts.

[1] See WJ Kamba 'Comparative law: A theoretical framework' (1974) 23(3) *The International and Comparative Law Quarterly* 485–519.

[2] See, for a discussion of the hierarchy of the courts, PT Damaseb *The Supreme Court of Namibia: Law, Procedure and Practice* (Juta & Co, 2021) chs 2, 3 and 4; PT Damaseb *Court Managed Civil Procedure of the High Court of Namibia: Law, Procedure and Practice* (Juta & Co, 2020) ch 2.

[3] Article 78(1).

A1.1 Supreme Court

The Supreme Court is primarily a court of appeal and review,[4] although, in terms of Art 79(2) of the Constitution, it may 'also deal with matters referred to it for decision by the Attorney-General under this Constitution, and with such other matters as may be authorised by Act of Parliament'.

The Attorney-General (A-G) is the principal legal adviser to the president and the government and is required by the Constitution to take all action necessary for protecting and upholding the Constitution.[5] The manner in which the A-G may invoke the Supreme Court's first-instance jurisdiction is set out in s 15 of the Supreme Court Act 15 of 1990, read with Rule 12 of the Rules of the Supreme Court.[6] Article 79(2) of the Constitution also envisages that parliament may bestow upon the Supreme Court additional jurisdiction – as, indeed, it did by making it the court of first and final instance in presidential election disputes.[7] This jurisdiction of the Supreme Court was invoked for the first time in the landmark case of *Itula & Others v Minister of Rural and Urban Development & Others*.[8]

The Supreme Court is headed by the Chief Justice and includes the Deputy Chief Justice and additional justices of appeal.[9]

A1.2 High Court

In terms of Art 80(2) of the Constitution, the High Court is a court of unlimited original jurisdiction to hear and adjudicate upon all civil disputes and criminal prosecutions, including cases which involve the interpretation, implementation and upholding of this Constitution and the fundamental rights and freedoms guaranteed thereunder.

It also has appellate and review jurisdiction over other inferior courts and tribunals.[10] The High Court is headed by the Judge President of the High Court, who is *ex officio* the Deputy Chief Justice of Namibia.[11]

---

[4] There is a distinction between review and appeal: the Supreme Court's appellate and review jurisdiction is given content in the Supreme Court Act 15 of 1990.

[5] Article 87*(b)* and *(c)*.

[6] See *Attorney-General v Minister of Justice & Others* 2013 (3) NR 806 (SC); Damaseb *Supreme Court* (note 2) at paras 4-004–4-009. Rule 12(1) states: 'Where the Attorney-General is, in terms of s 15 of the [Supreme Court] Act, entitled to approach the court directly for any relief or order as contemplated in that section, application to the Chief Justice must be made on petition, and in that event rules 4(1) to 14 [setting out the petition procedure], dealing with time limits and the number of copies required to be lodged, apply with necessary changes required by the context to such petition.'

[7] Electoral Act 5 of 2014, s 172.

[8] (A1/2019) [2020] NASC (5 February 2020).

[9] Article 79(1).

[10] Article 80(2) of the Constitution, read with s 16 of the High Court Act 16 of 1990.

[11] Article 80(1) of the Constitution.

Namibia's is a unitary High Court, unlike, for example, that of South Africa, which is made up of several provincial High Courts. In its current form, the High Court of Namibia is organised into a main division at Windhoek and the northern local division at Oshakati.[12] Section 4A(1) of the High Court Act 16 of 1990 leaves open the possibility of other regional divisions being created.

Unlike a magistrate's court, the Supreme Court and the High Court have *inherent jurisdiction*, which includes the power to regulate their own procedures and to make rules for that purpose.[13]

The inherent jurisdiction of the superior courts, it has been said, is 'the unwritten power without which the Court is unable to function with justice and good reason'. It includes the ability of the superior courts[14] to regulate their own proceedings and prevent an abuse of their process.[15]

A1.3 Appointment and removal from office

The judges of the superior courts are appointed by the president of the republic on the recommendation of an independent Judicial Service Commission (JSC) headed by the Chief Justice.[16] A superior court judge (except acting judges) retires at the age of 65 but their tenure may be extended by the president of the republic to 70 years.[17] In terms of Art 84 of the Constitution, a judge may be involuntarily removed from office only by the president on the recommendation of the JSC on the ground of mental incapacity or for gross misconduct. If the JSC considers that the question of removing a superior court judge ought to be investigated, it 'shall' establish a tribunal for that purpose in terms of Art 84(3) of the Constitution.

A1.4 Magistrate's courts

A magistrate's court[18] is a court of limited jurisdiction as it can exercise only such powers as are granted to it under statute. Its jurisdiction is statutorily defined in respect of criminal and civil causes.[19] It does not enjoy inherent jurisdiction in the same way as the superior courts. Magistrates are appointed by the Magistrate's Commission and are subject to the discipline of that body. The head of the magistracy

---

[12] Section 4A(1) of the High Court Act 16 of 1990.
[13] Article 78(4).
[14] J Taitz *The Inherent Jurisdiction of the Supreme Court* (Juta & Co Ltd, 1985) 1.
[15] Damaseb *Court Managed Civil Procedure* (note 2) at paras 2-040–2-042.
[16] Article 82 of the Constitution.
[17] Article 82(4).
[18] Comprising district courts and regional courts: Magistrate's Courts Act 32 of 1944.
[19] Damaseb *Court Managed Civil Procedure* (note 2) at paras 2-009–2-015.

is the Chief Magistrate, who, as a judicial officer, is not subject to political control or direction.[20]

In Namibia, judicial power vests in the courts alone,[21] which are independent and subject only to the Constitution and the laws made under it.[22] No member of the Executive or the Legislature or any other person may interfere with the Judiciary in the performance of its functions.[23]

The courts of Namibia are organically interwoven by the important constitutional principle of *stare decisis* or precedent (stand by things decided), which is founded on the hierarchy of the courts, with the Supreme Court at the apex. The Supreme Court's pre-eminence in that hierarchy is entrenched in Art 81 of the Constitution, which states:

> A decision of the Supreme Court shall be binding on all other Courts of Namibia and all persons in Namibia unless it is reversed by the Supreme Court itself or is contradicted by an Act of Parliament lawfully enacted.[24]

A2 *Stare decisis* in Namibia

Lord Mance and Turner give a helpful explanation of and rationale for the doctrine of *stare decisis* in the common-law tradition:[25]

> In the common law, where a legal principle falls to be identified and applied to resolve a dispute, then the later court (a) is bound by any earlier decision as to the applicable legal principle, if the earlier decision was by a higher court in the judicial hierarchy (being the highest court to have decided the point of law) and, where it is itself a court of appeal, (b) it is bound, if the earlier decision is by either a commensurate or the highest court in the judicial hierarchy. This is the doctrine of precedent *stare decisis* (stand by things decided) in its formal sense.

The essential nature of *stare decisis* or precedent in a constitutional democracy was highlighted by Cameron JA as follows:

> The doctrine of precedent, which requires courts to follow the decisions of coordinate and higher courts in the judicial hierarchy, is an intrinsic feature

[20] Magistrate's Commission Act 3 of 2003, s 11(1)*(a)*; *Mostert & Another v The Magistrates' Commission & Another* 2005 NR 491 (HC); *Van Rooyen & Others v State & Others (General Council of the Bar of South Africa Intervening)* 2001 (9) BCLR 915 (T); 2002 (5) SA 246 (CC); 2002 (2) SACR 222 (CC).

[21] Article 78(1): comprising a Supreme Court, a High Court and lower courts.

[22] Article 78(2).

[23] Article 78(2).

[24] For the application of the article, see *S v Likanyi* 2017 (3) NR 771 (SC).

[25] Lord J Mance & J Turner *Privy Council Practice* (Oxford University Press, 2017) 133 at para 5.01.

> of the rule of law, which is in turn foundational to our Constitution. Without precedent there would be no certainty, no predictability and no coherence. The courts would operate in a tangle of unknowable considerations, which all too soon would become vulnerable to whim and fancy. Law would not rule. The operation of precedent, and its proper implementation, are therefore vital constitutional questions.[26]

Namibia's courts are bound to respect the constitutional principle of *stare decisis*. The effect of precedent is that even the Supreme Court is bound by its own decisions, and it may depart from its own previous decisions only if it subsequently finds the decision to have been clearly wrong or its statement on a particular issue was *obiter*[27] in that it was not essential to the outcome of the dispute then before it. Whether or not a previous decision of the Supreme Court is found to be wrong, a judge of the High Court remains bound by such a decision. Although not binding, an *obiter* statement by the Supreme Court carries persuasive force both to the Supreme Court itself and to the courts below it. High Court judges are also bound by a decision of another judge of that court, unless the judge is satisfied that the decision is clearly wrong or is distinguishable.[28]

A2.1 Exceptions

The High Court and magistrate's courts may depart from a previous decision of the High Court only if the High Court's earlier decision was reached *per incuriam*,[29] it was only *obiter*, it is distinguishable or it was clearly wrongly decided.[30] The same principle applies to the Supreme Court in respect of its own decisions. The High Court may only not follow a Supreme Court decision if it is satisfied that the applicable statement of principle is *obiter* or is distinguishable from the facts before it.[31]

The doctrine of precedent practised in the common-law tradition finds no counterpart in the civil-law systems. The low priority of *stare decisis* in the common-law systems is best characterised by Lord Cross.[32]

---

[26] *True Motives 84 (Pty) Ltd v Mahdi & Others* 2009 (4) SA 153 (SCA) at para 100.

[27] *Digashu & Others v Government of the Republic of Namibia & Others* [SA7/2022] (May 2023). Even the House of Lords (and now the Supreme Court of the United Kingdom) followed the same approach.

[28] *Schroeder & Another v Solomon & Others* 2011 (1) NR 20 (SC) at 30A–C; *Digashu* (note 27); *Seiler-Lilles v GRN & Others*, unreported judgment (HC-MD-CIV-MOT-GEN 427 of 2018; HC-MD-CIV-MOT-REV 447 of 2017) [2022] NAHCMD 11 (20 January 2022).

[29] A decision is *per incuriam* if the court overlooks a statute or a binding authority which, if regard had been had to it, could have affected the outcome of a case: *TransNamib Ltd v Poolman & Others* 1999 NR 399 (SC) at 409C–H.

[30] *S v Katamba* 1999 NR 348 (SC) at 351B–E.

[31] *Digashu* (note 27); *Seiler-Lilles* (note 28).

[32] G Dworkin '*Stare decisis* in the House of Lords' (1962) 25(2) *The Modern Law Review* 163–178.

A3 Comparative law as a source of law

Hahlo and Kahn wrote: 'Ideas have wings. No legal system of significance has been able to claim freedom from foreign inspiration.'[33] In discussing the question of tortious (delictual) liability arising from asbestos and surveying the ways in which foreign courts dealt with the matter and seeking a proper approach to be adopted in England, Lord Bingham, with characteristic eloquence, in *Fairchild Glenhaven Funeral Services Ltd*, justified reliance on comparative precedent as follows:[34]

> [32] Development of the law in this country cannot of course depend on a headcount of decisions and codes adopted in other countries around the world often against a background of different rules and traditions. The law must be developed coherently, in accordance with principle, so as to serve, even-handedly, the ends of justice. If, however, a decision is given in this country which offends one's basic sense of justice, and if consideration of international sources suggests that a different and more acceptable decision would be given in most other jurisdictions, whatever their legal tradition, this must prompt anxious review of the decision in question. In a shrinking world (in which the employees of asbestos companies may work for those companies in any one or more of several countries) there must be some virtue in uniformity of outcome whatever the diversity of approach in reaching that outcome.

Comparative law assumes a place of pride in Namibia's legal system and comparativism in Namibia's judicial reasoning and decision-making is inevitable because of the country's constitutional design. In the first place, public international law is part of the body of Namibian law in terms of Art 144 of the Constitution:

> Unless otherwise provided by this Constitution or Act of Parliament the general rules of public international law and international agreements binding upon Namibia under this Constitution shall form part of the law of Namibia.

Article 143 of the Constitution entrenched all international agreements which were binding on Namibia at the date of independence, although the National Assembly may, in terms of Art 63*(d)*, resile from such agreements.

Pronouncements by foreign courts that share a common legal tradition with Namibia on the nature and effect of a rule of public international law would therefore be of persuasive force in Namibian courts. It has been said, for good reason, that relative to matters governed by treaties and international agreements, courts in nation-states should strive for uniformity. As Lord Lloyd aptly observed in *T v*

[33] HR Hahlo & E Khan *The South African Legal System and its Background* (Juta & Co, 1968) 484.

[34] *Fairchild Glenhaven Funeral Services Ltd* [2002] 3 All ER 305 (HL) at 334.

Secretary of State for the Home Department:[35] 'In a case concerning an international convention it is obviously desirable that decisions in different jurisdictions should, as far as possible, be kept in line with each other.'

The reception of international law into domestic law is subject to the important principle of subsidiarity, also referred to as the margin of appreciation doctrine. The essence of the principle is that international law has no superior status to that of domestic laws. The principle is neatly captured in the following statement by the South African Constitutional Court in *Zuma v Secretary of the Judicial Commission of Enquiry into Allegations of State Capture, Corruption and Fraud in the Public Sector including Organs of State & Others*:[36]

> [119] [F]ar from international law being reified to some superior status, crystallized as a structural, even constitutional, principle of international law is the doctrine of subsidiarity, and, more regionally-specific, the margin of appreciation doctrine.
>
> …
>
> The foundation of the principle of subsidiarity is the simultaneous recognition, at the international level, of legal pluralism and the centrality of individual sovereign States to the international legal order. As a principle, subsidiarity recognizes the centrality of State consent in creating legal obligations and the exercise of discretion in binding themselves thereto. It is a manifestation of an understanding, at the international level, that the main social function of international law is to supplement, not supplant, domestic law. Thus, latitude is granted to States, the conduits through which international law is given effect, in recognition of the fact that national institutions are better situated and equipped to implement this law domestically. And, far from reifying international law as some ultimate paragon, international for an exercise restraint and defer to the measures adopted by the member State.

This stands in sharp contrast to the position in Germany, where international law takes precedence over domestic law. Under Art 25 of the German Basic Law:

> The general rules of international law shall be an integral part of federal law. They shall take precedence over the laws and directly create rights and duties for the inhabitants of the federal territory.

[35] *T v Secretary of State for the Home Department* [1996] 2 All ER 865 (HL) at 889.

[36] *Zuma v Secretary of the Judicial Commission of Enquiry into Allegations of State Capture, Corruption and Fraud in the Public Sector including Organs of State & Others* 2021 ZACC 28 (17 September 2021).

That said, the Namibian Legislature has on occasion taken the conscious decision to domesticate certain international instruments. For example, the long title of the Children's Status Act states that the Act's purpose, among other things,

> is to give effect to the rights of children as contained in the Namibian Constitution and international agreements binding on Namibia and to give effect to the United Nations Convention on the Rights of the Child and the African Charter on the Rights and Welfare of the Child and other international agreements binding on Namibia.

Comparative law often exerts an indirect influence on judicial decision-making in Namibia – most notably in the interpretation and enforcement of the Bill of Rights. For example, the fundamental freedoms contained in Art 21(1) of the Constitution 'shall be exercised subject to the law of Namibia, in so far as such law imposes reasonable restrictions on the exercise of the rights and freedoms'. Similarly, where the Namibian Legislature makes inroads into the exercise of a fundamental right or freedom, Namibian courts are perforce required – when applying or interpreting a limitation or a restriction – to consider whether such limitation or restriction is necessary in a democratic society.[37] The way in which courts with constitutional architectures and constitutional values similar to Namibia's have grappled with such situations represents valuable persuasive precedent for the courts of Namibia. The law reports abound with such examples.[38]

The *Hahlo-Khan* credo – that legal cross-fertilisation is both inevitable and to be celebrated – has two implications. The first is that every sensible legal system – rather than reinvent the wheel – strives to adopt tried-and-tested formulas from other jurisdictions. The second consequence is that judicial pronouncements by courts in countries from which the model is borrowed would be a source of inspiration to a Namibian court applying the measure in question.

---

[37] Article 21(2).

[38] Article 21(1). See also *Kauesa v Minister of Home Affairs & Others* 1994 NR 102 (HC); *Trustco Group International Ltd & Others v Shikongo* 2010 (2) NR 377 (SC); *Medical Association of Namibia & Another v Minister of Health and Social Services & Others* 2017 (2) NR 544 (SC); *Free Press of Namibia (Pty) Ltd & Others v Nyandoro* 2018 (2) NR 305 (SC).

On Art 21(2): *Council of the Municipality of Windhoek v Petersen & Others* 1998 NR 8 (HC); *Fantasy Enterprises CC t/a Hustler The Shop v Minister of Home Affairs & Another* (Appeal 159 of 1996) [1998] NAHC 1 (1 April 1998); *Nasilowski & Others v Minister of Justice & Others* 1998 NR 96 (HC); *Afshani & Another v Vaatz* 2006 (1) NR 35 (HC); *Ex parte In re: Kamwi v Law Society of Namibia* 2009 (2) NR 569 (SC); *Trustco Group International Ltd & Others v Shikongo* 2010 (2) NR 377 (SC); *Director, General Namibia Central Intelligence Service & Another v Haufiku & Others* 2018 (3) NR 757 (HC); *Digashu* (note 27); *Seiler-Lilles* (note 28).

According to Kamba, citing an authoritative source: 'The chief function of comparative jurisprudence is to facilitate legislation and the practical improvement of the law.'[39] In the context of Namibia, that 'chief function' of comparative law has played a pivotal role in the reform of court rules and practices in the quest for improving access to justice. Prior to Independence and for a considerable length of time afterwards, Namibia, like its colonial ruler, South Africa, practised an orthodox adversarial system of civil justice in which litigants and their lawyers dictated the pace and intensity of litigation. In that paradigm, the judge was the passive neutral umpire who intervened primarily at the request of the litigants before court.

I described this orthodoxy and the resultant problem in the following terms:

> The most salient characteristic of the orthodox adversarial civil justice system is that the parties to litigation define the ambit of the dispute and decide what evidence to lead in order to prove or disprove a case. The role of the judge is that of a neutral and passive umpire with no real power or tools to expedite proceedings. The rules of court and practices underpinning the adversarial system thus place emphasis on litigants and their legal advisers as the prime drivers of litigation. Because of its emphasis on the interests of the litigants, the adversarial system is apt to be manipulated to frustrate an opponent and generally to cause delay.[40]

Impelled by the need to bring about an improvement in access to court, the Namibian Judiciary undertook benchmarking visits to several jurisdictions to assess the ways in which they dealt with the problems of access to court brought about by the orthodox adversarial system of civil justice. The upshot of this exercise was a complete overhaul of the rules of the High Court of Namibia, leading to the introduction of a system of judicial case management in which the court (or the judge) is the primary focus for moving a case expeditiously in the legal value chain.[41]

A4 Judicial cross-fertilisation in Namibia

Article 140 of the Constitution preserved the common law applicable at Independence. The common law of Namibia at the date of Independence was Roman-Dutch law, as introduced into South West Africa on 1 January 1920 by

[39] Kamba (note 1).

[40] Damaseb *Court Managed Civil Procedure* (note 2) at para 3-007.

[41] Rules of the High Court of Namibia, GN 4 of 2014, made in terms of s 39 of the High Court Act 16 of 1990.

virtue of s 1(1) of the Administration of Justice Proclamation 21 of 1919.[42] The consequence of that is that the decisions of the Appellate Division of South Africa and the decisions of the High Courts of South Africa (unless found to be clearly wrong or decided *per incuriam*) remain binding on the High Court of Namibia. The preservation of the Roman-Dutch common law also has the benefit that in matters of Roman-Dutch private law, Namibian courts can tap into the rich history of other Roman-Dutch jurisdictions in the region, such as Zimbabwe.

It is also trite that because of the colonial influence that the United Kingdom exerted over parts of the southern African region, the Roman-Dutch tradition in the sub-region has been greatly influenced by English law in the areas of the law of evidence, company law and public-law practices such as judicial review of administrative action. English law in those areas therefore remains a very influential source of law.

In terms of Art 81 of the Constitution, since the Appellate Division of South Africa is the constitutional predecessor of the Supreme Court of Namibia, decisions of the Appellate Division would have to be specifically overruled by the Supreme Court of Namibia and not by the High Court. The doctrine of *stare decisis* requires that unless there is very good reason not to do so, the Supreme Court will follow prior decisions of the Appellate Division. In keeping with its now settled jurisprudence to develop the common law,[43] the Supreme Court may also deviate from prior decisions of the Appellate Division.

Although, because of the historical connection between Namibia and South Africa, South African precedent is often cited in our courts, the Supreme Court has warned against slavish reliance on foreign authority. As Shivute CJ put it in *Attorney-General of Namibia v Minister of Justice & Others*:[44]

> [A]fter our country's Independence, Namibian courts have developed a reservoir of distinctly Namibian jurisprudence based on the Constitution and Namibian law. Decisions of foreign courts that are found to be persuasive due to similarity of applicable principles, provisions, issues and other circumstances relevant to matters at hand may, of course, be followed by our courts on principle rather than precedent.
>
> ...
>
> [E]ven where the wording in a foreign constitution is similar to that of a provision in the Constitution, caution should be exercised when

[42] For a detailed discussion of the operation of the Roman-Dutch common law in Namibia, see Damaseb *Court Managed Civil Procedure* (note 2) 298–301 at paras 12-018–12-028.

[43] *Minister of Safety and Security & Others v Mahupelo* 2019 (2) NR 308 (SC) and *JS v LC & Another* 2016 (4) NR 939 (SC).

[44] *Attorney-General of Namibia v Minister of Justice & Others* 2013 (3) NR 806 (SC) at para 8.

> considering the constitutionality of the provisions of a statute: ultimately the meaning and import of a particular provision of the Constitution must be ascertained with due regard to the express or implicit intention of the founders of the Constitution. Furthermore, as a general proposition, whilst foreign precedent is a useful tool to determine the trend of judicial opinion on similar provisions in jurisdictions which enjoy open and democratic societies such as ours, ultimately the value judgment that a Namibian court has to make in the interpretation of the provisions of the Constitution in as much as they may impact on the impugned provisions, must be based on the values and aspirations of the Namibian society.

That cautionary message applies with equal force to judgments from other jurisdictions. It is now settled in the rules of both the Supreme Court[45] and the High Court that it is the duty of a legal practitioner who places reliance on foreign case law to establish not only its relevance but also that reliance by the court on it would not be inconsistent with the Constitution or the laws of Namibia. It will suffice to quote the relevant High Court rule because the Supreme Court rule is couched in identical terms. High Court Rule 130 provides:

> Subject to Article 140(1) of the Namibian Constitution, where a legal practitioner in his or her heads of argument or any other written submissions or oral submissions relies on foreign authority in support of a proposition of law –
>
> (a) he or she must certify that he or she is unable after diligent search to find Namibian authority on the proposition of law under consideration; and
> (b) whether or not Namibian authority is available on the point, he or she must certify that he or she has satisfied himself or herself that there is no Namibian law, including the Namibian Constitution, that precludes the acceptance by the court of the proposition of law that the foreign authority is said to establish.[46]

A5 Concluding remarks

Part A sought to demonstrate that Namibia's constitutional architecture is designed to accommodate the reception of comparative law – both as a source of law and as an influence on judicial decision-making. Comparative law has undoubtedly enriched Namibia's jurisprudence post-independence and is destined to play an

---

[45] Supreme Court Rule 19.

[46] Regarding the importance of the rule, see *Westcoast Fishing Properties v Gendev Fish Processors Ltd & Another* 2013 (4) NR 1036 (HC) at paras 2 and 10.

influential role in the future development of our law. However, the courts are alive to the danger of importing foreign legal principles without taking into consideration Namibia's own legal framework and legal traditions. Judgments of the courts and the rules and practices of the courts have therefore been calibrated to ensure that foreign legal norms do not displace Namibia's domestic law.

Part B

B1 Namibia's judicial review mechanism

What is judicial review? It is the process by which an aggrieved person (either natural or juristic) seeks the intervention of a court having jurisdiction, to inquire into the lawfulness of a decision which is perceived to have a negative impact on a right enjoyed by that person. The American case of *Marbury v Madison Secretary of State*[47] is generally regarded as the *locus classicus* on judicial review.

In Namibia, judicial review takes one of two forms: scrutiny of legislation (both primary and subordinate) and scrutiny of administrative decision-making. Both spring from the role carved out for the Judiciary under the Constitution. As already stated in Part A of this chapter, in terms of Art 78(1)*(a)*–*(c)* of the Constitution, judicial power vests in the courts, except that lower courts do not possess the power of judicial review. Judicial power has been described as:

> 1. The authority vested in courts and judges to hear and decide cases and to make binding judgments on them; the power to construe and apply the law when controversies arise over what has been done or not done under it.[48]

Chief Justice Marshall iconically wrote in *Marbury v Madison*:[49]

---

[47] 5 US 137 at 140–243.

[48] BA Garner *Black's Law Dictionary* 11 ed (Thomson Reuters, 1999) 1012.

[49] In interpreting Art 3 of the US Constitution, which states:

Section 1 – The judicial power of the United States shall be vested in one supreme Court, and in such inferior Courts as the Congress may from time to time ordain and establish. The Judges, both of the supreme and inferior Courts, shall hold their Offices during good Behaviour, and shall, at stated Times, receive for their Services, a Compensation, which shall not be diminished during their Continuance in Office.

Section 2 – The judicial Power shall extend to all Cases, in Law and Equity, arising under this Constitution, the Laws of the United States, and Treaties made, or which shall be made, under their Authority;– to all Cases affecting Ambassadors, other public Ministers and Consuls;– to all Cases of admiralty and maritime Jurisdiction; – to Controversies to which the United States shall be a Party; – to Controversies between two or more States; – between a State and Citizens of another State; – between Citizens of different States; – between Citizens of the same State claiming Lands under Grants of different States, and between a State, or the Citizens thereof, and foreign States, Citizens or Subjects. In all Cases affecting Ambassadors, other public Ministers

> If an Act of the legislature, repugnant to the constitution, is void, does it, notwithstanding its invalidity, bind the courts and oblige them to give it effect? Or, in other words, though it not be law, does it constitute a rule as operative as if it was law? This would be to overthrow in fact what was established in theory; and would seem, at first view, and absurdity too gross to be insisted upon.
>
> ...
>
> It is emphatically the province and duty of the judicial department to say what the law is. Those who apply the rule to particular cases, must of necessity expound and interpret that rule. If two laws conflict with each other, the courts must decide on the operation of each. So, if a law be in opposition to the constitution: if both the law and the constitution apply to a particular case, so that the court must either decide that case conformably to the law, disregarding the constitution; or conformably to the constitution, disregarding the constitution, disregarding the law: the court must determine which of these conflicting rules governs the case. This is the very essence of judicial duty. If then the courts are to regard the constitution; and the constitution is superior to any ordinary act of the legislature; the constitution, and not such ordinary act, must govern the case to which they both apply.

Marbury v Madison is the United States' greatest contribution to constitutionalism. It asserts in stentorian terms the supremacy of the constitution and the pre-eminent role of the judicial branch to decide what is within the constitution and what is not and, most importantly, to set aside that which is not. The case confirms that the power of judicial review is the exclusive domain of the Judiciary. This is to be contrasted with the position in the United Kingdom, whose unwritten constitution is founded on the supremacy of parliament, in terms of which the courts lack the power to invalidate legislation duly and lawfully enacted.

In Namibia, Art 25 of the Constitution is the source of the superior courts' power to inquire into and to validate or invalidate legislation and decision-making that

---

and Consuls, and those in which a State shall be Party, the supreme Court shall have original Jurisdiction. In all the other Cases before mentioned, the supreme Court shall have appellate Jurisdiction, both as to Law and Fact, with such Exceptions, and under such Regulations as the Congress shall make. The Trial of all Crimes, except in Cases of Impeachment, shall be by Jury; and such Trial shall be held in the State where the said Crimes shall have been committed; but when not committed within any State, the Trial shall be at such Place or Places as the Congress may by Law have directed.

violate the fundamental rights and freedoms guaranteed under the Constitution. It states:25

> 25 (1) Save in so far as it may be authorised to do so by this Constitution, Parliament or any subordinate legislative authority shall not make any law, and the Executive and the agencies of Government shall not take any action which abolishes or abridges the fundamental rights and freedoms conferred by this Chapter, and any law or action in contravention thereof shall to the extent of the contravention be invalid …
>
> …
>
> (2) Aggrieved persons who claim that a fundamental right or freedom guaranteed by this Constitution has been infringed or threatened shall be entitled to approach a competent Court to enforce or protect such a right or freedom, and may approach the Ombudsman to provide them with such legal assistance or advice as they require, and the Ombudsman shall have the discretion in response thereto to provide such legal or other assistance as he or she may consider expedient.
>
> (3) Subject to the provisions of this Constitution, the Court referred to in Sub-Article (2) hereof shall have the power to make all such orders as shall be necessary and appropriate to secure such applicants the enjoyment of the rights and freedoms conferred on them under the provisions of this Constitution, should the Court come to the conclusion that such rights or freedoms have been unlawfully denied or violated, or that grounds exist for the protection of such rights or freedoms by interdict.
>
> (4) The power of the Court shall include the power to award monetary compensation in respect of any damage suffered by the aggrieved persons in consequence of such unlawful denial or violation of their fundamental rights and freedoms, where it considers such an award to be appropriate in the circumstances of particular cases.

Chapter 3 of the Namibian Constitution contains the fundamental rights and freedoms referred to in Art 25.[50] Article 5 gives a clear direction that those rights

[50] Fundamental human rights are the following: Art 6: protection of life; Art 7: protection of liberty; Art 8: respect for human dignity; Art 9: slavery and forced labour; Art 10: equality and freedom from discrimination; Art 11: arrest and detention; Art 12: fair trial; Art 13: Privacy; Art 14: Family;

> shall be respected and upheld by the Executive, Legislature and Judiciary and all organs of the Government and its agencies and, where applicable to them, by all natural and legal persons in Namibia, and shall be enforceable by the Courts in the manner hereinafter prescribed.

On the other hand, administrative decision-making can be challenged by aggrieved persons if it is suspected to be not in compliance with Art 18 of the Namibian Constitution, which states:

> Administrative bodies and administrative officials shall act fairly and reasonably and comply with the requirements imposed upon such bodies and officials by common law and any relevant legislation, and persons aggrieved by the exercise of such acts and decisions shall have the right to seek redress before a competent Court or Tribunal.

The power of judicial review of the superior courts is further entrenched by the supremacy clause contained in Art 1(6) of the Constitution to the effect that 'This Constitution shall be the Supreme Law of Namibia'. Therefore, any person aggrieved by any legislative or administrative decision-making has the right to approach a competent court for relief as long as the dispute concerned is justiciable in the sense that it is judicially cognisable and the court will assume jurisdiction and give a binding judgment on it. In *Somaeb v Standard Bank Namibia Ltd*[51] the Supreme Court held that a dispute that had previously been before court and on which a binding decision was given is not justiciable.

Relief may also be sought from the court in certain circumstances even if no consequential relief apart from a declaration of rights is sought. That is the effect of s 16*(d)* of the High Court Act 16 of 1990, in terms of which the High Court has jurisdiction in

> its discretion, and at the instance of any interested person, to enquire into and determine any existing, future or contingent right or obligation,

Art 15: Children's rights; Art 16: Property; Art 17: Political activity; Art 18: administrative justice; Art 19: Culture; Art 20: Education.

Fundamental freedoms are set forth in Art 21 as follows: freedom of speech and expression, press and other media; freedom of thought, conscience belief and academic freedom; freedom to practice any religion and to manifest such practice, right to assemble peaceably without arms; freedom of association including to form and join associations or unions, trade unions and political parties; right to withhold labour; right to move freely throughout Namibia to reside and settle in any part of Namibia and to leave and return to Namibia; right to practise any profession or carry on any occupation, trade or business.

[51] 2017 (1) NR 248 (SC).

> notwithstanding that such person cannot claim any relief consequential upon the determination.

This provision is the jurisprudential niche for the court's granting of declaratory orders.

Judicial decisions are not the subject of judicial review in the sense that those of the Legislature and Executive are. Instead, judicial decisions are subject to the appellate and review jurisdiction enjoyed by the courts either under the Constitution or in terms of statute. In addition, two clear examples have been recognised by Namibia's courts as being beyond the reach of the court's power of judicial review: decisions of ecclesiastical bodies[52] and disputes relating to voluntary organisations whose constitutive documents, such as a constitution binding the members, excludes the jurisdiction of the courts. Football disputes under the jurisdiction of FIFA are such an example.[53]

B1.1 Procedure

A constitutional challenge is ordinarily instituted by invoking Rule 65 of the High Court Rules. It is conducted by means of a notice of motion supported by affidavit. In the exceptional case where disputes of fact are anticipated, a party may proceed by way of action proceedings.

Where a person wishes to challenge an administrative decision in terms of Art 18 of the Constitution, Rule 76 of the High Court Rules provides for a special procedure by which the person seeking relief launches proceedings by identifying the offensive decision and its maker and requiring them to produce the record of the decision-making process. Once the record has been dispatched to the Registrar of the High Court and served on all interested parties, the applicant has the right to amplify the affidavit, after which the decision-maker may file an answering affidavit to justify the impugned decision. The applicant would still have the right to file a replying affidavit, after which the matter will be adjudicated and a binding decision given on the matter. In review proceedings, the court is not concerned with the correctness of the decision but whether it was lawfully made.

B1.2 Jurisdictions with historical ties to English law

Barring the inevitable difference in court structure, the judicial review model of Namibia resembles that of most of the common-law jurisdictions with historical ties to the English legal system. That would include all the English-speaking southern African countries,[54] East Africa and English-speaking West Africa. The difference in court structures is exemplified by those countries with a Constitutional Court at

[52] *New African Methodist Episcopal Church in the Republic of Namibia & Another v Kooper & Others* 2015 (3) NR 705 (HC); *Petrus v Roman Catholic Archdiocese* 2011 (2) NR 637 (SC).

[53] *Namibia Premier League v Namibia Football Association & Others* (SA 71/2018) [19 February 2020].

[54] South Africa, Zambia, Zimbabwe, Botswana, Lesotho, Kenya, Tanzania, Ghana, Nigeria and Malawi.

the apex (such as South Africa, Zambia and Zimbabwe) and those with a Supreme Court or a Court of Appeal at the apex.[55]

The common-law model, where the ordinary courts of the land exercise judicial review power over legislative and administrative decision-making, stands in sharp contrast to the mostly Continental European model, of which France is the most prominent. This model is also practised in most of French-speaking Africa (eg, Senegal) and the Lusophone jurisdictions such as Mozambique. I set out below the French model and the extent to which there are similarities to the African jurisdictions that fall into that mould. But before that I wish to deal with the unique position of the United Kingdom.

Although the common-law jurisdictions owe much of their legal tradition to England, the United Kingdom, with its unwritten constitution, represents a unique experiment in constitutional law review. Because of the absence of a written constitution and the time-honoured principle of the sovereignty of the UK parliament, legislation passed by this parliament cannot be challenged or set aside by the courts.[56] Administrative decision-making, on the other hand, is subject to the review jurisdiction of the ordinary courts of the United Kingdom.

B2 Comparison to other legal systems

As far as judicial review is concerned, a classic Continental European model is that of France. The French Constitution adopted on 4 October 1958 has at the apex of the judicial review process the *Counseil Constitutionel* (Constitutional Council) and below it the *Conseil d'Etat* (Council of State). In matters concerning criminal disputes and ordinary civil disputes, the apex court is the *Cour de Cassation* (Court of Cassation). Below it are the various appellate courts and at the base are the first-instance district courts.[57]

The courts which are under the ultimate supervisory jurisdiction of the Court of Cassation adjudicate over the full spectrum of criminal and civil disputes in the country. In contrast, challenges and questions relating to the constitutionality of legislation and the legality of administrative decisions are the exclusive preserve of the Constitutional Council and the Council of State.

The Constitutional Council is a unique institution which (although the French Constitution insulates it from political influence by denying membership to it from the Executive and the Legislature[58]) has very strong political representation on it.

---

[55] Botswana, Lesotho (with apex courts of appeal), Tanzania, Ghana, Nigeria, Kenya and Malawi (with apex supreme courts), to mention only some.

[56] AV Dicey *Introduction to the Study of the Law of the Constitution* 10 ed (Macmillan, 1959) 70.

[57] Sir Rupert Cross *Precedent in English Law* 3 ed (Clarendon Press, 1977) 12–22; R David & HP de Vries *The French Legal System. An Introduction to Civil Law Systems* (Oceana Publications for Parker School of Foreign and Comparative Law, Columbia University, 1958) 115.

[58] Article 75 of the 1958 Constitution.

Disputes that the common-law practitioner would expect to be adjudicated by the ordinary courts comprising professional judges, fall under the French Constitution, within the adjudicative competence of the Constitutional Council. The primacy of the Constitutional Council in France's constitutional architecture was recently highlighted by the pension reform controversy that arose when the French government decided to change the national retirement age from 62 to 64. The reform initiative was met with widespread protests and was ultimately declared by the Constitutional Council to be constitution-compliant. If such a dispute were to arise in Namibia or any other southern African country or the United States, it would be challenged and tested for its constitutionality in the ordinary courts of the land.

The adjudicative competence of France's Constitutional Council is as unique as its composition. All former presidents of the republic are *ex officio* members of the council. The president of the council is appointed by the president of the republic from among retired presidents of the republic and holds office for nine years.

The Council of State is another unique French creation unlike any known to the common-law tradition. It was established by Napoleon's Consulate Government in 1799 as a successor to the King's Council and performs the dual functions of a judicial body and an advisor to the government. As a judicial body, it has the mandate to adjudicate claims against the state and helps to draft important laws. It hears appeals on questions of law from lower courts and gives advisory opinions on the law referred to it by the lower courts. Below it are 42 administrative courts of first instance (*tribunaux administrative*) and eight administrative courts of appeal.

In France, therefore, the Council of State is the forum responsible for dispensing administrative justice. Its mission and mandate are described in the following terms on its official website:[59]

> The Council of State advises the Government on the preparation of bills, ordinances and certain decrees. It also answers the Government's queries on legal affairs and conducts studies upon the request of the Government or through its own initiative regarding administrative or public policy issues. The Council of State is the highest administrative jurisdiction – it's the final arbiter of cases relating to the executive power, local authorities, independent public authorities, public administration agencies or any other agency invested with public authority.
>
> …

[59] Association of Councils of State and Supreme Administrative Jurisdictions of the European Union *Report for France* (nd), https://www.acaeurope.eu/en/eurtour/i/countries/france/france_en.pd, accessed 18 August 2023.

> The Council of State has jurisdiction over disputes concerning public liberties, administrative police, taxes, public contracts, the civil service, public health, competition rules, environmental law, and urban and regional development.
>
> …
>
> The Council of State is responsible for the management of 42 administrative tribunals, 8 administrative courts of appeal and certain specialized courts such as the National Court of Asylum.

The official website also records that the Council of State comprises about 300 members and that its members are appointed to serve in either the litigation department or the advisory department. Some of its members sit as judges in the International Court of Justice (ICJ), the Court of Justice of the European Union or the European Court of Human Rights (ECHR).

Regarding judicial review, the legal systems of Senegal[60] and Mozambique[61] have much more in common with the French model than with the common-law tradition. In both, resort is had to the Constitutional Council to resolve the most important political disputes, such as the constitutionality of legislation and challenges to the outcomes of elections.

Unlike the adversarial process in the common-law tradition, the process of judicial review is inquisitorial and proactive and not reactive in the way that the adversarial common-law system is. In an adversarial system, the aggrieved individual approaches a court of competent jurisdiction by instituting legal proceedings against an identified person or body and bears the onus of presenting the evidence in support of their case and proving it on a balance of probabilities. The court assumes a neutral role and is not involved in the collection of the relevant evidence that will determine the outcome of a case. The inquisitorial system is the very opposite. Once a complaint has been brought to its attention, the relevant adjudicative forum is as much involved in the collection and evaluation of the evidence as the litigants.

B3 Concluding remarks

It has been demonstrated in Part B that judicial review in the common-law tradition is not the only model available in the world as a check on legislative and executive power. There are alternative models, such as the French one, that have been successfully adapted in African countries such as Mozambique and Senegal. Every civilised legal system laying claim to being a democracy recognises the separation of the Legislature, the Executive and the judicial functions in ordering national

[60] See the Constitution of Senegal, adopted in 2001 with amendments up to 2006, https://www.icnl.uploadsPDF.

[61] See the Constitution of the Republic of Mozambique, adopted on 21 December 2004, as amended in 2007. Translation by MOZLEGAL – Mozambique Legal Resource Portal, www.mozlegal.com.

affairs. There is an underlying assumption that the legislative and the executive roles should be kept in check to protect the rights of the governed. For this purpose, judicial power is vested in those who do not wield direct legislative or political power. In jurisdictions such as Namibia and other countries of the common-law tradition, the power of judicial review is assigned solely to unelected professionally trained judges who preside over ordinary courts of general jurisdiction. The French model, which has inspired much of Continental Europe and significant parts of Africa, practises a type of judicial review which combines ordinary courts and political players. Both models aim to achieve constitutional scrutiny of legislative power and a check on administrative power.

REFERENCES

Association of Councils of State and Supreme Administrative Jurisdictions of the European Union *Report for France* (nd), https://www.acaeurope.eu/en/eurtour/i/countries/france/france_en.pdf, accessed 18 August 2023.

Cross, Sir Rupert *Precedent in English Law* 3 ed (Clarendon Press, 1977).

Damaseb, PT *Court Managed Civil Procedure of the High Court of Namibia* (Juta & Co, 2020).

Damaseb, PT *The Supreme Court of Namibia: Law, Procedure and Practice* (Juta & Co, 2021)

David, R & De Vries, HP *The French Legal System; an Introduction to Civil Law Systems* (Oceana Publications for Parker School of Foreign and Comparative Law, Columbia University, 1958).

Dicey, AV *Introduction to the Study of the Law of the Constitution* 10 ed (Macmillan, 1959).

Dworkin, G '*Stare decisis* in the House of Lords' (1962) 25(2) *The Modern Law Review* 163–178.

Garner, Bryan A *Black's Law Dictionary* 11 ed (Thomson Reuters, 1999).

Hahlo, HR & Khan, E *The South African Legal System and Its Background* (Juta & Co, 1968).

Kamba, WJ 'Comparative law: A theoretical framework' (1974) 23(3) *The International and Comparative Law Quarterly* 485–519.

Lord Mance & Turner, J *Privy Council Practice* (Oxford University Press, 2017).

Taitz, J *The Inherent Jurisdiction of the Supreme Court* (Juta & Co, 1985).

CASES

Afshani & Another v Vaatz 2006 (1) NR 35 (HC)

Attorney-General v Minister of Justice & Others 2013 (3) NR 806 (SC)

Attorney-General of Namibia v Minister of Justice & Others 2013 (3) NR 806 (SC)

Council of the Municipality of Windhoek v Petersen & Others 1998 NR 8 (HC)

Digashu & Others v Government of the Republic of Namibia & Others [SA7/2022] (May 2023)
Director-General Namibia Central Intelligence Service & Another v Haufiku & Others 2018 (3) NR 757 (HC)
Ex parte In re: Kamwi v Law Society of Namibia 2009 (2) NR 569 (SC)
Fairchild Glenhaven Funeral Services Ltd [2002] 3 All ER 305 (HL)
Fantasy Enterprises CC t/a Hustler The Shop v Minister of Home Affairs & Another (Appeal 159 of 1996) [1998] NAHC 1 (1 April 1998)
Free Press of Namibia (Pty) Ltd & Others v Nyandoro 2018 (2) NR 305 (SC)
Itula & Others v Minister of Rural and Urban Development & Others (A1/2019) [2020] NASC (5 February 2020)
JS v LC & Another 2016 (4) NR 939 (SC)
Kauesa v Minister of Home Affairs & Others 1994 NR 102 (HC)
Marbury v Madison Secretary of State 5 US 137
Medical Association of Namibia & Another v Minister of Health and Social Services & Others 2017 (2) NR 544 (SC)
Minister of Safety and Security & Others v Mahupelo 2019 (2) NR 308 (SC)
Mostert & Another v The Magistrates' Commission & Another 2005 NR 491 (HC)
Namibia Premier League v Namibia Football Association & Others (SA 71/2018) [19 February 2020]
Nasilowski & Others v Minister of Justice & Others 1998 NR 96 (HC)
New African Methodist Episcopal Church in the Republic of Namibia & Another v Kooper & Others 2015 (3) NR 705 (HC)
Petrus v Roman Catholic Archdiocese 2011 (2) NR 637 (SC)
S v Katamba 1999 NR 348 (SC)
S v Likanyi 2017 (3) NR 771 (SC)
Somaeb v Standard Bank Namibia Ltd 2017 (1) NR 248 (SC).
T v Secretary of State for the Home Department [1996] 2 All ER 865 (HL)
TransNamib Ltd v Poolman & Others 1999 NR 399 (SC)
True Motives 84 (Pty) Ltd v Mahdi & Others 2009 (4) SA 153 (SCA)
Trustco Group InternationaL Ltd & Others v Shikongo 2010 (2) NR 377 (SC)
Van Rooyen & Others v State & Others (General Council of the Bar of South Africa Intervening) 2001 (9) BCLR 915 (T); 2002 (5) SA 246 (CC); 2002 (2) SACR 222 (CC)
Westcoast Fishing Properties v Gendev Fish Processors Ltd & Another 2013 (4) NR 1036 (HC)
Zuma v Secretary of the Judicial Commission of Enquiry into Allegations of State Capture, Corruption and Fraud in the Public Sector including Organs of State & Others 2021 ZACC 28 (17 September 2021)

LEGISLATION

Constitution of the Republic of France, 1958
Constitution of the Republic of Namibia, 1990

High Court Act 16 of 1990
Magistrate's Courts Act 32 of 1944
Magistrates Commission Act 3 of 2003
Rules of the High Court of Namibia, GN 4 of 2014
Supreme Court Act 15 of 1990

10

Liability in unjustified enrichment: a comparative overview of the Namibian, Continental European, English, Argentinean and Brazilian legal systems

Aimite Jorge

10.1 INTRODUCTION

The focus of this contribution is on the law of obligations, an area slightly neglected in research on the Namibian legal system. The chapter reflects on the liability in unjustified enrichment in selected jurisdictions: Namibia, Continental Europe, England and two South American countries, Argentina and Brazil. With the exception of Namibia, in all of the selected jurisdictions there have been some developments in this field of law in the past 20 years, or at least attempts to streamline the field so that its principles may respond more adequately to contemporary issues. Because there is a futuristic idea of a European Civil Code, with the creation of a single market in the European Union the need arose to harmonise certain rules, such as 'contract law', and for consumers to have at least a frame of reference regarding certain legal matters.

This initiative, which started with contract law, led to the creation of research groups, some of which ultimately focused on the entire private law of Europe. And in consequence of this initiative unjustified enrichment was also studied and a special book on this area of the law is included in the Model Principles, Draft Common Frame of Reference (DCFR) for private law. Emulating the same DCFR, England also enacted the monumental English Private Law in 2014 in which the law of restitution and unjust enrichment is also treated. Brazil revised its Civil Code in about 2002 and included a general principle against unjustified enrichment which was missing in the previous Civil Code. Namibia continues in the footsteps of developing its law of unjustified enrichment piecemeal through jurisprudence.

This chapter highlights the guiding principles on unjustified enrichment claims in the above selected jurisdictions and indicates some similarities and differences between the various jurisdictions on liability in unjustified enrichment.

The High Court of Namibia has delivered a series of summary judgments in cases involving persons previously associated with the Small and Medium Enterprise Bank (SME Bank), among which are *Bruni v Kahunda*,[1] *Bruni v Yatsua Investments CC*,[2] and *Bruni v Tulive Capital (Pty) Ltd*.[3] Apart from some insolvency and delictual aspects, which are not dealt with in this chapter, the decisions centred on claims against unjustified enrichment: the *condictio indebiti*. In short, these cases all state the basic principles of unjustified enrichment derived from Roman law and as enshrined in the laws of Namibia and South Africa.

In the pleadings of the cases, apart from *condictio indebiti*, the advocates also mentioned as alternative claims the *condictio sine causa* (commonly known as *condictio sine causa generalis*) and the *condictio furtiva*, and in some cases the *condictio ob turpe vel injustam causam*. Because of the shortcomings in some of the defendants' pleadings, the courts in the cases did not really deal with the other actions, nor did they deal with most of the defences arising under unjustified enrichment. Interestingly, both the plaintiffs' pleadings mentioned 'the defence of loss of enrichment', although the courts did not canvass this defence, nor did the defendants plead such a defence.

This chapter briefly analyses one of the Namibian cases that dealt in some detail with the *condictio indebiti* and highlights some 'fascinating' conceptualisations used in the cases, and in comparative analysis with some selected civil- and common-law jurisdictions. It points to some possibly confusing use of certain concepts in the analysis and application of the law of unjustified enrichment in Namibian law. After that, the chapter describes the structure and working of the law of unjustified or unjust enrichment in selected civil-law and common-law jurisdictions: Argentina, Brazil, Continental Europe and England.

10.2 NAMIBIAN CASES

All these Namibian cases – *Bruni v Kahunda*,[4] *Bruni v Yatsua Investments CC*[5] and *Bruni v Tulive Capital (Pty) Ltd*[6] – present similar facts on the issues of an unjustified enrichment claim. In essence, the facts of the cases generally arose

[1] *Bruni v Kahunda* [2020] NAHCMD 591.
[2] *Bruni v Yatsua Investments CC* [2020] NAHCMD 571.
[3] *Bruni v Tulive Capital (Pty) Ltd* [2020] NAHCMD 536.
[4] *Bruni* (note 3).
[5] *Bruni* (note 3).
[6] *Bruni* (note 3).

from the following: in the particulars of claim of all the cases, the plaintiffs sketch a situation in which certain individuals were referred to as the *dramatis personae*. One of these individuals, who was identified in one of the cases as Kamushinda, was at some point the Deputy Chairman of the Board of the SME Bank. Kamushinda, in conjunction with third-party entities, perpetrated fraud on a grand scale from the SME Bank. The investigations into the alleged fraudulent schemes led to the uncovering of more than N$247 545 004 which was misappropriated from the SME Bank. As a result of the theft, the SME Bank was forced into liquidation.

These amounts of money were transferred to various entities, some in Namibia and others in South Africa or elsewhere. Some of these entities were real but others were fictitious or false beneficiaries. One of the entities was referred to in one of the cases as Asset Movement and Financial Services CC (AMFS). Once the amounts were received by such entities (real, fictitious or false beneficiaries), they dealt with the money as if it were their own and they paid different sums to various individuals, some in South Africa and others in Namibia, each person receiving a considerable sum of money, in essence without any legal ground for the receipt of the payment.

On the claims based on the *condictio indebiti* in the plaintiffs' pleadings, each of the individuals (respondents) who was paid a certain amount in each case alleged a different 'reason' for having been paid, but ultimately all of the payments were categorised as 'undue payments', and therefore the use of the *condictio indebiti*.

In *Bruni v Kahunda*,[7] the following summary at paras [8] and [10] illustrates most of the cases:

> [8] The plaintiffs plead that the main perpetrators of the money laundering were the '*dramatis personae*' and one George Markides, who received approximately N$64 000 000 in cash from AMFS. Markides worked in close cooperation with the '*dramatis personae*' by laundering stolen money between the beneficiaries in Table 1 of the particulars of claim. Approximately N$250 000 000 was laundered through the bank accounts of false beneficiaries, whereafter approximately N$50 000 000 was re-laundered back to Namibia and which was handed out to the Namibian participants to the scheme. In order to understand how these payments were made, it is important to highlight how the payments system at the SME bank worked.

The payment system at the SME Bank worked in the following manner, as expressed at paras 9 and 10 of *Bruni v Kahunda*:

> The payment system: [9] The payment effected to the false beneficiaries followed its course through the Treasury Department of the Bank and can be briefly set out as follows:

[7] *Bruni* (note 1).

> (a) All preparation for payment would go through the Finance Department. Once the Finance Department has checked, verified and authorised, the CEO must approve the payment, and once the CEO has approved the payment, a document called a 'Payment Instruction' will be forwarded to the Treasury Back Office to effect payment.
>
> (b) At the Treasury Back Office, the payment instruction will be dealt with by three persons, namely: (i) the Treasury Inputter – being the person who physically loads the payment onto the system for payment to be effected; (ii) the Treasury Verifier – being the person who checks whether sufficient funds are available in the SME bank's bank account to meet the payment; and (iii) the Treasury Authorizer, the person who physically makes the payment by pressing a button on the system to effect the actual payment ('the Authorizer'). This 'third person' is also characterized in the case as the 'Button-pusher'.
>
> [10] Any person operating the Treasury Department will only receive a payment instruction indication to whom the payment must be made, the bank account number of the payee and the reason for the payment, all of which is confirmed by the signature of the CEO of the SME Bank or in his absence the Acting CEO. No supporting documents will accompany the payment instructions to the Treasury Department.

The focus of this chapter on the Namibian law is not that the *condictio indebiti* was wrongly applied in the Namibian cases cited above; rather, it is on some assertions in the cases(s) that may have misconstrued the law of unjustified enrichment. For instance, the assertion in the cases that the defendant had primarily to allege 'loss of enrichment' in his defence for the *condictio indebiti* to be defeated; and the erroneous characterisation at para [23] of *Bruni v Kahunda* (also repeated elsewhere) that the defendant was 'unjustly enriched'. For example, at para [24] the court repeats counsel's assertion, without any remarks, that the 'recipient [was] the ultimate recipient without herself giving any value'. The court continued that 'counsel argued that the transfer of the SME Bank's money to the defendant *prima facie* establishes the first defendant's enrichment and that proof of the transfer of the money gives rise to a presumption of enrichment and "the defendant has the onus to prove loss of enrichment", which she did not do'.

And again, that

> the payment on behalf of the plaintiff must be regarded as excusable as the money was paid in *bona fide* but in the mistaken belief that it was due and that AMFS then proceeded to act as a conduit paying the money over to the first defendant as the final recipient.

At para [28] in Bruni v Kahunda the court, citing African Diamond Exporters[8] and Le Riche v Hamman,[9] stated that

> in respect of a defence of non-enrichment, as was expressly pleaded in this matter, once a transfer *indebite* has been established, the onus would then shift to the defendant to prove that it was not enriched by the transfer. Where a defendant has disposed of a thing, to succeed with a defence of non-enrichment, the defendant would invariably be required to establish that the disposal was *bona fide.*

Because the judgments were delivered as summary judgments, although the reasons were provided later, the discussions of the defences regarding unjustified enrichment in these cases are very thin. Coupled with the judgments' being 'only summary judgments with little reasoning' is also the fact that counsel for the defendant (especially in *Bruni v Kahunda*) did not really advance any good arguments in their defence, coupled with the fact that often their assertions of the defences were so erratic that one cannot even know what their defence against the *condictio indebiti* claim was.

> For example, the plaintiff's pleadings assert (paraphrasing the court) that plaintiff's 'counsel argued that the transfer of the SME Bank's money to the defendant *prima facie* establishes the first defendant's enrichment and that proof of the transfer of the money gives rise to a presumption of enrichment and 'the defendant has the onus to prove loss of enrichment', which she did not do.

In this argument (which is assumed from the pleadings), the plaintiff was already alleging 'loss of enrichment' as a possible defence, but the defendant's counsel (Mr Rukoro) nevertheless argued that 'the plaintiffs were unable to prove the elements of the claim of *condictio indebiti*'.[10]

10.2.1 What are the elements of an enrichment claim in Namibian Law?

As stated above, the Namibian law of unjustified enrichment is based on the Roman law *condictiones*, which is succinctly captured in summary form in *Bruni v Kahunda*,[11] which cited Smuts J in *Van den Dries v The International University of Management*.[12]

---

[8] *African Diamond Exporters (Pty) Ltd Barclays Bank International Ltd* 1978 (3) SA 699 (A) at 713H–J.
[9] *Le Riche v Hamman* 1946 AD 648 at 657.
[10] *African Diamond Exporters* (note 8); *Le Riche v Hamman* (note 9).
[11] [2020] NAHCMD 591.
[12] [2014] NACHMD 159.

The essential requirements for an enrichment claim are that (*a*) the defendant must be enriched; (*b*) the plaintiff must be impoverished (a contentious assertion); (*c*) the defendant's enrichment must be at expense of the plaintiff; and (*d*) the enrichment must be unjustified (ie, *sine causa*). If the enrichment claim is based on the *condictio indebiti*, the issue of error may come into play (but not necessarily so). Whether the error must be 'excusable' is an element that is subject to debate, but it is not pertinent for the purposes of this chapter. Once the plaintiff has established their claim, then the defendant must have no defence for the claim to succeed.

10.2.2 What generally are the defences that can be raised against an enrichment claim?

Depending on the facts of the case, an enrichment claim could be resisted either *in toto* or in part and in different ways. A successful defence may fully defeat the claim or it may reduce the extent of the defendant's liability and in this way establish a specific measure of recovery. Defences in law in general may be of various natures:[13] positive or negative; total or partial; permanent or temporary; they may go to the root of the claim itself and in this way deny the claim's validity or they may relate to extrinsic facts subsequent to the facts giving rise to the claim to deny its effectiveness.[14] Defences may also be general in a wider sense or they may be general in a more restrictive sense; they may be peculiar to certain types of claim or specific to a certain field of law or to a certain subset of factual scenarios.[15]

Regardless of the nature of the defences, though, all of them have one thing in common: to exonerate fully the defendant from liability or reducing the liability to the extent that justice and legal rules allow. The recognition of some enrichment defences is dependent on the way the claim itself is perceived in a particular legal system, whereas others may be neutral to any formulation adopted. There is also no exhaustive list of defences and their nomenclature varies from jurisdiction to jurisdiction.

Whatever classificatory approach is used in the defences, the following are generally the possible defences encountered against an unjust(ified) enrichment claim:

- non-enrichment;
- loss of enrichment (or change of position or de-enrichment);
- estoppel;

[13] G Virgo *Principles of the Law of Restitution* 3 ed (Oxford Academic, 2015) 656–659 and 663–705; A Jorge *Change of Position in Comparative Perspective*, Doctoral thesis (University of Cape Town, 2009) 46–107

[14] ALI 'Restatement (Third) of Restitution and Unjust Enrichment' Reporter: Andrew Kull, 2011.

[15] Jorge (note 13) 46–47.

- counter-restitution (counter-restitution impossible);
- *prescription* (limitation);
- *res judicata* (dispute resolved);
- incapacity;
- illegality;
- bona-fide purchase from a third party;
- agency receipt (also called 'ministerial receipt' under English law), and
- passing on.[16]

If one follows a classificatory scheme related to the element of the enrichment claim to which each defence is related, non-enrichment, loss of enrichment (change of position), estoppel and probably counter-restitution go the question of the defendant's enrichment; passing on goes to the question whether the enrichment was at the claimant's expense,[17] and prescription (limitation), dispute resolved (*res judicata*), incapacity, illegality and 'bona-fide purchase' all go to the enquiry of the injustice of the enrichment.[18]

In the Namibian context, the defendant's defences to an enrichment claim can be related to any of the elements of the enrichment claim itself, as stated above:

- defendant can deny that they have been enriched;
- defendant can also defeat the claim by proving that the plaintiff is not 'impoverished' (although this element is contentious);
- the claim can also be defeated if the plaintiff can assert and prove that the enrichment of the defendant is not at the expense of the plaintiff, and,
- finally, the defendant can also defeat the claim if they can prove that the enrichment is *cum causa* (ie, it is based on a legal ground).

There can also be other defences, such as *res judicata*, illegality, bona-fide purchase from a third party, 'agency receipt' (also called 'ministerial receipt', under English law) and probably passing on.[19]

---

[16] In English law, for example, some new cases are trying to amplify the list, although the one just cited is not exhaustive. But new suggestions, such as that found in *CIR v Deutsch Morgan Grenfell Group PLC* [2005] EWCA Civ 78, [2006] 2 WLR 103 at paras 93 and 113, that the law should now consider defences such as 'settled understanding of the law', 'defence of compromise' and 'settlement of an honest claim' are not finding favour in the courts. The current title 18.146 (G) of *English Private Law* (2013), edited by Andrew Burrows, does not list these defences.

[17] P Birks *The Foundations of Unjust Enrichment: Six Centennial Lectures* (Larose et Tenin, 2002) 145; Virgo (note 13) 663–670.

[18] Birks (note 17) 145.

[19] C Webb *Reason and Restitution: A Theory of Unjust Enrichment* (Oxford University Press, 2016) 217–219.

10.2.3 What are the misconceptions of the enrichment claim in the *SME* cases, especially in *Bruni v Kahunda*?

The cases present a few misconceptions of the liability in an enrichment claim in Namibian law. Some misconceptions or misconstructions appear from the parties' pleadings, such as the plaintiff's pleading that the 'recipient must give value on the receipt' (para [24] of *Bruni v Kahunda*). Although this misconception from the plaintiff did not influence the judgment, it is noteworthy to mention that counsel's view here is being based not on Namibian law, but it is being influenced by English law (or even by a misconception of the English law). In the first instances that counsel's view is not based on Namibian law, the underlying thinking of counsel is that 'there was a contract between the parties' and that the recipient did not 'give value' to the contract, that is, the contract lacked consideration. If the contract 'lacked consideration' (that is why the recipient was being held liable on the claim against unjustified enrichment), the element of 'consideration' is not part of the Namibian law of contract. But, again, counsel's assertion is also erroneous, even if the contract 'lacked consideration', because the claim in unjustified enrichment is not based in the contract. Therefore, 'giving value' is not an element to be used to establish or defeat a claim in unjustified enrichment.

Another misconception in the cases (although this is also not from the court itself) is that sometimes the claim is characterised as 'unjust enrichment' instead of unjustified enrichment. For example, at para [23], the case states that 'defendant denied that she was unjustly enriched'. This presumes that enrichment liability in Namibia is based on 'unjust enrichment', when in fact it is based on 'unjustified enrichment'. A defendant can be 'unjustly enriched' but may not be liable on a claim in unjustified enrichment, if that 'unjust enrichment' has a valid legal ground.

The third misconception in the case is the implicit assumption that if the defendant is to defeat an enrichment claim, they must have 'lost the enrichment'. Here this misconception derives partly from the court itself. At para [28] the court states:

> In respect of a defence of non-enrichment, as was expressly pleaded in this matter, once a transfer *indebite* has been established, the onus would then shift to the defendant to prove that it was not enriched by the transfer. Where a defendant has disposed of a thing, in order to succeed with a defence of non-enrichment, the defendant would invariably be required to establish that the disposal was bona fide.

In the paragraph cited, whereas the court is clear that the defence of 'non-enrichment' was clearly pleaded in the case, and that such defence would succeed only if the defendant can prove that they have not been enriched (or is no longer enriched), the assertion in the second sentence that: '*where a defendant has disposed of a thing, in order to succeed with a defence of non-enrichment, the defendant would invariably be required to establish that the disposal was bona fide*', confused two different defences.

One is the 'defence of non-enrichment', which attaches to (or is directed at) the first element of the claim, that is to say, 'the defendant is enriched'; and the other is the defence of 'loss of enrichment' (or de-enrichment) itself. It is a misconstruction because nowhere in the case did the defendant ever plead or allege loss of enrichment. The defence of 'loss of enrichment' is relevant only if the defendant has already acknowledged enrichment (and the plaintiff has proved their claim), but then the defendant states that they are no longer enriched. Whereas the defence of 'non-enrichment' is attached to the first element of the claim, the defence of 'loss of enrichment' is a general defence that can defeat the entire claim, even if the plaintiff has proved that the defendant was enriched.

10.3 UNJUST ENRICHMENT IN CONTINENTAL EUROPE

10.3.1 Early evolution of enrichment liability in civilian systems based on Roman law

It is commonly acknowledged by most scholars that early Roman law did not have a general remedy for unjustified enrichment, but it offered three specific legal conceptions which can be seen as kindred to, or a specific manifestation of, the general notion of unjustified enrichment: the *condictio* (or, better, *condictiones*[20]), *negotiorum gestio* (mainly the *actio negotiorum gestiorum contraria*) and the *actio de in rem verso*.[21] The most common *condictio* was known as *condictio indebiti*, which enabled someone who had had money or goods delivered in error to reclaim the money or the goods. This *condictio* enabled the restitution of what had been performed based on a void contract and where no contract had been concluded between the parties, but where the performance was the consequence of a mistake.

[20] I use the plural here for convenience' sake, as the Roman *condictio* had various sub-species: *causa data causa non secuta, condictio indebiti, condictio ob turpe vel injustam causam*, etc.

[21] See P Gallo 'Unjustified enrichment: A comparative analysis' (1992) 40 *American Journal Comparative Law* 433–437; DH van Zyl 'The general enrichment action is alive and well' 1992a *Acta Juridica* 115; DH van Zyl 'Rethinking unjustified enrichment' 1992b *Acta Juridica* 203; J Hallebeek *The Concept of Unjust Enrichment in Late Scholasticism* (Gerard Noodt Instituut, 1996) 36. Various circumstances in which the *actio de in rem verso* would normally apply are mainly subsumed in the discussion of the *condictio sine causa specialis* in South African law, still adhering to the old *condictio* in its piecemeal form: F Giglio 'A systematic approach to "unjust" and "unjustified enrichment"' (2003) 23 *Oxford Journal for Legal Studies* 455, 458–460.

Then there was *negotiorum gestio*, which developed in close relation to agency (*mandatum*) and it enabled one who acted in an emergency in the interests of another, without previous authority, to be compensated for their altruistic behaviour. Essentially, the *actio negotiorum gestiorum contraria* was available only if the plaintiff had acted with the intention of binding the principal to themself. In some situations, however, the action against the principal (*actio negotiorum gestorium contratia*) could have the character of an enrichment action (D 3.5.5.5).

Finally, the *actio de in rem verso*, which was introduced in order to compel the father (*paterfamilias*) or the master to give back what he had obtained as a consequence of a contract executed by the son or a slave.[22] This action was developed because the ancient Romans did not recognise direct agency. The *condictiones*, which required a direct conveyance by the claimant to the defendant and the absence of a *causa* (basis) which could justify the retention of the thing by the defendant, were of no avail to an impoverished person where the transfer of wealth did not take place directly between the parties to the claim but where the defendant had benefited.

To remedy this imbalance, the action de *in rem verso* was introduced and through it the claimant could seize what the defendant had turned to his benefit (*in rem versus*). This action was by its nature based on equity and, to succeed in its terms, it did not matter whether the claimant was impoverished and the defendant enriched, but it looked for an equitable solution: that is, a solution according to justice, which took the general situation of both parties into consideration.[23] The main features of this new action were: (i) a three-party situation; (ii) the limitation of the extent of liability to the enrichment of the defendant, and (iii) an economic loss by the plaintiff.[24] Therefore, the defendant could not be made liable in unjustified enrichment beyond the concrete benefit which he had obtained from the transfer of wealth and which was still present in his assets. Furthermore, this action was not triggered by the invalidity of the basis of the transfer, as was the case with the *condictio*. In fact, an *actio de in rem verso* might be granted despite the existence of a valid cause.[25]

Given that classical Roman law did not acknowledge a general enrichment action,[26] later Roman law, mainly in the Middle Ages, progressively developed a

---

[22] Gallo (note 21) 433–437; Hallebeek (note 21) 36.

[23] Giglio (note 21) 459.

[24] For the *condictio* and history of this action see, generally, R Zimmermann *The Law of Obligations* (Oxford University Press, 1990) 834–857.

[25] Giglio (note 21) 459.

[26] See, eg, J du Plessis 'Towards a rational structure of liability for unjustified enrichment: Thoughts from two mixed jurisdictions' (2005) 122(1) *South African Law Journal* 142–181 and the authorities cited there). Du Plessis synthesises that view when, inter alia, he states: 'Although Roman

positive attitude towards generalisation,[27] principally with regard to restitution.[28] For example, the last title of the Digest (*De diversis regulis iuris antiqui*, mainly D 50.17.206) contains a general prohibition of unjustified enrichment (albeit without having the status of an enforceable rule of law); and similar statements can be found in D 12.6.14, where the principle is identified as being equitable according to nature. In D 2.15.8.22 norm is described as very equitable and the texts in D 14.3.17.4 and 5, D 23.3.6.2 and D 23.3.16 reflect the same disposition. Therefore, generally speaking, the civilian system of unjustified enrichment can be said to have emerged from Pomponius's maxim '*Jure naturae aequum est, neminem cum alterius detrimento et injuria fieri locupletiorem*'. (It is just and fair by nature that no one should be made richer at the expense of and injury to another.)[29]

Since the 12th century, the remedies mentioned above were progressively reinterpreted. *Negotiorum gestio* was developed to reach the *negotiorum gestio utilis*,[30] which, unlike the classical conception of the *negotiorum gestio*, no longer

lawyers at times stated that a *condictio* could be used to reclaim a specific thing or sum of money because it is in the hands of another without a *causa*, it unfortunately is rather difficult to establish clearly what this was supposed to mean ... and if one takes into account that Roman law in any event did not recognise unjustified enrichment as a source of obligation, it should be apparent that, from a modern perspective, it is difficult to obtain strong guidance from Roman law sources on what the notion of the absence of legal ground is supposed to mean.'

[27] 'Although there are some texts in the *Corpus Juris Civilis* which appear to indicate the contrary', Roman law did not manifest clearly any such positive attitude towards generalisation, and what in Grotius *Indeilinge* 3.30.18 appears to be a formulation of a general enrichment action with reference to Roman law is no more than a discussion of the *condictio sine causa specialis*. For a more detailed historical discussion of the issue in Germany, France, the Netherlands and eventually South Africa, see Van Zyl (1992a, note 21) 115.

[28] The interaction between the theological schools and the *ius commune* is mostly noticeable in this area. Although in Roman law the approach to unjust enrichment instances was conceived differently from the theological concept represented by the doctrine of restitution, the underlying idea in both notions is the same: no one is permitted to enrich themself at another's expense without justification.

[29] D 12.6.14 and D 50.17.206; Gallo (note 21) 438; Van Zyl (1992a, note 21) 115–118.

[30] For example, the early glossator Martinus Gosia and his followers tried to adopt as the general enrichment action a particular variant of the action for unauthorised administration: the *actio negotiorum gestorum utilis*. The difference from the normal remedy for managing another's affairs consists in the fact that it no longer requires the plaintiff to have acted with the intention of obligating another to themself. Martinus deduced this from the text in D 3.5.5.5 because there was room for such an action in the Roman system. For example, in D 3.5.5.5 the manager interferes with another's affairs simply in order to make a profit for himself. In spite of this malicious intention, he is nevertheless allowed to sue the principal, albeit not in order to obtain compensation but merely in order to obtain the amount of the enrichment, if any, which has accrued to the principal as a result of the manager's operation.

Even if the required intention to bind the principal is lacking, there are two other reasons which, according to Martinus, can justify granting the remedy: the principal himself could have required the intention to act in the interests of another (*animus aliena negotia gerendi*); and the *actio de in rem verso*[31] and the *condictio*[32] were extended far beyond their original field of application.[33]

The medieval lawyers concentrated their attention on three main problems: (i) a good faith improvement of the property of another; (ii) appropriation of value by using or disposing of the goods of another; (iii) indirect enrichment.[34] This tendency to extend the original remedies opened the way for the development of a general remedy against unjustified enrichment,[35] but its achievement took until the

been compelled to perform the same (management of another's affairs *re ipsa*) or the operation appeared eventually to be beneficial to the principal (management of another's affairs *ipso gestu*). See Hallebeek (note 21) 41.

[31] The first impetus to 'stretch' the applicability of the *actio de in rem verso* dates back to the periods of the early Glossators. We find, for example, that in C 4.26.7.3 an action is granted against a third party who is enriched by means of a contract entered into by an intermediary. Although this intermediary is a free person and not a slave or a son *in potestate* of the third party, some Glossators consider the action granted to be an *actio utilis de in rem verso*. See Hallebeek (note 21) 42.

[32] As in the case of *de in rem verso* already some early Glossators read, eg in D 12.1.32, a special use of the *condictio* which no longer required a *negotium* (dealing, transaction) between plaintiff and defendant. The text grants an action for the mere reason that my money has come into your hands and that it is right and equitable (*bonun et aequum*) that you should refund it. Despite that early flexibility, however, it was only in the 14th century that this special *condictio* ex D 12.1.32 was adopted as a general enrichment action. We find by this time, for example, Baldus, who speaks about a general equity (*aequitas generalis*) in the following terms: '*haec est etiam aequitas generalis, quocumque casu representata parit actionem generalem, scilicet certi condictionem, quod est notandum*' and later Commentators follow him. It is, however, acknowledged that this action was not by this time termed an enrichment action, but it qualified as *condictio sine causa, condictio certi generalis, condictio ex aequitate* or *actio in factum ex aequitate*. (see, generally, Hallebeek (note 21) 43–44. For the general teaching of Baldus on unjustified enrichment, see J Gordley *The Philosophical Origins of Modern Contract Doctrine* (Clarendon Press, 1991) 55–57.

[33] Gallo (note 21) 439; Van Zyl (1992a, note 21) 115 et seq.

[34] Gallo (note 21). One should note, for example, the jurists from the French School at Orleans that started soon after the period of the Ordinary Gloss granting enrichment remedies, which no longer clearly connected with a specific Roman quasi-contract. Following the example of Martinus, these jurists, among whom there was Pierre de Belleperche, based, for example, the *condictio incerti* or *condictio possessionis* on equity and they speak, for instance, about the *actio in factum ex aequitate*. This he is willing to grant in cases of necessary management of another's affairs when on the ground of C 2.18.28 it is not possible to bring the *actio negotiorum gestorum* because the manager acted against the principal's explicit prohibition. See, generally, Hallebeek (note 21) 42.

[35] Among those who advocated the general enrichment action either explicitly or implicitly in The Netherlands and/or France are: Grotius *Inleidinge* 3.30.18; Voet *Commentarius* 12.7.2; RJ Pothier *Appendice sur la gestion d'affaires* (an Appendix to his *Treatise on the Contract of Mandate*) (nd) 193, where Pothier says: '*Dans notre jurisprudence française, qui n'admet pas les subtilités de droit romain, et qui regarde la seule equité comme suffisante pour produire une obligation civile et pour*

very end of the 19th century.[36] The general action developed either from the *actio de in rem verso*[37] or through the *condictio sine causa specialis* or the extension of the action *negotiorum gestio*.

10.3.2 Current position on enrichment liability in Continental Europe

Many countries in Continental Europe (and other countries elsewhere inspired by the Napoleonic (French) and German codes) have adopted a general enrichment action incorporated either through the code or through jurisprudence. The *sine causa* approach represents its hallmark alongside the notion of 'transfer'.[38] *Sine causa* is understood as the 'absence of a legal ground', which implies that either the ground (*causa*) did not exist when the transaction occurred to sustain the validity of the 'transfer of the benefit' or, if it ever existed, it has since ceased to exist[39] (an *actio ob causam finitam*).

Obviously, civilian-law jurisdictions are not homogenous in their approach to unjustified enrichment. It is nonetheless true that all of them share the 'negative approach' to found a claim in unjustified enrichment. All of them begin from the proposition that every enrichment at another's expense either has an explanation known to the law (a *causa*) or it has not.[40] Enrichments are ordinarily received with the purpose of discharging an obligation or, if there is no such obligation, at least of

---

donner une action, il ne doit pas être douteux que ... celui qui a fait des impenses dont je profit doit avoir action contre moi, jusqu'à concurrence de ce que j'en profite.'

36 Gallo (note 21) 439.

37 Dawson, eg, says that the *actio de in rem verso*, in the course of the 18th century, escaped all the limitations adhering to the *condictio* and *actio negotiorum gestorum* and became a 'universal remedy for the prevention of unjust enrichment': J Dawson *Unjust Enrichment: A Comparative Analysis* (Little Brown & Company, 1951; reprinted 1999) 84–92, specially at 89–90.

38 'Transfer' here is used in a very loose sense to include both an active and a passive 'transfer'. It encompasses not only an actual 'transfer of the benefit from one person to another' but also an acquisition by 'omission', ie the saving of expenses which would have been incurred in the absence of the act complained about. It also includes an increase in liabilities on the part of the plaintiff while the defendant reduces their liabilities due to the fact complained about.

39 See further detail on the notion of *sine causa* in Jorge (note 13) ch 4. This chapter deals mainly with Brazilian law, but the notion of *sine causa* is dealt with in a wider perspective.

40 JG Lotz & FDJ Brand 'Enrichment' in WA Joubert & JA Faris (ed) *LAWSA* 9 ed (LexisNexis Butterworths, 2009) 209(*d*); Zimmermann (note 24) 834 and R Zimmermann 'Unjustified enrichment: The modern civilian approach' (1995) 15(3) *Oxford Journal of Legal Studies* 403–411; P Birks *Unjust Enrichment* 2 ed (Oxford University Press, 2005) 102–103; DP Visser *Unjustified Enrichment* (Juta & Co, 2008) 171ff; Du Plessis (note 26). Du Plessis observes that, although there is unanimity about the absence of legal ground (*cause*) in civilian-law in general, the meaning and content of that legal ground (*cause*) vary considerably within the civilian-law family. At 157 of his article, Du Plessis gives French and Dutch examples.

achieving some other objective – as, for example, making a gift, the satisfaction of a condition or the coming into being of a new contract.[41] If these outcomes succeed, then the enrichment is sufficiently explained, that is, it is obtained *cum causa*. If the enrichment turns out to have no such explanation, then it is inexplicable and therefore it cannot be retained.[42] The recipient is not entitled to it. It must be disgorged, otherwise the retention of it would be *sine causa*. The consensus among civilian-law systems, however, potentially ends here.

When defining what the measure of enrichment is – whether it is the object received itself or its value which should be returned and, if the enrichment ceased to exist, what should be done – civil-law countries start drifting apart again.

Differences also exist as to the moment of assessment of the enrichment measure: whether it is the moment the object was received or at *litis contestatio*. At the risk of over-simplification, one would say that what we actually find in civil-law jurisdictions today is, for convenience' sake, what one may broadly term as the 'Pothier' and the 'Glück-Windscheid' schools. The issue sometimes goes down to the structure of enrichment law itself.

To the Pothier school belong those who sustain the idea that enrichment law should emphasise 'value received' as the 'sole' measure of enrichment (in this way denying either implicitly or partially the 'loss of enrichment' (change of position) defence). The Glück-Windscheid[43] school covers all those countries which defend the idea that enrichment law should concentrate on the value surviving rather than the value received, save for exceptions.[44]

Obviously, there are intermediate positions between these two camps. The schools of thinking adopting Pothier's perspective of the field as a whole tend to deal extensively with *paiement de l'indue* (undue payment) apart from *negotiorum gestio*. Although there is diversity of thought in the Pothier school as to the place

---

[41] Current Canadian law calls all these situations and others 'juristic reasons': see *Garland v Consumer Gas Co* [2004] SCC 25; (2004) 237 DLR (4th) 385; *Kerr v Baranow* [2011] SCJ No 10 (a joint decision on two appeals, *Kerr v Baranow* 2009 BCCA 111 from British Columbia, and *Vanasse v Seguin* 2009 ONCA 595 from Ontario).

[42] In South African law, Visser (note 40) 173–174 poses the question whether one should consider only the *causa retinendi* or also the *causa dandi* and how to categorise the notion of *causa* in the face of the recognition that an invasion of rights can give rise to enrichment claims and in cases of contracts discharged by supervening impossibility.

[43] Current adherents of the Glück-Windscheid school align with what was concluded back in time by Glück *Ausführliche Erläuterung der Pandekten* ad D 12.6 (§ 835) and Windscheid *Lehrbuch* 2 § 424 that loss of enrichment applies both to a *genus* and to a *species* and, therefore, loss of enrichment can be pleaded in all cases.

[44] Among the limitations generally advocated, one would be that a *mala fide* recipient is always liable for value received and where the enrichment claim arose as part of an (invalid) reciprocal contract, value received is also the correct measure.

of all other enrichment situations[45] and the requirement of error, the general trend is that the nature of the enrichment claim does not depend on the type of benefit conferred. In other words, civil-law countries do not have different restitutionary remedies arising from the payment of money, the receipt of services and the delivery of goods.[46]

10.3.3 Harmonising rules on unjust or unjustified enrichment in European private law: Draft Common Frame of Reference

Since the early 2000s, a common effort has been underway by the Acquis Group[47] and the European Research Group on the 'harmonisation of European private law'. This group produced Outline Drafts known as Draft Common Frame of Reference (DCFR) in each area of private law, some of which potentially aimed at producing a 'European Civil Code'. In 2009 a DCFR (Outline edition) was produced and Book VII of that draft contained the basic rules for unjustified enrichment. In 2016 the Acquis Group finalised the Draft into a Model Law titled Principles, Definitions and Model Rules of European Private Law – Draft Common Frame of Reference.

In this DCFR, Book VII deals in detail with the Principles on Unjustified Enrichment. Thus, we find at Book VII-1:101 the basic rule guiding the law of unjustified enrichment in Continental Europe. Paragraph (1) of VII-1:101 states the general principle as follows: 'A person who obtains an unjustified enrichment which is attributable to another's disadvantage is obliged to that other to reverse the enrichment.' According to the comments and explanations that accompany para (1) of Book VII-1:101, it is stated that para (1) provides for a non-contractual obligation. It also clarifies that para (1) sets out a single general norm, that is to say, a rule of general application which provides the foundation of the claim recognised under Book VII of the DCFR of 2016. Nonetheless, it also provides that the basic rule enunciated in VII-1:101(1) is not free-standing. The application of the general rule is fleshed out and qualified by later provisions and therefore para (1) cannot be applied in isolation of the other chapters of Book VII.

The basic norm in VII-1:101(1) also sets out all the elements which must be present in order to support an enrichment claim. These elements are: 'a person' who is the debtor and 'another' who is the creditor of the enrichment claim. Then

[45] See, eg, the new Brazilian Civil Code of 2002 (Arts 876–886), which presents an enrichment law with a dual structure: 'undue payment' and 'enrichment *sine causa*'. See also the Dutch Civil Code (*BW*), which uses a similar structure.

[46] Zimmermann (note 24) 403, 411.

[47] The Acquis Group is a research body founded in 2002 and made up of legal scholars in the field of private law from each EU country. There are links to EU legislation concerning private law and European Court of Justice (ECJ) cases relating to contract law.

the potential debtor of the enrichment must have 'obtained' some benefits (ie, an enrichment); this enrichment must then be 'unjustified' and the 'potential creditor' must have sustained a disadvantage, and the enrichment must be attributable to this disadvantage.

In its turn, VII-2:101 (1–4) clearly delineates the circumstances in which an enrichment is unjustified. In para (1)*(a)* and *(b)* the DCFR provides that an enrichment is unjustified unless *(a)* the enriched person is entitled as against the disadvantaged person to the enrichment by virtue of a contract or other juridical act, a court order, or a rule of law; or *(b)* the disadvantaged person consented freely and without error to the disadvantage.

And para (4)(a*)–(c)* clarified that 'an enrichment is also unjustified if *(a)* the disadvantaged person conferred it (i) for a purpose which is not achieved; or (ii) with an expectation which is not realised'. And para (4)*(b)* that 'the enriched person knew of, or could reasonably be expected to know of, the purpose or expectation'. And para (4)*(c)* that 'the enriched person accepted or could reasonably be assumed to have accepted that the enrichment must be reversed in such circumstances'.

In Art VII-2:103, 'Consenting or performing freely', the DCFR sets out the circumstances in which a disadvantage person's consent is to be regarded as not having been given freely – namely, where the consent is affected by 'incapacity; fraud, threats or unfair exploitation'.[48]

The DCFR's official comments on VII-2:101 mention that the DCFR Book VII takes the 'absence of legal basis approach' and not the 'unjust factors' approach. The comment clearly states: 'This article (VII-2:102) takes a starting point notion that an enrichment is unjustified,[49] unless one of two broad exceptions [applies].' The broad exceptions are an enrichment supported either by contract (or other juridical act) with the disadvantaged person or a court order or a rule of law, or the disadvantaged person's consent. The DCFR comment then concludes that 'there is no catalogue of particular matters which trigger an absence of justification' (ie, 'unjust factor'). Therefore, the approach that supports such an idea of a catalogue of 'particular matters triggering an absence of justification' takes exactly the converse starting point, namely, that 'an enrichment is justified',[50] and looks to identify a reason for treating it otherwise.

As to the content of the obligation and defences, the DCFR provides that

[48] C von Bar & E Clive (eds) *Principles, Definitions and Model Rules of European Private Law – DCFR. Book VII-2* (Oxford University Press, 2016) 101–103; on VII-201 see Comments A–B at 3695–3709.

[49] This is the 'negative approach' I mentioned earlier, which underpins civil-law systems in enrichment liability.

[50] This is the 'positive approach' I mentioned earlier, which underpins most common-law systems, perhaps with the exception of Canada and a handful of South American states.

> if all the elements of the basic rule on VII-1:101(1) are established and the matter is not affected by defences (as provided for in chapter 6 of Book VII), then, the 'debtor' in an enrichment claim is obliged to 'reverse the enrichment'.

Chapter 7 of Book VII provides provisions which restrict the scope of the application of the basic rule.

In essence, the DCFR sets out the basic tenets of the enrichment claim in all Continental European countries, that is, the European civil-law systems.

10.4 UNJUST ENRICHMENT IN ENGLAND

10.4.1 Nomenclature of unjust enrichment in English law

The law of 'unjustified enrichment' in most common-law systems is called the law of restitution. More recently, some common-law jurisdictions have started using the dual description 'law of restitution and unjust enrichment'[51] (eg, the United States, with the introduction of the Restatement of the Law of Restitution and Unjust Enrichment in 2010). For some time, England used the description 'Law of Restitution' exclusively; later on, it began to emulate the dual description 'restitution and unjust enrichment'. But England has now firmly moved back to the description 'unjust enrichment',[52] as the new editions of Goff and Jones on restitution have now been retitled 'Law of Unjust Enrichment'.[53] But, for the time being, some common-law countries such as Australia and New Zealand (although they are rapidly changing) are still using the 'Law of Restitution' appellation,[54] or a mixture of restitution and unjust enrichment. But the law of restitution is now clearly termed 'unjust enrichment' in most common-law systems.[55]

---

[51] The appellation 'unjust enrichment' is still retained because English law in this area developed from equity, and the claim still has equitable features.

[52] However, there are still some who do not agree with this full move. See SA Smith 'The structure of unjust enrichment: Is restitution a right or a remedy?' (2003) 36 *Loyola of Los Angeles Law Review* 1037–1061.

[53] See C Mitchell 'Unjust enrichment' in A Burrows (ed) *English Private Law* (Oxford University Press, 2013) 18.1–18.3.

[54] But a recent book on the Australian law written by Barker and Grantham has changed its title fully to 'Law of Unjust Enrichment': K Barker & R Grantham *Law of Unjust Enrichment in Australia* (LexisNexis Butterworths, 2018).

[55] See T Cooksley 'The role of unjust enrichment in New Zealand' Victoria University of Wellington Legal Research Paper, Student/Alumni Paper 21 (2019), https://ssrn.com/abstract=3466517, discussing the full transition to unjust enrichment occurring in New Zealand and some voices still resistant to the full embrace of 'unjust enrichment' as the cause of action.

10.4.2 Early evolution of unjust enrichment in England and common-law systems based on English tradition

Common-law countries trace the foundations of their law of restitution (unjust enrichment) to the initial English extensions of *indebitatus assumpsit*,[56] into the quasi-contractual remedies of *quantum valebat, quantum meruit* and the action for *money had and received.* The recognition of *indebitatus assumpsit* itself as an action occurred sometimes earlier,[57] but it was firmly endorsed in *Slade.*[58]

These quasi-contractual remedies offered some sort of solution to restitutionary problems resembling 'unjust enrichment', but they contained no organising principle and, when available, they were subordinate to and always subject to contractual

[56] '*Assumpsit*' itself developed from the English 'action on the case', which is an English mimic of the Roman *actio in factum*. Although the *actio in factum* was mostly a form of words without specific content, its pattern could nevertheless in principle be adapted to any grievances. In the English version it took the form of the 'whereas' and the 'yet' clauses. The 'action on the case' could then be named in the various species. One such nameable species, when the name was taken from the 'whereas' clause, became the action on the promise (*assumpsit super se* = 'he undertook'), ordinarily expressed as: 'Whereas ... the defendant undertook (*assumpsit*) ... yet he wickedly ..., to the plaintiff's loss.'

The sub-form of *assumpsit* in the 'debt-promise' format is the '*indebitatus assumpsit*' (in Latin); '*indebitatus assumpsit* had in turn its sub-forms, according to the cause of the indebtedness. One such sub-form was 'money had and received to the use of the plaintiff'. See, generally, D Ibbetson 'Origins' *assumpsit* and debt in the early sixteenth century: The origins of the *indebitatus* count' (1982) 41(1) *The Cambridge Law Journal* 142–161; see also P Birks 'English and Roman learning in *Moses v Macferlan*' (1984) 37(1) *Current Legal Problems* 1–28, 25nn10–12 for other historical sources; RM Jackson *The History of Quasi-Contract in English Law* (Cambridge University Press, 1986) 27, 88 and 105. (All the citations in this chapter are taken from the reprinted version (Florida, 1986).)

[57] At least the year 1520 is the earliest date when legal historians have indicated the action on *assumpsit* was used the first time: see JB Ames *Lectures on Legal History and Miscellaneous Legal Essays* (Harvard University Press, 1913) 142. For a detailed historical account of the action, see Jackson (note 56) at 4ff and again at 40ff.

[58] (1602) 76 ER 1072. The development of *indebitatus assumpsit*, according to English legal historians, passed through the following phases: (i) a consideration that the defendant must be indebted and must make a subsequent promise to pay; (ii) in the Queen's Bench, the fact that the defendant was indebted on a simple contract was sufficient for the courts to imply a subsequent promise, specially from the time of *Edward v Burre* (1573) Dal 104, l.45), but often the Court of Exchequer Chamber reversed such judgments; (iii) *Slade*'s case ((1602) 76 ER 1072) endorsed the practice of the Queen's Bench; (iv) soon afterwards, the action was extended to cases where the defendant was not technically indebted but where there was a genuine contract. The action was not concurrent with debt immediately after *Slade*, since the action rested on a promise implied in fact, the implication being made from the acts of the parties; the idea of consent was whittled away slowly, so that the duties imposed primarily by law could therefore be enforced only towards the end of the 17th century. See, generally, Jackson (note 56) at 40ff.

principles.[59] These remedies were generally aimed at assisting a litigant in situations where they had performed a contract which was void because, for instance, a necessary element was lacking, such as full agreement on the consideration or the exact price.[60]

In brief, on the one hand, *quantum meruit* came to the assistance of, for example, an innkeeper entitling him to be paid for services actually rendered despite the lack of a previous agreement on the price to be paid. But, on the other hand, *quantum valebat* entitled, for instance, payment for their goods to those who had delivered them in execution of a contract considered unenforceable owing to the lack of determination of the amount of the consideration or for certain other reasons.[61]

The 'action for money had and received' developed mostly from the doctrine of waiver of tort.[62] This development occurred before Lord Mansfield came to the Bench in 1750,[63] although he is sometimes wrongly credited with its invention.[64]

---

[59] J Beatson *The Use and Abuse of Unjust Enrichment* (Clarendon Press, 1906) 2–3.

[60] JB Ames 'Purchase for value without notice' (1888) 2 *Harvard Law Review* 58: 'Services would be rendered, for example, by a tailor or other workman, an innkeeper or common carrier, without any agreement as to the amount of compensation. Such cases present no difficulty at present day, but for centuries there was no common-law action by which compensation could be recovered.' English writers and legal historians trace the origins of *assumpsit* to 1520, but its full endorsement occurred in 1602 in *Slade* (1602) 76 ER 1072 and that of *quantum meruit* and *quantum valebat* to 1609 and 1610 respectively in *Warbrooke v Griffin* (1609) 2 Brown 254 and *Six Carpenters* (1610) Re 147a. See CH Fifoot *History and Sources of the Common-law: Tort and Contract* (Stevens & Sons, 1949) 393ff; P Birks *Introduction to the Law of Restitution* (Oxford University Press 1985); P Birks 'English and Roman learning in *Moses v Macferlan*' (1984) 37(1) *Current Legal Problems* 1–28.

[61] Gallo (note 21) 435; Jackson (note 56) 27, 88 and 105.

[62] 'Waiver of tort' is a mechanism by which a claimant 'ratifies' the behaviour of the wrongdoer and asks for the money made by the wrongdoer as consequence of the tort (delict) instead of claiming damages. WA Keener *A Treatise on the Law of Quasi-contracts* (Baker Voorhis, 1893) 159 expressed such a notion in the following words: 'If anyone in the commission of a tort enriches himself by taking or using the property of another, the latter may, in some cases, instead of suing in tort to recover damages for the injury done, sue in *assumpsit* to recover the value of that which has been tortiously taken or used. The remedies in tort and *assumpsit* not being concurrent, a plaintiff is compelled to elect which remedy he will pursue; if he elects to sue in *assumpsit*, he is said to waive the tort.'

[63] For the authorities before Lord Mansfield, see H Cohen 'Change of position in quasi-contracts' (1932) 45 *Harvard Law Review* 1333, 1334n3, citing, among others, *Hussey v Fiddall* 12 Mod 324 (1770); *Lamine v Dorell* 2 Ld Raym 1216 (1706) (waiver of tort); *Hasser v Wallis* 1 Salk 28 (1708) (money had and received); *Holmes v Hall* Holt 36 (1695) (failing consideration); *Tomkins v Bernett* 1 Salk 22 (1693) (mistake).

[64] Several common-law writers hold that a remedy was developed in this sense by the possibility of waiving the tort, as acknowledged for the first time by Lord Mansfield. The same holding is also acknowledged by Gallo and he also thought that Lord Mansfield was the first to elevate the waiver of tort to the podium: Gallo (note 21) 435–437.

By that time it had been held that a plaintiff might waive a tort and sue in *assumpsit*; they could sue for money had and received to their use, for money paid on consideration which had failed and for money paid under mutual mistake.[65] The doctrine of waiver of tort was introduced in order to escape the rigidity and formalism of tort,[66] and that of contract law.

This system of waiver of tort introduced a more flexible mechanism into the common law. The evolution of the common law of restitution in the twin context of contract and tort gave rise to a system of restitutionary remedies which resembled more contractual and tortious configurations rather than a truly autonomous system of unjust enrichment remedies. That was the case because, for a quasi-contractual obligation in the old English law to be made, it did not require proof of unjust enrichment but the proof of a request or acceptance of the wares or services performed (*acceptio*).[67] This notion of request and acceptance still prevails to some extent in current common law. Its survival is made clearer when one considers the scenario of services rendered in the form of unrequested improvements to today's common law.

The standpoint of common law is that a person who improves the property they know belongs to another is viewed as a volunteer who is making a gift.[68] The improver's expectation of remuneration, if any were expected, merely indicates that in bestowing this gift, the improver is also taking the risk that the owner will pay for it.[69] The common law usually sees no reason to reverse the gift or re-allocate the risk through an award of restitution.[70] Because the improver knows that only

[65] Cohen (note 63) 1333–1334.

[66] In origin, tort liability came to an end as a consequence of the death of the wrongdoer (*actio personalis moritur cum persona*). In order to escape this rule, the waiver of tort was introduced to enable the ratification of the behaviour of the wrongdoer and ask for money obtained as a consequence of the tort instead of seeking damages. For example, in the case of conversion, if someone sells the goods of another – the owner waiving the tort – it is possible to be compensated even after the death of the wrongdoer; but it is still possible to waive the tort. In this way it is possible to choose between claiming damages or asking for the money obtained as a consequence of the wrong committed.

[67] Gallo (note 21) 433.

[68] This view, in my opinion, seems to echo a modified form of D 50.17.53, which reads: '*Cuius per errorem dati repetitio est, eius consulto dati donate est*' (repetition lies for what is given in error but what is given knowing (that is not due) it is a gift). It is enough here to twist the requirement of 'knowledge', assimilated as it is to the idea of gift to come, to such an approach.

[69] See, eg, *Greenwood v Bennett* (1973) 1 QB 195 (CA); and for unrequested improvement generally, see P Matthews 'Freedom, unrequested improvements and Lord Denning' (1981) 40(2) *The Cambridge Law Journal* 340–358.

[70] G Virgo *Restitution* (Oxford University Press, 1999) 39–40; G Virgo *Principles of Law of Restitution* (Oxford University Press, 2006) 55–58; G Virgo *Principles of the Law of Restitution* 3 ed (Oxford University Press, 2016) 70–77.

owners have the right to determine the condition of what they own, the improver is taken to know that the improvement cannot oblige the owner to pay for it. The improvement consequently counts as nothing more than a donative act. In other words, as Dagan[71] puts it,

> without a legal guarantee, a potential benefactor – who needs to decide whether to intervene before they are able to receive the beneficiary's binding commitment that they will indeed reimburse them – must take into account that their well-intentioned intervention could be abused.

This common-law approach to improvements is premised on a liberal value system because it regards negative liberty, or 'freedom from' forcible human interference, as the essential ingredient of personal development and autonomy (although it is not necessarily the ultimate value). Because each individual is distinct and unique, the common law thinks that every such individual should also be able to choose their goals voluntarily (and the means of achieving such goals) and should be held responsible for their choices. Any trespassing on that sphere of liberty should always be viewed with suspicion and should preferably be deterred.[72] On that basis, therefore, according to the common law,

---

[71] H Dagan 'Distributive foundations of corrective justice' (1999) 97 *Michigan Law Review* 138–166, 139, 140.

[72] The extreme anti-interventionist rules currently prevalent in most common-law jurisdictions know some exceptions: the doctrine does not apply in maritime salvage cases for which the law has a separate elaborate regime applying to those cases and whenever what is at stake is the preservation of life or health. Whenever rescuing life or preserving health is at stake, the common law generally has traditionally treated somewhat more liberally the benefactors in such cases than those who preserved only a proprietary or financial interest of another.

Fundamentally, the difference lies in the nature of the 'resource' involved. Between the civil law and the common law there is a fundamental difference not only between the nature of the resource involved, but especially regarding the significance of the intervention. Such a difference encompasses the 'ultimate success' test for one legal family and the 'reasonable diligence' test for the other. While it is a prerequisite of Anglo-American law to allow 'good Samaritan' claims – except in cases of life and limb – that the claimant's effort to protect or preserve the defendant's interest meets with actual success, as a fruitless intervention, even if reasonable, it cannot be said to produce any net value for the defendant (ie, an enrichment); and the reasonable person could, in any event, say that they would have been willing to pay only for a result, not an attempt, if one were to apply the 'bystander' test.

In contrast, under civil-law jurisdictions, the 'good Samaritan' is not required to demonstrate 'ultimate success' as long as they can show that they acted with 'reasonable diligence'. For further details on these issues, see S Eiseleen & G Pienaar *Unjustified Enrichment: A Casebook* 4 ed (LexisNexis, 2008); J Dawson '*Negotiorum gestio*: The altruistic intermeddler' (1961) 74 *Harvard Law Review* 817, 823; P Gallo 'Remedies for unjust enrichment in the history of Italian law and in

individuals should be entitled to control their resources, at least in so far as they do not actively harm others in exercising such control. As a corollary to such control, their actual consent – express or implied, but in all events actual and not legally imposed – should be the prerequisite of any legitimate transfer of or interference with any of their resources.[73]

As instances of unsolicited improvements and the benefits conferred by them threaten potential beneficiaries' control over their resources and in this way interfere ultimately with their free will, a legal system that takes seriously peoples' negative liberty must equally adopt the potential beneficiary's point of view. In so doing, such a legal system must require that these potential beneficiaries be the gatekeepers of their own affairs; and whoever officiously confers unrequested benefits upon them is, at best, to be viewed as a volunteer bestowing a gift or, at worst, as simply a risk-taker.

From the end of the 19th century, however, Anglo-American lawyers began to reconsider the whole field of restitution, starting with the pioneering historical research on *assumpsit*,[74] and other *quasi-contractual* analyses, especially in the United States.[75] They tried to unify all the quasi-contractual remedies described above. The process continued and accelerated throughout the last century with the landmark issue of the US *First Restatement of Restitution* in 1937, followed by other invaluable works both in the United States and in other common-law jurisdictions. Among these were Dawson *Unjust Enrichment* (1951); Goff & Jones *Law of Restitution* (1966);[76] Palmer *Law of Restitution* (1978); Birks *Introduction to the Unjust Enrichment* (1984); Virgo *Principles of Law of Restitution* (2006); Burrows *The Law of Restitution* (3 ed, 2011) and Burrows *A Restatement of the English Law of Unjust Enrichment* (2012). All these works, in one way or another, have emphasised the need for a unified principle for the entire law of restitution. Such a unifying principle has largely been found in the

the *Codice Civile*' in E Schrage (ed) *Unjust Enrichment: The Comparative Legal History of the Law of Restitution* (Duncker & Humblot, 1995) 275, 279.

[73] Dagan (note 71) 1161–1162.

[74] Ames (note 60) 58.

[75] See Cohen (note 63) 1333 for several works on quasi-contracts preceding the *Restatement of Restitution* of 1937. Among the most salient, the author cites Keener (note 62).

[76] R Goff & G Jones *The Law of Restitution* (Sweet & Maxwell, 1966) and all subsequent editions up to the 2007 edition reaffirm the same position that 'unjust enrichment' is at the foundation of the 'law of restitution'. Goff & Jones's book has now been retitled *The Law of Unjust Enrichment* 9 ed (Sweet & Maxwell, 2016).

general principle that no one should be enriched without reason at the expense of another,[77] a principle whose origin can be traced back to Roman law.[78]

10.4.3 Current status of unjust enrichment in English law

The clear recognition of the general enrichment principle in English law came in a unanimous judgment of the House of Lords in 1991: *Lipkin Gorman v Karpnale*.[79] This case recognised simultaneously the general principle against unjust enrichment and the general defence of change of position. The facts of the case are well known.

In short, the case was based on the following factual scenario: Cass, a solicitor (attorney) and partner at a law firm, was a gambling addict and a thief. He took £323 222.14 from his firm's client account and used this money to finance his gambling addiction at the defendant's club, the 'Playboy' club. It is thought he may have intended to return the money but, in the end, he was able to replace only £100 313.16. The balance of £222 908.48 could not be recovered from Cass. In total, he staked £561 014.06 at the club and won £378 294.06. The overall loss suffered by Cass over the period of his activities was calculated to be £174 745.00, of which it was agreed that £20 050.00 represented his own funds. Having the court accept that the club was liable to the solicitors in unjust enrichment, and in doing so recognising that this principle formed part of English law, the question was whether they should be liable for £200 000.00 or for £150 000.00. It was held that

[77] *Restatement of Restitution* § 1 (1937); P Birks *Unjust Enrichment* (Oxford University Press, 2005) P Birks 'Annual Miegunyah Lecture: Equity, conscience, and unjust enrichment' (1999) 23 *Melbourne University Law Review* 3–4; R Goff & G Jones *Law of Restitution* 5 ed (Sweet & Maxwell, 2002) ch 1; LD Smith 'The province of the law of restitution' (1992) 71 *Canadian Bar Review* 672. But also see, among others, the following authors who resist the generalisation of such a principle to the whole law of restitution: MP Gergen 'What renders enrichment unjust' (2011) 79 *Texas Law Review* 1763–2197; S Stoljar 'Unjust enrichment and unjust sacrifice' (1997) 50(5) *The Modern Law Review* 603–613; S Hedley 'Unjust enrichment as the basis of restitution – an overworked concept' (1985) 5(1) *Legal Studies* 56; S Hedley *Restitution: Its Ordering and Division (Modern Legal Studies)* (Sweet & Maxwell, 2001).

Atiyah is clearly opposed to the centrality of the notion of unjust enrichment, because despite recognising the importance of such a principle against unjust enrichment, he believes that it should not be elevated to a separate legal subject but viewed instead as a principle running through several existing subjects, such as property law, tort law and, most importantly, contract law: PS Atiyah *The Rise and Fall of Freedom of Contract* (Oxford University Press, 1985) 767–768.

[78] Pomponius D 12.6.14; D 50.17.206.

[79] *Lipkin Gorman v Karpnale* (1991) 2 AC 548, especially at 558 (*per* Lord Bridge), at 559 (*per* Lord Templeman), at 568 (*per* Lord Ackner) and 578 (*per* Lord Goff). Lord Griffiths concurred with Lord Templeman and Lord Goff. The case was again endorsed in *Banque Financière de la Cité v Parc (Bettersea) Ltd* [1999] 1 AC 221 (HL).

they were liable for the latter sum. This conclusion was based on the defence of change of position (loss of enrichment).

Lord Goff, whose judgment became more influential than that of Lord Templeman, as far as the defence of change of position is concerned, put the matter succinctly in this way:

> At the moment I do not wish to state the principle any less broadly than this: the defence (of change of position/(loss of enrichment)) is available to a person whose position has so changed that it would be inequitable in all the circumstances to require him to make restitution, or alternatively to make restitution in full.[80]

Since the House of Lords decision in the *Lipkin Gorman* case, the English law of restitution (now the law of unjust enrichment) in particular (and that of the whole common law, in general) has developed exponentially. Both the extent of the enrichment principle and its basis and the scope of the change of position defence and other defences have been scrutinised in subsequent cases and academic writing.

Judicially, cases subsequent to *Lipkin Gorman* such as *South Tyneside Metropolitan Borough Council v Skenska International Ltd*,[81] *Philip Collins v Davis*,[82] *Scottish Equitable v Derby*,[83] *Dextra Bank & Trust Co Ltd v Bank of Jamaica*,[84] *National Bank of New Zealand ltd v Waitaki International Processing (NI) Ltd*,[85] and many others, sought in one way or another to delineate the scope and operation of the law of unjust enrichment and the scope of the defence of change of position.

As regards the enrichment principle itself, cases such as *Hazell v Hammersmith & Fulham BC*,[86] *Westdeutsche Landesbank Girozentrale v Islington LBC* and *Kleinwort*

---

80 *Lipkin Gorman* (note 79) 580.

81 *South Tyneside Metropolitan Borough Council v Svenska International plc* [1995] 1 All ER 545.

82 *Philip Collins Ltd v Davis* [2000] 3 All ER 808.

83 *Scottish Equitable PLC v Derby* [2000] 3 All ER 793.

84 *Dextra Bank & Trust Co Ltd v Bank of Jamaica* (2002) 1 All ER (Comm) 192 (this is a Privy Council case, appealed from the Caribbean Dominions).

85 *National Bank of New Zealand Ltd v Waitaki International Processing (NI) Ltd* (1999) 2 *NZLR* 211 (a New Zealand case of general interest on the defence of change of position with its approach to negligence).

86 *Hazell v Hammersmith & Fulham BC* [1992] 2 AC 1 (HL). This case is said to have been the real 'trigger' of the full change in English law, because in it the House of Lords let it be known that billions of pounds had changed hands under void contracts (in both the closed swaps and the interrupted swaps). The House of Lords decided that the contracts of interest swaps made by the local authorities were not within the authorities' money management powers and were consequently void. For this reason, and with no exception, it required mutual restitution, with the effect that the winner, the party who had received the greater sum, had had to repay the winning difference. See, generally, P Birks *Unjust Enrichment* 2 ed (Oxford University Press, 2005).

Benson Ltd v Sandwell BC,[87] and *Guiness Mahon & Co Ltd v Kensington & Chelsea Royal London BC*[88] (commonly known as the 'swap' cases) sowed the seeds of some rapprochement of the common law with the civil law.

The mistake-of-law rule has also been abrogated[89] and, as often with the 'unjust factor' mistake or 'undue influence', failed squarely to explain the case of the restitution of illegally charged taxes in *Woolwich*,[90] triggering a potentially unparalleled revolution. Having the swap cases and others[91] recognise that the 'absence of basis' is the right explanation for understanding the swap cases, the English Judiciary provided the much-needed ammunition to Birks[92] (and probably others) finally to articulate the demise[93] of the 'unjust factor' approach as the basis of enrichment claims in English law. It did so by replacing it with the 'absence of basis' as the correct foundation of an enrichment claim at the top of the pyramid in his structure[94] – but a pyramid whose base can theoretically still encompass some of the traditional 'unjust factors'.[95]

However, since the death of Birks in 2004, the unjust factor approach has been revitalised and it is still prevalent under English law. It has been reaffirmed in the

---

[87] *Westdeutsche Landesbank Girozentrale v Islington LBC; Kleinwort Benson Ltd v Sandwell BC* [1994] 3 All ER 890 (CA); [1996] AC 699 (HL).

[88] *Guiness Mahon & Co Ltd v Kensington & Chelsea Royal London BC* [1999] QB 215 (CA).

[89] *Kleinwort Benson Ltd v Lincoln City Council* [1999] 2 AC 349.

[90] *Woolwich Equitable Building Society v IRC* [1993] 1 AC 70 (HL).

[91] *Woolwich Equitable Building Society* (note 90).

[92] Birks (note 86) 115–116.

[93] Although he cautioned that the new approach would be different from the civil interpretation, Birks himself described the potential 'demise' of the unjust factor approach in this way: 'The assertion of Englishness is not an outburst of chauvinism. It is merely a warning that, although the no basis approach is very civilian and although there is now guidance to be obtained from civilian jurisdictions, what has happened is not a passive reception of German and French law to fill a vacuum. Lord Mansfield did indeed do some borrowing of that kind from the *ius commune*.

'In contrast, the modern English judges have simply been drawn to an approach to "unjust" which, with hindsight, is both incompatible with the list of unjust factors with which they were previously managing and reflects the method which, in different sub-forms, is already familiar in civilian jurisdictions. This time there is no evidence in the cases of deliberate borrowing': Birks (note 86) 128. Thereafter, Birks devotes the whole of ch 6 (129–160) to the analysis of absence of basis. It is also instructive to read his own preface to the second edition dated 14 March 2004.

[94] Birks (note 86) 115–116.

[95] At this moment, some theorists are of the view that the 'unjust factor approach' has been completely discarded, with the only task remaining being that of realigning the interpretation of the precedents on which the whole system was based. But many others are still adamant that 'unjust factors' still have a vital role to play and that the English law of unjust enrichment is still firmly based on the positive approach. Krebs – a vehement defendant of the positive approach – notes, for example, that in the light of *Kleinwort Benson v Lincoln City Council* (1999) 2 AC 349 (HL), the argument in defence of the unjust factor approach might be too late.

recent monumental publication of A Burrows (ed) *English Private Law* (2013) at Title 18.[96] This is a collective work (with the companion book *English Public Law*) that organises English private law in a systematic manner, emulating to some extent the Justinian Digest (or the Blackstone Law of Scotland).

Thus far the development after *Lipkin Gorman v Karpnale (The Firm)*[97] is an ongoing process. Some milestones have already been reached while others are awaiting the opportunity to arise, as is typical of the common law. For example, in the conceptualisation of the change of position defence (loss of enrichment), *Philip Collins*[98] had already pointed out that the courts will not give defendants a particularly hard time to prove reliance where the evidential problems are insurmountable. This case therefore implies an interpretation of the change of position defence which is more generous to the defendant.

Svenska, on the other hand, was a test of the change of position defence in anticipatory reliance situations. The merits and demerits of anticipatory reliance are discussed elsewhere, but it suffices to note here that anticipatory reliance was firmly rejected in *Dextra Bank & Trust Co Ltd v Bank of Jamaica*.[99] *Scottish Equitable v Derby* represents the scenario where it is asked whether a general hardship can found the change of position defence in enrichment claims. The answer is clearly 'no'. What is required to found the change of position defence is a causal link between the original enrichment and the change of position (loss of enrichment).

New Zealand's *Waitaki*[100] is an example of an attempt by a legal system to try to balance the role of fault within the law of unjustified enrichment. It introduces the notion of comparative fault, but most academics and decisions in other common-law jurisdictions have rejected the *Waitaki* approach as undesirable and theoretically unsound. Many other landmarks have already been attained, some of which are now captured in Title 18 of *English Private Law* (2013) edited by Burrows.

The elements of enrichment liability under English law were also reaffirmed recently in the case of *Benedetti v Sawiris*,[101] in considering the following four questions relevant to a claim in unjust enrichment: (1) Has the defendant been

---

[96] A Burrows *English Private Law* (Oxford University Press, 2013) is a publication comprising 15 832 pages that deals with all aspects of English private law.

[97] For a good summary of the developments after *Lipkin Gorman*, see T Krebs *Restitution at the Crossroads* (Cavendish Publishing, 2001) 271–306. The same chapter is reproduced as a chapter in another compilation book: EJH Schrage (ed) *Unjust Enrichment and the Law of Contract* (Duncker & Humbolt, 2001) 295–336. Regarding the general principle against unjust enrichment, Krebs is in favour of maintaining the English 'unjust factor' approach. The same applies to McInnes: Canadian law is uncomfortable with the 'juristic reason' approach adopted in that jurisdiction.

[98] *Philip Collins Ltd v Davis* [2000] 3 All ER 808.

[99] (2002) 1 All ER (comm) 192.

[100] (1999) 2 NZLR 211, especially at 229.

[101] [2013] UKSC 50.

enriched? (2) Was the enrichment at the claimant's expense? (3) Was such enrichment unjust? (4) Are any defences available to the defendant? These questions in *Benedetti v Sawiris* and *Countryside Communications Ltd v ICL Pathway Ltd*,[102] *MSM Consulting Ltd v United Republic of Tanzania*,[103] and *Dowman Imports Ltd v 2 Toobz Ltd*,[104] were decided in the context of failed pre-services contracts. That is to say, 'services having been provided in anticipation of a contractual agreement which did not materialize', a situation similar to the civil law of *conductio ob causam finitam*.[105]

In this situation, in English law, the principles that apply are these: the court is likely to impose an obligation in unjust enrichment where the defendant has received an incontrovertible benefit (eg, an immediate financial gain or saving of expense) as a result of the claimant's services; or where the defendant has requested the claimant to provide services or accepted them (having had the ability to refuse them) when offered, in the knowledge that the services were not intended to be given freely.[106]

10.4.4 Concluding remarks

It is undeniable that if one looks comparatively at the history of the law of unjust or unjustified enrichment in the common law and civil law, some clear differences are noticeable. In spite of those developmental differences and some persistent voices to the contrary, particularly in English and Australian law,[107] there is now a

[102] [2000] CLC 324.

[103] [2009] EWHC 121 (QB).

[104] [2020] EWHC 291 (Comm).

[105] For other references in English law on this category of enrichment, see also ch 16 of Goff and Jones (2016) on *Unjust Enrichment* (9 ed) on this established category of unjust enrichment claim.

[106] *Dowman Imports Ltd v 2 Toobz Ltd* [2020] EWHC 291 (Comm) at para [33].

[107] As pointed out elsewhere above, not everyone in the common-law world agrees with the need for a general principle against unjustified enrichment as the foundation of the whole law of restitution. Until recently, the resistance was especially prominent in Australia, where the influence of writers such as S Stoljar, IM Jackman, R Gratham and C Rickett was heavily felt. See, for example, the approach in IM Jackman *The Varieties of Restitution* (1998). Three decades ago, Dickson ((1995) 54 *CLJ* 101, 126) equally noted that any direct comparison of the structure of unjust enrichment claims in common-law and civil-law systems is bound to be misleading because, he also thought, the principle against unjust enrichment serves different purposes in the two sets of systems.

Despite these dissonant voices, it is my view that the convergence is to a certain extent inevitable. This assertion gains greater force if one also considers, as already alluded to elsewhere in this work, that the unqualified sustainability of the 'unjust factor' approach is almost doomed. See the allusion made elsewhere in this work about the Canadian breakaway with the 'juristic reason', to which I shall return again at a later stage in this work. For fresh challenges to the 'unjust factor' approach in England, see, among others, S Worthington 'The new Birksian

growing consensus of a common ground. This common ground both legal families recognise, regardless of whether it is directly or indirectly acknowledged, that *iure naturae aequum est neminem cum alterius detrimento et iniuria fieri locupletiorem*[108] is the general foundation of unjust or unjustified enrichment claims.[109] It is acknowledged that this 'principle' is akin to representing an ideal rather than the exclusive and the most practical rule of law; and, if mechanically adopted, it may carry a legal system too far afield. This is because, by its terms, it gives an appearance of requiring a review of every transaction against an arithmetical standard, as it has the misleading semblance of mathematical simplicity. In any event, the sense of justice supports the conclusion drawn from simple arithmetic that a loss translated into another's gain is much more impressive than the loss would be alone.[110] English law has now concluded that 'unjust enrichment is a discrete source of rights and obligations and that the difference between unjust enrichment and restitution is the difference between event and response'.[111]

The essential differences between the two legal families are that the civil law of unjustified enrichment is based on a 'negative approach', whereas most of the common-law systems (especially that of England) are based on the 'positive approach'. That is to say, 'an enrichment is justified unless the claimant can point to a recognised unjust factor that would require to undo the enrichment' of the defendant. The negative approach, on the other hand, provides that an enrichment is unjustified and should be reversed if it is not supported by a legal ground.

---

approach to unjust enrichment' (2004) 12 *Restitution Law Review* 267 and Birks (2005). But now Barker and Grantham have essentially changed their minds, as evidenced in their new book, *Law of Unjust Enrichment in Australia* (LexisNexis Butherworths, 2018).

108 Pomponius D 50.17.206 or D 12.6.14 '*Jure naturae aequum est neminem cum alterius detrimento fieri locupletiorem*'.

109 See, eg, the development in French Law of the action described by Molinaeus as '*actio in factum ex aequitate*', which Pothier in *Appendice sur la gestion d'affaires* (Appendice to his *Treatise on the Contract of Mandate*) 191ff comments upon and refers to such *gestion d'affaires* by saying: '*dans notre jurisprudence française, … qui regarde la seule équité comme suffisante pour produire une obligation civile e pour donner une action, il ne doit pas être douté (douteux) que … celui qui a fait des impenses dont je profite doit avoir action contre moi, jusqu'à concurrence de ce que j'en profite.*'

For a similar approach in German law on the early use of the *actio de in rem verso* see the provisions in § 230 of the Prussian Code '*Allgemeines Landrecht*' of 1794 and § 233 on *negotiorum gestio*, which are said to have been used nearly interchangeably, and their application which virtually became a general enrichment action. See, generally, DL De Campos *A Subsidiariedade da Obrigação de Restituir o Enriquecimento* (Lisbon, 2003) 55–108; Van Zyl (1992a, note 21) 120n36. See equally B Nicholas 'Unjustified enrichment in the civil law and Louisiana law, Part I' (1962) 36 *Tulane Law Review* 605, 618–623.

110 J Dawson *Unjust Enrichment* (Little Brown & Company, 1951 [1999]) 7–8.

111 Mitchell (note 53) 18.1–18.3.

10.5 UNJUSTIFIED ENRICHMENT IN SELECTED SOUTH AMERICAN JURISDICTIONS (ARGENTINA AND BRAZIL)

10.5.1 Preliminary remarks

Unjustified enrichment in most South American countries is remotely based on the Roman law as mostly captured under the Napoleonic Code. But because some of the codifications occurred after the German BGB, most of these countries did not mechanically reproduce all the principles of the Napoleonic Code but re-examined them in the light of the much later German codifications and in the light of their own experiences.

For some countries, the Indicial Civil Codes of the late 1800s or the early 1900s have now been replaced with new enactments starting in the late 1990s and continuing until the early 2000s. This part deals only with two countries, Argentina and Brazil, and owing to space constraints, Argentinean law is presented in outline only and that of Brazil is discussed in more detail. Where it is necessary, though, cross-reference is made to the Argentinean law. These two codes are different, but the structure they follow on enrichment claims is slightly similar.

10.5.2 Unjustified enrichment in Argentina

The current law of unjustified enrichment in Argentina is found in the Argentinean Civil Code called the 'Código Civil y Commercial de la Nación' (National Civil and Commercial Code (CCCN)) of 2014 in Title 5, Chapter 4 of the CCCN. Title 5 is entitled 'Outras Fuentes de Obligaciones' (Other Sources of Obligations). The CCCN was approved by Law (Ley 26.994 de Congresso de la Nacion Argentina on 1 October 2014). Specifically, Title 5, Chapter 4 of the CCCN deals with 'enriquecimiento sin causa' (enrichment without cause). Article 1794 of the CCCN provides as follows:

> Any person that without a licit cause is enriched at another's expense is obliged, to the extent of his enrichment, to compensate (repay) the patrimonial detriment of the impoverished. If the enrichment consists in incorporation in his estate of a determined good, he must reverse it if it persists in his power at the time of the demand.

However, Art 1795 provides that the action is not applicable if the law allows the claimant another action to redress the impoverishment suffered. In essence, Art 1795 provides for the subsidiarity of the enrichment action.

The 'enrichment without cause' is recognised under Argentinean law as a classic figure of civil law, the purpose of which is to protect a person that has become impoverished in favour of another without legal justification.

Articles 1796–1799 of the CCCN (which is s 2 of Chapter 4) deal with 'undue payment', but they do so separately from Arts 1794–1795 (s 1 of Chapter 4), which to a certain extent indicates that the proposition in Art 1794 is not an all-encompassing provision as it would be under the German BGB.[112] This structure is akin to that in the French Code civil.[113]

These provisions in Arts 1794–1795 were not always in the Argentinean law, as the previous Civil Code, titled 'Código Civil Velezano de la Nación Argentina', did not have a specific provision of enrichment liability, but it was scattered in different articles such as Arts 499, 728, 748, 1000, 1165. However, recommendations that emanated from several law reform commissions and in the IV Congress of Civil Law,[114] in September 1969 had indicated the need to include in the Argentinean Civil Code a specific rule on unjustified enrichment similar to that in the German Civil Code or the Ante-Projects of Babylon, or similar to the Reform Projects of 1934 and the Reform Ante-Project of 1954.

This task was undertaken in the Ante-Projects of 1987 (in which Arts 2309 and 1310 did make basic reference to a general principle on enrichment liability). The reform of 1993 continued in the same footsteps of previous Ante-Projects, the 1998 Project of Civil Code, and it articulated in Arts 1723 and 1724 the basics of the current provision in the CCCN. In essence, the current Arts 1794–1795 developed from the *actio de in rem verso* because under the previous dispensation cases that did not fit the *condictio indebiti*, but also where the contract was not of help to decide those cases, were resolved under this heading.

But, interestingly, the Argentinean law of enrichment was until recently still classified alongside other institutes as a law of quasi-contracts. For a long time, though, several Argentinean academics decried the need to abandon the classification of quasi-contracts, which had been inherited from the old forms of action. In fact, even one of the most ardent defenders of the quasi-contract system, Marcelo López Mesa, acknowledged in his own writings that several Argentinean academics had for long advocated that 'the latest civilian orientations tend to abandon the category of quasi-contract, the persistence of which is due to a mere historical coincidence, which endured through codifications'.[115]

Despite these warnings, the idea of quasi-contract survived until the eve of the New CCCN. This system is articulated in 101 articles in the new Civil Code from Arts 1781 to 1881. Fortunately, the New Code adopts the terminology 'Other

[112] The rule in § 812 BGB (Bürgerliches Gesetzbuch), German Civil Code.

[113] French Civil Code, Art 1376.

[114] Proceedings of the Fourth National Congress of Civil Law, held in Córdoba, 22–27 September 1969, (Córdoba, 1971) T I, 70–71.

[115] LM Marcelo 'El cuasicontrato y el enriquecimiento sin causa en el nuevo Código Civil y Comercial Argentino' (2009) 13 *Anuario da Facultade de Dereito da Universidade da Coruña* 393–398.

sources of Obligations' instead of quasi-contracts. It is generally acknowledged in the Argentinean jurisprudence that enrichment liability in general, and enrichment without cause (in particular), is a classic figure of civil law. Both have the purpose of providing protection to that person who has become impoverished in favour of another without legal justification.[116] Despite abandoning the appellation of 'quasi-contracts', the general structure that was presented under the 'quasi-contract' in the Ante-Projects is generally predetermined. The scheme that the new Argentinean CCCN adopts is as follows:

Articles 1781 to 1790 '*Negotiorum gestio*'
Articles 1791 to 1793 'Useful employment'
Articles 1794 to 1795 'Enrichment without cause'
Articles 1796 to 1799 'Undue payment'
Articles 1800 to 1881 'Unilateral declaration of the will'.

And within this last category of the abandoned quasi-contracts, the new code regulates the following:

Articles 1800 to 1802 General provisions on the unilateral declaration of the will
Articles 1803 to 1806 Public promise of reward
Articles 1807 to 1809 Public competition
Articles 1810 to 1814 Unilateral guarantees
Articles 1815 to 1881 Securities.

Given some similarities of the Argentinean Code (CCCN) in the two elements 'enrichment without cause' (Arts 1794–1795) to the Brazilian Code Arts 884–885 and similarities of the Argentinean Code (CCCN, Arts 1796–1799) on undue payment to the Brazilian Code arts 876–883 (undue payment), this chapter will not describe in detail in the Argentinean Code provisions on 'undue payment' and 'enrichment *sine causa*'. Nevertheless, what is discussed under the Brazilian Code on these issues also applies implicitly to the Argentinean Code, except where there are marked differences.

The other articles listed above as being part of the general category in the scheme (Arts 1781–1793) negotiorum gestio and 'useful employment' (Arts 1800–1881) are not in the strictest sense part of the enrichment liability, although they may

[116] Example: *Amoroso Copello, Alfonso G v Telefonica de Argentina SA*, LL 2000-A, 572 (42.347) (Trelew Appeals Court).

have some aspects that may fall under enrichment liability. Therefore, those articles are not discussed in this chapter.

Article 1794 of the Argentinean Civil Code states the following: '*Toda persona que sin una causa lícita se enriquezca a expense's de otro, eats obligada, en la medida de su beneficio, a resarcir el detrimento patrimonial a favor del empobrecido*'. (Any person who, without a lawful cause, enriches himself at the expense of another, is obliged, to the extent of his benefit, to compensate the patrimonial detriment of the impoverished person.)

Article 1794 is followed by the qualification, 'if the enrichment consists of the incorporation of a specific asset into the patrimony of the recipient, he must restore it if it remains in his possession at the time of the claim.' On undue payment, the four Arts 1796–1799[117] are quite brief. Article 1796 provides as follows:

> *Pago indebido* (Undue payment)
> Cases in which payment is repayable, if:
>
> **ARTICLE 1796**
>
> a) The reason for the payment does not exist, or does not subsist, because there is no valid obligation; that reason for payment ceased to exist; or the payment was carried out in consideration of a future cause, which did not materialize.

[117] The original text in Spanish is as follows: SECCION 2a Pago indebido (undue payment). ARTICULO 1796. – Casos. El pago es repetible, si:

ARTICULO 1796

a) *la causa de deber no existe, o no subsiste, porque no hay obligación válida; esa causa deja de existir; o es realizado en consideración a una causa futura, que no se va a producir;*

b) *paga quien no está obligado, o no lo está en los alcances en que paga, a menos que lo haga como tercero;*

c) *recibe el pago quien no es acreedor, a menos que se entregue como liberalidad;*

d) *la causa del pago es ilícita o inmoral;*

e) *el pago es obtenido por medios ilícitos.*

ARTICULO 1797 – *Irrelevancia del error. La repetición del pago no está sujeta a que haya sido hecho con error.*

ARTICULO 1798 – *Alcances de la repetición. La repetición obliga a restituir lo recibido, conforme a las reglas de las obligaciones de dar para restituir.*

ARTICULO 1799 – *Situaciones especiales. En particular:*

a) *la restitución a cargo de una persona incapaz o con capacidad restringida no puede exceder el provecho que haya obtenido;*

b) *en el caso del inciso b) del artículo 1796, la restitución no procede si el acreedor, de buena fe, se priva de su título, o renuncia a las garantías; quien realiza el pago tiene subrogación legal en los derechos de aquél;*

c) *en el caso del inciso d) del artículo 1796, la parte que no actúa con torpeza tiene derecho a la restitución; si ambas partes actúan torpemente, el crédito tiene el mismo destino que las herencias vacantes.*

b) The person who does not have an obligation, has paid, or if he paid, he is not within the scope in which he pays, unless he did so as a third party.
c) The non-creditor receives the payment unless it is delivered as a gift.
d) The ground of the payment is illegal or immoral.
e) The payment is obtained by illegal means.

ARTICLE 1797 - Irrelevance of the error. The repetition of the payment is not subject to it being made in error.
ARTICLE 1798 - Scope of repetition. Repetition obliges the receiver to restore what was received, in accordance with the rules of the obligations to give to restore.
ARTICLE 1799 - Special situations. In particular:
a) the restitution by an incapable person or with restricted capacity cannot exceed the benefit that he/she has obtained;
b) in the case of subsection b) of article 1796, restitution does not proceed if the creditor, in good faith, deprives himself of his title, or renounces the guarantees; whoever makes the payment has legal subrogation in the rights of the former;
c) in the case of subsection d) of article 1796, the party who does not act clumsily has the right to restitution; and
d) if both parties act awkwardly, the credit has the same fate as the vacant inheritances.

10.5.3 Brazilian enrichment law

10.5.3.1 General observations

Brazilian enrichment law in general is codified and it is contained in Arts 876–885 of the relatively recent new Civil Code[118] of 2004. This enrichment law in general is captured under the umbrella title of '*atos unilaterais*'[119] (unilateral acts) in the new Civil Code 2004. The general description is differently formulated from that of the old 1916 Civil Code. The old Civil Code treated the same subject-matter under the heading of 'obligations arising from unilateral declarations of the will'.[120] The old description was influenced by the then predominant notion of quasi-contract inspired by the French codification. The nuanced use of the expression '*declaração*

[118] The new Civil Code was enacted in 2002, but came into effect in 2004. Therefore, I have used 2004 as the date of the code. The 2004 Civil Code replaced the 1916 Code, popularly known as the Bevilaqua Code.
[119] 'Unilateral acts'; for the appropriateness or otherwise of the choice for the heading 'unilateral acts', see C Michelon *Direito Restitutório* (Revista dos Tribunais, 2007).
[120] '*Obrigações por declaração unilateral da vontade*'.

unilateral da vontade' subtly reveals some contractual similarities that were mostly described as '*obrigações por declaração bilateral da vontade*' (obligations arising from bilateral declaration of the will).

However, despite the vital change, the central idea still remains the same: every legal aspect that is captured under enrichment liability or institutes akin to it is treated as though it emanates from a unilateral act. Therefore, the new Civil Code collects under the new heading four different categories of 'unilateral act': the promise of recompense,[121] *negotiorum gestio*,[122] undue payment and enrichment *sine causa*. The choice of the heading 'unilateral act' is also a clear manifestation of the Legislature's desire to differentiate these subjects from matters arising from contracts, because, under the general principles of contract, the manifestation of the free will of two or more parties immediately comes into play in assuming the obligation that is capable of triggering a legal response.

What motivated the Legislature to assemble undue payment, enrichment *sine causa* and the like under the heading of 'unilateral acts' is the fact that, prima facie, the obligation deriving from all of them is imposed by law and it does not depend upon the will of any of the parties. Therefore, for example, under promise of recompense,[123] the law imposes on the promissor the obligation to fulfil the promise, according to Art 854 of the new Civil Code.[124] Although the

[121] Several academics are unhappy that the drafters have brought 'promise of recompense' under this title. Others also criticise the reason for bringing in *negotiorum gestio* here. This was, for example, the view held by Caio Mario da Silva, author of the 1964 'Ante-Project of the Code of Obligations' (*O Anteprojeto do Código das Obrigações*), who tried again to include the institute of *negotiorum gestio* between the contracts. However, the Revising Committee altered that orientation and adopted that which appeared more preferable under a modern understanding of the institute. In effect, the project of the Code of Obligations assigned an autonomous title to *negotiorum gestio*, treating it as a source of obligations (Art 841ss). I think the former view has more substance than the latter, as almost every legal system recognises that enrichment liability often arises also from managing another's affairs, though without a mandate.

[122] Although the promise of recompense and *negotiorum gestio* appear under the umbrella term 'unilateral acts', they are not dealt with in this chapter as the actual enrichment liability starts with the sub-units on undue payment and enrichment *sine causa*.

[123] The concept of promise of recompense is described as the act of someone who, by public announcement directed to an indeterminate person, undertakes to gratify whoever fulfils a certain condition or performs a certain service. In these circumstances, it is obvious that the promissor undertook of his own free will the obligation and as soon as someone from the general public or the class to which the announcement is directed fulfils that condition or undertakes the service, the law will impose upon the promissor the obligation to fulfil the undertaking.

[124] The choice of the scheme also manifests another vision that permeates the whole new Civil Code, somewhat contrasted with the previous code, ie, under the new Civil Code the law is expected to fulfil a social function and the interests of society at large. The treatment of promise of recompense has its intricacies and complexities. Among the issues that may raise complex analysis are the revocability of the promise and its relationship with the binding aspect

treatment of recompense can reveal some minuscule features of an enrichment liability, enrichment law proper commences with the *negotiorum gestio* and grows progressively in importance until it is stated in a general principle.

10.5.3.2 A tripartite division and its underlying ideas

Despite the treatment of a promise of recompense under the same 'title', enrichment law proper under the new Civil Code starts with the treatment of the notion of *negotiorum gestio*[125] (which has a minuscule aspect of enrichment liability) and grows progressively from there until it is stated in a general principle of enrichment *sine causa*,[126] after consideration of its 'undue payment' aspect. This trio not only shares various elements in common but each one of them also has its own peculiarities. The same trio also appears in the Argentinean Code mentioned above.

(a) Negotiorum gestio (Articles 861–875)

Because *negotiorum gestio* manifests features of enrichment liability only when it presents itself in some instances akin to the forms of the old Roman *actio negotiorum gestiorum contraria*[127] (when it is the claim of the *gestor* against the *dominus*) and occasionally in instances of the old form of the *actio negotiorum gestorium directa* (the claim of the *dominus* against the *gestor*), it is mentioned only briefly here.

Negotiorum gestio is normally understood as the voluntary administration of another's affairs without a mandate,[128] which provides the reason for placing it among the unilateral acts.[129] In contrast, undue payment, which is discussed

that was alluded to earlier; the possibility of the act or the service required being realised by more than one person, or where the promise of recompense assumes the character of public tender in which various bidders will compete, for example, for the price, and in this way the *negotium* assumes an aleatory nature with the possibility of both (two people) winning and thereby having the prize conferred on them or being defeated and as a result suffering losses.

[125] For a relatively recent exposition of *negotiorum gestio* in Brazilian law see Michelon (note 119) 38–126, who devotes half of this book to this notion.

[126] Whereas *negotiorum gestio* is dealt with from Arts 861 to 875, 'undue payment' is dealt with from Arts 876 to 883 and 'enrichment *sine causa*' from Arts 884 to 886. Argentina reverses the order: it deals first with enrichment *sine causa* and after that with undue payment.

[127] See Michelon (note 119) 58–59. For the treatment and conception of *negotiorum gestio* in the common law and its current nuances and also in old Roman law and the development in the European *ius commune*, see the discussion in this thesis in chapter 1 above.

[128] For the treatment of mandate under Brazilian law see, among others, S Rodrigues '*Do mandato tácito*' (2005) 191 *Revista dos Tribunais* 579.

[129] Michelon (note 119) 30 considers that these three institutions were brought together under the title 'unilateral acts' because the new Civil Code adopted as its foundation of 'restitutionary law' the principle of 'static conservation of patrimonies' and not because the institutions manifest the common feature of 'unjustified enrichment' should the law not intervene. Admittedly,

immediately below, is often said to be nothing more than a species of the general notion of enrichment *sine causa*. Because by administering another's affairs without a mandate a party doing so will have conferred a benefit on the 'owner' which they did not request, or did not agree to have (but the owner might nevertheless have had their assets enhanced with such benefit or they might have been prevented from depletion), an unjustified enrichment claim could theoretically be made if the party refuses to compensate the *gestor*.

The approximation of *negotiorum gestio* to an enrichment claim was already evident under the old Brazilian Civil Code, because under the old provisions whoever administered another's business was under a duty to restore to the owner of that business everything they had acquired in such administration, regardless of what the cause was – subject, however, to the need to prove that were the owner in the same position as the *gestor*, the outcome of that administration would have been the same, that is to say, they would either have made the same profits or the same loss, as the case might have been. The foundation of *negotiorum gestio* in the old Code and the new Code remains the same, the two varying only in nuances.[130]

(b) Undue payment (Articles 876–883)

Undue payment is the subject-matter dealt with under Arts 876–883 of the new Civil Code. These provisions have remained virtually unchanged,[131] compared to what was already in the 1916 Code. The discussion in this chapter does not deal separately with each provision but briefly runs through the underlying principles, issues and structure of the institute. Obviously, not all Brazilian writers agree on the specific characterisation of this institute, whether it is self-standing or a species of general enrichment *sine causa*. For example, Sílvio Rodrigues[132] succinctly characterises the notion of undue payment in his treatment of the Brazilian law of enrichment under the new code as a species of the general enrichment *sine causa*. He says that from

---

though, he acknowledges that many other Brazilian writers think that that is indeed the case because all such institutions manifest features of enrichment *sine causa*. He also denies that Arts 884–886 of the new Civil Code have their foundations in principles of 'equity' and 'justice', not because of its falsehood but because, he says, 'equity, morality and justice have little explicative value' (31–33). But, again, in fact many Brazilian textbooks and case law (jurisprudence) assert that the general principle of enrichment *sine causa* is indeed based on equitable foundations as the provisions just cited are nothing but the manifestation of the Roman *actio de in rem verso* even if they have been now elevated to a higher principle of generalisation and systematisation.

[130] For a detailed discussion of the issue see Michelon (note 119) 39–129.

[131] The few changes made are the explicit inclusion of the obligations to fulfil within the scope of the institute (Art 881) and the possibility under Art 883 of payments effected to attain unlawful, immoral or prohibited aims to revert to charities.

[132] S Rodrigues *Dos Contratos e Atos Unilaterais* (Saraiva, 2003) 409–410.

a teleological perspective undue payment is just a chapter of the wider concept of enrichment *sine causa*.[133] As a species of the wider notion,[134] it shares not only its main features and manifestations, but presumably also the mechanisms of resisting such claims. In his brief treatment of the historical development '*do pagamento indevido*' (undue payment) from the Roman *condictiones*, he acknowledges that the *condictiones sine causa*[135] – as he generically calls all the *condictiones* – arose as a reaction to a system of abstract acts, because they were intended as a corrective means imposed by equity in order to avoid an act producing consequences different either from the parties' will or from the law, or else different from good morals.[136]

After describing the *condictiones* one by one, the Rodrigues finally remarks that

> in all other cases in which no specific *condictio* could be found, but equity imposed the restitution of the undue payment, it was certainly possible to have recourse to the generic idea of *condictio sine causa* to demand restitution.

It is therefore obvious from this analysis that Rodrigues, like many other Brazilian writers, recognises that the foundations of enrichment law lie firmly in equitable principles.[137]

---

133 *'O pagamento indevido constitui no plano teleológico, apenas, um capítulo de assunto mais amplo, que é o enriquecimento sem causa. Este repersenta o gênero do qual aquele não passa de espécie'.*

134 See, however, Michelon (note 119) 128–129, discussed below.

135 I believe that the author described the Roman *condictiones* in this way for brevity's sake, as there is a detailed analysis of the Roman *condictiones* one by one in the Brazilian legal literature undertaken mostly by Pontes de Miranda in (1959) 26 *Tratado de Direito Privado, Parte Especial* 131–155, though it would appear that the orientation of the discussion is essentially based on German legal literature.

136 S Rodrigues *Direito Civil – Volume 1* (Saraiva, 2003) 410–411.

137 JM Carvalho-Santos expressed the same idea in the following terms: *'A equidade a nosso ver, é o fundamento do não lucupletamento à custa de outrem'* (We are of the view that equity is the foundation of the idea that no one shall be enriched at another's expense' (*Código Civil Brasileiro Interpretado: Direito das Obrigações, XII* 13 e (1988) 382–383; CL Gonçalves *Tratado de Direio Civil 4* (1957) 607 also supported the same view when he says that there is no precise theory to justify an enrichment action other than the classic principles of justice and law *suum quique tribuere, neminem laedere* (dar a cada um o seu, e não lesar ninguém), because these principles do not reflect anything else other than rules of equity. Leonardo indirectly arrives at the same conclusion in his discussion of causality in the 'transmission of goods' in the Brazilian law as he remarks that 'given that the *negotium jurídico* on disposition of goods is directly related to the diminution of the active patrimony of the transferor in order to increase the assets of the receiver, causality must be seen as the rule and not the exception, mainly because the [Civil] Code in operation, explicitly and generally proscribes the enrichment *sine causa* according to article 884' (RX Leonardo *'Cessão de créditos: Reflexões sobre causalidade na transmissão de bens no direito Brasileiro'* (2005) 42 *Revista da Faculdade de Direito da UFPR* 133, 150). This analysis

The idea of equity emerges in the diverse formulations adopted to describe the various instances in which a reversal of enrichment is required. Michelon,[138] another prominent Brazilian author in this field, however, disagrees with the above position, stating that undue payment cannot be seen under the current Brazilian law as simply being a species of the wider notion of unjust enrichment. Michelon attempts to offer several explanations, among which are the difference in the prescription regime under undue payment and those under enrichment *sine causa*, and also the difference in the way each 'institute' determines the consequences of the action.

In summary, he says that the relation is not that of *genus* and species but that of a general rule and an exception to it. Unfortunately, he does not cite other Brazilian writers who support such a view on this point. Therefore, it cannot firmly be said that such position is the entrenched Brazilian view of the law. Be that as it may, the distinction between 'undue payment' and 'unjustified enrichment' (denominated enrichment *sine causa* in the current Brazilian Civil Code) is once again a certain manifestation of the 'Pothier School' to which references were made earlier – although, admittedly, more attenuated than the difference regarding the measure of enrichment. In the same way that there is no unanimity about the measure of enrichment, so there is also no unanimity about the relationship between 'undue payment' and enrichment *sine causa* in some other legal systems.

Adopting Pothier's presentation, the French Civil Code (for example) and those codes that in one way or another originally modelled their enrichment law on the French configuration, deal with the '*paiement de l'indu*' (*condictio indebiti*) quite extensively and tend to view it as 'completely separate' from the other forms of enrichment (see, eg, the Argentinean position described above).

Another example is the Dutch Civil Code (Nederlands Burgelijk Wetboek (BW)). The BW devotes nine sections to 'undue payment' (*onverschuldigde betaling*)[139]

---

reveals that, throughout its structure, the Code emphasises the notion of justice and equity and whenever justice would not be served, such as in circumstances that would enrich one person at the expense of another without a justification the law must offer redress.

[138] Rodrigues (note 136) 128–129.

[139] Sections 6:203–211 BW. These provisions are generally considered as '*betaling*' (payment) but their scope differs significantly from the one encountered in the old Dutch Code, which corresponded with the concept in the French Code civil. Therefore, under the new Dutch Code, the concept of 'payment' is wider: it includes a payment of money *strictu sensu* in addition to other forms of benefits such as, for example, transporting a stowaway or dredging a harbour, where restitution in kind is impossible. See MW Scheltma 'Restitution and mistaken payments' in Schrage (2001) 90.

In contrast, in French law, a benefit will be regarded as a 'payment' only when something – a property or a sum of money – is given that can be restored in kind (see, eg, M Billiau, J Ghestin & G Loiseau 'Répetition de l'indu' in *Encyclopédie Dalloz, Répertoire de Droit Civil IV* (Dalloz, 2020) 4.

(Art 6:203–211 BW) before it deals with other cases of 'unjustified enrichment'.[140] The Québec Code civil,[141] also follows similar lines (CCQ Arts 1491–1492 – undue payment) and (CCQ Arts 1493–1406 – unjustified enrichment). However, the current language of Arts 876–883 in the Brazilian Civil Code seems to have adopted a wider view of *paiement de l'indu*, while maintaining the dichotomy 'undue payment' and 'enrichment *sine causa*' because the legislative intention was to depart from the restrictive position embodied in the 1916 Code.

Whereas Art 876 of the new Brazilian Civil Code imposes upon the receiver (*accipiens*) the duty to restore what they have unduly acquired from the payer (*solvens*), the right of the *solvens* under this article is not to be construed as an unlimited one. This is because Art 877 immediately adds a caveat that 'whoever has voluntarily paid what was not due, is under the obligation to prove that he has done so by mistake'.[142] The language of Art 877 suggests that there may be two kinds of problem in this area of the law.

First, there is the issue of an undue payment that has been performed involuntarily and, second, the need to prove an error in the case where the performance was voluntary. Where the payment or performance was rendered involuntarily, few problems turn upon the issue, although the distinction must be drawn between an involuntary performance due to coercion and one devoid of it, or where sometimes the degree of coercion does not necessarily vitiate the performer's will. In spite of some divergences in the classification of the degree of coercion that will totally impair a free will, it is nonetheless safe to say that the degree of coercion does not necessarily vitiate the performer's will if such a coercion is what is usually termed as relative or compulsive (or still moral coercion), because such coercion reduces the freedom of the 'actor' (*o coagido*) but does not eliminate it altogether. For this reason, the adage *coatas voluntas, semper voluntas* is used in these circumstances.[143]

Consequently, a benefit such as a stowaway or dredging a harbour would not qualify as 'payment' under French law (ie, not claimable under *répetition de l'indu*). In such a case, it is possible to claim the benefit only under the action *de l'enrichissement sans cause* as recognised in *Boudier*. In essence, if one looks at Brazilian law (see C Michelon 'Native sources and comparative resources: Unjustified enrichment in Brazil after the 2002 Civil Code' 2014 *Restitution Law Review* 59–80), the position advocated is the same as that still prevailing in France. If that is the case, then the change operated under the new Civil Code is cosmetic.

[140] Section 6:212 BW – this is the 'unjust enrichment' clause in Dutch law.

[141] Code Civil de Québec (Québec Code civil).

[142] Art 877 – '*Aquele que voluntariamente pagou o indevido incumbe a prova de tê-lo feito por erro*'.

[143] Where there is a mere threat to use the course of the law in order to exact a performance from an existing right, such a threat does not qualify as coercion that renders a performance null and void. See Art 100 of the 1916 Code. This article in the Brazilian Civil Code also influenced the revision of the approach in the Portuguese law that now provides under Art 255(3) of its code

But where coercion is absolute or ablative, the performer is reduced to a mere automaton and any resulting act performed by them is legally considered as being null and void, that is, non-existent, or, more technically, it is an act *sine causa*. However, where the performance occurred voluntarily and free from any sort of coercion, it is the duty of the performer to prove that they did so by mistake.

(i) Undue payment and mistake: nature and assessment of error

As in many other jurisdictions, the notion of mistake has received some extensive coverage under the Brazilian law of enrichment. (The Argentinean law mentioned above has discarded the error requirement entirely under claims in undue payment.) The previous debate[144] about error of fact and error of law has been overcome and both are now admissible under Art 139(3) of the new Brazilian Civil Code. It is generally acknowledged that an error produces in the performer a false conception of the reality and invoking it does not frustrate the applicability of the law as long as such an error, if one of law, is substantial and it is the sole or the principal motive for the performance – be it a payment or any other juridical *negotium* – to have occurred.

Some nuanced difficulties still exist whether in the assessment of a mistake of law consideration should be given to the notion of excusability as it is done in the assessment of an error of fact (the excusability of error is also mentioned in the Namibian law discussed above, although it is a moot point there). It is sometimes

for the theory invoked by M Andrade that *'não consititui coação a ameaça do exercício normal de um direito'* [the threat of a normal exercise of a right does not constitute coercion]. See, generally, M Andrade *'Não se Considera Coação a Ameaça do Exercício Normal de um Direito'* (Mostrar Data De Publicaca, 2018); CA Mota-Pinto *Teoria Geral do Direito Civil* 3 ed (Coimbra, 1986); CR Gonçalves *Direito Civil Esquematizado, – Parte Geral: Contractos Em Especie – Direito das Coisas* (Editora Saraiva, 2016).

[144] The debate persisted throughout the project and up to the eve of the approval of the new Code. It was epitomised by the position defended by Professor Couto e Silva against that of José Carlos Moreira Alves, among others. (It should be remembered that Professor Couto e Silva was one of the collaborators in the drafting committee, as evidenced by the speech of Miguel Reale presenting the new code.)

In summary, while Couto e Silva objected to the position adopted by the project holding that the error of law would ultimately be confused with error over legal effects, the position of Moreira Alves, which finally triumphed, is inspired by the Italian Code (Art 1429(4) and others). It holds that the error of law must be substantial and that that will be the case 'if such error was the only motive or the principal reason for the transaction (or the *negotium*) and it does not result in the negation of the application of the law'. For details on these issues, see JCM Alves *A Parte Geral do Projecto Código Civil Brasileiro (The General Part of the Brazilian Civil Code Project)* (Saraiva, 1986) 45–55; PG Gonet-Branco *'Em torno dos vícios do negócio jurídico – a propósito do erro de fato e do erro de direito'* in D Fraciulli Netto et al (eds) *O Novo Código Civil: Estudos em Homenagem ao Professor Miguel Reale* (LTr, 2003) 129–146.

argued that such a requirement strengthens the applicability of the law, since the complainant alleging to have been mistaken is required to show that they applied all possible due diligence.[145] There is also the suggestion that the onus of proof in the assessment of such diligence should be more rigorous when an error invoked is that of law compared to the standard required when the error is one of fact, because of the importance of the laws.[146]

In addition to the above, there are some nuanced vestiges of a penal nature in some unjustified enrichment provisions in special laws. That is the case, for example, in the Consumer Code enacted under Lei 8.078 of 11 September 1990, which provides under the caveat to Art 42 (*parágrafo único*) that

> a consumer billed for an undue quantity has a right to restitution of that which was not due, in an amount equal to double of that which he paid in excess, increased by a monetary correction (adjustment) and legal interest, save in the case of a hypothesis of a justifiable mistake.[147]

The notion of the plaintiff's duty to prove that they have acted under mistake is in line with the main proposition that where the performer has transferred the assets or paid voluntarily and conscientiously, their act is to be understood as a free act with the concomitant consequences attaching to it. However, where such act is incapable of being classified as a free act, it may still reflect the so-called notion of an innocent simulation,[148] that encapsulates and hides within it a donative intent approach.[149] That being the case, the law comes to the help of whoever has paid

[145] S De Salvo-Venosa *Direito Civil: Part Geral, Obrigações e Responsabilidade Civil, Vol 2*, 17 ed (Altas, 2017) 428–436.

[146] Ibid.

[147] Artigo 42 – *da cobrança de dívidas. Na combrança de débitos, o consumidor inadimplente não será exposto a ridículo, nem será submetido a qualquer tipo de constrangimento ou ameaça. Parágrafo único – 'O consumidor cobrado em quantia indevida tem direito à repetição do indébito, por valor igual ao dobro do que pagou em excesso, acrescido de correcção monetária e juros legais, salvo hipótese de engano justificável'* (Emphasis added).

[148] See, eg, A Jorge *Ensaio Sobre o Enriquecimento Sem Causa* (Rede Virtual de Bibliotecas, 1891); Rodrigues (note 136) 413.

[149] Simulation as a legal concept is understood as the practice of an act or a *negotium* that hides the real intention. It occurs when the parties do not 'want' the *negotium* that they show to everyone; they want to produce only an external appearance, a semblance of truth, an illusion of the existence of the affairs to third parties. But in truth there is an opposition between the declared and the intended affairs.

There are different categories and classifications of simulations: innocent and malicious simulation, and relative and absolute simulation, depending on from which perspective the situation is accessed. If simulation is viewed from the perspective of good faith and bad faith, then the important categories are innocent simulation and malicious simulation. In the case of innocent

by mistake, avoiding in this way and for equitable considerations that they be unjustifiably impoverished.

In order to benefit from the protection of the law, the victim of the mistake is obliged to prove the error. In other words, where a performer alleges that they have voluntarily performed an undue obligation and that the law should come to their assistance in obliging the receiver to restore to them what was unduly performed or unduly transferred, the onus falls on them to prove that they have done so by mistake. Should they fail to do so, the courts will not come to their assistance. It is to be noted, however, that there is a reversal of onus of proof in the Consumer Code, mentioned above, which for practical and special reasons was enacted to counter a general trend in the industry.

(ii) Undue payment: enrichment and *causa* – general observations

Whereas the Brazilian law of enrichment proper is mostly premised on the notion of *causa* (but see below the drafting pitfalls on this issue), the law on undue payment does not prima facie appear strictly to require such an element, especially where an undue payment is the result of a mistake. There has, however, been some debate whether the notion of *causa* should be generalised, and in the cases concerning mistake some writers have advanced a position that the need to prove an error is an excessive demand on the performer. Some authors are of the view that the best approach should be that the performer or the *solvens* needs to show only the non-existence of the cause for the payment.[150] De Mendonça, for example, avers that whenever it is proved that what has been paid was not due, the logical inference to be drawn from that fact is that the payment was made by mistake. In such cases, therefore, once the *solvens* has proved the payment and the lack of *causa* for such payment, restitution should follow. The same line of thinking has been adopted by the DCFR (discussed above) and earlier continental writers such as Baudry-Lacantinerie[151] defended the same position.[152]

---

simulation, the 'declaration of affairs' does not harm anyone and it is therefore tolerated. And for this reason innocent simulation does not lead to the annulation or annulment of the act, because it does not cause trouble to third parties; therefore, the Brazilian legal order does not consider such simulation as a defect per se.

When the 'simulated' defect is unmasked, the *negotium* will be valid, as long as it is not contrary to law or does not harm third parties. In the case of malicious simulation, however, an intention exists to harm or cause damage by using the simulatory process (Art 162(2) of the new *Código Civil*). The effects are therefore different from innocent simulation. See, generally, S De Salvo-Venosa (note 145) 428–436.

[150] MI Carvalho e Mendonça *Doutrina e Práctica* I, 488n204.

[151] G Baudry-Lacantenerie & L Barde *Obligations* 3 ed (Tome Premier, 1906) 592.

[152] The position in Canada also seems to be heading in that direction, although still with fluctuations.

(c) Enrichment sine causa (Arts 884–886)

(i) Pathway from the old to the new Civil Code and some contentious issues

The other category of the Brazilian enrichment liability is described as enrichment *sine causa* (new Brazilian Civil Code, Arts 884–886). Technically speaking, this is the enrichment law proper and it is in this area that the new Code differs noticeably from the 1916 Code. Whereas the old Civil Code omitted a general principle of liability prohibiting an enrichment *sine causa*, the new Civil Code has stated this principle clearly.[153] The deficiencies in the earlier Brazilian enrichment law under the old Civil Code were that it was based solely on undue payment. This entailed the Civil Code objectively aligning the whole field as if it were all dependent upon a payment instead of on a more general principle. The new Civil Code partly overcomes that shortcoming: its Art 884 provides that 'whoever has been enriched at another's expense without just cause shall restore what he has unduly acquired, after updating (adjusting) the monetary values'.[154]

A caveat is, however, added to the provision (a slightly similar caveat also appears in the Argentinean Civil Code above in Art 1794):

> if the object of the enrichment claim consists in a specific thing, he who has received it is under a duty to restore it, and, if the thing does no longer subsist, its restitution shall be effected by its value at the time it was demanded.[155]

The Brazilian provision and its caveat do not provide much detail, but it seems certain that by negative inference the formulation adopted subtly envisages making a distinction between an enrichment that comes about through a fungible and one

[153] See also the Argentinean Civil Code above, CCCN Arts 1794–1795.

[154] Article 884 of the Civil Code 2002 (Título VIII – Direito das Obrigações – Dos Atos Unilaterais, Capitulo VI 'Do Enriquecimento Sem Causa'. The article reads in Portuguese: '*Aquele que, sem justa causa, se enriquecer à custa de outrem, será obrigado a restituir o indevidamente auferido, feita a atualização dos valores monetários.*' The Civil Code came into effect from 1 January 2003, although some parts are yet to enter into effect. Note, however, that, differently from Art 473 of the Portuguese Civil Code 1967 which speaks of '*sem causa justificativa*' (without a justified cause or, better, 'unjustified cause') [Full text: '*Aquele que, sem causa justificativa, enriquecer à custa de outrem, é obrigado a restituir aquilo com que injustamente se locupletou*'], the Brazilian provision speaks of '*sem justa causa*' (without a just cause). Note also the different wording of Art 2041 of the Italian Civil Code of 1942, which simply mentions 'without cause'. [Full text: 'A person who has enriched himself without cause at the expense of another shall, to the extent of the enrichment, indemnify the other for his correlative financial loss'.]

[155] For the implication of the expression 'its value at the time of the demand' see A Jorge 'Inflation in enrichment claims: Reflections on the Brazilian Civil Code' (2013) 6 *Journal of Civil Law Studies* 554–589.

that comes about through a non-fungible.[156] These notions seem to be built in and reflected in the language used. The same may be true for enrichment by services rendered, which does not seem to be recognised under any provision. Indeed, one must ask what is meant by a 'specific thing'. Is money, under such a formulation, a specific thing? Are shares specific things? Where does enrichment resulting from a performance of services fit into this caveat? Can one interpret the first part of the general enrichment action as being solely related to monetary claims because of the expression 'updating the monetary values'[157] attached to it, whereas the caveat (*parágrafo único*) is related to non-monetary claims? These questions would be the subject of another article.

This provision of Art 884 as a whole is followed by two other articles (Arts 885–886) which together form the whole new addition. However, the addition of these three new provisions to the enrichment law does not mean that under the old Civil Code one could not have recourse to provisions of the Civil Code to protect or defend one's interest if the case resembled a claim now sanctioned under the general enrichment *sine causa*. In the old Civil Code, the notion was partially covered under Art 964, which provided that 'whoever had received something not due to him, was obliged to restore it'. This provision was followed by an elucidation that 'the same obligation was incumbent upon someone who had conditionally received money before the condition was fulfilled'.

The main difference between the old and the new Civil Code is that the old version systematically treated the undue payment (*pagamento indevido*) feature of the enrichment law and accordingly a litigant could immediately and objectively refer to a clear provision in the law if aggrieved, whereas they could not do so if their claim was characterised under the so-called *actio de in rem verso*. The only way a litigant could protect their interest, or the court could help an aggrieved person in the absence of a general principle, was to refer to the general principles of the law by analogy – a technique which is allowed under Brazilian law. Absent

---

[156] Note, however, that Sílvio Rodrigues, in discussing the *condictio indebiti* under Arts 876 and 877, remarked that 'as regard to the *condictio indebiti* there is basically no difference whether the object that has been transferred is a movable or an immovable one, and whether it is fungible or non-fungible. The dispositions of Arts 876 and 877 apply to all of them alike. The *solvens* that has transferred an immovable to an *accipiens* on an undue payment can have it restored to him if he proves that he paid by mistake. The parties are returned to the position they had been in prior to the undue payment': Rodrigues (note 136).

This is not in contradiction to what we are saying above, because our emphasis is on the defence to a claim under Art 884 and the measure of the returnable enrichment under such provisions, although a cross-reference to the provisions in Arts 876 and 877 might create a contrary impression. Where a thing is lost or no longer in existence, there is no way of escaping from the fungibility and non-fungibility analysis to establish its value for the purposes of restitution.

[157] For an understanding of the expression 'updating monetary values' see Jorge (note 155) 554–589.

a general principle prohibiting enrichment *sine causa*, the Brazilian Legislature nevertheless dealt with various situations that today would fall under the heading 'enrichment *sine causa*' through the generic idea. But such cases had to be very specific. The new Civil Code has now resolved this issue, having included a general principle against unjustified enrichment.

Both the Brazilian and the Argentinean Civil Codes have introduced the general principle against unjustified enrichment. The main differences between them is that in the Argentinean Civil Code the general principle precedes the undue payment treatment, whereas in the Brazilian Civil Code the general principle appears after the treatment on undue payment. But both Civil Codes maintain the dichotomy 'undue payment' and 'payment *sine causa*'.

Both Civil Codes also maintain the subsidiarity of enrichment *sine causa*. For Brazil, it is Art 885, whereas for Argentina it is Art 1795. According to the Brazilian Commission on the Law of Obligations,[158] the Brazilian

> Article 885 dealing with the subsidiarity of the right to restitution based on the enrichment *sine causa* does not exclude the right to restitution of the enrichment either in the cases in which the alternative means given to the aggrieved to make up their losses encounter an obstacle of fact which hinders the elimination of the enrichment, or in the cases in which the alternative means offered to the aggrieved appear not to suffice to undo the totality of the enrichment.

A similar debate also appears in the Argentinean legal literature.

10.6 CONCLUSION

This chapter discussed liability in unjustified or unjust enrichment in several jurisdictions, namely, Namibia, Continental Europe, England and two South American countries, Argentina and Brazil. Whereas Continental Europe with its Model Law – DCFR has collectively opted for enrichment liability based on the 'negative approach' founded upon the concept of '*causa*' – that is to say, if a person enjoys enrichment by another where there is no legal ground, the law will oblige them to restore the enrichment – English law has opted for a positive approach – that is to say, the claimant in an enrichment claim must prove an unjust factor in order for the enrichment to be reversed.

[158] *Primeiras Jornadas de Direito Civil* – Council of Federal Justice – CJF – (Brasília, 2002), Enunciados: (Direito das Obrigações), Item 35 (which deals with Art 884 of the new Civil Code) and Item 36 (which deals with Art 886 of the new Civil Code).

Whereas the burden of proof rests with the defendant (respondent) in Continental Europe to prove that the enrichment is *cum causa* to avert the plaintiff's claim against unjustified enrichment, in English law the burden of proof lies with the claimant: they must point to an unjust factor in the enrichment of the defendant in order for the claim to succeed.

The commonality between all these legal systems is that English law has now clearly departed from calling the subject the 'law of restitution' in favour of adopting the nomenclature of 'unjust enrichment'. Therefore, English law has finally concluded that 'unjust enrichment is a discrete source of rights and obligations, and the difference between unjust enrichment and restitution is the difference between event and response'.[159]

The two South American countries discussed have generally recognised the general principle against unjustified enrichment in their new Civil Codes and general enrichment is subsidiary in both countries. In Argentina, 'enrichment *sine causa*' is provided for under '*disposiciones generals*' (general dispositions) and precedes undue payment. Undue payment, however, appears under a separate section, which may mean that the action of undue payment is not subsumed under the general principle.

In Brazil, 'enrichment *sine causa*', although a general principle, is provided for after 'undue payment'. Both legal systems have now abandoned the idea of 'quasi-contracts' when dealing with enrichment liability. But the formulation of the general principle against unjustified enrichment in Brazil is to a certain extent problematic because of its additional qualification of adjusting monetary values at the time a claim is instituted. This qualification may lead to an 'innocent party' being penalised under an enrichment claim.

Regarding Namibia, the country continues to develop this area of law piecemeal. However, some characterisations of the claim seem to be infusing English-law terminology in the institution of the claim, although the application and characterisations of the defences to an enrichment claim appear at times to be incoherent.

REFERENCES

Aimite, Jorge A 'Change of position in comparative perspective' Doctoral thesis (University of Cape Town, 2009).

ALI (2011). *Restatement (Third) of Restitution and Unjust Enrichment* (Reporter: Andrew Kull, 2011).

Alves, JCM *A Parte Geral do Projecto Código Civil Brasileiro [The General Part of the Brazilian Civil Code Project]* (Saraiva, 1986).

159 Mitchell (note 53) 18.1–18.3.

Americano, J & Ensaios, AJ *Sobre o Enriquecimento Sem Causa* (Doação, 1932).
Ames, JB 'The history of Assumpsit: II. Implied Assumpsit' (1888) 2 *Harvard Law Review* 53.
Ames, JB 'Purchase for value without notice' (1888) 2 *Harvard Law Review* 58.
Ames, JB *Lectures on Legal History and Miscellaneous Legal Essays* (Harvard University Press, 1913).
Atiyah, PS *The Rise and Fall of Freedom of Contract* (Oxford University Press, 1985).
Barker, K & Grantham, R *Law of Unjust Enrichment in Australia* (LexisNexis Butterworths, 2018).
Baudry-Lacantenerie, G & Barde, G *Obligations* 3 ed (Larose, 1906).
Beatson, J *The Use and Abuse of Unjust Enrichment* (Clarendon Press, 1906).
Billiau, M, Ghestin, J & Loiseau 'Répetition de l'indu' in *Encyclopédie Dalloz, Répertoire de Droit Civil IV* (Dalloz, 2001).
Birks, P 'English and Roman learning in *Moses v Macferlan*' (1984) 37(1) *Current Legal Problems* 1–28.
Birks, P *Introduction to the Law of Restitution* (Oxford University Press, 1985)
Birks, P 'Annual Miegunyah Lecture: Equity, conscience, and unjust enrichment' (1999) 23 *Melbourne University Law Review* 3–4.
Birks, P *The Foundations of Unjust Enrichment: Six Centennial Lectures* (Larose et Tenin, 2002).
Birks, P *Unjust Enrichment* 2 ed (Oxford University Press, 2005).
Burrows, A *English Private Law* (Oxford University Press, 2013).
Burrows, A, Barker, K, Mitchell, C, Worthington, S, Stevens, R, Krebs, T & Tettenborn, A 'The new Birksian approach to unjust enrichment' (2004) 12 *Restitution Law Review* 260–289.
Carvalho e Mendonça, MI Doutrina e pratica das obrigações, ou, tratado geral dos direitos de credito (Texto – Português, 1938).
Cohen, H 'Change of position in quasi-contracts' (1932) 45 *Harvard Law Review* 1333.
Cooksley, T 'The role of unjust enrichment in New Zealand' *Victoria University of Wellington Legal Research Paper, Student/Alumni Paper*, (21) (2019).
Council of Federal Justice, Brazil (CJF) *Primeiras Jornadas de Direito Civil.* Enunciados: Direito das Obrigações (Brasília, 2002).
Dagan, H 'Distributive foundations of corrective justice' (1999) 97 *Michigan Law Review* 138–166.
Dawson, JP *Unjust Enrichment: A Comparative Analysis* (Little Brown & Company, 1951[1999]).
Dawson, JP '*Negotiorum gestio*: The altruistic intermeddler' (1961) 74(5) *Harvard Law Review* 817.
De Campos, DL *A Subsidiariedade da Obrigação de Restituir o Enriquecimento Doctoral dissertation in Legal Sciences* (Faculty of Law, University of Coimbra, 2003).
De Carvalho, SJM *Código Civil Brasileiro Interpretado: Direito das Obrigações, XII* 13 ed (Freitas Bastos, 1988).
De Salvo-Venosa, S *Direito Civil – Parte Geral* 7 ed (Atlas, 2017).

De Salvo-Venosa, S *Direito Civil: Part Geral, Obrigações e Responsabilidade Civil, Vol 2*, 17 ed (Altas, 2017).

Dickson, B 'Unjust enrichment claims: A comparative overview' (1995) 54(1) *The Cambridge Law Journal* 101.

Du Plessis, J 'Towards a rational structure of liability for unjustified enrichment: Thoughts from two mixed jurisdictions' (2005) 122(1) *South African Law Journal* 142.

Eiseleen, S & Pienaar, G *Unjustified Enrichment: A Casebook* 4 ed (LexisNexis, 2008).

Ensaio, AJ *Sobre o Enriquecimento Sem Causa* (Saraiva, 1932).

Fifoot, CH *History and Sources of the Common-law: Tort and Contract* (Stevens & Sons, 1949).

Gallo, P 'Unjustified enrichment: A comparative analysis' (1992) 40 *American Journal Comparative Law* 433.

Gallo, P 'Remedies for unjust enrichment in the history of Italian law and in the Codice Civile' in E Schrage (ed) *Unjust Enrichment: The Comparative Legal History of the Law of Restitution* (Duncker & Humblot, 1995).

Gergen, MP 'What renders enrichment unjust' (2011) 79 *Texas Law Review* 1763.

Ghestin, J *Le Régime des Créances et des Dettes* (LGDJ Traités, 2005).

Giglio, F 'A systematic approach to "unjust" and "unjustified enrichment"' (2003) 23 *Oxford Journal for Legal Studies* 455.

Goff, R & Jones, G *The Law of Restitution* (Sweet & Maxwell, 1966).

Goff, R & Jones, G *Law of Restitution* 5 ed (Sweet & Maxwell, 2002).

Goff, R & Jones, G *The Law of Unjust Enrichment* 9 ed (Sweet & Maxwell, 2016).

Gonçalves, CR *Direito Civil Esquematizado, Parte Geral: Contractos Em Especie – Direito das Coisas* (Editora Saraiva, 2016).

Gonet-Branco, PG '*Em torno dos vícios do negócio jurídico – a propósito, do erro de fato e do erro de direito*' in D Fraciulli Netto et al (eds) *O Novo Código Civil: Estudos em Homenagem ao Professor Miguel Reale* (LTr, 2003).

Gordley, J *The Philosophical Origins of Modern Contract Doctrine* (Clarendon Press, 1991).

Hallebeek, J *The Concept of Unjust Enrichment in Late Scholasticism* (Gerard Noodt Instituut, 1996).

Hedley, S 'Unjust enrichment as the basis of restitution – an overworked concept' (1985) 5(1) *Legal Studies* 56.

Hedley, S *Restitution: Its Ordering and Division (Modern Legal Studies)* (Sweet & Maxwell, 2001).

Ibbetson, D 'Origins assumpsit and debt in the early sixteenth century: The origins of the indebitatus count' (1982) 41(1) *The Cambridge Law Journal* 142.

Jackman, IM *The Varieties of Restitution* (Federation Press, 1998).

Jackson, RM *The History of Quasi-Contract in English Law* (Cambridge University Press, 1986).

Jorge, A '*Change of position in comparative perspective*' Doctor of Laws in Philosophy thesis (University of Cape Town, 2009).

Jorge, A 'Inflation in enrichment claims: Reflections on the Brazilian Civil Code' (2013) 6 *Journal of Civil Law Studies* 554.

Keener, WA *A Treatise on the Law of Quasi-contracts* (Baker Voorhis, 1893).
Krebs, T *Restitution at the Crossroads* (Cavendish Publishing, 2001).
Leonardo, RX 'Cessão de créditos: Reflexões sobre causalidade na transmissão de bens no Direito Brasileiro' (2005) 42 *Revista da Faculdade de Direito da UFPR* 133.
Lotz, JG 'Enrichment' in WA Joubert & JA Faris (eds) *LAWSA* 2 ed (LexisNexis Butterworths, 2005).
Lotz, JG & Brand, FDJ 'Enrichment' in WA Joubert & JA Faris (eds) *LAWSA* 9 ed (LexisNexis Butterworths, 2009).
Marcelo, LM '*El cuasicontrato y el enriquecimiento sin causa en el nuevo Código Civil y Comercial argentino*' (2009) 13 *Anuario da Facultade de Dereito da Universidade* 393.
Matthews, P 'Freedom, unrequested improvements, and Lord Denning' (1981) 40(2) *The Cambridge Law Journal* 340.
Michelon, C *Direito Restitutório* (Revista dos Tribunais, 2007).
Michelon, C 'Native sources and comparative resources: Unjustified enrichment in Brazil after the 2002 Civil Code' 2014 *Restitution Law Review* 59.
Mitchell, C 'Unjust enrichment' in A Burrows (ed) *English Private Law* (Oxford University Press, 2013).
Mitchell, C, Mitchell, P & Watterson, S *Goff and Jones: The Law of Unjust Enrichment* 9 ed (Sweet & Maxwell, 2016).
Mota-Pinto, CA *Teoria Geral do Direito Civil* 3 ed (Coimbra, 1986).
Nicholas, B 'Unjustified enrichment in the civil law and Louisiana law, Part I' (1962) 36 *Tulane Law Review* 605.
Nicholas, B 'Unjustified enrichment in the civil law and Louisiana law Part II' (1962) 37 *Tulane Law Review* 49.
Pomponius, D 50.17.206 or D 12.6.14 '*Jure naturae aequum est neminem cum alterius detrimento fieri locupletorum*'.
Pontes de Miranda, 'Tratado de direito privado' (1959) *26 Parte Especial* 131–155.
Proceedings of the Fourth National Congress of Civil Law, held in Córdoba, 22–27 September 1969, Córdoba, 1971, T I, 70–71.
Rodrigues, S *Dos Contratos e Atos Unilaterais* (Saraiva, 2003).
Rodrigues, S *Direito Civil* 269 ed (Saraiva, 2003).
Rodrigues, S '*Do mandato tácito*' (2005) 191 *Revista dos Tribunais* 579.
Scheltma, MW 'Restitution and mistaken payments' in EJH Schrage (ed) *Unjust Enrichment and the Law of Contract* (Kluwer Law International, 2001).
Schrage, EJH (ed) *Unjust Enrichment and the Law of Contract* (Kluwer Law International, 2001).
Smith, LD 'The province of the law of restitution' (1992) 71 *Canadian Bar Review* 672.
Smith, SA 'The structure of unjust enrichment: Is restitution a right or a remedy?' (2003) 36 *Loyola of Los Angeles Law Review* 1037.
Stoljar, S 'Unjust enrichment and unjust sacrifice' (1987) 50(5) *The Modern Law Review* 603.
Van Zyl, DH 'Rethinking unjustified enrichment' 1992a *Acta Juridica* 203.
Van Zyl, DH 'The general enrichment action is alive and well' 1992b *Acta Juridica* 115.

Virgo, G *Restitution* (Oxford University Press, 1999).
Virgo, G *Principles of Law of Restitution* (Oxford University Press, 2006).
Virgo, G *Principles of the Law of Restitution* 3 ed (Oxford University Press, 2016/2017).
Visser, DP *Unjustified Enrichment* (Juta & Co, 2008).
Von Bar, C & Clive, E (eds) (2016). *Principles, Definitions and Model Rules of European Private Law - DCFR. Book VII, 2* (Oxford University Press, 2016).
Webb, C *Reason and Restitution: A Theory of Unjust Enrichment* (Oxford University Press, 2016).
Woodward, FC *The Law of Quasi Contracts* (Little Brown and Company, 1913).
Worthington, S 'The new Birksian approach to unjust enrichment' (2004) 12 *Restitution Law Review* 267.
Zimmermann, R 'Unjustified enrichment: The modern civilian approach' (1995) 15(3) *Oxford Journal of Legal Studies* 403.
Zimmermann, R *The Law of Obligations: Roman Foundations of the Civilian Tradition* (Juta & Co, 1990).

CASES

African Diamond Exporter (Pty) Ltd v Barclays Bank International Ltd 1978 (3) SA 699 (A)
Amoroso Copello, Alfonso G v Telefonica de Argentina SA, LL 2000-A, 572 (42.347) (Trelew Appeals Court)
Banque Financière de la Cité v Parc (Bettersea) Ltd [1999] 1 AC 221 (HL)
Benedetti v Sawiris [2013] UKSC 50
Bruni v Kahunda [2020] NAHCMD 591
Bruni v Tulive Capital (Pty) Ltd [2020] NAHCMD 536
Bruni v Yatsua Investments CC [2020] NAHCMD 571
CIR v Deutsch Morgan Grenfell Group plc [2005] EWCA Civ 78, [2006] 2 WLR 103
Countryside Communications Ltd v ICL Pathway Ltd [2000] CLC 324
Dextra Bank & Trust Co Ltd v Bank of Jamaica (2002) 1 All ER (Comm)
Direito Restitutório (2007) 128–129.
Dowman Imports Ltd v 2 Toobz Ltd [2020] EWHC 291 (Comm)
Edward v Burre (1573) Dal 104, l.45
Garland v Consumer Gas Co [2004] SCC 25; (2004) 237 DLR (4th)
Greenwood v Bennett (1973) 1 QB 195 (CA)
Guiness Mahon & Co Ltd v Kensington & Chelsea Royal London BC [1999] QB 215 (CA)
Hasser v Wallis 1 Salk 28 (1708)
Holmes v Hall Holt 36 (1695)
Hussey v Fiddall 12 Mod 324 (1770)
Kerr v Baranow 2009 BCCA 111
Kerr v Baranow [2011] SCJ No 10

Kleinwort Benson Ltd v Lincoln City Council [1999] 2 AC 349 (HL)
Lamine v Dorell 2 Ld Ray 1216 (1706)
Le Riche v Hamman 1946 AD 648 at 656
Lipkin Gorman v Karpnale (1991) 2 AC 548
MSM Consulting Ltd v United Republic of Tanzania [2009] EWHC 121 (QB)
National Bank of New Zealand ltd v Waitaki International Processing (NI) Ltd (1999) 2 NZLR 211
Philip Collins Ltd v Davis [2000] 3 All ER 808
Scottish Equitable plc v Derby [2000] 3 All ER 793
Six Carpenters (1610) Rep 147a
South Tyneside Metropolitan Borough Council v Svenska International PLC [1995] 1 All ER 545
Tomkins v Bernett, 1 Slk 22 (1693)
Van den Dries v The International University of Management [2014] NACHMD 159
Vanasse v Seguin 2009 ONCA 595
Vaux v Newman (1610) 8 Co Rep 146a, 147a (77 ER 695)
Warbrooke v Griffin (1609) 2 Brownl 254
Westdeutsche Landesbank Girozentrale v Islington LBC; Kleinwort Benson Ltd v Sandwell BC [1994] 3 All ER 890 (CA); [1996] AC 699 (HL)
Woolwich Equitable Building Society v IRC [1993] 1 AC 70 (HL)

LEGISLATION

Argentinean Code (Argentinean CCCN, Arts 1794–1795)
Brazilian Civil Code of 2002
Civil Code 2002 (Título VIII – Direito das Obrigações – Dos Atos Unilaterais, Capitulo VI 'Do Enriquecimento Sem Causa'
Code Civil de Québec (CCQ) (Québec Civil Code)
Dutch Civil Code (BW)
French Civil Code
German Civil Code
Italian Civil Code

11

Comparative law in Africa: an appraisal of the role of legal comparativism in the development of African law

Tapiwa V Warikandwa, Eugene L Libebe and Denis U Zaire

11.1 INTRODUCTION

One of the least researched and applied legal systems in the world is African law.[1] Little organised scholarship on African law is performed with a conscious purpose by individual African scholars or institutions as in the case of the scholarship and study of other legal systems such as European, American, Asian and Islamic law.[2] Several critical problems must first be clarified before approaching African law in the framework of comparative law. The assertion that Africa has many incomparable legal systems is not factual. Instead, African customs, which are becoming increasingly important in a decolonising and developing Africa, should be studied in their respective jurisdictions. For example, Namibia has 11 ethnic groups, each with its own distinct customary laws. These customary laws can be studied and compared with other cultural groupings in Namibia or other cultural groupings from other parts of Africa and the world. Legal scholars argue that, given the diversity of African laws, particularly customary law and traditions, such a study would be not only ineffective but also meaningless. In this regard Nigeria is mentioned: it contains more than 250 ethnic groups, each with its own customary

[1] CM Fombad 'Comparative research in contemporary African legal studies' (2018) 67(4) *Journal of Legal Education* 984–1004.

[2] Y Ghai 'Law, development and African scholarship' (1987) 50(6) *The Modern Law Review* 750–776.

traditions.[3] Learning about these many and varied customary laws, though, would be advantageous because they reflect African societal standards. A study driven by comparative law would correct the absurd situation in which Westernised national laws predominate in cities and yet customary law predominates in rural areas, notably regarding matters that are personal in nature. But laws in Africa must reflect the cultural values of the society in which they are enforced. When multiple cultural groups coexist, such as in Namibia, Nigeria and other African countries, comparative legal studies might uncover common practices that will be consolidated to constitute national laws. Imposing Roman, Roman-Dutch and English common law on African societies is both incorrect and deprives Africans of their natural state of being and cultural identity.

When approaching African law, it is necessary to consider the historical layers and the geographical splintering caused by colonialism. Historically, the legal traditions of Francophone, Lusophone and Anglophone Africa strove not only to take account of globalisation, but also to construct commercial and/or mercantile law. These legal systems assume that there were or are no African legal systems that govern(ed) trade between Africans and other ethnic groups and nationalities. But many economic activities took place in trading posts such as Zumbo, Sena, Tete and Sofala, where Africans established trade rules with Arabs and Europeans.[4] As a result, it is difficult to understand why Western forms of corporate law were later used to control trade among African countries.

It is therefore vital to recognise that, whereas the African continent resembles a patchwork of traditional religious Western common-law and civil–legal traditions, many of these combinations do not derive from the deliberate creation of African legal systems. Instead, they are influenced by the negative consequences of imposition by dominant colonial powers. Existing systems are finely balanced, frequently consisting of contradictory rules, and they necessitate the discovery of a balance and common ground between indigenous systems and colonially imposed Western and Asian legal systems. Legal comparativism could provide appropriate solutions to this difficulty by analysing and understanding the genesis, background and essence of these laws. Perhaps common ground can be found in seemingly irreconcilable disagreements between traditional, religious and Western legal systems.

As a result, this chapter demonstrates that adopting comparative law in Africa may lead to positive scientific outcomes. In the first place, adoption will help

---

[3] DE Agbiboa & AE Okem 'Unholy trinity: Assessing the impact of ethnicity and religion on national identity in Nigeria' (2011) 43(2) *Peace Research* 98–125.

[4] *Encyclopedia Britannica* 'European and African interaction from the 15th through to the 18th century' (2024), https://www.britannica.com/place/Southern-Africa/European-and-African-interaction-from-the-15th-through-the-18th-century.

Africans to understand both their own and other legal systems in use in their respective societies. Furthermore, it will help African countries to understand how to interact legally with the greater global or regional legal contexts. Therefore, it is emphasised that legal comparativism has value in Africa and can be used to expand the role of African law in comparative legal studies. This development will most likely help modern African countries to use legal comparativism as a means to an end. In this context, the aim of this chapter is to revolutionise and decolonise legal education in Africa. The use of comparative law in African judicial systems should therefore not be considered controversial; on the contrary, it should be encouraged.[5] It is widely acknowledged that, given the colonial backgrounds of most African countries, it would be difficult, if not impossible, for them to function in the legal realm if they had not used comparative-law principles to synthesise their countries' own multifaceted post-colonial legal systems. Comparative law is crucial to Africa because it entails the comparative study of laws and legal systems and their refinement in order to improve and standardise them. The importance of continuing legal education and research on legal comparativism is therefore emphasised. Legal comparativism is rapidly fading in Africa, particularly among jurists and/or comparative academics, and also from African law schools and/or faculty curricula.

11.2 OVERVIEW OF THE IMPORTANCE AND PURPOSE OF COMPARATIVE LAW IN AFRICA

Comparative legal study or legal comparativism refers to the comparison of legal systems with the aim of exploring historical and philosophical questions of law and building a better regime in international relations, among other objectives.[6] The term 'methodology' is derived from the noun 'method' and is described as 'a collection or system of procedures, concepts, and norms for controlling a certain field'.[7] From this definition it could be argued that the methodological approach to comparative legal studies covers the entire body of practice and procedures used in the researching, distinction and assessment of legal systems. Discussions about comparative-law methodology are important to the study of law in general, since comparison occurs in all aspects of life and influences all kinds of human decision-making. For the purposes of this chapter, the theoretical instruments, frameworks

[5] KA Mingst 'Judicial systems of sub-Saharan Africa: An analysis of neglect' (1988) 31(1) *African Studies Review* 135–147.

[6] C Valcke 'Comparative law as comparative jurisprudence: The comparability of legal systems' (2004) 52(3) *The American Journal of Comparative Law* 713–740.

[7] *The American Heritage Dictionary of the English Language* 4 ed (Houghton Mifflin, 2000).

and procedures used in the analysis of other legal systems are referred to as the methodological approach to comparative legal studies. When referring to Africa, the methodological approach to comparative legal studies refers to the process by which African countries study their legal systems (which are primarily customary laws) and compare them to other legal systems (ie, Western, Asian and Islamic).[8] There is much convergence in the approaches adopted by African countries in the study of their laws and these approaches may be similar to those of other jurisdictions, such as those of America, Europe and Asia.[9] However, no two legal systems are exactly the same and it is accordingly challenging to find a common methodology for comparative legal studies. Because of this, comparing Africa as a whole to the United States, which has a single legal system, does not indicate that African countries and the United States do not use similar methodological techniques in comparative legal studies.

Comparative legal studies is a prominent academic field that has received insufficient attention internationally, particularly in Africa.[10] This is true despite the fact that globalisation has increased interconnections between states and that this current milieu is considered to be a favourable period for comparative legal studies. A significant portion of the comparative legal literature has almost entirely been excluded Africa from the research plan.[11] Except for South Africa, the vast majority of African law schools or faculties and legal education programmes or curricula do not have a comparative-law component.[12] As a result, it is not surprising that court decisions, which rarely use comparative law as a guide or tool for adjudication, reflect this unsatisfactory state of affairs. Many African legal systems may consequently face the same fate as comparative legal studies across the continent. The fact that common, civil and customary law are all components of African law makes it challenging for those in charge of enforcing and interpreting the law to comprehend the complexities of these several systems and the ways in which they interact.[13] Since an effective comparison of two systems necessitates at least a fundamental comprehension of how the systems operate, this presents a challenge to African comparativists. In addition, the limited works on comparative legal studies in Africa may never be published due to Africa's lack of involvement

[8] CN Okeke *Comparative Law in Africa: Methodologies and Concepts. Book Chapters by GGU Law Authors, Bk 26* (Golden Gate University School of Law, 2015).

[9] Ibid.

[10] WJ Kamba 'Comparative law: A theoretical framework' (1974) 23(3) *The International and Comparative Law Quarterly* 485–519.

[11] Fombad (note 1) 984–1004.

[12] Ibid.

[13] M Ndulo 'African customary law, customs, and women's rights' (2011) 18(1) *Indiana Journal of Global Legal Studies* article 5.

in the processes of the formation of laws. If Africa's methodological approach to comparing legal studies includes the consideration of African legal systems, then some people's rejection of the existence of African law will have an effect on comparative legal studies in Africa.[14]

Improved legal comprehension, legal reform and international unification and standardisation are essential goals of comparative law.[15] These objectives are connected because, once the way in which a legal system operates is understood, it can be used as a model to reform others or be considered a part of a unified legal system. The comparison of legal norms has been practised for centuries, even though the label 'comparative legal studies' is relatively recent. In reality, comparison has always been a part of human intellectual processes – it is difficult to imagine legal education and practice that does not include at least an element of comparison. Understanding the law or a legal system necessitates revealing the complete apparatus on which that law or legal system is grounded. At times, possessing knowledge of many legal subjects might be extremely beneficial to this quest. A crucial component of legal comparativism is keeping track of amendments to national and international laws. The comparative method is not only important but absolutely necessary when applying foreign law to domestic law in order to resolve any conflict of laws.[16] In the 21st century, globalisation presents challenges to comparative-law jurists, lawyers and lecturers in law schools or faculties and also to comparative lawyers. This is because comparative-law jurists, lecturers and lawyers must stay up-to-date on foreign legislation in order to advise their clients or teach law students the legal requirements of cross-border transactions.

Moreover, understanding the diverse legal systems in Africa will help the population to deal with the many difficulties that plague them and will assist governments in making better policy decisions. By understanding both a specific African country's law and a foreign law, a legal comparativist acquires a broader perspective on the interaction of diverse legal systems and is better prepared to deal with the inherent complex legal challenges and dilemmas.

The purpose of comparative legal studies is legal reform, which focuses on the way one legal system influences another. This gives birth to the contentious notion

---

[14] SF Joireman 'Inherited legal systems and effective rule of law: Africa and the colonial legacy' (2001) 39(4) *The Journal of Modern African Studies* 571–596. See also Okeke (note 8) bk 26; Fombad (note 1) 984–1004.

[15] PI Bhat 'Comparative method of legal research: Nature, process and potentiality' (2015) 57(2) *Journal of the Indian Law Institute* 147–173; see also R Michaels *Comparative Law* (nd), https://scholarship.law.duke.edu/cgi/viewcontent.cgi?article=3014&context=faculty_scholarship, accessed 20 August 2023.

[16] HC Gutteridge 'Comparative law and the conflict of laws' (1943) 29 *Transactions of the Grotius Society* 119–141.

of legal borrowing: legal borrowing can be a powerful weapon for legal change in practically every legal system,[17] but it necessitates the use of a tool for legislative comparison.[18] However, this method of legal comparativism has a few drawbacks of its own. One notable drawback is that of the increase in 'copy and paste' legal drafting in Namibia, Africa and the rest of the world. This approach to legislative drafting carries an inherent risk of imposing one country's legal culture on another. This is particularly true of the post-colonial strategies adopted by Western countries, which constantly impose laws on African countries, leading to the Westernisation of legal systems and acculturation. These problems arise during the legal borrowing process.

African legislators, judges and legal drafters are mostly driven by a reliance on Western-influenced (and at times -sponsored) political and economic agendas when changing or enhancing a particular piece of legislation or a legal system. African laws, particularly customary laws, are always considered as being out of date and so they require complete replacement by laws from so-called civilised (Western) countries.[19] African legal experts (in this case judges, academics and lawyers) who declare that specific practices recognised by African customary laws are outdated and out of step with contemporary African societies never leave such matters to society to determine.[20] However, public consultation would be a beneficial tool in making such decisions. As a result, these illogical conclusions are typically not supported by solid scientific or legal arguments from an African context but are based on Western perspectives instead. The decisions are typically supported by fictitious arguments which assert that because African countries are said to have underdeveloped legal systems (customary law is frequently considered outdated and useful only in rural, rather than urban, areas), they must rely on case law or common law from particular Western jurisdictions. This explains why, in the majority of modern African societies, legal transformation is frequently imposed on the public in order to further the reform agents' imperialist political and economic interests. This is the reason why, during the period of Western countries' colonisation of African countries, customary law – which had previously mostly governed the conduct of the indigenous African people – became subordinate to

---

[17] J Goldsmith & D Levinson 'Law for states: International law, constitutional law, public law' (2009) 122(7) *Harvard Law Review* 1791–1868.

[18] J Lafranque *Judicial Borrowing: International & Comparative Law as Nonbinding Tools of Domestic Legal Adjudication with Particular Reference to Estonia* (nd), https://core.ac.uk/download/pdf/216908301.pdf, accessed 20 August 2023.

[19] B Bwire 'Integration of African customary legal concepts into modern law: Restorative justice: A Kenyan example' (2019) 9(1) *Societies* 17.

[20] MO Hinz 'The ascertainment of customary law: What is ascertainment of customary law and what is it for? The experience of the Customary Law Ascertainment Project in Namibia' (2012) 2(7) *Oñati Socio-legal Series* [online] 85–105.

the foreign law that the colonialists imposed on the population.[21] Surprisingly, the same trend that existed during the colonial period continues in post-colonial 21st-century African countries. This leads to the application of customary law being subject to its conformity with common-law principles and the constitution.

The repugnancy doctrine, which has become the tool or standard for assessing the legal sustainability of some African customs, was easily applied in some African countries to strike down any aspect of customary law that did not comply with the Western norm of 'natural justice, equity and good conscience' (eg South Africa and Nigeria). As a result, the reformative potential of the repugnancy doctrine has been called into question. The repugnancy doctrine has since been adopted by other post-colonial African states. It claims that in order to serve the comparative-law objective of legal reform, any changes made to the legal frameworks of African countries must be founded on solid, well-considered policies and be a result of comparative law, as opposed to simply emanating from the leaders' parochial considerations. According to Fombad, one of the challenges in many (African) countries has been the ways in which African leaders have rendered constitutions ineffective by frequently ignoring or unilaterally modifying them when it is expedient for them to do so.[22] Reform requires comparison, and there may be differences among reformers over which comparisons to make and which components of one legal system to adopt from another. It is critical that these disagreements be resolved. After all, the goal of comparative legal studies is to find the most appropriate and just solution to a problem out of all conceivable options.

Comparative legal studies are crucial to harmonising and unifying legislation internationally:[23] laws become uniform and certain when they are unified and harmonised. Although the concept of legal unification has its roots in ancient times, it was not until the 19th century – when a surge in national interest in comparative legal studies occurred – that unification took place on a significant scale.[24] For instance, the Hague Conventions on the Uniform Laws of the International Sale of Goods and the United Nations Commission on International Trade Law (UNCITRAL) were both created during this time. It is therefore vital for African nations to unite to build a unified front to deal with these issues at a time when they are all facing the same challenges, including human rights violations, poverty and corrupt leadership.

---

[21] Ndulo (note 13) 87–120.

[22] Fombad (note 1) 984–1004.

[23] HE Yntema 'Comparative research and unification of law' (1942) 41(2) *Michigan Law Review* 261–268; see also M Fontaine 'Law harmonisation and local specificities – a case study: OHADA and the law of contracts' (2013) 18(1) *Uniform Law Review* 50–64,

[24] AN Allott 'Towards the unification of laws in Africa' (1965) 14(2) *The International and Comparative Law Quarterly* 366–389.

Legal unification might be a helpful tool for Africa in this sense. However, given the African community's chronic tensions and xenophobic tendencies, arriving at successful legal unification is doubtful. Legal unification has a number of disadvantages, including the potential for legal ambiguity and the requirement of repealing particular laws. While Europe continues to struggle with some aspects of legal unification, Africa can benefit from the European community's experience in determining the best course of action to take in order to achieve some level of legal uniformity.

Attempts at legal unification have already been made in some African countries. For instance, the *Organization Pour L'harmonisation en Afrique du Droit des Affaires en Afrique* (OHADA) seeks to harmonise trade laws across its member nations. These objectives are shared by the East African Community (EAC). The unification argument seems to consider legal plurality as a problem that needs to be solved, notwithstanding its appeal. Because a watertight legal union is not possible in reality, comparative legal studies can be used only to a limited extent to achieve continental and/or global legal unification.

Furthermore, if unification is the ultimate goal of comparative legal studies, then conflicts of law must be overcome. When multiple jurisdictions are involved, this conflict may become more apparent since conflict exists not only between statutory and customary law, but also between two (or more) legal systems. When determining which law or set of laws should govern a group of states, say African states, it is possible that the laws of certain states would be neglected or that some legal systems would be prioritised, resulting in the imposition of laws on those states. A negotiated solution aimed at achieving a win–win strategy, in contrast, would be encouraged to provide an inclusive legal unification approach and method in Africa and the world. Careful balancing of the interests of the states pursuing legal harmonisation is necessary for unification. Another fundamental objective of comparative law is the maintenance or improvement of its status as an independent field of study.[25] This is disputed, though, as it is unclear whether comparative law constitutes an independent subject.

11.3 COMPARATIVE LAW IN AFRICA: NECESSITY OR LUXURY IN 21ST-CENTURY LEGAL EDUCATION AND PRACTICE?

The first step in studying comparative law in Africa is to understand the purposes served by its study on the continent. Many comparative-law scholars concur that

[25] R Michaels *The Functional Method of Comparative Law* (nd), https://scholarship.law.duke.edu/cgi/viewcontent.cgi?article=2033&context=faculty_scholarship, accessed 20 August 2023.

studying comparative law requires both the intellectual effort of evaluating the relationships between different legal systems and the study of legal history and jurisprudence. One common purpose is to maintain an awareness of the diverse legal rules applicable to a number of states. This enables comparative-law scholars to track the growth of regional laws and legal systems. Furthermore, specialists in international law can use comparative law to assess how well Africa is applying both public and private international law. Cross-national research has made major contributions to the study, application and change of law throughout the past century.

Improving knowledge and modifying laws are two of the primary goals of comparative legal studies. Before delving into the purpose of comparative law in Africa, it is vital to define the terminology and the method of study used. Nations such as Canada or the United States are easy to categorise for the purposes of conducting comparative research. Despite the fact that each of these nations has its own set of laws, the overarching legal framework is uniform and comparable. In contrast, Africa is home to more than 54 governments, each with its own culture and legal system. It is difficult and impractical to compare the African continent to the United States as a whole, though. An analogous comparative legal analysis would be extremely broad and complex, but not useless, due to Africa's continental diversity.[26]

After taking these precautions, we can proceed to the objectives of a comparative legal investigation of African law.

The development of a state's legal systems or their reformulation is an often-stated reason for studying comparative law. This includes the legal, economic and social aspects of development. It is also important to note that the Namibian Constitution does not provide a clear legal basis for Namibian courts to apply foreign law using comparative legal methods – in contrast to Art 144 of the Namibian Constitution, which expressly accepts international law.[27] Instead, Namibian courts have developed a preference for international case law and comparative legal systems.[28] However, the late Taslim Olawale Elias, a former judge of the International Court of Justice (ICJ) and the Supreme Court of Nigeria, best exemplified the objective

[26] CN Okeke 'African law in comparative law: Does comparativism have worth?' (2011) 16(1) *Roger Williams University Law Review* article 1; see also M Reimann 'The progress and failure of comparative law in the second half of the twentieth century' (2002) 50(4) *The American Journal of Comparative Law* 671–700.

[27] K Kariseb 'Reflections on judicial cross-fertilisation in the adjudication of human rights and constitutional disputes in Africa: The case of Namibia' (2021) 35(1) *Speculum Juris* 19–32.

[28] See the Namibia Supreme Court's decision in *Ex parte: Attorney-General in re: Constitutional Relationship between Attorney-General and the Prosecutor-General* (SA 7 of 1993) [1995] NASC 1 (13 July 1995).

of comparative law in Africa.[29] Judge Elias was a comparative-law specialist who emphasised that in order for an African country to establish a more comprehensive legal framework, it must first undergo legal reform, evaluate diverse legal theories, and investigate the nature and purpose of law.

Judge Elias modernised and amended several Nigerian laws.[30] However, Elias J's comparative study did more than only advance the Nigerian legal system. He believed that comparative legal studies could foster dialogue and improve interactions among Africans with divergent views on the rule of law. The conviction of Elias J implied that many of Africa's problems could be resolved only by Africans themselves. Therefore, in order to achieve this developmental aim, African states had to form powerful coalitions. The Organisation of African Unity (OAU), today known as the African Union (AU), and its Protocol of Mediation, Conciliation, and Arbitration were therefore established, with Elias J a party to the drafting of these agreements.[31] Recent events, such as the adoption of the Africa Continental Free Trade Agreement (AfCFTA), have bolstered Elias J's aspirations for Africa. His convictions contradict some Africans' belief that implementing Western legal systems will solve the continent's problems.[32] Despite the fact that many African countries have adopted Western legal systems, they continue to face a number of challenges. It may therefore be time for Africans to make full use of Elias J's comparative legal studies perspective on African development.

Depending solely on foreign aid will not improve the conditions of African countries in any area of human need. African countries can succeed only when they start cooperating with one another and learning how to support one another in economic, social and legal ways. Judge Elias was able to pinpoint acceptable shared legal grounds for developing regional organisations such as the recently adopted AfCFTA within Africa through the study of comparative law. However, it is difficult to divide Africa into African states. The majority of African state borders were drawn by colonial powers along longitude lines, disregarding ethnic and tribal locations. And many Africans first identify with their tribe or homeland before identifying with the country they share a border with. In addition, many instances exist where clans or tribes are split apart by state lines – for example, between Namibia and Angola and between Zimbabwe and Mozambique – to name

[29] Okeke (note 26) article 1; see also C Landauer 'Taslim Olawale Elias: From British colonial law to modern international law' in J von Bernstorff & P Dann (eds) *The Battle for International Law: South–North Perspectives on the Decolonization Era, The History and Theory of International Law* online ed (Oxford Academic, 2019).

[30] Ibid.

[31] Ibid.

[32] Ibid.

only two examples. Furthermore, there are many communities with varying legal systems within the same state.

To be realistic, explaining an African country's traditional or tribal law would necessitate bringing together diverse tribal and ethnic laws for a plausible but complex investigation. Whereas tribal legal systems exist in every African country, they serve as diverse and innovative functions as any country's legal system. The dynamic potential for studying these traditional and tribal legal systems creates methodological obstacles in studying African legal systems.[33] But teaching comparative law to law students serves a practical instructional purpose.[34] Studying comparative law exposes students to other legal systems and ways of reasoning. Students typically have a greater knowledge of the dynamics, advantages, disadvantages and reforms taking place in their own legal systems due to comparative-law education.

Comparative law encourages the confrontation of opposing ideas and the cognitive dissonance that might lead to original thought. It forces African countries such as Namibia to design an alternative legal and normative framework that allows legal academics, judges and legal practitioners to recognise the deficiencies or defects in the current framework. This informs legal experts and those working in the legal profession about alternative theories that more accurately reflect who we are and what we strive to be. The highest objective of comparative-law research in Africa might be attained in this manner. By studying different legal systems, regardless of where they live in the world, law students may be better equipped to identify jurisprudential shortcomings in their own domestic law and argue for its reform. And comparative law can provide useful suggestions for advancing international and human rights legislation. Moving away from the old Eurocentric approach to comparative-law studies and comprehending traditional legal systems, which are more effective in many African countries, would be extremely beneficial to law students.

Another interesting area for comparative study is international law and its application in Africa. Countries in Africa, such as South Africa, have transformed their entire legal systems to adhere to international law. Other African countries also routinely receive warnings for significant violations of international law. These realities imply that comparative-law research is critically important now because the expansion and dynamism of those institutions' legislative, administrative and judicial responsibilities create new demands on international law.

---

[33] A Porter 'Africana legal studies: A new theoretical approach to law & protocol' (2022) 27 *Michigan Journal of Race & Law* 249.

[34] JN Hazard 'Comparative law in legal education' (1951) 189(2) *The University of Chicago Law Review* 264–279.

11.4 INTEGRATING SEVERAL AFRICAN LEGAL FRAMEWORKS INTO A SINGLE, ALL-INCLUSIVE FRAMEWORK

Owing to their distinct indigenous and colonial histories, several African countries have a patchwork of legal systems. Lord Denning once remarked that

> African laws are an assortment of fragments, much like a jigsaw or a mosaic: all must be placed together to form a cohesive unit, and updated to suit modern conditions.[35]

It is crucial that African countries use comparative law to decide whether or not to incorporate a specific body of law into their legal systems. It is difficult to put the puzzle pieces together without first examining the contours and shapes of each piece. Comparative law gives these African countries' governments the freedom to choose how disputes can be resolved, which laws they have to follow in particular areas and whose judicial systems they should use.[36]

Comparative law also indicates a government's policy decisions and value judgements through the laws it enacted. For instance, for the most part, African family law has retained components of customary law, Islamic law or, in the case of Kenya, Hindu law.[37] In Nigeria, Sharia law is now being implemented more liberally to include other offences such as drinking and promiscuity.[38] Nonetheless, because customary law permeates these countries' legal systems, their courts must be prepared to deal with it efficiently because it may be necessary to apply it, particularly at the appellate level, when necessary.[39] Regrettably, Kenya dissolved all of its indigenous courts. However, regardless of Kenya's dissolving its indigenous courts, there are still attempts afoot to codify customary law in Africa. Since it was initially unwritten, attempts have been made to codify customary law, including the Restatement of African Law Project, which conducted a thorough examination and documentation of the different customary laws in use in African countries.[40]

Customary or native law had to be codified before it could be used in courts. This was a difficult and time-consuming task, with varying degrees of success among the participating nations. The documents were made official in Kenya and used as evidence in court. However, as Menski points out, African leaders' perspectives

---

[35] Okeke (note 26) article 1.

[36] Joireman (note 14) 571–596; see also TA Aguda 'The judiciary in Africa' (1985) 9(1) *The Fletcher Forum* 13–35.

[37] Okeke (note 26) article 1.

[38] Ibid.

[39] Ibid.

[40] Ibid.

vary on how far their citizens have departed from traditional legal systems outside of state-centred judicial structures.[41] Menski continues that residents regularly uphold traditional law outside of the formal court system through village tribunals and that this is 'open knowledge' in Nigeria.[42] Owing to challenges faced in attempts to codify customary or native law in Africa, Kibwana, of the Centre for Human Rights at the University of Pretoria, South Africa, elaborated on the goals of comparative law. Owing to the fact that African legal systems are established on imposed law, African legal pedagogy is preoccupied with learning, researching and teaching foreign or imported laws.[43] This is a major problem from an African perspective.

The majority of comparative law focuses on imparting legal principles from the 'Western world'.[44] Consequently, African laws imported from the West to deal with 'local impediments' may not work as intended and African countries' experiences might be leveraged to develop more effective universal legal solutions. Such perspectives are critical to the decolonisation and transformation of African society, and Namibia and other African countries could draw significant lessons from these observations. Africa and African states are accountable for developing locally acceptable solutions to their challenges and appropriate laws which suit their environments. Legal comparativism can help them to find best practices from other jurisdictions; however, it is the responsibility of African legal drafters, legal academics, legal practitioners and legislators to create laws that are appropriate to regional African contexts.

Contrasting African legal systems that are 'similarly fitted in economic, cultural, social, and historical settings' may be more effective in resolving the continent's legal challenges. Comparative legal studies in African countries frequently focus on comparisons between close countries or constrained geographic areas rather than on a more comprehensive and systematic perspective. We therefore submit to the view that comparative legal studies based on comparisons between adjacent countries or regions are a good place to start, but focusing on a broader range appears to be more advantageous, especially now that the AU has been promoting continental solidarity and interdependence in many areas of current interest. The establishment of a common market for trade through the AfCFTA agreement is a prominent example of such a strategy.

---

[41] Ibid.

[42] Ibid.

[43] GP Fletcher 'Comparative law as a subversive discipline' (1998) 46(4) *The American Journal of Comparative Law* 683–700.

[44] EJ Eberle 'The method and role of comparative law' (2009) 8 *Washington University Global Studies Law Review* 451.

11.5 EFFECT OF COLONIALISM ON COMPARATIVE-LAW STUDIES IN AFRICA

Every time there is a discussion on comparative legal studies in Africa, the subject of colonialism must be brought up.[45] In pre-colonial African legal systems, the dominance of customary law in governing indigenous people was a prominent feature.[46] A combination of legal positivist prejudice and a colonial mentality that did not view customary law as proper law therefore led to a negative attitude towards it. The same attitude to customary law still exists in post-colonial Africa, hence the recent calls to decolonise legal education in Africa, especially in southern Africa. This is not surprising, given that Western countries have often classified Africans and their laws as 'uncivilised'. This has had an adverse effect on Africa's participation in comparative legal studies.

The colonialists' use of the repugnancy doctrine may be the only instance of some form of comparative work performed on Africa's indigenous laws by Europeans with the objective of diminishing those laws; but the question has been raised in this chapter whether the repugnancy doctrine constitutes reform for the purposes of comparative legal studies.[47] In the South African context, the repugnancy doctrine lasted longer than its usefulness and the courts now apply customary law with reference to the Constitution and any legislation dealing with customary law.[48]

Although the colonial regimes and governments were overthrown in Africa, the eradication of African customary law appears to be continuing covertly under the auspices of globalisation. The accepted legal systems to which the application of African customary law must be subjected are constitutionalism and common law. In contrast to Western legal systems such as Roman-Dutch law and English common law, African value systems such as ubuntu are still merely acknowledged as aspects of African philosophy and not substantive legal principles. Achieving tangible African legal changes will require expert African legal comparativists to keep African traditional legal systems relevant in the comparative legal studies field. This is attributed to the fact that customary law is at present only superficially included in comparative legal studies.

It is undeniable that the damage done to African laws and their study after independence does not appear to have been undone. Therefore, it is not surprising

[45] Fombad (note 1) 984–1004; see also SE Merry 'Law and colonialism' (1991) 25(4) *Law & Society Review* 889–922.

[46] Joireman (note 14) 571–596.

[47] M Demian 'On the repugnance of customary law' (2014) 56(2) *Comparative Studies in Society and History* 508–536.

[48] EA Taiwo 'Repugnancy clause and its impact on customary law: Comparing the South African and Nigerian positions – some lessons for Nigeria' (2009) 34(1) *Journal of Juridical Science* 89–115.

that the erroneous beliefs that post-colonial Africans lack appropriate religious, cultural and legal traditions to cling to and that the only practical solution is to modernise Africa and shape Africans into Western stereotypes continue to permeate the continent and the entire world. Whereas the stereotyping of African legal traditions has arguably become politically unacceptable, much damage has been done and continues to be done and some developments have become irreversible during the post-colonial era. The contemporary fallacies about African laws which greatly influence legal studies, together with associated historical misconceptions, have had a considerable impact on the way African legal systems are studied. Even African indigenous peoples have come to regard their own traditional customs as archaic. Decolonising African legal education is accordingly necessary to ensure that Africans study law from an Afrocentric perspective using African legal philosophy.[49]

11.6 METHODS OF COMPARATIVE LEGAL STUDIES

In order to analyse, review, determine, explain, comprehend and evaluate legislation using acceptable legal procedures, one must possess the necessary skills and knowledge. Such analysis or review should be conducted thoroughly, considering the complexities of law as a subject of study. To carry out this duty appropriately and efficiently, objectivity and neutrality are required. As a result, whether the legislation is written or not, it must be analysed in its entirety and as it is given, as in the case of customary law. An investigation into how such law (in this case, customary law) functions and is applied in a certain society should also be conducted. This section therefore discusses the different methods of conducting comparative legal studies, starting with the historical method.

11.6.1 Historical method

Knowledge of the law is essential to an adequate appreciation of comparative legal studies.[50] Because this genre is concerned with the comparison of laws or legal systems, it is only natural that a study of the history of the many laws to be compared should be conducted.[51] This covers the concept of the historical method or approach

---

[49] KB Motshabi 'Decolonising the university: A law perspective' (2018) 40(1) *Strategic Review for Southern Africa* 104.

[50] P Legrand 'Comparative legal studies and commitment to theory (review of *A Modern Approach to Comparative Law*, by P de Cruz)' (1995) 58(2) *The Modern Law Review* 262–273.

[51] Fombad (note 1) 984–1004.

to comparative legal studies, because it has been stated that 'comparative law without the history of law is an impossible endeavour'.[52] The history is significant because it reveals why a certain legal system works for the country or countries who adopt it. For example, the particular history of the English parliamentary system explains why the monarchy has survived in England.[53] And Namibia, a former apartheid regime colony, followed the colonial-imposed parliamentary system of governance.[54] However, Namibia abandoned the parliamentary system of government when it gained independence and became a republic in 1990.[55] It replaced it with a form of government based on constitutional supremacy that was better suited to its new status as a republic and to its cultural and social past. In post-colonial Namibia, customary law has continued to form a major source of law, as is the case in other African countries, despite the attempts of the Western countries to disparage it. The historical past of many African countries is not unrelated to this. In Namibia, customary law remains one of four sources of law, together with statutes, common law and international law. African customary law is based on normative principles that have historical roots in community development. When a country wishes to borrow some aspects of another legal system, the historical approach takes on practical significance because what works for a Western country such as England may not work for Namibia, an African country. The simple reason for this assertion is that England and Namibia are two countries with different histories. Therefore, the historical method is used either to resurrect long-forgotten but still valuable concepts or to look into the effects that a legal provision has had on human conduct in a specific society. Nonetheless, in 21st-century African society, studying a Western country's history and foreign ideals might help the country to understand and deal with some difficulties, such as those relating to globalisation.

11.6.2 Functional approach to comparative legal studies

In contemporary legal society, when comparing laws, a functional approach is employed.[56] This means that, in addition to looking at what the rules state, there is a need to analyse the issues dealt with by different legal systems. The functional approach to comparative legal studies is goal-oriented, supports a variety of social

---

[52] Ibid.

[53] Ibid.

[54] G Bauer 'Namibia in the first decade of independence: How democratic?' (2001) 27(1) *Journal of Southern African Studies* 33–55.

[55] Ibid.

[56] P Mahy 'The functional approach in comparative socio-legal research: Reflections based on a study of plural work regulation in Australia and Indonesia' (2016) 12(4) *International Journal of Law in Context* 420–436.

purposes and is not bound to resolving the challenges peculiar to a given geographic entity. For this reason, the functional approach has dominated comparative legal research in the world.[57] Functionalism is based on the notion that, despite the diversity of human civilisations, many of their challenges can be dealt in similar ways, with equivalent results for the benefit of all.[58] This functionalist hypothesis holds that when the common problems of various states are resolved, the legal systems of the globe might unite.

Garbarino has shown how the functional approach can be used to deal with the tax issues facing diverse nations.[59] Concerns may be raised at the idea that governments face similar difficulties because some legal problems may be specific to a particular legal system or set of legal systems. However, as the African proverb goes, 'only a fool would refuse quinine merely because it did not grow in their backyard.'[60] This means that the earlier criticism does not alter the fact that another legal system may still offer a solution to such legal problems. The functional approach is practical in nature because it focuses on what legal rules and principles can achieve rather than on what they say. Another premise of the functional approach is that legal systems solve practical problems in the same way. As a methodology for comparative legal studies, the pragmatic undertone of functionalism appears to stand out.

11.6.3 Legal harmonisation and unification

Harmonisation and unification are not only the goals of comparative legal studies; they also appear to be the technique.[61] Attempts are currently underway to establish a single legal framework or set of laws to govern people in a certain area. Harmonisation and unification are often achieved through the negotiation of bilateral and multilateral treaties to minimise disparities in the same legal disciplines and generate identical laws in some areas between the agreed countries.

11.6.4 Method of reviewing customary or natural law

Although customary law is recognised in the African countries and represents the majority of their laws, the concerns surrounding customs in Africa have yet to be

---

[57] Ibid.

[58] Ibid.

[59] C Garbarino 'An evolutionary approach to comparative taxation: Methods and agenda for research' (2009) 57(3) *The American Journal of Comparative Law* 677–709.

[60] Fombad (note 1) 984–1004.

[61] A Rosett 'Unification, harmonization, restatement, codification, and reform in international commercial law' (1992) 40(3) *The American Journal of Comparative Law* 683–697.

resolved. Africa comprises at least 54 countries.[62] This could mean that the African continent has around the same number of customs, if not more. Customary law, by definition, is primarily unwritten and varies from one location to another. Also, it is subject to modification. And whereas some countries consider customary law to be an issue of fact that must be proven via evidence, others believe it to be a question of law.

For comparative legal studies in Africa, particularly in the context of harmonisation and unification, these disparate treatments of customary law and other customary-law issues have significant implications. Achieving meaningful harmonisation of customary law in Africa may require that all of the continent's different customary laws be treated in the same way: that is, as a legal issue. A renowned African scholar, Elias, made this demand, urging all independent Commonwealth African nations to follow Ghana's example and treat customary law as a legal issue.[63] This idea has drawn criticism, though, for its propensity to exaggerate patriotism and nationalism. This is because, without codifying the many customary-law principles already in place in African jurisdictions, this cannot be accomplished. This undertaking not only seems challenging, if not impossible, but it will also have an impact on the way customary law evolves. This is possibly one of the most obvious ways in which legal diversity prevents harmonisation.

11.6.5 Economic analysis method or approach

Growing discontent with the functional method led to the development of the economic approach.[64] This approach is focused on creating a paradigm for an appropriate legal solution and considers 'efficiency' to be such a paradigm. This method therefore has a connection to the functional approach. An application of economic principles is essential and notions of fairness are downplayed in order to analyse legal regulations correctly. Having '... less waste, reduced transaction costs, better resource allocation, or greater freedom for individuals to engage' would be considered characteristics of an efficient legal system.[65]

Competition between legal systems occurs during the legal transplantation process and only the most effective systems ultimately triumph or, rather, become hegemonic. In theory, this would appear to be advantageous for the entire world, but

[62] Ndulo (note 13) 87–120.

[63] D Forde 'Tropical African studies. A report on the Conference Organized by the International African Institute in Conjunction with the University of Ibadan, 5–11 April 1964' (1965) 35(1) *Journal of the International African Institute* 30–97.

[64] KC Schwartzman & KA Taylor 'What caused the collapse of apartheid?' (1999) 27(1) *Journal of Political & Military Sociology* 109–139.

[65] Fombad (note 1) 984–1004.

given the imbalance of economic strength between industrialised and developing nations, on the one hand, and their counterparts, on the other, it is clear that the latter may not be able to compete.

Nonetheless, the economic method might be useful for developing African nations in formulating a common economic code that would regulate their trade. This perspective examines instances of legal transplantation and the convergence and divergence of legal systems as a product of this competition – presuming, of course, that there is a competitive market for the delivery of law. The economic perspective emphasises the usefulness and economic effectiveness of legislation and its associated regulations.

11.6.6 Law and cultural approach

The cultural method of comparative legal studies affirms that every culture is unique, in contrast to the functional approach's assertion that legal regimes face comparable issues.[66] Following this approach, each legal system has its own unique cultures and traditions. The cultural approach emphasises variations in legal systems to this extent. And since laws are a manifestation of culture, it is important to take culture into account when comparing different laws.[67] The requirement that a comparativist should employ the technique of 'cultural immersion', which immerses comparative law in the 'political, historical, economic, and linguistic contexts that shaped the legal system, and in which the legal system operates', reflects the cultural undertone of comparative legal studies.[68]

Given that the cultural approach acknowledges cultural differences and may even try to conserve them, it would seem that legal unification is inimical to the maintenance of these distinctions. In this regard, Legrand has noted that 'it is time we stand back and re-evaluate' when the forces of unification endanger what gives a people their cultural uniqueness.[69] Because the cultural method is used solely to identify and characterise cultural differences, it may not be either normative or reformative. The challenge of identifying the true components of a legal culture is one of the issues with the cultural approach: for the cultural method to succeed as an industry, it is therefore first necessary to identify the elements of a legal culture.

---

66 VV Palmer 'From Lerotholi to Lando: Some examples of comparative law methodology' (2005) 53(1) *The American Journal of Comparative Law* 261–290.

67 Ibid.

68 Ibid.

69 P Legrand 'John Henry Merryman and comparative legal studies: A dialogue' (1999) 47(1) *The American Journal of Comparative Law* 3–66.

11.6.7 Critical method

Because it is Eurocentric and has a strong hegemonic–ideological bent, traditional comparative legal studies has attempted to incorporate the non-Western world into Western systems.[70] The movement to deconstruct comparative law of its Eurocentric garb is known as the critical approach to comparative legal studies. Frankenberg (as quoted by Oderkerk) – a proponent of the critical technique – envisages it being used as a three-step procedure.[71] He contends that the first step is to take the complex factual circumstances out of their social context and place them in a legal framework.[72] In order to identify the political objectives concealed behind the legal decision-making process, the second stage necessitates its dismantling. The third phase entails reintroducing the cultural context to the legal framework it had been previously separated from. African nations are the group of non-Western governments that the critical method aims to engage as participants in comparative legal studies.

11.6.8 Convergence and non-convergence approaches

According to the convergence theory, legal systems exist in numerous configurations but share a fundamental structure.[73] Supporters of this strategy claim that whereas legal systems may not be completely comparable, they do share certain basic characteristics. Markesinis (as quoted by Legrand) suggests that comparative legal studies should focus on the parallels that exist between various legal systems because there are already enough variances across the globe.[74] The functional method is therefore a subset of the convergence approach because it maintains that all legal issues, regardless of differences in social structures and developmental phases, are universal and are covered by all legal systems.

Contrary to the convergence approach, the non-convergence approach focuses on the variations between legal systems. The non-convergence comparativist believes that law is a living component of a larger culture and that focusing on superficial similarities between legal systems would be a mistake since doing so would ignore the cultural specificity of legal systems. The non-convergence model is accordingly applied in the cultural approach.

[70] JT Gathii 'International law and eurocentricity' (1998) 9 *European Journal of International Law* 184–211.

[71] M Oderkerk 'The need for a methodological framework for comparative legal research: Sense and nonsense of "methodological pluralism" in comparative law' (2015) 79(3) *Rabels Zeitschrift für Ausländisches und Internationales Privatrecht/The Rabel Journal of Comparative and International Private Law* 589–623.

[72] Ibid.

[73] B Buzan 'From international system to international society: Structural realism and regime theory meet the English school' (1993) 47(3) *International Organization* 327–352.

[74] Legrand (note 50) 262–273.

11.7 MODIFICATION OF LEGAL EDUCATION

Kibwana (as quoted by Okeke) has advised that priority be given to research on unique African comparative law across the continent.[75] Kibwana's suggestions have included researching: the effectiveness of imported foreign laws in Africa; the effectiveness, continuation and development of the application of customary law in Africa's contemporary systems, and the distinctions across legal systems.[76] He has also outlined specific actions for growing the field of African comparative law.[77]

Kibwana promoted the establishment of pan-African associations of law instructors and students in order to institutionalise this kind of comparative research; this resulted in the continuing interchange of publications, contests, personnel and consistent legal research on the subject.[78] He also advocated the inclusion of African comparative law as a required course in all African law schools.[79] The application of customary law, which is consistently taught in Western legal curricula, is a distinctive aspect of African comparative law. Accordingly, the author, Menski (as quoted by Okeke), has indicated: 'Promising models of teaching on customary laws exist in Namibia and several South African colleges.'[80]

Some Namibian lawyers received their early legal education in Europe and the United States. It is, however, clear that US and UK training is insufficient for efficient legal practice in Namibia, given the variety of sources of law that apply there. In southern Africa, especially in Namibia, African legal education was adjusted to include the study of the required legislation in addition to the common law. The same position was adopted in Kenya on the advice of Lord Denning. When Nigeria established the Legal Education Act in 1962, coursework on local customary law, Muslim law and the Nigerian court system was added to the mandatory legal education for attorneys in that country.

11.8 LEGAL REFORM

There are many instances of these nations' adopting comparative law to implement legal reform. According to Kibwana, Africa may steer clear of the difficulties the West ran into when considering the comparative Western legal culture.[81] In June 1985, for instance, South Africa repealed the statute outlawing inter-racial sex.

[75] Okeke (note 26) article 1.
[76] Ibid.
[77] Ibid.
[78] Ibid.
[79] Ibid.
[80] Ibid.
[81] Ibid.

At a fundamental level, the development of the 'one person, one vote' democratic ideal and the lessons learned from the abolitionist campaign served as a partial model for South Africa's protracted fight for equality.[82] Human rights and idealised social structures, have remained hotly contested issues in South Africa since the end of apartheid. It is clear that South Africa has accepted the idea that diversity and plurality are crucial to the population's well-being and that global homogeneity would be unwise. This is known as the 'to survive as a rainbow nation' philosophy. Okeke observes that South African law is 'not turning out as a carbon copy of Western legal systems' since it incorporates the diversity present in its mixed legal system.[83]

Nigeria and Kenya, too, have employed comparative law to advance legal reform, a process driven by both domestic concerns and the global impact of globalisation. Anti-corruption legislation is one pertinent example:[84] Nigeria has considered a number of ways of combating corruption, including consultations, open hearings and trips to other nations such as Ethiopia, Zimbabwe and Zambia, and also Hong Kong.[85] This endeavour led to the weaknesses in their anti-corruption legislation being identified, the unification of those laws and the appointment of an independent agency tasked with enforcing the legislation. Owing to corruption infractions, the International Monetary Fund (IMF) and Scandinavian nations suspended aid to Kenya in 1997:[86] before they would consider resuming their aid programmes, these donors demanded that the necessary adjustments be effected.

In response, Kenya was forced to compare its laws to other, more effective laws in order to de-monopolise, deregulate, privatise, prosecute and govern for improved human rights, accountability and rule clarification.[87] Reviewing the reasons why a particular law might be effective in one country but not in another was also required because certain reforms failed to resolve the issues. This is a crucial objective of comparative law that is applicable in the African setting.

Mubangizi reviewed the comparative laws of four African nations in order to offer advice on how to defend socio-economic rights under their constitutions.[88] He considered examples from the African continent and shared them with other nations in the area. His article exhorts many African nations to share their

[82] Ibid.
[83] Ibid.
[84] Ibid.
[85] Ibid.
[86] Ibid.
[87] Ibid.
[88] JC Mubangizi 'A comparative discussion of the South African and Ugandan Human Rights Commissions' (2015) 48(1) *The Comparative and International Law Journal of Southern Africa* 124–143.

knowledge with one another, particularly given that they are in transitional phases of development.[89]

11.9 HARMONISATION OF LAWS

The harmonisation of trade rules in particular is a significant issue for these developing nations due to the growing regionalisation and globalisation of commerce.[90] In determining whether it would be advantageous for it to join a treaty such as the Organisation pour l'Harmonisation en Afrique du Droit des Affaires (OHADA), for instance, Nigeria must assess the impact of the treaty laws on national laws, decide on the best course of action for its development and consider any trade-offs.[91] Whereas signing such a treaty offers greater commercial prosperity, it is critical to consider the local legal context when assessing the demands of modernising the law, such as accepting arbitration rather than judicial adjudication for company-law matters.[92] Kenya, a member of the East African Community (EAC), which also includes Somalia, Tanzania and Uganda, promotes commerce and economic progress among its residents through comparative law.[93] The EAC was created in 1967 and was briefly disbanded in 1977.

Since Tanzania is a former German colony, the regional economic development pact called for the harmonisation of laws among nations with different histories. In 2000, a revised EAC treaty came into effect and Rwanda joined the original three nations. In the light of Read's observation that 'African legal systems are particularly dysfunctional in the field of Family Law, where African forms of social organization have resisted harmonisation', it is obvious that one of the main objectives of comparative law in African nations is to resolve 'legal conflicts arising from the frequent combination of "customary" forms of law with statutory laws', for instance, in marriage and succession laws.[94] When regional cooperation is required or desired, comparative law is also helpful to these nations. For instance, when tackling environmental challenges, African nations should therefore naturally

---

[89] Ibid.

[90] Economic Commission for Latin America and the Caribbean (ECLAC) *International Trade and Inclusive Development: Building Synergies* (2014), https://repositorio.cepal.org/bitstream/handle/11362/37040/1/S1420266_en.pdf, accessed 20 August 2023.

[91] CM Fombad 'Some reflections on the prospects for the harmonization of international business laws in Africa: OHADA and beyond' (2013) 59(3) *Africa Today* 51–80; see also N Enonchong 'The harmonization of business law in Africa: Is article 42 of the OHADA Treaty a problem?' (2007) 51(1) *Journal of African Law* 95–116.

[92] Fombad (note 91) 51–80.

[93] Ibid.

[94] Ibid.

compile and harmonise relevant regulations to ensure environmentally sound development.

Another instance is the fact that currently in South Africa Muslim marriages are not regarded as legitimate: even though Muslims make up around one-and-a-half million of South Africa's population, their unions are not recognised by the law.[95] As a consequence, when problems in such marriages emerge, some couples seek formal legal remedies through the civil-law system, but the majority do not.

11.10 EFFICIENT PROBLEM-SOLVING

Comparative law can help with creative problem-solving in the case of legal matters.[96] For instance, Kenya needed to find a solution to a sharply split administration in a unitary system following the unrest of the closely fought presidential elections in 2007.[97] The final solution – an extra-constitutional power-sharing arrangement that gave the opposition seats in the cabinet and a prime ministerial position – was modelled on coalition governments that were formed in emergency situations, such as that in the United Kingdom during the Great Depression. The Kenyan parliament has pledged to continue with legal reform and alter the constitution.

Another issue that could be dealt with through the use of comparative law is the assessment of domestic risks and the impact of supranational legislation. For instance, Wiwa, an Ogoni leader, challenged the business and environmental practices of multinational corporations in Nigeria in the case of *Wiwa v Dutch Petroleum Co* 226 F3d 88 (2nd Cir 2000), particularly the activities of Shell Nigeria, a division of the Dutch company, Royal Dutch Shell. The deceased's next of kin brought a lawsuit under the US Alien Tort Claims Act after the Ogoni leaders were executed by Nigeria's military regime after a fabricated trial. According to the plaintiffs, Shell Nigeria participated in the executions. The case was initially dismissed for *forum non conveniens*, but the Second Circuit Court of Appeals overturned that decision, ruling that the case should proceed in the United States because the Act 'seems to reach claims for human rights abuses occurring abroad' and also because some of the plaintiffs were residents of the United States. Countries and the businesses

[95] R Denson 'Non-recognition of Muslim marriages: Discrimination and social justice' 2009 *Obiter* 244–285.

[96] C Engel 'Challenges in the interdisciplinary use of comparative law' (2021) 69(4) *The American Journal of Comparative Law* 777–797; see also HJ Ault & MA Glendon 'The importance of comparative law in legal education: United States goals and methods of legal comparison' (1976) 27(4) *Journal of Legal Education* 599–608.

[97] FO Owuor 'The 2007 general elections in Kenya: Electoral laws and process' (2007) 7(2) *Journal of African Elections* 113–128.

operating in them displayed a lack a comprehensive understanding of the way supranational laws would judge their behaviour and how these laws can affect the risk involved in activities in the country without a comparative-law perspective.[98] For instance, there are a number of areas where the development of South African law indicates the impact of foreign legal systems. The first is consumer protection, which has British influences. As a result, the previous perspective that contracts were regarded as 'sacred' changed and now the law ensures consumer protection and equitable remedies in the case of unfair contract conditions.

Property ownership is another instance of this. A 'complete analysis of systems prevailing in other countries providing for the ownership of a piece of a building' was conducted since a number of traditional property ownership schemes were problematic. As a result, 'sectional titles' may now be held and recorded under new legislation. The advent of the time-share concept and associated regulations to facilitate that market's development has been another trend.

The case of South Africa's offer of amnesty to persons on all sides of previous conflicts who had abused human rights is another instance of where the influence of precedent from other legal systems is obvious. But South Africa is neither the first nor the last state to make use of amnesty regimes: Zimbabwe has adopted some form of amnesty in attempts at resolving internal conflict.[99]

'Detailed consideration of foreign alternatives is a typical aspect of tax reform' in South Africa.[100] To fulfil its goals of national tax parity, the government has implemented a comparative capital gains tax policy.

The arrest warrant issued for the president of Sudan by the International Criminal Court (ICC) is one recent incident that requires the attention of all African countries. African leaders are scrutinising one another and the situations in which other leaders have been caught to identify the best course of action and response. The publication of some of the conversations that ensued from the issuing of the ICC warrant demonstrates the fact that comparative law includes the application of current international law. However, there have been complaints that the ICC was selectively targeting Africa.[101]

---

[98] S Hartmann, T Lindner, J Müllner et al 'Beyond the nation-state: Anchoring supranational institutions in international business research' (2022) 53 *Journal for International Business Studies* 1282–1306.

[99] M du Plessis & J Ford 'Transitional justice: A future Truth Commission for Zimbabwe?' (2009) 58(1) *The International and Comparative Law Quarterly* 73–117.

[100] TJ Steenekamp & JA Döckel 'Taxation and tax reform in LDCs: Lessons for South Africa' (1993) 10(3) *Development Southern Africa* 319–333.

[101] R Lough 'African Union accuses ICC prosecutor of bias' *Reuters*, 30 January 2011; see also P Kastner 'Africa – a fertile soil for the International Criminal Court?' (2010) 85(1/2) *Die Friedens-Warte* 131–159.

11.11 DIFFERENTIATION

When a government believes that observing global legal trends from a comparative-law perspective would have a different impact on their own country, they may decide to differentiate national laws or modify laws in a different way.[102] A regional neighbour's interpretation of this particular legislation may be more in line with the objectives of African countries, notwithstanding the Western countries' influence on a significant portion of African law. The objectives of comparative law can occasionally be more focused on a particular area. One region may have certain problems or customs that are more prevalent in it than elsewhere. One such matter is female genital circumcision (FGC). FGC is a popular practice throughout the Middle East and Africa, including Côte d'Ivoire in the past. Several laws, both traditional and more recent, govern and, in some situations, specifically forbid the practice. Comparing the relevant laws between Africa and the West in this situation would be less helpful because FGC is more prevalent in the setting of African countries than it is in the developed world.

11.12 COMPARATIVE LAW AND NAMIBIA

The complex legal system of Namibia demonstrates legal pluralism: owing to its colonial past, it is a hybrid legal system that incorporates South African law, Roman-Dutch common law, English common law and customary rules from Africa and post-independence states. In general, Namibia is a member of the common-law family of legal systems. The apartheid policy, which involved the segregation of and discrimination against Namibia's non-white people, must be taken into account in order for Namibia's history to be considered fully. But even though that system is no longer in effect, it is unlikely that its traces have completely vanished from Namibia's socio-political scene.

The Namibian Constitution's Art 144, which requires courts or tribunals to take international law into account while interpreting the Bill of Rights, is a noteworthy feature of the current Namibian legal system. These courts or tribunals are required to interpret cases in accordance with international law and may also consider foreign legislation. This clause has been hailed as evidence that 'African countries are becoming open to and responsive to outside normative influences',[103] along with similar clauses in the constitutions of certain other African nations. It does not

[102] U Karpen 'Comparative law: Perspectives of legislation' (2013) 17 *Anuario Iberoamericano de Justicia Constitutional* 141–185.

[103] M Welz 'External influence' in M Welz (ed) *African since Decolonization: History and Politics of a Diverse Continent* (Cambridge University Press, 2021).

appear that the Namibian courts have applied this clause, though. A body of laws, standards and norms commonly recognised in international relations is known as international law. It establishes common legal duties to serve as guidance for nations to follow on international matters such as trade, the environment, human rights and foreign policy. International law generally serves the objective of helping nations to maintain orderly, consistent and stable international relations. By approving and domesticating many international human rights accords, international law has also been used over time to deal with internal challenges in many nations.

The Namibian Constitution and international law are clearly related. For instance, the 1948 International Declaration of Human Rights served as the foundation for much of Namibia's Bill of Rights. Moreover, Art 144 of the Namibian Constitution specifically incorporates international law into Namibian law. The general principles of public international law and any international agreements binding upon Namibia under this Constitution must be a component of Namibian law, unless otherwise established by the Constitution or by an Act of Parliament.

The fact that international law is one of the sources of Namibian law is one of the significant ramifications of Art 144. This was confirmed in the *Mwilima* case,[104] where the Supreme Court referred to Art 144 as a 'special mechanism' that introduces international treaties such as the International Covenant on Civil and Political Rights into the law of Namibia. Conversely, international law must abide by Namibia's Constitution in order to be recognised. This means that wherever a clause in a treaty or another rule of international law conflicts with a clause in the Namibian Constitution, the clause in the Constitution will take precedence. A treaty will also be enforceable in Namibia in accordance with Art 144 only if the pertinent international and constitutional conditions under the law of treaties and the Namibian Constitution have been met.

Moreover, Art 144 upholds the Roman-Dutch common-law assertion that Namibia has always been subject to the broad principles of international law. For example, in the pre-Independence *Binga* decision,[105] the court stated that where the terms of legislation are not clear and are reasonably capable of having than one meaning, an international treaty on the topic becomes relevant, because there is a presumption that the Legislature did not intend to act in breach of international law.

There are two methods by which nations might implement international law. First, international law is regarded as a component of a state's internal legal structure in a monist legal system. Second, and in contrast, in a dualist legal system, international law is distinct from domestic law and must be approved by legislation

---

[104] *Government of the Republic of Namibia & Others v Mwilima & Others* (SA 29 of 2001) [2002] NASC 8 (7 June 2002).

[105] *Binga v Cabinet for South West Africa & Others* (250/1984) [1988] ZASCA 22 (24 March 1988).

before it can have an impact on national rights and obligations. Namibia has a monist legal system, while it actually features aspects of dualism because foreign agreements become Namibian law only if they are recognised by Namibia. Although the Namibian Constitution allows for the direct execution of international treaties, doing so without a domestic legal framework being in place is frequently difficult.

For instance, in the *Frank* case, despite having been in a long-term same-sex relationship with a Namibian resident, the applicant was refused permanent residence in the country. Several advisory opinions on the definition of 'sex' under the International Covenant on Civil and Political Rights and other treaties over the years have concluded that this term encompasses sexual orientation as a category for protection. The Namibian Supreme Court, however, decided to disregard the case law of international human rights law in *Frank* and determined that the term 'sex' does not include sexual orientation. The court declared further, using the stringent interpretation of Zimbabwean courts, that the term 'spouse' refers solely to those who are partners in legally registered heterosexual marriages.

Reflecting on the application of international human rights law in Namibia's jurisprudence, the Supreme Court relied on the *Namunjepo* judgment,[106] which stated:

> Whilst it is extremely instructive and useful to refer to, and analyse, decisions by other Courts such as the International Court of Human Rights ... the one major and basic consideration in arriving at a decision involves an enquiry into the contemporary norms, aspirations, expectations, sensitivities, moral standards, relevant established beliefs, social conditions, experiences and perceptions of the Namibian people.

Another example is the case of *Tsumib*,[107] where the High Court was requested to determine whether to grant permission to the eight applicants to appear before the court on behalf of the Hai||om People in a claim to what they consider to be their ancestral land. These applicants claimed that, because of their close association with the primary defendant, the Namibian government, the Hai||om Traditional Authority would be the most qualified to bring the case.

In the absence of any statutory provisions on the restitution of ancestral land rights in Namibia, the applicants relied on comparative case law and international human rights law in support of their application for representative action. However, the court ignored international law, ruling instead that if it were to allow the applicants

---

[106] *Namunjepo & Others v Commanding Officer Windhoek Prison & Another* (SA 3 of 1998) [1999] NASC 3 (9 July 1999).

[107] *Tsumib & Others v Government of the Republic of Namibia & Others* (SA 53 of 2019) [2022] NASC 6 (16 March 2022).

to proceed with the action, it would aid them in circumventing the rights given to the Hai||om Traditional Authority under the Traditional Authorities Act. As a result, the applicants were left without a remedy as to how they could assert their rights under both international human rights law and Namibian constitutional law.

These cases suggest that Namibian courts are sometimes hesitant to apply international human rights law, especially if it is seen to be in conflict with longstanding practices or traditions in the country – even where those traditions have the potential to limit the human rights of applicants. In addition, Namibian courts are more likely to refer to the decisions of other jurisdictions such as Canada, India, South Africa and Zimbabwe than to apply a provision from an international human rights treaty – which could be partly because legal practitioners who present cases to the courts are typically more comfortable with citing comparative case law than with presenting arguments based on international law.

However, Namibia is a signatory to several international human rights laws, which places a duty on the courts to apply them when appropriate. But it would appear that courts often favour the application of statutory law or comparative case law over international human rights law. While this is perhaps understandable, the failure of the judiciary to consider and apply the vast body of international human rights law in Namibia more frequently is a lost opportunity. The direct application of international human rights law is not only in line with the Namibian Constitution but will also afford more significance and protection to the human rights of all Namibians.

11.13 CONCLUSION

There is little doubt that comparative legal studies in Africa has a bright future. Those African legal scholars who are involved in the teaching and disseminating of comparative legal studies will play a crucial role in determining whether this possibility is converted into something 'actual' or meaningful. The more likely it is that these researchers will be motivated to advance the field of comparative legal studies, the brighter its future will be. To make this happen, however, there is one major issue that needs to be remedied: African academics must overcome their reliance on, and in some cases their obsessive loyalty to, the legal frameworks and procedures of the former colonial powers. A regrettable colonial attitude that has left African scholars with an engrained inferiority complex regarding their own capacities is revealed in the deference they display to foreign ideas on researching and teaching law. The causes of this unsatisfactory situation are easy to identify. The top professors and researchers who were in charge of creating the curricula for the existing law schools at the time (ie, during the immediate post-colonial years) had themselves received legal education according to Western ideas of what constituted respectable legal systems and standards. This ideology held that African perspectives on legal issues did not merit consideration, which had the result that African academics in charge of creating the curricula for law institutions continued to minimise or disregard the importance of African customary or traditional law. Even policy-makers and practitioners lacked greater exposure or sophistication. In reality, the vast majority of top attorneys across the board, including those in the Judiciary, appeared to have narrow, localised views of the law and legal education. Until the middle of the 1980s, when legal scholars educated in other non-common-law jurisdictions managed to overcome the formidable barrier preventing them from taking part in the development of their national legal systems, a negative attitude prevailed towards the handling of legal issues in other legal systems – through comparative legal systems.

REFERENCES

Agbiboa, DE & Okem, AE 'Unholy trinity: Assessing the impact of ethnicity and religion on national identity in Nigeria' (2011) 43(2) *Peace Research* 98–125.

Aguda, TA 'The judiciary in Africa' (1985) 9(1) *The Fletcher Forum* 13–35.

Allott, AN 'Towards the unification of laws in Africa' (1965) 14(2) *The International and Comparative Law Quarterly* 366–389.

The American Heritage Dictionary of the English Language 4 ed (Houghton Mifflin, 2000).

Ault, HJ & Glendon, MA 'The importance of comparative law in legal education: United States goals and methods of legal comparison' (1976) 27(4) *Journal of Legal Education* 599–608.

Bauer, G 'Namibia in the first decade of independence: How democratic?' (2001) 27(1) *Journal of Southern African Studies* 33–55.

Bhat, PI 'Comparative method of legal research: Nature, process and potentiality' (2015) 57(2) *Journal of the Indian Law Institute* 147–173.

Buzan, B 'From international system to international society: Structural realism and regime theory meet the English (1993) 47(3) *International Organization* 327–352.

Bwire, B 'Integration of African customary legal concepts into modern law: Restorative justice: A Kenyan example' (2019) 9(1) *Societies* 17.

Demian, M 'On the repugnance of customary law' (2014) 56(2) *Comparative Studies in Society and History* 508–536.

Denson, R 'Non-recognition of Muslim marriages: Discrimination and social justice' 2009 *Obiter* 244–285.

Du Plessis, M & Ford, J 'Transitional justice: A future truth commission for Zimbabwe?' (2009) 58(1) *The International and Comparative Law Quarterly* 73–117.

Eberle, EJ 'The method and role of comparative law' (2009) 8 *Washington University Global Studies Law Review* 451.

Economic Commission for Latin America and the Caribbean (ECLAC) *International Trade and Inclusive Development: Building Synergies* (2014), https://repositorio.cepal.org/bitstream/handle/11362/37040/1/S1420266_en.pdf, accessed 20 August 2023.

Encyclopedia Britannica 'European and African interaction from the 15th through to the 18th century (nd), https://www.britannica.com/place/Southern-Africa/European-and-African-interaction-from-the-15th-through-the-18th-century.

Engel, C 'Challenges in the interdisciplinary use of comparative law' (2021) 69(4) *The American Journal of Comparative Law* 777–797.

Enonchong, N 'The harmonization of business law in Africa: Is article 42 of the OHADA Treaty a problem?' (2007) 51(1) *Journal of African Law* 95–116.

Fletcher, GP 'Comparative law as a subversive discipline' (1998) 46(4) *The American Journal of Comparative Law* 683–700.

Fombad, CM 'Some reflections on the prospects for the harmonization of international business laws in Africa: OHADA and beyond' (2013) 59(3) *Africa Today* 51–80.

Fombad, CM 'Comparative research in contemporary African legal studies' (2018) 67(4) *Journal of Legal Education* 984–1004.

Fontaine, M 'Law harmonisation and local specificities – a case study: OHADA and the law of contracts' (2013) 18(1) *Uniform Law Review* 50–64.

Forde, D 'Tropical African studies. A report on the conference organized by the International African Institute in Conjunction with the University of Ibadan, 5–11 April 1964' (1965) 35(1) *Journal of the International African Institute* 30–97.

Garbarino, C 'An evolutionary approach to comparative taxation: Methods and agenda for research' (2009) 57(3) *The American Journal of Comparative Law* 677–709.

Gathii, JT 'International law and Eurocentricity' (1998) 9 *European Journal of International Law* 184–211.

Ghai, Y 'Law, development and African scholarship' (1987) 50(6) *The Modern Law Review* 750–776.

Goldsmith, J & Levinson, D 'Law for states: International law, constitutional law, public law' (2009) 122(7) *Harvard Law Review* 1791–1868.

Gutteridge, HC 'Comparative law and the conflict of laws' (1943) 29 *Transactions of the Grotius Society* 119–141.

Hartmann, S, Lindner, T, Müllner, J & Puck, J 'Beyond the nation-state: Anchoring supranational institutions in international business research' (2022) 53 *Journal for International Business Studies* 1282–1306.

Hazard, JN 'Comparative law in legal education' (1951) 18(2) *The University of Chicago Law Review* 264–279.

Hinz, MO 'The ascertainment of customary law: What is ascertainment of customary law and what is it for? The experience of the Customary Law Ascertainment Project in Namibia' (2012) 2(7) *Oñati Socio-legal Series* 85–105.

Joireman, SF 'Inherited legal systems and effective rule of law: Africa and the colonial legacy' (2001) 39(4) *The Journal of Modern African Studies* 571–596.

Kamba, WJ 'Comparative law: A theoretical framework' (1974) 23(3) *The International and Comparative Law Quarterly* 485–519.

Kariseb, K 'Reflections on judicial cross-fertilisation in the adjudication of human rights and constitutional disputes in Africa: The case of Namibia' (2021) 35(1) *Speculum Juris* 19–32.

Karpen, U 'Comparative law: Perspectives of legislation' (2013) 17 *Anuario Iberoamericano de Justicia Constitutional* 141–185.

Kastner, P 'Africa – a fertile soil for the International Criminal Court?' (2010) 85(1/2) *Die Friedens-Warte* 131–159.

Lafranque, J 'Judicial borrowing: International & comparative law as nonbinding tools of domestic legal adjudication with particular reference to Estonia' (nd), https://core.ac.uk/download/pdf/216908301.pdf, accessed 20 August 2023.

Landauer, C 'Taslim Olawale Elias: From British colonial law to modern international law' in J von Bernstorff & P Dann (eds) *The Battle for International Law: South-North Perspectives on the Decolonization Era, The History and Theory of International Law* online ed (Oxford Academic, 2019).

Legrand, P 'Comparative legal studies and commitment to theory (review of *A Modern Approach to Comparative Law*, by P de Cruz)' (1995) 58(2) *The Modern Law Review* 262–273.

Legrand, P 'John Henry Merryman and comparative legal studies: A dialogue' (1999) 47(1) *The American Journal of Comparative Law* 3–66.

Lough, R 'African Union accuses IIC prosecutor of bias' *Reuters*, 30 January 2011.

Mahy, P 'The functional approach in comparative socio-legal research: Reflections based on a study of plural work regulation in Australia and Indonesia' (2016) 12(4) *International Journal of Law in Context* 420–436.

Merry, SE 'Law and colonialism' (1991) 25(4) *Law & Society Review* 889–922.

Michaels, R 'Comparative law' (nd), https://scholarship.law.duke.edu/cgi/viewcontent.cgi?article=3014&context=faculty_scholarship, accessed 20 August 2023.

Michaels, R 'The functional method of comparative law', https://scholarship.law.duke.edu/cgi/viewcontent.cgi?article=2033&context=faculty_scholarship, accessed 20 August 2023.

Mingst, KA 'Judicial systems of sub-Saharan Africa: An analysis of neglect' (1988) 31(1) *African Studies Review* 135–147.

Motshabi, KB 'Decolonising the university: A law perspective' (2018) 40(1) *Strategic Review for Southern Africa* 104.

Mubangizi, JC 'A comparative discussion of the South African and Ugandan Human Rights Commissions' (2015) 48(1) *The Comparative and International Law Journal of Southern Africa* 124–143.

Ndulo, M 'African customary law, customs, and women's rights' (2011) 18(1) *Indiana Journal of Global Legal Studies* article 5.

Oderkerk, M 'The need for a methodological framework for comparative legal research: Sense and nonsense of "methodological pluralism" in comparative law' (2015) 79(3) *Rabels Zeitschrift Für Ausländisches Und Internationales Privatrecht/The Rabel Journal of Comparative and International Private Law* 589–623.

Okeke, CN 'African law in comparative law: Does comparativism have worth?' (2011) 16(1) *Roger Williams University Law Review* article 1.
Okeke, CN *Comparative Law in Africa: Methodologies and Concepts. Book Chapters by GGU Law Authors* (Golden Gate University School of Law, 2015) Book 26.
Owuor, FO 'The 2007 general elections in Kenya: Electoral laws and process' (2007) 7(2) *Journal of African Elections* 113–128.
Palmer, VV 'From Lerotholi to Lando: Some examples of comparative law methodology' (2005) 53(1) *The American Journal of Comparative Law* 261–290.
Porter, A 'Africana legal studies: A new theoretical approach to law & protocol' (2022) 27 *Michigan Journal of Race & Law* 249.
Reimann, M 'The progress and failure of comparative law in the second half of the twentieth century' (2022) 50(4) *The American Journal of Comparative Law* 671–700.
Rosett, A 'Unification, harmonization, restatement, codification, and reform in international commercial law' (1992) 40(3) *The American Journal of Comparative Law* 683–697.
Schwartzman, KC & Taylor, KA 'What caused the collapse of apartheid?' (1999) 27(1) *Journal of Political & Military Sociology* 109–139.
Steenekamp, TJ & Döckel, JA 'Taxation and tax reform in LDCs: Lessons for South Africa' (1993) 10(3) *Development Southern Africa* 319–333.
Taiwo, EA 'Repugnancy clause and its impact on customary law: Comparing the South African and Nigerian positions – some lessons for Nigeria' (2009) 34(1) *Journal of Juridical Science* 89–115.
Valcke, C 'Comparative law as comparative jurisprudence: The comparability of legal systems' (2004) 52(3) *The American Journal of Comparative Law* 713–740.
Welz, M 'External influence' in M Welz (ed) *African since Decolonization: History and Politics of a Diverse Continent* (Cambridge University Press, 2021).
Yntema, HE 'Comparative research and unification of law' (1942) 41(2) *Michigan Law Review* 261–268.

CASES

Ex parte Attorney-General in re: Constitutional Relationship between Attorney-General and the Prosecutor-General (SA 7 of 1993) [1995] NASC 1 (13 July 1995)
Binga v Cabinet for South West Africa & Others (250/1984) [1988] ZASCA 22 (24 March 1988)
Government of the Republic of Namibia & Others v Mwilima & Others (SA 29 of 2001) [2002] NASC 8 (7 June 2002)
Namunjepo & Others v Commanding Officer Windhoek Prison & Another (SA 3 of 1998) [1999] NASC 3 (9 July 1999)
Tsumib and Others v Government of the Republic of Namibia and Others (SA 53 of 2019) [2022] NASC 6 (16 March 2022).

12

Decolonial theory: a critical analysis of the ways in which legal transplant manifests coloniality – a comparative study of southern African and southern Asian states

Pilisano Masake and Eugene L Libebe

12.1 INTRODUCTION

Legal transplant can be effectuated in various ways: through colonialism, globalism and internationalism, to mention a few.[1] Decolonial theory, among other theories, acknowledges that colonialism disrupted the pre-colonial legal philosophies – of which the African and Asian legal philosophies are not an exception. It is common cause that Africa and Asia were subjected to colonial rule. The disruption of the organically created legal philosophies at the behest of colonialism led to a legal paradigm shift: the introduction of colonial laws. This legal paradigm shift, among other actions, witnessed the transplanting of laws from the colonial masters into the colonies. The concept of *legal transplant* is compound: it comprises *legal*[2] and *transplant*. And it raises issues related to its conceptual meaning – for example, What does the concept of *legal* that precedes *transplant* mean? Is there a distinction

[1] D Nelken 'Comparatists and transferability' in P Legrand & R Munday (eds) *Comparative Legal Studies: Traditions and Transitions* (Cambridge University Press, 2003) 437–466.

[2] 'Legal' is a commonly accepted adjective that means 'relating to law' or 'permitted by law'.

between *law*[3] and *legal* – in particular, *legal* as understood in the context of *legal transplant*? What is it that is transplanted? Is it *law* or *legal*?

This chapter's authors recognise the distinctive intellectual meaning of these concepts; however, and despite these distinctions, they find the distinction less fertile and for this reason, as is demonstrated below, they adopt the view that legal transplant implies the movement and reception of law and legal institutions from one jurisdiction, community or legal system to another, regardless of the method adopted for their movement and reception. In the context of colonialism, legal transplant involves the laws which were applied by the colonial masters in their jurisdictions, or legal systems, being made applicable to and enforced in the colonies. This aspect of the conceptual meaning of legal transplant is central to this discourse and is discussed in detail below. These transplanted colonial laws in fact came to be the pinnacle of coloniality. However, this assumption does not diminish the fact that any legal transplant which adopts any other method of movement and reception other than colonialism cannot manifest coloniality – these postulations are articulated below.

At the present time, portions of these transplanted colonial laws are still in force. This assertion informs and confirms coloniality. Understood in the context of decolonial theory, it presupposes that the disparagement of colonialism did not bring an end to the effects and/or impact of colonialism. The assumption here is clear: the attainment of political independence by the colonised succeeded through the freedom of *being*. In contrast, the effect and impact of colonialism subsists in and continues to influence state affairs in the present politically independent states. In this way, coloniality is construed as being the source of disarray, inequality, powerlessness, ignorance, the continuation of oppression, psychological trauma and odious debts, to state only a few negative outcomes.[4] Premised on this assumption, the authors of this chapter critically assess the impact of the transplanted laws with a specific focus on the way in which legal transplant may manifest as coloniality. The chapter proceeds from a distinct normative imperative of decolonial theory. It is based on a working presupposition that to counter coloniality effectively the need exists to transcend decolonisation and to implement a decoloniality agenda defiantly. Furthermore, it proceeds from the belief that in order for decoloniality to be effective indigenous people need to resist any form of centricity materially. The

[3] Commonly understood, the concept of law means 'a system of rules which a particular state recognizes as regulating conduct of members, and which may be enforceable and it provide for sanctions': K Jayasuriya 'Globalisation, law, and the transformation of sovereignty: The emergence of global regulatory governance' (1999) 6 *Indiana Journal of Global Legal Studies* 425.

[4] PH Masake & EL Libebe 'Colonialism, coloniality and decolonisation of legal education: Perspectives from universities in Southern African Development Community' (2019) 11(1) *Namibia Law Journal* 270–294.

argument is that any form of centricity may assume ignorance and potentially risk obscuring pluriversality. As a result, it may reinforce coloniality.

Applying comparative methodologies, the authors examine the pre- and post-colonial laws and practices in southern Africa[5] and southern Asia.[6] The regions under investigation are comparable based, among other factors, on their common rich history of colonial rule at the behest of British colonial masters. Our interest is not limited to recounting the rich and sour history of colonial rule, but to use such history to evaluate critically the ways in which the transplanted laws shaped and/or continue to inform the legal, political and social spheres in these regions. This includes considering the adverse consequences and determining whether any interventions were adopted to realise the decoloniality agenda (and their effectiveness).

12.2 DECOLONIAL THEORY IN PERSPECTIVE

Decolonial theory is a critical school of thought that, as described by Mignolo, advocates

> the openness and freedom of thought and ways of life; the cleanliness of the coloniality of being and knowledge; the detachment of the rhetoric of modernity and its imperial imaginary.[7]

As construed in this context, decolonial theory is related to decolonisation. And it traces its conception to the writing and works of Latin American scholars who engaged with the epistemological distinctiveness of coloniality in the colonising state in contrast to colonised states (colonies). From the Latin American perspectives, decolonial theory, to a large extent, is perceived to have been modelled by liberation theories, hegemony theory and the sour history.[8] This is considered in the context of persisting underdevelopment, a lack of economic independence, and political

[5] Countries such as Angola, Botswana, eSwatini, Lesotho, Malawi, Mauritius, Mozambique, Namibia, Rwanda, Seychelles, South Africa, Tanzania, Zambia, and Zimbabwe.

[6] Countries such as Bangladesh, Brunei Darussalam, India, Malaysia, Maldives, Pakistan, Singapore and Sri Lanka.

[7] W Mignolo *The Darker Side of Western Modernity: Global Futures, Decolonial Options* (Duke University Press, 2011) 30.

[8] S Marzagora 'The humanism of reconstruction: African intellectuals, decolonial critical theory and the opposition to the "posts" (postmodernism, poststructuralism, postcolonialism)' (2016) 28(2) *Journal of African Cultural Studies* 161–178.

upheaval and unrest that has plagued the majority of the Latin American states.[9] The presupposition embedded in the concept of decoloniality, which informs decolonial theory, is the recognition that 'ours is an asymmetrical world order, that is sustained not only by colonial matrices of power but also by specific pedagogies and epistemologies of equilibrium that continue to produce alienated Africans who are socialised into hating the Africa that produced them, and liking the Europe and America that rejects them'.[10] With the foregoing, the departure points in decolonial discourses are often characterised as 'the existential realities of suffering, oppression, repression, domination and exclusion'.[11] In deference to the decolonial theory, it is necessary to provide a concise attribution of coloniality. In essence, it is important to highlight the point that, prior to unpacking decolonial theory, there are several questions that may linger and that may have to be addressed, including these: What is coloniality? How is coloniality different from colonialism, capitalism or neo-colonialism? Is there any link between coloniality and decolonial theory? With these questions, the rationale of providing the description of coloniality cannot be understated: that is, without the spectre of coloniality, the debate that underpins decolonial theory falls away altogether. In the light of this, decolonial theory is an antidote to coloniality.

The theory of coloniality as construed from the writings of scholars such as Maldonado-Torres is summarised as follows:[12]

> [a] long-standing pattern of power that emerged because of colonialism, but define culture, labour, inter-subjective relations, and knowledge production well beyond the strict limits of colonial administrations. Thus, coloniality survives colonialism. It is maintained alive in books, in the criteria for academic performance, incultural patterns, in common sense, in the self-image of peoples, inaspirations of self, and in so many aspects of our modern experience. In a way, as modern subjects we breathe coloniality all the time and every day.

What emerges from this description of coloniality is the realisation that the effects of the post-colonial era brought to the fore the theory of coloniality.

---

[9] S Harding 'Latin American decolonial social studies of scientific knowledge: Alliances and tensions' (2016) 41(6) *Science, Technology, & Human Values* 1063–1087.

[10] OS Afolabi 'Globalisation, Decoloniality and the question of knowledge production in Africa: A critical discourse' (2020) 18(1) *Journal of Higher Education in Africa* 93–110; SJ Ndlovu-Gatsheni 'Why decoloniality in the 21st century?' (2020) 48 *The Thinker* 10–15, 11.

[11] SJ Ndlovu-Gatsheni, 'Decoloniality as the future of Africa' (2015) 13 *History Compass*, 485–496, 492.

[12] N Maldonado-Torres 'On the coloniality of being: Contributions to the development of a concept' (2007) 21 *Cultural Studies* 243; see also I Shai 'The right to development, transformative constitutionalism and radical transformation in South Africa: Post-colonial and de-colonial reflections' (2019) 19 *African Human Rights Law Journal* 494–509.

Grosfoguel postulates that coloniality renders it possible for us to comprehend the full-scale impact of the existence of and the continuation of various forms of colonial administration. These could be synchronised with colonial culture as practised, the application of colonial laws and the retention of colonial structural formation. In other words, legal transplant is not an exception.[13] The assumption here is clear: coloniality is understood as an extension of colonialism or hegemony and domination imposed on another (ie, former colonies). Adopted from the typology developed by Horvath, the characteristics of colonialism may fall in three categories: colonialism *(a)* with the object of exterminating the colonised; *(b)* viewed as an assimilative relationship (cultural doner vs cultural host), and *(c)* without acculturation but possibly including cultural exchange.[14] Grosfoguel, though, stated differently, makes a similar observation to that of Horvath; he explains that colonialism entails:[15]

> The presence of a colonial administration such as the period of classical colonialism. Colonial situation is explained with reference to the cultural, political, sexual, spiritual, epistemic and economic oppression or exploitation of subordinate racialised/ ethnic groups by dominant racialised/ethnic groups.

There is no disagreement that most of the colonies were at some point politically liberated from the hounds of the colonial masters – in this sense it was the achievement of the decolonisation of *being*. However, the impact of colonialism, as demonstrated above, continues to haunt the colonies through the coloniality phenomenon – in this sense, the coloniality of *knowledge* and *power*. The stench of colonialism, drawing from Horvath's typology, lies, for instance, in colonialism, where the objective of assimilative relationships accounts for much legal transplant from the cultural donor during the colonial era, the colonial master states, into or as received by the cultural hosts, the colonies. An example in point here is the reception of Roman-Dutch law and English common law that the colonial masters imposed on the states of the Global South. An elaborate account of these examples is provided below. However, suffice to reiterate that one of the conduits of harmful legal transplant was colonialism. In addition, there is a link, as is demonstrated below, between the transplant of laws that took place during the colonial era and their present manifestation as coloniality in the former colonies. The acknowledgement

[13] R Grosfoguel 'The epistemic decolonial turn: Beyond the political-economy paradigms' (2007) 21(2) *Cultural Studies* 211–223.

[14] RJ Horvath 'A definition of colonialism' (1972) 13(1) *Current Anthropology* 45–57.

[15] Grosfoguel (note 13) 213.

of coloniality, as shown above, renders the decolonial discourse even more relevant nowadays.[16]

According to Noxolo, the emergence and justification of postcolonial and decolonial theories, respectively, is based on concrete theoretical and practical experiences that continue to manifest in the former colonies.[17] As observed by Noxolo regarding these experiences, inevitably,

> each is an analysis of the brutal inequalities at the heart of the global system, and neither is thoroughly open to appropriation by those who benefit from those inequalities, even when they do share post-colonised or decolonial identities.[18]

Decolonial theory presents important features and creates opportunities for conversations and jurisprudence about the nature of decolonial comparative law and what it could achieve. The objective, as drawn from decolonial perspectives, is to advance the case for the recognition of legal pluralism and equality. It is therefore imperative that decolonial comparative law guard against reinforcing hegemony, domination, inequality and legal transplants that give effect to coloniality.

Notwithstanding the reverence afforded to the decolonial theory, there are impediments, including its disparagement, a hangover from the decolonial theorists, as observed by Harding, in the form of mimicry. Harding observed that

> [m]ost of the decolonial theorists advocate for attention to indigeneity and indigenous knowledge, to the poor, and to hindmost guard theory that stays close to the cause of social justice. However, none of these intellectuals are themselves poor, and it is not apparent that any have peasant or indigenous origins.[19]

Moreover, many of the theorists nowadays hold elite positions in elite locations (in universities mostly in the Western world). Therefore, if decolonial comparative law is to be theorised predominantly by scholars in the West or the North, it is likely to maintain the epistemological hegemony of the Global North and the West, which will hinder pluriversality. These setbacks adversely affect the decolonial theory,

[16] J Schacherreiter 'Postcolonial theory and comparative law: On the methodological and epistemological benefits to comparative law through postcolonial theory' (2016) 49(3) *Verfassung und Recht in Übersee/Law and Politics in Africa, Asia and Latin America* 291–312.

[17] P Noxolo *Decolonial Theory in a Time of the Re-colonisation of UK Research* (Royal Geographical Society, 2107) 342, https://rgs-ibg.onlinelibrary.wiley.com/doi/epdf/10.1111/tran.12202, accessed 20 August 2023.

[18] Noxolo (note 17) 42.

[19] Harding (note 9) 1073.

since decolonial theory, by its very design, strikes at the heart of this hegemony and legal transplants cannot be an exception. The next section highlights the underlying meanings of and debates on legal transplants in comparative law and examines the way legal transplants may manifest as coloniality through the lens of decolonial comparative law – a view that is peculiar to the Global South.

12.3 COMPARATIVE LAW AND LEGAL TRANSPLANTS

In comparative-law discourses it is often very important to understand the theoretical framework, the meaning and the functions of comparative law. Comparative law is the systematic application of comparison to law:[20] the objective or question of comparison strongly influences the decision as to which legal system, practice, institution or law may be compared to and also the methodology that may be adopted.[21] The functions of comparative law include but are not limited to judicial process,[22] law reform, legislation, academic studies, international law[23] and understanding, and unification and harmonisation. Kamba makes a qualified postulation, descriptively, when describing the imperative nature and scope of comparative law:

> Comparative law is indispensable to the legal theorist/philosopher – (i) for the formulation of general theories of law: generalisation must proceed by way of bringing together a number of particular instances of law ie, legal systems, and (ii) for the testing of these general theories, for instance, how universal is the Western idea of law – with its close association with specialised agencies for its making, interpretation, application and enforcement? How far do the traits of Western legal systems represent the characteristics of legal orders in all societies? The answers to these questions can only be given satisfactorily by comparative legal research.[24]

There is a close relationship between legal transplant and the study of comparative law.[25] Legal transplant, the unfertile questions identified in the introduction section

[20] WJ Kamba 'Comparative law: A theoretical framework' (1974) 23(3) *The International and Comparative Law Quarterly* 485–519.
[21] Kamba (note 20) 488.
[22] Especially in cases of first impression.
[23] For example, Art 38(1)(*c*) of the Statute of the International Court of Justice.
[24] Kamba (note 20) 494.
[25] S Zongling 'Legal transplant and comparative law' (1999) 51(4) *Revue Internationale de Droit Comparé* 853–857.

above, is a concept and topic of interest particular to comparative law. To 'transplant', according to the *Oxford Dictionary*, means

> to take an organ form one person, animal or part of the body and put in into or onto another; or to move a growing plant and plant it somewhere else; or to move something to a different place or environment.[26]

In comparative law, transplant is kind of metaphor, although the term has been used in the context of botany (forestry) and fields of medicine. Transplant therefore implies displacement.[27] This term, introduced as a metaphor by Watson, has been heavily criticised but has established itself as the keyword for the phenomenon of transnational legal influences.[28] At the formal level, transplants are the official promulgation of borrowed law.[29] The infamous cases are countries such as Japan and Turkey, which absorbed all codes of law from Europe.[30] Legal transplants involve the diffusion of rules, codes or practices from one country to another: a country can borrow from another country or can have an alien system imposed on it.[31] It is a concept that

> denotes the transfer or movement and reception of laws, principles, rules, cords, practices or doctrines from one legal environment or society to another, generally but not always to effect an improvement in the recipient's socio-legal order.[32]

The classic examples here, in the Global South, are the reception and application of Roman-Dutch law and English law in South Africa, Namibia and most of southern Africa. The reception of Roman law in Western Europe during the Middle Ages is also an illustration of successful legal transplantation.[33] According to Friedman, much of the transplanting of law has occurred throughout history by way of

---

[26] *Oxford Advanced Learner's Dictionary: International Student's Edition* 9 ed (Oxford University Press, 2015) 1609.

[27] P Legrand 'The impossibility of legal transplants' (1997) 4(2) *Maastricht Journal of European and Comparative Law* 111–124.

[28] Schacherreiter (note 16) 301. See also A Watson *Legal Transplants: An Approach to Comparative Law* (University of Georgia Press, 1993).

[29] L Friedman 'Some comments on Cotterrell and legal transplants' in D Nelken & J Feest (eds) *Adapting Legal Cultures* (Hart Publishing, 2001) 93.

[30] Friedman (note 29) 93.

[31] Friedman (note 29) 94.

[32] TW Bennett *Ubuntu: An African Jurisprudence* (Juta & Co, 2018) 15.

[33] Zongling (note 25) 854.

conquest and colonisation.[34] For example, the common law is a worldwide system because the British had a global empire; this law took hold in British-formed settlements and colonies in Africa and Asia.

It is important to distinguish various categories of legal transplant. Solinas identifies two broad categories: the hegemonic at the one extreme, and, at the other, the non-hegemonic legal transplant.[35] The hegemonic category presupposes imposed legal transplant; in contradistinction, the non-hegemonic category relatively implies the voluntary diffusion of the legal system from one legal environment to the other. As is demonstrated below, both of these categories of legal transplant are relevant to decolonial discourse, albeit with varied distribution. Scholars are yet to be *ad idem* on the typology of legal transplant; equally, there appears to be no consensus on the objective of legal transplant: the list is endless, and may include cost-saving, legitimisation,[36] filling a legal *lacuna*, advancing legal hegemony or coloniality, harmonisation and law reform,[37] to mention only a few. Regarding these objectives, it is argued that legal transplant is paradoxical, that is, it may either be in the best interests of the receiving nation or it may be harmful. This could be construed as a manifestation of coloniality if and when the evidence depicts such transplant as having been imposed or received by the former colony and that it was facilitated by a colonial order or it advanced the hegemony of the legal system from the colonial master, or was imposed by states to exercise domination over weaker states.

Transnational legal influences, including legal transplants, play an integral part in categorising the legal systems into legal families.[38] The analysis of legal transplants is therefore pivotal in order to overcome essentialist conceptions of legal cultures because it emphasises mutual influences between legal systems during their historical development.[39] This analysis reveals that legal transplants are characterised by multiple influences, differences and ambivalences that may well even manifest in coloniality.

This work critically analyses whether the European legal transplants have in fact influenced the law of southern Africa and south and south-east Asian states

---

[34] Friedman (note 29) 94; see also Legrand (note 27).

[35] M Salinos 'The nature of legal transplants – inspirations from postcolonial scholarship' (2016) 22 *New Zealand Association of Comparative Law* 179–216.

[36] K van Wallenndael 'Legal transplants: Profitable borrowing or harmful dependency? The use of legal transplant framework for the adoption of EU law: The case of Croatia' in A Filipiak, E Kania, J van den Bosch & R Wisniewski (eds) *Evolving Dependency Relations* (Revolution Research Centre, 2014) 75–98.

[37] H Xanthaki 'Legal transplants in legislation: Defusing the trap' (2008) 57(3) *The International and Comparative Law Quarterly* 659–673.

[38] Schacherreiter (note 16) 312.

[39] Schacherreiter (note 16) 311.

so profoundly that these legal systems as a whole can be classified as belonging to Western or European legal families and in this way lead to a conclusion on whether legal transplant manifests in coloniality. Furthermore, analysis could indicate whether – despite the European legal transplants – African and Asian legal systems are so fundamentally different that they constitute their own legal family, dispelling the opinion that legal transplant manifests in coloniality. On this point, Schacherreiter makes the following observation:

> The phenomenon of legal transplants demonstrates the permeability of legal systems, their mutual influences, and the resulting similarities and differences. Thus, the study of legal transplants can help break up homogenizations and rigid dichotomies, thereby contributing an integral part to overcoming ethnocentrism and cultural individualisation.[40]

Watson considers legal transplants to be the main source of legal change and development and concludes from his studies about the European reception of Roman law that legal transplants can happen even between very different societies and relatively independently of social context.[41] Legrand, by way of contrast, considers it impossible that a legal rule together with its significance can be transferred perfectly from one legal culture to another: this is because different legal cultures will attribute completely different meanings to the rule in question. In his opinion, all that remains of the legal rule are the words, devoid of their original meaning.[42]

According to Schacherreiter, both approaches are problematic because they hardly attribute any significance to exchange and dialogue between different legal systems and cultures.[43] Legrand's approach denies the possibility of mutual understanding and dialogue, denying as it does in principle the possibility of legal transplants between legal cultures because they attribute completely different meanings to the same rule. Watson's contrasting position, namely, that transplants can be implemented independently of different social, legal and cultural contexts, denies the necessity of such a dialogue.[44] In practice, Watson's position contrasts with this these, reinforcing approaches that propagate reforms in countries on the periphery or semi-periphery by seeking recourse from European or US legal models without taking into account the peripheral countries' own specific contexts.[45] This

[40] Schacherreiter (note 16) 301; see also Bennett (note 32) 15.
[41] Schacherreiter (note 16) 301.
[42] Ibid.
[43] Ibid.
[44] Schacherreiter (note 16) 302.
[45] Legrand (note 27) 111.

position has been criticised with regard to the reforms in the former socialist states after 1990 and the US-dominated reforms in Latin America.[46]

In the context of decolonial theory we concur to a certain extent with Legrand's approach because it stresses the differences between legal cultures and warns against assuming that one's own legal models, as successful as they may be in one's own legal system, are capable of meeting the requirements of another legal culture. He explicitly demands that the 'Other' not be equated to the 'Self' but rather allows 'the realisation of its own view of the world'.[47] However, Legrand's stance is also problematic because it links legal cultures to nation-states and presents these as fundamentally distinct and walled off from one another, but internally uniform. This leads to a radical cultural relativism that presents different legal cultures as monolithic national blocks incapable of dialogue and mutual understanding.[48]

Another voice on this matter is that of Kahn-Freund, who refers to a view stated by Montesquieu that an organic law which is created to regulate a specific situation or country is appropriate only to that particular situation or country, to the exclusion of other situations or countries. However, if such a law becomes appropriate and applicable to other situations or countries, then that should not be viewed as a norm; it should instead be construed as a coincidence.[49] Kahn-Freund's other point is that the application of comparative law transcends mere knowledge of the law of a particular foreign state: indeed, it should include an understanding of the social, economic, cultural and political context of that particular foreign state (to mention only a few aspects), otherwise the practice of comparative law will be a case of misuse.[50]

Watson, however, challenges Kahn-Freund's idea about legal transplant. According to his view,

> history clearly shows that successful transplantation from a very different legal system has frequently been accomplished. Besides, systematic knowledge of foreign systems is not necessary.[51]

Compared to Watson's view, Kahn-Freund's is more scientific, decolonising and decolonial. Kahn-Freund based his arguments on Montesquieu's statement that developments of law are 'the necessary relations arising from the nature of things', that is, that law is inseparable from natural, social, economic and cultural

[46] Watson (note 28) 1.
[47] Legrand (note 27) 111.
[48] Ibid.
[49] Zongling (note 25) 854.
[50] Ibid; O Kahn-Freund 'On uses and misuses of comparative law' (1974) 7(1) *Modern Law Review* 1.
[51] Watson (note 28) 1.

conditions.[52] Similarly, Legrand cautions against the use of comparative analysis when such use is purely based on legalistic spirit and ignores other factors, such as the cultural and political context of such law.[53]

From a comparative-law standpoint, if legal transplants manifest as coloniality, then we have a useful way of thinking about how the transfer of law(s) or concepts from one legal system to another can affect the laws and social order in the recipient system. According to Bennett, South African lawyers are used to legal transplants because they have a long history of borrowing from common- and civil-law jurisdictions to fill what is perceived to be lacunae or deficiencies in the local law.[54] In *The Citizen 1978 (Pty) Ltd &Others v McBride (Johnstone & Others, Amici Curiae)* Mogoeng J cautioned that 'we should be slow to take from comparable jurisdictions, which do not necessarily share the same history and experience with us'.[55] This caution from Mogoeng J illuminates an observation that the transplantation discourse, more often than not, is traditionally analysed from the legislative perspective but not by the judicial or executive branches of government. However, experience has demonstrated that lawyers and judges tend to integrate foreign law into domestic case law (ie, as precedents) without legislative oversight.[56]

The next section provides a deductive account of selected fields or indicators of the ways in which legal transplant is constructed to manifest as coloniality. The unit of analysis, didactically speaking, recognises several indicators; however, the emphasis here is on four aspects: practising colonial culture, the application of colonial laws, the retention of colonial structural formations, and globalisation (internationalism).

12.4 HOW LEGAL TRANSPLANT MANIFESTS AS COLONIALITY: EXCERPTS

It is common knowledge that the Global South endured the ruthless paws of colonialism, of which the southern African and south and south-east Asian states were not exceptions. With a historical background that is rooted in colonialism, it is highly probable that coloniality may manifest itself after colonialism. There are countless ways in which coloniality may manifest itself; however, for the purposes of this chapter, the focus is on legal transplant. In the preceding discussion, the

[52] Zongling (note 25) 855.

[53] Legrand (note 27) 68.

[54] Bennett (note 32) 23.

[55] *The Citizen 1978 (Pty) Ltd & Others v McBride (Johnstone & Others, Amici Curiae)* 2011 (4) SA 191 (CC) para 243.

[56] R Leckey 'Review of comparative law' (2017) 26(1) *Social & Legal Studies* 3–24.

linkage between legal transplant and coloniality was laid out. However, it is important to provide concrete examples of such a linkage. With this objective in mind, in this section several points are made that focus on factors such as practising colonial culture, applying colonial laws, adopting or retaining colonial structural formations, and globalisation or internationalism. These factors illustrate the ways in which legal transplant may manifest as coloniality.

12.4.1 Practising colonial culture: questioning hybridisation

It is debatable whether there is a relationship between law and culture, and also between law and the social environment. It is, however, agreed that there is a connection between cultural practices and the evolution of common law. Stated differently, common law, as deduced from the classical natural-law theories, traces its roots to the morality and cultural practices of a given society.[57] The pro-relationship scholars contend that law attains its full meaning and effect when it is organically created. Furthermore, they hold that, if it is organically created, law ought to consider or attempt to respond to the social, political and economic issues of the society within which it is created. Salinos postulates that 'the law does not take place through borrowing because law mirrors, and it is responsive to, situated linguistic, cultural and moral national framework'.[58] In contrast to this view is the presupposition, with reference to historical evidence, that the law evolves independently and it is not influenced by the society it contemplates to serve. For this reason, law may be transplanted from one jurisdiction or legal system to another. These contrasting views need not be extended any further, as were those of Watson and Legrand as discussed above.

The importance of reiterating these views here is to render us alive to the debate and to the realisation that, prior to colonialism, nations in the Global South had rich linguistic and cultural heritages that informed their social, political and economic cohesion.[59] However, the uncontested view is that the influence of the Global South's cultural practices or their invaluable their role in the societies in the Global South was obliterated by the imposition or transplantation of the etymology, customs and cultural practices of the colonial masters. This harmful legal transplant still subsists in most of the former colonies – the continuation of the application of customary law as received from the West is one such example. Regarding language, the former colonial masters' languages, such as French, Portuguese and English,

[57] R Cotterrell 'Common law approaches to the relationship between law and morality' (2000) 3(1) *Ethical Theory and Moral Practice* 9–26.

[58] Salinos (note 35) 180.

[59] Masake & Libebe (note 4) 272.

as an instrument of hegemony, have been ordained in the present as scientific languages of instruction in most parts of the world, if not universally. The practice of prescribing these languages as the medium of instruction has permeated all of the southern African and southern Asian states. This unfettered hegemony enjoyed by French and English has rendered local languages virtually meaningless.

It is with incredulity that the postcolonial scholars have opted to occupy the middle ground. Their doing so is an injustice to Global South customary and cultural philosophies instead of their adopting approaches such as those of the Afrocentric constructions of tracing the African *lingua franca* and legal or cultural philosophies and ascertaining them first with a view to solving domestic issues. Regarding the Afrocentric assertions about the obliterated African languages and cultural practices, among other considerations, the Global South acknowledges, in the words of Masake and Libebe (2019), that 'there is a need to trace the pre-colonial African legal philosophies and to understand how these philosophies informed the political, social and economic cohesion'.[60]

The middle ground referred to above means advocating the hybridisation theory. The presupposition here is that because of the cultural contact that occurred between the cultural donor and the cultural host – whether as a result of colonialism, assimilation or acculturation – it is difficult to disentangle with certainty the entangled cultures. Furthermore, it is held that, because of this cultural contact, tracing the pure culture is improbable. Instead of ascertaining the lost values of languages, customs and culture that resulted from cultural contact, those in the Global South prefer the easy way out: the middle ground, the hybridisation of cultures. This stance argues that the result of cultural contact is the creation of a different and new species and therefore such new cultural species need to be treated as independent cultures. Solinos explains the hybridisation theory in the following terms:

> The claim for a hierarchical purity of cultures is untenable in colonial situations and that the copying of colonisers' culture and value is not a simple reproduction of the same traits. … hybrid culture is more than the result of fusion of features of colonial and indigenous background: it is a new creation in its own right.[61]

The hybridisation assertion is challenged, though, because it attempts to look no further than buttressing coloniality. The premise of this challenge lies in the assumption that when hybridisation is accepted, it becomes irrelevant to ascertain the lost languages and cultural practices of both the donor and the host. For instance,

[60] Masake & Libebe (note 4) 270.
[61] Salinos (note 35) 180.

instead of ascertaining the cultural practices that were obliterated by harmful legal transplant, the society becomes complacent to the colonially imposed customs and cultural practices – as is evident currently.

To apply the argument above to the Global South: its common customs and cultural practices favoured communion and here individuality was uncommon. Family ties fairly extended beyond the unit of husband, wife and children to include the entire village and community. These Global South pre-colonial customs and cultural practices were slayed by the legal transplant (cultural contact) that was imposed by the colonial masters, who favoured capitalism. With capitalism, individualism flourished and family ties were drastically reduced to husband, wife and children. For instance, in South Africa and Namibia the colonial regimes introduced segregationist laws in order to negate communion. The effect of segregationist laws accounts for the loss of the traditional values that favoured communion. In the context of southern Asian states, these same laws account for the collapse or negation of the Indus Valley Civilisation. The consequence was the proliferation of loathing, racial discrimination, injustice, miseducation, irreversible ignorance, to mention but a few outcomes – which are currently observed as a depiction of coloniality.

12.4.2 Practising colonial culture: application of colonial laws

In order to answer the question whether the application of colonial laws in the former colonies exemplifies coloniality, it is necessary to ask whether the colonial regimes imposed harmful colonial laws. And are these harmful colonial laws still in existence? And if they exist, what is their current impact or effect? Do they still have legal force? These questions, which arise in connection with legal transplant, may fairly be extended to enquire about the nature of the reception of these legal transplants in the former colonies.

It is uncontested that the colonial masters imposed on the former colonies a number of laws and legal institutions. In point is Roman-Dutch law, English common law and even the promulgation of colonial laws that were linked to the colonial masters' social and cultural context that were applied in the former colonies. These promulgated laws were not linked to the social and cultural contexts of the colonies. This is evident in, for instance, s 17(6) of Proclamation 15 of 1928 (Namibia), which discriminates against marital regimes consummated in the north of the country compared to those consummated in the south of the country. Moreover, legal reform has failed to cure this injustice: the courts have continued to grapple with deploying constitutional value judgements but have failed to cure the defect itself.[62] This colonial law, as with many other colonial laws, still has force.

[62] *Mofuka v Mofuka* 2003 NR 1 SC.

A distinction in the context of reception is needed here. As elucidated above, during the colonial era, the reception of the transplanted laws was aligned to the advancement of the hegemony (ie, harmful legal transplanting that manifested as coloniality). This is different from the reception that is observed in the post-colonial era, where the reception would be classified as and/or aligned with a less harmful legal transplant. A legal transplant in the post-colonial era could be accepted for such purposes as legal reform, dispute resolution or filling a legal lacuna, for instance. In this context, legal transplant is not considered harmful, although to a lesser extent it may prove to be hegemonical.

The consequence of legal transplant in such circumstances is disguised as legal pluralism at the expense and in defiance of the true legal pluralism. Tuori has explained legal pluralism as follows:

> legal pluralism was initially a concept of comparative law that was used to describe situations where several legal systems may apply; however, the notion has since been primarily linked with legal anthropology and indigenous law.[63]

According to Bekker et al, legal pluralism in South Africa exists as a result of prevailing cultural pluralism, but what this legal pluralism actually encompasses is not entirely clear.[64] Legal pluralism in the narrow sense refers to the co-existence of various officially recognised state laws, or 'state-law pluralism',[65] whereas in the broader sense it is 'a feature of a social field and not an attribute of a legal system or order'.[66]

In the context of southern Asia, it is a local field with a rich diversity of indigenous laws that are aligned with religion: the Muslims, Hindus and Sikhs, to mention only a few, at the one extreme, and at the other, English law. This diversity presupposes legal pluralism – at least from the perspectives of southern Asian scholars. In contradistinction, the Eurocentric perspective, a hegemonically driven endeavour as articulated by Menski, considers the indigenous southern Asian laws as inferior; he summarises this hegemonic proposition as follows:

---

[63] K Tuori 'The disputed roots of legal pluralism law' (2011) 9(2) *Culture and the Humanities* 331, 330–351; see also MB Hooker *Legal Pluralism: An Introduction to Colonial and Neo-colonial Laws* (Clarendon Press, 1975); L Sheleff *The Future of Tradition: Customary Law, Common Law, and Legal Pluralism* (Frank Cass, 2000).

[64] JC Bekker, C Rautenbach & NMI Goolam *Introduction to Legal Pluralism in South Africa* 2 ed (LexisNexis Butterworths, 2006) 5.

[65] For example, in the South African and Namibian contexts state law is largely Roman-Dutch law influenced by English common law, as adapted, applied and developed through legislation and judicial decisions.

[66] Bekker et al (note 64) 5–6.

> English law is ... a uniform legal system which does not recognise the personal laws of different communities. ... Only English law is law, all these ethnic paraphernalia are customs and are therefore inherently inferior. As the result you cannot have conflicts of laws, only problems created by the fact that Southern Asians continue to adhere to their customs.[67]

The narrow conception of legal pluralism flows from the positivist school of thought and Western perceptions of what is moral and in the best interests of the public. In southern African jurisdictions, the recognition of customary or indigenous law and common law is one not based on equality. In essence, common law is recognised as superior and dominant, whereas customary law retains a subordinate position. With this inequality, the case for disguised legal pluralism predominates: the common law and legislation, based mainly on Roman-Dutch and English law, prevail when there is a conflict of laws. This practice exemplifies a harmful dependency on colonisers' legal systems and in this sense it is an example of the manifestation of coloniality.

In southern Africa, moreover, Western law is still the dominant system and legal developments continue to be directed and influenced by Western values. In this region, as is the case with its southern Asian counterparts, state-law pluralism fails to explain adequately the social reality in these states.[68] Decolonial discourse runs counter to this manifestation in that it depicts coloniality, at least from our perspective.

Combining legal theory (or decolonial theory in the present study) and comparative law strikes at the narrow application of comparative methods and emphasises the need to recognise legal pluriversality and variance. Menski notes that, notwithstanding decolonisation, the law and legal system (legal education) in the former colonies are still largely Eurocentrically constructed, with a specific focus on state-made law to the exclusion of indigenous contributions.[69] This is particularly the case in southern Africa. It is uncontested, for example, that the law schools in Namibia, South Africa, Zimbabwe and Zambia are mainly dominated by Western philosophy or methodologies (English law or Roman-Dutch law) at the expense of the African legal philosophies. The fact that these law schools continue in the post-colonial era to teach legal curricula that are based on the colonial masters' legal philosophies implies that legal practitioners who are miseducated

[67] W Menski *Legal Pluralism and South Asian Minorities in Britain* (nd) 1, https://www.academia.edu/35295870/Legal_pluralism_and_South_Asian_minorities_in_Britain, accessed 20 August 2023.

[68] Bekker et al (note 64) 5.

[69] W Menski *Comparative Law in a Global Context: The Legal Systems of Asia and Africa* (Cambridge University Press, 2006) 6.

and graduate from these law schools will continue, in their ignorance, to advocate coloniality.

Given this reality, it is necessary to reverse coloniality through a decolonial agenda. Decolonial perspectives advance the case for a scientific pluralism as opposed to disguised legal pluralism – the latter being a perfect manifestation of coloniality.[70] In this regard, Harding notes that 'it is both impossible and undesirable to unify the sciences in the ways US logical positivism imagined'.[71] What is required is the recalculation of the legal curricula and for legal curricula to be devised that effectively educate and appreciate legal pluralism. The presence of African or Asian law as a separate family of laws continues to be denied and defined away, whereas theoretical scholarship on African and Asian laws can play a significant role in developing global jurisprudence. Comparative law, too, has struggled to accept that laws which emerge in African and Asian states are proper laws to be taken seriously.[72]

It is not surprising, therefore, that after attaining independence and adopting constitutions, most southern African and southern Asian countries adopted and continue to apply colonial legislation or law. Legal reforms have failed to decolonise law. In the face of this glaring failure, the assumption is that former colonies still transplant laws, rules and principles from their colonial masters. This situation can, of course, be attributed to the forces of colonisation, imperialism and coloniality. Despite the fact that customary law is, to a lesser extent, recognised in southern Africa as a source of law, it has not enjoyed the same status as the imported laws that have come to form the theoretical foundations of African law. The neglect of African laws and principles has facilitated the ways in which legal transplants have manifested as coloniality. Decolonial comparative theory ought therefore to rescue this situation through the inclusion of African and Asian narratives or methodologies in legal discourse and the application of the law. As Bennett notes, South African lawyers are used to legal transplants because they have a long history of taking from common law and civil-law jurisdictions to fill what is perceived as to be lacunae or deficiencies in the local law.[73] What could have rendered this situation possible could have been appropriate training, acculturation, etc.

Given that most legal systems in southern Africa and southern Asia are dominated by ingredients of either English law or Roman-Dutch law, the courts have lost an opportunity to apply African or Asian law in most cases. This is also because both legislation and policies are dominated by Eurocentric norms and

---

[70] S Harding 'Latin American decolonial social studies of scientific knowledge: Alliances and tensions' (2016) 41(6) *Science, Technology, & Human Values* 1063.

[71] Harding (note 70) 1070.

[72] Menski (note 69) 380.

[73] Bennett (note 32) 23.

values, a blind eye being turned to indigenous norms and values. Therefore, most scholars and lawyers tend to be accustomed to these Western ideas of law and in the process they, either consciously or unconsciously, apply colonial laws.

The founding comparative-law scholars were not interested in African law, which explains the absence of Africanism in even comparative-law jurisprudence. Accordingly, the law as applied in most of southern Africa has mainly been modernised along Western lines. After colonisation, most of the political landscapes changed, but a legal discourse founded on African philosophies, ontologies, epistemologies or contexts did not follow suit. This has largely led to the application and theorisation of the laws and methods of the colonial administrations. Okupa has also noted critically that the study of African indigenous law has been carried out by Western anthropologists, who attempted to interpret such laws without the engagement or contribution of the authors of such African indigenous law.[74]

12.4.3 Practising colonial culture: retention of colonial structural formations as a manifestation of coloniality

It is an uncontested fact that the Global South endured colonialism. During the colonial era, the colonial masters created institutions and systems which were similar to those practised in the colonial masters' territories. The implications of the installation of colonial institutions were that the indigenous institutions and systems were not only not fully recognised but were also largely disregarded and/ or destroyed. For instance:

- the transplanting and reception of civil courts and penal systems, which accounts for the destruction of indigenous dispute-resolution systems;
- the creation of artificial African borders and the delimitation of the African state territories (the question of national borders), and
- the installation of colonial miseducation, which accounts for the obliteration of the Global South's indigenous knowledge and education systems.

These institutions and systems were retained and still exist in the former colonies. By way of explanation, there is the question of the African borders. Prior to 1885 in what became colonies, particularly in Africa, there were African territories. The history of the scramble for Africa has not been challenged, that is, it is a commonly held historical fact that the infamous Berlin Conference of 1885, which was convened by the European leaders (colonial masters), produced a Western-imposed

[74] E Okupa *International Bibliography of African Customary Law* (LIT and International African Institute, 1998) 177.

demarcation of the African borders and African territories as we know them today. The partitioning of the African territories was one of the colonial masters' powerful weapons (ie, a divide-and-conquer strategy) which was deployed against the former colonies. As fate would have it, those territories as were drawn up at that infamous conference are the accepted territories of the former colonies today. But whereas the former colonies liberated themselves politically, the decolonisation agenda failed to liberate the African borders or territories. What does this mean for Africa, of which southern Africa is not an exception, particularly in the context of a decolonial agenda? Does the partitioning of Africa in the present manifest itself as coloniality? The answer has to be in the affirmative. This is buttressed by the undisputed fact that the act of partitioning the African territories was deployed as a system that effectuated colonialism, and in this manner the present remnants of the African territories are a manifestation of coloniality. It is unfortunate that there is no agenda, at least from the Afrocentric perspective, that contemplates liberating the African borders to be reset to the status that existed prior to the 1885 Berlin Conference. The lack of African political will to decolonise the African borders is a living indictment on Africa's complacency towards a fundamental injustice.

It is worth noting that the current practice, at least that which is common in African states as part of a decolonial agenda, is a symbolic or a renaming exercise. Here, several names of places of great importance – streets, buildings, venues – continue to be changed and renamed by replacing colonial with indigenous names. This includes the fall of the Rhodes statue in South Africa, the fall of the '*Reiterdenkmal*' or 'Rider of South West' in Namibia and the renaming of the former Caprivi region as the Zambezi region, to mention only three instances. The motivation behind the removal of statues or the renamings is to denounce any colonially installed matter; however, the question whether symbolic condemnation will bear the desired fruits remains to be seen. Mukoma wa Ngugi, in his opening remarks at the Writers Unlimited Literature Festival held in The Hague in 2020, cautioned against relegating the decolonial agenda to mere symbolic decolonisation, arguing that decolonisation should transcend symbolism and aspire to the decolonisation of both philosophy and materials. To buttress his assertion, he raised the question of the unresolved historical inequality that underlay decolonisation. Ngungi expressed his sentiments as follows:[75]

> But here is the question. Consider all the unresolved historical inequalities where slavery becomes indentured servitude as Indians are imported into British colonies, colonialism becomes neocolonialism, and neo-colonialism

[75] M Wa Ngugi *The Pitfalls of Symbolic Decolonisation*, https://africasacountry.com/2020/01/the-pitfalls-of-symbolic-decolonization, accessed 20 August 2023.

opens up to unequal globalization. Also consider the inherited trauma still suffered by communities all over the world that have been, generation after generation, at the brunt end of global exploitation. Can what we in the West are calling decolonization in philosophical and material terms, really address historical inequalities?

These questions should form the launch pad of decolonial theory. However, in the context of the retention of colonial structural formations, it is apparent that the decolonisation agenda has failed to achieve its objective.

12.4.4 Globalisation, (de)coloniality and legal transplants

With the forces of globalisation, theoretical actuality confronts a new challenge.[76] Some argue that the emphasis on transplants or borrowings tends to obscure what is really happening: modernisation and industrialisation.[77] These transform society and create new needs and problems that require legal solutions; therefore, countries adapt, beg, borrow or steal law from jurisdictions that have encountered similar problems previously. An apt example here is the institution of the International Monetary Fund (IMF). The IMF exemplifies an institution that advocates the internationalisation of laws – for instance, for a state to be eligible for lending funds it must meet certain preset conditions. If a state that intends to lend funds fails to adapt to and meet the preset conditions, it is likely to be disqualified. It is worth noting that these preset conditions are copied from the practices of the industrialised states (which are mainly the former colonial master states). The effect of adapting to these preset conditions is implicitly to call on the borrowing state to reform its legal environment[78] in order to conform to the dictates or prescriptions of the superpowers or the former colonial masters.

According to Menski, the unequivocal acceptance, without critical thinking, of the practice of universalism, globalism and internationalism is a cause for concern. It goes beyond imagination that the world will ever achieve a specific level of identification – individualism – that is, one world order, rule, culture or practice

[76] O Acha 'The places of critical universalism: Postcolonial and decolonial approaches in context' in C Roldán, D Brauer & J Rohbeck (eds) *Philosophy of Globalization* (De Gruyter, 2018), http://www.jstor.com/stable/j.ctvbkk12k.10, accessed 20 August 2023.

[77] Friedman (note 29) 94.

[78] M Goretti, D Kihara & R Salgado *Is South Asia Ready to Take Off? A Sustainable and Inclusive Growth Agenda* (2019) 33, https://www.imf.org/en/Publications/Departmental-Chapters-Policy-Chapters/Issues/2019/10/29/Is-South-Asia-Ready-for-Take-Off-A-Sustainable-and-Inclusive-Growth-Agenda-47125, accessed 20 August 2023.

that ought to be followed.[79] Legrand has pointed out that the 'globalisation of the world cannot change the reality of varied historical traditions'.[80]

The point here is that, whereas global uniformity is an idealistic notion, it takes away experiences of human existence and is repressive in nature. In other words, whose values, norms or rules should be chosen to dominate the world? Melissaris concludes:[81]

> The study of the law must be directed towards the discovery of alternative perceptions of the world and justice and of different practices of solving practical problems by accommodating competing interests as well as meeting the prerequisites of substantive justice. The question of law and justice then becomes one concerning our whole way of life, how we perceive and place ourselves in our surrounding.

This passage also reminds legal comparatists that during the comparative process one ought to search for substantive justice through examining alternative practices to solve practical problems. Furthermore, the reception of mainstream Western laws, both pre- and post-independence, particularly in Africa, has led to the complex pluralisation of laws worldwide.

12.5 METHODOLOGICAL CHALLENGES TO DECOLONIAL COMPARATIVE RESEARCH

The question regarding which methodology may be adopted or recommended in comparative law in general, and specifically in decolonial research, remains unsettled. The dominant, although unsatisfactory, approach to comparative law has been centred on the objective of the research and the research question that ought to be solved – the traditional approach. In essence, this traditional approach implies that the factors which determine a comparative methodology revolve around the research objective and the research question. The example of the research objective could include but is not limited to harmonisation, legal reform, an 'instrument of learning and knowledge'[82] and judicial process,[83] to mention only a few.

---

[79] Menski (note 69) 3.
[80] Ibid.
[81] E Melissaris 'The more the merrier? A new take on legal pluralism' (2004) 13(4) *Social and Legal Studies* 57–79.
[82] PJ Glen 'The deconstruction and reification of law in Franz Kafka's *Before the Law* and *The Trial*' (2007) 17(23) *Southern California Interdisciplinary Law Journal* 59.
[83] Kamba (note 20).

Notwithstanding the traditional approach, the recent literature leads one to the conclusion that there are multiple methods that may be adopted, either individually or concurrently, when conducting comparative research.[84] The implication of this is that innumerable methodologies may be applicable provided that they attempt to relate to the objective and/or the research question. The assertion here is that it is unrealistic to recommend or prescribe one standard methodology that may be adopted as '*the*' decolonial research methodology. Van Hoecke agrees with this. He recommends instead what he terms a 'toolbox', a notion that dispels what he has termed a 'fixed methodological road map'.[85] The purpose of the toolbox is to acknowledge and buttress the importance of multiple methods that may be adopted or applied when conducting a comparative-law study of any nature – of which decolonial research is not an exception.

Considering, from the orthodox approach, that at the centre of the question of decolonial comparative methodology lie the binary factors of *(a)* research objective and *(b)* research question, the questions that linger may include this: How do the research objective and the research question influence the type of methodology that may be adopted? An attempt at answering this question, from the Global South context, is imperative. Take, for example, divorce as the variable. The question here is whether the state law requirements for divorce should be reviewed and abolished in post-colonial Namibia. For obvious reasons, as stated above, because Namibia was colonised and during colonial rule the pre-colonial laws were obliterated and the colonial masters imposed the colonial laws that regulated marriage and divorce – it would be imperative to adopt a legal–anthropological and/or a legal–historical research methodology to deal with this question. This is because the question should attempt to compare the African indigenous (customary) law with the state-'imposed' law. To establish the exact tension between the African indigenous law on marriage and divorce – which, significantly, is followed by most of the indigenous people – on the one hand, and, on the other, the Western (state) law, which is exclusive, the researcher may prefer to adopt an anthropological and/or a historical research methodology. The essence here is that these methodologies, by their nature, can place the law in its proper context. In this regard, context is crucial to understanding or solving this tension between the two systems.

[84] Glen (note 82) 59; W Twining 'Globalization and comparative law' (1999) 6(3), *Maastricht Journal of European and Comparative Law* 217–243.

[85] M van Hoecke 'Methodology of comparative legal research' (2015) 1, https://www.lawandmethod.nl/tijdscrift/lawandmethod/2015/12/RENM-D-14-00001.pdf, accessed 23 August 2023.

On methodology and considering undertaking comparative research between African indigenous law and Western-imposed law in Africa, Van Hoecke expressed the opinion that

> when comparing official state law in African countries with local customary law, one will notice that they show a tension between tradition and modernity, between Western law only followed by the elite and African law as the large majority of the population perceive it. Hence, an anthropological approach (methodology) that puts the law in context will be necessary for explaining this tension, for understanding it and for finding solution for it.[86]

Moreover, some of the decolonial questions may require comparative research that transcends one's own legal system. For example, the question is whether legal transplant manifests as coloniality in the Global South. It may be necessary not only to compare legal systems in the Global South but to extend the comparison to Latin America, which was also exposed to colonialism and coloniality. Therefore, to respond to this question effectively at a methodological level, one could adopt a combination of methodologies. These could include but not be limited to these alternatives: functional, anthropological, historical, structural, dialectical,[87] law-in-text, comparative, sociological, analytical or common core.[88]

With the multiplicity of possible applicable methodologies with which to conduct decolonial comparative research, it is argued that each question or object of comparison should be considered on its merits and on a case-by-case basis. The implication is that a one-size-fits-all methodology may amount to defeating the very essence of decolonial comparative research.

Considering the discussion above, it is worth providing a snapshot of some of the methodologies identified above and attempting to set down some of the steps that may be taken when applying such a specific methodology in decolonial discourses.

12.4.1 Functional method

The functional method is accredited to Rabel and its point of departure is the unqualified statement that legal problems are similar from one legal system to the other.[89] That is, in each legal system one may find instances of common legal challenges such as theft, homicide and rape. It is said to be an unqualified statement

[86] Van Hoecke (note 85).

[87] G Samuel *An Introduction to Comparative Law Theory and Method* (Hart, 2014) 19–26.

[88] Van Hoecke (note 85).

[89] K Zweigert & H Kötz *An Introduction to Comparative Law* 3 ed (Oxford University Press, 1998).

because the functional method is silent on the context of the legal system in question, that is, the historical, political, cultural and sociological factors that influenced the adoption of the rules, laws or concepts of a given legal system. Through this statement, the functional method implicitly recognises the possibility that the rules or concepts between one legal system and another may be drafted in different ways. Premised on this recognition, the functional method presupposes that inasmuch as the laws, rules or concepts may be dissimilar between one legal system and another, they are set to resolve like legal glitches in a comparable manner.[90] The focus is specifically on the result or outcome as opposed to the process that is undertaken for the purposes of achieving the result or outcome. With this limited focus, the functional method may not be effective when the object of comparative research is to determine the way rules attempt to resolve legal challenges.[91] Van Hoecke correctly noted that the functional method attempts to 'isolate the solutions from practical problems'.[92] This isolation, among other factors, is vehemently criticised.

The functional method has attracted criticism: for example, it is criticised for not being a method; for being a misnomer; for treating law as a solution to all challenges; for assuming that challenges in different settings are similar and that they can be solved in a similar manner.[93] Notwithstanding these criticisms levelled against it, the functional method is useful and may provide great insight into comparative research. One instance of such usefulness is the invocation of the theory of functional equivalent.

At this juncture, it is worth noting that Van Hoecke has summarised the relevance of the functional method as follows:[94]

> the functional method is looking for such *functional equivalent* at the level of the solutions. If, in view of the research question, such as which solution is given in countries A, B and C to a legal problem P? or which institution in system B performs an equivalent function to the one under survey in system A? Only the result counts and if this legal solution is the same in the compared countries, then the researcher may conclude that the law is the same in those countries.[95]

---

[90] Hoecke (note 85).

[91] JC Reitz 'How to do comparative law' (1998) 46(4) *The American Journal of Comparative Law* 617–636.

[92] Hoecke (note 85).

[93] R Michaels, 'The functional method of comparative law' in M Reimann & R Zimmermann (eds) *The Oxford Handbook of Comparative Law* (Oxford Academic, 2006).

[94] Hoecke (note 85).

[95] EA Örücü 'Methodology in comparative law' in M Smits (ed) *Elgar Enclopedia of Comparative Law* (Edward Elgar Publishing, 2006) 443.

Drawing on the discussion above, it is agreed that the functional method may be useful to a certain extent; however, it has its own challenges and shortcomings. The identified shortcomings buttress the assumption that there is no one-size-fits-all method that can be adopted in comparative research. In this context, each method should be applied only when it is shown be able to yield the desired process or result. For instance, in decolonial research, one may adopt the functional method if the objective of such decolonial research is, for example, to determine the impact of legal transplanting that is effectuated through coloniality. This matter is results-oriented and it may fit well into the functional method.

From the outset, we reiterate the position that there are no prescribed rules regarding the steps that may be adopted to conduct legal comparison. Otherwise stated, there is no consensus on the rules or steps for carrying out a comparative-law study.[96] However, the absence of settled rules should not be construed as being a bar to suggesting or developing guidelines for the purposes of conducting decolonial comparative research. It is within this construction that we set out to suggest the steps below.

In decolonial comparative research, depending on the method adopted, the suggested built-in procedural steps that may be undertaken could include these nine:

- Step 1 – provide the reason for comparing (why?);
- Step 2 – provide what to compare;
- Step 3 – set the level and extent of comparison;
- Step 4 – make a choice of the jurisdiction, community, institution, system or person that you intend to compare with (where/who?);
- Step 5 – extract and interpret the rules;
- Step 6 – articulate the similarities and differences – the functional equivalent;
- Step 7 – explain the causes and effects of the similarities and differences;
- Step 8 – articulate the adoption-ability of foreign rule or law; and
- Step 9 – identify and select the appropriate methodology.

These steps are aligned to the theoretical underpinning that the objective and/or question of research has the potential to inform the type of methodology that may be adopted in comparative research, of which decolonial comparative research is not an exception. Furthermore, these steps are flexible enough, with necessary amendment where required, to be applicable to most of the methodologies described.

[96] Reitz (note 91); LM LoPucki 'A rule-based method for comparing corporate laws' (2018) 94 *Notre Dame Law Review* 263.

12.5 CONCLUSION

Most theoretical approaches in comparative law tend to be Eurocentric and parochial, failing to adopt a global plurality-conscious perspective. This is so not only among lawyers, but also among academics. Criticism of the ways in which legal transplants manifest as coloniality in the lens of comparative law – that is, as philosophical, methodological, political and cultural transplants that emerge from and are embedded in the historical European colonisation – is essential to understanding the aggressive strategies used by the West to impose symbolic and material domination globally in the name of universal reason.[97]

In order to borrow or transplant foreign law successfully, judicial and legislative bodies and legal scholars should study carefully the natural, cultural and social conditions of the foreign countries. In sum, legal transplanting may in certain qualified ways be a useful exercise; however, equally, it may be very harmful as it may lead to the effectuation of coloniality. Therefore, comparative lawyers need to be cautious and critical when considering transplanting laws from one jurisdiction to another.

In this chapter it was demonstrated that the harmful legal transplanting that took place at the behest of colonialism still haunts the Global South today. For example, in the present former colonies, among other negatives, the colonial culture is still practised and it is dominantly misplacing and/or obliterating indigenous cultures. And whereas English is a colonial language, it remains the dominant language of instruction in southern Africa. Furthermore, the colonial laws are still valid and in force in the former colonies. These examples serve as the tip of the iceberg, forming as they do part of a larger picture of the way legal transplants have resulted in coloniality. However, the impact of coloniality in the Global South is both irreversible and unparalleled; therefore, to remedy this travesty effectively, the fully fledged implementation of the promises of decolonial theory has become a highly desirable objective.

REFERENCES

Acha, O 'The places of critical universalism: Postcolonial and decolonial approaches in context' in C Roldán, D Brauer & J Rohbeck (eds) *Philosophy of Globalization* (De Gruyter, 2018), http://www.jstor.com/stable/j.ctvbkk12k.10, accessed 20 August 2023.

---

[97] See M Morana, E Dussel & CA Jauregui 'Colonialism and its replicants' in M Morana, ED Dussel & CA Jauregui (eds) *Coloniality at Large: Latin America and the Postcolonial Debate* (Duke University Press, 2008).

Bekker, JC, Rautenbach, C & Goolam, NMI *Introduction to Legal Pluralism in South Africa* 2 ed (LexisNexis, Butterworths, 2006).

Bennett, TW *Ubuntu: An African Jurisprudence* (Juta & Co, 2018).

Cotterrell, R 'Common law approaches to the relationship between law and morality' (2000) 3(1) *Ethical Theory and Moral Practice* 9.

Friedman, L 'Some comments on Cotterrell and legal transplants' in D Nelken & J Feest (eds) *Adapting Legal Cultures* (Hart Publishing, 2001).

Glen, PJ 'The deconstruction and reification of law in Franz Kafka's *Before the Law* and *The Trial*' (2007) 17(23) *Southern California Interdisciplinary Law Journal* 59.

Goretti, M, Kihara, D & Salgado, R *Is South Asia Ready to Take Off? A Sustainable and Inclusive Growth Agenda* (2019), https://www.imf.org/en/Publications/Departmental-Chapters-Policy-Chapters/Issues/2019/10/29/Is-South-Asia-Ready-for-Take-Off-A-Sustainable-and-Inclusive-Growth-Agenda-47125, accessed 20 August 2023.

Grosfoguel, R 'The epistemic decolonial turn: Beyond the political-economy paradigms' (2007) 21(2) *Cultural Studies* 211.

Harding, S 'Latin American decolonial social studies of scientific knowledge: Alliances and tensions' (2016) 41(6) *Science, Technology, & Human Values* 1063.

Hooker, MB *Legal Pluralism: An Introduction to Colonial and Neo-colonial Laws* (Clarendon Press, 1975).

Horvath, RJ 'A definition of colonialism' (1972) 13(1) *Current Anthropology* 45.

Jayasuriya, K 'Globalisation, law, and the transformation of sovereignty: The emergence of global regulatory governance' (1999) 6 *Indiana Journal of Global Legal Studies* 425.

Kahn-Freund, O 'On uses and misuses of comparative law' (1974) 37(1) *Modern Law Review* 1.

Kamba, WJ 'Comparative law: A theoretical framework' (1974) 23(3) *The International and Comparative Law Quarterly* 485–519.

Leckey, R 'Review of comparative Law' (2017) 26(1) *Social & Legal Studies* 3.

Legrand, P 'The impossibility of legal transplants' (1997) 4(2) *Maastricht Journal of European and Comparative Law* 111.

LoPucki, LM 'A rule-based method for comparing corporate laws' (2018) 94 *Notre Dame Law Review* 263.

Maldonado-Torres, N 'On the coloniality of being: Contributions to the development of a concept' (2007) 21 *Cultural Studies* 243.

Marzagora, S 'The humanism of reconstruction: African intellectuals, decolonial critical theory and the opposition to the "posts" (postmodernism, poststructuralism, postcolonialism)' (2016) 28(2) *Journal of African Cultural Studies* 161.

Masake, PH & Libebe, EL 'Colonialism, coloniality and decolonisation of legal education: Perspectives from universities in Southern African Development Community' (2019) 11(1) *Namibia Law Journal* 270.

Melissaris, E 'The more the merrier? A new take on legal pluralism' (2004) 13(4) *Social and Legal Studies* 57.

Menski, W *Comparative Law in a Global Context: The Legal Systems of Asia and Africa* (Cambridge University Press, 2006).

Menski, W *Legal Pluralism and South Asian Minorities in Britain* (nd), https://www.academia.edu/35295870/Legal_pluralism_and_South_Asian_minorities_in_Britain, accessed 20 August 2023.

Michaels, R 'The functional method of comparative law' in M Reimann & R Zimmermann (eds) *The Oxford Handbook of Comparative Law* (Oxford Academic, 2006).

Mignolo, W *The Darker Side of Western Modernity: Global Futures, Decolonial Options* (Duke University Press, 2011).

Morana, M, Dussel, E & Jauregui, CA 'Colonialism and its replicants' in M Morana, ED Dussel & CA Jauregui (eds) *Coloniality at Large: Latin America and the Postcolonial Debate* (Duke University Press, 2008).

Nelken, D 'Comparatists and transferability' in P Legrand & R Munday (eds) *Comparative Legal Studies: Traditions and Transitions* (Cambridge University Press, 2003).

Noxolo, P *Decolonial Theory in a Time of the Re-colonisation of UK Research* (Royal Geographical Society, 2017), https://rgs-ibg.onlinelibrary.wiley.com/doi/epdf/10.1111/tran.12202, accessed 202 August 2023.

Okupa, E *International Bibliography of African Customary Law* (LIT and International African Institute, 1998).

Örücü, EA 'Methodology in comparative law' in M Smits (ed) *Elgar Enclopedia of Comparative Law* (Edward Elgar Publishing, 2006).

Oxford Advanced Learner's Dictionary: International Student's Edition 9 Ed (Oxford University Press, 2015) 1609.

Reitz, JC 'How to do comparative law' (1998) 46(4) *The American Journal of Comparative Law* 617–636.

Salinos, M 'The nature of legal transplants – inspirations from postcolonial scholarship' (2016) 22 *New Zealand Association of Comparative Law* 179.

Samuel, G *An Introduction to Comparative Law Theory and Method* (Hart, 2014).

Schacherreiter, J 'Postcolonial theory and comparative law: On the methodological and epistemological benefits to comparative law through postcolonial theory' (2016) 49(3) *Verfassung und Recht in Übersee/Law and Politics in Africa, Asia and Latin America* 291.

Shai, I 'The right to development, transformative constitutionalism and radical transformation in South Africa: Post-colonial and de-colonial reflections' (2019) 19 *African Human Rights Law Journal* 494.

Sheleff, L *The Future of Tradition: Customary Law, Common Law, and Legal Pluralism* (Frank Cass, 2000).

Tuori, K 'The disputed roots of legal pluralism law' (2011) 9(2) *Culture and the Humanities* 330.

Twining, W 'Globalization and comparative law' (1999) 6(3) *Maastricht Journal of European and Comparative Law* 217.

Van Hoecke, M *Methodology of Comparative Legal Research* (2015) 1, https://www.lawandmethod.nl/tijdscrift/lawandmethod/2015/12/RENM-D-14-00001.pdf, accessed 23 August 2023.

Van Wallenndael, K 'Legal transplants: Profitable borrowing or harmful dependency? The use of legal transplant framework for the adoption of EU law: The case of Croatia' in A Filipiak, E Kania, J van den Bosch & R Wisniewski (eds) *Evolving Dependency Relations* (Revolution Research Centre, 2014).

Wa Ngugi, M *The Pitfalls of Symbolic Decolonisation* (nd), https://africasacountry.com/2020/01/the-pitfalls-of-symbolic-decolonization, accessed 20 August 2023.

Watson, A *Legal Transplants: An Approach to Comparative Law* (University of Georgia Press, 1993).

Xanthaki, H 'Legal transplants in legislation: Defusing the trap' (2008) 57(3) *The International and Comparative Law Quarterly* 659.

Zongling, S 'Legal transplant and comparative law' (1999) 51(4) *Revue Internationale de Droit Comparé* 853.

Zweigert, K & Kötz, H *An Introduction to Comparative Law* 3 ed (Oxford University Press, 1998).

CASES

Mofuka v Mofuka 2003 NR 1 SC

The Citizen 1978 (Pty) Ltd & Others v McBride (Johnstone & Others, Amici Curiae) 2011 (4) SA 191 (CC)

LEGISLATION

Statute of the International Court of Justice, 24 October 1945

13

Comparative law and the transformation of legal education in the 21st century: lessons for Namibia

Tapiwa V Warikandwa

13.1 INTRODUCTION

Although it is crucial that judges, legal scholars, practitioners and law students obtain instruction that is specifically geared towards solving the challenges of the contemporary world, the unknown can be frightening and it may seem superfluous to devote time to comparative law. How is comparative law to be accommodated in overloaded curricula where room is being sought for an ever-increasing number of new topics such as e-commerce, law and technology, communications law and law on terrorism? When offered, comparative-law courses are rarely taken by many students at institutions that teach law, especially at the undergraduate level. Nonetheless, it is undeniably true that judges and other legal professionals are now more closely connected to international law, foreign attorneys and overseas clients.[1] As a result, the subject of teaching foreign law is becoming ever more crucial. The two methods of comparative law adopted by comparative lawyers – normative enquiry and contextual or jurisprudential research – are reflected in the way that comparative law is taught.[2] The two variant techniques used throughout this work and this sub-topic of the comparative-law theme match each other quite well.

[1] H Gutteridge 'The value of comparative law' 1931 *Journal of the Society of Public Teachers of Law* 27–31.

[2] G Wilson 'Comparative legal scholarship' in M McConville & W Hong Chui (eds) *Research Methods for Law* (University Press, 2007) 87–103.

It is difficult to prove that the application of international law and harmonised national legislation is necessary to solve today's transnational problems, despite there appearing to be a trend in law schools around the world to improve the teaching of law in general and comparative law in particular.[3] Accordingly, the pertinent questions to be asked are these: How is comparative law being taught in schools of comparative law, and how ought it to be taught? What effects do recent global trends, particularly globalisation and multiculturalism, have on the comparative law classroom? This chapter discusses how to teach comparative law as a theoretical subject that is interwoven with cultural studies; emphasises the practical aspects of the subject and even contends that it should not be taught as a standalone course.

Comparative law is primarily an academic discipline. Its achievements depend on how it is taught, what is taught, and what is expected of it. Comparative law must be regarded as a distinct category of law.[4] It may be that problems faced today in institutions that teach law and which are related to the status of comparative-law courses arise from the crisis in which comparative law finds itself. As we have seen, its working assumptions and methodology are being challenged nowadays and the need to build a theoretical base is stressed.[5] The importance of this subject increases with the increasing interest in the peculiarities of localisms, in appreciating cultural differences and the particular and yet working towards commonality and the universal. For these reasons, comparative lawyers are busy rethinking their subject.[6] To provide insight, comparative law must be taught as a theoretical subject, perhaps under the name 'comparative jurisprudence', 'comparative analysis of law' or 'comparative legal studies'.[7] It should be the autonomous, general, theoretical core course of any programme.

In teaching comparative law, the traditional teaching methods, including lectures and seminars, backed up by problem-focused examinations and essays, are considered to be the most appropriate. This is particularly the case when the legal systems covered are from the same or similar socio-legal traditions.[8] However, when the systems are not from such traditions, area and case study analysis within a theoretical framework would be more appropriate. Comparative-law teaching should focus on an exploration of the historical, jurisprudential and cultural

[3] P Zumbansen 'Transnational law, evolving' in J Smits (ed) *Elgar Encyclopedia of Comparative Law* (Edward Elgar, 2012) 898–925; see also P Zumbansen 'Transnational legal pluralism' 2010 *Transnational Legal Theory* 141–189.

[4] C Valcke 'Global law teaching' (2004) 54 *Journal of Legal Education* 160–182.

[5] E Örücü (ed) *Mixed Legal Systems at New Frontiers* (Wiley, 2010).

[6] CJ Wallace 'Law, culture and Euro-crime: Using spiral to teach French law' (2014) 48 *Law Teacher* 154–165.

[7] C Valcke 'Comparative legal education in Canada' (2005) 39 *Thémis* 483–505; see also Valcke (note 4) 162–163.

[8] G Samuel *An Introduction to Comparative Law Theory and Method* (Hart Publishing, 2014) 36.

backgrounds of the legal systems or legal institutions studied.[9] It may be true that many law teachers are sceptical of cultural analysis and prefer normative enquiry, but an increasing number of them, and therefore legal education institutions, are now trying to focus students' minds on social, historical, cultural and economic contexts.[10]

In the common-law world, the historical legacy of largely vocational training persists, with little contact between lawyers and social scientists.[11] The reasons for the lack of interest and confidence in theory and the relative lack of methodological debate are partly cultural and partly institutional. In the civilian world, where law is seen as a social science, the constraints of the curricula dictate that comparative legal studies has not been prioritised. Different constructions are put forward on what comparative law could be. Kamba proposed the use of four questions as a basis of establishing a useful theoretical framework within which to build an understanding of what constitutes comparative law:[12]

(1) What does the term comparative law mean?
(2) Why does, or should, one engage in comparative legal study or research?
(3) What is it that the legal comparatist compares? and
(4) How should meaningful and effective comparison be carried out?

This chapter responds to these questions and outlines the significance of comparative law in the contemporary legal education system in Africa.[13]

13.2 COMPARATIVE LAW AS A CONCEPT: AN OUTLINE OF THE BACKGROUND

The term 'comparative law' has been defined in different ways. It describes the comparison of various laws; it is not a distinct body of law. This is clearer from the term in German (*Rechtsvergleichung*, 'comparison of laws') than from the term in

---

[9] C Gane & RH Huang (eds) *Legal Education in the Global Context – Opportunities and Challenges* (Routledge, 2016).

[10] J Husa 'Turning the curriculum upside down: Comparative law as an educational tool for constructing the pluralistic legal mind' (2009) 10 *German Law Journal* 913–928.

[11] C Stolker *Rethinking the Law School: Education, Research, Outreach and Governance* (Cambridge University Press, 2014).

[12] WJ Kamba 'Comparative law: A theoretical framework' (1974) 23(3) *The International and Comparative Law Quarterly* 485–519; see also M van Hoecke & M Warrington 'Legal cultures, legal paradigms and legal doctrine: Towards a new model for comparative law' (1998) 47(3) *The International and Comparative Law Quarterly* 495–536.

[13] Kamba (note 12) 485–519.

other languages (comparative law, *droit comparé*).[14] The method of comparison is an integral part of thinking and knowing. The comparative technique must therefore be viewed as an instrument or mechanism with which to achieve breakthroughs and advances in all the natural and social sciences. McDougal defines comparative law as 'a literature that is voluminous, obsessively repetitious and sterile ....'[15] Comparative law may therefore be defined as the study of and research on law by the systematic comparison of two or more legal systems; or parts, branches or aspects of two or more legal systems.[16] It is a type or body of legal knowledge and/or an autonomous branch of legal science.[17] It is a science whose key objective is to discover concepts and principles common to all civilised systems of law. It is a legal science which seeks to discover the causes that underlie the origin, development and extinction of legal institutions.[18]

Comparative law searches for collocations, coincidences and sequences in legal systems. It is the systematic use of a comparative technique and includes the study and research aimed at the discovery of universal concepts and principles or aimed at the discovery, formulation or verification of natural laws regarding legal phenomena.[19] It does not constitute a distinct branch of national law nor does it comprise normative prescriptions for regulating human conduct and relationships. It has no rules or principles.[20] Moreover, the systematic use of the comparative method does not result in legal norms. In contemporary law schools, law students in legal aid clinics, candidate attorneys, legal practitioners, legal academics, judiciary officials and other legal technocrats face a plethora of legal systems as they advise clients or conduct legal research in the 21st century.[21] The inescapable growth of multilateral trade and the emergence of trade arrangements such as the Africa Continental Free Trade Area (AfCFTA) have multiplied the domestic variations of the common- and civil-law traditions that lawyers must deal with. An increasing number of issues that overlap temporal and religious law have arisen in both religious and non-religious societies.

---

[14] G Soriano-Barabino *Comparative Law for Legal Translators* (Peter Lang, 2016) 141–183.

[15] MS McDougal 'The comparative study of law for policy purposes: Value clarification as an instrument of democratic world order' (1952) 1(1/2) *The American Journal of Comparative Law* 24–57.

[16] J Husa *A New Introduction to Comparative Law* (Hart Publishing, 2015) 58–95.

[17] J Bell 'Legal research and the distinctiveness of comparative law' in M van Hoecke (ed) *Methodologies of Legal Research* (Hart Publishing, 2011) 155–176.

[18] M Rheinstein 'Teaching tools in comparative law' (1952) 1 *American Journal of Comparative Law* 95, 98.

[19] AW Heringa & P Kiiver *Constitutions Compared: An Introduction to Comparative Constitutional Law*, 3 ed (Intersentia, 2012).

[20] O Kahn-Freund 'Comparative law as an academic subject' (1966) 82 *Law Quarterly Review* 40, 41; see also HC Gutteridge *Comparative Law* 2 ed (Cambridge University Press, 1949) 2.

[21] B Grossfeld *The Strength and Weakness of Comparative Law* (Clarendon Press, 1990) 2.

Many legal problems are reaching transnational and international proportions, to the extent that they must either be considered within a regional legal system or be tossed into the loose structure of international law. The law schools in Africa and probably elsewhere in the world have chosen to deal with these issues piecemeal through a loose amalgam of law-school courses under an international law heading. However, in Namibia, the sole school of law housed in the country's premier institution of higher learning, the University of Namibia, offers comparative law (course code LJCO 3861) as an elective module in the old and new Bachelor of Laws Honours (LLB) programmes. The module has nevertheless not been offered since 2022 and was also not on offer in 2023, regardless of its status as an elective. However, comparative law (course code L6912BC) was offered as an elective in the new Master of Laws programme for the first time in the 2023 academic year. In principle, even though comparative law is listed as an elective in the school of law at the university, it is at times not offered to students even though it is a key module that offers a bridge to other modules such as Constitutional law, Jurisprudence, International Economic Law, Public International Law, Mining law, Research Methodology, Criminal law, Bachelor of Laws Research Projects, just to name a few. In principle, Comparative Law touches on the other modules and is a bridge between legal courses but is studied independently. In acknowledging the significance of comparative law in legal education, Kamba, as far back as 1974, reasoned that '[t]here is no doubt that the days are over when comparative law represented an academic pastime good only to add a scholarly touch to footnotes in learned articles'.[22] However, the course in comparative law as it is currently offered at the university and by many law schools or faculties in Africa needs to be restructured from its current bias towards Roman-Dutch law, English common-law and so-called civilised nations' laws into an introduction to the broad diversity of legal systems in Africa and then other parts of the world. There is no doubt that comparative law is an essential offering in every law school's curriculum. This is irrespective of the current trend in Africa of minimising its significance through not offering it as an independent module.[23] Fombad argued that

> [the]situation in Africa, however, is worryingly different. A cursory look at the law curriculum in South African universities reveals the fairly disturbing trend in South Africa and, in fact, in most African universities, namely that comparative law as a subject of study has either been quietly relegated to the dustbin of history or left in the limbo of electives.[24]

---

[22] Kamba (note 12) 485.

[23] HP Glenn 'Against method?' in M Adams & D Heirbaut (eds) *The Method and Culture of Comparative Law* (Hart Publishing, 2014) 177–188.

[24] CM Fombad 'Comparative research in contemporary African legal studies' (2018) 67(4) *Journal of Legal Education* 984–1004.

The law school in Namibia and other law schools or faculties do not seem to appreciate the significance of comparative law, let alone the undying need to expand the place of studying African indigenous legal systems as part of comparative law. Apart from being recognised as a compulsory module, the study of comparative law must be decolonised to enable law students in Namibia and elsewhere in Africa to benefit from place-based learning as a critical pedagogical tool in legal education. The module must be offered as a compulsory and not a mere elective module. The aspect of a decolonised approach to comparative legal studies is regarded by short-sighted law advisers and students at schools of law or faculties of law as an unnecessary course for intellectuals. This seeming contradiction is due in large part to the conflict between viewing comparative law as a primary way for students to think outside the box of Roman-Dutch law and English common law and also viewing it as substantively irrelevant to the areas of law in which we expect our students to practice.

Globalisation seems to be fuelling the process of expanding the place of comparative law in legal education in the world. This has prompted Nelken to argue that

> amidst the current processes of borrowing, imitation and imposition of law and increasing global interdependence (both desired and undesired), comparative law is truly coming into its own.[25]

Strangely, the effects of globalisation in Africa seem to be causing institutions to attach minimal significance to adopting a place-based learning approach to legal studies on the continent. This implies that whereas globalisation is increasing the significance of comparative law in the world, in Africa the significance of comparative legal education is diminishing. This contradiction may have been fostered by the Westernisation of comparative law in African law schools or faculties. This can be attributed to the fact that globalisation, which is associated with Westernisation, appears to be prioritising the so-called laws of civilised nations such as those in America and Europe and to some extent Islamic law over African indigenous legal systems and/or laws. Making comparative law a vehicle for comparing civil and criminal procedure in the common and civil law and the standard Namibian law-school methods leads to the vast majority of students not studying comparative law. Students' perceptions of comparative law are then rendered erroneous because the discipline is not connected to their African way of life and therefore becomes

[25] D Nelken 'Comparative law and comparative legal studies' in E Örücü & D Nelken (eds) *Comparative Law: A Handbook* (Hart Publishing, 2007) 3; see also E Örücü 'Developing comparative law' in E Örücü & D Nelken (eds) *Comparative Law: A Handbook* (Hart Publishing, 2007) 44, 62.

irrelevant to their lives simply because their perceptions are highly Westernised or Islamic.

New decolonised approaches to teaching comparative law in Namibia and the rest of Africa must therefore be developed to close the existing relevancy gap while also expanding students' legal horizons. The inexorable shift to transnational and global legal practice also demands a comparable shift in the methods of teaching comparative law in African law schools or faculties. It is in this sense that the study of comparative law should also include a study of comparative cultures, one that exposes students to a panoply of legal systems, including traditional African indigenous legal systems and/or customary laws. Most African students may not be interested in learning the details of Western civil and criminal procedure, contracts, torts or European civil law. Instead, they would want to study more of the African indigenous laws and compare them to aspects of Western laws. The current approach to comparative-law education is that most African law students who have never been out of their home countries or regions are forced to study the legal systems of Western countries in detail. They then have to imagine how such laws operate in the Western context. Here the students can use only cultural images as vehicles to transport them culturally beyond the written word. This has often forced students studying comparative law in Africa to examine written materials visually in order to stimulate discussion about significant legal issues that exist in diverse Western cultures within and beyond the civil–common law dichotomy.

Many lecturers of the module in Africa often teach comparative law using the legal structure and operation of Western legal systems and/or laws. This misguided gravitation to Western-oriented civil or criminal procedure, contracts, property, torts or constitutional and administrative law often renders comparative law unappealing to contemporary law students, especially those in southern Africa, where calls for the decolonisation of legal education have reached a crescendo through mantras such as the #RhodesMustFall and #FeesMustFall movements. Accompanying indigenisation policies have been crafted and adopted by southern African governments. This has been coupled to calls to teach Liberation History together with Global Citizenship in secondary schools and universities in the region. At the University of Namibia, for instance, this started in February 2023 through the rollout of the core semester modules. These modules are taught for a period of five weeks and end before the commencement of mainstream lectures in the first week of March of every academic year.

It is therefore clear that by decolonising and transforming southern African law, students in the region are made more comfortable with learning foreign or Western law together with their indigenous African laws. Instead of having to apply the mental processes used to train law students in Western and Islamic environments, law students in Namibia are comfortable with the content and processes of African legal systems laws precisely because the systems feel so familiar to them. African students do not really have to wrestle with the foreign law (much less the culture) of another society because, although they will ultimately gain some technical knowledge, the absence of context renders the knowledge dry and virtually meaningless. In the process of teaching comparative law in Namibia and other parts of Africa, it is therefore important to expose students to the great legal and cultural differences between African and radically different societies such as those of Europe, America and Asia. Unfortunately, because most students are unfamiliar with the history, culture and legal practices in their own African contexts and both the Western and the Asian societies, they are unable to bridge the vast divide between that which is familiar to them and the sterile description of the unfamiliar. It is therefore not surprising that most law students, academics, judges, legal practitioners and other parties interested in legal studies in Africa are unable to take the next step of relating the substantive issues raised in foreign laws to the context of African law and society.

13.3 FUNCTIONS OF COMPARATIVE LAW

Comparative law has many functions to fulfil in the legal fraternity.[26] This section discusses its main functions. In the main, it serves to facilitate legislation and the practical improvement of law. However, the functions of comparative law are explored under different themes, as set out in this section: comparative law in legal education; legal research and comparative law, and legal research and its significance to formulating legislation and legal reforms.

13.3.1 Comparative law in legal education

Comparative law is a crucial component of academic studies in Namibia and elsewhere in the world. The term 'academic' in this chapter refers to the teaching and study of law. The conception of legal education determines the role of comparative law. Legal education in the contemporary era is important because technological advances and rapid industrialisation have led to socio-economic transformation which has created complex socio-economic problems. Comparative law is also important because the law has become intricate and requires more specialisation. Furthermore, the law in Namibia, Africa and the rest of the world is now a vehicle for promoting and guiding

[26] J Husa 'Interdisciplinary comparative law – between Scylla and Charybdis' (2014) 9 *Journal of Comparative Law* 28–42; see also J Smits 'European legal education, or: how to prepare students for global citizenship?' (2011) 45 *Law Teacher* 163–180; J Smits *Contract Law: A Comparative Introduction* (Edward Elgar, 2014).

socio-economic change. Owing to its importance, legal education must therefore cultivate the attributes and skills needed by lawyers such as:

(a) the ability to reason methodically;
(b) the capacity to think independently;
(c) having a critical and questioning attitude.

It must also provide students with sound knowledge and a proper understanding of the principles and techniques of national law. Furthermore, students must receive a broad-based legal education. Comparative law has the potential to fulfil the attributes and functions as alluded and referred to in this section. Comparative law therefore opens up legal students' minds to different legal possibilities in Namibia. If a student is confined to the study of their own law in their own cultural environment, there is a strong tendency to accept without questioning the norms, concepts and institutions of their own legal system.[27] There is also a tendency to think that solutions in one's own legal order are the only possible ones. The solitary study of one's own legal system leads to an idealisation of one's own legal institutions and to treating them as inherent in the general nature of law.

Learning to 'think like a lawyer' makes for a nice slogan, but exactly how would that be achieved? In essence, learning by studying and practising comparative law is an interactive chain of processes where the law student embraces the experiences gained in the study of foreign law in a way that results in changes in their professional thought patterns and their legal and cultural attitudes.[28] It makes sense to point out that the comparison, even in ambitious academic research, in comparative law does not normally mean operating with watertight research results and exact methods, but instead it is a continuous learning process.[29] To many, part of the intellectual appeal of comparative law is specifically due to this incompleteness. Husa argued that '[c]omparative law as an academic discipline is a very personal subject, giving its proponents great liberty to choose their interests'.[30] Moreover, this liberty offers opportunities for individual learners to interact with legal cultures: first, getting to know the basic approaches and solutions of the 'other law'; second, establishing an educational–dialogical interaction with foreign models seems to be a decent way to

[27] K Zweigert & H Kötz *An Introduction to Comparative Law* 3 ed (Oxford University Press, 1998) 21–24.

[28] J Squelch & D Bentley 'Preparing law graduates for a global world' (2017) 51 *Law Teacher* 2–16.

[29] LO Natt Gant II 'Deconstructing thinking like a lawyer: Analyzing the cognitive components of the analytical mind' (2007) 29 *Campbell Law Review* 413–480.

[30] J Husa 'Comparative law in legal education – building a legal mind for a transnational world' (2018) 52(2) *The Law Teacher* 201–215.

promote transnational legal study and peaceful coexistence between different legal cultures and the mentality of inquisitive cosmopolitanism.[31]

Obviously, there are difficulties and complications inherent in this kind of educational approach to law teaching. Yet, in spite of the hindrances, comparative law is at present a well-known and acknowledged constituent part of legal disciplines, which in different fields of law is used routinely as an auxiliary approach.[32] It has its own legitimate objects, distinctive methodologies and a distinctive epistemology that differs from that of other legal studies. Notwithstanding this, the strengthening of Asia and the rise of the Islamic world can bring new epistemic barriers to replace the old ones if the approach is distinctively Western. This seems to call for more a diverse understanding of how to 'think like a lawyer'. Accordingly, developments such as transnational legal pluralism or the globalisation of law have become more important than they were back in the 20th century. As a consequence, it makes sense not to start legal education and teaching processes today that focus exclusively on domestic law, since doing so may lock the legal minds of law students epistemically in such a manner that it becomes arduous later to deal with competing and overlapping plural normativities and transnational law.

The idea of a pluralistic legal mind has been attached to the 'other law', but it is crucial to see that the processes of legal influences also work the other way around: Western law also learns from other legal cultures. This means, among other things, that modern pluralism-conscious law education should not be only about Western approaches. Indeed, it is important to realise that the Western concept of 'law' is 'not the only complex institutional form of normativity'. Despite this, the Western cultural sphere is inevitably increasing its influence on Asian and African cultures and citizens in particular, not only through political and commercial contacts, but also by means of the internet, the entertainment industry and social media. It is hardly likely that these developments would not be reflected in the sphere of law. And yet, embracing the variety of law found in the world seems to be a very fit didactic approach for non-ethnocentric comparative law-based education. No originality can be claimed here: Gutteridge pointed out more than 80 years ago that the 'comparative method lends itself to the study of any branch of legal learning'.[33] However, this pedagogic idea has not actually been followed in the shaping of legal curricula. Obviously, a comparative-law-based learning process also requires legal imagination and not an overtly doctrinal domestic mental framework.

---

[31] NB Rapoport 'Is 'thinking like a lawyer' really what we want to teach?' (2002) 1 *Journal of the Association of Legal Writing Directors* 91–108.

[32] VV Palmer 'From Lerotholi to Lando: Some examples of comparative law methodology' (2005) 53 *American Journal of Comparative Law* 261–290.

[33] Husa (note 30) 201–215.

The dimensions which are referred to in this chapter deal with novel developments such as globalisation, pluralism, hybridity and transnational law, which are examples of events, phenomena and discussions that break new ground in a legal education that is not as restricted by national borders as before.[34] But, as stated above, this development is not a one-way process: the West does learn from other cultural spheres through interactive processes. Importantly, comparative law-based education helps law students to grasp legal contradictions and to live with them.[35] It is about subjecting the law student to pluralistic forms of law and the polycentricism of a transnational legal world. For someone learning to 'think like a lawyer' for a global world, a comparative-law approach to legal education makes sense: legal systems or other forms of organised normativities are not monolithic and coherent but overlapping and mixed.[36] Why should the model of legal education therefore not embrace the idea also when considering the pedagogical vision, the accompanying didactic solutions, and shaping law curricula?

These ideas are not as far-fetched as one might presume at first. A notable example of such a curriculum is the University of Namibia's new Bachelor of Laws Honours programme (LLB), which commenced in March 2023. The underlying idea in this programme is an attempt to take into account an increasingly global world so that the curriculum comprises learning about not only the national law of Namibia, but also and to a large extent the world's main legal systems. Importantly, in this programme, students are immersed in foreign legal materials from the very start of their studies. In other words, this LLB programme is global and/or transnational in its pedagogic approach: basic legal questions are first learnt through the study of Africa and the world's major legal models. What is lacking, though, is a multilingual approach: that is, Namibia's LLB programme has yet to teach classes through the medium of English plus any other relevant languages, such as Afrikaans and Swahili. However, international mobility is a key part of the degree programme and subjects such as Global Citizenship Education are now part of the core semester modules in law. It is not argued here that this kind of approach would not give rise to various challenges or that problems would not be inherent in it. But this particular programme is a fitting illustration of a genuinely global approach to shaping a law curriculum for a globalising world and relying on the pedagogic use of comparative-law materials instead of advanced comparative-law

[34] W Menski 'Remembering and applying legal pluralism: Law as kite flying' in SP Donlan & LH Urscheler (eds) *Concepts of Law: Comparative, Jurisprudential and Social Science Perspectives* (Ashgate, 2014) 91–108.

[35] P Legrand 'Foreign law: Understanding understanding' (2011) 6 *Journal of Comparative Law* 67–177.

[36] P Ancel 'Towards a new model of legal education: The special case of Luxembourg' in C Jamin & W van Caenegem (eds) *The Internationalisation of Legal Education* (Springer, 2016) 195–208.

scholarship.[37] Essentially, new phenomena such as transnational law or global law share the same basic epistemic assumption with comparative law: they are not bound to the jurisdiction of any state in a legal and – what is more important – an epistemic sense.

13.3.2 Legal research and comparative law

Comparative law is indispensable to the legal researcher or the legal philosopher.[38] This can be attributed to the fact that in the process of formulating general theories of law, generalisation must proceed by way of bringing together a number of particular legal systems.[39] Furthermore, in testing the general theories in so far as the Western idea of law is universal, questions have to be raised regarding the manner in which and the extent to which such a system represents the characteristics of legal orders in all societies, especially those in Africa. Here, comparative law offers the best answers. It therefore is not surprising that comparative law is very important to the concept of legal research.[40] Legal research is the process one uses to identify the laws – including statutes, regulations and court opinions – that apply to the facts of one's case.[41] In most instances, the purpose of legal research is to find support for a specific legal issue or decision. Legal research is therefore conducted in varying contexts and circumstances. Such contexts and circumstances are discussed in this section, beginning with drafting legislation and undertaking legal reforms.

13.3.3 Legal research and its significance in formulating legislation and legal reforms

One of the key functions of legal research in so far as comparative law is concerned is to facilitate the formulation or drafting of legislation and to ensure the practical improvement of the existing laws in Namibia. Following the Second World War, comparative law was increasingly used by different countries in the world as a vehicle for formulating and reforming legislation. It is therefore not surprising that in the contemporary era comparative law continues to play a key role in the creation of new rules and solutions or in modifying or abolishing existing ones. It also establishes the

[37] J Engberg 'Word meaning and the problem of a globalized legal order' in P Tiersma & L Solan (eds) *The Oxford Handbook of Language and Law* (Oxford University Press, 2012) 175–186.

[38] J Smits *The Mind and Method of the Legal Academic* (Edward Elgar, 2012) 141–148.

[39] JS Bruner 'Going beyond the information given' in *Contemporary Approaches to Cognition* (Harvard University Press, 1957) 218–238.

[40] J Dewey *Experience and Education* (Macmillan, 1938).

[41] HP Glenn *Legal Traditions of the World: Sustainable Diversity in Law* 5 ed (Oxford University Press, 2014).

appropriate technique for drafting or formulating legislation and is instrumental in ascertaining the practicability and enforceability of any proposed law.

13.4 COMPARATIVE LAW AND THE JUDICIAL PROCESS

Comparative law plays a key role in national judicial processes. It is useful when magistrates or judges preside over cases of first impression. In systems of common-law tradition, gaps occur in cases which are not plainly covered by legislation or binding judicial precedents.[42] In civil-law systems, gaps can occur due to the absence of code provisions directly in point. Acquiring knowledge of the law and practice of foreign courts may not only suggest possible and preferable solutions but also indicate possible but also undesirable solutions.

Comparative law may also be useful in the process of explaining national-law concepts and principles of foreign origin.[43] Many systems of law have to varying degrees imported or have had imposed on them principles, concepts and institutions from other legal systems.[44] The hybrid or mixed systems of in particular jurisdiction on sub-Saharan Africa provide a striking and even more fascinating mixture of the elements of various Western systems and indigenous customary systems of law. Comparative law therefore becomes a useful tool with which to clarify, understand and ascertain an intelligent application of foreign concepts and principles in domestic courts.

Comparative law can also be useful in applying foreign law in national courts under the conflict of laws.[45] The increase in multilateral trade, regional trade and rapid globalisation has led to an ever-increasing number of transactions which cut across national boundaries. National courts have therefore become heavily involved in settling disputes which contain elements of foreign law. Courts therefore have to determine their competence to deal with a dispute, that is, whether they have jurisdiction; or, if they are competent, which system of law governs such a dispute.[46]

---

[42] AM Slaughter 'On thinking like a lawyer' 2002 *Harvard Law Today*, http://www.princeton.edu/~-slaughtr/Commentary/On%20Thinking%20Like%20a%20Lawyer.pdf, accessed 20 August 2023.

[43] A Watson 'Legal transplants and European private law' (2000) 4(4) *Electronic Journal of Comparative Law* 12; see also A Watson 'From legal transplants to legal formants' (1995) 43 *American Journal of Comparative Law* 469–476.

[44] G Frankenberg 'Stranger than paradise: Identity and politics in comparative law' (1997) 2 *Utah Law Review* 259–274.

[45] HW Micklitz 'On the politics of legal methodology' (2014) 21 *Maastricht Journal of European and Comparative Law* 589–595.

[46] SP Donlan & LH Urscheler 'Concepts of law: An introduction' in SP Donlan & LH Urscheler (eds) *Concepts of Law: Comparative, Jurisprudential, and Social Science Perspectives* (Routledge, 2014) 1–17.

Comparative law can help with resolving such issues. Moreover, in the case of Namibia, Arts 143 and 144 of the Namibia Constitution make provision for reliance on international legal norms and standards when dealing with legal matters in Namibia. However, the import of these provisions is not that the international law must per se vitiate against the best interests of Namibians but that it must advance their best interests.

13.5 COMPARATIVE LAW AND THE UNIFICATION AND HARMONISATION OF LAWS

Comparative legal studies contribute to the unification and harmonisation of laws. The recent developments regarding regional integration and the creation of a common market for trade in Africa through the AfCFTA, the creation of multilateral legal frameworks for trade and other legal disciplines and the process of globalisation all create a basis for unifying and harmonising laws in Africa and the rest of the world. Unification signifies the process by which two or more different legal provisions or systems are supplanted by a single provision or system: it creates an identity of legal provisions. Harmonisation is designed to effect an approximation or co-ordination of different legal provisions or systems by eliminating major differences and creating minimum requirements or standards. Unification and harmonisation are necessitated by the existence of a large number of diverse legal systems in the world and for this reason either can occur at the international, regional or national level.

13.6 COMPARATIVE LAW AND INTERNATIONAL LAW

Comparative law serves as an aid to ascertaining, creating, formulating and applying principles of international law. For example, Art 38:1 of the Statute of the International Court of Justice (ICJ) provides that the court shall apply:

A. International conventions, whether general or particular, establishing rules expressly recognised by the contesting states;
B. ....
C. The general principles of law recognised by civilised nations;
D. ...

The phrase 'general principles of law recognised by civilised nations' refers to those principles that find expression in the municipal laws of various nations. Such principles can be ascertained by the comparative method.

13.7 COMPARATIVE LAW, LEGAL EDUCATION AND A GLOBALISING WORLD

A connection may exist between comparative law, legal education and globalisation. This could suggest that comparative law has the potential to contribute to offering quality legal education in a globalising world. However, it is important to note that learning law and comparing law appear to be quite different things. Scholars who speak of teaching are seldom those who discuss the methodology and epistemology of comparative law.[47] Besides, theoretical writing about comparative law covering its epistemology and methodology tends to report warnings and endless lists of difficulties.[48] In fact, it is virtually a miracle that anyone well aware of the difficulties dares to do comparative legal research at all. Accordingly, the snobbish message from the scholarship is typically that 'comparative law is always forbidding and difficult'. This is not an inspiring message for legal educators. What is more, it is an unhelpful message. If comparative law is considered to be a specialised field of legal research, these warnings make sense. However, if reference is being made to legal education and teaching, the situation may be quite the opposite. Comparative law can and, indeed, ought to be developed as an important pedagogical tool. And its educational use must be aligned to the undying need to rethink approaches to legal education in law schools in Africa and the rest of the world.

From the perspective of comparative law and in pursuit of the best interests of legal education today and in the future in Namibia and the rest of Africa, the need exists to turn the law curriculum on its head. However, it may not be enough to do so if law teachers were to cling to an over-theorised and exclusive conception of comparative law. To underline the value of comparative law for the purposes of legal education does not mean underestimating the difficulties that ambitious comparative research faces, though. But if we deal purely with comparative law and its purpose and function in our teaching, the theoretical debate about comparative legal research does not offer much educational argument or course material. To be sure, epistemological obstacles to the understanding of foreign law in Africa are significant, since there are different epistemic structures of understanding. On this point, Legrand argued that

> no understanding and no narrative ever capture[s] the whole of the foreign law-text, interpretation is revealed to be not only an act of memory (meaning is recoverable), but also an act of mourning (some meaning is irrecoverably lost).[49]

---

[47] C Nicholson 'The relevance of the past in preparing for the future: A case for Roman law and legal history' (2011) 17 *Fundamina* 101–114.

[48] N Howson 'Can the West learn from the rest? The Chinese legal order's hybrid modernity' (2009) 32 *Hastings International & Comparative Law* 815–830.

[49] P Legrand 'Comparative legal studies and commitment to theory' (2005) 58(2) *The Modern Law Review* 143–283.

Undoubtedly, comparative legal research is challenging, but the education-related question is this: Can we separate comparative-law research and the accompanying theory from comparative law applied for the purposes of teaching law? The answer to this appears to be straightforward because in education the typical set of core questions in the theoretical debates about comparative law is not really relevant (eg, What is meant by 'comparison', 'understanding' or 'tradition', etc?).[50] For pedagogical purposes, it seems to be a useful distinction to separate educating lawyers from educating researchers. This, however, seems to require developing some kind of comparative-law pedagogics which deals with different kinds of question than those pertinent to the theory and methodology of comparative law. But what kind of pedagogics could this be?

Comparative-law pedagogics may be defined tentatively as 'the art of teaching legal thinking through other law'.[51] Accordingly, it would not be about the epistemological and methodological problems of comparative-law research but rather about the principles of teaching foreign law and non-national law (ie, the other law) for non-research-based purposes. This would lead to acquiring a better understanding of one's own legal system (ie, teaching legal thinking, not 'reading law' as such) and developing a critical approach to one's own law, starting with questions instead of answers. Learning outcomes would be, ultimately, to have a deeper understanding of the legal problems lawyers tend to face and unexpected ideas for solving them (ie, building awareness).[52] In short, this would mean a move away from 'reading law' to learning legal thinking, that is, how to 'think like a lawyer'.

The suggested separation of research and teaching may give rise to justified objections, though, because academic teaching is supposed to be based on research.[53] To be sure, there is nothing wrong with the classical academic ideal that underlines the connection between research and teaching; but the real issue here is how to deploy research-based knowledge for teaching students to 'think like a lawyer' in an efficient manner. The question therefore boils down to this: How to shape the curriculum?

Now, the goal in scientific research is normally to arrive objectively at the truth, or at least at a deep understanding. But the goal in teaching is perhaps less complicated, that is, learning. To simplify the matter a great deal, legal education seems to be about the process of acquiring legal knowledge and skills (eg, acquaintance with a range of information, awareness of multiple legal approaches). Learning outcomes are skills and knowledge which are acquired

[50] Ibid.

[51] Ibid.

[52] Ibid.

[53] J Dewey 'John Dewey in the 21st century' (2017) 9(1) *Journal of Inquiry & Action in Education* 91–102.

by a systemic study of law (ie, following the curriculum). Against this backdrop, comparative-law-based learning would mean, first and foremost, acquiring skills and knowledge through the general study of different (perhaps competing) laws or normativities.

By and large, comparative-law-based teaching can rely on the idea of turning the curriculum on its head: instead of placing national law at the forefront (ie in the first year), one should start with foreign laws and different approaches to similar types of legal problem. This idea draws on Dewey's pedagogical basic idea, that is, 'learning by doing'.[54] Dewey's pedagogical theory refers to an experiential way of learning. Essentially, this kind of learning involves learning through experiencing and reflecting on non-national approaches to legal questions.[55] Moreover, it also points out that the process of comparing laws is, to a large extent, about learning by doing. This would require law schools to integrate strong comparative-law elements into their curricula, therefore offering insights into the workings of foreign legal systems (state-based and other types) from the very beginning of a student's legal education. In turn, these insights may be applied to one's own legal system in the sense that foreign solutions and approaches illuminate what is typical in one's own law, as a result yielding also a more profound understanding of one's own law.[56] Moreover, it makes sense to underline the point that comparative law itself is not a monolith but something which has a variety of dimensions, uses and functions. On a more practical note, many diverse comparative- and foreign-law materials are available on the internet. Consequently, certain comparative-law text types may be used in legal education as non-nationally oriented teaching materials.

What would be the practical consequences if we were to rely on 'learning by doing' and comparative law? This is a complicated question, but we can at least point out certain basic outcomes. One of the most underrated features of the comparative-law methodology is its ability not only to promote a higher quality of research, but also to encourage positive attitudes to experiential learning. Crucially, the study of comparative law should not be regarded exclusively as a form of rigorous non-national legal research; it ought rather to be viewed also as a kind of continuous learning process in which the learner interacts epistemologically with the other law. Comparative law, if it is understood as being a teaching aid, has potential as an educational tool in legal education, as we shall see in the following section.

[54] Ibid.
[55] Ibid.
[56] Ibid.

13.8 TOWARDS COMPARATIVE-LAW-BASED LEARNING IN NAMIBIA AND AFRICA

Comparative law may be a didactic approach that could be applied for the purposes of modern teaching in African law schools.[57] In the first place, the pedagogical interest at the base of comparative law seems to be related to acquiring a better understanding of one's own legal system and to developing a critical approach to one's own law. However, there is more to it than merely learning to understand one's own law better: learning many approaches to the same legal problem, or at least to similar types, tends to open learners' minds to a broader epistemic structure than what is possible if the education takes place primarily from the perspective of one system only. Both of these educational dimensions naturally diminish often implicit ethnocentric attitudes and facilitate epistemically non-national legal minds and the transnational conception of law. In a world that is globalising more and more vehemently, such information that contributes to an understanding of the views and legal concepts of others tends to be beneficial. This is so because the legal world of today consists of a plurality of legally significant normativities. Zumbansen makes the important point that transnationalisation concerns the law curriculum in general; it is not a question of educating only those lawyers who work in the international fields of law.[58] Instead, the problem for the current law curriculum is that there is a gap between 'first-year courses and the crème de la crème curriculum specialisation restricted to upper-year course selections'.[59]

Essentially, the practrice of comparing laws (and other similar types of organised normativity) requires an ability to understand foreign law in the form it takes in the basic legal cultural assumptions.[60] For a scholarly comparatist, it is a question of possessing the ability to draw conclusions that are at least potentially legally correct also in the sphere of foreign law, and of possessing skills in legal thinking in general and knowing the legal language that is typical of a particular foreign legal culture. The situation is different in the case of learning because the aims are different from research.

Even while the benefits of turning the curriculum on its head seem undeniable from the perspective of transnational and globalising law, actually injecting foreign law and the underlying principles and doctrines of the other law into the law curriculum can pose a multitude of problems. For instance, the further apart the

[57] J Basedow 'Comparative law and its clients' (2014) 62(4) *American Journal of Comparative Law* 821–857.

[58] P Zumbansen 'Transnational law, evolving. comparative research in law & political economy' Research Paper No 27/2011.

[59] Ibid.

[60] Husa (note 30) 201–215.

legal systems or other normativities in question are in a legal–cultural sense, the more significant a role the contextual information assumes.[61] This is illustrated, for example, by the collision of Islamic and Western concepts of justice: discussion on mere principles is difficult enough because there are such significant differences in the basic concepts and approaches to law. In such cases, knowledge of the concepts and origins of Islamic law is cognitively and often also strategically useful to a Western lawyer. Discussion and rendering one's own points of view comprehensible become easier when one possesses contextual knowledge. For instance, the Islamic legal culture is one of the major legal cultures of the world and so possessing general knowledge about it cannot be anything but useful for a Western lawyer. In fact, the mere existence of relatively numerous Muslim populations in non-Muslim countries creates a need for knowledge of Islamic law: when the cultures of the people meet, then their legal cultures also meet. An example which demonstrates that reconciliation between legal cultures is not entirely impossible is the Islamic banking principles and practices. Islamic banking embodies the pluralistic nature of today's legal world that exposes lawyers and legal cultures to a range of sometimes competing, sometimes fusing and mixing, normativities.[62] Moreover, to take another example, the judge who is having to apply the marital right to property to a Muslim family will benefit greatly from acquiring a rudimentary knowledge of Islamic law: they will then understand argumentation that is based on Islamic law and are at least to some extent more capable of estimating the significance of such arguments from the point of view of the party who presents them.[63] However, this does not mean accepting those arguments or granting them a role as sources of law; instead, it is about understanding foreign legal culture-based arguments more fully. Moreover, the abovementioned Islamic financial principles and practice which operate according to Islamic law are a powerful example of a situation in which understanding non-Western religious law has proved to be highly profitable.[64] Then again, one should perhaps not draw too far-reaching conclusions from banking law, because the reconcilability of Sharia law with Western law in the area of marital law or other aspects of private law is obviously more questionable.[65]

[61] Ibid.

[62] R Wilson 'Challenges and opportunities for Islamic banking and finance in the West: The United Kingdom experience' (1999) 41 *Thunderbird International Business Review* 421–444; see also R Cranston 'Theorizing transnational commercial law'(2007) 42 *Texas International Law Journal* 597–617; P Wesley-Smith *An Introduction to the Hong Kong Legal System* 3 ed (Oxford University Press, 1999); A Belouafi & A Chachi 'Islamic finance in the United Kingdom: Factors behind its development and growth' (2014) 22 *Islamic Economic Studies* 37–78.

[63] Wilson (note 62) 421–444.

[64] Ibid.

[65] Ibid.

However, we do not need to move beyond the sphere of Western law in order to understand the point made here. It is, for example, considerably easier for a civil servant who gets involved in European administrative law to operate successfully as part of a multicultural legal environment if their primary epistemology is not limited to their own legal system.[66] Crucially, we are talking here about the legal mind, not the domestic doctrine on sources of valid applicable law. Foreign legal cultures can be taken into consideration as evidence of the beliefs held by parties, even if they would not be given legal significance as a source of law. In addition, the study of comparative-law material (foreign rules, doctrines, cases, ideas, etc) plays a significant role in developing law graduates' ability to think globally.[67] And this may not mean anything which would be terrifyingly difficult or utterly complex. Becoming acquainted with the laws and different legal cultures of other countries serves to improve one's ability for legal thinking; moreover, argumentation becomes more versatile when different normative points of view are taken into consideration. If students are offered the models of one country or legal culture only, their initial knowledge capacity for versatile argumentation is weakened. In this sense, comparative-law teaching material opens up legal thinking but, to be sure, it does not mean that foreign law would gain the position of a source of law. More importantly, the process of interacting with other law shapes one's way of 'thinking like a lawyer'. Using the other law in legal teaching serves its purpose well if and when learning law is no longer simply 'reading law' but learning to 'think like a lawyer' in a world where different legal cultures and bodies of law necessarily interact with one another.

13.9 TEACHING COMPARATIVE LAW

From the perspective of learning law, teaching comparative law may have a key role to play for the transnational or global legal mind. An effective law curriculum of today that is suited to globalisation is one which can stimulate students to learn legal thinking generally, not only the legal rules of a single jurisdiction. Globalisation is, of course, a debatable concept, yet in this chapter it refers broadly but not exclusively to the globalisation of law or global law, which is normally defined as the law of non-state governance systems. These are typically legal orders that develop beyond the scope of the sovereignty of a state. For example, this kind of global law may

[66] The Commission on European Contract Law *Principles of European Contract Law I, II* and *III* (The Hague, Kluwer, 2000, The Hague, Kluwer, 2003); see also JEC Brierley & RA Macdonald (eds) *Quebec Civil Law: An Introduction to Quebec Private Law* (Emond Montgomery, 1993).

[67] L Heuschling *Etat de Droit, Rechtsstaat, Rule of Law* (Dalloz, 2002); see also K Gammelgaard & E Holmøyvik *Writing Democracy: The Norwegian Constitution 1814–2014* (Berghahn Books, 2015).

develop through processes in international forums such as the United Nations (eg the International Criminal Court) or geographically in a more limited sense, such as the Council of Europe. Or it may occur in a less formal manner so that it grows out of the common practices of a profession – such as international arbitrators or in transnational business communities (ie, a new *lex mercatoria*). Commercial law, in particular, is globalising as states and transnational companies agree to various forms of standard regulations, rules and legal practices. In any event, the globalisation of law opens up a new role for comparative law in law teaching, leading to pressure being exerted on the reshaping of curricula.

Comparative law and/or foreign law, and even an approximate knowledge of different non-national approaches to similar types of legal question, may be a valuable tool with which to construct a pluralistic legal mind that is prepared to look beyond the borders of legal systems. Non-national laws, customs and legal doctrines are useful learning materials for anyone who seeks to cultivate a pluralistic legal mind. It is relevant here to emphasise that this is not merely a distant dream but, as the examples of McGill University (Canada), Maastricht University (Netherlands), Tilburg University (Netherlands), Hanse Law School (Germany/Netherlands), Peking School of Transnational Law (China) and Luxembourg University show, these ideas are already being put to use in plurality-conscious legal education. And yet traditional law curricula still seem to hold the upper hand even while we can witness new developments and ideas emerging that embrace the ideas of transnational and/or global law.

Essentially, comparative-law material and foreign language studies are of great pedagogical importance in a world where the role of state law is on the decline. But this does not mean that it would become meaningless; instead, it means that legal systems are increasingly influencing one another and in this sense state law has become largely subject to globalisation. However, this does not mean that scholarly focused comparative law is not relevant because pedagogical needs are different from purely scholarly ones. And it is noteworthy that a particularly profound study of foreign law is not needed for educational purposes: if a student becomes acquainted with both the history and the general grounds and typical features of, say, common law through reading the comparative-law literature, it becomes easier for them to approach the laws of the United Kingdom, Canada, New Zealand and the United States and also the laws of all the countries that have been influenced by common law. More generally, the significance of non-national legal general knowledge should not be belittled in the present-day world. And, considering the obvious fact that law and legal ideas do travel when people travel, the global world of law is also a world of migrating law. Along similar lines, it would not be a healthy idea to educate all lawyers for a mono-epistemic mindset any longer. This is because world in which law students act 'wisely' by concentrating on the technicalities of national law and 'keep body and mind at home' has passed – but our curricula have not changed accordingly.

The key argument of this chapter holds that the objectives of pedagogical comparative interests are better realised if comparative law is not given a minor role in or labelled as a jurisprudential curiosity of the legal academia but is instead included from the very beginning in the learning of law. There are good reasons for this in the very nature of law, which has never stopped at national borders, as legal history shows us. Legal norms and doctrines travel just like other technical or commercial inventions; it is almost impossible to stop them because a human being is instinctively interested in different solutions, and our capacity to adopt social and other innovations is ample. And, yes, sceptics undoubtedly have a point when they are doubtful about matters such as the simplified assumptions of similarity of legal transplants or the legal convergence of European law. Yet the reality of human capability to learn and adapt ought not to be denied: the legal historical evidence of this is overwhelming. There is, it would appear, a quintessential lesson for legal education here: law travels, rendering all national systems anything but purely domestic.

But what does all this mean in practice? Turning the curriculum on its head seems to make sense, but what kind of an education should be given to first-year and second-year law students without their getting entangled in the serious difficulties that accompany scholarly research on comparative law? This is, perhaps surprisingly, not so formidable an obstacle as one might think because we are dealing with basic legal ideas, principles and doctrines. It is, for instance, considerably easier to understand the basic institutional decisions of constitutional law if one is acquainted with a number of other basic models (eg, British parliamentarianism, US presidentialism with its separation of powers, French semi-presidentialism). In the same way, several of the most central principles (eg, the principle of liberal constitutionalism or the Western rule-of-law principle) are non-national by nature. Accordingly, principles adopted in different countries can be used to facilitate the interpretation of law and the theory of public law in other countries and non-national organisations, although the principles in question would not be exactly the same. Or, for instance, the Norwegian application of the principle of *Rechtsstaat* (*Rettsstat*) Law could be perceived with more insight if it were related, for example, to the German or English version of the same basic legal idea: there are similarities and differences between them. There are many possibilities of which especially comparative-law scholars are aware; the challenge lies in producing such material that works well for first- and second-year law students and does not become entangled in any of the unsolvable theoretical dilemmas plaguing comparative-law scholarship.

Accordingly, for example, to comprehend contract law it is beneficial if one recognises the difference in the concept of a contract between civil law and common law. And there are differences in attitudes to some basic legal–cultural factors: Why is bona fides important in Continental Europe but not so important on the other side of the Channel? Why is a literal interpretation of contracts in favour in the United Kingdom? Why are commercial practices of such significance in English common law? Or why, in Hong Kong, which is part of the People's Republic of China, is the law based on the precepts, principles and framework of English common law? Or why, in order to understand Quebec's law, it is important to grasp that the roots of Quebec's private law are founded in the French civil law? An example of this kind of teaching material is Smits' book, *Contract Law*, which introduces certain key principles of contract law by comparing solutions from different jurisdictions. Contract law is presented first and foremost in a comparative light and without starting from a certain legal system.

Sceptics may question, no doubt, and criticise this kind of educational 'reduced' comparative law, but it is not based on a whim. In fact, this kind of pluralist-conscious legal education can be based on pedagogical theory. Such theory giving support to the use of comparative or foreign law in teaching is based on so-called constructivism, which refers to the idea according to which an effective law curriculum stimulates students to learn legal thinking (ie, it does not offer ready answers). Here, the materials used in teaching are regarded as a stimulus that sets the learner's learning process in motion; that is, the stimulus itself (the substance of law) is not as important as the cognitive process that it sets in motion. Basic textbooks on foreign law and uncomplicated comparative-law introductions would, in fact, provide useful material for this kind of learning process. It should go without saying that this kind of introductory material does, of course, not meet the criteria of in-depth comparative legal research.

Importantly, it is crucial to separate research results from learning results and research methods from didactic tools. In practice, this means that comparative law and/or foreign law and even an approximate knowledge of different foreign approaches to similar types of question offer pedagogical tools for constructing a pluralistic legal mind that is prepared to look beyond the borders of legal systems (ie, an epistemic attitude) and to think outside the national box. In summary, we should be moving from 'reading law' to 'learning legal thinking' in this comparative-law pedagogics. And turning the law curriculum on its head can make a significant educational contribution towards achieving this aim.

13.10 CONCLUSION

Globalisation and parallel phenomena, such as transnational law and global law, are challenging nationally oriented ways of defining and understanding legal education. Consequently, it has become clear that law graduates must be prepared for working in a non-national global context. Furthermore, the legal education of today should meet this challenge. This chapter has discussed some aspects of the use of comparative law in pluralism-conscious legal education. Learning to 'think like a lawyer', as this expression was used above, refers to acquiring certain basic skills, such as being able to perform (normative) legal reasoning on the basis of rules, principles and doctrines. This learning also entails being able to make legal arguments on any side of a question at hand, learning about different sources of law, learning about alternative approaches and their strengths and weaknesses in addition to learning that there are arguments on both sides, learning to reject some arguments and to embrace others, and learning to combine passion with principle and even reason with judgement.

It has been argued in this chapter that by means of teaching foreign law (or the 'other law') it is possible to transfer the focus of legal learning away from learning detailed domestic rules and instead concentrating on general principles and features. It was claimed that more significance ought to be placed on the transnational dimensions of law as part of legal education in all branches of law. Through the 'other law' it becomes didactically possible to proportion the familiar to the unfamiliar – this may generate new knowledge and novel insights about law as a non-national phenomenon. This, however, also puts pressure on the nature of the teaching materials used in a law curriculum which has been turned on its head. Turning the curriculum on its head means changing the order and focus of subjects in the curriculum so that the legal curriculum would meet the changes that have occurred and are occurring because of globalisation. Placing non-national and problem-based materials at the beginning rather than at the end of a curriculum would make it easier to focus on the epistemic aspects of learning law for a world in which the borders of states have lost much of their earlier significance in the eyes and practice of legal professions. Even though all of this is certainly challenging, it is hardly an insurmountable obstacle for today's law teachers.

More generally, comparative-law-based materials and teaching ought to be regarded as the stimulus that sets a learner's learning process in motion, that is, the stimulus (substance) is not as important as the cognitive process that the stimulus is igniting. In this regard, Bruner has noted:

> The most characteristic thing about mental life, over and beyond the fact that one apprehends the events of the world around one, is that one constantly goes beyond the information given.[68]

No doubt this sounds rather grand, but the idea is simply this: on the basis of many approaches to similar types of legal problem, law students are able to combine (or synthesise) overlapping and competing materials and in this limited sense they are

[68] Bruner (note 39).

learning to 'think like lawyers' and go beyond the materials presented to them by building on them.

On the downside, pedagogics centred on comparative law is not without its problems. To turn the curriculum on its head is a rather dramatic move in the somewhat conservative and nation-state-oriented academic world of legal education. One of the most obvious hazards is the possible creation of an illusion of knowledge. This is because comparative-law pedagogics does not offer genuine deep-level knowledge but rather simulated information. As a result, law students may generate imaginative information that they may mistakenly regard as legally valid knowledge of foreign law. To be sure, this kind of comparative-law teaching does not turn the law graduate into an expert on foreign law but, instead, it equips them with an open and inquisitive legal mind. From there it follows, of course, that this is the price that must be paid if the goal of deep cultural knowledge in research-oriented comparative law is transformed into a 'lighter' use for educational purposes: moulding the mind of a law student instead of producing deep-level and culturally sensitive knowledge about foreign law.

In the end, we are talking about a simulated learning experience. Simulation in this context refers to learning scenarios in which foreign law is reconstructed and simplified for learning purposes and made to look, feel or behave like the 'other law' so that it can be studied or otherwise used to teach law graduates to cope with the plurality of legal sources.

To conclude, pedagogical usage of comparative or foreign law makes it possible to educate transnationally oriented lawyering minds instead of nationally restricted lawyering memories. However, for this to take place, it would require comparative-law scholars to step down from their ivory tower and participate more actively in shaping a globalisation-compatible law curriculum and legal pedagogics.

REFERENCES

Ancel, P 'Towards a new model of legal education: The special case of Luxembourg' in C Jamin & W van Caenegem (eds) *The Internationalisation of Legal Education* (Springer, 2016).

Basedow, J 'Comparative law and its clients' (2014) 62(4) *The American Journal of Comparative Law* 821–857.

Bell, J 'Legal research and the distinctiveness of comparative law' in M van Hoecke (ed) *Methodologies of Legal Research* (Hart Publishing, 2011).

Belouafi, A& Chachi, A 'Islamic finance in the United Kingdom: Factors behind its development and growth' (2014) 22 *Islamic Economic Studies* 37–78.

Brierley, JEC & Macdonald, RA (eds) *Quebec Civil Law: An Introduction to Quebec Private Law* (Emond Montgomery, 1993).

Bruner, JS 'Going beyond the information given' in *Contemporary Approaches to Cognition* (Harvard University Press, 1957).

Commission on European Contract Law *Principles of European Contract Law I, II* and *III* (The Hague, Kluwer, 2000. The Hague, Kluwer, 2003).

Cranston, R 'Theorizing transnational commerciallaw' (2007) 42 *Texas International Law Journal* 597–617;

Dewey, J *Experience and Education* (Macmillan, 1938).

Dewey, J 'John Dewey in the 21st century' (2017) 9(1) *Journal of Inquiry & Action in Education* 91–102.

Donlan, SP & Urscheler, LH 'Concepts of law: An introduction' in SP Donlan & LH Urscheler (eds) *Concepts of Law: Comparative, Jurisprudential, and Social Science Perspectives* (Routledge, 2014).

Engberg, J 'Word meaning and the problem of a globalized legal order' in P Tiersma & L Solan (eds) *The Oxford Handbook of Language and Law* (Oxford University Press, 2012).

Fombad, CM 'Comparative research in contemporary African legal studies' (2018) 67(4) *Journal of Legal Education* 984–1004.

Frankenberg, G 'Stranger than paradise: Identity and politics in comparative law' (1997) 2 *Utah Law Review* 259–274.

Gammelgaard, K & Holmøyvik, E *Writing Democracy: The Norwegian Constitution 1814–2014* (Berghahn Books, 2015).

Gane, C & Huang, RH (eds) *Legal Education in the Global Context – Opportunities and Challenges* (Routledge, 2016).

Glenn, HP 'Against method?' in M Adams & D Heirbaut (eds) *The Method and Culture of Comparative Law* (Hart Publishing, 2014).

Glenn, HP *Legal Traditions of the World: Sustainable Diversity in Law* 5 ed (Oxford University Press, 2014).

Grossfeld, B *The Strength and Weakness of Comparative Law* (Clarendon Press, 1990).

Gutteridge, H 'The value of comparative law' 1931 *Journal of the Society of Public Teachers of Law* 27–31.

Gutteridge, HC *Comparative Law* 2 ed (Cambridge University Press, 1949).

Heringa, AW& Kiiver, P *Constitutions Compared: An Introduction to Comparative Constitutional Law* 3 ed (Intersentia, 2012).

Heuschling, L *Etat de Droit, Rechtsstaat, Rule of Law* (Dalloz, 2002).

Howson, N 'Can the West learn from the rest? The Chinese legal order's hybrid modernity' (2009) 32 *Hastings International & Comparative Law* 815–830.

Husa, J 'Turning the curriculum upside down: Comparative law as an educational tool for constructing the pluralistic legal mind' (2009) 10 *German Law Journal* 913–928.

Husa, J 'Interdisciplinary comparative law – between Scylla and Charybdis' (2014) 9 *Journal of Comparative Law* 28–42.

Husa, J *A New Introduction to Comparative Law* (Hart Publishing, 2015).

Husa, J 'Comparative law in legal education – building a legal mind for a transnational world' (2018) 52(2) *The Law Teacher* 201–215.

Kahn-Freund, O 'Comparative law as an academic subject' (1966) 82 *Law Quarterly Review* 40, 41.
Kamba, WJ 'Comparative law: A theoretical framework' (1974) 23(3) *The International and Comparative Law Quarterly* 485–519.
Legrand, P 'Comparative legal studies and commitment to theory' (2005) 58(2) *The Modern Law Review* 143–283.
Legrand, P 'Foreign law: Understanding understanding' (2011) 6 *Journal of Comparative Law* 67–177.
McDougal, MS 'The comparative study of law for policy purposes: Value clarification as an instrument of democratic world order' (1952) 1(1/2) *American Journal of Comparative Law* 24–57.
Menski, W 'Remembering and applying legal pluralism: Law as kite flying' in SP Donlan & LH Urscheler (eds) *Concepts of Law: Comparative, Jurisprudential and Social Science Perspectives* (Ashgate, 2014).
Micklitz, HW 'On the politics of legal methodology' (2014) 21 *Maastricht Journal of European and Comparative Law* 589–595.
Natt Gant II, LO 'Deconstructing thinking like a lawyer: Analysing the cognitive components of the analytical mind' (2007) 29 *Campbell Law Review* 413–480.
Nelken, D 'Comparative law and comparative legal studies'in E Orucu & D Nelken (eds) *Comparative Law: A Handbook* (Hart Publishing, 2007).
Nicholson, C 'The relevance of the past in preparing for the future: A case for Roman law and legal history' (2011) 17 *Fundamina* 101–114.
Örücü, E 'Developing comparative law' in E Örücü & D Nelken (eds) *Comparative Law: A Handbook* (Hart Publishing, 2007).
Örücü, E (ed) *Mixed Legal Systems at New Frontiers* (Wiley, 2010).
Palmer, VV 'From Lerotholi to Lando: Some examples of comparative law methodology' (2005) 53 *American Journal of Comparative Law* 261–290.
Rapoport, NB 'Is "thinking like a lawyer" really what we want to teach?' (2002) 1 *Journal of the Association of Legal Writing Directors* 91–108.
Rheinstein, M 'Teaching tools in comparative law' (1952) 1 *American Journal of Comparative Law* 95, 98.
Samuel, G *An Introduction to Comparative Law Theory and Method* (Hart Publishing, 2014).
Slaughter, AM 'On thinking like a lawyer' 2002 *Harvard Law Today*, http://www.princeton.edu/~slaughtr/Commentary/On%20Thinking%20Like%20a%20Lawyer.pdf, accessed 20 August 2023.
Smits, J 'European legal education, or how to prepare students for global citizenship?' (2011) 45 *Law Teacher* 163–180.
Smits, J *The Mind and Method of the Legal Academic* (Edward Elgar, 2012).
Smits, J *Contract Law: A Comparative Introduction* (Edward Elgar, 2014).
Soriano-Barabino, G *Comparative Law for Legal Translators* (Peter Lang, 2016).
Squelch, J & Bentley, D 'Preparing law graduates for a global world' (2017) 51 *Law Teacher* 2–16.

Stolker, C *Rethinking the Law School: Education, Research, Outreach and Governance* (Cambridge University Press, 2014).

Valcke, C 'Global law teaching' (2004) 54 *Journal of Legal Education* 160–182.

Valcke, C 'Comparative legal education in Canada' (2005) 39 *Thémis* 483–505.

Van Hoecke, M & Warrington M 'Legal cultures, legal paradigms and legal doctrine: Towards a new model for comparative law' (1998) 47(3) *The International and Comparative Law Quarterly* 495–536.

Wallace, CJ 'Law, culture and Euro-crime: Using spiral to teach French law' (2014) 48 *Law Teacher* 154–165.

Watson, A 'From legal transplants to legal formants' (1995) 43 *American Journal of Comparative Law* 469–476.

Watson, A 'Legal transplants and European private law' (2000) 4(4) *Electronic Journal of Comparative Law* 12.

Wesley-Smith, P *An Introduction to the Hong Kong Legal System* 3 ed (Oxford University Press, 1999).

Wilson, G 'Comparative legal scholarship' in M McConville & W Hong Chui (eds) *Research Methods for Law* (Edinburgh University Press, 2007).

Wilson, R 'Challenges and opportunities for Islamic banking and finance in the West: The United Kingdom experience' (1999) 41 *Thunderbird International Business Review* 421–444.

Zumbansen, P 'Transnational legal pluralism' (2010) 1 *Transnational Legal Theory* 141–189.

Zumbansen, P 'Transnational law, evolving. comparative research in law & political economy' Research Paper No 27/2011, 2011.

Zumbansen, P 'Transnational law, evolving' in J Smits (ed) *Elgar Encyclopedia of Comparative Law* (Edward Elgar, 2012).

Zweigert, K & Kötz, H *An Introduction to Comparative Law* 3 ed (Clarendon Press, 1998).

LEGISLATION

The Namibian Constitution, 1990

14

African customary law and comparative law in contemporary Africa: a Namibian perspective

Eugene L Libebe and Samuel K Amoo

14.1 INTRODUCTION

No African country is free of African traditions or free of at least some elements that belong to Western modernity and the effects of colonisation.[1] Africa's colonial experience often demands that a distinction be drawn between indigenous African law and African customary law. Whereas indigenous laws are surviving the precolonial norms which people still observe in their ancient forms, customary laws are adaptations of these ancient norms to legal, religious, economic and cultural changes.[2] African customary law is usually used as a generic term to denote the various laws of the indigenous peoples of southern Africa.[3] Writers on the jurisprudence and legal systems of traditional African societies acknowledge that before the advent of colonialism African communities had, and still have, their own

---

[1] See AN Allott 'What is to be done with African customary law? The experience of problems and reforms in Anglophone Africa from 1950' (1984) 28(1/2) *Journal of African Law* 56–71; see also M Hinz 'Traditional governance and African customary law: Comparative observations from a Namibian perspective' in N Horn & A Bosl (eds) *Human Rights and the Rule of Law in Namibia* (Macmillan, 2008).

[2] See AC Diala 'Curriculum decolonisation and revisionist pedagogy of African customary law' (2019) 22 *PER/PELJ* 1.

[3] JC Bekker, C Rautenbach & NMI Goolam *Introduction to Legal Pluralism in South Africa* 2 ed (Butterworths, 2006) 5; see also C Himonga & C Bosch 'The application of African customary law under the Constitution of South Africa: Problems solved or just beginning?' (2000) 117 *South African Law Journal* 306.

laws and legal systems regulating the affairs and behaviours of society.[4] African customary law extensively covers areas such as criminal and civil liability, marriage, inheritance, succession and land-tenure systems.[5] These are often described in the contemporary literature as either customary law or indigenous law. Customary law is plural (since it is an aggregate of the laws of a particular tribal community), diverse and unwritten because its primary source is oral tradition.[6]

African customary law is somewhat controversial, thanks to the dissonance between the past and the present.[7] The social settings in which Africans interact have changed over time.[8] These changes have been characterised by a tense relationship between indigenous customs and statutory laws with colonial origins.[9] Indigenous customs have communal, welfarist features, whereas statutory laws have industrial, individualistic features. Statutory laws do not take sufficient account of the differences between African social settings in the past and present; and the foundational values that underpin indigenous African customs are often disregarded.[10] From the age of discovery in the 15th century to the colonisation of African states in the 20th, African customary law was degraded to pave the way for modern models of law. This can be attributed to the introduction of Westernised legal systems by the European settlers and of religious systems such as Christianity and Islam that have their own specific sets of laws.[11] The introduction of canon law by the missionaries led to the conversion of tribesmen from their indigenous laws.[12] The colonial administrations accorded limited recognition to customary law by

[4] SK Amoo *An Introduction to Namibian Law: Materials and Cases* (UNAM Press, 2008); see also M Gluckman 'Judicial process among the Barotse' in P Bohannan (ed) *Law and Warfare: Studies in the Anthropology of Conflict* (The Natural History Press, 1967).

[5] TW Bennett *A Sourcebook of African Customary Law for Southern Africa* (Juta & Co, 1991) 1–484.

[6] Amoo (note 4) 2–3.

[7] A Diala *Understanding the Relevance of African Customary Law in Modern Times*, (2020), https://theconversation.com/understanding-the-relevance-of-african-customary-law-in-modern-times-150762, accessed 20 August 2023.

[8] According to Diala (note 7), a scholar on customary law in Africa, scholars and policy-makers misunderstand the nature of African customary law because they ignore the ways in which socio-economic changes create dissonance between the way Africans observed indigenous customs in the past versus the present.

[9] Diala (note 2).

[10] Ibid.

[11] L Owino 'Application of African customary law: Tracing its degradation and analysing the challenges it confronts' (2016) 1(1) *Strathmore Law Review* 145.

[12] Ibid. The first missionary in Africa is claimed to have been George Schmidt, who arrived in Table Bay, South Africa, in 1737. He established a mission station for the KhoiKhoi, baptising five of them in 1742. They were the first indigenous African people to be converted to Christianity: South African history, http://www.sahistory.org.za/dated-event/first-missionary-arrives-cape, accessed 20 August 2023.

subsuming it under the received law and by subjecting it to the repugnancy clause tests of equity, good conscience, morality or incompatibility with the provisions of written law.[13] According to Professor Amoo, the problem that the courts of most African jurisdictions which had these 'repugnancy preconditions' faced was the standard they were required to employ in order to interpret those preconditions to rule on the admissibility and enforcement of a particular customary law.[14]

This chapter seeks to promote a discussion and an understanding of the role and nature of African customary law and explores its continued relevance from a comparative law perspective. It also incorporates an overview of customary law in Namibia. As a reflection on and a consideration of the virtues of African customary law, this contribution argues for the foundational values of customary and indigenous laws as building blocks of legal integration and comparative law from Afrocentric perspectives.

14.2 COLONIALISM AND THE NATURE AND RECOGNITION OF AFRICAN CUSTOMARY LAW

Customary law comprises the laws, practices and customs of particular indigenous peoples and local communities. Customary law is intrinsic to the way of life and customs of indigenous peoples and local communities.[15] What has the status of 'custom' and what amounts to 'customary law' will often depend to a large extent on the way in which indigenous peoples and local communities themselves perceive norms or values, and on how they function as indigenous peoples and local communities. This work does not seek to define and characterise customary law, which would itself be the subject of an extended study. As this chapter also does not attempt to define customary law, some general comments on its characteristics and recognition are worth noting. The idea of 'customary law' discussed here concerns the laws, practices and customs of indigenous peoples and local communities in the African context.

The nature and recognition of customary law as we know it today must be understood in the context of colonialism. Many agree that colonialism was largely a struggle over natural resources and human resources and authority, and also cultural and moral legitimacy.[16] Colonisers enforced their authority by means

---

[13] Amoo (note 4) 103.

[14] Ibid.

[15] Word Intellectual Property Organization (WIPO) *Customary Law, Traditional Knowledge and Intellectual Property: An Outline of the Issues*, https://www.wipo.int/export/sites/www/tk/en/resources/pdf/overview_customary_law.pdf, accessed 20 August 2023.

[16] C Himonga et al *African Customary Law in South Africa: Post-apartheid and Living Law Perspectives* (Oxford University Press, 2015) 6–7.

of physical and legal coercion; and in the process they failed to recognise and undermined the legitimacy of African laws, leadership, traditions and institutions. Colonisers believed in the superiority of their own culture as against local values and these cultural attitudes were embedded into law to legitimise their rule and laws.[17] An appreciation of colonial history is therefore essential to understanding the concept of African customary law.[18] An analysis of customary law from a historical perspective links the concept of customary law to colonial and apartheid legal cultures.[19] According to Luluaki,

> [c]ustomary law is a colonial invention aimed primarily at facilitating and entrenching the colonial agenda in the management and control of colonised peoples and bringing them closer within the larger colonial and latterly neo-colonial legal, economic and cultural whole.[20]

There is no single or uniform system of customary law that applies to all indigenous communities in Africa; however, there are some similarities in other areas and in the principles of the customary laws of various communities. A customary law is generally taken to mean a certain pattern of behaviour consistently observed over a period of time, one that creates an expectation in the wider community that it will be repeated in the future. This expectation may then come to be expressed as an obligatory right and duty.[21] Customary laws and traditional institutions in Africa constitute comprehensive legal systems that regulate the entire spectrum of activities from birth to death. Once the sole source of law, customary rules now exist in the context of pluralist legal systems with competing bodies of domestic constitutional law, statutory law, common law and international human rights treaties.[22]

According to Gluckman, the jurisprudence and legal systems of traditional African societies acknowledged, and owned before the advent of colonialism, their own laws and legal systems regulating the behaviours of individuals in a

---

[17] Ibid.

[18] In *Alexkor Ltd v Richersveld Community* 2004 (5) SA 460 (CC), the Constitutional Court reminded courts to bear in mind the historical perspective when considering issues of customary law and, further, that courts today have to bear in mind the extent to which indigenous law in the pre-democratic period was influenced by the political, administrative and judicial context in which it was applied.

[19] *Alexkor Ltd* (note 18) at 24.

[20] As cited in Himonga et al (note 16) 24.

[21] TW Bennett 'Comparative law and African customary law' in M Reimann & R Zimmermann (eds) *The Oxford Handbook of Comparative Law* 2 ed (Oxford Handbooks, 2019).

[22] See J Fenrich, P Galizzi & TE Higgins (eds) *The Future of African Customary Law* (Cambridge University Press, 2011).

society.[23] These laws covered both civil and criminal liability, marriage, inheritance, succession and issues regarding land tenure, among others. Customary law is both plural and diverse; and it is largely unwritten, as its primary source is oral tradition.

In the famous case of *Van Breda v Jacobs*,[24] the court stipulated four tests required for a custom to have the authority of law. These are:

i The custom must be reasonable;
ii The custom must have been in existence for a long time;
iii The custom must be generally recognized and observed by the community; and
iv The content of the customary rule must be clear and certain.

However, in other common-law jurisdictions in colonial Africa, such as the Gold Coast (now Ghana), Nigeria, Zambia and Tanzania, because of the juxtaposition of the received law emanating from the legal systems of the metropolitan countries alongside the customary law of indigenous African communities, different standards of recognition were applied. The tests of recognition meant that the colonial administration accorded limited recognition to customary law and subjected it to so-called repugnancy clauses. Faced with the problem of accommodation, the colonial administration accorded limited recognition to customary law by subsuming it under the received or foreign law and by subjecting it to the all-too-familiar repugnancy clause test of equity, good conscience and morality.

Typical comparative examples are Zambia and Tanzania. In Zambia, for example, under the provisions of the Native Courts Ordinance, Cap 158, s 14(1)*(a)* and s 12(1)*(a)* of the Local Courts Act 1966 of Zambia, courts could apply customary law only as far as such law 'was repugnant to natural justice or incompatible with the provisions of any written law'. In *R v Matengu*,[25] Zambian courts applied this provision.

In Tanzania, Art 24 of the Tanganyika Order in Council of 1920 provides that in all customary-law cases involving civil or criminal law, '... courts could only apply such law so far as it is applicable and is not repugnant to justice and morality or inconsistent with any Order in Council or Ordinance ...'[rephrased].

Namibia has since replaced repugnancy clauses with constitutional provisions that render a particular customary law unenforceable on the grounds of '... its

---

[23] Amoo (note 4); see also TW Bennett 'Legal anthropology and comparative law: A disciplinary compromise?' (2010) 21(1) *Stellenbosch Law Review* 4–25.

[24] *Van Breda v Jacobs* 1921 AD 330.

[25] *R v Matengu* 1951 LRNR 148.

inconsistency with the Constitution or a provision of a statute' – Art 66 in the case of Namibia.[26]

Diala and Kangwa emphasise that constitutionalism in sub-Saharan Africa evolved from imperial European laws which were imposed on Africa's agrarian political economies through legal transplants.[27] Being historical continuities of imperial laws, state laws have a rule-obsessed approach to law, with its attendant problems in delivering justice.[28] Significantly, colonial legal transplant in Africa was accompanied by radical socio-economic changes, whose persistent patterns of power, philosophy and conduct are referred to as the 'coloniality of power'.[29] Therefore, the astounding extent to which coloniality affects the normative behaviours of Africans often calls for and demands a reassessment of the status of African customary laws.

14.3 RELEVANCE OF AFRICAN CUSTOMARY LAW

African indigenous justice systems and customary laws reflect those values that have been enshrined over time by the ancestors.[30] The laws and values such as ubuntu are often passed from one generation to the next through various ways, such as folklore, musicology and idioms.[31] Most African societies are embedded in the socio-cultural philosophies and values of ubuntu. From a socio-cultural perspective, ubuntu is a multi-dimensional and relational worldview of African ontological values of, inter alia, common humanity, interconnectedness, humility, sharing, communalism, dignity, obedience and responsibility to one another.[32] In

[26] Article 66 provides that both the customary law and the common law of Namibia in force on the date of Independence shall remain valid to the extent to which such customary or common law does not conflict with this Constitution or any other statutory law. Furthermore, that subject to the terms of this Constitution, any part of such common law or customary law may be repealed or modified by Act of Parliament and the application thereof may be confined to particular parts of Namibia or to particular periods. Although customary law is recognised, it has a test or standard it has to pass; therefore, customary law is also subordinate to the Constitution itself.

[27] A Diala & B Kangwa 'Rethinking the interface between customary law and constitutionalism in sub-Saharan Africa' 2019 *De Jure Law Journal* 189–206.

[28] Ibid.

[29] Ibid.

[30] P Ongyango *African Customary Law: An Introduction* (African Books Collective, 2013); see also C Mapaure 'Reinvigorating African values for SADC' (2011) 1 *SADC Law Journal* 148, 152; E Okupa 'Is African customary law just?' in M Hinz (ed) *In Search of Justice and Peace: Traditional and Informal Justice Systems in Africa*. (Namibia Scientific Society, 2010) 341.

[31] Ibid.

[32] M Mluleki 'The African concept of ubuntu/Botho and its socio-moral significance' (2005) 3 *Black Theology* 215–237; see also O Elechi et al 'Restoring justice (ubuntu): An African perspective'

the famous case of *S v Makwanyane & Another*,[33] the South African Constitutional Court, *per* Madala J, stated that ubuntu carries ideas of humaneness, social justice and fairness, and places emphasis on communality and the interdependence of the members of a community; in this way ubuntu recognises a person's status as a human being who is entitled to unconditional respect, dignity, value and acceptance from community members.[34]

According to Diala, statutory laws do not take sufficient account of the differences between African social settings in the past and the present. The foundational values that underpin indigenous African customs are often disregarded.[35] Therefore, the meaning and relevance of African customary law can be understood through dialogue between indigenous customs and state laws. This will provide scholars and policy-makers with a theoretical path to legal integration in Africa.[36] Verhelst make a case for customary law being retained in a number of fields because it is the body of law best suited to African society.[37] Accordingly, the law must express the value system of the society it seeks to serve.[38] Customary law, which was generated by African society and which developed within it, is just that type of *corpus juris*; it reflects the cultural and societal patterns of the population to which it applies. This is not the case with foreign law.[39] The imposition of a foreign legal system may result either in the failure of the law to receive acceptance and enforcement or in the unnecessary and harmful wrenching of the social fabric of the society concerned.[40] This in turn might lead either to the undermining of the authority of the law or to the disruption of society.

Furthermore, it is generally accepted that customary law should be adapted to the requirements of a society in search of speedy economic and social development.[41] It would be arguable that if the law should reflect the values and

(2010) 20 *International Justice Review* 73, 75; N Ndeunyema *Re-invigorating Ubuntu through Water: A Human Right to Water Under the Namibian Constitution* (Pretoria University Law Press, 2021) 64–71.

[33] *S v Makwanyane & Another* 1995 (3) SA 391 (CC).

[34] *S v Makwanyane* (note 33) at para 224.

[35] Diala (note 7) 190.

[36] Ibid.

[37] T Verhelst 'Safeguarding African customary law: Judicial and legislative processes for its adaptation and integration' Occasional Paper No 7 (African Studies Centre, University of California, Los Angeles, 1968).

[38] Most, if not all, African societies are embedded in the philosophies and values of ubuntu.

[39] Verhelst (note 37) 6.

[40] Ibid.

[41] M Gluckman *Les Aspects Juridiques du Developpement Economique/Legal Aspects of Economic Development* 59 (Association Internationale des Sciences Juridiques/International Association of Legal Sciences, 1966).

ethos of a given society, then only that law can transform that society, be it socially, economically, technologically, spiritually or otherwise. This process may involve adjustments to or the modification of its substantive rules or its form; however, the process of modification is not alien to the nature of customary law. 'Customary law is not a petrified body of law, it is living law which has shown its ability to evolve in relation to changing conditions.'[42] In the application of their laws and lore, African communities have embraced restorative values in resolving conflicts and in responding to wrongdoing. Civil and penal practices in these communities have embraced restorative justice as it is understood today.[43] Restorative justice can be defined as

> processes whereby parties with a stake in a specific offence collectively resolve how to deal with the aftermath of the offence and its implications in the future. African customary law has always emphasised the welfare of the community over the individual and accordingly the individual was forced to make decisions for the betterment of the community.[44]

For example, the Xhosa community of South Africa believes in ubuntu, which translates to 'I am because we are', or humaneness, as discussed above.

Basically, traditional African communities used a justice system which was akin to that used today.[45] Parties were allowed to argue their case and present evidence before a number of adjudicators. Punishment or justice was meted out to the wrongdoer once guilt was ascertained. The only differences perhaps are that punishment was restorative as opposed to retributive and the verdicts did not hinge on argument but truth.[46] Customary law and social norms were applied in adjudication, with different communities applying their own specific laws and norms, much like the jurisdictional use of law today.[47]

In addition, customary law is an important source of law which can be used to dispose of disputes easily and with expediency as it does not have difficult procedural technicalities.[48] Furthermore, customary law can serve as a fundamental legal basis or source of law for indigenous peoples' and local communities' legal rights over traditional knowledge and cultural heritage.[49] African customary laws

---

[42] Ibid.
[43] Owino (note 11) 143; see also Elechi et al (note 32) 20.
[44] Owino (note 11) 144.
[45] Ibid.
[46] Ibid.
[47] Ibid.
[48] See Hinz (note 1).
[49] See WIPO (note 15).

and practices are central to the very identity of many indigenous peoples and local communities, including many aspects of their life. African customary laws define the rights and responsibilities of peoples and communities on important aspects of their life, culture and worldview; and customary law can relate to the use of and access to natural resources, rights and obligations relating to land, inheritance and property, conduct of spiritual life, maintenance of cultural heritage and knowledge systems, and many other matters.[50] Customary law defines or characterises the very identity of the community itself, fulfilling the right to one's culture and heritages.[51]

14.4 CUSTOMARY LAW AS A COMPARATIVE-LAW TOOL

Since the start of the European colonisation of Africa, and even in its aftermath, perceptions of the continent's indigenous systems of customary law have been decidedly Eurocentric, a bias that has also marked comparative law.[52] Therefore, when one explores the position of African customary law in comparative legal studies, it is very and immediately evident that Eurocentric laws provide the standards for comparison. European legal scholars, who for most of the 19th and 20th centuries were working from the positivist perspective that dominated European thinking, assumed that the law emanated from the command of a sovereign and was therefore rational and purposeful.[53] Therefore, custom was seen as a primitive regime, one less worthy of study than true law, and it was relegated to anthropology.[54] Given all these problems and preconceptions, it should come as no surprise that the study of African customary law was a latecomer to comparative law.[55] However, it could also be a major game-changer.

During the 1950s, when one of the primary tasks of comparative law was to classify laws into family groups, David – whose vision was more expansive than that of most – subsumed customary laws under civil, common and socialist law, systems which he regarded as the world's main legal families.[56] Furthermore, not only has anthropology provided most of the raw data from which texts on customary law

---

[50] BM Tobin 'Why customary law matters: The role of customary law in the protection of indigenous peoples' human rights' PhD Thesis (Irish Centre for Human Rights, University of Galway, 2011); WIPO (note 15).

[51] WIPO (note 15); see also P Kuruk 'The role of customary law under *sui generis* frameworks of intellectual property rights in traditional and indigenous knowledge' (2007) 17(1) *Indiana International and Comparative Law Review* 67–118.

[52] Bennett (note 21) 23.

[53] Ibid.

[54] Bennett (note 21) 4–25.

[55] Ibid.

[56] Ibid.

are written, but it has also been the most valuable source of critical reflection on the purposes and methods of enquiry.[57] Any student of customary law therefore needs to be aware of shifts in thinking within the discipline of anthropology, because these have exerted a strong influence on perceptions of the subject in comparative law.[58] On methodology and considering undertaking comparative research between the African indigenous law and Western-imposed law in Africa, Hoecke,[59] expressed the view that

> when comparing official state law in African countries with local customary law, one will notice that they show a tension between tradition and modernity, between Western law only followed by the elite and African law as the large majority of the population perceive it. Hence, an anthropological approach (methodology) that puts the law in context will be necessary for explaining this tension, for understanding it and for finding solution for it.

Mancuso maintains that African law can serve as a comparative-law model or an African legal model having its own features and characteristics.[60] According to him, such a model also presents elements of what could be considered to be out of the pure African reality

> the holistic approach of the African dispute resolution system with its mediatory characteristics not forced within rigid rules of procedure, the communitarian approach taking into consideration a definitely larger number of interests than in the individualistic Western formulation are elements that could be interesting even out of Africa, especially considering the present situation where law is a tool to be used to facilitate economic development, and that it should be therefore as flexible as possible.[61]

Furthermore, the cultural method or approach to comparative law ascribes uniqueness to every culture, therefore every system possesses specific legal traditions and cultures.[62] The cultural approach emphasises differences in legal

---

[57] TW Bennett 'The meeting of comparative law and legal anthropology in Africa' in S Mancuso & CM Fombad (ed) *Comparative Law in Africa, Methodologies and Concepts* (Juta & Co, 2015) 132–141.

[58] Bennett (note 21) 134.

[59] M van Hoecke *Methodology of Comparative Legal Research* (2015), http://www.bjutijdschriften.nl, accessed 22 July 2024.

[60] S Mancuso 'Comparative law in the African context' in S Mancuso & CM Fombad (eds) *Comparative Law in Africa, Methodologies and Concepts* (Juta & Co, 2015) 21–33.

[61] Ibid.

[62] See O Brand 'Conceptual comparisons: Towards a coherent methodology of comparative legal studies' (2007) 32 *Brooklyn Journal of International Law* 405, 409; CN Okeke 'Methodological

systems. Law is then viewed as an expression of culture and the cultural context of law should be considered when engaging in comparative exercises.[63] It is this very cultural undertone of comparative legal studies that is reflected in the call that a comparativist must use a technique of 'cultural immersion', which gets comparative law enmeshed in the political, historical, economic and linguistic contexts that moulded the legal system and in which the legal system operates.[64]

We need to be mindful that comparative law is a meta-legal discipline that should ideally be aimed at the objective study of all legal systems, including African systems. It nevertheless takes on this task laden with assumptions about law, research methods and subjects for research, all of which have traditionally been dictated by Western legal scholars.[65] However, the living form of African customary law, with its associated empirical research method, does not fit easily into the mould of Western law or typical legal scholarship, a mismatch that poses a decided challenge for the comparatist.[66] The point here is that, whereas global uniformity is an idealistic idea, it takes away experiences of human existence and is repressive in nature. In other words, whose values, norms, or rules should be chosen to dominate the world? Melissaris concludes:[67]

> The study of the law must be directed towards the discovery of alternative perceptions of the world and justice and of different practices of solving practical problems by accommodating competing interests as well as meeting the prerequisites of substantive justice. The question of law and justice then becomes one concerning our whole way of life, how we perceive and place ourselves in our surrounding.

This passage also reminds legal comparatists that during the comparative process one ought to search for substantive justice through examining alternative practices to solve practical problems. African jurisprudence is one such alternative practice through which to solve practical socio-economic and legal problems.

---

approaches to comparative legal studies in Africa' in S Mancuso & CM Fombad (eds) *Comparative Law in Africa, Methodologies and Concepts* (Juta & Co, 2015) 47.

63 Okeke (note 62) 47.

64 Ibid; see also VG Curran 'Cultural immersion, difference and categories in US comparative law' (1998) 46 *American Journal of Comparative Law* 43; EJ Eberle 'The method and role of comparative law' (2009) 8 *Washington University Global Studies Law Review* 451–452.

65 Bennett (note 21).

66 Ibid.

67 E Melissaris 'The more the merrier? A new take on legal pluralism' (2004) 13(4) *Social and Legal Studies* 57–79.

14.5 REVIEW OF CUSTOMARY LAW AS A SOURCE OF LAW IN NAMIBIA

With the dawn of Independence on 21 March 1990, customary law together with common law became recognised as sources of law in Namibia's legal system. According to Art 19 of the Bill of Rights,

> every person shall be entitled to enjoy, practice, profess, maintain and promote any culture, language, tradition or religion subject to the terms of this Constitution and further subject to the condition that the rights protected by this Article do not impinge upon the rights of others or the national interest.[68]

Specifically, Art 66 of the Namibian Constitution provides for customary and common law as follows:

> **Article 66 Customary and Common Law**
>
> (1) Both the customary law and the common law of Namibia in force on the date of Independence shall remain valid to the extent to which such customary or common law does not conflict with this Constitution or any other statutory law.
> (2) Subject to the terms of this Constitution, any part of such common law or customary law may be repealed or modified by Act of Parliament, and the application thereof may be confined to particular parts of Namibia or to particular periods.

This constitutional recognition is subject to consistency with the rights and principles embedded in the Namibian Constitution.[69] For example, whereas corporal punishment was to a certain extent practised under customary law, the court in *S v Sipula*[70] discussed the application of corporal punishment by a traditional court and found that it was inconsistent with the fundamental rights and values in the Constitution, such as respect for human dignity entrenched in Art 8 of Chapter 3 on the Bill of Rights. Furthermore, in *Myburgh v Commercial Bank of Namibia*,[71] the court held that the recognition of a particular principle under

[68] Article 19 of the Namibian Constitution.

[69] In *Witbooi & Others v Minister of Urban and Rural Development & Others* 2022 (2) NR 383, the High Court held that customary law favouring members of a patrilineal line over members of a matrilineal line for chieftainship would violate Art 10(2) of the Namibian Constitution.

[70] *S v Sipula* 1994 NR 41 (HC).

[71] *Myburgh v Commercial Bank of Namibia* 1999 NR 287.

common law (and by implication under customary law) must be determined by the basic test whether or not it has 'fallen foul' of the Constitution or any statutory law. In *LM v JM & Others*,[72] in respect of a constitutional challenge to customary law, the court stressed the need to tender evidence to establish customary law and to establish unconstitutionality. The constitutional recognition of customary law as a source of law in Namibia assumes its application by the existing judicial structures, which until 2003 did not specifically deal with the status of traditional courts and traditional authorities within the justice system.[73]

Furthermore, the problem of recognising the jurisprudence of traditional courts arose in *S v Haulondjamba*.[74] In this case the High Court found it irregular for a decision of a tribal court to be confirmed and incorporated in the sentence of a magistrate's court, the reason being that tribal judgments should stand on their own.

The vacuum of uncertainty of the traditional courts' jurisprudence was filled by the promulgation of the Community Courts Act of 2003.[75] The Act gives the traditional authorities the necessary statutory recognition and jurisdiction over the application of customary law. It places the community courts under the mainstream of the judicial structures of Namibia. It provides further that community courts are courts of record and their proceedings must be recorded in writing by the clerk of the courts.[76] A community court must have jurisdiction to hear and determine any matter relating to a claim for compensation, restitution or any other claim recognised by the customary law, but only if the cause of action of such a matter arose within the area of jurisdiction of that community court; or the person or persons to whom the matter relates are, in the opinion of that community court, closely connected to the customary law.[77] The advantages of community courts include, inter alia:

(i) expedience in practice and procedure;
(ii) community courts are easily accessible and often situated within communities;
(iii) punishment and sentencing in community courts are more victim-focused as opposed to punitive, and
(iv) they are largely reconciliatory and restorative.[78]

---

72 *LM v JM & Others* 2016 (2) NR 603 (HC).
73 Amoo (note 4).
74 1993 NR 103 (HC).
75 Community Courts Act 10 of 2003.
76 Section 18(1) of Community Courts Act 10 of 2003.
77 Section 12; see *Adcock v Mbambo* (A 87/2010) [2012] NAHCMD 35 (24 October 2012) (jurisdiction of traditional court in terms of s 3 read together with s 1: definitions of 'member' and 'traditional community').
78 Amoo (note 4).

Traditional authorities are recognised under both the Constitution[79] and the Traditional Authorities Act.[80] In terms of the Constitution, the Traditional Authorities Council is mandated to 'advise the President on all matters relating to land inter alia in the country'.[81] A traditional authority is the primary custodian of customary law,[82] and in the context of land it exercises the right to allocate land under the Communal Land Reform Act, together with the Communal Land Boards.[83] In terms of the Communal Land Reform Act, in considering the allocation of land, the traditional authorities are enjoined to comply with the customary laws of a particular traditional community.[84] In terms of s 1 of the Traditional Authorities Act customary law means

> the customary law, norms, rules of procedure, traditions and usages of a traditional community in so far as they do not conflict with the Namibian Constitution or with any other written law applicable in Namibia.

In addition, the Council of Traditional Leaders Act[85] provides for the establishment of the Council of Traditional Leaders and defines its powers, duties and functions; and it provides for matters incidental to these.

Other relevant legislation includes the Access to Biological and Genetic Resources and Associated Traditional Knowledge Act.[86] This Act regulates access to biological or genetic resources and associated traditional knowledge and innovation, practices and technologies associated with biological and genetic resources and traditional knowledge. It also aims to protect the rights of the local communities over biological and genetic resources and associated traditional knowledge; to provide for a fair and equitable mechanism for benefit sharing; to establish the necessary

---

[79] Article 102(5) of the Namibian Constitution.

[80] The Traditional Authorities Act 25 of 2002. The Act provides for the establishment of traditional authorities and the designation, election, appointment and recognition of traditional leaders; to define the powers, duties and functions of traditional authorities and traditional leaders; and to provide for matters incidental thereto.

[81] See the Council of Traditional Leaders Act 13 of 1997. See *Witbooi* (note 69) on the distinction between a traditional authority and a traditional council.

[82] Article 102(5) of the Namibian Constitution.

[83] The Communal Land Reform Act 5 of 2002. The Act provides for the allocation of rights in respect of communal land; to establish Communal Land Boards; to provide for the powers of Chiefs and Traditional Authorities and boards in relation to communal land, and to make provision for incidental matters.

[84] Ibid.

[85] The Council of Traditional Leaders Act 13 of 1997; the Council of Traditional Leaders Amendment Act 31 of 2000.

[86] The Access to Biological and Genetic Resources and Associated Traditional Knowledge Act 2 of 2017.

administrative structures and processes for the implementation and enforcement of such principles, and to provide for incidental matters.[87]

The Nature Conservation Amendment Act[88] also amended the Nature Conservation Ordinance of 1975 so as to provide for an economically based system of sustainable management and use of game in communal areas and to provide for matters incidental to that. Section 1 of the Act recognises and defines communal land, conservancies, wildlife, etc. This has added another layer to the administration of traditional authorities and communal natural resource governance which also has implications for aspects of cultural heritage.

In addition, Professor Manfred Hinz (former Dean of the Faculty of Law at the University of Namibia) made great contributions to customary-law jurisprudence and projects in Namibia and African customary law in general. One of the key projects was the ascertainment (not the codification) of customary law in Namibia.[89] This work undertook to ascertain the customary laws of various traditional authorities in Namibia.[90] Recognised traditional authorities in Namibia were expected to ascertain the customary law applicable in their respective communities after consultation with the members of their community and to note the most important aspects of such law in written form.[91]

Future research and scholarship should undertake comparative studies of traditional governance, justice systems or customary laws in Namibia and other southern African jurisdictions, and beyond. This would shape, inform and contribute to the comparative-law discourse in various ways, both in Africa and globally.

14.6 CONTEMPORARY CHALLENGES TO CUSTOMARY-LAW APPLICATION AND PRACTICE

Menski[92] notes that, notwithstanding decolonisation, the law and legal system (legal education) are still largely Eurocentrically constructed with a specific focus on state-

[87] See the Preamble.

[88] The Nature Conservation Amendment Act 5 of 1996.

[89] See MO Hinz & NE Namwoonde (eds) *Customary Law Ascertained, 1. The Customary Law of the Owambo, Kavango and Caprivi Communities* (Namibia Scientific Society, 2010); MO Hinz & A Gairiseb (eds) *Customary Law Ascertained, 2. The Customary Law of the Bakgalagari, Batswana ba Namibia and Damara Communities of Namibia* (UNAM Press, 2014); MO Hinz & A Gairiseb (eds) (2016). *Customary Law Ascertained, 3. The Customary Law of the Nama, Ovaherero, Ovambanderu, and San Communities of Namibia* (UNAM Press, 2016).

[90] Ibid.

[91] Ibid. This project was facilitated by the Human Rights and Documentation Centre (HRDC) of the University of Namibia through the former Dean of the Law Faculty, Professor Manfred Hinz.

[92] W Menski *Comparative Law in a Global Context: The Legal Systems of Asia and Africa* (Cambridge University Press, 2006) 6.

made law to the exclusion of indigenous contributions.[93] This is particularly so in southern Africa. It is uncontested, for example, that the law schools in Namibia, South Africa, Zimbabwe and Zambia are mainly dominated by Western philosophy and methodologies (English law or Roman-Dutch law) at the expense of the African legal philosophies. The fact that these law schools continue, in the post-colonial era, to teach legal curricula that are preoccupied with the colonial masters' legal philosophies implies that legal practitioners who are miseducated and graduates from these law schools will continue, ignorantly, to advocate coloniality.

Yet it would be remiss to assume that the application of customary law both now and in the future is not fraught with difficulties. African societies have developed vastly since the pre-colonial period whereas customary law has not. Its unwritten nature, lack of precedence, inherent favouritism towards the male gender, etc, are definite contributions to its lack of pliability in modern legal systems. Furthermore, by definition, living systems of law are not directly available to outsiders. To be of any value to courts or law- and policy-makers, the law must be discovered by way of empirical research or by the evidence of expert witnesses. In either case, the process is costly and time-consuming, with the result that, for better or worse, legal professionals needing to refer to customary law are usually forced to make do with official or academic versions.[94]

The streamlining of community courts within the broader ambit of the Judiciary poses challenges between customary law and practice under the community courts and the practices and procedures of the higher courts. For example, community courts are often informal in nature or orientation, and often conducted without records, which can pose challenges for victims on appeal to higher courts, which require evidential proof. In practice, community courts exercise jurisdiction over criminal matters such as theft, murder or rape.[95] One of the principles of criminal justice is that no one can be prosecuted for an offence which is not written and that any criminal matter requires representation. Legal representation, however, is not allowed in the community courts, which hinders and compromises the fair trial rights of persons as contemplated under the Namibian Constitution.[96]

---

[93] Ibid.

[94] Bennett (note 21).

[95] Although community courts are not allowed to try persons accused of murder or rape, families can turn to traditional authorities for what is regarded as a *wiping of tears*. For example, in 2021, the family of a deceased who was found floating in the Kavango River with a number of his body parts, including his testicles, missing, had turned to the Mbunza Traditional Authority Community Court for recourse.

[96] Article 12(1)*(e)* provides: 'All persons shall be afforded adequate time and facilities for the preparation and presentation of their defence, before the commencement of and during their trial, and shall be entitled to be defended by a legal practitioner of their choice.'

In its original form, customary law existed in oral traditions. The process of transcribing the law into written form caused it to undergo certain significant changes due partly to the effect of writing and partly to the views of the authors, which were shaped by contemporary theories in jurisprudence and anthropology.[97] Critical to understanding the content of the customary laws of Africa, therefore, are the two primary influences on its production: transcription to writing and the prejudices and preconceptions of the authors, who were all too often European.[98] The founding comparative-law scholars were not interested in African law, which accounts for the absence of Africanism in even comparative-law jurisprudence. The law as applied in most of southern Africa has mainly been modernised along Western lines. After colonisation, most of the political landscapes changed, but not a legal discourse founded on African philosophies, ontologies, epistemologies or contexts. This has largely led to the application and theorisation of laws and methods of the colonial administration. Professor Okupa critically noted that the study of African indigenous law has been carried out by Western anthropologists who attempted to interpret such laws without the contribution of the authors of such African indigenous law.[99]

14.7 CONCLUSION

Despite customary law being recognised in most of Africa as a source of law, it has not enjoyed the same status as the imported laws that have formed the theoretical foundations of African law. The neglect of African laws and principles has facilitated the way in which legal transplants manifest coloniality and has deprived the comparative-law discourse of the great contributions of the African justice systems. Customary law and decolonial comparative theory ought to rescue this situation through the inclusion of African narratives and methodologies in the legal discourse and application of the law.

We propose further that African constitutions should integrate customary laws with state law by adopting the foundational values of indigenous laws as constitutional principles. These easily ascertainable values include ubuntu or humaneness, family continuity, preservation of the ancestral home, the duty of care owed to family members by the family head, and land governance. Customary laws naturally evolve with changing circumstances and so we recommend that empirical

[97] Bennett (note 21).

[98] Ibid.

[99] E Okupa *International Bibliography of African Customary Law: Ius non scriptu. IAI Monographs 4. London: International African Institute; Hamburg: Lit Verlag,* (Cambridge University Press , 1998) 177.

and participatory assessments of the contemporary status and content of customary laws be carried out.[100]

African customary law and indigenous justice systems are a critical tool in and component of the development and processes of comparative law and decolonisation. The foundational values and precepts of African customary or indigenous laws such as ubuntu make a significant contribution to a progressive and transformative approach to the development of African jurisprudence and globally. Therefore, in this context, African laws can make great contributions to comparative-law approaches and methodologies.

REFERENCES

Allott, AN 'What is to be done with African customary law? The experience of problems and reforms in Anglophone Africa from 1950' (1984) 28(1/2) *Journal of African Law* 56–71.

Amoo, SK *An Introduction to Namibian Law: Materials and Cases* (UNAM Press, 2008).

Bekker, JC, Rautenbach, C & Goolam, NMI *Introduction to Legal Pluralism in South Africa* 2 ed (LexisNexis, Butterworths, 2006).

Bennett, TW *A Sourcebook of African Customary Law for Southern Africa* (Juta & Co, 1991).

Bennett, TW 'Legal anthropology and comparative law: A disciplinary compromise?' (2010) 21(1) *Stellenbosch Law Review* 4–25.

Bennett, TW 'The meeting of comparative law and legal anthropology in Africa' in S Mancuso & CM Fombad (ed) *Comparative Law in Africa, Methodologies and Concepts* (Juta & Co, 2015).

Bennett, TW 'Comparative law and African customary law' in M Reimann & R Zimmermann (eds) *The Oxford Handbook of Comparative Law* 2 ed (Oxford Handbooks, 2019).

Brand, O 'Conceptual comparisons: Towards a coherent methodology of comparative legal studies' (2007) 32 *Brooklyn Journal of International Law* 405, 409.

Curran, VG 'Cultural immersion, difference and categories in US comparative Law' (1998) 46 *American Journal of Comparative Law* 43;

Diala, AC 'Curriculum decolonisation and revisionist pedagogy of African customary law' (2019) 22 *PER/PELJ* 1.

[100] M Kane et al. (2005). *Reassessing Customary Law Systems as a Vehicle for providing Equitable Access to Justice for the Poor.* New Frontiers of Social Policy, Arusha Conference, http://landwise-production.s3.amazonaws.com/2022/03/Kane_Reassessing-customary-law-systems-as-a-vehicle-for-providing-equitable-access-to-justice-for-the-poor_2005-1.pdf, accessed 20 August 2023.

Diala, A *Understanding the Relevance of African Customary Law in Modern Times* (2020), https://theconversation.com/understanding-the-relevance-of-african-customary-law-in-modern-times-150762, accessed 20 August 2023.

Diala, A & Kangwa, B 'Rethinking the interface between customary law and constitutionalism in sub-Saharan Africa' 2019 *De Jure Law Journal* 189–206.

Eberle, EJ 'The method and role of comparative law' (2009) 8 *Washington University Global Studies Law Review* 451–452.

Elechi, O et al 'Restoring justice (ubuntu): An African perspective' (2010) *International Justice Review* 20.

Fenrich, J, Galizzi, P & Higgins, TE (eds) *The Future of African Customary Law* (Cambridge University Press, 2011).

Gluckman, M *Les Aspects Juridiques du Developpement Economique/Legal Aspects of Economic Development* 59 (Association Internationale des Sciences Juridiques/International Association of Legal Sciences, 1966).

Gluckman, M 'Judicial process among the Barotse' in P Bohannan (ed) *Law and Warfare: Studies in the Anthropology of Conflict* (The Natural History Press, 1967).

Himonga, C & Bosch, C 'The application of African customary law under the Constitution of South Africa: Problems solved or just beginning?' (2000) 117 *South African Law Journal* 306.

Himonga, C et al (eds) *African Customary Law in South Africa: Post-Apartheid and Living Law Perspectives* (Oxford University Press, 2015).

Hinz, M 'Traditional governance and African customary law: Comparative observations from a Namibian perspective' in N Horn & A Bosl (eds) *Human Rights and the Rule of Law in Namibia* (Macmillan, 2008).

Hinz, MO & Gairiseb, A (eds) *Customary Law Ascertained, 2. The Customary Law of the Bakgalagari, Batswana ba Namibia and Damara Communities of Namibia* (UNAM Press, 2014).

Hinz, MO & Gairiseb, A (eds) *Customary Law Ascertained, 3. The Customary Law of the Nama, Ovaherero, Ovambanderu, and San Communities of Namibia* (UNAM Press, 2016).

Hinz, MO & Namwoonde, NE (eds) *Customary Law Ascertained, 1. The Customary Law of the Owambo, Kavango and Caprivi Communities* (Namibia Scientific Society: Windhoek, 2010).

Kane, M, Oloka-Onyango, J, Tejan-Cole, A & Leone, S *Reassessing Customary Law Systems as a Vehicle for Providing Equitable Access to Justice for the Poor.* New Frontiers of Social Policy, Arusha Conference, 2005, http://landwise-production.s3.amazonaws.com/2022/03/Kane_Reassessing-customary-law-systems-as-a-vehicle-for-providing-equitable-access-to-justice-for-the-poor_2005-1.pdf, accessed 20 August 2023.

Kuruk, P 'The role of customary law under *sui generis* frameworks of intellectual property rights in traditional and indigenous knowledge' (2007) 17(1) *Indiana International and Comparative Law Review* 67–118.

Mancuso, S 'Comparative law in the African context' in S Mancuso & CM Fombad (eds) *Comparative Law in Africa, Methodologies and Concepts* (Juta & Co, 2015).

Mapaure, C 'Reinvigorating African values for SADC' (2011) 1 *SADC Law Journal* 148, 152.

Melissaris, E 'The more the merrier? A new take on legal pluralism' (2004) 13(4) *Social and Legal Studies* 57–79.

Menski, W *Comparative Law in a Global Context: The Legal Systems of Asia and Africa* (Cambridge University Press, 2006).

Mluleki, M 'The African concept of ubuntu/Botho and its socio-moral significance' (2005) 3 *Black Theology* 215–237.

Ndeunyema, N *Re-invigorating Ubuntu Through Water: A Human Right to Water under the Namibian Constitution* (Pretoria University Law Press, 2021).

Okeke, CN 'Methodological approaches to comparative legal studies in Africa' in S Mancuso & CM Fombad (eds) *Comparative Law in Africa, Methodologies and Concepts* (Juta & Co, 2015).

Okupa, E 'Is African customary law just?' in M Hinz (ed) *In Search of Justice and Peace: Traditional and Informal Justice Systems in Africa* (Namibia Scientific Society, 2010).

Okupa, E *International Bibliography of African Customary Law: Ius non scriptu. IAI Monographs 4. London: International African Institute; Hamburg: Lit Verlag* (Cambridge University Press, 1998) 177

Ongyango, P *African Customary Law: An Introduction* (African Books Collective, 2013).

Owino, L 'Application of African customary law: Tracing its degradation and analysing the challenges it confronts' (2016) 1(1) *Strathmore Law Review* 143.

Tobin, BM 'Why customary law matters: The role of customary law in the protection of indigenous peoples' human rights' PhD Thesis (Irish Centre for Human Rights, University of Galway, 2011).

Van Hoecke, M *Methodology of Comparative Legal Research* (bjutijdschriften, 2015), http://www.bjutijdschriften.nl.

Verhelst, T 'Safeguarding African customary law: Judicial and legislative processes for its adaptation and integration' Occasional Paper No 7 (African Studies Centre, University of California, Los Angeles, 1968).

World Intellectual Property Organization (WIPO) *Customary Law, Traditional Knowledge and Intellectual Property: An Outline of the Issues*, https://www.wipo.int/export/sites/www/tk/en/resources/pdf/overview_customary_law.pdf, accessed 20 August 2023.

CASES

Adcock v Mbambo (A 87/2010) [2012] NAHCMD 35 (24 October 2012)

Alexkor Ltd v Richersveld Community 2004 (5) SA 460 (CC)

LM v JM & Others 2016 (2) NR 603 (HC)

Myburgh v Commercial Bank of Namibia 1999 NR 287

R v Matengu 1951 LRNR 148

S v Haulondjamba 1993 NR 103 (HC)
S v Makwanyane & Another 1995 (3) SA 391 (CC)
S v Sipula 1994 NR 41 (HC)
Van Breda v Jacobs 1921 AD 330
Witbooi & Others v Minister of Urban and Rural Development & Others 2022 (2) NR 383 (HC)

LEGISLATION

Access to Biological and Genetic Resources and Associated Traditional Knowledge Act 2 of 2017
Communal Land Reform Act 5 of 2002
Community Courts Act 10 of 2003
Council of Traditional Leaders Act 13 of 1997
Council of Traditional Leaders Amendment Act 31 of 2000
Namibian Constitution of 1990
Nature Conservation Amendment Act 5 of 1996
Traditional Authorities Act 25 of 2002

15

Comparing in the ascertainment of customary law: jurisprudential remarks

Manfred O Hinz

15.1 INTRODUCTION: RECALLING THE 'MONSTER-STATEMENT' IN METHODOLOGICAL PERSPECTIVE

The 'monster-statement' to which this chapter's introduction refers has already been the subject of scientific elaboration[1] and will conveniently lead to the focus of this chapter. It was in a workshop with traditional[2] leaders on human rights in the Constitution of Namibia some years ago that one of the participating leaders – he represented one of the Otjiherero-speaking communities – raised his hand, stood up and spoke about the problems he and many in his community had with the fundamental rights and freedoms enshrined in the Constitution. He concluded his intervention by saying: 'Human rights are monsters.' He said so and again took his seat.

I do not exactly remember how we, the organisers of the workshop – a guest from the United Nations in Geneva and the author of this chapter – responded, but it is certain that we spent time after the workshop overcoming our surprise and unlocking the background to the 'monster-statement'. It became clear that it was not an instantaneously uttered emotional eruption but a message founded on something that had to be looked at seriously. The person who made the monster-statement was a well-respected leader, a leader with experience, a serious person who did not thoughtlessly say what he said. It took time until a plausible explanation was found for the surprising qualification of human rights.

---

[1] W Menski 'Fuzzy law and the boundaries of secularism' (2010) 13(3) *Potchefstroom Electronic Law Journal* 30–50; FM Engelbronner-Kolff, MO Hinz & JL Sindano (eds) *Traditional Authority and Democracy in Southern Africa* (New Namibian Books, 1998) 289.

[2] This chapter uses the terms 'traditional', 'traditional community', 'traditional authority' and 'traditional leader' with the same meanings as in legislation enacted in Namibia, such as the Traditional Authorities Act 25 of 2000.

What exactly did we do when we searched for the something behind the statement? We established (or at least tried to establish) two socio-political frameworks: the socio-political framework with which arguments about human rights are usually associated and the socio-political framework in which customary law operates. We placed the two frameworks against each other and compared them. We learnt from this comparison how different and, to some extent, exclusive the two frameworks were. The framework in which human rights are operated supports offensive, even aggressive claims in teaching and legally pursuing the universality of human rights; the framework of customary law is primarily remedial, even takes note of societal circumstances which would normally be dismissed as irrelevant under general law.

We therefore interpreted the monster-statement from the point of view of both legal and political anthropology. We did not simply state that declaring human rights monsters violates the spirit and meaning of the Constitution and would therefore be beyond acceptance. In evaluating these socio-political frameworks, we distanced ourselves from our convictions and allowed for a comparative approach. We understood that the normative expectation of human rights and the statement that human rights are monsters flowed from observations we had to attend to. Such attention would open the way for the exchange of reasoned arguments. Methodologically speaking, we practised comparative jurisprudence in a very special way!

The goal of this chapter is to submit arguments for the thesis that the employment of comparative jurisprudence in its rather recent manifestation – which one may call postmodern comparative jurisprudence – is a methodologically indispensable tool in ascertaining customary law and accommodating it in plural legal orders. Jurisprudentially interpreted, postmodern comparative jurisprudence is essential to legal anthropology and its contribution to anthropological jurisprudence.

In view of this thesis, it might be helpful to note the definitions of three conceptualisations which guide this chapter:

(a) **Legal anthropology** emerged as a branch of anthropological research interested in questions about the maintenance of order in non-Western societies, which were not subjects of specialised disciplines such as Asian studies and Oriental studies. As it developed, legal anthropology extended its scope. It was the discovery of the fact that all societal orders depended to a great degree on rules, which were not created by the respective central government of the society but by various societal agents. It was the conceptualisation of this plurality of law in the theory of legal pluralism that opened the way for legal anthropology to research law in all kinds of society.[3]

[3] See on this, in particular, F von Benda-Beckmann 'Riding or killing the centaur: Reflections on the identities of legal anthropology' in M Freeman & D Napier (eds) *Law and Anthropology* (Oxford University Press, 2009) 13–46.

(b) **Anthropological jurisprudence** is part of jurisprudence in the usually defined manner, but it focuses on the fact that it is not determined by Western legal philosophy. Anthropological jurisprudence notes that different cultures have developed their own different understandings of societal order, law and justice. Anthropological jurisprudence is the jurisprudential reflection of a globalising world. Processes that lead to the enactment of laws, which are related to the plurality of legal orders existing in a society, and also the decisions of courts, which deal with conflicts based on the same plurality, play an important part in the development of anthropological jurisprudence.[4]

(c) **Comparative jurisprudence** is what is commonly called 'comparative law'. However, comparative law is, as Schlesinger and the co-authors of their book on comparative law have already said, a 'misnomer' because 'neither the comparative method, nor the insights gained through its use, can be said to constitute a body of binding norms'. Although the term 'comparative law' is widely accepted,[5] the term 'comparative jurisprudence' is preferred in this chapter.

What is postmodern comparative jurisprudence? Menski offers the following convincing definition of postmodern analysis in his introduction to *Hindu Law*:

> A postmodern legal analysis takes a pluralistic approach to law. It recognizes it as a complex amalgam of state-produced, religious, and social rules which are forever in competition with each other and interact systematically.[6]

Such an approach to law is pursued in the more recently published textbooks on comparative jurisprudence, which do not restrict themselves any more to the description and analysis of classical legal families,[7] but reach out instead to, for example, the general law of African countries. Although it is law widely received

---

[4] See MO Hinz 'Jurisprudence and anthropology' (2003) 26 *Anthropology Southern Africa* 114–118; W Fikentscher *Law and Anthropology* 2 ed (CH Beck/Hart Publishing, 2016). Fikentscher took a central sentence from Hinz as one of the mottos of his book. The concept of anthropological jurisprudence is close to 'general jurisprudence' as submitted by W Twining *General Jurisprudence. Understanding Law from a Global Perspective* (Cambridge University Press, 2009).

[5] RB Schlesinger & HW Baade et al *Comparative Law. Cases – Text – Materials* 5 ed (Foundation Press, 1988) 1; see also U Kischel *Rechtsvergleichung* (CH Beck, 2015). Kischel at 27ff submits that the German term '*Rechtsvergleichung*' (comparing of law) is more correct while, focusing on comparing, he avoids qualifying the process and the result of comparing as law.

[6] W Menski *Hindu Law. Beyond Tradition and Modernity* (Oxford University Press, 2003) 18; see also W Menski *Comparative Law in a Global Context. The Legal Systems of Asia and Africa* 2 ed (Cambridge University Press, 2006) 85.

[7] For example, K Zweigert & H Kötz *Introduction to Comparative Law. 1 – The Framework* 2 ed (Clarendon Press, 1987).

from the former European colonisers, the general law of African countries developed their own perceptions, the inherited law of the African traditional communities (customary law) and the relationship between general and inherited laws.[8]

This chapter describes in its part 5.2 the use of legal comparison in the development of legal and political anthropology since its early development to where anthropological jurisprudence stands today. On the basis of the observations in part 5.2, part 5.3 considers the Namibian customary-law ascertainment project; part 5.4 illustrates the successful or missed employment of comparative jurisprudence in reaching solutions in law-making, law reform and Court decisions. The last part (part 5.5) returns to comparative jurisprudence as a methodological tool with which to achieve a reasoned ascertainment of customary law and, with this, to the thesis stated above.

15.2 CHANGING SCOPE OF COMPARISON IN THE DEVELOPMENT OF LEGAL ANTHROPOLOGY

The following allows a focus only on some aspects of the development of legal anthropology: the early discovery of other cultures when the European Enlightenment started, the subsequent evolutionist theorising of the discoveries, the response of structural functionalism, the methodological problematisation of empirical research in the Bohannan–Gluckman debate, the conceptualisation of legal pluralism and the recognition of legal pluralism in the Namibian context.

Comparing societies and comparing rules applied in societies was prompted by the development of critical thinking as it became apparent in the time of the European Enlightenment. Montesquieu[9] wrote that whenever he reached an area which he had not visited before, he looked out for the highest place. He climbed it to learn about the geographical and socio-political environment of the area.[10] The 'discovery' of communities with people different from the mainstream population of Europe and socio-political orders also different from what was accepted as God-given led not only to systematic destructive inroads into these communities and the oppression of their people, but also to attempts that challenged the hitherto prevailing monistic view of the world. For this view of the world, Europe and European values were dominated by the version of Christianity applied at that time. Scholars who collected ethnographical material from communities in all parts of the world described the rules maintained in these communities and compared the

[8] See Menski (note 6) 85; HP Glenn *Legal Traditions of the World. Sustainable Diversity in Law* 5 ed (Oxford University Press, 2007); Kischel (note 5); M Reimann & R Zimmermann (eds) *The Oxford Handbook of Comparative Law* 2 ed (Oxford University Press, 2019).

[9] 1689–1755.

[10] Quoted from H Stubbe-da Luz *Montesquieu* (Rowohlt, 1998) 53.

differences between them and what was in place in Europe. Although they did not necessarily express appreciation for what they found, they confirmed that there were human beings behind the reported differences, human beings created by God and part of the same group of beings to whom all human beings belonged![11]

The long-lasting and powerful theoretical reaction to the discovered differences is the construction of evolutionist interpretations according to which the Western world was the world of modernity. The Western world was seen as the result of historical development to which deviating forms of society reflected earlier stages of society: the Western way of life stood for achieved progress while the way of life of American Indians, Africans and others reflected primitivism. Maine, Bachofen, Morgan, Marx, Engels and others offer evolutionist theories which compare the different ways of life and organise the results of the comparison into an order, starting with so-called primitive forms of socio-political organisation and leading to complex forms.[12] At the top end there is the modern, capitalist or, as in the Marxist vision, communist society, all of them marking the end of history.

The evolutionist interpretation of the differing modes of society found its way into European legal projects related to the growing importance of colonialism. The law project conducted on behalf of the then Imperial German government is seen to be of particular importance to this chapter. The aim of the project was to gather data on the law applied in the then German colonies. The larger part of the data assembled was collected in German East Africa (now Tanzania) and German South West Africa (now Namibia). Standardised questionnaires were the instrument for the collection of the data.

The use of standardised questionnaires was an established practice in anthropology, as can be seen by the widely employed British *Notes and Queries on Anthropology*, which was published in 1874.[13] However, a legal questionnaire was drafted by Post, who was one of the first German lawyers with an interest in legal anthropology. His aim was to establish a foundation of law by focusing on legal ethnographical data in a comparative manner.[14] Post's questionnaire and

---

[11] As, eg, in Sebastian Münster's *Cosmographia* published in 1544. See on this W Petermann *Die Geschichte der Ethnologie* (Hammer, 2004) 73ff.

[12] Cf M Harris *The Rise of Anthropological Theory. A History of Theories of Culture* (Thomas Y Crowell, 1968) 142ff, 180ff.

[13] British Association (1874).

[14] See on Post and also on his legal questionnaire, HJ Hildebrandt (ed) *A Post and the Anthropology of Law. A Forgotten Pioneer. Einleitung in das Studium der ethnologischen Jurisprudenz von Albert Hermann Post* (Edition Re, 1989). Responses to the questionnaire sent out by Post are collected in RR Steinmetz *Rechtsverhältnisse von eingeborenen Völkern in Afrika und Ozeanien. Beantwortungen des Fragebogens der Internationalen Vereinigung für vergleichende Rechtswissenschaft und Volkswirtschaftslehre zu Berlin* (Julius Springer, 1903). This collection contains three Namibian reports: one each on the Ovaherero, the Nama and the Ondonga.

later submissions influenced the questionnaire drafted by the commission of the German Colonial Office (*Reichskolonialamt*) of 1908.[15] This commission was presided over by Kohler, who was also a professor of law and, like Post, attracted to legal anthropology.[16]

The interest in the law of the people in the colonies was summarised by Zwierlein in the following observation:[17]

> The colonial powers had, in most cases, a genuine practical interest in knowing the legal relationships of the indigenous people because there was more or less in all colonial territories the rule that European law directly only applied to the Europeans while the law of the indigenous people was applicable to indigenous conflicts – at least as long as it did not contradict the fundamental principles of the law of the colonialists.

The author of this statement goes on to say that this approach was based on the paradoxical assumption that, on the one hand, the so-called primitive people could not be seen to be at the same level of civilisation as the Europeans and therefore were to be treated under their respective laws; but, on the other, they were, in pursuit of colonial interests, also to be subjected to the law of the coloniser.

Kohler believed in the universality of legal history, according to which the legal orders of primitive peoples (*Naturvölker*) expressed the forms and structures of past developmental stages of civilised peoples (*Kulturvölker*).[18]

While Meyer, one of the members of the commission, looked forward to 'legislative work' on the materials, some colonial officers were of the opinion that the responses to the questionnaires would certainly contribute to the immediate

---

[15] It is interesting to note that the questionnaire and the responses to it were used for research on customary law when German East Africa was under British rule. Cf A Redmayne 'Research on customary law in German East Africa' (1983) 27(1) *Journal of African Law* 22–41.

[16] Father Wilhelm Schmidt, a leading anthropologist at the time, was one of the members of the commission. Further on the commission see H Sippel 'Die Reichstags-Kommission zur Erforschung des, Eingeborenenrechts' in U von Heyden & J Zeller (eds) *Macht und Anteil an der Weltherrschaft. Berlin und der deutsche Kolonialismus* (Unrast Verlag, 2005) 101–108 and also H Sippel 'Der deutsche Reichstag und da Eingeborenenrecht: Die Erforschung der Rechtsverhältnisse der autochthonen Völker in den deutschen Kolonien' (1997) 61(4) *The Rabel Journal of Comparative and International Private Law* 714–738.

[17] C Zwierlein 'Übersetzungen ohne Original – Die Erfassung des Rechts der Naturvölker per Fragebogen in den deutschen Kolonien 1907–1914' (2012) 34 *Zeitschrift für Neuere Rechtsgeschichte* 219–245 (translated by the author of this article).

[18] Cf J Kohler 'Zur vergleichenden Rechtswissenschaft und ihrer Literatur' (1981) 23(1) *Kritische Vierteljahresschrift für Gesetzgebung und Rechtswissenschaft* 1–24.

'sociological basics', but that not much of the collected law would survive the attempts at establishing a 'higher culture' in the colonies.[19]

The questionnaire elicited 77 responses. Most of them were sent from German East Africa and South West Africa.[20] Although there is evidence that the responses were communicated back to the authorities of the colonies before 1914, it is held that they did not really have an impact on the courts and the administration.[21]

With the loss of its colonies, the legal project lost importance. However, the anthropologist Adam and the former governor of Samoa, Schultz-Ewerth, published two volumes summarising and evaluating the results of the questionnaire project in 1929–1930.[22]

What does the way the questionnaire was worded and used and what do the collected data tell us? Lyall is of the opinion that the responses to the questionnaires would provide 'much valuable material' for historians and anthropologists about the legal relationships of the reported societies.[23] This statement is debatable, though, given the evolutionist approach that guided the questionnaire project. The implied evolutionist assumption prevented research from observing societies in their own right, including the fact that societies were the product of and subject to change and, in fact, existed today, that is, at the same time as the societies from which the researcher originate. Therefore, the responses to the questionnaires will hardly have the value that Lyall suggested. Instead, the analysis of the responses to the questionnaires lies somewhere else. It adds, in a specific way, to the knowledge about the ideological obstinacy of this phase of legal anthropology and, with this, to what has become known as *orientalism*, that is, the exclusive interpretation of the world from a Western perspective.[24]

---

[19] See the quotations in: Zwierlein (note 17) 226f.

[20] Twenty-seven responses from South West Africa are available in a collection prepared by the Namibian Bibliographical Data Project *Beantwortung des Fragebogens über die Rechte der Eingeborenen in den deutschen Kolonien* (Namibian Bibliographical Data Project, 1988). An additional response appeared in M Krafft 'Aus dem deutsch-südwestafrikanischen Schutzgebiete. Die Rechtsverhältnisse der Ovakuanjama und der Ovandonga' (1914) 27(1) *Miteilungen aus den deutschen Schutzgebieten* 3–35.

[21] Zwierlein (note 17) 229.

[22] E Schultz-Ewerth & L Adam (eds) *Das Eingeborenenrecht. Sitten und Gewohnheitsrechte der Eingeborenen der ehemaligen deutschen Kolonien in Afrika und in der Südsee. Ostafrika* (worked on by B Ackermann) (Strecker und Schröder, 1929) and E Schultz-Ewerth & L Adam (eds) *Das Eingeborenenrecht. Sitten und Gewohnheitsrechte der Eingeborenen der ehemaligen deutschen Kolonien in Afrika und in der Südsee. Togo, Kamerun, Südwestafrika, die Südseekolonien* (worked on by A Schlettwein et al) (Strecker und Schröder, 1930).

[23] A Lyall 'Early German legal anthropology: Albert Hermann Post and his questionnaire' (2008) 52(1) *Journal of African Law* 114–138.

[24] See on this Zwierlein (note 17) 245 – on *orientalism*; cf E Said *Orientalism* (Routledge & Kegan Paul, 1978).

The phase of colonialism, which is characterised by the more or less systematic establishment of state-like administrations after the First World War, coincided with the development of structural–functional approaches and approaches related to this in anthropology.[25] These approaches displaced the classical expressions of evolutionism and opened up new perceptions in understanding societies.

African Political Systems by Fortes and Evans-Pritchard, published in 1940, is an outstanding example of structural–functional anthropology. It was based on field work, that is, work with and in communities. The book was published in the hope that it would 'be of interest and of use to those who have the task of administering African peoples'.[26] It was, indeed, of interest, as it informed colonial administrators that the societies in the colonies had functioning legal and political structures. The collected research showed that these legal and political structures were, in some cases, very different from what the colonisers had in mind on the basis of their experience at home.

The research offered by *African Political Systems* expected that colonial administrations would apply a comparative view before deciding on administrative acts. Colonial administrators were expected to learn that, in executing their administrative tasks, they were well advised to undertake comparative work, that is, by investigating whether what they wanted to implement corresponded or responded to the rules existing in the societies to which the tasks were addressed before deciding; and also about how to implement the decisions.[27]

---

[25] See T Asad 'Two European images of non-European rule' in T Asad (ed) *Anthropology & the Colonial Encounter* (Humanity Books, 1973); Petermann (note 11) 882ff, 905; and RA Paul 'Colonialism, capital, and the rise of the structural–functionalist school of British anthropology' (2016) 27(2) *History and Anthropology* 210–219.

[26] So in note of the editors, M Fortes & EE Evans-Pritchard (eds) *African Political Systems* (Oxford University Press, 1940) VII.

[27] To what extent research of structural–functional anthropology influenced colonial administration is a field on its own. The case of Namibia is different from that of other parts of Africa insofar as it became, after the end of German colonialism, *de facto* part of South Africa. One consequence of this was that the customary law of its communities was basically seen and treated as in South Africa. The South African Black Administration Act 38 of 1927 was translated into the South West African Native Administration Proclamations (11 of 1922 and 15 of 1928). The implementation of the recommendations of the so-called Odendaal Commission introduced the South African bantustan system into Namibia: see Republic of South Africa, 1964.

The South African application of the policy of apartheid prompted wide-ranging research on the customary law and government of the South African communities. Gordon has shown that this research by legal *volkekundiges* (the Afrikaans term for South African legal anthropologists who belonged to the South African school of anthropology named *volkekunde*; see on this WD Hammond-Tooke *Imperfect Interpreters. South Africa's Anthropologists 1920–1990* (Witwatersrand University Press, 1997) 119ff) was, although to some extent empirically minded, ideologically more influenced by German promoters of the evolutionist theory than by (British)

African Political Systems and other research work undertaken in the same spirit paved the way for understanding societies and the rules that guarantee their functioning as entities in their own right. Comparing, therefore, meant noting the differences and, very generally speaking, relating them to each other. But in which sense? The comparison did not result in manifestations of societal organisations, which followed each other as predicted in evolutionist concepts. Instead, it prompted questions about the approach to comparing: What would be compared with what, how would they be compared and subsequently what could be the criteria for critically assessing the compared differences?

In dealing with this kind of question, comparative jurisprudence changed its focus away from comparing individualised functions of rules to exploring the position of rules in their societal environment. This was an approach for which contextualised comparison is the key word.[28] In his analysis of contextualising comparative jurisprudence, Kischel gives, on the one hand, credit to researching the functions of rules, but in addition he submits that the contextualising approach 'requires the comprehensive reflection of all relevant legal and non-legal factors and insights in each individual examination'.[29] It is obvious that contextualising is, in particular, important when the rules to be compared are rules of very different legal systems.[30]

Legal anthropology contributed substantially – even if it was not widely acknowledged – to comparative jurisprudence as a contextualising method with what has become known as the Gluckman–Bohannan debate. In his work on the law of the Tiv of Nigeria,[31] Bohannan pays attention to a specific problem that legal anthropologists have when writing about the law of a community under research. The ethnographer, according to Bohannan,[32]

---

structural-functional anthropology: R Gordon 'The white man's burden: *Ersatz* customary law and internal pacification in South Africa' (1989) 2(1) *Journal of Historical Sociology* 41–65. This applies also to Namibia, although the socio-political structure of Namibian communities and their customary law remained less researched because Namibia was more important as a militarily secured buffer zone between the South African mainland and its northern neighbours and not as a social reality to be administratively controlled like the communities in South Africa: cf R Gordon 'The stat(u)s of Namibian anthropology: A review' (2000) 16 *Cimbebasia* 1–23 and R Gordon *South Africa's Dreams. Anthropologists and Apartheid in Namibia* (Berghahn, 2021).

[28] See here the various contributions to Part II of Reimann & Zimmermann (note 8) and, in particular, Kischel (note 5) 92ff, 108ff and 164ff. It may be noted that both works on comparative jurisprudence deal not only with the legal systems usually analysed in textbooks on comparative jurisprudence, but also have chapters on African law.

[29] Kischel (note 5) 187 (translation by the author of this article).

[30] Cf F von Benda-Beckmann & K von Benda-Beckmann *Gesellschaftliche Wirkung von Recht. Rechtsethnologische Perspektiven* (Dietrich Reimer, 2007) 21ff.

[31] P Bohannan *Justice and Judgement among the Tiv of Nigeria* (Oxford University Press, 1957).

[32] Ibid.

> must report accurately the ideas and institutions of the people he has studied, in a language (English) in which most of the words and concepts of social control have been pre-empted by jurists and given precise and technical meaning.

In order to achieve accurate reporting, Bohannan distinguishes between 'folk systems' and 'analytical systems'. People 'create meaningful systems out of the social relationships in which they are involved'. These systems are folk systems.[33] What 'sociologists and anthropologists create by more or less scientific methods' are analytical systems.[34] An analytical system 'is a systematisation of ethnographic fact (including the folk system) for purposes of analysis'.[35] The 'key to the folk system – almost the only key – is the language in which it is stated'.[36] The problem with this key, however, is to what it will lead when we use it.

Bohannan's work was published two years after Gluckman's legal research in the Barotse community of Zambia.[37] Gluckman's *Judicial Process among the Barotse* is praised as one of the classics of legal anthropology.[38] The two books, the reviews of the books and the responses to them by Gluckman and Bohannan are the main texts of the Gluckman–Bohannan debate. Gluckman's first response appeared as an amendment to the second edition of the book on the Barotse.[39] Gluckman defends the approach in his book and calls it a 'myth' that he 'forced the concepts and processes of Barotse law into a [Procrustean] mould of English terminology and, as some apparently hold, of Roman-Dutch law'. Instead:[40]

> I have very occasionally, when discussing a trial and after showing a principle of Barotse law in that trial, stated that the principle can be compared with

[33] Ibid.

[34] Ibid.

[35] Bohannan (note 31) 5.

[36] Ibid.

[37] M Gluckman *The Judicial Process among the Barotse of Northern Rhodesia* (Manchester University Press, 1955).

[38] N Rouland *Legal Anthropology* (Athlone, 1994) 38.

[39] Where Gluckman also refers to reviews of his book. The added chapter is titled 'reappraisal': see M Gluckman *The Judicial Process among the Barotse of Northern Rhodesia* 2 ed (Manchester University Press, 1973) 367ff; see, further, SF Moore 'Descent and legal position' in L Nader (ed) *Law in Culture and Society* (Aldine Publishing Company, 1969) 374–400; M Gluckman 'Concepts in the comparative study of tribal law' in L Nader (ed) *Law in Culture and Society* (Aldine Publishing, 1969) and P Bohannan 'Ethnography and comparison in legal anthropology' in L Nader (ed) *Law in Culture and Society* (Aldine Publishing, 1969), but also the reprint of the second edition of M Gluckman *The Judicial Process among the Barotse of Northern Rhodesia* 2 ed (Manchester University Press, [1967] 1973) contributed a further preface to this edition.

[40] Gluckman (1967, note 39) 377.

> one in Roman (and hence Roman-Dutch, and here English) law. ... But the whole of my analysis is concerned to show that, even if the principles of law be similar in the different systems, they are 'permeated' by quite different economic and social conditions. This being so, it is nevertheless important to state that there are similar principles.

And:[41]

> It is almost impossible to write in English about a foreign system of law without using English words.

We use English in describing folk systems and we use English when we move in analytical systems.[42] As long as we take note of data from a social-cultural context, which is not the context of the researcher, translations are unavoidable. As problematic as translations may be, though, they nevertheless contribute to mutual understanding. Translations are the first result of comparison: they may lead to terms which express differences, but also commonalities, eventually even universalities.

A critical view of the work of the Gluckman–Bohannan debate may hold that the first translated too early and too much and the latter used too many Tiv terms. Either conclusion, however, should not deviate from the further existing need 'to proceed with the painstaking collection of indigenous legal terms and expressions'.[43]

However, the 'painstaking' business of collecting data in different cultures today is different from the work of the time in which the Gluckman–Bohannan debate occupied the methodological discourse. Translation today is different from translation at the time of Gluckman and Bohannan. Translations from so-called indigenous languages into world languages, such as English or French, have been complemented by translations from English or French into exactly those traditionally orally used languages. It is the practice in many countries to have publications which offer information and reports in English and, taking Namibia as an example, in Oshiwambo, Otjiherero, Silozi and other African languages of the country. This means that the distinction that structural-functional anthropology makes between folk systems – the systems applied by indigenous people and investigated by Europeans in European languages – and analytical systems, used only by these Europeans, has lost its meaning. What appears today is a complex mixture of what was distinguished as analytical and folk systems. Science and research in counties

---

[41] Gluckman (1969, note 39) 354.

[42] See Von Benda-Beckmann (note 3) 28ff, who correctly holds that 'absolutely objective and value free' categories are not possible.

[43] Rouland (note 38) 145.

such as Namibia contribute to the understanding and interpretation of social and legal life in their own ways.[44] What used to be called 'folk systems', the analytical systems of which were solely seen to be part of the work of analysts from outside, now have their own analytical systems.[45]

The very far-reaching and, to date, the last challenge to comparative jurisprudence applied to legal anthropological work is linked to the fact of legal plurality and the conceptualisation of legal pluralism. Irrespective of any rules existing in a society to provide for a hierarchically constructed system of legal rules,[46] it is, by now, a fact that societies consist of networks of sub-central entities that generate rules in their own right.[47] Research in the Bukovina region (which today belongs partly to Ukraine and partly to Romania) by the Austrian professor of law, Ehrlich, during the first half of the 20th century revealed that certain communities – Ehrlich named 'nine tribes' (*neun Stammesgesellschaften*) – in Ehrlich's terminology, preferred their 'living law' (*lebendes Recht)* to the law of the empire.[48]

Ehrlich's work prompted the first prominent controversy about legal pluralism. It was an exchange of views between Kelsen and Ehrlich. The Kelsen–Ehrlich controversy remained, however, bound to legal theory – the methodological foundation of the sociology of law – until legal anthropologists working in colonised territories applied Ehrlich's concept to their research and, as a consequence, added wide-ranging material to the conceptualisation of legal pluralism.[49]

---

[44] Interpreting the interpreters is a title-made motto of a Namibian analysis (Horn 2017) of Namibian constitutional case law!

[45] The next sub-section returns to this.

[46] As, eg, suggested by Hans Kelsen *Reine Rechtslehre* (Mohr Siebeck, 2008).

[47] J Griffith 'What is legal pluralism?' (1986) 24 *Journal of Legal Pluralism* 1–55.

[48] E Ehrlich *Recht und Leben – Gesammelte Schriften zur Rechtstatsachenforschung und zur Freirechtslehre* (Duncker & Humblot, 1967) 43. Ehrlich is a collection of articles, originally published in different journals and different years. Ehrlich's articles *Die Erforschung des lebenden Rechts* and *Das lebende Recht der Völker der Bukowina* in: Ehrlich (1967) 11ff and 43ff were originally published in 1911 and 1912.

[49] On the Kelsen–Ehlich controversy, see Kelsen in SL Paulsen *Hans Kelsen und die Rechtssoziologie* (ed). *Auseinandersetzung mit Hermann U, Kantorowicz, Eugen Ehrlich und May Weber* (Scientia Verlag, 1992) and E Ehrlich 'Entgegnung' (1916) 41 *Archiv für Sozialwissenschaft und Sozialpolitik* 844–849, but also M Rehbinder *Die Begründung der Rechtssoziologie durch Eugen Ehrlich* (Duncker & Humblot, 1967) 89ff; and B Van Klink 'Facts and norms: The unfinished debate between Eugen Ehrlich and Hans Kelsen' in M Hertogh (ed) *Living Law. Reconsidering Eugen Ehrlich* (Hart Publishing, 2009) 127–155.

Many scholars have contributed to the further conceptualisation of legal pluralism; only the following refer: Griffith (note 47); F von Benda-Beckmann 'Rechtspluralismus: Analytische Begriffsbildung oder politisch-ideologisches Program?' (1994) 119 *Zeitschrift für Ethnologie* 1–16; F von Benda-Beckmann 'Who's afraid of legal pluralism?' (2002) 47 *Journal of Legal Pluralism* 37–82; W Menski *Comparative Law in a Global Context. The Legal Systems of Asia and Africa* 2 ed (Cambridge University Press, 2006) 82ff; MO Hinz (ed) *In Search of Justice and*

Moore termed the entities which are part of a system of social entities and create rules on their 'own semi-autonomous social fields'. According to Moore, the

> semi-autonomous social field is defined and its boundaries identified not by its organization (it may be a corporate group, it may not) but by a processual characteristic, the fact that it can generate rules and coerce or induce compliance to them.[50]

It is obvious that the generation of rules by semi-autonomous fields which are related to an overarching society – for instance, a state with governmental functions – may lead to conflicts prompted by contradictory rules set by the state. In this regard, Moore states:[51]

> One of the most usual ways in which centralized governments invade the social fields with their boundaries is by means of legislation. But innovative legislation or other attempts to direct change often fails to achieve their intended purposes; even when they succeed wholly or partially, they frequently carry with them unplanned and unexpected consequences. This is partly because new laws are thrust upon going social arrangements in which there are complexes of binding obligations already in existence.

While Moore's notion of semi-autonomous social fields, the rules created in these fields and the interaction between these rules and the rules of the state informed and guided empirical research, legal pluralism acquired a new quality with its legal, even constitutional, confirmation. The fact that, for example, most, if not all, African states harbour social entities, traditional communities that, in one way or the other, reach back to pre-colonial forms of government, prompted developments to recognise these communities as part of the societies as they exist today. Traditional communities are, seen from the perspective of legal pluralism, as modern as what is usually called 'modern' with respect to the modern societal system. For this reason,

Peace: Traditional and Informal Justice Systems in Africa (Namibia Scientific Society, 2010); MDA Freeman *Lloyd's Introduction to Jurisprudence* 9 ed (Sweet & Maxwell, 2014) 926ff; R Seinecke *Das Recht des Rechtspluralismus* (Mohr Siebeck, 2015) and also J Beyer 'Das Recht der Andere. Rechtsethnologie zwischen Pluralität und Alterität' in C Boulanger, J Rosenstock & T Singelnstein (eds) *Interdisziplinäre Rechtsforschung. Eine Einführung in die geistes- und sozialwissenschaftliche Befassung mit dem Recht und seiner Praxis* (Springer, 2019). The current debate about legal plurality is heavily occupied with the question whether and to what extent the application of Islamic law in secular states can be tolerated.

[50] SF Moore *Law as Process. An Anthropological Approach* (James Currey, 2000) 57 – the quoted text was originally published in 1973 (Moore (2000) 54).

[51] Ibid.

the proponents of legal pluralism speak of modernities, modernity in the plural, in order to stress the point that none of the social fields is supreme simply because it represents the more desirable form of government.[52]

15.3 NAMIBIAN CUSTOMARY-LAW ASCERTAINMENT PROJECT

With Independence, the political order established in Namibia may be referred to in order to illustrate the legal recognition of legal pluralism. Article 103 of the Constitution of Namibia recognises traditional communities incidentally in establishing the Council of Traditional Leaders as a state organ with (albeit) restricted responsibilities. Article 66(1) of the Constitution confirms the customary law of traditional communities as part of the law of Namibia with the same quality as the general common law. Section 3(3)*(c)* of the Traditional Authorities Act[53] lists as one of the tasks of traditional authorities 'to make customary laws'. However, the description of the confirmation of legal plurality of Namibia would be incomplete without the reference to constitutional and other statutory limitations of the confirmation of customary law. Article 66(1) of the Constitution limits the validity of customary law to its compliance with the Constitution and any other statutory law. This limitation is repeated in the Traditional Authorities Act and the Community Courts Act.[54]

It was soon after the enactment of the Constitution of Namibia that the government appointed a commission to investigate the position of traditional authorities and the extent to which these authorities were accepted by the people. The commission submitted its report in 1991 and stated in clear terms that traditional authorities did not only exist in all parts of the country, but enjoyed support as the local leaders in their regions.[55] This message and the detailed findings of the commission were the background to which the Traditional Authorities Act of 1995[56] and the Council of Traditional Leaders Act of 1997[57] were enacted. With the execution of the Traditional Authorities Act, traditional communities, respectively the leaders of the communities were officially recognised and gazetted.[58] The

[52] Cf J Comaroff & J Comaroff 'Introduction' in J Comaroff & J Comaroff (eds) *Modernity and Its Malcontents. Ritual and Power in Postcolonial Africa* (University of Chicago Press, 1993).

[53] Act 25 of 2000.

[54] See s 1 of the Traditional Authorities Act 25 of 2000 and s 1 of the Community Courts Act 10 of 2003.

[55] Republic of Namibia (1991) 73ff.

[56] Act 17 of 1995.

[57] Act 13 of 1997.

[58] Section 6 of the Traditional Authorities Act 25 of 2000.

investigation into traditional leaders by the commission of inquiry was followed by an investigation into the administration of justice by traditional authorities. The Community Courts Act and the gazetting of community courts[59] were the statutory and administrative reactions to the findings on traditional courts.[60]

The project to ascertain the customary law of the Namibian traditional communities[61] illustrates the practice in support of the legal confirmation of legal plurality and the use of comparative jurisprudence in the process of confirmation. The first interest behind ascertaining was to contribute with certainty about the law that might be applied to the members of the various communities and the public in general. The philosophy behind ascertaining is to consider societal processes, to reflect on the law, to consider its function when it was first applied and the societal changes that occurred, and to become involved in a discourse on the relationship between the inherited law and the new constitutional order. The project supported the possibility of discussing law and the law of a particular community by distributing already received pieces of self-stated law and, therefore, inviting communities to attend comparing discussions.[62]

The concept of self-stating stands in contrast to codification, which occurred, for example, in South Africa,[63] and also in contrast to restatement, as was done by the School of Oriental and African Studies of the University of London under Allott.[64] In the approach to self-stating customary law, the communities were requested to write up those aspects of their customary law which they found important to have in writing. Members of the communities responded to this request by using their own languages and also provided the project with English translations.

---

59 Section 4 of the Community Courts Act 10 of 2003.

60 See MO Hinz & S Joas 'Customary law in Namibia: Development and perspective' *Working Paper No 303, 2 series* (CASS Papers, 1995a).

61 Cf the three volumes MO Hinz & NE Namwoonde (eds) *Customary Law Ascertained: 1. The Customary Law of the Owambo, Kavango and Caprivi Communities of Namibia* (Namibia Scientific Society, 2010); Hinz (note 49); MO Hinz & A Gairiseb *Customary Law Ascertained, 2. The Customary Law of the Bakgalagari, Batswana and Damara Communities of Namibia* (UNAM Press, 2013); and MO Hinz & A Gairiseb Customary Law Ascertained, 3. *The Customary Law of the Nama, Ovaherero, and San Communities of Namibia* (UNAM Press, 2016).

62 See MO Hinz 'What is ascertainment of customary law, what is it for and what is the work ahead?' in Hinz & Gairiseb (note 61) 3–18; and MO Hinz 'Customary law ascertained – project completed?' (2019) 119(1) *Namibia Law Journal* 47–65. Hinz (2019) also discusses first critical comments about the approach of the project, which is not repeated here.

63 Cf TW Bennett *Customary Law in South Africa* (Juta & Co, 2004) 5.

64 See A Allott 'International development in customary law. The restatement of African law project and thereafter' in TW Bennett & M Rünger (eds) *The Ascertainment of Customary Law and the Methodological Aspects of Research into Customary Law*. Proceedings of workshop, February/March 1995 (Republic of Namibia: Law Reform and Development Commission, 1996).

The project of self-stating reflected the Gluckman–Bohannan debate in a special way. As already noted, versions of the law in two languages could be requested because the 'good old time' is past of the anthropologist communicating with their community in the language of the community and members of the communities basically not able to communicate in English (or whatever European language). The role of participating legal anthropologists was reduced to that of coordinators: they were basically not more than the receivers of products.

Gordon noted the Namibian customary law ascertainment project in his view on post-millennial anthropology in Namibia and commented on it in the following way:[65]

> The project, with its focus on 'ethnic groups' (as defined largely by the Odendaal Commission), is reminiscent of projects carried out by the South African ethnologists under the aegis of the erstwhile Department of Bantu Administration and Development.

Unfortunately, Gordon did not consider what the Report by Commission of Inquiry into Matters Relating to Chiefs, Headmen and other Traditional or Tribal Leaders[66] confirmed as the ethnic reality of the country and what the Namibian Parliament recognised in the Traditional Authorities Act and other laws. This confirmation and legal recognition informed the customary-law ascertainment project. In its ascertaining of customary law it followed its own approach, which is substantially different from that of the colonial questionnaire projects and also of the projects conducted by government-employed anthropologists of the then apartheid South Africa and Namibia.[67]

At this point a remark may be added that calls again for the distinction between folk and analytical systems. Folk systems have also absorbed concepts from the culture of the European analysers and, by making them part of their own understanding, changed the meaning of the absorbed concepts or gave them an additional meaning.

In their submissions on the self-stated Namibian customary law, some Namibian communities used ownership to describe the relationship to land in traditional communities.[68] Just looking at the appearance of the words, this could be interpreted

---

[65] R Gordon '(Sm)othering others? Post-millennial anthropology in Namibia' (2015) 18 *Journal of Namibian Studies* 7–23.

[66] Republic of Namibia (1991).

[67] The fact that the United Nations Development Programme employed the Namibian approach to customary law to ascertain the customary law in South Sudan may be mentioned as a reference to the Namibian approach: see MO Hinz '"... *to develop the customary laws into the common law of the Sudan ...*". Customary Law in Southern Sudan: A strategy to strengthen Southern Sudanese customary law as a source of law in an autonomous legal system'. Report (United Nations Development Programme and Ministry of Legal Affairs and Constitutional Development, 2009).

[68] See, eg, s 10(1) of the Laws of the Zeraua: Hinz & Gairiseb (note 62) 403.

as not being in line with the Communal Land Reform Act, according to which communal land is not owned according to ownership defined under general law. Communal land – so says the Communal Land Reform Act – is vested 'in the State in trust for the traditional communities'.[69] What users of communal land get are rights to use land. The use is defined by customary law, which will not allow for the selling or buying of communal land.[70]

The responsible researchers for *Customary Law Ascertained* did not intervene in the use of the concept of 'ownership' in the self-stated customary law. And this was not only because it was part of the philosophy of the project not to intervene – not even in cases of suspected unconstitutionality[71] – but also because they understood that the originally foreign concept of 'ownership' was used to underscore that rights to communal land were expected to be protected in the same way as rights of ownership under general law. Calling customary land rights 'rights of ownership' was meant to call against the view inherited from colonial times that inroads into customary land rights were basically generally possible only because the state claimed to be owner as provided for under general law.

Another example is the naming of the self-stated 'customary law'. The Ondonga Traditional Authority decided to use the Oshiwamboised Afrikaans word for rule: *wet*. This led to making it *oVeta* (*ooVeta* in plural) in the title of its self-stated customary law. The Oshiwambo word for laws, *ooMpango*, was added in brackets after *ooVeta*.[72] This was most probably done due to the fact that a written version of customary law was not part of the inherited understanding of customary law. Therefore, it was appropriate to choose a foreign word for this new appearance of law. *ooMpango* was added to inform the reader and all who listened to references to the *ooVeta* that the *ooVeta* document had the quality of *ooMpango*.

15.4 COMPARATIVE JURISPRUDENCE AND ASCERTAINING CUSTOMARY LAW IN LAW-MAKING AND DECISIONS OF COURTS

The law-maker and courts have the authority to confirm ascertained customary law. The authoritative confirmation is the final step in the process of ascertaining customary law. This last step in the ascertainment of customary law differs from what happens before. The ascertainment of customary law for *Customary Law Ascertained*

---

[69] See s 17(1) of the Communal Land Reform Act 5 of 2002, as amended.

[70] Cf s 21 of the Act.

[71] MO Hinz 'What is ascertainment of customary law, what is it for and what is the work ahead?' in MO Hinz & A Gairiseb (eds) *Customary Law Ascertained: 3. The Customary Law of the Nama, Ovaherero, and San Communities of Namibia* (UNAM Press, 2016).

[72] See Traditional Authority of Ondonga *Ooveta (Oompango) dhOshilongo shOndonga. The Laws of Ondonga* 2 ed (Evangelical Lutheran Church in Namibia, 1994).

is empirical work; legally confirming ascertainment is normative. However, in order to reach the point of confirmation, comparative jurisprudence plays a role. The process of confirming customary law requires a new dimension in the use of comparative jurisprudence. As the report about the analysis of the monster-statement in the introduction to this chapter demonstrated, the need to contextualise applies also to constitutional norms and norms of general law. Only then, and after comparing the results of what may be called cross-contextualisation, can a suitable foundation for the decision about the validity of customary law be achieved.

The examples selected for the following section refer, first, to two matters related to acts that regulate the application of customary law; second, to the preparation of law reform to accommodate claims for ancestral land, and, third, to two judgments by Namibian courts. The factual or possible role of comparative jurisprudence is considered in all the examples.

15.4.1 Harmonising the laws

The Traditional Authorities Act, the Community Courts Act and the Communal Land Reform Act translated the constitutional confirmation of traditional government into a detailed statutory framework. Harmonisation and consolidation were important goals of the enactments, the remaining fragmented regulations having been provided.[73] Despite the legitimate interest in harmonising and consolidating, the law-makers employed the empirical material in work mandated by the government and took note of what was part of the societal reality regarding practice but also taking expectations into account.[74] These Acts established new provisions where the repeal of discriminatory provisions inherited from the time of South African occupation left matters open.[75] They changed provisions where the new democratic and human rights-oriented new order required such changes.

(a) Traditional leadership

According to the original version of the Traditional Authorities Act, a traditional community was entitled to have one chief or one senior traditional councillor and such number of councillors as may be designated in accordance with the Act. 'Chief' meant chief as designated in terms of the Act.[76] The Amendment Act of 1997[77] and

[73] Cf the list of repealed Acts *per* s 33 of the Community Courts Act.

[74] See, as mentioned above, Republic of Namibia (1991) and Hinz & Joas (note 60).

[75] Schedule 8 to the Constitution refers.

[76] Sections 1 and 2(1) of the Traditional Authorities Act 17 of 1995.

[77] Act 8 of 1997.

the subsequent new Traditional Authorities Act now in force[78] enacted changes with respect to the definition of 'chief' and the government structure of traditional communities. The Amendment of 1997 entitled the traditional community to have one chief and also senior traditional councillors and traditional councillors as may be designated according to the Act.[79] 'Chief' received a new definition: it was to mean 'the supreme traditional leader of a traditional community'.[80] In case a traditional community did not have a chief, it was given the opportunity to designate a senior traditional councillor as 'the supreme traditional leader'.[81] The Traditional Authorities Act in force added a further change by giving traditional communities the power to establish their traditional authority consisting of 'the chief or head of that community' and of senior traditional councillors and traditional councillors in accordance with the Act.[82] The definitions section,[83] now has two separate definitions of 'chief' and 'head', but both meaning 'supreme traditional leader' of the community.

The *Report of the Commission of Inquiry into Matters to Chiefs, Headmen and Other Traditional or Tribal Leaders*,[84] informed the law-makers that there were communities which knew a paramount chief, there were communities that had one supreme leader to whom they referred in many cases with titles which are usually translated as king or queen, and there were communities with less hierarchically structured forms of government. In San groups, for example, members with special personal qualities would be given leadership positions.[85] For the Oshiwambo-speaking community of Uukwaludhi, the report held that this community had two senior headmen who formed the highest authority.[86] Parts of the Otjiherero-speaking communities and the Damara maintained, apart from the positions of chiefs, the position of paramount chief.[87]

Whereas the original version of the Traditional Authorities Act at least still distinguished between communities with a chief and communities with a senior headman at the highest level of the traditional authority, the later versions abandoned this arrangement and simplified the construction of 'authority' calling its highest level 'chief'. The version in force reintroduced a new distinction nominally because there is no explanation of the difference between head and chief. With this, there is

[78] Act 25 of 2000.
[79] Section 2(1) of Act 8 of 1997.
[80] Section 1.
[81] Section 2(1).
[82] Section 2(1) of the Traditional Authorities Act 25 of 2000.
[83] Section 1.
[84] Republic of Namibia (1991).
[85] Republic of Namibia (note 84) 12.
[86] Republic of Namibia (note 84) 14.
[87] Republic of Namibia (note 84) 15ff.

no space to consider that the differences in traditional government as reported by the Commission of Inquiry into Matters to Chiefs, Headmen and Other Traditional or Tribal Leaders reflect differences in the provision of structures for more or less participation of the members of the communities. It is certainly a consequence of this that communities which previously did not know royal families with the right to have one of their members to rule the community now claim to have royal families. Claims of this nature could be observed in San communities.[88] San communities were traditionally communities without centralised authority according to the classification in African political systems.

That the Traditional Authorities Act did not recognise the position of paramount chief has created confusion with respect to the two sets of communities in which the position of paramount chief is, at least partly, maintained. When the process of recognising traditional leaders started after the first version of the Traditional Authorities Act was in force, the Damara communities applied for the recognition of their paramount chief, Justus //Garoëb, as chief and under him as senior councillors the extant chiefs of Damara communities.[89]

This concession to the legally required construction of traditional authority did not last long, though. The original application was withdrawn and the senior councillors or chiefs applied for recognition as chiefs. Justus //Garoëb did not disappear as paramount chief or king. He held his, albeit disputed, position beyond the confines of the Traditional Authorities Act.[90] The Herero paramount chief, Kuaima Rirukao, received recognition as chief after a long political and even legal battle.[91] His successor, the now late Advocate Vekuii Rukoro,[92] was elected paramount chief by his community and was also recognised as chief.[93] The name of the community of Riruako and Rukoro is *Ovaherero Traditional Authority*, which signals it to be the traditional authority of the Ovaherero. This is not the case, though: the Ovaherero Traditional Authority is one of several other Otjiherero-speaking communities.[94]

---

[88] See MO Hinz 'Traditional governance of the San in Namibia. San law ascertained: challenge to tradition or inventing new traditions?' Paper for the Conference on Hunting and Gathering Societies, Vienna, unpublished (2015).

[89] Recognition of Designation of Traditional Leaders, GN 65 of 1998.

[90] Announcement of Appointment of Traditional Leaders of Certain Traditional Communities, GN 64 of 2002.

[91] The application for recognition was subject to an unsuccessful court case: cf *Kuaima Riruako v Minister of Regional, Local Government and Housing*, High Court judgment (unreported, case no A 336/2001).

[92] Rukoro passed away on 18 June 2021.

[93] Proclamation of 1 December 2016, Proclamation 10 of 2016; Proclamation of 16 January 2017, Proclamation 1 of 2017 and Proclamation of 15 August 2018, Proclamation 15 of 2018.

[94] See Hinz (2016) 257ff.

It can be assumed that the drafters of the Traditional Authorities Act were guided more by the interest in a unified and simple construction of traditional government and therefore they did not give attention to what the comparison of the empirical reality indicated. Had they been open to information reflecting the reality and compared the different forms of traditional government, they would have provided the legal space to accommodate the reality; and the problems that were prompted by the decision of the makers of the law would have been avoided.

(b) Jurisdiction

The Community Courts Act regulates the jurisdiction of the community courts in a very novel manner. The relevant first part of s 12 reads:

> A community court shall have jurisdiction to hear and determine any matter relating to a claim for compensation, restitution or any other claim recognized by the customary law ...

The rule on jurisdiction was developed in response to broadly established legal anthropological comparative jurisprudence.[95] This jurisprudence took note of the law and practice in other African countries and of empirical research in Namibia. The research revealed the overall importance of compensation in terms of customary law.[96] The importance of customary compensation ranges from the very basic rule that the theft of one head of cattle has to be compensated for by paying two head of cattle. In order to 'wipe the tears'[97] of the family of a murdered person, compensation is achieved by paying ten or 12 head of cattle. Only by paying this kind of compensation can justice equating reconciliation and peace be accomplished.

---

[95] Cf Hinz & Joas (1995a). The author of this chapter was responsible for an empirical inquiry into traditional courts while he was legal adviser to the Ministry of Justice after the Independence of Namibia. He visited Botswana and Zimbabwe to consult experts and traditional leaders and held consultations with the traditional communities of each country. This publication was amended over the years to meet the legal developments with respect to traditional authorities, customary law and the administration of customary law and served as a textbook on customary law. (The latest 7 ed appeared in 2002.) See also the case study on the customary law of the Sambyu community by FM D'Engelbronner-Kolff *A Web of Cultures: Dispute Resolution Processes amongst the Sambyu of Northern Namibia* (Shaker Publishing, 1997) and Hinz (2006). MO Hinz & HK Patemann (eds) *The Shade of New Leaves. Governance in Traditional Authority: A Southern African Perspective* (Lit, 2006).

[96] So noted in Hinz & Joas (note 60) 181.

[97] Words used by interviewees to underscore the meaning of compensation under customary law: Hinz & Joas (note 60) 181.

The analysis of the law, practice and jurisprudence in Botswana and Zimbabwe revealed the difficulties that existed in determining the jurisdiction of traditional courts in applying the accepted distinction between civil and criminal cases, the civil cases being those between subjects of private law, the criminal cases being those between the state and the individual wrongdoer. The following quotation from Schapera's handbook of Tswana law and custom illustrates this difficulty:[98]

> It must be noted … that many civil injuries are on occasions also treated as crimes … The man who steals an ox from another may be required to pay him two or more, and is thrashed as well if he is in the habit of stealing, … In the same way certain crimes, especially against bodily security, may on occasions also give rise to civil remedies. The man who assaults another is generally fined, the fines belonging to the Chief. But the general tendency in recent years has been to award part, if not all, of the fine as compensation to the victim; ….

In assessing customary compensation, its peculiarities must be borne in mind:[99] it could be approached from the distinction between civil and criminal law mentioned above and interpreted as part of civil law. It is obvious that this customary compensation will not be met by applying s 300 of the Criminal Procedure Act,[100] because the compensation under s 300 is compensation for 'damage to or loss of property' subject to proof according to the rules of evidence.[101] Furthermore, the perceptions of general and customary law on what is a case of civil law and what is a case of criminal law differ. This is a provocative result of comparative jurisprudence. It calls for a legal response, which would either be to overrule customary compensation or to replace the perception of general law with the perception of customary law in the application of the latter. Section 12 of the Community Courts Act has done the latter by focusing the jurisdiction of community courts on matters 'relating to a claim for compensation, restitution or any other claim recognised by the customary law'.

However, the legislative decision in favour of customary law did not consider whether a person sentenced to compensation under customary law for a crime committed by them could, in addition to the trial before a community court, be tried in a state court. This is, in particular, a matter of concern in cases of rape and murder, serious crimes for which customary law has very clear rules for

[98] I Schapera *A Handbook of Tswana Law and Custom* 2 ed (Frank Cass, 1995) 46.
[99] To this and the following Hinz & Joas (note 95) 182f.
[100] Act 51 of 1977, as amended.
[101] See more details on this in Hinz & Joas (note 95) 181f.

compensation[102] and the state has a special interest in the prosecuting. Therefore, the questions emerge: Is customary compensation part of civil law? And, because of this, does it allow for an additional trial in terms of criminal law? The fact that compensation under customary law is standardised – that is, it is not dependent on the amount of calculated damage – proves that customary compensation contains a punitive element.

Section 12 of the Community Courts Act did unfortunately not learn from comparative jurisprudence to avoid a possible constitutionally prohibited double punishment in terms of Art 12(2) of the Constitution. The self-stated laws of the Kwangali, for instance, contained a rule[103] which could have led to a constitutionally acceptable solution. This rule linked the sentence by a state court in the case of murder to the customary trial for compensation. The provision held that the amount of compensation should depend on the sentence in such a way that it can be reduced according to the years to be spent in jail.

15.4.2 Commission of Inquiry into Claims of Ancestral Land Rights and Restitution

Namibia's Second National Land Conference, held in 2018, took stock of what had happened to solve the land question in the years after the first land conference of 1991. The government's Concept Paper for the Second National Land Conference identified a list of matters to be considered by the second land conference and among them were the claims for restitution of ancestral land.[104] The appointment of the Commission of Inquiry into Claims of Ancestral Land Rights and Restitution by the President of Namibia was the response to the recommendation to attend to these claims.[105]

The terms of reference of the commission covered all possible aspects related to ancestral land and included some of the tasks to be covered:

- the generation of a common understanding of ancestral land rights;
- the establishment of the size of lost ancestral land;

[102] Cf the customary-law workshop of Owambo traditional leaders (Ongwediva workshop 1994), which decided to unify the rules of the Oshiwambo-speaking communities on compensation for killing a person to 10 head of cattle (88f).

[103] See MO Hinz & S Joas Developing customary law: Self-stated laws of Namibian communities and customary law consultative meetings with traditional leaders. Windhoek: CASS Papers, Working Documents No 31 (1995b) 47.

[104] Government of the Republic of Namibia (2018) 6ff.

[105] GN 59 of 2019; see also Proclamation 5 of 2019 declaring the Commissioner Act 8 of 1947 applicable to the Commission of Inquiry. The commission was chaired by High Court Judge Shafimana Ueitelle.

- the measures to restore social justice;
- the determination of claims for ancestral land vis-à-vis the principles and standards of human rights as guaranteed in the Constitution;
- the renaming of places with colonial names;
- the erection of monuments in remembrance of the victims of genocide.

Part of the terms of reference was also to draft legislation on how to cater for ancestral land claims.

The commission worked from March 2019 until June 2020 and submitted its report in July 2020.[106] It held public hearings; commissioned three studies, one on the history of land dispossession, one on legal aspects of the claims for ancestral land and one on the National Resettlement Programme;[107] invited the public to submit contributions; conducted fact-finding missions, and held retreat sessions to review the collected material. The report is a very comprehensive assessment of the problem of ancestral land. The commission approached the tasks given to it with a close understanding of the international debate on ancestral land and in line with the case law in which ancestral land claims were discussed and decided by courts.[108] In its final summary, the commission expressed that it[109]

> is of the firm conviction that claims of ancestral land rights and restitution are genuine, and that they have been largely a reaction to a land reform process that has been perceived to fall short of addressing the genuine needs of landless communities in the country. The inquiry of the Commission has heightened expectations for restitution among affected communities. The heightened expectation translates to a need by the Government to regard the issue as a serious national concern that requires urgent attention, action and prioritization through policy, legislation and programmes.

Taking a methodological stand, it is, indeed, the wealth of material from comparative jurisprudence on ancestral land claims that guided the work of the Commission of

[106] Republic of Namibia (2020) – see in particular 9ff and Appendix B.

[107] See W Werner 'History of land dispossession in Namibia' in Republic of Namibia *Report of the Commission of Inquiry into Claims of Ancestral Land and Restitution* (Republic of Namibia, 2020) Appendix F; J Nakuta 'Ancestral and, human rights and the law' in Republic of Namibia *Report of the Commission of Inquiry into Claims of Ancestral Land and Restitution* (Republic of Namibia, 2020) Appendix G and Namibia Statistics Agency *Results of the Resettlement Farmers' Analysis* (Republic of Namibia, 2020).

[108] Such as, eg, *Mabo v Queensland* (No 1) [1988] HCA at 69; *Mabo v Queensland* (No 2) [1992] HCA 23; *Alektor Ltd v Richtersveld Community* 2003 (12) BCLR 1301 (CC); *Sesana v Attorney-General* (2006) AHRLR 183 (BwHC).

[109] Republic of Namibia (note 107) 272.

Inquiry, guided the report and assisted in reaching the forward-looking final result of the report: the draft of the Ancestral Land Rights Claims and Restitution Bill.[110] The comparative material will be of further assistance when the draft Bill will be handed to the law-maker, but also the administration of the expected Act.

15.4.3 Legal pluralism

The fact that the legal system of Namibia is pluralistic is a challenge for the courts: it is up the courts to decide about the application of the law when the law of the state and customary law are both relevant to the solution of the conflict but provide for different solutions. How the courts employ or do not employ comparative jurisprudence in assessing the finally applicable law and its interpretation will be demonstrated by the reports of two cases.[111] The cases have been selected because they were seen to be two good examples that illustrate the relevance of comparative jurisprudence to achieving just and fair solutions of conflicts.

(a) MM v VT *case*

In *MM v VT* the High Court of Namibia had to decide whether a wife married in community of property and now in divorce proceedings could claim that a customary land right granted to her husband was part of the joint estate.[112] The court denied this, interpreting customary land rights as being comparable to usufructs, which give the holder the personal right to enjoy the benefits of the object of usufruct but excludes, for example, its sale.[113] From this, the judge in the case declared as follows:[114]

> It appears to me, from the provisions of the Act[115] that a customary land right may not be allocated to more than one person jointly. Therefore, the concept of joint holdership, as claimed by the defendant, does not find support in the provisions of the Act.[116] Had the legislator intended the same, it would have said so either expressly or by necessary implications.

---

[110] Republic of Namibia (note 107) Appendix J.

[111] The following is based on MO Hinz & A Schmidt *The Constitution: Supreme Law of Namibia* 2 ed (Konrad Adenauer Stiftung 2023).

[112] *MM v VT* 2017 (3) NR 743 (HC).

[113] *MM* at 32ff.

[114] *MM* at 35.

[115] The reference is to the Communal Land Reform Act.

[116] In a footnote, the judgment calls for comparison with s 9(8) of the Flexible Land Tenure Act 4 of 2012, according to which 'a "starter title right" may not be held by more than one person'.

This argument deserves a critical comment: the right to land under customary law may have similarities with usufruct, but it is not convincing, from assessed similarities, to assume that the customary-law land right as a whole is like usufruct. And, although the practice of allocating customary land rights may show that the majority of applications are applications of (single) men, there is nothing in the Communal Land Reform Act to support the statement that joint application is excluded. In interpreting the silence of the Act, one should understand that the Communal Land Reform Act is a piece of partial codification of customary law. This means that, in a case where the Act is silent, the ascertained customary law is requested.

The judge in the *MM v VT* case did not do this! Had he done it, he would have either found a rule that the woman has a right to the land held by her husband or a rule that supports the position of the man. The first possible finding would have led the judge to decide in favour of the woman. The second possible finding would have required the court to raise the question whether the rule could be confirmed as being in line with the Constitution. Here, comparative jurisprudence would have helped the judge to answer this question. The discussion about the rights of widows to customary land after the decease of their right-holding husbands[117] should have led the court to consider whether this law is constitutionally problematic as possibly discriminating against the women requesting a divorce.

The fact that what is recognised as discriminatory in the case of the termination of a marriage resulting from the death of a husband remained on the books until the Ondonga Traditional Authority,[118] the Oshiwambo-speaking communities,[119] and eventually the Communal Land Reform Act ruled against the discrimination[120] does not stand against the expectation that courts had decided against the discriminatory rules of customary law if a case had been brought to them. Irrespective of such speculation, there is now the clear statutorily confirmed position that the economic consequences after the end of a marriage by death must recognise that men and women have equal rights with respect to the remaining estate. This applies to people living in communities that follow a matrilineal order (such as the Oschiwambo-speaking communities) or any other order of descent. The comparison of the

[117] Cf Extract of minutes of the customary-law workshop in Ongwediva, 25–26 May 1993 (Traditional Authority of Ondonga (1994); *Ooveta (Oompango) dhOshilongo shOndonga The Laws of Ondonga* 2 ed (Evangelical Lutheran Church in Namibia, 1994) 88f; and MO Hinz 'Law reform from within: Improving the legal status of women in northern Namibia' (1997) 36 *Journal of Unofficial Law and Legal Pluralism* 69–79.

[118] See s 9 of the Laws of Ondonga (Traditional Authority of Ondonga, 1994): the repealed version of s 9 is published in the footnote to the section.

[119] *MM* (note 112) at 38.

[120] Section 16 of the Communal Land Reform Act 5 of 2002.

legal situation of a marriage ending by the death of one partner and the ending by divorce should have led the court to accept the constitutionally required equal treatment of the cases.[121]

(b) *Kashela v Katima Mulilo Town Council case*

In the second case, *Kashela v Katima Mulilo Town Council,*[122] the Town Council of Katima Mulilo claimed to have full rights over communal land transferred to it while the appellant in the case held that her customary land right remained in existence and was to be respected by the Town Council. The Supreme Court decided in favour of the applicant.[123] The details of the case are set out below.

The father of the appellant had a customary right to a piece of land, which was transferred to the Town Council of Katima Mulilo in terms of the Local Authorities Act[124] in 1995. Despite the transfer, the father of the appellant continued to live on the land, as he had done before. He died in 2001. His daughter, the appellant, took over from her father as heir according to the customary law of the Mafwe traditional community. It was after this that the Katima Mulilo Town Council rented out portions of the land and offered these portions for sale. The appellant objected to this. The Supreme Court identified two questions to be answered in its judgment:[125]

> what obligations or liabilities did KTC [Katima Mulilo Town Council] assume when that land was declared KTC's land and became its property? ... assuming that the late Mr Andrias Kashela [the father of the appellant] retained or acquired any rights over the land upon its proclamation as town land, did those rights survive his death and pass on to the heir?

---

[121] The case of *MM v VT* was unfortunately followed with just repeating a paragraph from this case in *WWB v Johannes Aipanda*, High Court judgment (unreported case no I 402/2014) at 81. Reference can also be made to the *LM v JM* High Court judgment (unreported, case no A 22/2013), in which the claim of a woman married under customary law of the Maharero Traditional Community against her eviction from the common home after divorce and against the denial of her having a share in a joint estate was dismissed, but also to the *M v M* High Court judgment, case no A/22/2013.

[122] *Kashela v Katima Mulilo Town Council* 2018 (4) NR 1160 (SC).

[123] Setting aside the judgement of the High Court in *Kashela v Katima Mulilo Town Council & Others* (1157 of 2012) [2017] NAHCMD 49 (1 March 2017).

[124] Act 23 of 1992, as amended.

[125] *Kashela* (note 122) at 57.

In its answer, the Supreme Court referred to Schedule 5 to the Constitution and the words in its sub-Art 3, according to which the transfer of rights is bound to 'obligations' and 'trust'. This language, averred the court,[126]

> aimed at recognizing that in such land there are interests short of rights in the black-letter law sense. That is so because the legal framework that governed communal land prior to Independence treated it as trust land.

The transfer to the state did not terminate the obligation:[127]

> The state, as owner of land, in the context of Schedule 5, has 'obligations' which a private owner does not have. It has to use the land for the public good.

That the land in question ceased to be communal land does not lead to a loss of the protection given by Schedule 5 of the Constitution. The land was transferred to the government 'subject to any existing rights … obligations over the property', as stated in Schedule 5. The court concluded[128] that the appellant

> acquired a right of exclusive use and occupation of the land in dispute upon passing of her father and … [it] survived and attached to the land even after the proclamation as town land.

The Supreme Court reached its vote without entering into a discussion whether customary land rights were rights protected under Art 16 of the Constitution. The lawyer representing the appellant submitted arguments to this effect.[129] The Court did not dismiss these arguments, but was, nevertheless, reluctant to base its conclusion on them, preferring the less challenging reference to Schedule 5 of the Constitution. It was less challenging because the Court achieved the desired protection of customary land rights without opening for other obligation following the application of Art 16 to customary land rights. This was because in particular compensation in the case of expropriating made inroads into customary land rights. Until this point, the interpretation of customary land rights as rights protected under Art 16 was for the Supreme Court 'perhaps, an undue emphasis on art 16'.[130]

---

[126] *Kashela* (note 122) at 72.
[127] *Kashela* (note 122) at 76.
[128] *Kashela* (note 122) at 81.
[129] *Kashela* (note 122) at 28–32.
[130] *Kashela* (note 122) at 69.

The use of the word 'perhaps' appears to be an indication that the nature and concept of rights under customary land law will remain on the agenda for argumentation if other cases reach the Court. However, what the Supreme Court has offered to date is certainly an important step in the direction of the need to substantiate customary rights to land.

In a recent scholarly review of the *Kashela* case, though, it was stated that the *Kashela* judgment could have 'added much substance to its conclusion by seeking wider jurisprudential support'. [131] The jurisprudential support the author of the review had in mind includes the case law mentioned in the section on ancestral land above. Referring to such case law would certainly have widened the scope of the decision. It would most probably have replaced the word 'perhaps' as used by the Court with the confirmation of rights on land under customary law as rights in terms of Art 16 of the Constitution.

15.5 CONCLUSION: COMPARATIVE JURISPRUDENCE AND INTERPRETATION

It is noteworthy to refer in the conclusion of this chapter to the jurisprudence of South Africa, where the courts have contributed directly to the judicial employment of comparative jurisprudence.

The search for living law in the sense of Ehrlich has occupied the minds of South African Courts in several cases.[132] In *Shilubana v Nwamitwa*,[133] the Constitutional Court of South Africa devoted several paragraphs to the problem of how to ascertain living customary law. The Court identified three factors to be observed. First, the Court says[134]

> It will be necessary to consider the traditions of the community concerned.... An inquiry ... will therefore invariably involve a consideration of the past practice of the community. Such a consideration also focuses the inquiry on

[131] G Barrie 'The concept of "indigenous land tenure" surfaces in Namibia: A comparative overview – *Agnes Kahimbi Kashela v Katima Mulilo Town Council* (SA 15/2017) [2018] NASC 409 (16 November 2018)' (2021) 42(1) *Obiter* 175–185.

[132] See C Himonga & C Bosch 'The application of African customary law under the Constitution of South Africa' (2000) 117 *South African Law Journal* 306–341; F Osman 'The ascertainment of living customary law: An analysis of the South African Constitutional Court jurisprudence' (2019) 51(1) *The Journal of Legal Pluralism and Unofficial Law* 98–113.

[133] Case CCT 03/07 [2008] ZACC 9.

[134] Case CCT 03/07 (note 133) at 44.

> customary law in its own setting rather than in terms of the common law paradigm, …

Second:[135]

> It is important to respect the right of communities that observe systems of customary law to develop their law. The right of communities under section 211(2)[136] includes the right of traditional authorities to amend and repeal their own customs.

Third:[137]

> courts must be cognizant of the fact that customary law, like any other law, regulates the lives of the people. The need for flexibility and the imperative to facilitate development must be balanced against the value of legal certainty, respect for vested rights, and the protection of constitutional rights.

The Court did not deal with the question of how and by whom these three requirements in ascertaining customary law should be applied. Is proof to be reached in line with the law of evidence and with the understanding that the ascertainment of a rule of customary law is ascertainment of a fact and, with this, burdening the proof on the litigant referring to the rule to be proved? In another case,[138] the South African Constitutional Court responded to this question by saying in the *Mayelane v Ngwenyama* case that[139]

> it is the function of a court to decide what the content of customary law is, as a matter of law not fact. It does not depend on rules of evidence: a court must determine for itself how best to ascertain that content.

The fact that the Court did not provide further arguments in support of its view and scholarly critical comments shows that still more discussion is needed.[140] However, the three quoted requirements for ascertaining customary law meet the observations submitted in this article, derived from the analysis of the history of legal anthropology, the use of comparative jurisprudence in legal anthropology and

135 Case CCT 03/07 (note 133) at 45.
136 Of the Constitution of South Africa, 1996, as amended, originally referred to as Act 108 of 1996.
137 *Shilubana v Nwamitwa* (note 133) 9 at 47.
138 *Mayelane v Ngwenyama* Case CCT 57/12 [2013] ZACC 14.
139 *Mayelane* (note 138) 61. Judge Zondo was not in agreement with this; see his separate opinion at 98.
140 See Osman (note 132).

the employment (or non-employment) in practising law. The examples from past completed law-making and current law reform underscore the help comparative jurisprudence is able to offer. The court cases reported prove how comparative jurisprudence contributed or could have contributed to achieving just solutions of conflicts. South African case law has moved scholarly reflections on comparative jurisprudence as submitted in this article to a hitherto not existing level of authority.

This result allows us to return to the thesis stated in the introduction to this chapter: one may convincingly state that the employment of comparative jurisprudence was traditionally very much at the discretion of researchers and also of the appliers of law; today, this has to be revisited. Responses to questions about the law in the constitutionally accepted pluralistic order require openness to comparative jurisprudence in the contextualising interpretation of law. Only in accepting this will anthropological jurisprudence progress: only then will the rules created in semi-autonomous fields enjoy the respect that societally created rules deserve. And, what's more, the rules of general law (including the rules of a constitution) will not be interpreted any more as *monsters*.

REFERENCES

Allott, A 'International development in customary law. The restatement of African law project and thereafter' in TW Bennett & M Rünger (eds) *The Ascertainment of Customary Law and the Methodological Aspects of Research into Customary Law* (Proceedings of workshop, February–March 1995) (Republic of Namibia: Law Reform and Development Commission, 1996).

Asad, T 'Two European images of non-European rule' in T Asad (ed) *Anthropology & the Colonial Encounter* (Humanity Books, 1973).

Barrie, G 'The concept of "indigenous land tenure" surfaces in Namibia: A comparative overview – *Agnes Kahimbi Kashela v Katima Mulilo Town Council* (SA 15/2017) [2018] NASC 409 (16 November 2018)' (2021) 42(1) *Obiter* 175–185.

Bennett, TW *Customary Law in South Africa* (Juta & Co, 2004).

Beyer, J 'Das Recht der Andere. Rechtsethnologie zwischen Pluralität und Alterität' in C Boulanger, J Rosenstock & T Singelnstein (eds) *Interdisziplinäre Rechtsforschung. Eine Einführung in die geistes- und sozialwissenschaftliche Befassung mit dem Recht und seiner Praxis* (Springer, 2019).

Bohannan, P *Justice and Judgement among the Tiv of Nigeria* (Oxford University Press, 1957).

Bohannan, P 'Ethnography and comparison in legal anthropology' in L Nader (ed) *Law in Culture and Society* (Aldine, 1969).

British Association for the Advancement of Sciences *Notes and Queries on Anthropology for the Use of Travellers and Residents in Uncivilized Lands* (Edward Stanford, 1874).

Comaroff, J & Comaroff, J 'Introduction' in J Comaroff & J Comaroff (eds) *Modernity and Its Malcontents. Ritual and Power in Postcolonial Africa* (University of Chicago Press, 1993).

D'Engelbronner-Kolff, FM *A Web of Cultures: Dispute Resolution Processes amongst the Sambyu of Northern Namibia* (Shaker Publishing, 1997).

D'Engelbronner-Kolff, FM, Hinz MO & Sidano J (eds) *Traditional Authority and Democracy in Southern Africa* (New Namibia Books, 1998).

Ehrlich, E 'Entgegnung' (1916) 41 *Archiv für Sozialwissenschaft und Sozialpolitik* 844–849.

Ehrlich, E *Recht und Leben – Gesammelte Schriften zur Rechtstatsachenforschung und zur Freirechtslehre* (Duncker & Humblot, 1967).

Fikentscher, W *Law and Anthropology* 2 ed (CH Beck/Hart Publishing, 2016).

Fortes, M & Evans-Pritchard, EE (eds) *African Political Systems* (Oxford University Press, 1940).

Freeman, MDA *Lloyd's Introduction to Jurisprudence* 9 ed (Sweet & Maxwell, 2014).

Glenn, HP *Legal Traditions of the World. Sustainable Diversity in Law* 5 ed (Oxford University Press, 2014).

Gluckman, M *The Judicial Process among the Barotse of Northern Rhodesia* (Manchester University Press, 1955).

Gluckman, M *The Judicial Process athe Barotse of Northern Rhodesia* 2 ed (Manchester University Press, [1967] 1973).

Gluckman, M 'Concepts in the comparative study of tribal law' in L Nader (ed) *Law in Culture and Society* (Aldine, 1969).

Griffith, J 'What is legal pluralism?' (1986) 24 *Journal of Legal Pluralism* 1–55.

Gordon, R 'The white man's burden: *Ersatz* customary law and internal pacification in South Africa' (1989) 2(1) *Journal of Historical Sociology* 41–65.

Gordon, R 'The stat(u)s of Namibian anthropology: A review' (2000) 16 *Cimbebasia* 1–23.

Gordon, R '(Sm)othering others? Post-millennial anthropology in Namibia' (2015) 18 *Journal of Namibian Studies* 7–23.

Gordon, R *South Africa's Dreams. Anthropologists and Apartheid in Namibia* (Berghahn, 2021).

Government of the Republic of Namibia 'Concept paper. Second national land conference' (Government of the Republic of Namibia, 2018).

Hammond-Tooke, WD *Imperfect Interpreters. South Africa's Anthropologists 1920–1990* (Witwatersrand University Press, 1997).

Harris, M *The Rise of Anthropological Theory. A History of Theories of Culture* (Thomas Y Crowell, 1968).

Hildebrandt, HJ (ed) *A Post and the Anthropology of Law. A Forgotten Pioneer. Einleitung in das Studium der ethnologischen Jurisprudenz von Albert Hermann Post* (Edition Re, 1989).

Himonga, C & Bosch, C 'The application of African customary law under the Constitution of South Africa' (2000) 117 *South African Law Journal* 306–341.

Hinz, MO 'Law reform from within: Improving the legal status of women in northern Namibia' (1997) 36 *Journal of Unofficial Law and Legal Pluralism* 69–79.

Hinz, MO 'Jurisprudence and anthropology' (2003) 26 *Anthropology Southern Africa* 114–118.

Hinz, MO 'Customary Law in Southern Sudan: A strategy to strengthen Southern Sudanese customary law as a source of law in an autonomous legal system' Report (United Nations Development Programme and Ministry of Legal Affairs and Constitutional Development, 2009).

Hinz, MO (ed) *In Search of Justice and Peace: Traditional and Informal Justice Systems in Africa* (Namibia Scientific Society, 2010).

Hinz, MO 'Traditional governance of the San in Namibia. San law ascertained: Challenge to tradition or inventing new traditions?' Paper for the Conference on Hunting and Gathering Societies, Vienna (2015, unpublished).

Hinz, MO 'What is ascertainment of customary law, what is it for and what is the work ahead?' in MO Hinz & A Gairiseb (eds) *Customary Law Ascertained: 3. The Customary Law of the Nama, Ovaherero, and San Communities of Namibia* (UNAM Press, 2016).

Hinz, MO 'Customary law ascertained – project completed?' (2019) 11(1) *Namibia Law Journal* 47–65.

Hinz, MO & Gairiseb, A *Customary Law Ascertained: 2. The Customary Law of the Bakgalagari, Batswana and Damara Communities of Namibia* (UNAM Press, 2013).

Hinz, MO & Gairiseb, A *Customary Law Ascertained: 3. The Customary Law of the Nama, Ovaherero, and San Communities of Namibia* (UNAM Press, 2016).

Hinz, MO & Joas, S. (1995a). Customary law in Namibia: Development and perspective. Windhoek: CASS Papers, Working Documents No 29.

Hinz, MO & Joas, S. (1995b). Developing customary law: Self-stated laws of Namibian communities and customary law consultative meetings with traditional leaders. Windhoek: CASS Papers, Working Documents No 31.

Hinz, MO & Joas, S 'Customary law in Namibia. Development and perspective 7 ed (CASS Papers, 2002) Working Documents No 48.

Hinz, MO & Namwoonde, NE (eds) *Customary Law Ascertained: 1. The Customary Law of the Owambo, Kavango and Caprivi Communities of Namibia* (Namibia Scientific Society, 2010).

Hinz, MO & Patemann, HK (eds) *The Shade of New Leaves. Governance in Traditional Authority: A Southern African Perspective* (Lit, 2006).

Hinz, MO & Schmidt, A. *The Constitution: Supreme Law of Namibia* 2 ed (Konrad Adenauer Stiftung, 2023).

Horn, N *Interpreting the Interpreters. A Critical Analysis of the Interaction between Formalism and Transformative Adjudication in Namibian Constitutional Jurisprudence* (Konrad Adenauer Stiftung, 2017).

Kelsen, H *Reine Rechtslehre* (Mohr Siebeck, 2008).

Kischel, U *Rechtsvergleichung* (CH Beck, 2015).

Kohler, J 'Zur vergleichenden Rechtswissenschaft und ihrer Literatur' (1981) 23(1) *Kritische Vierteljahresschrift für Gesetzgebung und Rechtswissenschaft* 1–24.

Krafft, M 'Aus dem deutsch-südwestafrikanischen Schutzgebiete. Die Rechtsverhältnisse der Ovakuanjama und der Ovandonga' (1914) 27(1) *Miteilungen aus den deutschen Schutzgebieten* 3–35.

Lyall, A 'Early German legal anthropology: Albert Hermann Post and his questionnaire' (2008) 52(1) *Journal of African Law* 114–138.

Menski, W *Hindu Law. Beyond Tradition and Modernity* (Oxford University Press, 2003).

Menski, W *Comparative Law in a Global Context. The Legal Systems of Asia and Africa* 2 ed (Cambridge University Press, 2006).

Menski, W 'Monsters, legal pluralism and human rights in Africa' in MO Hinz (ed) *In Search of Justice and Peace: Traditional and Informal Justice Systems in Africa* (Namibia Scientific Society, 2010).

Moore, SF 'Descent and legal position' in L Nader (ed) *Law in Culture and Society* (Aldine Publishing Company, 1969).

Moore, SF *Law as Process. An Anthropological Approach* (Lit/James Currey, 2000).

Nader, L (ed) *Law in Culture and Society* (Aldine Publishing Company, 1969)

Nakuta, J 'Ancestral and, human rights and the law' in Republic of Namibia *Report of the Commission of Inquiry into Claims of Ancestral Land and Restitution* (Republic of Namibia, 2020).

Namibia Statistics Agency *Results of the Resettlement Farmers' Analysis* (Republic of Namibia, 2020).

Namibian Bibliographical Data Project *Beantwortung des Fragebogens über die Rechte der Eingeborenen in den deutschen Kolonien* (Namibian Bibliographical Data Project, 1988).

Osman, F 'The ascertainment of living customary law: An analysis of the South African Constitutional Court jurisprudence' (2019) 51(1) *The Journal of Legal Pluralism and Unofficial Law* 98–113.

Paul, RA 'Colonialism, capital, and the rise of the structural–functionalist school of British anthropology' (2016) 27(2) *History and Anthropology* 210–219.

Paulsen, SL *Hans Kelsen und die Rechtssoziologie Auseinandersetzung mit Hermann U Kantorowicz, Eugen Ehrlich und May Weber* (Scientia Verlag, 1992).

Petermann, W *Die Geschichte der Ethnologie* (Hammer, 2004).

Redmayne, A 'Research on customary law in German East Africa' (1983) 27(1) *Journal of African Law* 22–41.

Rehbinder, M *Die Begründung der Rechtssoziologie durch Eugen Ehrlich* (Duncker & Humblot, 1967).

Reimann, M & Zimmermann, R (eds) *The Oxford Handbook of Comparative Law* 2 ed (Oxford University Press, 2019).

Republic of Namibia *Report by Commission of Inquiry into Matters Relating to Chiefs, Headmen and Other Traditional or Tribal Leaders* (Government of Namibia, 1991).

Republic of Namibia *Report of the Commission of Inquiry into Claims of Ancestral Land and Restitution* (Republic of Namibia, 2020).
Republic of South Africa *Report of the Commission of Enquiry into South West Africa Affairs, 1962–1963* (Republic of South Africa, 1964).
Rouland, N *Legal Anthropology* (Athlone, 1994).
Said, E *Orientalism* (Routledge & Kegan Paul, 1978).
Schapera, I *A Handbook of Tswana Law and Custom* 2 ed (Frank Cass, 1955).
Schlesinger, RB, Baade, HW, Damaska, MR & Herzog PE *Comparative Law. Cases – Text – Materials* 5 ed (Foundation Press, 1998). Schultz-Ewerth, E & Adam, L (eds) *Das Eingeborenenrecht. Sitten und Gewohnheitsrechte der Eingeborenen der ehemaligen deutschen Kolonien in Afrika und in der Südsee. Ostafrika* (worked on by B Ackermann) (Strecker und Schröder, 1929).
Schultz-Ewerth, E & Adam, L (eds) *Das Eingeborenenrecht. Sitten und Gewohnheitsrechte der Eingeborenen der ehemaligen deutschen Kolonien in Afrika und in der Südsee. Togo, Kamerun, Südwestafrika, die Südseekolonien* (worked on by A Schlettwein, J Lips, B von Zastrrow, M Schmidt, H Vedder, H Trimborn, R Thurnwald & E Schultz-Ewerth) (Strecker und Schröder, 1930).
Seinecke, R *Das Recht des Rechtspluralismus* (Mohr Siebeck, 2015).
Sippel, H 'Der deutsche Reichstag und da Eingeborenenrecht: Die Erforschung der Rechtsverhältnisse der autochthonen Völker in den deutschen Kolonien' (1997) 61(4) *The Rabel Journal of Comparative and International Private Law* 714–738.
Sippel, H 'Die Reichstags-Kommission zur Erforschung des, Eingeborenenrechts' in U Heyden & J Zeller (eds) *Macht und Anteil an der Weltherrschaft. Berlin und der deutsche Kolonialismus* (Unrast Verlag, 2005).
Steinmetz, RR *Rechtsverhältnisse von eingeborenen Völkern in Afrika und Ozeanien. Beantwortungen des Fragebogens der Internationalen Vereinigung für vergleichende Rechtswissenschaft und Volkswirtschaftslehre zu Berlin* (Julius Springer, 1903).
Stubbe-da Luz, H *Montesquieu* (Rowohlt, 1998).
Traditional Authority of Ondonga *Ooveta (Oompango) dhOshilongo shOndonga. The Laws of Ondonga* 2 ed (Evangelical Lutheran Church in Namibia, 1994).
Twining, W *General Jurisprudence. Understanding Law from a Global Perspective* (Cambridge University Press, 2009).
Van Klink, B 'Facts and norms: The unfinished debate between Eugen Ehrlich and Hans Kelsen' in M Hertogh (ed) *Living Law. Reconsidering Eugen Ehrlich* (Hart Publishing, 2009).
Von Benda-Beckmann, F 'Rechtspluralismus: Analytische Begriffsbildung oder politisch-ideologisches Programm?' (1994) 119 *Zeitschrift für Ethnologie* 1–16.
Von Benda-Beckmann, F 'Who's afraid of legal pluralism?' (2002) 47 *Journal of Legal Pluralism* 37–82.
Von Benda-Beckmann, F 'Riding or killing the centaur: Reflections on the identities of legal anthropology' in M Freeman & D Napier (eds) *Law and Anthropology* (Oxford University Press, 2009).

Von Benda-Beckmann, F & Von Benda-Beckmann, K *Gesellschaftliche Wirkung von Recht. Rechtsethnologische Perspektiven* (Dietrich Reimer, 2007).

Werner, W 'History of land dispossession in Namibia' in Republic of Namibia *Report of the Commission of Inquiry into Claims of Ancestral Land and Restitution* (Republic of Namibia, 2020).

Zweigert, K & Kötz, H *Introduction to Comparative Law 1 – The Framework* 2 ed (Clarendon Press, 1987).

Zwierlein, C 'Übersetzungen ohne Original – Die Erfassung des Rechts der Naturvölker per Fragebogen in den deutschen Kolonien 1907–1914' (2012) 34 *Zeitschrift für Neuere Rechtsgeschichte* 219–245.

CASES

Alektor Ltd v Richtersveld Community 2003 (12) BCLR 1301 (CC)
Kashela v Katima Mulilo Town Council & Others (1157 of 2012) [2017] NAHCMD 49 (1 March 2017)
Kashela v Katima Mulilo Town Council 2018 (4) NR 1160 (SC)
LM v JM (unreported, case no A 22/2013)
Mabo v Queensland (No 1) [1988] HCA
Mabo v Queensland (No 2) [1992] HCA 23
Mayelane v Ngwenyama Case CCT 57/12 [2013] ZACC 14
MM v VT 2017 (3) NR 743 (HC)
Sesana v Attorney-General (2006) AHRLR (BwHC)
Shilubana v Nwamitwa Case CCT 03/07 [2008] ZACC 9
WWB v Johannes Aipanda (unreported, case no I 402/2014)

LEGISLATION

Announcement of Appointment of Traditional Leaders of Certain Traditional Communities, GN 64 of 2002
Black Administration Act 38 of 1927 (South Africa)
Commissions Act 8 of 1947 (South Africa)
Communal Land Reform Act 5 of 2002
Community Courts Act 10 of 2003
Constitution of the Republic of Namibia 1990
Council of Traditional Leaders Act 13 of 1997
Criminal Procedure Act 51 of 1997
Flexible Land Tenure Act 4 of 2012
Local Authorities Act 23 of 1992
Native Administration Proclamation 11 of 1922

Native Administration Proclamation 15 of 1928
Proclamation of 1 December 2016
Proclamation 10 of 2016
Proclamation of 16 January 2017
Proclamation 1 of 2017
Proclamation of 15 August 2018
Proclamation 5 of 2019 declaring the Commissioner Act 8 of 1947 applicable to the Commission of Inquiry
Recognition of Designation of Traditional Leaders, GN 65 of 1998
Traditional Authorities Act 13 of 1997
Traditional Authorities Amendment 31 of 2000

16

Comparative constitutional law: application of the Bill of Rights

Samuel K Amoo

16.1 INTRODUCTION

The Bill of Rights, which in most written constitutions contains the fundamental rights and freedoms of a jurisdiction, evolved historically from the Magna Carta of 1215, the United States Bill of Rights of 1791, the Universal Declaration of Human Rights of 1948 and the writings of naturalists such as Grotius,[1] Montesquieu,[2] and Locke,[3] from the 16th to the 18th centuries. In the context of constitutional law and human rights jurisprudence, a Bill of Rights is associated with the concept of constitutional government, which is premised on and articulated through the principles of constitutionalism. Constitutionalism is defined by Nwabueze as follows:

> Government is universally accepted to be a necessity, since man cannot fully realise himself – his creativity and his whole personality – except within an ordered society. Yet the necessity for government creates its own problem for man, the problem of how to limit the arbitrariness inherent in government and to ensure that its powers are to be used for the good of society. It is this limiting of the arbitrariness of political power that is expressed in the concept of constitutionalism. Constitutionalism recognises the necessity for

[1] H Grotius *De Jure Belli Pacis* Transl FM Kelsey (Clarendon Press, 1925/[1646]).
[2] C Montesquieu *Spirit of the Laws* Transl & edit AM Cohler, BC Miller & HM Stone (Cambridge University Press, 1989/[1750])
[3] J Locke *Treatise on Civil Government in Two Treatises on Government 1698* (P Laslett ed) (Cambridge University Press, 1988/[1698]).

> government but insists upon a limitation being placed upon its powers. It connotes in essence therefore a limitation on government; it is the antithesis of arbitrary rule; its opposite is despotic government, the government of will instead of law.[4]

Constitutionalism therefore goes beyond a government according to the terms of a constitution; it implies limited government. This limitation on government recognises both the provision and guaranteeing of individual rights and freedoms, which is a *sine qua non* for the attainment of constitutionalism.

Traditionally, constitutional rights, including fundamental human rights and freedoms, apply in the public sphere but not in the private sphere. In other words, private actors were not bound by human rights. Although often associated with the natural rights theory, the distinction between the public and the private in the application of human rights 'antedates modern liberalism by more than two millennia'.[5] The traditional position has also been maintained in international law. Therefore, non-state actors, such as transnational corporations, cannot be found liable in international law for violating human rights.[6]

16.2 DISTINCTION BETWEEN HORIZONTAL AND VERTICAL APPLICATION

Among the most fundamental issues in constitutional law is the scope of application of individual rights provisions and their reach into the private sphere. This issue is also currently one of the most important and hotly debated in comparative constitutional law, where it is known under the rubric of 'vertical' and 'horizontal' effect. These alternatives refer to whether constitutional rights regulate only the conduct of government actors in their dealings with private individuals (vertical) or also relations between private individuals (horizontal).[7] Between these polar positions of the vertical and horizontal effect of constitutional rights lies a third position that has come to be known as the 'indirect horizontal effect'. In essence, this intermediate or hybrid position is that although constitutional rights apply

---

[4] BO Nwabueze *Constitutionalism in the Emergent States* (C Hurst & Co Publishers Ltd, 1973) 1.

[5] M Thorton 'The cartography of public and private' in M Thorton (ed) *Public and Private: Feminist Legal Debates* (Oxford University Press, 1995).

[6] DM Chirwa 'The horizontal application of constitutional rights in a comparative perspective' (2006) 10(2) *Law, Democracy and Development* 21–48.

[7] S Gardbaum 'The horizontal effect of constitutional rights' (2003) 102 *Michigan Law Review* 387–459.

directly with respect to the government only, they are nonetheless permitted to have some degree of indirect application to private actors.[8]

16.2.1 Purely vertical approach

This is the familiar position that individual rights bind, or impose constitutional duties on, only the government and not private actors. Rights regulate only the conduct of government actors in their dealings with private citizens but not the relations between private citizens. The animating idea informing the vertical approach is the perceived desirability of a public–private division in the scope of constitutional rights, leaving the private sphere free from constitutional regulation. The well-known justifications for this division lie in the values of liberty, autonomy and privacy.[9]

16.2.2 Horizontal approach

According to this approach, constitutional rights provisions impose constitutional duties on private actors, regulating interpersonal relations; and private actors may sue each other for violations of these duties. The horizontal position expressly rejects a public–private division in constitutional law.[10] Given the limited possibility of creating a more equal and just society in the medium term,[11] by requiring individuals to uphold their moral duties towards one another and to cooperate in realising a new vision for a shared future, horizontality reaffirms the human dignity of those who bear such duties as much as it does those who benefit from their performance. Horizontality requires that, in a dispute between private parties, a court must interpret and balance rights in the Bill of Rights, to the extent that they are implicated in the dispute, in order to determine whether and to what extent each party bears human rights obligations.[12] This is a logical precursor to determining whether the law or conduct in question is in accordance with the requirements of the Constitution. Viewed in this way, the rights in the Bill of Rights are always horizontal. There remains, however, concern about developing substantive law in order to give content to the rights in the Bill of Rights, and particularly to the duties imposed by those rights on private persons.[13]

---

[8] Gardbaum (note 7) 387.
[9] Gardbaum (note 7) 394.
[10] Gardbaum (note 7) 387.
[11] N Friedman *Human Rights and the South African Common Law: Revisiting Horizontality* (University of Oxford, Centre for Socio-legal Studies, 2012) 10.
[12] Friedman (note 11) 17.
[13] Friedman (note 11) 21.

16.3 APPLICATION BY SELECTED JURISDICTIONS

In this section reference is made to selected jurisdictions in Africa, Europe and North America to explore their jurisprudence on the application of a Bill of Rights. It starts with a discussion on the developments in Namibia regarding the discourse.

16.3.1 Namibia

Chapter 3 of the Namibian Constitution deals with the protection of fundamental rights and freedoms. Article 5 provides for the protection of the fundamental rights and freedoms, stating that

> [t]he fundamental rights and freedoms enshrined in this Chapter shall be respected and upheld by the Executive, Legislature and Judiciary and all organs of the Government and its agencies and, where applicable to them, by all natural and legal persons in Namibia and shall be enforceable by the Courts in the manner hereinafter prescribed.

The wording of Art 5 clearly and unequivocally indicates that the Bill of Rights of the Namibian Constitution is to be applied both vertically and horizontally. Since the establishment of the Superior Courts of Namibia following the enactment of the Namibian Constitution, the Superior Courts have interpreted and applied the provisions of the Namibian Constitution in a few landmark cases involving alleged violations of the rights of individuals by both state actors and non-state actors – that is, cases involving both the vertical and the horizontal application of the Bill of Rights.

The vertical application of the Bill of Rights can be found in the decisions of the Superior Courts in landmark cases such as *Kauesa v Minister of Home Affairs*,[14] *Chairperson of the Immigration Selection Board v Frank & Another*,[15] *Günther Kessl v Ministry of Lands and Resettlement & 2 Others*,[16] and *Government of the Republic of Namibia v Sikunda*.[17] In the *Kauesa* case, the Supreme Court was called upon to determine whether reg 58(32), in its attempt to impose restrictions on the right to freedom of speech and expression, falls within the ambit Art 21(2) of the Namibian Constitution. Article 21, which deals with the fundamental freedoms under sub-art (1), provides that all persons shall have the right to *(a)* freedom of speech and

[14] (SA 5 of 1994) [1995] NASC 3.
[15] (SA 8 of 1999) [2001] NASC 1.
[16] Case Nos 27/2006 and 266/2006.
[17] (SA 5 of 2001) [2002] NASC 1.

expression, which shall include freedom of the press and other media. Sub-art 21(2) reads as follows:

> The fundamental freedoms referred to in Sub-Article (1) hereof shall be exercised subject to the law of Namibia, in so far as such law imposes reasonable restrictions on the exercise of the rights and freedoms conferred by the said Sub-Article, which are necessary in a democratic society and are required in the interests of the sovereignty and integrity of Namibia, national security, public order, decency or morality, or in relation to contempt of court, defamation or incitement to an offence.

Regulation 58(32) provides as follows:

> 58 A member shall be guilty of an offence and may be dealt with in accordance with provisions of the Act and these Regulations if he:
>
> ...
>
> (32) comments unfavourably in public upon the administration of the Force or any other Government department.

The issue for determination by the court was whether the restrictions imposed by reg 58(32) were reasonable and proportionally connected to its objectives. The court acknowledged that the rights and freedoms under Art 21(1) have limitations and added that the restrictions must be necessary in a democratic society; and that not only must they be necessary in a democratic society but that they must also be required in the interests of the sovereignty and integrity of Namibia, national security, public order, decency or morality, or in relation to contempt of court, defamation or incitement to commit an offence. Limitations are imposed in order that the rights enshrined in the Constitution should not interfere with the rights and freedoms of others.

The Supreme Court held that reg 58(32) published under Government Notice R203 in *Government Gazette* 791 dated 14 February 1964 did not specify the ascertainable extent of the limitation, was inconsistent with Art 21(1) and (2) of the Namibian Constitution and therefore was invalid and without force and effect in law.

In the cases of *Chairperson of the Immigration Selection Board v Frank & Another,*[18] and *Günther Kessl v Ministry of Lands and Resettlement & 2 Others,*[19] the superior courts of Namibia developed the application of the principles of

---

[18] *Government of the Republic of Namibia* (note 17).

[19] *Government of the Republic of Namibia* (note 17).

administrative justice as embodied under Art 18 of the Namibian Constitution. These decisions have contributed to the Namibian jurisprudence of administrative justice, which is a constitutional right under the Bill of Rights.

Under the common-law principles of administrative law, the exercise of administrative discretion is subject to judicial review and extrajudicial adjudication. The principle enjoins administrative officials and bodies to comply with certain legal rules in the exercise of administrative discretion as granted by law. Under the principles of judicial review of administrative action, an individual aggrieved by the exercise of administrative discretion or administrative action has the right to judicial redress. This makes the right justiciable under the common law: the courts accordingly have the jurisdiction to review that administrative discretion or action and make an appropriate order. In Namibia, therefore, the common-law right to judicial review and extrajudicial adjudication granted to the individual has been elevated to a fundamental human right protected by the Constitution.[20]

Article 18 of the Namibian Constitution provides that administrative bodies and administrative officials shall act fairly and reasonably and comply with requirements imposed upon such bodies and officials by the common law and any relevant legislation. Persons aggrieved by the exercise of such acts and decisions must have the right to seek redress before a competent court or tribunal. This article falls under the entrenched provisions of the Bill of Rights and therefore, under the Namibian legal system, the jurisdiction of the courts to review administrative action is entrenched. And the justiciability of this right by any person aggrieved by the exercise of administrative discretion falls within the regime and protection of the Constitution.[21]

The cases of *Chairperson of the Immigration Selection Board v Frank & Another*,[22] and *Günther Kessl v Ministry of Lands and Resettlement & 2 Others*[23] involved applications by non-state actors to the courts for orders of nullity to set aside the decisions and actions of the Executive branch of government. The superior courts in both cases granted the orders of nullity as a consequence of the failure of the Executive to comply fully with the requirements of Art 18 of the Namibian Constitution.

The case of *Government of the Republic of Namibia v Sikunda*,[24] involved an application for a declaration by the court that the decision of the Minister of Home Affairs ordering the removal of one Jose Domingo Sikunda from Namibia and declaring him *persona non grata* by virtue of the provisions of Part VI, s 49(I) of the Immigration Control Act 7 of 1993 be set aside. The Supreme Court held inter alia that the procedures used by the appellant (the State) to detain Sikunda were indeed

[20] SK Amoo *An Introduction to Namibian Law: Materials and Cases* (UNAM Press, 2018) 318.
[21] Amoo (note 20) 319.
[22] *Chairperson of the Immigration Selection Board* (note 15).
[23] *Chairperson of the Immigration Selection Board* (note 15).
[24] *Chairperson of the Immigration Selection Board* (note 15).

tainted with irregularity and illegality to the extent that they constituted a grave infringement of his fundamental rights.

These cases involved the applications of aggrieved persons or non-state actors to the courts for review of the exercise of an executive discretion or power granted by law – that is, the vertical application of the Bill of Rights.

The case of *Hipandulwa v Kamupunya*,[25] involved a horizontal application of the Bill of Rights. The plaintiff had instituted an action in the High Court against the defendant for damages for pain, suffering, humiliation, mental anguish and infringement of her dignity and personality. The defendant had assaulted the plaintiff and had deprived her of food and water. He had chained her to a pole and had unlawfully detained her for an indefinite period. The chain of events had occurred over a period of two months and the plaintiff had claimed damages.

Levy J held that the defendant had acted in an inhuman and barbaric manner out of sheer malice and that his unlawful conduct constituted not only an unlawful detention and deprivation of the basic right of liberty, but also that the manner in which it had been perpetrated was a continuing assault and an invasion of her right to bodily integrity and a violation of her right to mental and intellectual well-being. It was further held that the Namibian common law recognises the right of every person to liberty and to human dignity and that Arts 7 and 8 of the Namibian Constitution have entrenched these common-law rights. In principle, this is a good example of the horizontal application of the Bill of Rights.

16.3.2 United States

According to Chirwa,[26] the US Constitution is emblematic of traditional constitutions in the sense that it is intended to bind the state only. It does not permit the application of rights to non-state actors. The human rights provisions under the Constitution have no direct application between private actors. Gardbaum[27] adds that, in the United States, this fundamental issue has long been considered fully and resolved by a constitutional axiom.[28] With the exception of the Thirteenth Amendment,[29] both the text and authoritative precedent[30] make it clear that with

[25] 1993 NR (HC) 254.

[26] Chirwa (note 6) 21–48.

[27] Gardbaum (note 7) 388.

[28] The state action doctrine.

[29] US Constitution Amendment. XIII, sub-section 1 reads: 'neither slavery nor involuntary servitude, except as a punishment for crime whereof the party shall have been duly convicted, shall exist within the United States nor any place subject to their jurisdiction.'

[30] The textual provision underlying the state action doctrine is the 'no state shall' language of the second clause of the Fourteenth Amendment. The standard precedent cited for definitively

respect to its individual rights provisions the Constitution binds only government actors and not private individuals. Gardbaum continues that, according to US constitutional theory, private actors are not bound by constitutional rights unless the conduct of those rights qualifies as 'state action'. In *Virginia v Rives* 100 US 313 (1879), the US Supreme Court stated that

> the provisions of the Fourteenth Amendment of the Constitution all have reference to State action exclusively, and not to any action of private individuals.

Chirwa[31] adds that this principle was reiterated in the *Civil Rights* cases (*supra*), where it was held that 'it is state action of a particular character that is prohibited'. Individual invasion of individual rights is not the subject-matter of the Fourteenth Amendment.

Gardbaum[32] writes that the fact that private actors are not bound by constitutional rights in no way entails that such rights do not govern their legal relations with one another, and thereby affect what they can lawfully be authorised to do, and which of their interests, choices and actions may be protected by law. Although, to be sure, he adds, the state action doctrine forecloses the most direct way in which the constitution might regulate private actors, by imposing constitutional duties on them. Itdoes not rule out other indirect ways, however.

(a) Exceptions

Chirwa[33] contends that the jurisprudence on state action defies coherence and its scope has been the subject of a long, drawn-out academic debate. He states that some private conduct may in some cases be considered as state action and therefore is subject to constitutional rights. These are:

- Private conduct regulated directly by government. In *Jackson v Metropolitan Edison Co* 415 US, 912, 94S, CL 1407 US 1974, the Supreme Court held that a sufficiently close nexus between the state and the challenged action of the required entity must be established for the action of the latter to be treated as that of the state itself.
- A private decision exercised under the coercive power of the state or where the latter has provided such significant encouragement, either overtly or covertly, that the choice could in law be deemed to be that of the state.[34]

interpreting this language as imposing constitutional duties only on government and not private actors is the *Civil Rights Cases* 109 US 3 (1883).

[31] Chirwa (note 6) 21–48.

[32] Gardbaum (note 7) 387.

[33] Chirwa (note 6) 21–48.

[34] *Peterson v City of Greenville* Supreme Court US 373 244 (1963).

- Acts performed by non-state actors with the participation or involvement of the state 'through any arrangement, management, funds or property' may also constitute state action.[35]
- Private conduct in which there is no apparent state involvement may also constitute state action if it relates to functions or powers normally exercised by the government.[36]

Chirwa[37] adds that these decisions demonstrate that, despite the strong adherence to the traditional conception of rights as injunctions against the state, US courts recognise that private conduct may be subject to constitutional rights in certain limited circumstances. It should be noted that the manner in which constitutional rights reach private conduct is indirect, because it is the state that is held responsible. Chirwa states further that the duty to protect constitutional rights is not recognised in US constitutional law. According to Strickland,[38] the state generally has no constitutional obligation to intervene in private disputes either to protect individuals from harm inflicted by other private entities or to force the wrongful private entities to compensate the victims of their wrongdoing.

Chirwa[39] refers to the case of *Shelley v Kraemer* 334 US 1, which, he writes, represents the closest that US courts have come to recognising the duty to protect. This case has been roundly criticised by those who consider constitutional rights to be of no relevance to private relations and it has hardly been invoked again. Furthermore, he adds that the US Constitution is limited regarding the application of its rights to private relations. Constitutional rights have no direct application to non-state actors. Rather, they can bind non-state actors indirectly only where their conduct can be attributed to a state. The rules of attribution of state conduct are very limited, meaning that the indirect application of constitutional rights to private relations is also circumscribed. Furthermore, he contends that the US constitutional jurisprudence does not give full recognition to the state's duty to protect constitutional rights, which has also limited the extent to which non-state actors may be held indirectly accountable for human rights through the state. What is important to note is that this jurisprudence establishes that the conduct of private actors can, in limited cases, be constrained by constitutional rights.

[35] *Cooper v Aaron* 1958, 358 US 14.

[36] *Marsh v Alabama* 326 US 501.

[37] Chirwa (note 6) 21–48.

[38] HC Strickland 'The state action doctrine and the Rehnquist court' (1991) 18 *Hastings Constitutional law Quarterly* 587.

[39] Chirwa (note 6) 21–48.

16.3.3 Canada

Similarly to the US Constitution, the Canadian Charter, writes Chirwa,[40] does not contain an express provision regarding its application in the private sphere. However, s 32(1) of the Charter provides as follows:

This charter applies

(a) To the Parliament and government of Canada in respect of all matters within the authority of Parliament, including all matters relating to the Yukon territory and Northwest Territories; and
(b) to the legislature and government of each province in respect of all matters within the authority of the legislature of each province.

Chirwa refers to the case of *Retail Wholesale and Department Store Union v Dolphin Delivery Ltd,* (1986) 2 SCR, 573, 9 BCLR (2d) 273, 595 in which the Canadian Supreme Court adopted a restrictive interpretation of this section to hold that Charter rights do not bind private persons. The facts of this matter are as follows:

The respondent (Dolphin Delivery Company) was a private company engaged in the courier business. The appellants (a trade union and some of its members) advised the respondent that its place of business would be picketed unless it agreed to stop doing business with Super Courier, with whom the appellants were involved in an unresolved labour dispute. In response, the respondent made application for an injunction to restrain the threatened picketing, which was granted. The basis of granting the injunction was that the threatened secondary picketing amounted to the common-law tort of inducing a breach of contract.

The appellants' appeal to the Court of Appeal was dismissed. In the appeal to the Supreme Court, the issue for consideration was whether secondary picketing by members of a trade union in a labour dispute is a protected activity under s 2*(b)* of the Canadian Charter, which guarantees freedom of expression and therefore not the proper subject of injunction to restrain it.

The Supreme Court found it easy to hold that picketing sought to be restrained as it involved freedom of expression. However, since the parties to this matter were private, the question arose whether Charter rights had application to private litigation and common law. Judge McIntyre, who wrote the opinion of the court, stated that s 32(1) of the Charter was conclusive as regards the actors to whom the Charter was applicable. The learned Judge held that the actors bound by the Charter were the Legislature, the Executive and the administrative branches of government. With respect to these, the Charter would apply 'whether or not their action is invoked in public or private litigation'.[41]

---

[40] Chirwa (note 6) 26.
[41] Chirwa (note 6) 27.

Furthermore, as the respondent was a private company, the appellants could not plead freedom of expression as a defence to the injunction. Having denied the possibility of direct horizontal application of the Charter, the Supreme Court considered the question whether the Charter applied indirectly to private litigation through the Charter's application to the Judiciary and to common law. The court rejected the contention.

The above decision presents certain conclusions. Chirwa[42] contends that this dictum means that in so far as litigation involves private actors, the Judiciary is not bound to apply or consider the human rights provisions in the Charter, unless it can be shown that there is some government connection to the litigation at hand. The prime basis for this holding, he adds, was that s 32(1) of the Charter does not mention the Judiciary as an actor to whom it applies. This leaves another possibility open.

Considering this, Chirwa[43] argues that it can therefore be said that the constitutional rights have indirect application to private relations in Canada in the sense that they can be considered as values that can inform the development of the common law. Another possibility is that they can also be relied upon in private litigation where either party invokes a provision in legislation that is inconsistent with any of those rights.

Significantly, unlike under the state action doctrine, it is the private party that is sued and held responsible for the conduct in issue, meaning that, although the manner in which constitutional rights are considered is said to be indirect, in effect, the private party is held directly responsible for the human rights violation. Chirwa concludes that, apart from enforcing the obligations of non-state actors by suing the state, the courts in Canada have conceded, albeit in a limited way, that constitutional rights also have relevance to private litigation. Furthermore, where the litigation involves legislation, Charter rights will have direct application. However, in contrast, Charter rights will be considered as Charter values where the issues raised in the private litigation concern common law.[44]

16.3.4 South Africa

According to Friedman[45] at the time when South African law journals were brimming with writing about the effect of human rights on the private law, the debate was about the *form* of that impact, namely, whether human rights would influence the development of the private law indirectly.[46] The ancillary question

[42] Ibid.
[43] Ibid
[44] Chirwa (note 6) 29.
[45] Friedman (note 11) 10.
[46] The author suggests that it was always clear from both the Interim Constitution of 1993 and the final Constitution of 1996 that human rights were intended to shape the private law in some way or another.

was whether this would be done by influencing the development and interpretation of the law or whether human rights would be of direct horizontal application.

(a) Backdrop of interpretation

Friedman writes that the South African Constitution confirms the country's tragic past not only idealistically, but also realistically. Furthermore, it recognises that the pervasive injustices of apartheid not only have to be eliminated from public life, but also have to be rooted out of the private sphere. He contends that, seen against the backdrop of South Africa's past, the demand for horizontality is immediately apparent and that the South African Constitution adopted in 1996 expressly recognises that non-state actors are bound by constitutional rights.[47]

(b) Section 8(2) of the South African Constitution

Van Huyssteen,[48] contends that in the light of the main tenets of interpretation advanced by the Constitutional Court in *Du Plessis v De Klerk*,[49] direct horizontal application of the basic rights protected in Chapter 2 of the Constitution to private relations regulated by private law is possible.[50]

Friedman[51] points out that s 8(2) of the final Constitution removed the ambiguities about horizontality which existed under the interim constitutional order in that it states expressly that

> [a] provision of the Bill of Rights binds a natural or a juristic person.

Furthermore, he contends that there can be no doubt that s 8(2) renders rights in the Bill of Rights binding on individuals as a matter of law. The implications of

[47] Section 8 provides: '(1) The Bill of Rights applies to all law, and binds the legislature, the executive, the judiciary and all organs of the state. (2) A provision of the Bill of Rights binds a natural or a juristic person if, and to the extent that, it is applicable, taking into account the nature of the right and the nature of any duty imposed by the right. (3) When applying a provision of the Bill of Rights to a natural or juristic person in terms of subsection (2) 'a court – *(a)* in order to give effect to a right in the Bill, must apply, or if necessary develop, the common law to the extent that legislation does not give effect to that right; and *(b)* may develop rules of the common law to limit the right, provided that the limitation is in accordance with section 36(1).'

[48] LF van Huyssteen 'The horizontal application theory and its influence on freedom of agreement in the law of contract – a South African perspective' (1998) 2(2) *Law, Development and Democracy* 209–217.

[49] *Du Plessis v De Klerk* 1996 (3) SA 850 (CC) at 876–903.

[50] Whether a right is directly enforceable in terms of the Constitution and whether a new remedy may be created in the process will, of course, depend on the nature of the right and of the duty imposed by the right.

[51] Friedman (note 11) 11.

this section must not be misunderstood. To qualify this, Friedman,[52] points out that, despite the fact that s 8 unambiguously imposes human rights obligations on individuals, it also makes the obvious point that individuals do not bear those obligations in the same way as the state does, and not necessarily in respect of all rights: whether they bear duties, and the extent of those duties, depends on the nature of the right involved. Therefore, while it is difficult to imagine circumstances in which a private individual might infringe the right of another to a fair criminal trial, it is easy to see how the individual might infringe another's right to freedom of expression or to freedom from discrimination.[53]

The direct application of human rights was definitively confirmed by O'Regan J in *Khumalo v Holomisa*,[54] where the learned Judge held that the right to freedom of expression is of direct horizontal application to the law of defamation. Friedman[55] contends that, by implication and in principle, that holding also extends to the area of private law.

16.3.5 Germany

Gardbaum[56] writes that between these polar positions of the vertical and horizontal effect of constitutional rights lies a third position that has come to be known as 'indirect horizontal effect'. In essence, this intermediate or hybrid position is that, although constitutional rights apply directly only with respect to the government, they are nonetheless permitted to have some degree of indirect application to private actors.[57] According to Lewan,[58] constitutional rights have an indirect horizontal effect because they influence but do not directly govern or control private-law disputes between individuals. The courts have a duty to take constitutional values into account when adjudicating purely private litigation, but they are not bound to ensure the full compatibility of the relevant private law with constitutional rights, because the latter do not apply directly to the case. Gardbaum adds that, like the US Constitution, the German Constitution,[59] does not contain an explicit provision concerning the direct application of 'basic rights' to non-state actors. However, Art

[52] Ibid.
[53] Ibid.
[54] (2002) ZACC 12; 2002 (5) SA 401 (CC) at para 30.
[55] *Khumalo* (note 54).
[56] Gardbaum (note 7) 573.
[57] Gardbaum (note 7) 387.
[58] KM Lewan 'The significance of constitutional rights for private law: Theory and practice in West Germany' (1968) 17 *International Comparative Law Quarterly* 571, 599.
[59] Basic Law for the Republic of Germany (Grundgesetz GG), promulgated on 23 May 1949.

1(3) of the German Constitution provides expressly that 'basic rights' shall bind the Legislature, the Executive and the Judiciary as directly applicable law.

Chirwa[60] writes that the absence of an express provision led to the emergence of two main schools of thought: one school arguing that basic rights had direct horizontal application but no indirect application and the other propounding the opposite view.

(a) Doctrine of Drittwirkung

Gardbaum writes that, in a series of decisions in the 1950s, first the various federal civil courts and eventually the Federal Constitutional Court (FCC) developed the doctrine that has come to be known as *Drittwirkung*,[61] which has remained foundational ever since. In essence, he adds, this doctrine holds that, although constitutional rights bind only government organs, they apply directly to all private law and so have an indirect effect on private actors whose legal relationships are regulated by that law.

(b) Luth *case*[62]

According to Gardbaum,[63] constitutional rights, as declared by the FCC in the landmark *Luth* decision[64] of 1958, form 'an objective order of values'. He recounts that the court went on to state:

This value system, which centers upon human dignity and the free unfolding of personality within the social community, must be looked upon as a fundamental constitutional decision affecting the entire legal system ... it naturally influences private law as well; no rule of private law may conflict with it, and all such rules must be construed in accordance with its spirit.

Chirwa[65] adds that the *Luth* case is regarded as a 'linchpin of German constitutional law', especially on the issue of the horizontal effect of basic rights. He continues that the FCC, while endorsing the idea that the primary purpose of basic rights is to safeguard the liberties of the individual against interferences by public authority, states:

> It is equally true, however, that the Basic Law is not a value-neutral document. Its section on basic rights establishes an objective order of values, and this order strongly reinforces the effective power of basic rights … Thus, it is

---

[60] Chirwa (note 6) 32.

[61] Also known as the third-party effect of Constitutional Rights doctrine.

[62] BVerfGE 7, 198. I. Senate (1 BvR 400/51).

[63] Gardbaum (note 11) 403.

[64] *Luth*, BVerfGE 7, 198 (205).

[65] Chirwa (note 6) 32.

> clear that basic rights also influence [the development of] private law. Every provision of private law must be compatible with this system of values, and every such provision of private law must be compatible with this system of values, and every such provision must be interpreted in its spirit.

One can draw certain conclusions from the above. In the light of this, Chirwa[66] writes that basic rights serve the function of influencing the development of private law in Germany and, as a result, bind private actors indirectly. This influence, the court suggested, would be through those provisions of private law that contain mandatory rules of law which form part of the *ordre public*. He adds that these are rules which for reasons of the general welfare also are binding on private legal relationships and are removed from the dominion of private intent. Furthermore, this influence could also occur through the interpretation of general clauses in private law, such as 'good morals'. Chirwa writes that it was held that the duty to consider basic rights when applying and interpreting substantive rules of private law emanates from Art 1(3) of the Constitution, which states that basic rights shall bind, among other actors, the Judiciary. Therefore, if a judge fails to apply these standards and ignores the influence of constitutional law on the rules of private law, they violate objective constitutional law. Chirwa adds that where the formation of public opinion on a matter important to the general welfare is concerned, private and especially individual interests must, in principle, yield.

The above indicates that, for those countries where the constitutions do not expressly provide for it, basic rights have strong indirect horizontal application. It must be understood that it is indirect because a private person may not commence a constitutional action against another private person. Most writers suggest that one has to rely on private law to redress violations of human rights. Furthermore, as seen above, the cases brought before the Constitutional Court are argued as if a lower court had violated the right in issue rather than the private action involved in the litigation. An important point to note is that, despite these technical points, the FCC has held quite clearly that private-law courts have a duty to consider human rights if called upon to do so by the parties in the case at hand. If they fail to do so, the aggrieved person may initiate a constitutional complaint before the FCC.

16.4 CONCLUSION

The US courts, through the doctrine of state action, acknowledge that non-state actors are indirectly bound by human rights. Similarly, Canadian courts have

---

[66] Ibid.

experienced particular difficulty in maintaining the public–private distinction in applying constitutional rights.[67] However, the Canadian Supreme Court held in *Dolphin Delivery* (*supra*) that Charter rights have no application to the common law in private litigation, unless some government connection to the issues at hand can be established. In other cases, however, it held that the Charter values are relevant to private disputes. It becomes clear that this jurisprudence arguably lacks consistency because the public–private distinction in the application of human rights to private conduct is difficult to defend conceptually. Taking guidance from Chirwa, it is important to note that, despite an inclination to the conventional position, Canadian courts have acknowledged that private actors can, in certain circumstances, be bound by constitutional rights indirectly. An instance given by the writers above is where the common law is considered by the courts in the light of the Charter values when resolving private disputes. The above also demonstrates a move towards the recognition of the duty to protect human rights. The recognition of this duty might require courts to intervene to protect parties to private litigation from violations of their rights by other parties, as in the case of Germany. Compared to the position in the United States and Canada, basic rights have a wider reach in Germany: there is no need to prove state action before invoking basic rights. All laws have to be construed and interpreted against the backdrop of basic rights. Furthermore, German courts, unlike those in the United States and Canada, are bound to consider basic rights when resolving purely private disputes.[68] Furthermore, in Germany, this recognition that non-state actors are bound by constitutional rights has occurred through the doctrine of *Drittwirkung*, which posits that basic rights influence the development of private law. The cases decided by the FCC effectively establish that basic rights have a strong indirect effect on private actors. Failure by a court to consider a basic right in private litigation amounts to a dereliction of duty on the part of the court which entitles the aggrieved party to apply to the FCC to set aside the decision of that court.

The South African Constitution shares the similarities with the German Constitution. There is a distinction, though, in that the South African Constitution expressly states that non-state actors can be bound by constitutional rights, depending on the nature of the right and the duty in question. Furthermore, it expressly recognises that the Judiciary is bound by these rights. Another aspect that sets it apart from the German Constitution is that, in order to enforce a constitutional right in issue, courts are enjoined to apply the common law or develop it in order to give effect to that right. These are broad powers, and the fact that no direct constitutional claims can be brought to enforce the obligations of private actors in relation to constitutional

[67] Chirwa (note 6) 32.

[68] Ibid.

rights should not be seen as a claw-back clause on the explicit recognition in the constitution of the horizontal application of these rights.

The wording of Art 5 of the Namibian Constitution clearly and unequivocally indicates that the Bill of Rights is to be applied both vertically and horizontally. Furthermore, the Namibian case law discussed above supports this assertion that constitutional rights have not only vertical effect and application but also direct horizontal effect and application.

REFERENCES

Amoo, SK *An Introduction to Namibian Law: Materials and Cases* (UNAM Press, 2018).

Chirwa, DM 'The horizontal Application of Constitutional Rights in a Comparative Perspective' (2006) 10(2) *Law, Democracy and Development* 21–48.

Friedman, N Human Rights and the South African Common Law: Revisiting Horizontality. (University of Oxford: Centre for Socio-legal Studies, 2012).

Gardbaum, S 'The horizontal effect of constitutional Rights' (2003) 102 *Michigan Law Review* 387–459.

Grotius, H *De Jure Belli Pacis* (transl FM Kelsey) (Clarendon Press, 1652 [1925]).

Lewan, KM 'The significance of constitutional rights for private law: Theory and practice in West Germany' (1968) 17 *International Comparative Law Quarterly 571, 599.*

Locke J *Treatise on Civil Government in Two Treatises on Government* (P Laslett ed) (Cambridge University Press, 1698).

Montesquieu, C *Spirit of the Laws* Transl & edit AM Cohler, BC Miller & HM Stone (Cambridge University Press, 1750/[1989]).

Nwabueze, BO *Constitutionalism in the Emergent States* (C Hurst & Co Publishers Ltd, 1973).

Strickland, HC 'The state action doctrine and the Rehnquist court' (1991) 18 *Hastings Constitutional law Quarterly* 587.

Thorton, M 'The cartography of public and private' in M Thorton (ed) *Public and Private: Feminist Legal Debates* (Oxford University Press, 1995).

Van Huyssteen, LF 'The horizontal application theory and its influence on freedom of agreement in the law of contract – a South African perspective' (1998) 2(2) *Law, Development and Democracy* 209–217.

CASES

BVerfGE 7, 198. I. Senate (1 BvR 400/51)

Chairperson of the Immigration Selection Board v Frank & Another (SA 8 of 1999) [2001] NASC 1.

Civil Rights Cases 109 US 3 (1883)

Cooper v Aaron 1958, 358 US 14
Du Plessis v De Klerck 1996 (3) SA 850 (CC)
Government of the Republic of Namibia v Sikunda (SA 5 of 2001) [2002] NASC 1
Günther Kessl v Ministry of Lands and Resettlement & 2 Others Case Nos 27/2006 and 266/2006
Hipandulwa v Kamupunya 1993 NR (HC) 254.
Kauesa v Minister of Home Affairs (SA 5 of 1994) [1995] NASC 3
Marsh v Alabama 326 US 501
Peterson v City of Greenville, Supreme Court US 373 244 (1963)

LEGISLATION

Basic Law for the Republic of Germany (Grundgesetz.GG) promulgated on 23 May 1949
Canadian Charter of 17 April 1982
Constitution of the Republic of South Africa of 8 May 1996
Namibian Constitution of 21 March 1990
US Constitution of 17 September 1787

17

Expropriation: a comparative study of the jurisprudence of Ghana, Namibia, South Africa and Zimbabwe

Samuel K Amoo

17.1 INTRODUCTION

In a speech marking the formal opening of the Accra conference on legal education and of the Ghana Law School, the late Dr Kwame Nkrumah emphasising the need for a legal system to be identified with the ethos of society stated as follows:

There is a ringing challenge to African lawyers today. African law in Africa was declared foreign law for the convenience of colonial administrations, which found the administration of justice cumbersome by reason of the vast variations in local and tribal customs. As a result, African law had to be proved in court by experts; but no law can be foreign to its own land and country, and African lawyers, particularly those in the independent African states, must quickly find a way to reverse this judicial travesty. The law must fight its way forward in the general reconstructions of African action and thought and help to remould the generally distorted African picture in all other fields of life. This is not an easy task, for African lawyers will have to do effective research into the basic concepts of African law, clothe such concepts in living reality and give Africans a legal standard upon which African legal history in its various compartments could hopefully be built up. Law does not operate in a vacuum. Its importance must be related to the overall importance of the people, that is to say, the state.[1]

---

[1] K Nkrumah 'Ghana: Law in Africa' (1962) 6(2) *Journal of African Law* 103–112.

17.1.1 State sovereignty and development

One of the essential elements of statehood is the occupation of a territorial area within which a state's law operates. Over this area, supreme authority is vested in the state. Therefore, the concept of territorial sovereignty arises which signifies that in this territorial domain jurisdiction is exercised by the state over persons and property to the exclusion of other states. In general terms, the origin of expropriation can be traced to state sovereignty, by virtue of which the state is empowered to exercise the right of expropriation over private property in the public interest. This state sovereignty vests the control of the natural resources in the state. Under international law, the nationalisation of private property by the state, or expropriation, is allowed, but subject to the condition that nationalisation or expropriation is effected in the public interest and subject to the payment of compensation. The United Nations Resolution on Permanent Sovereignty over Natural Resources, 1962, which was adopted in the case of *Texaco v Libya*,[2] provides as follows:

> Nationalisation, expropriation or requisition shall be based on grounds or reasons of public utility, security, or the national interest which are recognized as overriding purely individual or private interests, both domestic and foreign. In such cases the owner shall be paid appropriate compensation in accordance with the rules in force in the state taking such measures in the exercise of its sovereignty and in accordance with international law. In any such case where the question of compensation gives rise to a controversy, the national jurisdiction of the state taking such measures shall be exhausted.

17.1.2 Doctrine of eminent domain

Under the doctrine of eminent domain, the state is given the power to expropriate private property for infrastructural development or public utility such as the construction of bridges railways, roads, etc. Therefore, traditionally, under the doctrine of eminent domain, the power of the state to expropriate is limited. The eminent domain concept is incorporated in municipal legislation but there is no uniformity in these pieces of legislation with regard to the purpose of expropriation. There are two models. In the first, the power to expropriate is limited to infrastructural development. In the second, however, the purpose of expropriation is formulated in an open-textured manner, generally in terms of public interest, and in most cases no precise definition is given of what constitutes public interest. What constitutes public interest, however, is not defined under international law and it is, therefore, subject to the municipal laws of a particular jurisdiction.

[2] *Texaco v Libya* 1977 53 ILR 389.

17.1.3 Procedural requirements and the protection of the rights of an individual and the determination of compensation

Since expropriation involves the deprivation of the right of an individual, it is important that procedural mechanisms and requirements are put in place to prevent any potential abuse of the power to expropriate. Mere substantive rules are not enough; procedural rules are equally important. The procedure involved in the process of expropriation therefore becomes a legal requirement in the sense that it is aimed at ensuring procedural justice, transparency, recognition of the rule of law and the protection of individual rights.

The details of the procedure may vary from jurisdiction to jurisdiction and are stipulated in the relevant legislation, but the most important criterion is that of compliance with the principles of natural justice and reciprocity. This implies that an individual whose property is to be expropriated is involved, to a certain degree, in the expropriation process and must be given a fair hearing not only with regard to the amount of compensation, but also with regard to the decision concerning expropriation. These measures are necessary to reduce the possibility of corruption, the irregular promotion of individual interests and the arbitrary use of state power.

This chapter is a comparative study of the laws in selected jurisdictions on eminent domain or public interest, the determination of compensation and the procedural mechanisms employed in the process of the exercise of the power by the state and the protection of the fundamental rights of individuals whose property is earmarked for expropriation.

17.2 DEFINITION

Expropriation may be defined as the power of the state compulsorily but lawfully, and for reasons considered to be in the public interest, to acquire ownership or some of the powers contained in ownership in respect of property to the extent that the owner is deprived of the power to use or alienate their property in the manner that they may wish to do. Expropriation constitutes a limitation on the right of ownership. Silberberg[3] defines it as follows:

> Expropriation in the strict sense means that the owner is deprived of his right of ownership in his property which then becomes vested in the state or some other public authority or corporation authorized by the state to acquire ownership of the property. In the wider sense expropriation includes

[3] DG Kleyn et al *Silberberg and Schoeman's The Law of Property* 3 ed (Butterworths, 1992) 316; MO Hinz, SK Amoo & D van Wyk (eds) *The Constitution at Work: 10 Years of Namibian Nationhood* (Unisa, 2002) 256–267.

> measures less than the deprivation of ownership, for instance temporary acquisition of the thing for a particular purpose ....

17.2.1 State sovereignty and the doctrine of eminent domain

(a) Doctrine of eminent domain under municipal laws of selected jurisdictions

One of the essential elements of statehood is the occupation of a territorial area within which state law operates. Over this area supreme authority is vested in the state. Therefore, the concept of territorial sovereignty arises which signifies that within this territorial domain jurisdiction is exercised by the state over persons and property to the exclusion of other states.[4] In general terms, the origin of expropriation can be traced to state sovereignty; by virtue of this sovereignty the state is empowered to exercise the rights of sovereignty over its natural resources (including the power to expropriate). With regard to the exercise of state sovereignty over land, the particular land-tenure system of a state is a product of the political and economic ideology of the society. The legal framework may be taken as an expression of that ideology defining the rights and duties in relation to land and the procedure for its acquisition, use and procedure.

In the context of land expropriation, however, international law prescribes certain norms. In the Namibian context, the legal authority to expropriate is provided for in Art 16(2) of the Namibian Constitution. This article empowers the state, or any competent body or organisation authorised by law, to expropriate property in the public interest subject to the payment of just compensation.

As stated earlier, the power given to the state to expropriate private property in the public interest is derived from state sovereignty, which vests the control of the natural resources in the state. Under the doctrine of eminent domain, the state is given the power to expropriate private property for infrastructural development or public utility, such as the construction of bridges railways, roads, etc.

Seervai,[5] in discussing Arts 19(1)*(f)* and 31 of the Indian Constitution which deal with the right of citizens to acquire, hold and dispose of movable and immovable property, points out that the sovereignty of the state involves three elements: the power to tax, 'police power' and the 'power of eminent domain'. The author then refers to the definition of 'police power' as

> the inherent power of a government to exercise reasonable control over person and property within its jurisdiction in the interest of general security,

[4] JG Shearer & IA Shearer *Starke's Introduction to International Law* 11 ed (Butterworths, 1994) 144.

[5] SV Manohar *Constitutional Law of India* 3 ed (Law & Justice Publishing Co, 2010).

> health, safety, morals and welfare, except where legally prohibited (as by constitutional provision).

The accepted definition for 'eminent domain' is 'the power of the sovereign to take property for public use without the owner's consent upon making just compensation'. The distinction between the exercise of the state's police power and its power of eminent domain is similar to that in South African expropriation law.[6] This distinction between the state's police power and its power of eminent domain is also found in the property jurisprudence of Namibia, specifically under Arts 16 and 100 of the Namibian Constitution. Articles 16(1) and 100 can be compared to the state's police powers and Art 16(2) to its powers of eminent domain.

Traditionally, under the doctrine of eminent domain, the power of the state to expropriate is limited. The eminent domain concept was incorporated into legislation but there was no uniformity in these pieces of legislation regarding the purpose of expropriation. There were two models. In the first, the power to expropriate was limited to infrastructural development. In the second, however, the purpose of expropriation was formulated in an open-textured manner, generally in terms of public interest, and in most cases no precise definition was provided of what constitutes public interest.

Under international law, the nationalisation of private property by the state, or expropriation, is allowed, but subject to the condition that nationalisation or expropriation is effected in the public interest and subject to the payment of compensation. What constitutes public interest, however, is not defined under international law and is therefore subject to the municipal laws of a particular jurisdiction. The UN Resolution on Permanent Sovereignty over Natural Resources, 1962, which was adopted in the case of *Texaco v Libya*,[7] provides as follows:

> Nationalisation, expropriation or requisition shall be based on grounds or reasons of public utility, security, or the national interest which are recognized as overriding purely individual or private interests, both domestic and foreign. In such cases the owner shall be paid appropriate compensation in accordance with the rules in force in the state taking such measures in the exercise of its sovereignty and in accordance with international law. In any such case where the question of compensation gives rise to a controversy, the national jurisdiction of the state taking such measures shall be exhausted.

[6] See in this regard: D Davis, H Cheadle & N Haysom *Fundamental Rights in the New Constitution: An Overview of the New Constitution and a Commentary on Chapter 3 on Fundamental Rights* (Juta & Co, 1994) 243.

[7] *Texaco* (note 2).

But, as Dunning states it:

> The relationship between the state and the development process has an important bearing on the purpose limitation in the law of eminent domain. In the past, the public purpose doctrine has meant that the state could only take property by eminent domain where that property was needed for 'public' activities. Compulsory acquisition was limited to traditional state activities – such as defence, highways, and education. But the modern African government seeking active economic development acts in all spheres. The state either engages directly in production or takes important action to enable private persons to produce and develop. When the state has a dominant and rapidly increased production, any productive purpose becomes a public purpose.[8]

(b) Namibia

As mentioned earlier, the traditional concept of public interest as contemplated in the context of eminent domain includes infrastructural development and public utility. The provisions of the Namibian Constitution relating to the power of the state to acquire private property compulsorily are provided for under Art 16.[9] The purpose limitation in the eminent domain clause is an entrenched provision: Art 100 of the Namibian Constitution vests sovereign ownership of the natural resources of Namibia in the state.[10] Article 16, however, acknowledges private ownership but empowers the state to acquire private property compulsorily in the public interest subject to the payment of just compensation. Article 16 states further that an Act of Parliament should be promulgated for the exercise of the power of expropriation.

---

[8] HC Dunning 'Law and economic development in Africa: The law of eminent domain' (1968) 68 *Columbia Law Review* 1286–1315; KL Kaarst & KS Rosenn *Law and Development in Latin America: A Case Book* (University of California Press, 1975) 1298–1299.

[9] Article 16 of the Namibian Constitution provides as follows: '(1) All persons shall have the right in any part of Namibia to acquire, own and dispose of all forms of immovable and movable property individually or in association with others and to bequeath their property to their heirs or legatees: provided that Parliament may by legislation prohibit or regulate as it deems expedient the right to acquire property by persons who are not Namibian citizens.

(2) The state or a competent body or organ authorized by law may expropriate property in the public interest subject to the payment of just compensation, in accordance with requirements and procedures to be determined by Act of Parliament.'

[10] Article 100 of the Namibian Constitution states that land, water and natural resources below and above the surface of the land and in the continental shelf and within the territorial waters and the exclusive economic zone of Namibia belong to the state if they are not otherwise lawfully owned.

The article does not define 'public interest'; therefore, the determination and definition of 'public interest' lie within the subjective jurisdiction of the state. It is a legal requirement that falls within the sphere of political definition.

Since the Constitution leaves the definition of public interest undefined and open-textured, the attempts at a definition are to be found in particular pieces of legislation. Currently in Namibia, depending on the relevant portfolio, pieces of legislation have been promulgated to empower the state or an appropriate authority to expropriate private property for various purposes.

In the context of the constitutional and political history of Namibia, land resettlement and agrarian reform will legitimately come within the definition of public interest. It is in this context that one can see the justification for the promulgation of the Agricultural (Commercial) Land Reform Act 6 of 1995. In this Act, public interest has been defined to include agricultural and resettlement purposes in the context of the government's land-reform and poverty-alleviation programme.

The purpose of the Act is to provide for the acquisition of agricultural land by the state for the purpose of land reform and for the allocation of such land to Namibian citizens who do not own or otherwise have the use of any or of adequate agricultural land. The Agricultural (Commercial) Land Reform Act 6 of 1995 regulates the purchase and redistribution of privately owned farms. The relevant sections of the Act in respect of acquiring agricultural land and the expropriation of such land are s 14, which provides for the purchase of agricultural land by the state on a willing buyer, willing seller basis, and s 20, which provides for the expropriation of such land and the requirements for that. The Act also provides for the appointment, composition, powers and duties of the Land Reform Advisory Commission. The technical commission on commercial farm land was mandated to investigate the entire land-tenure situation in Namibia and to make recommendations as far as *absentee foreigners* are concerned.

The Act was promulgated as the legislative tool for the implementation of the government's land-reform programme. In the context of legislative restrictions on the right of ownership the Act imposes dual restrictions. The first type of restriction entails a pre-emptive right, the so-called willing buyer, willing seller option granted to the minister, in terms of s 17(3). The second type of restriction arises from the minister's power to expropriate agricultural land for the purposes of land reform, resettlement of the landless and poverty alleviation in terms of s 14, but subject to the requirements and procedures provided in ss 14 and 20. These requirements include the payment of compensation and the public interest provision.

The Act gives the minister two options: the power to acquire land (1) either on the basis of the willing buyer, willing seller option or (2) by compulsory acquisition. Section 14 of the Act grants the minister the general authority to acquire, out of moneys appropriated by parliament for that purpose, agricultural land for the implementation of land reform and resettlement policies. It is therefore clear that expropriation is not the only option; it is the last option.[11] Section 14(2) provides as follows:

The Minister shall under this subsection acquire:

(a) any agricultural land offered for sale to the Minister in terms of section 17(4) whether or not the offer is subsequently withdrawn;
(b) any agricultural land which has been acquired by a foreign national, or by a nominee owner on behalf of or in the interest or in the interest of a foreign national, in contravention of section 58 or 59; or
(c) any agricultural land which the minister considers to be appropriate for the purposes contemplated in that subsection classified as under-utilized and in terms of subsection (3);
(d) any agricultural land or portion or portions of such land classified as excessive land in terms of subsection (3); or
(e) any agricultural land acquired by a foreign national, or by a nominee owner on behalf or in the interest of a foreign national, in contravention of section 58 or 59.

These provisions have been amended by s 2*(b)* of Act 14 of 2003 as follows:

(1) The Minister may under subsection (1) acquire –
(2) *(a)* any agricultural land offered for sale to the Minister in terms of section 17(4), whether or not the offer is subsequently withdrawn;
(b) any agricultural land which has been acquired by a foreign national, or by a nominee owner on behalf or in the interest of a foreign national, in contravention of section 58 or 59; or
(c) any agricultural land which the Minister considers to be appropriate for the purposes contemplated in that subsection.

These requirements appear to accord with international standards. In *Texaco v Libya*[12] it was held that the nationalisation of property by the state or expropriation is allowed, but subject to the condition that nationalisation or expropriation is implemented in the public interest, subject to the payment of just compensation. Similar provisions are to be found in the 1962 UN General Assembly Resolution on Permanent Sovereignty over Natural Resources, which states inter alia that expropriation must be based on grounds for or reasons of public utility, security

[11] See s 20(1) of the Agricultural (Commercial) Land Reform Act 6 of 1995.
[12] *Texaco* (note 2).

or the national interest which are recognised as overriding purely individual and private interests.

The state's power to expropriate agricultural land which is exercised by the minister under the Act to advance the government's land-reform and poverty-alleviation programmes was considered by the court in *Gunther Kessl v Ministry of Lands and Resettlement & Others*,[13] which was described as a 'test case' by Muller J. In this case, the applicants applied for an order to review and set aside the decision of the Ministry of Lands and Resettlement to expropriate certain farms belonging to the applicants in the Otjozondjupa Region of the Republic of Namibia. The applicants initially conceded that the Government of the Republic of Namibia has the right to expropriate farms under certain conditions and therefore only two main issues needed to be considered by the court. First, the question whether the *audi alteram partem* principle was relevant in expropriation cases such as those before the court and, second, whether the procedure that was followed in all these three cases before the court was in conformity with the law.

As stated earlier, since the Act in principle imposes restrictions on the constitutional right of ownership, the court reiterated the principle that an Act or statute which provides for actions that may infringe fundamental rights should be interpreted restrictively in such a manner as to place the least possible burden on subjects or to restrict their rights as little as possible. The rights of the public should be properly balanced against those of subjects by adhering to the requirement of 'public interest' in Art 16(2) and the provisions of s 14 of the Act.

On the issue of the relevance of the *audi alteram partem* principle in expropriation cases such as those under consideration, the court held that Art 16(2) is not a self-contained or 'walled-in' provision that excludes the application of the *audi alteram partem*[14] principle, which was therefore held to be applicable. In the context of the Act, the exercise of the powers of expropriation granted to the minister was therefore subject to the provisions of Art 18 of the Namibian Constitution and the common-law grounds for review of administrative discretion.[15] In terms of Art 18 the minister may act only within the limits of their statutory discretion and should apply their mind to the requirements of the enabling Act. In order to expropriate land, it must be done within the provisions of the Act and involves a double-barrelled process: first, in terms of s 14 and then in terms of s 20. This provision is peremptory and must be complied with *before* the minister takes a decision. Furthermore, the court held that under the provisions of s 20(6) the commission is

[13] *Gunther Kessl v Ministry of Lands and Resettlement & Others* 2008 (1) NR 167 (HC).

[14] The decision in *West Air Aviation & Others v Airports Company Limited & Another* 2001 NR 256 (HC) in respect of the applicability of the *audi alteram partem* principle was confirmed.

[15] *Immigration Selection Board v Frank* 2001 NR 107 (SC).

obliged to consider the interests of the persons employed and lawfully residing on the land and the families of such persons residing with them. This factor becomes a variable in the determination of what constitutes public interest.[16]

The Land Reform Advisory Commission established under s 2 of the Act is mandated to make recommendations to the minister or advise the minister in relation to any power conferred upon the minster by the Act. The court held that such consultation between the minister and the commission was a prerequisite before embarking upon the s 20 expropriation process, and that such consultation should take place at the s 14 stage when a determination whether there was a willing buyer and a willing seller must be made and *before* the minister decides to purchase a particular farm. The requirements of this provision go beyond a mere consultation; they demand genuine consultation.

Under the authority granted by these provisions and other relevant laws, the minister, on behalf of the government has to date acquired 461 000 hectares of land, including 22 605 hectares which were donated. Total government expenditure has been N$52 451 355,79 for the purchase of 79 farms and it must be emphasised that all of these farms were purchased on a willing buyer, willing seller basis. During the National Development Plan 1 (NDP1) the government spent N$45 921 168,79 and a total number of 22 083 people were resettled. It is, however, now estimated that about 34 000 Namibians have been settled through the government's resettlement programme,[17] and the ministry intends acquiring an additional 360 000 hectares of land in the next five years and approximately 1 080 people will be resettled.

The criteria used by the ministry for selecting people to be resettled are embodied in the Government Resettlement Policy. This policy places people to be resettled into three categories. The first group consists of Bushmen and any landless formerly disadvantaged Namibians; the second group consists of landless livestock owners, and the third group comprises people with an income but who do not own any land. The resettlement programme aims at improving the living standards of previously disadvantaged Namibians. Therefore, the resettlement schemes are not restricted to the provision of land for agrarian purposes only: the resettlement schemes have a broader social agenda. They include the provision of training facilities and housing. People who are resettled hold the land under leasehold titles of 99 years.

The power to expropriate privately owned farms is the other option granted to the ministry by the Act. Under s 20,[18] in terms of which the minister, acting on the

[16] See also *Aonin Fishing (Pty) v Ministry of Fisheries and Marine Resources* 1998 NR 47.

[17] As stated in *The Namibian*, 30 August 2000.

[18] Section 20 provides as follows: '(1) Where the Minister decides to acquire any property for the purposes of section 14(1) and the Minister, acting on the recommendation of the Commission, and the owner of such property are unable to negotiate the sale of such property by mutual

recommendation of the commission, and the owner of the property are unable to negotiate the sale of the property by mutual agreement, the ministry may provide for the condition that the exercise of the power to expropriate be subject to the payment of compensation.

(c) Ghana

The Ghanaian Constitution guarantees the right to property and ownership of property. Under Art 18(1) every person has the right to own property either alone or in association with others. Article 20(1) provides that no property of any description or interest in or right over any property shall be compulsorily taken possession of or acquired by the state unless the following conditions are satisfied:

(a) The taking of the possession or acquisition is necessary in the interest of defence, public safety, public order public morality public health town and country planning or the development or utilization of property in such a manner as to promote the public benefit; and
(b) The necessity for the acquisition is clearly stated and is such as to provide reasonable justification for causing any hardship that may result to any person who has an interest in or right over the property.

The Constitution under subsec 2 mandates that compulsory acquisition of property by the state shall be made only under a law which makes provision for the prompt payment of fair and adequate compensation and a right of access to the High Court by any person who has an interest in or a right over the property, whether direct or on appeal from any other authority, for the determination of their interest or right and the amount of compensation to which they are entitled. The Constitution furthermore places an obligation on the state by prescribing that where a compulsory acquisition duly authorised by the state results in the displacement of any inhabitants, the state is under an obligation to provide suitable alternative land to the affected inhabitants with due regard for their economic well-being and social and cultural values. The Constitution clearly provides that any property which is compulsorily acquired in the public interest shall be used only in the public interest for which it was acquired. Where the property is not used in the public interest, the affected individual or owner of the property immediately before the compulsory acquisition shall be given the first option for acquiring the property. Upon such

agreement, or the whereabouts of the owner of such property cannot be ascertained after diligent inquiry, the Minister may, subject to the payment of compensation in accordance with provisions of this Act, expropriate such property for such purpose.'

re-acquisition they shall refund the whole or part of the compensation paid to them or such other amount as is commensurate with the value of the property at the time of the re-acquisition.

(d) South Africa

The South African Constitution contains grounds for expropriation which are also more elaborate and specific, in comparison to the Namibian provisions, and include the traditional ground of eminent domain. The South African Constitution's s 25(2)*(a)* states that property may be expropriated for a public purpose or in the interest of the public and its s 25(4)*(a)* explains that the public interest includes the nation's commitment to land reform to bring about equitable access to all South Africa's natural resources. The public purpose requirement can be interpreted in at least three different ways:

- very narrowly to restrict expropriations to actual public use;
- slightly wider to include almost any public benefits that exceed actual public use; or
- very widely to include almost any purpose that is vaguely beneficial to the public weal.

The public purpose requirement in s 25(2) has a double function: to control the justification and authority for expropriations in the way that constitutional property clauses usually do; and, further, to ensure that this normal function of the property clause does not impede or frustrate expropriations that form part of land and other similar reforms to which the Constitution commits itself.[19]

The South African constitutional provision gives the South African government the power to acquire land for land resettlement and reform. Apart from the constitutional provisions pertaining to compensation, the Restriction of Land Rights Act 22 of 1994 provides for the restitution of rights to land for persons or communities dispossessed of such rights after 19 June 1913 as a result of past racially discriminatory laws or practices. For the purpose of claiming restitution, this Act also established the Land Claims Court.

(e) Zambia

In Zambia, as in Namibia, the colonial government divided land into Crown land, trust and native reserves. The law applicable to state land was the English land law; all land in the reserves and trust areas was held under customary land law. This division was effected by the Northern Rhodesia Order in Council of 1924. This proclamation was followed by the enactment of the Public Lands Acquisition

[19] AJ Van der Walt 'Constitutional property law' (2011) 1 *Annual Survey of South African Law* 245–292.

Ordinance of 1929, which applied only to state land. Under s 53 of this Ordinance of 1929, the governor was empowered

> to acquire any lands required for any public purpose for an estate in fee simple, or for a term of years as he may think proper, paying such consideration or compensation as may be agreed upon or determined under the provisions of the Ordinance.[20]

After independence, however, the Zambian government felt that the then existing legislation relating to land had certain inadequacies located specifically in the provisions of Clause 18 of the Constitution. Clause 18 provided for compensation in the event of expropriation, but compensation had to be paid and certain conditions had to be satisfied. The circumstances under which compulsory acquisition could be allowed fell generally within the scope of the orthodox definition of the right of eminent domain. These circumstances were substantially identical to those given under s 53 of the Northern Rhodesia Public Lands Acquisition Ordinance of 1929, which after independence became known as the Public Lands Acquisition Act.

In addition to these conditions, it was provided that the government had to pay adequate compensation immediately after expropriation and that provision had to be made for the guarantee of the remittance of money outside the country free from any deduction, charge or tax made or levied in respect of its remission. This clause was entrenched and could be repealed only by a referendum. In 1969 a referendum was held to amend Clause 18 of the independence Constitution. It was argued that since the existing laws of expropriation embodied in Clause 18 of the Constitution and the Public Lands Acquisition Act were designed to serve the economic interests of the colonial government and were therefore obsolete as a result of the shift in emphasis of economic planning towards rapid development and state participation, the existing laws of expropriation had to be repealed.

The government made it an objective of the new Public Lands Acquisition Act[21] to eliminate powerful landlords, on the one hand, and tenants and workers, on the other. The Act denied the right of compensation in respect of undeveloped or unused land except for unexhausted improvements. But even for unexhausted

[20] The definition of 'public purpose' included the following: 'Any land (1) for the exclusive use of the Government or Federal Government or for general public use; (2) for or in connection with sanitary improvements of any kind including reclamations; (3) for or in connection with the laying out of any new municipality, township in Government station or the extension or improvements of any existing municipality, township or Government station; (4) for obtaining control over land contiguous to, or required for or in connection with any port, airport, railways, roads, or other public works of convenience, constructed or about to be undertaken by the Government or Federal Government.'

[21] Public Lands Acquisition Act cap 296 of the Laws of Zambia.

improvements no compensation was payable if the land was unused land belonging to an absentee landowner. In addition, it is interesting to note that the power to acquire land was not restricted only to cases where it was needed for a public purpose. In fact, 'public purpose' was eliminated from the Act. Section 3 of the Act reads as follows:

> Subject to the provisions of the Act, the President may, whenever he is of the opinion that it is desirable or expedient in the interest of the Republic so to do, compulsorily acquire any property of any description ....

This provision was more liberal than the equivalent provision of the earlier Act. For 'public purpose' the latter Act substitutes 'interest of the Republic',[22] which is not defined in the Act and which is determined only at the discretion of the President.

(f) Zimbabwe

In Zimbabwe, the land question was one of the issues that had to be settled at the Lancaster House Conference. The Lancaster House Constitution that brought an end to colonial rule in Rhodesia had under Part III an enshrined provision that protected fundamental rights to private property and restricted the right of the state to compulsorily acquire land for agriculture or resettlement. Any compulsory acquisition had to be accompanied by prompt and adequate compensation[23] and it was negotiated and agreed that the British government had to make funds available for that purpose. The circumstances under which the state could compulsorily acquire property in the public interest were clearly defined in the Constitution. Property could not be acquired compulsorily except under the authority of law and only after reasonable notice of the intention to acquire the property has been given to any person owning the property or who would be affected by such acquisition.[24] The purposes for which land could be compulsorily acquired included the interests of defence, public safety, public morality, public health and town and country planning. Land acquired in this manner should be used for a purpose beneficial to the public generally or a section of it. The provision specified further that under-used land could be acquired only for the settlement of land for agricultural purposes.[25] The entrenched provision, including the provision that reserved 20 seats for whites, could not be amended before ten years after the implementation of the Constitution.

---

[22] Section 3.

[23] See s 11*(c)* of the Constitution of Zimbabwe Amendment Act 20 of 2013.

[24] See s 16(1)*(a)* and also L Tshuma & K Makamure *Land Policy in Zimbabwe: The Legal Framework* (Harare, 1990).

[25] See s 16(1)*(b)* of the Public Lands Acquisition Act cap 296 of the Laws of Zambia.

In 1990 the Constitution, including s 16, was amended to give the state more power to remove some of the restrictive provisions and to give it more leverage in its authority to acquire property compulsorily for agricultural and resettlement purposes. This amendment affected the requirements relating to the payment of compensation. The amendment required that compensation be paid, but that the compensation had to be 'fair' and be made available 'within a reasonable time'. The amendment implied that 'fair compensation' is necessarily less than adequate compensation, which is market-related, and that the state would be in a better position to acquire land since it would not be compelled to pay 'promptly' but within a 'reasonable time'.

The amendment was followed by the Lands Acquisition Act of 1992. Section 3 of the Act empowers the President to acquire any land compulsorily where:

(1) the acquisition is reasonably necessary in the interest of the defence, public safety, town and country planning or the utilization for that or any other property for a purpose beneficial to the public generally or to any section of the public;
(2) any rural land where the acquisition is reasonably necessary for the utilization of that purpose or any other land –

    (i) for resettlement for agriculture or other purpose; or
    (ii) for purpose of land reorganization; and
    (iii) for the relocation of persons dispossessed in consequence of the utilization of land for a purpose referred in subparagraph (i) and (ii).

The new Lands Acquisition Act provided for compensation, but for fair compensation within a reasonable time, and it also brought in the concept of deprivation.[26] After the referendum that rejected the draft constitution, the constitutional provisions relating to land acquisition were amended to include some of the provisions of the draft constitution.[27] The amended law makes provision for compensation, but compensation

[26] In the case of *Davies v Minister of Lands, Agriculture and Water Development* 1996 (9) BCLR 1209 (ZS) the Supreme Court of Zimbabwe, in its interpretation of s 11(*c*) of the Land Acquisition Act, chap 20: 10 (Zimbabwe), drew a distinction between an acquisition and deprivation and held that s 11(*c*) did not afford protection against deprivation of property by the state where the act of deprivation fell short of compulsory acquisition or expropriation. It held further that no compensation was required for a deprivation of rights in property and that it was not every deprivation which amounted to a compulsory acquisition of property. Nor did every deprivation require that compensation be paid.

[27] See s 3 of the Constitution of Zimbabwe Amendment Act 16 of 2000.

is not automatic. It gives the government the power to acquire agricultural land compulsorily for the resettlement of people in accordance with the programme of land reform. This position is informed by the principles that are also reiterated in the 2013 Constitution,[28] with due regard to the fact that the people of Zimbabwe, as a consequence of colonialism, were unjustifiably dispossessed of their land and other resources without compensation and consequently took up arms to regain their land and political sovereignty. Accordingly, the people of Zimbabwe must be enabled to reassert their rights and gain ownership of their land. The Act[29] therefore imposes on the former colonial power the obligation to pay compensation for agricultural land compulsorily acquired for resettlement through a fund established for this purpose. Therefore, if the former colonial power fails to pay compensation through such fund, the government of Zimbabwe has no obligation to pay compensation for agricultural land compulsorily acquired for resettlement. Furthermore, the amended provision states that even where compensation is to be paid, the following factors must be considered in the assessment of any compensation that may be payable:

(a) the history of the ownership, use and occupation of the land;
(b) the price paid for the land when it was last acquired;
(c) the cost or value of improvements on the land;
(d) the current use to which the land and any improvements on it are being put;
(e) any investment which the state or the acquiring authority may have made which improved or enhanced the value of the land and any improvements on it;
(f) the resources available to the acquiring authority in implementing the programme of land reform;[30]
(g) any financial constraints that necessitate the payment of compensation in installments over a period of time; and
(h) any other relevant factor that may be specified in an Act of Parliament.[31]

In 2005 the Constitutional Amendment Act 17 was promulgated. It introduced further amendments to the Constitution. First, the right of persons aggrieved by the government's land policy to have recourse to the courts when their land had been acquired under s 18 of the Constitution was removed. It effectively ousted judicial jurisdiction from determining land-acquisition disputes. Second, two other clauses legitimised previous and current land acquisition without compensation. These were *ex post facto* provisions which were to apply retrospectively in order to accord

[28] Article 72(7) of the Constitution of Zimbabwe Amendment Act 20 of 2013.

[29] See s 16(A) as amended by s 3 of the Constitution of Zimbabwe Amendment Act 16 of 2000.

[30] [2008] SADCT 2.

[31] Section 16(A)(2) of the Constitution of Zimbabwe as amended by the Constitution of Zimbabwe Amendment Act 16 of 2000.

legality to illegally acquired and/or occupied farms. The changes were designed to legitimise the activities during the Fast Track Land Reform Programme (FTLRP), which were then illegal under law. These amendments were challenged before the regional court, the Southern African Development Community Tribunal (SADC Tribunal). In the case of *Mike Campbell (Pyt) Ltd et al v Republic of Zimbabwe* the tribunal ruled that the white farmers had been racially discriminated against in the execution of the land-reform programme and that this conduct by the Government of the Republic of Zimbabwe was in violation of SADC principles. It also ruled that the farmers were entitled to compensation for the loss of their land. However, the Zimbabwean government refused to pay compensation for the land, arguing that the obligation to pay compensation to the farmers rested on the British government in its capacity as the former colonial power.[32]

The property provisions of the 2013 Constitution[33] separated property rights strictly so-called from agricultural land.[34] Whereas property rights are couched in traditional terms that are protected and justiciable, the provisions relating to agricultural land do not have such provisions. The provisions governing property rights hold that no person may be compulsorily deprived of their property rights unless (1) they are given reasonable notice; (2) they are paid fair and adequate compensation, and (3) the acquiring authority applies to the courts to confirm the acquisition if it is contested. If the court does not confirm the acquisition, a person may apply to the court for the prompt return of their property. The provisions also allow a person to challenge in a court of law the legality of the acquisition and the amount of compensation and also to ask for prompt compensation.[35] These rights do not apply to agricultural land.[36] Under the provisions of s 72, the state may acquire agricultural land for a public purpose, which includes resettlement. As the acquiring authority, the state must publish a notice in the *Gazette* identifying the land that is being compulsorily acquired. It also provides that the state will acquire full title in the land with effect from the date of publication of the notice. The existing title deed will be endorsed and cancelled immediately, vesting the title to the land in the state. The mere publication of the notice completes the process of acquisition. As compared to the constitutions of other jurisdictions discussed above, persons aggrieved by the compulsory acquisition are not entitled to compensation. Compensation is payable only for improvements. There is no right of access to the courts for the determination of any question relating to acquisition, except

[32] See s 16A of the Constitution of Zimbabwe and s 72(7) of the Constitution of Zimbabwe Amendment Act 20 of 2013.

[33] Constitution of Zimbabwe Amendment Act 20 of 2013.

[34] Sections 71 and 72.

[35] See s 71 in the Appendix at the end of this chapter.

[36] See s 72 in the Appendix at the end of this chapter.

for compensation for improvements. The acquisition cannot be challenged on the ground that it was discriminatory. These provisions therefore grant constitutional legitimacy to the provisions of the previous constitution that were struck down by the SADC Tribunal for being discriminatory and in violation of international norms and the rule of law.

17.3 CONSEQUENCES OF EXPROPRIATION AND LAND RESETTLEMENT

17.3.1 Protection of individual rights: procedural requirements and determination of compensation

(a) Procedural requirements and protection of individual rights

The individual's right to own property and the protection of that right are recognised as fundamental rights of the individual under international law. This right can be found in most constitutions and international conventions. Article 17 of the Universal Declaration of 1948 provides that everyone has the right to own property alone as well as in association with others; and no one may be arbitrarily deprived of property. In terms of Art 5*(d)*(v) of the International Convention on the Elimination of all Forms of Racial Discrimination, state parties undertake to eliminate racial discrimination in all forms and to guarantee the right of everyone to own property either alone or in association with others.[37] The protection of this right is contained in various provisions, such as substantive-law provisions, provisions for the payment of compensation, procedural requirements to guarantee the application of the rules of administrative justice in the exercise of the powers of expropriation, and procedural mechanisms meant to safeguard against the abuse of the power to expropriate.

Since this right is recognised as a fundamental right in most jurisdictions, it is enshrined in and guaranteed by the Constitution; and therefore the power to deprive an individual of this right can be granted by the law only on justifiable grounds. It is for this reason that in earlier constitutions the right to expropriate could be justified only on grounds of public utility and was subjected to the purpose limitation in the eminent domain clause. The determination of what constitutes public utility is a political one and therefore the individual might not be competent to make any pronouncement on the validity of that decision. But the individual must be involved in the process of deciding what property must be subject to expropriation – for

[37] See also Art 1 of the First Protocol to the European Convention for the Protection of Human Rights and Fundamental Freedoms of 1950; Art 23 of the American Declaration of the Rights and Duties of Man of 1948; Art 21 of the American Convention on Human Rights of 1969, and Art 14 of the African Charter on Human and People's Rights of 1981.

example, they must be given the opportunity to suggest alternative land equally suitable for expropriation under the public utility justification.

In most southern African countries which achieved independence through liberation wars it is common knowledge that colonial land policies and land-tenure systems constituted the major causes of the liberation struggles. Therefore, at the time of independence governments had to embark on land-reform and resettlement programmes to correct the injustices of the past. In the context of the laws of expropriation the traditional public utility rationale for expropriation was found wanting. The orthodox grounds for expropriation had accordingly to be expanded to accommodate resettlement and agrarian reform. In Namibia, for example, land resettlement and agrarian reform have come under the domain of public interest in the context of the provision of Art 16 and the government can therefore exercise the powers of expropriation for its resettlement and agrarian reform schemes. Confronted with such onerous provisions justifying the deprivation of their rights, an individual can be assured of equity and justice only if the right to compensation is assured.

Since expropriation involves the deprivation of the right of the individual, it is important that procedural mechanisms and requirements are put in place to prevent any potential abuse of the power to expropriate. Mere substantive rules are not enough; procedural rules are equally important. The procedure involved in the process of expropriation therefore becomes a legal requirement in the sense that it is aimed at ensuring procedural justice, transparency, recognition of the rule of law and the protection of individual rights.

The details of the procedure may vary from jurisdiction to jurisdiction and may be stipulated in the relevant legislation, but the most important criterion is that of compliance with the principles of natural justice and reciprocity. For example, this implies that the individual whose property is to be expropriated is involved, to a certain extent, in the expropriation process and given a fair hearing not only with regard to the amount of compensation, but also with regard to the decision concerning expropriation as a fair hearing is necessary to reduce the possibility of corruption, the irregular promotion of individual interests and the arbitrary use of state power. Article 16(2) of the Namibian Constitution clearly stipulates that the power to expropriate can be exercised only following the promulgation of an Act of Parliament. Therefore, the power becomes statutory and discretionary in nature and must be exercised subject to the provisions of Art 18 of the Namibian Constitution, which enjoins administrative officials to comply with the principles of natural justice in the execution of administrative and executive powers. This was confirmed in *Gunther Kessl & Others v Ministry of Lands and Resettlement*[38] by Muller J, where the learned judge held that Art 16 of the Namibian Constitution

[38] See note 37.

does not stand alone. This means, therefore, that the requirements of Art 18 are applicable to the exercise of the powers of expropriation granted to the minister by the Agricultural (Commercial) Land Reform Act 6 of 1995 and that the conduct of the administrative official, the minister, must be both fair and reasonable and legitimate. The ultimate objective is to ensure that the power to expropriate is not abused. These procedural rules are meant to ensure that in the exercise of the power of expropriation the individual is protected through the due process of law. Under the Namibian Constitution, the exercise of this power will be subjected to the provisions of Art 18 of the Constitution, which demand the application of the principles of natural justice. The Agricultural (Commercial) Land Reform Act has provisions to that effect. It also contains provisions to ensure that the power to expropriate is not concentrated in the hands of only one person. The power is exercised in consultation with the Land Reform Advisory Commission and, as mentioned previously, the determination of the amount of compensation, in the event of a disagreement, is subject to the jurisdiction of the Lands Tribunal, which was established under s 63 of the Act.

The two requirements of Art 18 are, first, that the principle of natural justice must be satisfied in order to ensure some involvement of the owner whose property is to be considered for expropriation and, second, that the owner must be given a fair hearing. This should apply not only in the context of assessing the amount of compensation, but also in the decision to expropriate the property concerned. As stated by Muller J in *Gunther Kessl & Others v Ministry of Lands and Resettlement*,[39] before the minister can take a decision to expropriate, they are duty-bound to apply the principle of *audi alteram partem*. This implies that they must afford the landowner an opportunity to be heard in order to persuade them that they should not take the decision to expropriate their property. Subjecting the Executive's power of expropriation to the concept of reciprocity implies the justifiability of rights and judicial review of the powers of expropriation.

(b) General application of limitation provisions

Since expropriation amounts to deprivation of one of the fundamental rights provided for by Chapter 3 of the Namibian Constitution (Art 16(1)), any legislation purporting to vest the power of expropriation in the state or an organ of state must be of general application in compliance with the provisions of Art 22 of the Namibian Constitution. In terms of Art 22, the limitation of any fundamental right or freedom is lawful only if it is provided for in legislation and if the limitation is generally applicable and not aimed at a particular individual. The latter two

[39] See note 37.

requirements were confirmed in the case of *Cultura 2000 & Another v Government of the Republic of Namibia & Others*[40] with regard to Art 22(*a*).

(c) Role of the Judiciary

Property rights, land reform and the protection of individual rights represent prototypical or classic illustrations of the relationship between the three branches of government and, more specifically, the extent to which the Judiciary can fetter executive powers or the powers of government. These constitutional provisions discussed above can be meaningful and represent a protection of the rights of the individual only where there is a strong, impartial and independent Judiciary that can restrain the exercise of legislative and executive powers. This was one of the concerns of the Lancaster House Conference.

The Namibian Judiciary in its relatively short span of existence has demonstrated its resolve to maintain its independence of the other branches of government in interpreting the Constitution in a purposive manner in order to uphold the fundamental principles of the Constitution, especially in the area of property rights and land reform. The same can be said of the South African Judiciary, especially the Constitutional Court. The history of the post-independence Zimbabwean Judiciary demonstrates an example of a Judiciary that can be induced to transform itself from being a liberal protector of human rights to one that is distinctly pro-government in so far as the land-reform exercise is concerned (the post-2000 Supreme Court starting from the externally induced resignation of Chief Justice Gubbay).

17.3.2 Determination of compensation

Expropriation also involves the deprivation of the rights of the individual and, more especially, their entitlements of ownership. Consequently, therefore, both in law and on grounds of equity, an individual must be compensated for their loss. This is a principle recognised under international law, as stated in the case of *Texaco v Libya*.[41] Most municipal laws authorising the state to expropriate private property incorporate the right to compensation in the relevant laws. However, the contentious issue has been the determination of the amount of compensation. Under international law, compensation has to be prompt, adequate and effective. This standard is commonly referred to as the Hull doctrine, which is accredited to

[40] *Cultura 2000 & Another v Government of the Republic of Namibia & Others* 1992 NR 110 (HC); 1993 NR 328 (SC); 1993 (2) SA 12 (NHC). This principle was also affirmed in the case of *Gunther Kessl v Ministry of Lands and Resettlement & Others* 2008 (1) NR 167.

[41] *Gunther Kessl* (note 40).

and named after the United States Secretary of State, Cordell Hull, who in reliance on the prevailing international norm, wrote his famous letter to the Mexican government asking Mexico for 'prompt, adequate and effective compensation for the expropriated land of United States nationals'. The Hull formula has been translated to mean that compensation should be paid in a currency that can be readily used, reflecting the full value of the expropriated property and incorporating future lost profits and interest, if payment is not effected within a reasonable time after expropriation. This criterion does not, however, find automatic translation and incorporation into the provisions of municipal legislation, which falls under the domain and jurisdiction of the government of the day.

In Namibia, s 25 of the Agricultural (Commercial) Land Reform Act 5 of 1995 provides for variables to be taken into consideration when determining compensation. These include the current value of the property and any improvements made by the state.

Section 25(1) of the South African Constitution of 1996 gives and protects the rights of the individual to own property. However, s 25(2) empowers the state to expropriate property provided that it is done:

- in terms of a law of general application;
- for a public purpose or in the public interest, and
- subject to compensation determined in the prescribed manner.

The spirit of these provisions is reflected by s 25(3) of the Constitution, in terms of which the compensation and the time and manner of payment must be just and equitable and must reflect an equitable balance between the public interest and the interest of those individuals affected by the expropriation. However, notwithstanding this spirit of the compensation provision, s 25(3) specifically provides that when compensation is being assessed, regard must be had to all the relevant circumstances, including:

- the current use of the property;
- the history of the acquisition and use of the property;
- the market value of the property;
- the extent of direct state investment and subsidy in the acquisition and beneficial capital improvement of the property, and
- the purpose of the expropriation.

The significance of these factors in the Zimbabwean and South African Constitutions is that in assessing the amount of compensation the court will not only have to be guided by the market value of the property, but will have to take these specified factors into consideration.

The payment of compensation is one of the requirements in customary international law for the validity of the power to expropriate private property by a sovereign state. This right to expropriate is within the competence of a sovereign state, but the compensation requirement imposes a legal restriction on this competence.[42] In *Texaco v Libya*[43] the requirement that was adopted as a rule of public international law is that the expropriating sovereign state must pay 'prompt, adequate and effective compensation'. The 1962 Resolution on Permanent Sovereignty over Natural Resources also makes provision for the payment of compensation. It provides that in a case of expropriation, 'the owner shall be paid appropriate compensation.'

In *Texaco v Libya*[44] it was stated further that the standard of 'appropriate compensation' in the resolution 'codifies positive principles', but there is no one uniform standard for the quantum of compensation under municipal law. The expropriation laws of Zambia, Zimbabwe, Namibia and South Africa all make provision for the payment of compensation. In the case of Zambia, the government was required to pay 'adequate compensation' and in the case of Zimbabwe, the Lancaster House Constitution provided for the payment of 'prompt and adequate' compensation. This was amended to 'fair compensation', but only for improvements. The South African Constitution makes provision for the payment of 'just and equitable' compensation and stipulates the factors[45] that must be considered in the assessment of compensation. Article 16(2) of the Namibian Constitution inter alia provides that the state may expropriate property 'subject to the payment of just compensation'. One is therefore obliged to conclude that the amount of compensation is a political decision that is within the competence of the government of the day. If this is accepted as a valid conclusion, this matter must be justiciable – the jurisdiction of the courts in this matter must not be ousted.

The Namibian Agricultural (Commercial) Land Reform Act 6 of 1995[46] empowers the minister, upon the recommendation of the Land Reform Advisory Commission, to offer the owner concerned, in the appropriation notice, the amount of compensation for the property which is being expropriated. In assessing the amount of compensation, the Act stipulates under s 25(5)*(a)* and *(b)* that the

---

[42] In some jurisdictions, such as Zimbabwe, South Africa and the United States, the distinction is drawn between expropriation of property and deprivation of property. The former involves the payment of compensation, but deprivation has been held not to involve the payment of compensation. In the United States, expropriation falls under eminent domain and deprivation is known as 'police power'.

[43] *Texaco* (note 2).

[44] *Texaco* (note 2).

[45] See s 25(1), (2) and (3) of the South African Constitution.

[46] See ss 23 and 25.

minister must take into consideration the enhancement of the value of the property in consequence of its use and the improvements made after the date of notice on or to the property in question, provided that the amount does not exceed the aggregate of the amount which the land would have realised if sold on the date of notice in an open market by a willing seller to a willing buyer and an amount to compensate any actual financial loss caused by the expropriation.[47] The Act also provides that if the parties fail to reach an agreement regarding the amount of compensation, compensation is to be determined by the Lands Tribunal on the application of any party and resettlement is to be effected by arbitration in terms of the Arbitration Act 42 of 1965.[48] The Act is silent on the individual's right of appeal to the courts, but it does not specifically oust this right either.

17.3.3 Social and economic consequences of expropriation

The decision to expropriate is a political one but it has some legal, economic and social implications that affect not only the individual but also the budget of the nation. In Zimbabwe, for example, it was reported in *The Herald* of 21 August 2000 that more than 240 000 farm workers were likely to lose their jobs after the conclusion of the acquisition of more than 3 000 commercial farms for resettlement. The newspaper added, however, that the government intended resettling these farm workers. Furthermore, it must be noted that expropriation without compensation erodes the confidence that the banks have in title deeds. It reduces title deeds to mere pieces of paper.

17.4 CONCLUSION

Under international law, states have a sovereign right over their natural resources. Public international law also recognises an individual's right to property. The problem that could result from these potentially conflicting rights could be resolved by the application of the principle that the right of the community overrides the right of the individual. On this premise, the power of the state to extinguish an individual's right to property could be justified only on the ground of public utility; and where expropriation is justified on this ground, the individual must be compensated for the deprivation of their rights. The demands of natural justice and equity enjoin the expropriating authority to comply with the principles of natural justice since, in essence, the right to expropriate is discretionary.

In most southern African countries that achieved independence through liberation wars, it is common knowledge that colonial land policies and land-tenure systems

---

[47] See s 25(1)(*a*)(i) and (ii).

[48] See s 27(1), (2) and (3).

constituted the major causes of the liberation struggles. Therefore, at the time of independence, governments had to embark on land reform and resettlement programmes to correct the injustices of the past. In the context of the laws of expropriation the traditional public utility rationale for expropriation was found wanting. The orthodox grounds for expropriation had to be expanded to accommodate resettlement and agrarian reform. In Namibia, for example, land resettlement and agrarian reform have come under the domain of public interest in the context of the provision of Art 16 and the government can therefore exercise the powers of expropriation for its resettlement and agrarian reform schemes. Confronted with such onerous provisions justifying the deprivation of their rights, an individual can be assured of equity and justice only if the right to have redress before a competent court is assured. But the protection of the rights of the individual requires the existence of an independent Judiciary that is able to fetter the exercise of discretionary powers given to governments. And implicit from the statement by the late Dr Kwame Nkrumah, is the underlying imperative that these expropriation laws must give effect to the legitimate aspirations of the ordinary citizen.

REFERENCES

Cheadle, MH, Davis, DM & Haysom, NRL *South African Constitutional Law: The Bill of Rights* (LexisNexis Butterworths, 2005).

Davis, D, Cheadle, H & Haysom, N *Fundamentals Rights in the New Constitution: An Overview of the New Constitution and a Commentary on Chapter 3 on Fundamental Rights* (Juta & Co, 1994).

Dunning, HC 'Law and economic development in Africa: The law of eminent domain' (1968) 68 *Columbia Law Review* 1286–1315.

Hinz, MO, Amoo, SK & Van Wyk, D (eds) *The Constitution at Work: 10 Years of Namibian Nationhood* (Unisa, 2002).

Karst, KL & Rosenn, KS *Law and Development in Latin America: A Case Book* (University of California Press, 1975).

Kleyn, DG et al *Silberberg and Schoeman's, The Law of Property* 3 ed (Butterworths, 1992).

Manohar, SV *Constitutional Law of India* 3 ed (Law & Justice Publishing Co, 2010).

Nkrumah, K 'Ghana: Law in Africa' (1962) 6(2) *Journal of African Law* 103–112.

Starke, JG & Shearer, IA *Starke's International Law* 11 ed (Butterworths, 1994).

Tshuma, L & Makamure, K *The Legal Framework,* Conference on Land Policy in Zimbabwe after Lancaster, Harare, 1990.

Van der Walt, AJ 'Constitutional property law' (2011) 1 *Annual Survey of South African Law* 245–292.

CASES

Aonin Fishing (Pty) v Ministry of Fisheries and Marine Resources 1998 NR 47

Cultura 2000 & Another v Government of the Republic of Namibia & Others1992 NR 110 (HC); 1993 NR 328 (SC);1993 (2) SA 12 (NHC)
Davies v Minister of Lands, Agriculture and Water Development 1996 (9) BCLR 1209 (ZS)
Gunther Kessl v Ministry of Lands and Resettlement & Others 2008 (1) NR 167(HC)
Immigration Selection Board v Frank 2001 NR 107 (SC)
Texaco v Libya (1977) 53 ILR 389
West Air Aviation & Others v Airports Company Limited & Another 2001 NR 256 (HC)

LEGISLATION

African Charter on Human and People's Rights of 1981
Agricultural (Commercial) Land Reform Act 6 of 1995
American Convention on Human Rights of 1969
American Declaration of the Rights and Duties of Man of 1948
Constitution of the Republic of South Africa, 1996
Constitution of Zimbabwe Amendment Act 16 of 2000
Constitution of Zimbabwe Amendment Act 20 of 2013
First Protocol to the European Convention for the Protection of Human Rights and Fundamental Freedoms of 1950
Namibian Constitution of 1990
Public Lands Acquisition Act Cap 296 of the Laws of Zambia

APPENDIX

71 Property rights

(1) 'Property' means property of any description and any right or interest in property.
(2) Subject to section 72, every person has the right, in any part of Zimbabwe, to acquire, hold, occupy, use, transfer, hypothecate, lease or dispose of all forms of property, either individually or in association with others.
(3) Subject to this section and to section 72, no person may be compulsorily deprived of their property except where the following conditions are satisfied –
  (a) the deprivation is in terms if a law of general application;
  (b) the deprivation is necessary for any of the following reasons –
    (i) in the interests of defence, public safety, public order, public morality, public health or town and country planning; or
    (ii) in order to develop or use that or any other property for a purpose beneficial to the community;
  (c) the law requires the acquiring authority –
    (i) to give reasonable notice of the intention to acquire the property to everyone whose interest or right in the property would be affected by the acquisition;

   (ii) to pay fair and adequate compensation for the acquisition before acquiring the property or within a reasonable time after the acquisition; and
   (iii) if the acquisition is contested, to apply to a competent court before acquiring the property, or not later than thirty days after the acquisition, for an order confirming the acquisition;
- (d) the law entitles any person whose property has been acquired to apply to a competent court for the prompt return of the property if the court does not confirm the acquisition; and
- (e) the law entitles any claimant for compensation to apply to a competent court for the determination of –
   (i) the existence, nature and value of their interest in the property concerned;
   (ii) the legality of the deprivation; and
   (iii) the amount of compensation to which they are entitled; and to apply to the court for an order directing the prompt payment of any compensation.

72 Rights to agricultural land

(1) In this section 'agricultural land' means land used or suitable for agriculture, that is to say for horticultural, viticulture, forestry or aquaculture or for any purpose of husbandry, including –
   (a) the keeping or breeding of livestock, game, poultry, animals or bees; or
   (b) grazing of livestock or game; but does not include Communal Land or land within boundaries of an urban local authority or within a township established under a law relating to town and country planning or as defined in a law relating to land survey; 'land' includes anything permanently attached to or growing on land; 'piece of agricultural land' means a piece of agricultural land registered as a separate piece of land in a Deeds Registry.

(2) Where agricultural land, or any right or interest in such land, is required for a public purpose, including –
   (a) Settlement for agricultural or other purposes;
   (b) Land reorganization, forestry, environmental conservation or the utilisation of wildlife or their natural resources; or
   (c) The relocation of persons dispossessed as the result of the utilisation of land for a purpose referred to in paragraph (a) or (b); the land, right or interest maybe compulsorily acquired by the State by notice published in the Gazette identifying the land, right or interest, whereupon the land, right or interest vests in the State with full title with effect from the date of publication from the notice.

(3) Where agricultural land, or any right or interest in such land, is compulsorily acquired for a purpose referred to in subsection (2) –
   (a) Subject to section 295(1) and (2), no compensation is payable in respect of its acquisition, accept for improvements effected on it before its acquisition;
   (b) No person may apply to court for the determination of any question relating to compensation, accept for compensation for improvement effected on the land before its acquisition, and no court may entertain any such application; and
   (c) The acquisition may not be challenged on the ground that it was discriminatory in contravention of section 56.

(6) An act of parliament may make it an offence for any person, without lawful authority, to possess or occupy agricultural land referred to in this section or other State land.

(7) In regard to the compulsory acquisition of agricultural land for the resettlement of people in accordance with a programme of land reform, the following factors may be regarded as of ultimate and overriding importance –
   (a) Under colonial domination the people of Zimbabwe were unjustifiably dispossessed or their land and other resources without compensation;
   (b) The people consequential took up arms in order to regain their land and political sovereignty, and this ultimately resulted in the Independence of Zimbabwe in 1980;
   (c) The people of Zimbabwe must be enabled to re-assert their rights and regain ownership of their land; and accordingly –
      (i) The former colonial power has an obligation to pay compensation for agricultural land compulsorily acquired for resettlement, through an adequate fund established for the purpose; and
      (ii) If the former colonial power fails to pay compensation through such a fund, the government of Zimbabwe has no obligation to pay compensation for agricultural land compulsorily acquired for resettlement.

This section applies without prejudice to the obligation of the former colonial power to pay compensation for land referred to in this section that has been acquired for resettlement purposes.

18

Bail jurisprudence of Ghana, Namibia, Zambia and South Africa[1]

Samuel K Amoo

18.1 INTRODUCTION

Topics such as bail jurisprudence more often than not conjure up emotions of security concerns about the 'bad guy who must be kept off the streets'. Most often, we tend to forget about the cardinal principle of the presumption of innocence in criminal justice. The contemporary international policies and measures adopted by some states to combat international terrorism testify to the dangers of actual pre-trial punishment. The root cause of this, it is submitted, is the concentration of excessive powers over security matters in the Executive. Refusal of the right to bail assumes that our criminal justice systems are perfect and that individuals detained for allegedly committing serious offences will be charged and tried in accordance with the precepts of the due process of the law. Yet, empirically, evidence proves the contrary: there are cases in certain jurisdictions of torture in detention camps[2] and the inability of the state to bring detained persons for trial within reasonable period of time.

---

[1] Different versions of this chapter have been published as 'The bail jurisprudence of Ghana, Namibia, South Africa and Zambia' 2008 *Forum on Public Policy: A Journal of the Oxford Round Table*; *Gale Academic OneFile* and (2010) 2(2) *The Namibian Law Journal*.

[2] See, eg, s 1005 of the Detainee Treatment Act of 2005 of the United States, which provides that 'no court, justice or judge shall have jurisdiction to hear or consider ... an application of a writ of *habeas corpus* filed by or on behalf of an alien detained by the Department of Defense at Guantanamo Bay; and the Military Commissions Act of 2006 which eliminates the constitutional due process right of *habeas corpus* for detainees at Guantanamo Bay and elsewhere by allowing the US government to hold hundreds of prisoners for more than five years without charges'.

Security concerns traditionally fall under the jurisdiction of both the Legislature and the Executive, but the determination of bail applications forms part of the due process of the law which belongs to the domain of the Judiciary. The question regarding which organ of state has the final say in bail applications is a question of choices. Bail jurisprudence involves the balancing of the values relating to the rights of the individual against the security of the state; it involves the balancing of the dictates of positivism and rationality and how these choices have an impact on the individual and society. Essentially, it is a cultural phenomenon, since the values of society dictate the content of bail jurisprudence. Nagel has stated the position as follows:[3]

> The basic purpose of bail, from society's point of view, has always been and still is to ensure the accused's reappearance for trial. But pretrial release serves other purposes as well, purposes recognized over the last decade as often dispositive of the fairness of the entire criminal proceedings. Pretrial release allows a man accused of crime to keep the fabric of his life intact, to maintain employment and family ties in the event he is acquitted or given a suspended sentence or probation. It spares the family the hardship and indignity of welfare and enforced separation. It permits the accused to take an active part in planning his defense with his counsel, locating witnesses, proving his capability of staying free in the community without getting into trouble.

These interests may legitimately be placed under the jurisdiction of all three organs of state. However, since the right to bail involves constitutional and human rights considerations, the most suitable and appropriate organ of state to be vested with that function is the Judiciary. This is the submission of this chapter. In criminal justice jurisprudence, the right to bail has often been discussed in the context of the presumption of innocence and the right to liberty. As stated by Mahomed J (as he then was) in *S v Acheson*:[4]

> An accused person cannot be kept in detention pending his trial as a form of anticipatory punishment. The presumption of the law is that he is innocent until his guilt has been established in Court. The Court will therefore ordinarily grant bail to an accused person unless this is likely to prejudice the ends of justice.

It is therefore submitted that the better approach to the jurisprudence of bail is a holistic one; it is an approach that must look at bail, or the right to apply for bail, as

[3] SS Nagel (ed) *The Rights of the Accused in Law and Action* (Sage Publications, 1972) 177–178.
[4] *S v Acheson* 1991 (2) SA 805 (Nm) at 822A–B.

part of the rights of the accused to the due process of the law and therefore forms part of the human rights discourse.

As stated by Hiemstra CJ in the case of *Smith v Attorney-General, Bophuthatswana*, '[e]very man is entitled to "due process of the law". This principle is so ancient that it can be traced back to the *Magna Carta*.'[5]

Due process of the law in human rights jurisprudence under both international and municipal laws is an all-embracing concept and in the context of bail, as indicated earlier, it includes the right to liberty, a fair trial and the presumption of innocence. Bail may be defined as security to procure the release of a person from legal custody together with an undertaking that they shall appear at the time and place designated and submit themself to the jurisdiction and judgment of the court. Bail application proceedings are normally pretrial proceedings, and one of the reasons why discussion of the right to bail as a human rights issue should be held in the general context of due process of the law rather than in the limited confines of the presumption of innocence.

Furthermore, the issue of guilt or criminal liability is not determined in the course of a bail application. The presumption in criminal trial proceedings is a factor that determines and allocates the burden of proof; but placed in the context of the due process of the law the cumulative impact of the presumption of innocence and the right to freedom before conviction permits the unhampered preparation of a defence and serves to prevent the inflicting of punishment prior to conviction.

There are no specific international human rights standards on the right to bail; there are only generic provisions on the right to liberty and due process of the law which are incorporated into constitutions, which include the 48-hour rule. The detailed provisions relating to the procedure and the guidelines (both mandatory and discretionary) to be followed by the courts in the judicial process fall within the ambit of the Legislature and of state sovereignty. Legislative intervention has almost invariably taken the form of criminal procedure legislation, the contents of which appear to have been motivated by concerns of security, the right of the accused person or the arrestee and due process of the law. But it is submitted that in jurisdictions where an automatic right to bail is denied on grounds of the nature of an offence, the legislative intervention is motivated more by security concerns than the protection of the rights of the individual.

The demands of sovereignty place on states and governments inter alia the responsibility to protect and defend the integrity of the state and maintain peace and security. Among the institutions and mechanisms employed by states is the criminal justice system that provides for the legal framework of the powers exercised by law-enforcement agencies and judicial officers. Penal laws and their enforcement, in

[5] 1984 (1) SA 182 (B) at 200F–G.

particular, impinge on the rights of the individual, especially with regard to the rights of personal liberty, freedom of movement and privacy, etc. The concern about the potential abuse of the rights of the individual in the process of the enforcement of the penal laws by the state security apparatus and law-enforcement agencies has resulted in legislative intervention at both the international (in the form of international covenants) and the national levels aimed at protecting the rights of the individual. International Bills of Rights have affected municipal jurisdictions to the extent that most contemporary jurisdictions have incorporated the International Bill of Rights,[6] and treaty norms in their constitutions and domestic legal systems.

The right to bail falls under the general rubric of the right of personal liberty. For this reason, international instruments have provisions protecting the rights of personal liberty of the individual both during pre-trial and trial proceedings. These international instruments include the Universal Declaration of Human Rights, the African Charter on Human and Peoples' Rights and the International Covenant on Civil and Political Rights (ICCPR). The provisions they contain have been internalised in the municipal laws of most countries, as illustrated here:

Universal Declaration of Human Rights

> Article 9
> No one shall be subjected to arbitrary arrest, detention or exile.
>
> Article 10
> Everyone is entitled in full equality to a fair and public hearing by an independent and impartial tribunal, in the determination of his rights and obligations and of any criminal charge against him.
>
> Article 11(1)
> Everyone charged with a penal offence has the right to be presumed innocent until proved guilty according to law in a public trial at which he has had all the guarantees necessary for his defence.

African Charter on Human and Peoples' Rights

> Article 6
> Every individual shall have the right to liberty and to the security of his person. No one may be deprived of his freedom except for reasons and conditions

[6] The International Bill of Human Rights consists of the Universal Declaration of Human Rights, the International Covenant on Economic, Social and Cultural Rights, and the International Covenant on Civil and Political Rights and its two Optional Protocols.

previously laid down by law. In particular, no one may be arbitrarily arrested or detained.

Article 7*(d)* states that every individual has the right to be tried within a reasonable time by an impartial court or tribunal.

International Covenant on Civil and Political Rights (ICCPR)

Article 9

1) Everyone has the right to liberty and security of person. No one shall be subjected to arbitrary arrest or detention. None shall be deprived of his liberty except on such grounds and in accordance with such procedure as are established by law.
2) Anyone who is arrested shall be informed, at the time of arrest, of the reasons for his arrest and shall be promptly informed of any charges against him.
3) Anyone arrested or detained on a criminal charge shall be brought promptly before a judge or other officer authorized by law to exercise judicial power and shall be entitled to trial within a reasonable time or to release.
4) Anyone who is deprived of his liberty by arrest or detention shall be entitled to take proceedings before a court, in order that the court may decide without delay on the lawfulness of his detention and order his release if the detention is not lawful.

As a general application of the basic principles of the law of treaties, in international law the parties to these international treaties are states and international organisations and therefore such international standards and norms become binding on state parties either through the constitutional technique of legislative incorporation or automatic incorporation.[7] These constitutions guarantee the civil and political rights of every citizen and also the democratic values of human dignity, equality and freedom; and in the Bill of Rights provisions such rights as the right to fair hearing, including the right to be heard, to appeal, to be presumed innocent, to be defended by counsel of one's choice and to have a trial within a reasonable time by an impartial court or tribunal are both entrenched and justiciable.

International covenants such as the International Covenant on Civil and Political Rights (the ICCPR) and the Protocols provide not only for these rights but also for the mechanisms for redress and appropriate remedies that are available to

[7] V Leary *International Labour Conventions and National Law* (Martinus Nijhoff Publishers, 1982).

a victim of a human rights violation. State parties to such covenants are bound to these international instruments and therefore any alleged violations of individual rights are governed by the provisions of not only the municipal laws of a particular jurisdiction but also international law. The Human Rights Committee established under the ICCPR, for example, is mandated to monitor and supervise the implementation of the rights set out in the ICCPR. At the continental level, such treaty bodies as the African Court on Human and Peoples' Rights, and the African Commission on Human and Peoples' Rights,[8] are mandated to protect and defend the rights of the individual against violations by state agencies.

However, it must be added that under international law, as a general rule, there is no formal obligation on states to ratify a particular international covenant or a protocol and therefore, for example, the invocation of the jurisdiction of the Human Rights Committee, mentioned above, will require prior ratification of the Protocol establishing the committee. The limitations of the binding effect of international conventions and the lack of enforcement mechanism by which to hold signatories accountable are recognised in the jurisprudence of international law. Furthermore, under international law, individuals seeking the jurisdiction of international tribunals have *locus standi* only where the state has acceded to the jurisdiction of the particular international organisation and the individual has exhausted all available domestic remedies[9] to enforce compliance.

This seeming inefficacy of the enforcement mechanisms under international law does not mean, however, that states can indulge in violations of rights with impunity. There exist in modern international relations and especially in human rights jurisprudence such mechanisms and instruments of compliance, such as sanctions against and isolation of the recalcitrant and delinquent state, exerted by the international community and international human rights watchdogs, such as Amnesty International, to enforce compliance. Steiner and Alston[10] describe the concept as follows:

> Human rights violations occur within a state, rather than on the high seas or in outer space outside the jurisdiction of any one state. Ultimately, effective protection must come from within the state. The international human rights system does not typically place delinquent states in political bankruptcy and through some form of receivership take over the administration of a country in order to assure the enjoyment of human rights – although the measures implemented by the international community in Bosnia-Herzegovina after

[8] The Protocol establishing the African Court on Human and Peoples' Rights entered into force on 25 January 2004.

[9] There are a large number of cases on the exhaustion of domestic remedies, such as *Attorney-General of The Gambia v Jawara* Case Nos 147/95 and 149/96.

[10] HJ Steiner & P Alston *International Human Rights in Context: Law, Politics and Morals* (Oxford University Press, 2000) 987.

> the 1995 Dayton Peace Agreement and especially in Kosovo represent steps in that direction. Rather the international system seeks to persuade or pressure states to fulfil their obligations through one or another method – either observing national law (constitutional or statutory) that is consistent with the international norms, or making the international norms themselves part of the national legal and political order.

Under international law, the international standards and norms contained in international treaties and conventions become binding on states upon accession of the instruments and acceptance of the jurisdiction of the particular international organisation. However, if the provisions of a treaty or an international instrument are considered to be self-executing and an individual has the standing to do so, the individual may invoke the provisions of a treaty before national courts in automatic incorporation in the absence of implementing legislation. Individuals have *locus standi* before the institutions if all available domestic remedies have been exhausted. This international rule of exhaustion of local remedies before taking to international remedies is one of the basic rules in international law. The objective of the rule is to afford a respondent state the first opportunity to correct a harm and to make redress. A person whose rights have been violated should therefore first make use of domestic remedies to right a wrong rather than first raise the issue with an international committee, court or other tribunal.[11] However, if no domestic remedies are available or there is an unreasonable delay on the part of the national courts in granting a remedy,[12] then a person is justified in having recourse to international remedies. The rule of local remedies should not constitute an unjust impediment to access to international remedies.

The foregoing seeks to establish that the right to bail is a human right recognised under both international law and municipal law and that the process of determining whether bail should be granted lies within the remit of the Judiciary which exercises this mandate in compliance with the imperatives of the due process of the law.

The next section deals with the various models or approaches of bail systems and their consistency with human rights standards.

18.2 JURISPRUDENCE OF THE RIGHT TO BAIL UNDER MUNICIPAL LAW

18.2.1 Models of bail system

There are three models and/or approaches to the right to bail as a human right that balance the right of the individual to liberty and the security of the community. The first model or approach is premised on a policy and a constitutional position that

[11] See, in general, the doctrine of the margin of appreciation.

[12] See, eg, *Attorney-General of The Gambia* (note 9), and many others.

makes the Legislature the repository of the determination of the right to bail and leaves the Judiciary to implement broad legislative directives. A legislative directive invariably includes mandatory refusal of bail in certain offences and the Judiciary is left with the discretion to determine the granting or refusal of bail with the primary objectives of promoting the due process of law and securing the presence of the accused or the arrestee before the jurisdiction and judgment of the court.

The second model or approach is premised on the constitutional position that grants the Judiciary the sole determination of the right to bail. This approach is not prescriptive in the case of bailable and non-bailable offences: the accused or arrestee has the prima facie constitutional right to apply for bail, irrespective of the seriousness of the alleged offence.

The first model or approach is adopted by countries such as Zambia, India and certain states in the United States; the latter is applied by countries such as Ghana and Namibia. Prior to the decision of Supreme Court in *Martin Kpebu v Attorney General,*[13] Ghana adopted the first model or approach as provided for in s 96(7) of the Criminal Procedure Code (Act),[14] as amended; it drew a distinction between bailable and non-bailable offences that had not been declared unconstitutional.

A third model or approach may be described as amalgam of the first two. Here, the power over determining matters relating to bail is generally vested in the Judiciary. There is no legislated mandatory refusal of bail and the law does not draw a distinction between bailable and non-bailable offences. However, there is a legislative intervention in the form of legislative guidelines that the courts must follow in the exercise of their discretion to grant or refuse bail in serious or scheduled offences. This is the South African model.

18.2.2 First model or approach

As stated earlier, bail jurisprudence aims at achieving a balance between personal liberty and state security or the interests of society. Consequently, the first model or approach is premised on three tenets: security concerns emanating from state sovereignty; the protection of the rights of the individual, and the promotion of due process of the law. Under this model or approach, legislative intervention is exercised by the promulgation of legislation which deals with the procedural and substantive principles relating to bail. The justification for legislative intervention

---

[13] *Martin Kpebu v Attorney-General* (J1/13/2015) [2016] GHASC 15 (5 May 2016).

[14] Section 96(7) of Act 30 reads as follows: A court shall refuse to grant bail:
(a) In a case of treason, subversion, murder, robbery, narcotics, hijacking, piracy, rape, defilement or escape from lawful custody; or
(b) Where a person is being held for extradition to a foreign country.

has been based on security concerns and therefore the Legislature has been recognised as the legitimate organ of state to be vested with the jurisdiction to make broad pronouncements on matters relating to bail. In the interests of state security and securing the presence of the accused before the jurisdiction of the courts, the Legislature has thought it prudent to draw a distinction between bailable and non-bailable offences. The former consist of less-serious non-scheduled offences over which the courts have unfettered discretion to make pronouncements on whether or not bail must be granted. This notwithstanding, the courts exercise this discretion guided by certain imperatives and values developed through case law.

The latter consist of serious or scheduled offences in which the courts are mandated to refuse bail. This approach is adopted by Zambia (and was adopted by Ghana prior to the *Martin Kpebu* case). But in order to temper any injustices that this approach may cause to the accused person, under relevant Zambian constitutional provisions supported by relevant case law, the courts have the power to grant bail to the accused if they are not tried within a reasonable time in cases of statutory non-bailable offences. But this approach tends to confuse release on bail and the accused's right to be brought to trial within a reasonable time. The fact is that release on bail is not a substitute for an accused's right to be brought to trial within a reasonable period. In all such cases, the fundamental issue is the constitutionality of these legislative interventions regarding their consistency and compliance with international human rights standards. Under this head we discuss the Zambian model or approach below.

This model or approach traces its legitimacy to the fact that the power to determine the general policy, principles and rules of law governing the granting or refusal of bail is vested in the Legislature. But in human rights bail jurisprudence the protection of the liberty of the accused potentially stands to be compromised if this power is vested in the Legislature. This is a human rights issue which traditionally falls under the jurisdiction of the courts and therefore the most acceptable approach that will be consistent with international norms and standards will be that of the automatic legal right to appeal – the determination of which will be at the discretion of the courts. This approach will cater adequately for all the concerns mentioned earlier that determine the content of bail jurisprudence. In the case of *Smith v Attorney-General, Bophuthatswana*, for instance, Hiemstra CJ stated as follows:

> In America there is a lively controversy between those who would award the Court a constitutional policymaking function and those who want to limit its constitutional interpretation. Before a Court has established itself as an unchallenged third force in a country it would be wiser to limit itself to interpretation, which nevertheless is imaginative and designed to keep open

> the horizon of individual liberty. There will be an ongoing debate in the courts about definitions and priorities, all the time aiming, not at freedom from law, but at freedom through the law.[15]

Freedom through the law involves due process of the law. In the context of bail jurisprudence, it encapsulates these basic tenets: first, that a bail application falls within the judicial process and therefore within the jurisdiction of the courts; second, that the accused has the right to trial within a reasonable time, failure of which leads to their being entitled to release. These basic tenets are premised on the accused's automatic right to apply for bail.

Release on bail has at times been obfuscated by the accused's right to be brought to trial within a reasonable period of time. But the two define two different principles: this is because release on bail is not a substitute for an accused's right to be brought to trial within a reasonable period. Release on bail on account of failure to prosecute a case within a reasonable time is not a proactive provision because it seeks only to deal with the issue after the fact.

The automatic right to apply for bail is not specifically provided for by, for example, the constitutions of Ghana and Zambia. This is subject to the interpretation of the relevant provisions of the constitutions. And the courts in both countries, (in the case of Ghana before the *Martin Kpebu* case) in their interpretations of these provisions, have adopted a holistic approach by relying on legislation that denies the accused the right to apply for bail in offences statutorily classified as non-bailable.[16] This mandatory denial of bail coupled with the fact that the constitutional right to release deals with the issue after the fact implies that the right to liberty of an accused stands tremendously compromised, since the accused is subjected to punitive conditions before trial. In order to remove these uncertainties, it is submitted that the jurisdiction to determine bail should be granted to the Judiciary and that appropriate provisions should accordingly be incorporated into the constitutions. It is therefore submitted further that the correct jurisprudential approach to bail applications is that the courts of law should adjudicate these matters and that, as a matter of principle, there should be no legislative or executive attempts to curtail or oust the jurisdiction of the courts.[17]

(a) Zambia

The Zambian position, as described earlier, falls under the first model or approach and the sources of the legal principles and rules governing the granting or refusal

---

[15] *Smith v Attorney-General, Bophuthatswana* 1984 (1) SA 196 (B) at 200D–E.

[16] In the case of Ghana this was the position before the *Martin Kpebu* case (note 13).

[17] See, generally, *S v Ramgobin* 1985 (3) SA 587 (N); *S v Ramgobin* 1985 (4) SA 130 (N); *Bull v Minister of Home Affairs* 1986 (3) SA 870 (Z).

of bail are the Constitution, the Criminal Procedure Code[18] and case law. In the context of the right to bail, the Constitution of Zambia makes provisions for the right to liberty,[19] a fair trial and the presumption of innocence.[20] The Constitution of Zambia encapsulates the constitutional rule that the defendant is presumed to be innocent until they are proven guilty. From this rule flows the proposition that the defendant must not be subjected to unnecessary pre-trial deprivation of their freedom.

This is contemplated under Arts 13(3) and 18(1) of the Constitution of Zambia; moreover, s 33(1) of the Criminal Procedure Code[21] provides that arrested persons are to be taken before a competent court without undue delay and if not tried within reasonable time, they should be released either conditionally or unconditionally.

These are the fundamental provisions relating to bail and the protection of the rights of a detained or an accused person. The remainder of the legislative principles are contained in the Criminal Procedure Code. In essence, the primary policy is that in the interests of the security of the community or society and of guaranteeing the completion of criminal proceedings and promoting due process of the law, a person charged with a scheduled offence such as murder, treason, aggravated robbery or rape is not eligible for bail. The Zambian Legislature has accordingly legislated for bailable and non-bailable offences. As stated earlier, in the case of the latter, the courts are mandated to refuse bail under s 123 of the Criminal Procedure Code.

The right to bail is therefore guaranteed under Zambia's Constitution and international law. However, s 123 of the Criminal Procedure Code provides for specific offences that may not be bailable.[22] The effect of this is that the accused person in such an instance is condemned unheard, as they stand to be subjected to an unreasonable period of detention. Furthermore, the provisions in the Criminal Procedure Code curtailing the discretion of the courts to grant bail in the specified instances can be considered to be unconstitutional as they are inconsistent with Arts 13(3) and 18(1) of the Constitution that require any accused person charged

[18] Chapter 88 of the Laws of Zambia.

[19] Article 13 of the Constitution of Zambia.

[20] Article 18.

[21] Chapter 88 of the Laws of Zambia.

[22] See s 123 of the Criminal Procedure Code: '(1) When any person is arrested or detained, or appears before or is brought before a subordinate court, the High Court or Supreme Court he may, at any time while he is in custody, or at any stage of the proceedings before such court, be admitted to bail upon providing a surety or sureties sufficient, in the opinion of the police officer concerned or court, to secure his appearance, or be released upon his own recognizance if such officer or court thinks fit: Provided that any person charged with – (i) murder, treason or any other offence carrying a possible or mandatory capital penalty; (ii) misprision of treason or treason-felony; or (iii) aggravated robbery; shall not be granted bail by either a subordinate court, the High Court or Supreme Court or be released by any Police Officer.'

with an offence to be afforded a fair hearing before an independent tribunal within a reasonable time. In addition, the offending provisions can be regarded as unconstitutional as they attempt to curtail the unlimited jurisdiction of the High Court to hear all civil and criminal matters, which is guaranteed under Art 94(1) of the Constitution.

The automatic denial of bail negates the spirit of the provisions of the Constitution because such an accused person is *ab initio* denied the opportunity to appear before an impartial tribunal and present reasons why they believe they should be granted bail.

The Constitutional Court of Zambia has to date not pronounced itself on the constitutionality of s 123 of the Criminal Procedure Code. This could be due to the fact that the issue of bail involves applying the presumption of innocence in the Bill of Rights, over which the Court has no (original) jurisdiction. In terms of Arts 28, 128 and 134 of the Constitution of Zambia, matters concerning the Bill of Rights in Part III of the Constitution are a preserve of the High Court. The jurisdiction of the Constitutional Court covers all matters except those contained in the Bill of Rights.[23]

However, in *Chetankumar Satkal Parekh v The People*[24] the Supreme Court stated that

> there [was] nothing in the Constitution which invalidates a law imposing a total prohibition on the release on bail of a person reasonably suspected of having committed a criminal offence, provided that he is brought to trial within a reasonable time.

In summary, therefore, under Zambian bail jurisprudence, the determination of whether or not an accused has the right to apply for bail depends on the classification of the offence. The courts have an unfettered discretion to entertain applications for bail in offences prescribed as bailable and to make determinations on the applications, taking into consideration a mixture of factors. However, in cases involving serious offences prescribed as non-bailable, the courts are mandated to refuse such applications. Under the so-called 'constitutional bail concept', an accused is entitled to bail if the trial does not take place within a reasonable period. However, as stated earlier, under this regime the rights of the accused stand to be compromised and susceptible to being violated.

(b) Ghana

Prior to the *Martin Kpebu* case, the Ghanaian model or approach was exhaustively discussed by Prof Ocran JSC in the case of *The Republic of Ghana v Kevin Dinsdale*

[23] See *Hichilema & Others v Government of the Republic of Zambia* (2020) ZMSC 37: *Hichilema & Others v Government of the Republic of Zambia* (2017/CCZ 006) and (2017/HP 0888).

[24] *Chetankumar Satkal Parekh v The People* (1995–1997) ZR 78.

Gorman,[25] which dealt inter alia with the court's discretion to grant bail fettered by the provisions of s 96(7) of the Criminal Procedure Code (Act 30) as amended by s 7 of the Criminal Procedure Code (Amendment Act 633 of 2002) and amended further by s 41(1)*(a)* of the Anti-Terrorism Act 762 of 2008. The relevant paragraphs of this section read as follows:

A court shall refuse to grant bail:

(a) In a case of treason, subversion, murder, robbery, narcotics, hijacking, piracy, rape, defilement or escape from lawful custody; or
(b) Where a person is being held for extradition to a foreign country.

In its determination of the constitutionality of s 96(7) of the Criminal Procedure Code (Act 30), the court highlighted the underpinnings of the bail jurisprudence of Ghana as follows:[26]

> Undergirding our principles for arriving at decisions on applications for bail is the effective enforcement of our criminal law guided by due process considerations, which constitute the procedural aspects of our commitment to the liberty of the individual. A true system of justice must indeed reflect both aspects of criminal jurisprudence. If not, one of two consequences will follow: either the law-enforcement agencies of the state will ride roughshod over the rights of the accused: or criminals would have had a field day in the system as they roam the streets in full liberty and with contempt for the efficacy of our criminal enactments.

With respect to the bail jurisprudence of Ghana, the court stated:[27]

> Drawing on our general analysis of the law above, we summarize our holdings as follows:
>
> 1. The constitutional presumption of innocence embedded in article 19(2)*(c)* of the 1992 Constitution does not import an automatic right to bail.
> 2. The constitutional duty of the court under article 14(4) of the Constitution, to grant bail to the accused if he is not tried within a reasonable time, is applicable irrespective of the nature of the accusation or the severity of the punishment upon conviction.

---

[25] *The Republic of Ghana v Kevin Dinsdale Gorman* Criminal Appeal No J3/3/2004; *Goram & Others v The Republic* (2003–2004) 2 SCGLR 784.

[26] *Goram & Others* (note 25) at 795.

[27] *Goram & Others* (note 25) at 808–809.

3. In the cases falling outside the direct duty to grant bail under article 14(4), there is a constitutional presumption of grant of bail drawn from the spirit of the language of articles 14(1) and (3), and 19(2)*(c)*, in further protection of persons charged with offences in situations which do not mandate the grant of bail.
4. The said constitutional presumption of the grant of bail is rebuttable; and it is in fact rebutted by a statutory provision that expressly disallows bail, such as the circumstances outlined in section 96(7) of the Criminal Procedure Code.
5. Outside the strictures of section 96(7) of the Code and article 14(4) of the Constitution, the presumption of the grant of bail is still extant, and is exercised under judicial discretion, which is itself fettered by other provisions of section 96.
6. There is no *prima facie* inconsistency between the relevant provisions of the Code and the 1992 Constitution.
7. Considerations of the nature of an accusation and the severity of punishment upon conviction, as part of the decision not to grant bail under sections 96(5) and (6), are constitutional; and that the gravity of an offence may be viewed as an aid in understanding and categorizing the nature of an accusation.

In essence, therefore, regarding the constitutionality of s 96(7), the subsection is not inconsistent with the letter and spirit of the Constitution.

The above position of the Supreme Court in the *Gorman* case has, however, been reversed by the decision of the Supreme Court in the *Martin Kpebu* case.[28] In this case, the plaintiff, Martin Kpebu, a private legal practitioner, sued in the Supreme Court under Arts 2(1) and 130(1) of the 1992 Constitution for a declaration that s 96(7) of the Criminal Procedure Code, (Act) s 30, as amended by s 7 of the Criminal Procedure Code (Amendment) Act, 2002 (Act) 633 and further amended by s 41(1)*(a)* of the Anti-Terrorism Act 762 of 2008, contravenes Arts 14(1),[29] 15(2)[30] and 19(2)*(c)*[31] of the 1992 Constitution. In support of his claim, the

[28] *Martin Kpebu* (note 13).

[29] '(1) Every person shall be entitled to his personal liberty and no person shall be deprived of his personal liberty except in the following cases and in accordance with procedure permitted by law –.

[30] **Respect for Human Dignity** (1) The dignity of all persons shall be inviolable. (2) No person shall, whether or not he is arrested, restricted, or detained, be subjected to –*(a)* torture or other cruel, inhuman, or degrading treatment or punishment; *(b)* any other condition that detracts or is likely to detract from his dignity and worth as a human being.'

[31] Section 19(2)*(c)*(i): 'A person charged with a criminal offence shall be given a fair hearing within a reasonable time by a court. be presumed to be innocent until they are proved or has pleaded guilty; …

(3) A person who is arrested, restricted or detained –*(a)*for the purpose of bringing him before a court in execution of an order of a court; or *(b)* upon reasonable suspicion of his having

plaintiff referred to Art 19(2)*(c)* of the 1992 Constitution, which provides that 'a person charged with a criminal offence shall be presumed to be innocent until he is proved or pleaded guilty'.

The plaintiff submitted further that bail was directly linked to individual liberty, which is guaranteed by Art 14 of the 1992 Constitution and that the no-bail provision under s 96(7) of Act 30 as amended by Act 633 raised constitutional challenges when viewed against the automatic presumption of innocence until proven guilty or confession to the commission of a crime.

Unlike in the *Gorman* case, where the Supreme Court was not called upon to interpret the provisions of Arts 14(4),[32] and 19(2)*(c)*, the Supreme Court in its landmark decision in the *Martin Kpebu* case[33] interpreted Art 19(2)*(c)* of the 1992 Constitution and held that s 96(7) was inconsistent with an individual's freedom of liberty as stated in Art 14(1)*(g)*,[34] and therefore the mandatory provision of s 96(7) stood to be declared unconstitutional and consequently null and void.

For reasons of brevity, only two elements of the decision of the court that need to be emphasised are given here: first, that whatever pronouncement the court made in reference to the constitutionality of s 96(7) of the Criminal Procedure Code Act 30 in the *Gorman* case had been made *per incuriam* as the court was not called upon to determine that issue; and, second, that s 96(7) of Act 30 as variously amended is inconsistent with Art 19(2) of the Constitution of Ghana.

(c) Namibia

Namibia's attainment of sovereignty and self-determination ushered in a new constitutional dispensation characterised by constitutional supremacy as opposed to legislative sovereignty, the rule of law and respect for human rights. These values have engendered a new jurisprudence in Namibia and the Namibian Superior Courts have used these values as the basis of their judgments in cases involving the interpretation and implementation of the Bill of Rights of the Constitution of Namibia. The respect for the internalization or domestication of international

committed or being about to commit a criminal offence under the laws of Ghana, and who is not released, shall be brought before a court within forty-eight hours after the arrest, restriction or detention.'

[32] Section 14(4): 'Where a person arrested, restricted or detained under paragraph *(a)* or *(b)* of clause (3) of this article is not tried within a reasonable time, then, without prejudice to any further proceedings that may be brought against him, he shall be released either unconditionally or upon reasonable conditions, including in particular, conditions reasonably necessary to ensure that he appears at a later date for trial or for proceedings preliminary to trial.'

[33] *Martin Kpebu* (note 13).

[34] Article 14(1) Every person shall be entitled to his personal liberty and no person shall be deprived of his personal liberty except in the following cases and in accordance with procedure permitted by law – *(g)* upon reasonable suspicion of his having committed or being about to commit a criminal offence under the laws of Ghana.

human rights norms in the domestic laws has also had its impact on the criminal justice system and in particular on the bail jurisprudence of Namibia.

The Namibian model or approach is premised on the constitutional position advocated by Hiemstra J in the case of *Smith v Attorney-General, Bophuthatswana*,[35] namely, that the universal method of safeguarding individual liberty is to entrust it to an independent Judiciary operating in public and compelled to give reasons. The jurisdiction over the right to grant or refuse bail is consequently left entirely to the discretion of the courts. The sources of bail jurisprudence in Namibia comprise the Constitution of Namibia and the Criminal Procedure Act,[36] to the extent that they are relevant to Namibia, and case law. In terms of Namibian bail jurisprudence, there is no distinction between bailable and non-bailable offences: the rights to liberty, bail and lawful detention in terms of the 48-hour rule are protected by the Bill of Rights of the Constitution. There are no statutory limitations to the right to bail, therefore: the matter is solely within the discretion of the courts, which exercise this discretion taking into consideration the guidelines as stated in the case of *S v Acheson*.[37] The relevant constitutional provisions are as follows:

> **Article 7 Protection of Liberty**
> No persons shall be deprived of personal liberty except according to procedures established by law.
>
> **Article 11 Arrest and Detention**
> 1) No persons shall be subject to arbitrary arrest or detention.
> 2) No persons who are arrested shall be detained in custody without being informed promptly in a language they understand of the grounds for such arrest.
> 3) All persons who are arrested and detained in custody shall be brought before the nearest Magistrate or other judicial officer within a period of forty-eight hours of their arrest or, if this is not reasonably possible, as soon as possible thereafter, and no such persons shall be detained in custody beyond such period without the authority of a Magistrate or other judicial officer.
>
> **Article 12 Fair Trial**
> (1) *(a)* In the determination of their civil rights and obligations or any criminal charges against them, all persons shall be entitled to a fair and

[35] *Smith* (note 15) at 200E–F.
[36] Act 51 of 1977. This Act is applicable to Namibia but not all of the amendments automatically apply in Namibia.
[37] *S v Acheson* (note 4).

> public hearing by an independent, impartial and competent Court or Tribunal established by law: provided that such Court or Tribunal may exclude the press and/or the public from all or any part of the trial for reasons of morals, the public order or national security, as is necessary in a democratic society.
> *(b)* A trial referred to in Sub-Article *(a)* hereof shall take place within a reasonable time, failing which the accused shall be released.
> *(c)* ...
> *(d)* All persons charged with an offence shall be presumed innocent until proven guilty according to law, after having had the opportunity of calling witnesses and cross-examining those called against them.

In the case of *S v Acheson*,[38] Mahomed AJ (as he then was) stated the position of the Namibian jurisprudence of bail in the context of the fundamental values underlying the Namibian Constitution.

The accused in this matter was Mr Donald Acheson, an Irish citizen who was charged with the murder of Advocate Anton Lubowski on 12 September 1989. When the matter was called on 18 April 1990, Mr Heyman, who appeared for the state, applied for an adjournment. He indicated that he sought a lengthy adjournment and that the accused should be kept in custody in the interim. In order to put the relevance of the case in context, a summary of the material facts found by the Court during the hearing on 18 April are summarised below.

The accused was arrested on 13 September 1989 and he had been in continuing custody since that day. Although the initial arrest on 13 September 1989 was on the allegation of murder, he was on 15 September 1989 detained as a prohibited immigrant in terms of the Admission of Persons to the Republic Regulations Act of 1972.

An application to set aside the accused's detention in terms of this Act was successful in the Supreme Court on 6 November 1989, but the accused was immediately arrested again on the allegation that he had murdered Mr Lubowski. An unsuccessful application for bail was made to the magistrate on 13 November 1989. An appeal to the Supreme Court against that refusal of bail also failed.

On 10 January 1990 the accused again appeared before the magistrate, where he pleaded not guilty pursuant to the provision of s 119 of the Criminal Procedure Act 51 of 1977. The state requested a postponement until 15 February 1990 so as to enable the Attorney-General to make his decision as to the further prosecution of the matter in terms of s 122 of the Criminal Procedure Act. The defence objected to such a lengthy postponement while the accused was to be kept in custody and the magistrate decided to adjourn the matter until 25 January 1990.

---

38 *S v Acheson* (note 4).

On 25 January the accused again appeared before the magistrate. The prosecutor informed the court that the Attorney-General had decided to arraign the accused on the charge of murder in the Supreme Court on 18 April 1990. After that, the accused was served with a formal indictment charging him with the murder of Mr Lubowski together with a summary of substantial facts and a list of witnesses to be called by the state.

The above facts therefore indicate that the accused had been in custody for more than seven months after he had first been taken into custody. The court took cognisance of the period of detention and pronounced itself on the bail jurisprudence of Namibia, setting out the factors that a court must consider in determining whether to grant bail. The court held that an accused person cannot be kept in detention pending their trial as a form of anticipatory punishment. The presumption of the law is that they are innocent until their guilt has been established in court. The court will therefore ordinarily grant bail to an accused person unless this is likely to prejudice the ends of justice. The factors which the court considers in deciding this issue include the following:

1. Is it more likely that the accused will stand his trial or is it more likely that he will abscond and forfeit his bail? The determination of that issue involves a consideration of other sub-issues such as: –

> first, how deep are his emotional, occupational and family roots within the country where he is to stand trial; what are his assets in that country; what are the means that he has to flee from the country; how much can he afford the forfeiture of the bail money; what travel documents he has to enable him to leave the country; what arrangements exist or may later exist to extradite him if he flees to another country; how inherently serious is the offence in respect of which he is charged; how strong is the case against him and how much inducement there would therefore be for him to avoid standing trial; how severe is the punishment likely to be if he is found guilty; how stringent are the conditions of his bail and how difficult would it be for him to evade effective policing of his movements.
>
> The second question which needs to be considered is whether there is a reasonable likelihood that, if the accused is released on bail, he will tamper with witnesses or interfere with the relevant evidence or cause such evidence to be suppressed or distorted. This issue again involves an examination of other factors such as: whether or not he is aware of the identity of such witnesses or the nature of such evidence; whether or not the witnesses concerned have already made their statements and committed themselves to give evidence or whether it is still the subject-matter of continuing

investigations; what the accused's relationship is with such witnesses and whether or not it is likely that they may be influenced or intimidated by him; whether or not any condition preventing communication between such witnesses and the accused can effectively be policed.

A third consideration is how prejudicial it might be for the accused in all the circumstances to be kept in custody by being denied bail. This would involve again an examination of other issues such as, for example, the duration of the period for which they have already been incarcerated, if any; the duration of the period during which they will have to be in custody before their trial is completed; the cause of any delay in the completion of their trial and whether or not the accused is partially or wholly to be blamed for such a delay; the extent to which the accused needs to continue working in order to meet their financial obligations; the extent to which they might be prejudiced in engaging legal assistance for their defence and in effectively preparing for their defence if they remain in custody, and the health of the accused.

18.2.3 Third model or approach

(a) South Africa

The sources of the bail jurisprudence South Africa are the Constitution of South Africa,[39] the Criminal Procedure Act[40] and case law.

As may be evident from the above provisions, the South African Constitution, under s 12, guarantees individual liberty, including the right to freedom and security of the person. The protections are extended to arrested, detained and accused persons. These guarantees, however, are not absolute in the sense that they are circumscribed in accordance with the limitations clause. In the case of the right to bail, for example, an arrested person has the right to be released from detention if the interests of justice permit it, subject to reasonable conditions.

As stated earlier, the South African bail laws do not draw a distinction between bailable and non-bailable offences. However, for security concerns, the Legislature has intervened by providing legislative guidelines that the courts have to consider in the exercise of their discretion in bail applications in order to satisfy the constitutional limitations of 'reasonable and justifiable in an open and democratic society based on human dignity, equality and freedom, considering all relevant factors', and the interests of justice.

[39] For the relevant sections of the South African Constitution, see the Appendix at the end of this chapter.

[40] Criminal Procedure Act 51 of 1977.

Under the provisions of s 60(11)*(b)*, which applies only to serious violent crimes enumerated in Schedule 6,[41] of the Criminal Procedure Act 51of 1977, the accused is required to adduce evidence which satisfies the court that exceptional circumstances exist which in the interests of justice permit their release.

The South African bail scheme, in general, takes detailed account of the state's legitimate interests in protecting the integrity of the criminal justice system and public safety between the time of arrest and trial, giving the courts a broad discretion to detain individuals who pose an identifiable risk to the interests of justice. Not only does the Constitution's 'interests of justice' standard permit the detention of any individual whose liberty would threaten the interests of justice between the time of arrest and trial, but the statutory provisions that guide the application of this constitutional standard give thorough consideration to the state's interests, enumerating in great detail those factors relevant to assessing any dangers to the public safety, risks of flight, threats of interference with witnesses or evidence, jeopardy of the criminal justice system and exceptional threats to public order pending trial.[42]

The constitutionality of these provisions has been challenged in court: first, on the grounds that they circumscribe the jurisdiction of the courts and usurp the judicial prerogative to interpret the 'interests of justice' standard and, second, that s 60(11)*(b)* also imposes a reverse onus on the accused to prove that the granting of bail will be in the interests of justice. Commenting on the bail system of South Africa, Axam writes that

> in the bail context, as in the criminal trial context, a reverse onus raises a presumption against the individual's liberty interests, permitting the state to deprive an individual of his liberty by relying on his failure to rebut a legal presumption in the state's favour, instead of by affirmatively establishing factual grounds to justify the deprivation.[43]

The South African bail jurisprudence was discussed in the cases of *S v Dlamini*, *S v Dladla Others*, *S v Joubert* and *S v Schietekat*.[44] All four of these separate cases dealt with issues relating to bail proceedings and were accordingly dealt with in a

[41] For the contents of Schedule 6 of the Criminal Procedure Act, see the Appendix at the end of this chapter.

[42] Section 60(4)–(9) of the Criminal Procedure Act 51 of 1977.

[43] HS Axam 'If the interests of justice permit: Individual liberty, the limitation clause, and the qualified constitutional right to bail' (2001) 17 *South African Journal of Human Rights* 330.

[44] *S v Dlamini* Case No 1 CCT 21/98; *S v Dladla & Others* Case No 3 CCT 22/98; *S v Joubert* Case No 3 CCT 2/99; *S v Schietekat* Case No 4 CCT 4/99, 1999 (4) SA 623 (CC).

single judgment. In all the cases, the court had to deal with the legal principles that applied to the granting of bail.

Section 35 of the Bill of Rights provides that a detained person has the right to be released from detention 'if the interests of justice permit'.[45] The Criminal Procedure Act has developed procedures and guidelines that would regulate the granting of bail. The court had to consider whether the procedures (including the admission of evidence), guidelines and criteria were consistent with the right granted in s 35.

In three of these matters – *S v Schietekat, S v Joubert* and *S v Dladla & Others* – the court had to consider the constitutionality of the provisions of the Criminal Procedure Act in so far as they related to the granting of bail. It was argued that, in setting out the criteria that a court could consider in determining what constituted 'the interests of justice', the Legislature was usurping the function of the court in determining what was in the interests of justice. According to the argument, this violated the separation of powers doctrine.

The court rejected this argument and found that the criteria laid down by the Legislature constituted a proper exercise of its legislative function and that it did not relieve the court of making its own evaluation or looking at any other factor it deemed relevant. At most it was in the nature of a checklist that could assist, but not necessarily bind, the court.

A further challenge was premised on the argument that some of the bail provisions amounted to 'lynch law' in that they elevated the sentiments of the community above the interests of the detainee. These provisions relate to factors such as whether the release of an accused person will lead to a sense of shock and outrage on the part of the community.

The court found, with reluctance, that the relevant provisions passed constitutional muster in that, while they did indeed limit the right to be released on reasonable conditions, they were saved by the limitation clause.

The court also held that applying the constitutional principles establishing the granting or refusal of bail is a judicial function. The court attempted to show how the application of constitutional norms to the law and practice of bail did not complicate the task of judicial officers but crafted it. The institution of bail was intended to maximise personal liberty. Section 35(1)*(f)* of the Bill of Rights envisaged three things: the limitation on liberty caused by an arrest; a circumscribed right to be released from custody, and that the interests of justice permit such a release.

The court drew a distinction between bail and the trial process and postulated that the bail process is significantly different from the trial process and, accordingly, in a bail hearing the question of the guilt or otherwise of the accused, while it may have some relevance, was not the central issue – that issue was whether the interests

---

[45] See s 35(1)*(f)*.

of justice required the release of a detainee. In deciding on bail, a court had to act as proactively and inquisitorially as might be necessary and was further required to weigh up the pros and cons of bail judicially.

It held, furthermore, that there is a fundamental difference between the objective of bail proceedings and that of a trial. In a bail application, the enquiry is not really concerned with the question of guilt. That is the task of the trial court. The court hearing a bail application is concerned with the question of possible guilt only to the extent that it may have a bearing on where the interests of justice lie in regard to bail. The focus at the bail stage is to decide whether the interests of justice permit the release of the accused pending trial; and that entails in the main protecting the investigation and prosecution of the case against hindrance.

18.3 SUBMISSIONS AND RECOMMENDATIONS

(a) Eligibility for bail

The institution of bail traces its origins to international conventions that protect and guarantee the fundamental rights of the individual to liberty, the presumption of innocence and due process of the law. These basic international norms and conventions have been internalized, or domesticated, in the municipal laws of states. The general pattern of internalisation is the incorporation of the basic rights in the Bills of Rights of the constitutions of the various states and the determination of detailed provisions relating to procedure and the substantive rules of bail are left to the Legislature and the Judiciary to determine.

In the regime of eligibility for bail, three models have been discussed. The first model is that which imposes a mandatory prohibition on the granting of bail in the case of offences that are classified as non-bailable. This is the model adopted by Zambia,[46] (and Ghana prior to the *Martin Kpebu* case[47]). Under this bail regime, however, there is the phenomenon of constitutional bail by which, as stated in the case of *Chetankumar Satkal Parekh v The People*,[48] the Supreme Court of Zambia held that constitutional bail could be granted under Art 13(3) of the Constitution of Zambia in cases where bail was not available if it could be shown that the case had been unreasonably delayed through no fault of the accused.

This position of the bail jurisprudence of Zambia that draws the distinction between bailable and non-bailable offences is derived from a statutory provision – to be more specific, s 123 of the Criminal Procedure Code – and not from the

[46] See s 123 of the Criminal Procedure Code of Zambia.

[47] *Martin Kpebu* (note 13).

[48] *Chetankumar Satkal Parekh* (note 24).

Constitution. Consequently, there is no automatic and mandatory grant of bail in the case of non-bailable offences. In such cases, the courts are mandated to disallow bail. This position notwithstanding, the right to bail is available to the accused in accordance with the provisions of Art 13(3)*(b)* of the Constitution of Zambia if they are not tried within a reasonable time. Article 13(3)*(b)* reads as follows:

> (3) Any person who is arrested or detained –
> (a) for the purpose of bringing him before a court in execution of an order of a court; or
> (b) upon reasonable suspicion of his having committed, or being about to commit, a criminal offence under the law in force in Zambia; and who is not released, shall be brought without undue delay before a court; and if any person arrested or detained under paragraph *(b)* is not tried within a reasonable time, then, without prejudice to any further proceedings that may be brought against him, he shall be released either unconditionally or upon reasonable conditions, including in particular such conditions as are reasonably necessary to ensure that the appears at a later date for trial or for proceedings preliminary to trial.

As stated earlier, the South African bail laws do not draw a distinction between bailable and non-bailable offences. However, for security concerns, the Legislature has intervened by providing legislative guidelines that the courts have to consider in the exercise of their discretion in bail applications in order to satisfy, first, the constitutional limitations of 'reasonable and justifiable in an open and democratic society based on human dignity, equality and freedom, considering all relevant factors' and, second, the interests of justice contained under paragraph *(b)* if the accused is not tried within a reasonable time. Then, without prejudice to any further proceedings that may be brought against them, they shall be released either unconditionally or upon reasonable conditions, including in particular such conditions as are reasonably necessary to ensure that they appear at a later date for trial or for any proceedings preliminary to trial.

The pre-*Martin Kpebu*[49] Ghanaian bail jurisprudence drew a distinction between bailable and non-bailable offences. The decision in the *Goram* case,[50] however, added another element to the discretion to grant bail in situations where a trial is not commenced within a reasonable time and the offence is 'severe'. In this case, bail may be granted even in the face of the severity of an offence if there are other considerations in the combination of stipulated factors that satisfy

[49] *Martin Kpebu* (note 13).
[50] *The Republic of Ghana* (note 25).

the court that the defendant is likely to appear to stand trial. The decision in the *Martin Kpebu* case has reversed the decision in the *Goram* case as the pre-*Martin Kpebu* law recognises the distinction between bailable and non-bailable offences as unconstitutional as it does not accord with the tenor and spirit of the Constitution of Ghana.

Under the Namibian model or approach, the bail system is underpinned by the human rights values of the new dispensation. Consequently, the Constitution provides the basic human rights of the right to liberty and due process of the law, but the procedural aspects of the principles relating to bail are contained in the relevant legislation, that is, the Criminal Procedure Act.[51] In all cases involving bail applications the courts are guided by certain considerations and factors in assessing the promotion of the interests of justice and the protection of the right of the individual. In Namibia these guidelines are not statutory; they are case-law guidelines developed by the courts themselves, as stated in the *Acheson* case.[52] There is no mandatory legislative denial of bail in certain specified offences. The jurisdiction regarding bail applications is entirely vested in the courts. This implies that all accused persons have the initial right to bail but the final determination of the application will depend on the facts of a particular case – and the primary determining factor is the promotion of the interests of justice. The virtue and advantages of this model are that, first, it accords with the tenor and spirit of international conventions and standards. Second, it confirms the jurisdiction of the courts as the custodian of human rights and therefore the appropriate organ of state to be vested with the jurisdiction over pronouncements of bail. Third, considering the view that the system of bail is part of the judicial process, it is fit and proper that legislative intervention in such matters is left to the bare minimum of regulation on procedural matters rather than substantive matters which in such cases involve the rationality of limitations clauses in human rights and bail jurisprudence.

The South African bail laws do not draw a distinction between bailable and non-bailable offences. However, for security concerns, the Legislature has intervened by providing legislative guidelines that the courts have to consider in the exercise of their discretion in bail applications in order to satisfy the constitutional limitations of 'reasonable and justifiable in an open and democratic society based on human dignity, equality and freedom, considering all relevant factors' and the interests of justice.

---

[51] Criminal Procedure Act 51 of 1977; but note that not all of the provisions of the Act are relevant to Namibia.

[52] *S v Acheson* (note 4).

18.4 CONCLUSION

The discussion in this chapter is an exposition of the bail jurisprudence of selected jurisdictions to ascertain their consistency and compliance, or otherwise, with human rights standards. The central issue at hand is the constitutionality of the statutory provisions of jurisdictions that impose a mandatory denial of bail in offences classified as 'serious' and non-bailable. In view of the exposition on the three models as presented above, the only models that very closely approximate international standards in their promotion of human rights standards are the Namibian and Ghanaian post-*Martin Kpebu* approaches. The Zambian model, it is submitted, is inconsistent with the spirit and tenor of international standards. There is the so-called constitutional bail or the derivative constitutional presumption and the right to bail in the event of unreasonable delay in prosecuting a case, which arguably are meant to temper the rigours of that particular bail system. However, as explained earlier, these provisions are not proactive; they are based on interpretative conjectures and seek to deal with the issue of the liberty of the individual after the fact. This position compromises the right to liberty of the accused because such detention subjects the accused to punitive conditions before conviction and tends to constitute a possible violation of the generality of the right to a fair trial and due process of the law.

In the bail jurisprudence of these jurisdictions, the factors that are to be considered before granting bail are statutory, but these are matters that form part and parcel of the judicial process. In a jurisdiction that belongs to the common-law tradition, the system of judicial precedents enables the courts to play a proactive role in developing the law by seeking appropriate jural postulates and *ratio decidendi* in the determination of issues based on the adduced evidence. Legislative intervention at times stifles this initiative and the pro-active role of the courts and therefore it can legitimately be argued as constituting the usurpation of judicial function by the Legislature.

Bail systems involve balancing the fundamental rights of an accused person against those of the security of the community, guided by the due process considerations that are meant to protect the liberty of the individual. What is accordingly required in each case would be a proper and considered determination of the factors relevant to determining the granting of bail rather than a court's doing so, as is the case in jurisdictions that adopt the first model. This would mean having the court give up its judicial role and allowing it to be replaced by legislative guidelines or the sentiments of a community or the public at large. Important as these factors are, they do not relieve the judicial officer of their responsibility to apply their mind to all the relevant facts in the process of deciding whether to grant bail or not.

This chapter does not attempt to prescribe. Instead, it is intended to be an exposition of the bail jurisprudence of the various jurisdictions discussed and to provide the basis for appropriate recommendations to approach the issue of the constitutionality of bail jurisprudence in selected jurisdictions. With respect to the lack of jurisdiction of the Constitutional Court of Zambia to hear cases implicating the Bill of Rights as per the Constitution of Zambia, Amendment Act 2 of 2016, it is respectfully submitted that this is a huge anomaly in the Zambian constitutional architecture and, it is hoped, one that will be attended to in the next round of constitutional reforms.

REFERENCES

Axam, HS 'If the interests of justice permit: Individual liberty, the limitation clause, and the qualified constitutional right to bail' (2001) 17(3) *South African Journal on Human Rights* 330.

Leary, V *International Labour Conventions and National Law* (Martinus Nijhoff Publishers, 1982).

Nagel, SS (ed) *The Rights of the Accused in Law and Action* (Sage Publications, 1972).

Steiner, HJ & Alston, P *International Human Rights in Context: Law, Politics and Morals* (Oxford University Press, 2000).

CASES

Bull v Minister of Home Affairs 1986 (3) SA 870 (Z)
Chetankumar Satkal Parekh v The People (1995–1997) ZR 78
Hichilema & Others v Government of the Republic of Zambia (2017/CCZ 006) and (2017/HP/0888)
Hichilema & Others v Government of the Republic of Zambia, (2020) ZMSC 37
Kpebu v Attorney-General (J1/13/2015) [2016] GHASC 15 (5 May 2016)
Martin Kpebu v Attorney-General (J1/13/2015) [2016] GHASC 15 (5 May 2016)
S v Acheson 1991 (2) SA 805 (Nm)
S v Dladla & Others Case No 3 CCT 22/98 1999 (4) SA 623 (CC)
S v Dlamini Case No 1 CCT 21/98 1999 (4) SA 623 (CC)
S v Joubert Case No 3 CCT 2/99 1999 (4) SA 623 (CC)
S v Ramgobin 1985 (3) SA 587 (N)
S v Ramgobin 1985 (4) SA 130 (N)
S v Schietekat Case No 4 CCT 4/99 1999 (4) SA 623 (CC)
Smith v Attorney-General, Bophuthatswana 1984 (1) SA 182 (B)
The Republic of Ghana v Kevin Dinsdale Gorman Criminal Appeal No J3/3/2004; (2003–2004) 2 SCGLR 784

LEGISLATION

Criminal Procedure Act 51 of 1977
Criminal Procedure Code of Zambia

Detainee Treatment Act of 2005
International Covenant on Civil and Political Rights. Adopted by the United Nations General Assembly on 16 December 1966, https://www.ohchr.org/en/instruments-mechanisms/instruments/international-covenant-civil-and-political-rights
International Covenant on Economic, Social and Cultural Rights. Adopted by the United Nations General Assembly on 16 December 1966
Military Commissions Act of 2006
The Constitution of Zambia, 1991
The International Bill of Human Rights consists of the Universal Declaration of Human Rights. International Bill of Human Rights. Universal Declaration of Human Rights, https://www.ohchr.org/en/what-are-human-rights/international-bill-human-rights
The Protocol establishing the African Court on Human and Peoples' Rights entered into force 25 January 2004

APPENDIX

Constitution of the Republic of South Africa

12. Freedom and security of the person

1. Everyone has the right to freedom and security of the person, which includes the right:
   a. not to be deprived of freedom arbitrarily or without just cause;
   b. not to be detained without trial;

35. Arrested, detained and accused persons

1. Everyone who is arrested for allegedly committing an offence has the right
   ...
   d. to be brought before a court as soon as reasonably possible, but not later than:
      i. 48 hours after the arrest; or
      ii. the end of the first court day after the expiry of the 48 hours, if the 48 hours expire outside ordinary court hours or on a day which is not an ordinary court day;
   e. at the first court appearance after being arrested, to be charged or to be informed of the reason for the detention to continue, or to be released; and
   f. to be released from detention if the interests of justice permit, subject to reasonable conditions.
2. Everyone who is detained, including every sentenced prisoner, has the right
   a. to be informed promptly of the reason for being detained;
   b. to choose, and to consult with, a legal practitioner, and to be informed of this right promptly;

c. to have a legal practitioner assigned to the detained person by the state and at state expense, if substantial injustice would otherwise result, and to be informed of this right promptly;
d. to challenge the lawfulness of the detention in person before a court and, if the detention is unlawful, to be released;
e. to conditions of detention that are consistent with human dignity, including at least exercise and the provision, at state expense, of adequate accommodation, nutrition, reading material and medical treatment; and

...

3. Every accused person has a right to a fair trial, which includes the right
   a. to be informed of the charge with sufficient detail to answer it;
   b. to have adequate time and facilities to prepare a defence;
   c. to a public trial before an ordinary court;
   d. to have their trial begin and conclude without unreasonable delay;
   e. to be present when being tried;
   f. to choose, and be represented by, a legal practitioner, and to be informed of this right promptly;
   g. to have a legal practitioner assigned to the accused person by the state and at state expense, if substantial injustice would otherwise result, and to be informed of this right promptly;
   h. to be presumed innocent, to remain silent, and not to testify during the proceedings;

36. Limitation of rights

1. The rights in the Bill of Rights may be limited only in terms of law of general application to the extent that the limitation is reasonable and justifiable in an open and democratic society based on human dignity, equality and freedom, taking into account all relevant factors, including
   a. the nature of the right;
   b. the importance of the purpose of the limitation;
   c. the nature and extent of the limitation;
   d. the relation between the limitation and its purpose; and
   e. less restrictive means to achieve the purpose.
2. Except as provided in subsection (1) or in any other provision of the Constitution, no law may limit any right entrenched in the Bill of Rights.

Schedule 6 of the Criminal Procedure Act 51 of 1977

Schedule 6 provides:

Murder when

(a) it was planned or premeditated;

(b) the victim was –
  (i) a law enforcement officer performing his or her function as such whether on duty or not, or a law enforcement officer who was killed by virtue of his or her holding such a position; or
  (ii) a person who has given or was likely to give material evidence with reference to any offence referred to in Schedule 1;
(c) the death of the victim was caused by the accused in committing or attempting to commit or after having committed or having attempted to commit one of the following offences:
  (i) rape or
  (ii) robbery with aggravating circumstances; or
(d) the offence was committed by a person, group of persons or syndicate acting in the execution or furtherance of a common purpose or conspiracy.

Rape –
(a) when committed
  (i) in circumstances where the victim was raped more than once whether by the accused or by any co-perpetrator or accomplice,
  (ii) by more than one person, where such persons acted in the execution or furtherance of a common purpose or conspiracy
  (iii) by a person who is charged with more having committed two or more offences of rape; or
  (iv) by a person, knowing that he has acquired immune deficiency syndrome or the human immunodeficiency virus;
(b) where the victim –
  (i) is a girl under the age of 16 years
  (ii) is a physically and disabled woman who, due to her physical disability is rendered particularly vulnerable.
  (iii) Is a mentally ill woman as contemplated in s 1 of the Mental Health Act 18 of 1973;
(c) involving the infliction of grievous bodily harm

Robbery involving
(a) the use by the accused or any co-perpetrators or participants of a firearm
(b) the infliction of grievous by the accused or any co-perpetrators or participants, or
(c) the taking of a motor vehicle.

Indecent assault on a child under the age of 16 years, involving the infliction of grievous bodily harm.

19

Jurisprudence of the right to trial within a reasonable time in Namibia and Zambia[1]

Samuel K Amoo

19.1 INTRODUCTION

The alleged violation of the rights of individuals detained for a long time before trial has become phenomenal and has raised global concerns. One has in mind the interns in the infamous Guantanamo Bay detention facility. In the Zambian case of the *People v John Chisimba*,[2] for example, the victim was arrested on an alleged charge of murder in 1994. In 1998 he was examined by a specialist psychiatrist and neurologist to determine whether he was fit to stand trial, it was concluded that he was and a report was sent to the court in May 2004. Despite the report having been received, the victim did not stand trial until June 2006, when the applicant applied for constitutional bail, which was granted. During the bail hearing, it emerged that the prosecution had misplaced the victim's file and that resulted in the delay in trial.

In what is commonly referred to in Namibia as the Caprivi Treason Trial, the accused were arrested in August 1999 and charged with some 275 counts of inter alia high treason, murder, sedition, public violence and attempted murder following an armed attack launched in the Caprivi Region of Namibia. Bail applications were denied by the courts because of the nature of the offences. Amnesty International in its report refers to alleged violations of the accused's pre-trial rights and concludes that these alleged violations may seriously undermine their right to a fair hearing in accordance with international standards articulated in the International Covenant

[1] Another version of this chapter was published in the *Namibia Law Journal* issue of July 2010.

[2] *People v John Chisimba* 2 TO/O9/95.

on Civil and Political Rights (ICCPR) and the African Charter on Human and Peoples' Rights (ACHPR).[3] Concerns have also been raised about the duration of the trial. The Government of the Republic of Namibia in its Report to the United Nations Secretary-General responded to these allegations[4] and one obvious reason given for the prolonged duration of the trial was the complex nature of the case.[5]

19.2 REVIEW OF THE APPLICABLE INTERNATIONAL HUMAN RIGHTS TREATIES AND CONVENTIONS

19.2.1 Maintaining peace and security

The demands of sovereignty place on states and governments inter alia the responsibility to protect and defend the integrity of the state and to maintain peace and security. Among the institutions and mechanisms employed by states is the criminal justice system that provides for the legal framework of the powers exercised by law-enforcement agencies and judicial officers. Penal laws and their enforcement, in particular, impinge on the rights of the individual, especially with regard to the rights of personal liberty, freedom of movement and privacy, etc. The concern about the potential abuse of the rights of the individual in the process of the enforcement of the penal laws by the state security apparatus and law-enforcement agencies has resulted in legislative intervention at both international (in the form of international covenants) and national levels aimed at protecting the rights of the individual. The International Bill of Rights has affected municipal jurisdiction to the extent that most contemporary jurisdictions have incorporated the International Bill of Rights[6] and treaty norms into their constitutions and domestic legal systems. For example, with regard to the right to a fair trial, both the ACHPR and the ICCPR have provisions protecting the rights of the individual to a fair trial and these provisions have been internalised in the municipal of laws of most countries. The provisions are as follows:

---

[3] Amnesty International 'Namibia: Justice delayed is justice denied: The Caprivi treason trial', 4 August 2003, 42/001/2003.

[4] Reports submitted by the Government of the Republic of Namibia under Art 9 of the International Convention on the Elimination of Racial Discrimination CERD/C/NAM/12, 18 July 2007.

[5] See also SK Amoo 'The bail jurisprudence of Ghana, Namibia, South Africa and Zambia' 2008 *Forum on Public Policy: A Journal of the Oxford Round Table* 1–29.

[6] The International Bill of Human Rights consists of the Universal Declaration of Human Rights, the International Covenant on Economic, Social and Cultural Rights, and the ICCPR and its two Optional Protocols.

Article 7*(d)* of the African Charter on Human and Peoples' Rights states that every individual has the right to be tried within a reasonable time by an impartial court or tribunal.

The ICCPR states in Article 9(3) that anyone arrested or detained on a criminal charge shall be brought promptly before a judge or other officer authorized by law to exercise judicial power and shall be entitled to trial within a reasonable time or to release.

(a) Standards and norms contained in international treaties and conventions

Under international law, the international standards and norms contained in international treaties and conventions become binding on states upon accession of these instruments and acceptance of the jurisdiction of the particular international organisation. However, if the provisions of a treaty or an international instrument are considered to be self-executing and an individual has the standing to do so, the individual may invoke the provisions of a treaty before national courts on automatic incorporation in the absence of implementing legislation. Individuals have *locus standi* before the institutions if all available domestic remedies have been exhausted. This international rule of the exhaustion of local remedies before resorting to international remedies is one of the basic rules in international law. The objective of the rule is to enable the respondent state the first opportunity to correct the harm and to make redress. Therefore, a person whose rights have been violated should first make use of domestic remedies to right a wrong rather than first raise an issue with an international committee, court or other tribunal.[7] However, if no domestic remedies are available or there is an unreasonable delay on the part of the national courts in granting a remedy, then a person is justified in having recourse to international remedies. The rule of local remedies should not constitute an unjust impediment to access to international remedies.[8]

19.3 INTERNATIONAL COVENANT ON CIVIL AND POLITICAL RIGHTS

As stated under para 19.2.1 above, the international human rights treaties or conventions and treaty bodies that inter alia protect and enforce the right of the individual to a trial within a reasonable time are the ICCPR, the ACHPR, the Human Rights Committee, the African Commission on Human and Peoples' Rights and the African Court on Human and Peoples' Rights.

[7] See, eg, *Attorney-General of The Gambia v Jawara* Case Nos 147/95 and 149/96, and many others.

[8] *Attorney-General of The Gambia* (note 7).

The ICCPR states in Art 9(3) that

> anyone arrested or detained on a criminal charge shall be brought promptly before a judge or other officer authorized by law to exercise judicial power and shall be entitled to trial within a reasonable time or to release.

This provision must not to be seen as standing on its own. The efficacy and application of this provision will be fully appreciated if it is discussed in a holistic context and in conjunction with the complementary provisions under Arts 1 and 2 of the Optional Protocol. Articles 1 and 2 of the Optional Protocol read as follows:

> Article 1
> A State Party to the Covenant that becomes a Party to the present Protocol recognizes the competence of the Committee to receive and consider communications from individuals subject to its jurisdiction who claim to be victims of a violation by that State Party of any of the rights set forth in the Covenant. No communication shall be received by the Committee if it concerns a State Party to the Covenant which is not a Party to the present Protocol.
>
> Article 2
> Subject to the provisions of article 1, individuals who claim that any of their rights enumerated in the Covenant have been violated and who have exhausted all available domestic remedies may submit a written communication to the Committee for consideration.

19.3.1 Comments on Article 1

Reference is made to the Human Rights Committee that is established under Art 28 of the ICCPR. The jurisdiction of the committee is stated under Art 40 of the Covenant and it requires states party to submit reports on measures taken to give effect to the undertakings of the Covenant and on the progress made in the enjoyment of rights declared by the Covenant. The reports are transmitted to the committee for consideration, which then has to study them. The same article instructs the committee to transmit such general comments as it may consider appropriate to these states party. The other aspect of the jurisdiction of the committee which is particularly relevant to this case is the jurisdiction provided for by Art 2 of the Optional Protocol.

The Human Rights Committee is a treaty body whose jurisdiction may be described as quasi-judicial. With respect to individual communications, it has the jurisdiction to receive communications from individuals who claim to be victims of a violation by a state party to the Optional Protocol of any of the rights set forth in the Covenant. After being notified of the communication, the state party must submit to the committee explanations or statements clarifying the matter. The committee then examines the communications and after that forwards its views to the individual and the state concerned. The views of the committee may include the payment of compensation or the release of a prisoner. But it must be noted that there is no provision setting forth the precise legal effect of the views of the committee or what follow-up should take place if the committee's views are ignored.

19.3.2 Comments on Article 2

Article 2 requires that, in addition to effective protection of Covenant rights, states party must ensure that individuals also have accessible and effective remedies to vindicate those rights. States party are also enjoined to establish appropriate judicial and administrative mechanisms for dealing with claims of rights violations under domestic law. The enjoyment of the rights recognised under the Covenant can be effectively assured by the Judiciary in many different ways, including the direct applicability of the Covenant, the application of comparable constitutional or other provisions of law, or the interpretive effect of the Covenant in the application of national law. Administrative mechanisms in particular are required to give effect to the general obligation to investigate allegations of violations promptly, thoroughly and effectively through independent and impartial bodies. A failure by a state party to investigate allegations of violations could in and of itself give rise to a separate breach of the Covenant. The cessation of an ongoing violation is an essential element of the right to an effective remedy.

Article 2 also requires that states party make reparation to individuals whose Covenant rights have been violated. Without reparation made to individuals whose Covenant rights have been violated, the obligation to provide an effective remedy, which is central to the efficacy of Art 2, is not discharged. In addition to explicit reparation in specific instances of violations, the Covenant generally entails appropriate compensation. Reparation can involve restitution, rehabilitation and measures of satisfaction, such as public apologies, public memorials, guarantees of non-repetition and changes to relevant laws and practices, and bringing the perpetrators of human rights violations to justice. Victims of violations of rights suffering from long periods of detention, as in the case of an accused, are entitled to such reparation.

International human rights jurisprudence indicates that, in general, the purposes of the Covenant would be defeated without an obligation integral to Art 2 to take measures to prevent a recurrence of a violation of the Covenant. Accordingly, it has been a frequent practice of the Human Rights Committee in cases under the Optional Protocol to include in its views the need for measures, beyond a victim-specific remedy, to be taken to avoid a recurrence of the type of violation in question. Such measures may require changes to the state party's laws or practices[9] and they are encouraged in jurisdictions that have the notoriety of violations of rights to a fair trial and, in the context of this article, a trial within a reasonable time.

19.4 AFRICAN CHARTER ON HUMAN AND PEOPLES' RIGHTS AND THE PROTOCOL

The continental human rights regime under whose jurisdiction cases of alleged violations of the right to a speedy or reasonable time to trial may be redressed is the ACHPR and the Optional Protocol. Art 7*(d)* of the ACHPR states that every individual has the right to be tried within a reasonable time by an impartial court or tribunal. However, this provision does not operate in a vacuum: its application and enforceability are be found in the jurisdiction of the ACHPR and the Protocol to the ACHPR on the Establishment of an African Court on Human and Peoples' Rights.

Article 30 of the ACHPR establishes the African Commission on Human and Peoples' Rights, the primary function of which is the promotion and protection of human and peoples' rights in Africa. The *modus operandi* employed by the commission includes the submission of communications by both states party and individuals or what is also referred to as 'non-state communications'.

With regard to cases such as *John Chisimba*,[10] the most appropriate procedure will be individual communications. This procedure, however, has certain limitations which may affect the satisfactory redress of such matters and which must therefore be highlighted. As stated by Steiner and Alston,[11] the ACHPR does not expressly define an objective for the individual complaints procedure. In *Free Legal Assistance Group* (a 1996 decision involving Zaire),[12] the commission established that the objective of the communications procedure is 'to initiate a positive dialogue, resulting in an amicable resolution between the complainant and the state concerned, which remedies the prejudice complained of'.[13] The attainment of this objective, the commission continued, was dependent on 'the good faith of the parties concerned,

[9] See the Human Rights Committee, General Comment No 31(80) The Nature of the General Legal Obligation Imposed on States Party to the Covenant Adopted on 29 March 2004 (2187th meeting).

[10] *People* (note 2).

[11] HJ Steiner & P Alston *International Human Rights in Context* (Oxford University Press, 2000) 925–926.

[12] *Free Legal Assistance Group & Others v Zaire* Comm No 25/89.47/90, 56/91, 100/93.

[13] *People* (note 2).

including willingness to participate in a dialogue'.[14] The commission therefore recognises that the bottom line of the communications procedure is the redress of any violations complained of. In order to enable it to attain this objective, it is prepared to seek an amicable settlement between the parties, which must fulfil two-pronged subjective and objective criteria. Subjectively, the parties must be satisfied with the result – a difficult standard to meet, given that the interests and aims of the victims and perpetrators of violations are often at odds. Objectively, both parties are called upon to act in good faith so as to bring about a resolution which 'remedies the prejudice complained of'.[15]

Another limitation of the objectives established by the commission for the communications procedure is that they are dependent on the volition and good faith of the state party – the respondent in this case – and therefore may not be entirely consistent with the obligation of the states party under Art 1 of the ACHPR to recognise the rights, duties and freedoms enshrined in it and to 'undertake to adopt legislative and other measures to give effect to them'.[16] Where efforts to reach an amicable resolution fail, the commission is then forced to reach a decision on the merits.[17] Article 56(5) also renders the invoking of this procedure subject to the general international-law principle of the exhaustion of domestic remedies. But, as pointed out by Steiner and Alston,[18] in practice the commission has been willing to allow wide margins of exception to this requirement, especially in situations in which massive violations of human rights are alleged.

Pityana[19] also points out that the commission's decisions lack enforceability as they are not judicial decisions. Moreover, too many of the commission's decisions are ignored routinely by states. Furthermore, the commission lacks not only the authority to enforce its own decisions; it also does not have the resources to undertake follow-up activities and to monitor compliance with its decisions. The matter could be placed before the assembly, but the assembly itself has not so far had any legislative framework by which it can demand compliance from Member States.

The African Court on Human and Peoples' Rights was established in 1998 by a Protocol which entered into force on 1 January 2004 upon its ratification by 15 Member States. The Protocol under Art 2 asserts that the court must complement the protective mandate of the ACHPR. Given the limitations of the commission, this must be understood to mean that it will reinforce and make more complete the objectives

---

[14] *People* (note 2).

[15] *People* (note 2).

[16] *Free Legal Assistance Group & Others* (note 12).

[17] See the 1994 Decision in the Mekongo Communication Against Cameroon.

[18] Steiner & Alston (note 11) 927.

[19] NB Pityana 'Reflections on the African Court on Human and Peoples' Rights' (2004) 4 *African Human Rights Law Journal* 121–129.

of the Charter. Under Art 3, the court has jurisdiction over all cases and disputes submitted to it concerning the interpretation and application of the Charter, the Protocol and other relevant human rights instruments ratified by the states concerned.

Regarding *locus standi,* the court may entitle relevant non-governmental organisations (NGOs) with observer status to appear before the commission and individuals to institute cases directly before it in accordance with Art 34(6) of the Protocol. This article demands that the states party must have made a declaration at the time of the ratification of the Protocol or at any time after that in which they accept the competence of the court to receive cases under Art 5(3) of the Protocol. In the absence of any such declaration, therefore, individuals have to submit their complaints first to the African Commission. The Protocol is silent on the question of the exhaustion of local remedies but it may be presumed that the general principles of international law will apply to subject individuals who seek the jurisdiction of the court to satisfying the exhaustion of the local remedies principle.

A judgment of the African Court on Human and Peoples' Rights is binding on states party to the Protocol.[20] These states party undertake, in terms of Art 30, to comply with the judgment in any case where they are parties within the time stipulated by the court and to guarantee its execution. In other words, the states take primary responsibility for the execution of the judgments of the court. Should the affected parties fail to do so, other persuasive and coercive means are available to the AU: the court submits its reports to a regular session of the assembly[21] and the provision goes on to state that the report must in particular specify the cases in which a state has not complied with the court's judgment.[22] This provision in effect transfers the secondary responsibility for ensuring compliance with the rulings of the court to the collective of the heads of state and government. This could serve as a kind of peer-review mechanism.[23] As a monitoring mechanism, the judgments of the courts are notified not only to the parties in dispute, but also to the Council of Ministers, which must monitor its execution on behalf of the assembly.[24]

19.5 APPLICATION OF INTERNATIONAL HUMAN RIGHTS CONVENTIONS AND STANDARDS

The ICCPR and the ACHPR contain provisions that protect the right of the individual to a trial within a reasonable time and under these treaties there are

[20] Article 30 of the Organization of African Unity (OAU), *Protocol to the African Charter on Human and Peoples' Rights on the Establishment of an African Court on Human and People's Rights,* 10 June 1998 (hereinafter the Protocol).

[21] Article 31 of the Protocol.

[22] Ibid.

[23] Pityana (note 19).

[24] Article 29.2 of the Protocol.

treaty bodies that have been established and empowered with the jurisdiction to enforce compliance with the obligations of the treaties. In Zambia, international instruments are not self-executing and require legislative implementation to take effect. The position in Namibia is rather more complex: Namibia has adopted both the monist and the dualist approaches with respect to the implementation of international treaties. The Executive concludes or accedes to international treaties, which then will require ratification by the National Assembly: ratification does not imply the automatic integration of treaty obligations as part of the law of Namibia. The nature of the treaty obligations will determine whether parliament will regard a particular international instrument as self-executing or not after ratification. Both Namibia and Zambia have ratified the ICCPR[25] and are also parties to the First Optional Protocol to the ICCPR providing for individual complaint procedures.

First and foremost, therefore, it must be emphasised that Zambia is bound by the treaty obligations under Art 2 to make available to the victim the remedies stated above if a violation of the victim's right is successfully established. Second, in the event of the victim's dissatisfaction with the local legal system for reasons stated above, the victim or applicant can avail themself of the individual communications procedure under the jurisdiction of the Human Rights Committee. As stated earlier, the committee has the jurisdiction to examine communications from individuals who claim to be victims of a violation of any of the rights proclaimed in the Covenant, including the right to trial within a reasonable period.

At the regional or continental level, both Namibia and Zambia are also parties to the ACHPR.[26] The Zambian Constitution has incorporated international human rights standards and these include the right to a fair trial, which is justiciable. Both Namibia and Zambia are therefore bound by the treaty obligations under the Charter just as much as they are bound by the treaty obligations of the ICCPR. The victim or applicant is therefore entitled to invoke the jurisdiction of the African Commission on Human and Peoples' Rights and avail themself of the individual communications procedure.

These international instruments that provide for these rights, however, do not define what constitutes 'within a reasonable time' or 'a speedy trial' and therefore reference will have to be made to other sources to determine what constitutes 'a speedy trial'. These sources will include relevant legislation and case law, but it must be explained that there is greater reliance on case law than legislative sources in this chapter, due to a lack of access to these latter sources, if they are available.

[25] Namibia and Zambia acceded to the ICCPR on 10 April 1984.

[26] Zambia signed the African Charter on Human and Peoples' Rights on 17 January 1983 and ratified it on 10 January 1984.

19.5.1 Establishing a violation of rights under international conventions and treaties bodies

Establishing a successful case of infringement and violation of rights will necessitate the adducing of sufficient evidence to satisfy the requirements of both substantive and procedural law in order to establish that the delay complained of exceeds what is reasonable. Furthermore, evidence will have to be adduced to quantify the damage and/or loss occasioned as a result of the violations with regard to the claim for compensation.

(a) Substantive considerations

Determining what constitutes 'reasonable time' has been discussed in judicial decisions of certain jurisdictions, the most notable of which is perhaps the case of *R v Askov*,[27] where the issue involved alleged violations of constitutional rights. This case reviews the relevant authorities, especially cases of the Supreme Court of the United States and Canada, and lays down standards for establishing a speedy trial or a trial within a reasonable time. These standards have been followed by superior and constitutional courts in a number of jurisdictions, including Zimbabwe[28] and Namibia.[29] The standards are discussed extensively in the cases mentioned in this section, but a summary of the factors is given here in order to put them in context. *R v Askov* lays down four factors to consider when determining 'reasonable time':

(i) the length of the delay;
(ii) the explanation for the delay (this includes evidence relating to the conduct of the Crown or the state, systemic or institutional delays and the conduct of the accused);
(iii) the waiver, and
(iv) prejudice to the accused.

The court held that the first factor is the triggering mechanism or threshold determination of the excessiveness of the delay and that if that delay appears prima facie excessive, the court must then consider the three remaining factors to determine whether the accused has been deprived of the Sixth Amendment. In the Zimbabwean case of *In re Mlambo*,[30] in determining a violation of the rights of the accused to trial within a reasonable time, Gubbay CJ followed the factors laid down

[27] *R v Askov* (1990) 2 SCR 1199; (1991) 49 CRR 1 (Supreme Court of Canada).
[28] *In re Mlambo* 1992 (4) SA 144 (ZS); 1992 (2) SACR 245 (ZS).
[29] *S v Heidenrich* 1996 (2) BCLR 197 (NmH); 1998 NR 229.
[30] *In re Mlambo* (note 28).

in the *Askov* case and stated that additional evidence would have to be established to determine whether a violation of human rights could be claimed. He stated:

> I have no hesitation in holding that the time frame is designed to relate far more to the period prior to the commencement of the hearing or trial that to whatever period may elapse after the accused has tendered a plea. This meaning is wholly consonant with the rationale of s 18(2) – that the charge from which the reasonable time enquiry begins, must correspond with the start of the impairment of the individual's interest in the liberty and security of his person. *The concept of 'security' is not restricted to physical integrity, but includes stigmatisation, loss of privacy, anxiety, disruption of family, social life and work.* I may say that this view accords with the interpretation given to the materially similar wording of Article 6 para 1 of the European Convention by the European Court of Human Rights. [Emphasis added]

In the case of *R v Askov*,[31] Lamer J, as he then was, also expressed similar views and referred to these vexations, as described above by Gubbay CJ, as 'all strictly individual rights'. In the case under consideration, the presiding judge ruled that there had been an inordinate delay as the accused had been in detention for more than 12 years. Therefore, there was incontrovertible evidence to satisfy the triggering mechanism that the delay was prima facie unreasonable or, in the words of Powell J in *Barker v Wingo*,[32] 'presumptively prejudicial'. However, in order to conclude that the effect of the lengthy delay is such as to deny the applicant the right to a fair hearing in this case there is the need to balance the other factors against it.

Further evidence will also have to be adduced to prove that the inordinate delay led to the impairment of the accused's interests in the liberty and security of their person and therefore constituted a violation of their rights. In the light of the above, therefore, proof of violation will include evidence to establish, for example, stigmatisation, loss of privacy, anxiety, and disruption of family life, social life and work occasioned as a result of the inordinate delay and long period of detention.

19.5.2 Procedural considerations

The burden of proof required will be the standard required in civil proceedings, which is on the balance of probabilities; and with regard to the question of *locus standi* there must be evidence of the exhaustion of local remedies. This will include both judicial and extrajudicial remedies, as in the case of Zambia, which entailed

[31] *R v Askov* (note 27).

[32] *Barker v Wingo* (1972) 407 US 514 at 530.

placing the matter before the Zambian Human Rights Commission, unless it can be established that the prevailing conditions are such that it can be legitimately claimed that the victim will not receive justice under the local legal system, including the reasons stated in para 19.2.1.2 These procedural considerations will apply to applications to both the Human Rights Committee and the African Commission.

With respect to petitions before the African Court, it is imperative that the petition be directed against a state party which has made a declaration under Art 34.6 of the Protocol authorising direct access for individuals and NGOs with Observer Status before the African Commission. In order to be admissible under Art 56.2 of the Charter, the petition must invoke the provisions of the ACHPR allegedly violated, in this case Art 7*(d)* of the Charter.

19.6 JURISPRUDENCE OF THE RIGHT TO A FAIR TRIAL UNDER MUNICIPAL LAW

19.6.1 Right to a hearing within a reasonable time

Article 18(1) of the Zambian Constitution, which deals with the protection of law, provides as follows:

> If any person is charged with a criminal offence, then, unless the charge is withdrawn, the accused shall be afforded a fair hearing within a reasonable time by an independent and impartial court established by law.

Article 12(1)*(b)* of the Constitution of Namibia has a similar provision which provides as follows:

> A trial referred to in Sub-Article *(a)* hereof shall take place within a reasonable time, failing which the accused shall be released.

The term 'reasonable time' has not been defined in the various constitutions, but has been considered in a number of cases from various jurisdictions. In the English case of *Hickey v Raymond and Reid*,[33] Lord Watson observed:

> The condition of reasonable time has been frequently interpreted and has invariably been held to mean that a party upon whom it is incumbent duly fulfils his obligation not withstanding protracted delay, so long as such

[33] (1893) AC 22 at 32 and 33.

> delay is attributable to cause beyond his control, and he has neither acted negligently nor unreasonably.

Perhaps the most comprehensive consideration of what amounts to a 'speedy trial' or a fair hearing within a 'reasonable time' is to be found in the judgment of Cory JJ of the Supreme Court of Canada in the case of *R v Askov*.[34] The case involved the interpretation of what constitutes unreasonable delay in the context of s 11*(b)* of the Canadian Charter of Rights and Freedoms, which provides that 'any person charged with an offence has the right to be tried within a reasonable time' (the facts are stated below).[35] The provisions of s 11*(b)* of the Canadian Charter of Rights and Freedoms are couched in the same terms as the provisions of Art 18(1) of the Zambian Constitution and Art 12(1)*(b)* of the Namibian Constitution stated above.

In laying down the factors to be considered in determining 'reasonable time', the Court reviewed the position of the law in both the United States and Canada and discussed in detail the *raison d'être* of the right to a fair trial within a reasonable time. Corry J explained the position of the law as follows:

> *(a) Judicial consideration of the principle of providing a trial within a reasonable time*
> (i) United States
> In the United States the Sixth Amendment ensures that '[i]n all criminal prosecutions, the accused shall enjoy the right to a speedy and public trial'. The United States Supreme Court considered the issue in *Barker v Wingo*,

---

[34] *R v Askov* (note 27).

[35] In *R v Askov* (note 27), the appellants were charged with conspiracy to commit extortion in November 1983. A, H and M were also charged with several related offences and detained in custody for almost six months before being released on recognisances. G was released on a recognisance shortly after his arrest. All counsel agreed on a date early in July 1984 for the preliminary hearing, but it could not be completed until September. A trial was then set for the first available date in October 1985. The case could not be heard during that session and was held over for trial to September 1986, almost two years after the preliminary hearing. When the trial finally began, the appellants moved to stay the proceedings on the ground that the trial had been unreasonably delayed. The trial judge found that the major part of the delay following appellants' committal stemmed from institutional problems and granted the stay. The Court of Appeal found: (1) no misconduct on the part of the Crown; (2) no indication of any objection by the appellants to any of the adjournments, and (3) no evidence of any actual prejudice to the appellants. It accordingly set aside the stay and directed that the trial proceed. But the Supreme Court found that the delay was prima facie excessive; indeed, that it was grossly excessive. The court found further that the defence had never caused the delay nor agreed to it: the delay was caused by the prosecution. Taking all those factors into consideration, the court concluded that the delay could not be justified and was therefore unreasonable.

> 407 US 514 (1972). In that case, Barker, who was charged with murder, was brought to trial five years after the murder was committed. The delay was caused by the necessity of trying an accomplice beforehand. This prerequisite trial was extremely complicated; the accomplice was tried no less than six times. During this ongoing process, Barker initially had agreed to continuances or adjournments. He only began to assert his right to a speedy trial three-and- a-half years after the charges were laid.
>
> The court held that a flexible approach should be taken to cases involving delay and that the multiple purposes or aims of the Sixth Amendment must be appreciated. Powell J, giving the reasons for the court, recognised the general concern that all persons accused with crimes should be treated according to fair and decent procedures. He particularly noted that there were three individual interests which the right was designed to protect:
>
> (i) to prevent oppressive pre-trial incarceration;
> (ii) to minimize the anxiety and concern of the accused; and
> (iii) to limit the possibility that the defence will be impaired or prejudiced.

However, Powell J[36] went on to observe that, unlike other constitutional rights which have only an individual interest, the right to a speedy trial involved the added dimension of a societal interest. He found that a delay could result in increased financial cost to society and, in addition, could have a negative effect upon the credibility of the justice system. Furthermore, it was noted that a delay could work to the advantage of the accused. For example, fostering a delay could become a defence tactic designed to take advantage of failing memories or missing witnesses or could permit the accused to manipulate the system in order to bargain for a lesser sentence. Specifically, he stated[37] that the right to a speedy trial was

> a more vague concept than other procedural rights. It is, for example, impossible to determine with precision when the right has been denied. We cannot definitely say how long is too long in a system where justice is supposed to be swift but deliberate. As a consequence, there is no fixed point in the criminal process when the State can put the defendant to the choice of either exercising or waiving the right to a speedy trial.

In order to balance the individual right and the communal aspect of the Sixth Amendment, the US Supreme Court adopted an approach of ad hoc balancing 'in which the conduct of both the prosecution and the defendant are weighed'.[38] The

---

[36] *R v Askov* (note 27).
[37] *R v Askov* (note 27) at 521.
[38] *R v Askov* (note 27) at 530.

balancing is undertaken by reference to four factors, identified by Powell J as the test for infringement of the right to a 'speedy trial'. They are as follows:

(a) the length of the delay;
(b) the reason for the delay;
(c) the accused's assertion of the right; and
(d) prejudice to the accused.

The first factor is the triggering mechanism or threshold determination of the excessiveness of the delay. If that delay appears prima facie excessive, the court must then consider the three remaining factors to determine whether the accused has been deprived of the Sixth Amendment right.

After his definition and exposition of the factors which should be taken into consideration on an application for a stay of proceedings, Powell J proceeded to explain that before that step is undertaken, it is necessary to determine what may be distilled from the cases as to the purpose or aim of s 11*(b)*.

19.6.2 Purpose of section 11*(b)*

Powell J[39] explained that s 11*(b)* focuses explicitly on the individual interest of liberty and security of the person. Like other specific guarantees provided by s 11, this paragraph is primarily concerned with an aspect of fundamental justice guaranteed by s 7 of the Charter. He stated:

> There could be no greater frustration imaginable for innocent persons charged with an offence than to be denied the opportunity of demonstrating their innocence for an unconscionable time as a result of unreasonable delays in their trial. The time awaiting trial must be exquisite agony for accused persons and their immediate family. It is a fundamental precept of our criminal law that every individual is presumed to be innocent until proven guilty. It follows that on the same fundamental level of importance, all accused persons, each one of whom is presumed to be innocent, should be given the opportunity to defend themselves against the charges they face and to have their name cleared and reputation re-established at the earliest possible time.

Furthermore, he added that community interest has a dual dimension:

> First, there is a collective interest in ensuring that those who transgress the law are brought to trial and dealt with according to the law. Second, those

[39] *R v Askov* (note 27).

individuals on trial must be treated fairly and justly. Speedy trials strengthen both those aspects of the community interest. A trial held within a reasonable time must benefit the individual accused as the prejudice which results from criminal proceedings is bound to be minimized. If the accused is in custody, the custodial time awaiting trial will be kept to a minimum. If the accused is at liberty on bail and subject to conditions, then the curtailments on the liberty of the accused will be kept to a minimum. From the point of view of the community interest, in those cases where the accused is detained in custody awaiting trial, society will benefit by the quick resolution of the case either by reintegrating into society the accused found to be innocent or if found guilty by dealing with the accused according to the law. If the accused is released on bail and subsequently found guilty, the frustration felt by the community on seeing an unpunished wrongdoer in their midst for an extended period of time will be relieved.

There are as well important practical benefits which flow from a quick resolution of the charges. There can be no doubt that memories fade with time. Witnesses are likely to be more reliable testifying to events in the immediate past as opposed to events that transpired many months or even years before the trial. Not only is there an erosion of the witnesses' memory with the passage of time, but there is bound to be an erosion of the witnesses themselves. Witnesses are people; they are moved out of the country by their employer; or for reasons related to family or work they move from the east coast to the west coast; they become sick and unable to testify in court; they are involved in debilitating accidents; they die and their testimony is forever lost. Witnesses too are concerned that their evidence be taken as quickly as possible. Testifying is often thought to be an ordeal. It is something that weighs on the minds of witnesses and is a source of worry and frustration for them until they have given their testimony.

19.6.3 Factors to be considered in determining whether or not there has been an infringement of the right to a 'speedy trial'

As stated by Powell J in *R v Askov*,[40] the four factors that have generally been recognised as constituting the test for determining the infringement of the right to a speedy trial are:

- the length of the delay;
- the reason for the delay;

[40] *R v Askov* (note 27).

- the accused's assertion of the right, and
- prejudice to the accused.

It might be useful to expand on the requirements and applications and of these factors.

(a) Length of the delay

Prima facie evidence of an unreasonably prolonged delay will necessitate an enquiry into a possible infringement of the individual's right to a speedy trial or a trial within a reasonable time. In certain jurisdictions, such as the United States, this factor constitutes the triggering mechanism or threshold for determining the excessiveness of a delay. In other jurisdictions it is a factor to be balanced against the others. However, very lengthy delays may be such that they cannot be justified for any reason.

(b) Explanation for the delay

This category may be subdivided into and discussed as either systemic delay or the conduct of the accused:

(i) Conduct of the Crown or state (or delay attributable to the Crown)

Generally speaking, this category will comprise all possible factors that could be causing a delay which flow from the nature of the case, the conduct of the state, including officers of the state, and the inherent time requirements of the case. Delays attributable to the actions of the state or its officers will weigh in favour of the accused. For example, adjournments initiated by the state, the unavailability of judges and the misplacement of files by the prosecution are examples of the actions or the lack of actions of Crown officers that may weigh against the state in the assessment of the reasonableness of a delay.

It is under this heading that the complexity of a case should be considered. Complex cases, such as Caprivi Treason Trial, which require longer time for preparation, greater expenditure on resources by Crown officers and the longer use of institutional facilities will justify delays longer than those that would be acceptable in more straightforward cases.

(ii) Systemic or institutional delays

Delays occasioned by inadequate resources or systemic or institutional limitations must weigh against the state. Various variables will determine this factor and they must be determined objectively. The state bears the onus of justifying inadequate resources that result in systemic delays, because it is the responsibility of the state to bring the accused to trial. The courts have always insisted that the lack of institutional resources cannot be used as a reason to justify a continuing unreasonable postponement of trials. In *Mills v The Queen*,[41] Lamer J noted:

> In an ideal world there would be no delays in bringing an accused to trial and there would be no difficulties in securing fully adequate funding, personnel and facilities for the administration of criminal justice. As we do not live in such a world, some allowance must be made for limited institutional resources.

However, Lamer J added that the lack of institutional facilities can never be used as a basis for rendering the right to trial within a reasonable time meaningless. In the same case he stated:[42]

> It is imperative, however, that in recognizing the need for such a criterion we do not simply legitimate current and future delays resulting from inadequate institutional resources. For the criterion of institutional resources, more than any other, threatens to become a source of justification for prolonged and unacceptable delay. There must, therefore, be some limit to which inadequate resources can be used to excuse delay and impair the interests of the individual.

(iii) Conduct of the accused (or delay attributable to the accused)[43]
As stated previously, it is the responsibility of the state to bring the accused to trial within a reasonable time. The courts in the *Askov*[44] and *Mills*[45] cases explained that it follows from this responsibility and the right to trial within a reasonable time that any enquiry into the conduct of the accused should in no way absolve the state of its responsibility to bring the accused to trial.

Nonetheless, there is a societal interest in preventing an accused from using the guarantee as a means of escaping trial. It should be emphasised that an enquiry into the actions of the accused should be restricted to discovering those situations in which the accused's acts either directly caused the delay or the acts of the accused are shown to be a deliberate and calculated tactic employed to delay the trial. These direct acts on the part of the accused, such as seeking an adjournment to retain new counsel, must, of course, be distinguished from those situations where the delay was caused by factors beyond the control of the accused or a situation where

[41] *Mills v The Queen* [1986] 1 SCR 863 at 935.
[42] Mills (note 41) at 935.
[43] Corry J in *R v Askov* (note 27).
[44] Corry (note 43).
[45] *Mills* (note 41).

the accused did nothing to prevent a delay caused by the state; and the burden of proving that the direct acts of the accused caused the delay falls accordingly upon the state.

The court added the proviso that this would be true except in those cases where the effects of the accused's action are so clear and readily apparent that the intention of the accused to cause a delay is the inference that must be drawn from the record of their actions.

(c) Waiver

The accused may be deemed to have waived their rights to a trial within a reasonable time by consenting to or concurring in a delay, and this aspect must be considered. However, for a waiver to be valid it must be informed, unequivocal and freely given. The accused must have full knowledge of the rights and the effects the waiver will have on those rights. The failure of an accused to assert the right does not give the state licence to proceed with an unfair trial. Failure to assert the right would be insufficient in itself to impugn the motives of the accused. Instead, there must be something in the conduct of the accused that is sufficient to give rise to an inference that the accused has understood that they had a right to trial within a reasonable time, understood its nature and has waived the right provided by the Constitution. Although no particular magical incantation of words is required to waive a right, the waiver must nevertheless be expressed in some manner. Silence or a lack of objection cannot constitute a lawful waiver. The matter was put in these words by Dickson J, as he then was, in *Park v The Queen*:[46]

> No particular words or formula need be uttered by defence counsel to express the waiver and admission. All that is necessary is that the trial judge be satisfied that counsel understands the matter and has made an informed decision to waive .... Although no particular form of words is necessary, the waiver must be express. Silence or mere lack of objection does not constitute a lawful waiver.

The burden of showing that a waiver should be inferred falls upon the state. An example of a waiver or concurrence that could be inferred is the consent by counsel for the accused to a fixed date for trial.

(d) Prejudice to the accused

There is a general – and in the case of very long delays – an often virtually irrebuttable presumption of prejudice to the accused resulting from the passage of time. But

[46] [1981] 2 SCR 64 at 73–74.

where the Crown can demonstrate that there was no prejudice to the accused flowing from a delay, then such proof may serve to excuse the delay. It is also open to the accused to call evidence to demonstrate actual prejudice to strengthen their position that they have been prejudiced as a result of the delay.

The issue of what constitutes a fair hearing within a reasonable time was also considered in the Zimbabwean case of *In re Mlambo*.[47] The applicant was arrested in 1986 and charged with theft. He appeared in court and was released on bail after two weeks in custody. He subsequently appeared in court on 12 occasions until August 1987, when his legal representative complained about the lengthy delay in bringing the matter to trial and made strong representations that a date for trial be set. In response, the prosecutor promptly withdrew the charges and the applicant was advised that he could be charged at a later stage. In August 1990 the applicant was summonsed to appear in court on substantially the same charges. His legal representative wrote on several occasions to the clerk of the court requesting copies of various documents which the state intended to produce at the trial. When the date of trial arrived and the copies of documents had not been provided, the applicant's legal representative sought a postponement of the trial, which was granted. At the resumed hearing the applicant's counsel asked the Court to stay the proceedings on the grounds that the applicant's rights under s 18(2) in the Declaration of Rights in the Constitution of Zimbabwe had been infringed by the delay in bringing the matter to trial. The prosecution made no attempt to explain the delay and the magistrate dismissed the application. On the following day, the matter resumed before another magistrate, who agreed to refer the matter to the Supreme Court in terms of s 24(2) of the Constitution.

The court held that a reasonable time was necessary for the state to be ready for a trial, which period varied from case to case, and that the distinction between what was a reasonable period and what was not a reasonable period could not be drawn too sharply. Gubbay CJ, delivering the judgment of the Full Bench of the Supreme Court, endorsed the approach of the European Court of Human Rights in *Eckle v Germany (Federal Republic)*[48] and *Foti v Italy*.[49] He restated the factors as follows:

> In *Fikilini v Attorney-General* 1990 (1) ZLR 105 (SC) at 112G this Court approved of the factors identified by Justice Powell in his landmark judgment in *Barker v Wingo*,[50] as amongst those to be considered in

[47] *In re Mlambo* (note 28).
[48] (1985) 5 EHRR 1.
[49] (1983) 5 EHRR 313.
[50] *Barker* (note 32).

assessing whether an accused has been deprived of his constitutional right to a speedy trial.

He stated these factors[51] as follows:

> The length of the delay is to some extent a triggering mechanism. Until there is some delay which is presumptively prejudicial, there is no necessity for inquiry into the other factors that go into the balance. Nevertheless, because of the imprecision of the right to speedy trial, the length of delay that will provoke such an inquiry is necessarily dependent upon the peculiar circumstances of the case. To take but one example, the delay that can be tolerated for an ordinary street crime is considerably less than for a serious, complex conspiracy charge.

Closely related to length of delay is the reason the government gives to justify the delay. Here, too, different weights should be assigned to different reasons. A deliberate attempt to delay the trial in order to hamper the defence should weigh heavily against the government. A more neutral reason such as negligence or overburdened courts should weigh less heavily, but it should nevertheless be considered since the ultimate responsibility for such circumstances must rest with the government rather than with the defendant. Finally, a valid reason, such as a missing witness, should serve to justify an appropriate delay.

Prejudice is also a factor to be considered with respect to the defendant. Prejudice, of course, should be assessed in the light of the interests of defendants which the right to a speedy trial was designed to protect. Three such interests are: (1) to prevent oppressive pre-trial incarceration; (2) to minimise the anxiety and concern of the accused, and (3) to limit the possibility that the defence will be impaired. Of these, the most serious is the last, because the inability of a defendant to prepare adequately for their case skews the fairness of the entire system. If witnesses die or disappear during a delay, the prejudice is obvious. There is also prejudice if defence witnesses are unable to recall accurately events of the distant past. Loss of memory, however, is not always reflected in the record because what has been forgotten can rarely be shown.[52]

---

[51] *In re Mlambo* (note 28) at 530–532.

[52] See also *United States v Van Neumann* 474 US 242 (1986) at 247.
These factors received the *imprimatur* of the Privy Counsel in *Bell v Director of Public Prosecutions of Jamaica & Another* [1985] 2 All ER 585.

19.7 ONUS

As stated previously, it is for the applicant to persuade the court that the delay complained of exceeds what is reasonable: *Fikilini v Attorney-General.*[53] The degree of persuasion required of them is to show that the delay is prima facie unreasonable or, in the words of Powell J in *Barker v Wingo,*[54] 'presumptively prejudicial'. It is that which triggers the enquiry into the other factors that go into the balance. It is the threshold at which the court may look to the state for an explanation. It is, of course, neither possible nor desirable to identify precisely the length of delay which will trigger the enquiry: each case is to be viewed in the light of its own particular circumstances in order to determine whether the delay is prima facie unreasonable.

19.8 ASSESSMENT OF REASONABLENESS

In the Zambian *John Chisimba* case,[55] for example, the overall length of the delay was 12 years, which is more than adequate to trigger an enquiry. It is 'presumptively prejudicial'. It is submitted in the premise, therefore, that the disposition of the *John Chisimba* case will ultimately turn on the proof of the other factors such as

(1) The explanation for the delay, particularly systemic or institutional delay and delays attributable to the accused;
(2) waiver, and
(3) prejudice to the accused.

Considering the length of the delay and the explanation of it, one is obliged to conclude that the state's conduct is indicative of a sustained lack of concern to proceed as quickly as possible against the accused. The explanation for the delay is that the prosecution had misplaced the victim's file. It is submitted that this is as totally unacceptable as it is reprehensible. That the entire delay was attributable to the actions of the state weighs heavily in favour of the accused. Unless, therefore, there is some strong basis to counter this factor which becomes clear from an examination of other factors, it will not prove possible to tolerate it.

Next to be set in the scale is the frequency and force of the objection to the delay. Here evidence must be adduced to establish that there was nothing in the conduct of the victim or their defence counsel that can be viewed as a waiver of the applicant's constitutional guarantee. It must be proved that concerted efforts were

[53] 1990 (1) ZLR 105 (SC) at 117D–E.
[54] *Barker* (note 32) at 530.
[55] *People* (note 2).

made by the victim or their counsel to object to the delay. With regard to the fourth factor, evidence must be elicited from the applicant to the effect that the delay had caused them actual prejudice. This may relate to the unavailability of witnesses and other evidence that collectively impair the accused's ability to present an adequate defence to establish the prejudice. It must also be borne in mind that a very long delay such as this inherently gives rise to a strong presumption of prejudice to an accused. As stated by Hannah J:[56]

> The right, therefore, recognises that, with the passage of time, subjection to a criminal charge gives rise to restrictions on liberty, inconveniences, social stigma and pressures detrimental to the mental and physical health of the individual. It is a truism that the time awaiting trial must be agonising for accused persons and their immediate family. I believe that there can be no greater frustration for an innocent person charged with an offence than to be denied the opportunity of demonstrating his lack of guilt for an unconscionable time as a result of delay in bringing him to trial. The right recognises, also, that an unreasonable delay may well impair the ability of the individual to present a full and fair defence to the charge. Where the State can demonstrate that there was no prejudice flowing from the delay, then such proof may serve to excuse it.

In the *John Chisimba* case, for example, balancing all the factors leads one irresistibly to submit that the effect of this extraordinarily lengthy delay is such as to deny the applicant or victim the right to a fair hearing of their case. Justice so delayed is an affront to the individual, to the community and to the very administration of justice. The charge against the victim or accused was murder and, therefore, far from trivial; and there can be no doubt that it would be in the best interests of society to proceed with the trial of those who are charged with the commission of serious crimes. Yet that trial can be proceeded with only if the guarantee under s 18(1) of the Zambian Constitution has not been infringed. In this case, it had been grievously infringed.

19.9 APPROPRIATE REMEDY

As stated previously, both the constitutions of Namibia and Zambia protect and guarantee the right of the accused to a fair trial within a reasonable time and a cause of action for alleged violations of the right will necessitate an application for

[56] *S v Heidenrich* (note 29) at 235A–C.

a declaration of the violations. Moreover, the order for the remedies will have to be made to the courts in both countries that have jurisdiction over constitutional matters, which will be the High Court and the Supreme Court respectively.

In criminal-law jurisprudence there are two schools of thought on the appropriate remedy to be ordered in cases of violation of the right to a fair trial: either an order for a stay of prosecution (ie, an order to abort the trial) or an order for a speedy trial. In *R v Askov*, the court granted a stay of proceedings. In the *Mlambo* case, the court granted a permanent stay of proceedings but added that an order that the charge be dismissed would be tantamount to a pronouncement of innocence. In the Namibian case of *S v Heidenrich*[57] Hannah J stated that

> once the main objective of the sub-article 12(1)*(b)* of the Constitution of Namibia, which provides that the accused shall be released in the event of the violation of right, has been identified as being not only to minimise the possibility of lengthy pre-trial incarceration and to curtail restrictions placed on an accused who is on bail but also to reduce the inconvenience, social stigma and other pressures which he is likely to suffer and to advance the prospect of fair hearing, then it seems to me that 'release' must mean release from further prosecution for the offence with which he is charged. It is only by giving the term this wider meaning that the full purpose of the sub-article is met. Release from custody or from onerous conditions of bail meets part of purpose of the sub-article.

In another Namibian case, *S v Uahanga & Others*,[58] the accused had originally been charged in March 1995. After that, the matter had been postponed several times. By the time the matter was to be heard in October 1995, the state requested a further postponement. When the matter was postponed in July, it had been recorded that the postponement to October was to be the final postponement. On the day in October when the matter was to be heard, witnesses were available but there seemed to be a problem with the availability of prosecutors. It appeared that at least two prosecutors were not involved in trials, but the state alleged that it could not proceed and the magistrate acquitted the accused, invoking Art 12 of the Namibian Constitution, which provides for the right to a speedy trial. On appeal, the court held that the accused were entitled to a speedy trial in terms of Art 12 of the Namibian Constitution. The delay had not been unduly long, but the court held that the explanations for the continual postponements had been unsatisfactory.

[57] *S v Heidenrich* (note 29).
[58] 1998 NR 160.

The court found that the conduct of the prosecution had been slovenly and that the accused had been correctly acquitted.

However, in *Van As & Another v Prosecutor-General*,[59] a Three Bench High Court, in interpreting 'release' in Art 12(1)*(b)* of the Namibian Constitution, which provides to the effect that where a criminal trial has not taken place within a reasonable time, the accused may be released, the court held that 'release' in Art 12(1)*(b)* could not be equated to 'acquit' and that it merely meant that an accused would be released but did not preclude the prosecution from rearresting the accused at a later stage and reviving the proceedings. The court added, however, that this interpretation did not lose sight of the fact that the prosecution should not be allowed to benefit from its ineptitude. The court accordingly held that Art 12(1)*(b)* did not provide for a permanent stay of criminal proceedings.

The Supreme Court's interpretation of 'release' in Art 12(1)*(b)* in the case of *Margaret Malama-Kean v The Magistrate of the District of Oshakati NO and the Prosecutor-General NO*[60] is the latest and most comprehensive formulation of the nature and forms of release as contemplated by the framers of the Constitution. The court confirmed that those criminal courts which are competent courts with the necessary jurisdiction should have the power and the responsibility in an appropriate case of unreasonable delay to order a permanent stay of prosecution as at least one of its discretionary powers. The court went further to indicate that a permanent stay of prosecution is not the only order contemplated as constituting the discretionary powers of the criminal courts. It argued further that a particular form that an order for release from a trial will take will depend not only on the degree of prejudice caused by the failure of the trial to take place within a reasonable time, but also the jurisdiction of the court considering the issue and making the order. O'Linn AJA, delivering the judgment of the court, described the various forms of release as follows:[61]

> However, the entire effect of an order stating 'shall be discharged from the trial' remains unclear. It is clear that the remedy provided in art 12(1)*(b)* – 'shall be released' is couched in mandatory and peremptory terms. Nevertheless, it does not seem to me that only one form of release from the trial would meet the peremptory requirement. The following forms of release from the trial, will in my view all be legitimate forms meeting the peremptory requirement:

[59] 2000 NR 271.

[60] Case No SA 04/2002.

[61] *Margaret Malama-Kean* (note 60).

(i) A release from the trial prior to plea on the merits, which does not have the effect of a permanent stay of the prosecution and is broadly tantamount to a withdrawal of the charges by the State before the accused had pleaded.

This form of release will encompass:[62]

(a) Unconditional release from detention if the accused is still in detention when the order is made for his/her release;
(b) Release from the conditions of bail if the accused had already been released on bail prior to making the order;
(c) … sub-article 12(1)*(b)* …
  (ii) An acquittal after plea on merits:
  (iii) A permanent stay of prosecution, either before or subsequent to a plea on the merits.

In the South African case of *McCarthy v Additional Magistrate, Johannesburg*[63] the court decided that a party asserting an unreasonable delay in prosecution was required to show more than average systemic delay and that an indefinite stay of prosecution would seldom be granted in the absence of extraordinary circumstances.

19.10 CONCLUSION

Both Namibia and Zambia are sovereign states with supreme courts as the final courts of appeal and therefore foreign authorities are only persuasive, not binding. But the authorities referred to above are not from the courts of only one jurisdiction. These authorities all confirm that stay of proceedings is an appropriate remedy to be ordered in a case of violation of the right to a fair trial. Considering the length of the delay – for example, in the Zambian case – coupled with the non-availability of the case records, it is inconceivable that the state would wish to continue with the proceedings. Constitutional bail has already been granted by the trial court and therefore further detention of the victim in a case of this nature will amount to the court's disobeying its own orders and an affront to the criminal justice system of Zambia. Appropriate remedies provided for by the Criminal Procedure Code of Zambia must be investigated and ascertained because the municipal laws of certain jurisdictions such as South Africa and Namibia have specific legislative provisions relating to remedies to be granted in cases of violation of the right to a fair trial.

[62] *Margaret Malama-Kean* (note 60).
[63] 2000 (2) SACR 542 (SCA).

Victims of violations of the right to a speedy trial are also entitled to invoke the civil jurisdiction of the Superior Courts to apply for a declaration of the violation of their rights and compensation. But, in practice, to succeed in a claim for compensation, sufficient evidence must be adduced to establish quantifiable loss. Evidence such as job loss, loss of conjugal and matrimonial rights and deprivation of family life will be relevant and necessary.

Both Namibia and Zambia are signatories to both the ICCPR and the ACHPR. Furthermore, Zambia, for example, has internalised the norms and standards of the International Bill of Rights in its domestic laws – more particularly, the Constitution of Zambia, Art 18(1) which protects the right to a fair trial within a reasonable time. It is submitted, therefore, that the Zambian law-enforcement agencies are bound not only by the treaty obligations of the abovementioned international instruments, but also the provisions of their own Constitution, the supreme law of the land, to give effect to these standards and norms.

The application of the principles of law dealing with the right to a fair trial within a reasonable time to the *Chisimba* case, for example, will lead to the conclusion that there was obviously an unreasonable delay by the state and therefore the triggering threshold requirement is satisfied. If sufficient evidence is adduced to establish prejudice to a trial, then a clear case of the infringement of the rights of the victim exists. In the case of Mr Chisimba, therefore, he was entitled to approach the Constitutional Court of Zambia for redress. The remedies of stay of proceedings and release should be available to the victim in this case.

Regarding applications to the treaty bodies whose protocols Zambia has ratified, the victim prima facie has jurisdiction before these treaty bodies but with the proviso that the exhaustion of domestic remedies requirement must first be complied with, except where, of course, no domestic remedies are available or there is an unreasonable delay on the part of the Zambian courts in granting remedy.

REFERENCES

Amnesty International 'Namibia: Justice delayed is justice denied: The Caprivi treason trial', 4 August 2003, 42/001/2003.

Amoo, SK 'The bail jurisprudence of Ghana, Namibia, South Africa and Zambia' 2008 *Forum on Public Policy: A Journal of the Oxford Round Table* 1–29.

Government of the Republic of Namibia *Reports submitted under Article 9 of the International Convention on the Elimination of Racial Discrimination* CERD/C/NAM/12, 18 July 2007.

Leary, V *International Labour Conventions and National Law* (Martinus Nijhoff Publishers, 1982).

Pityana, NB 'Reflections on the African Court on Human and Peoples' Rights' (2004) 4 *African Human Rights Law Journal* 121–129.

Steiner, HJ & Alston, P *International Human Rights in Context* (Oxford University Press, 2000).

CASES

Attorney-General of The Gambia v Jawara Case Nos 147/95 and 149/96
Barker v Wingo (1972) 407 US 514
Bell v Director of Public Prosecutions of Jamaica & Another [1985] 2 All ER 585
Decision in the Mekongo Communication against Cameroon, 1994
Eckle v Germany (Federal Republic) (1985) 5 EHRR 1
Fikilini v Attorney-General 1990 (1) ZLR 105 (SC)
Foti v Italy (1983) 5 EHRR 313
In re Mlambo 1992 (4) SA 144 (ZS); 1992 (2) SACR 245 (ZS)
Margaret Malama-Kean v The Magistrate of the District of Oshakati NO and the Prosecutor-General NO Case No SA 04/2002
McCarthy v Additional Magistrate, Johannesburg 2000 (2) SACR 542 (SCA)
Mills v The Queen [1986] 1 SCR 863
People v John Chisimba 2TO/O9/95
R v Askov (1990) 2 SCR 1199; (1991) 49 CRR 1 (Supreme Court of Canada)
S v Heidenrich 1996 (2) BCLR 197 (NmH); 1998 NR 229
S v Uahanga & Others 1998 NR 160
United States v Van Neumann 474 US 242 (1986)
Van As & Another v Prosecutor-General 2000 NR 271

LEGISLATION

African Charter on Human and Peoples' Rights on January 17, 1983 and ratified it on 10 January 1984
Human Rights Committee, General Comment No 31(80) The Nature of the General Legal Obligation Imposed on States Party to the Covenant Adopted on 29 March 2004 (2187th meeting)
International Convention on the Elimination of Racial Discrimination CERD/C/NAM/12, 18 July 2007
International Covenant on the Civil and Political Rights on 10 April 1984
The Protocol establishing the African Court on Human and Peoples' Rights entered into force 25 January 2004
UN General Assembly, International Covenant on Economic, Social and Cultural Rights, 16 December 1966, United Nations, Treaty Series
UN General Assembly, Universal Declaration of Human Rights, 10 December 1948, 217 A (III)

20

Law on adultery: a comparative overview of seven jurisdictions

Eugene L Libebe, Tapiwa V Warikandwa and Samuel K Amoo

> Therefore shall a man leave his father and his mother,
> and shall cleave unto his wife: and they shall be one flesh.
>
> Genesis 2:24[1]

20.1 INTRODUCTION

This chapter is a comparative overview of the law on adultery in seven jurisdictions: Namibia, South Africa, Zimbabwe, Nigeria, Botswana, the United States and Indonesia as a basis for suggesting a frame of reference that would inform comparative law in Africa.[2] Court cases in Namibia, Zimbabwe and South Africa have involved reaching decisions on whether third-party claims for adultery are

[1] *The Remnant Study Bible King James Version* (Remnant Publications Inc, 2010).

[2] See also TV Warikandwa & EL Libebe (2021). 'Namibia Superior Courts' findings on adultery claims: A case of undermining African jurisprudence?' in TV Warikandwa & J Baloro (eds) *Namibia's Supreme Court at 30 Years – A Review of the Superior Court's Role in the Development of Namibia's Jurisprudence in the Post-Independence Era* (Konrad Adenauer Foundation, Supreme Court of Namibia/University of Namibia, 2021) 357–375; EL Libebe 'Analysis of the Namibian Superior Courts' judgments on the action for adultery against a third party: The implications on African customary laws and jurisprudence' in A Nhemachena, TV Warikandwa & SK Amoo (eds) *Social and Legal Theory in the Age of Decoloniality (Re-)Envisioning Pan-African Jurisprudence in the 21st Century* (Langaa Research & Publishing CIG Mankon, 2018) 399–420.

still an acceptable legal norm in contemporary African societies. Most African societies recognise third-party claims for adultery.[3] It is no wonder, then, that in the Zimbabwean case of *Timothy Chinyadza v Melton Phiri*, Kudya J defined *contumelia* as follows:

> *Contumelia* is equated to the injury, hurt, insult and indignity inflicted upon a plaintiff by adultery committed by a defendant with his or her spouse.[4]

In the case of *Njodzi v Matiwone*, Mwayera J made the following point:

> One does not require a magnifying glass to scrutinize and come up with a conclusion that *contumelia*, that is injury, hurt, insult and indignity occurs, to an innocent spouse where the other commits adultery.[5]

In such instances, the injury is so obvious that there would be no justification in not seeking legal redress for the wrongful hurt occasioned. Strangely, South African and Namibian apex court decisions have found that the delictual action of an innocent spouse based on adultery committed by a spouse has become outdated and can no longer be sustained in the law of these two jurisdictions.[6] In principle, therefore, adultery is no longer actionable at law, which effectively means that adulterers are not legally liable for their immoral conduct anymore. In South Africa (similarly as in Namibia), the courts have pronounced clearly that the criminal offence of adultery had been abrogated by disuse.[7] The same sentiments were echoed by Kentridge AJ (as he then was) in *Du Plessis & Others v De Klerk & Another*, quoting *R v Salituro* (1992) 8 CRR 2nd 173, when he remarked:

> Judges can and should adapt the common law to reflect the changing, social, moral and economic fabric of the country. Judges should not be quick to perpetuate rules whose social foundation has long since disappeared ....[8]

From a comparative-law perspective, it is pertinent to question which methodology and processes the South African and Namibian judges followed in determining that third-party claims for adultery are outdated in a country where customary law remains fundamental. Yes, courts have a duty to develop the common law whenever

[3] *Mangole v Rapuleng* 1990 BLR 450 (HC).
[4] *Timothy Chinyadza v Melton Phiri* HH 76–2009 at 4.
[5] *Njodzi v Matione* (HC 11253 of 2014, HH 37 of 2016) 2016 ZWHHC 37 (14 January 2016) at 4.
[6] *RH v DE* (Case No 594/2013) [2014] ZA SCA 133; *Van Straten v Bekker* (I 6056-2014) [2016] NAHCMD 24 (25 August 2016).
[7] *DE v RH* (CCT 182/14) [2015] ZACC 18.
[8] [1966] ZACC 10, 1996 (3) SA 850 (CC).

it is warranted and in conformity with the interests of justice and society. However, it is also common knowledge that public policy is now infused with constitutional values, norms and aspirations. It is apparent that public policy often represents the legal convictions of a community and reflects those values that are held dearly by a society. Therefore, in deciding whether a delictual claim for adultery damages is outdated or otherwise, while learning about foreign jurisdictions' decisions, the court decisions should be contextualised to reflect the legal convictions and societal values of the African society, particularly through the lens of ubuntu and living customary laws and lore. African countries' moral fabric is engraved in each country's culture, religion and traditional values or heritages. Any development of the common law ought therefore to be underpinned by the African philosophy of ubuntu and customary-law precepts in line with the interests of justice and constitutional values. The institution of marriage is deeply entrenched in African countries' cultures, traditions and religions; and its protection has been propagated by the courts in unambiguous language.[9] Furthermore, the courts have frowned upon the wrongfulness of adultery in so far as it is a threat to the institution of marriage. Malaba J (as he then was), in the *Mungate* case, held that '[a]dultery is still prohibited by public opinion as an act of sexual incontinence'.[10]

This chapter provides an overview and a comparative analysis of the law and court decisions on adultery claims from third parties in seven jurisdictions in southern Africa and elsewhere. The chapter begins by examining the law on third-party claims for adultery in general and proceeds with an analysis of the Namibian and South Africa positions (which are somewhat similar), contrasting them with differing court decisions in other jurisdictions, such as Zimbabwe, Nigeria, the United States and Indonesia. The chapter concludes by arguing that the African philosophy of ubuntu and living customary laws and lore must come to the aid of courts as frames of reference and inform comparative law in Africa.

20.2 LAW ON THIRD-PARTY CLAIMS FOR ADULTERY

The action for adultery is part of a group of actions, based on the *action iniuriarum*, which are connected to the institution of marriage. The group also comprises the action for breach of promise to marry. From a historical perspective, Roman law punished adultery as a crime but did not accommodate an action in private law.[11]

---

[9] See *Katsumbe v Buyanga* 1991 (2) ZLR 256 and *Mapuranga v Mungate* 1997 (1) ZLR 64.

[10] *Mapuranga* (note 9).

[11] M Carnelley *Laws on Adultery: Comparing the Historical Development of South African Common Law Principles with those in English Law*. 2013, http://www.scielo.org.za/pdf/funda/v19n2/01.pdf, accessed 21 August 2023.

As to Roman-Dutch law, support for the proposition that it made provision for a private-law action for adultery is hard to find among our old authorities.[12] The action for adultery against a third party has its origin in an archaic English action called 'criminal conversation', which was abolished in England in 1970.[13] The action was rooted in the antiquated notion of a husband's property rights in his wife – essentially viewing wives as mere chattels who are to provide services.[14] The action was not only abolished in England as no longer justifiable, but shortly afterwards in most common-law jurisdictions which had inherited that action.[15]

In Namibia, the action formed part of the common law applied before Independence and it continued to be applied after Independence by virtue of Art 140 of the Constitution.[16] The abolition of the action for criminal conversation in England was followed in other common-law jurisdictions, which inherited that action from English law. In New Zealand and Australia, this happened in 1975, in Scotland in 1976, in Ontario in 1978 and subsequently in almost all the provinces of Canada.[17] In the United States the action has been abolished or severely restricted in 42 states and the District of Columbia either by what has been called 'anti-heart balm statutes' or by decisions of the state Supreme Courts.[18] North Carolina appears to be one of the last remaining states where tort claims for adultery are still recognised.[19] The reasons for the abolition in these jurisdictions include that the action is regarded as no longer in conformance with considerations of *morality*, that it has grave disadvantages and that, on balance, its continued existence is no longer justifiable.[20] Whereas the courts in both Namibia and South Africa concur with this stance, it is difficult to reconcile it in the African context –most African societies perceive adultery as immoral. Although it is maintained that the courts find fewer or the same answers from other jurisdictions to same legal problems, it is improbable that ideals in Eurocentric jurisdictions are similar to and consistent with Afrocentric ideals. Moreover, a complete disregard of Afrocentric or ubuntu ideals and values hinders the development of Pan African jurisprudence. In the process, our courts will continue to import judgments and miss opportunities to develop unique laws that reflect the values and morals of the people from an

[12] *RH v DE* (note 6) at para 22.
[13] *RH v DE* (note 6) at para 26; see also *Pritchard v Pritchard and Sims* [1966] 3 All ER 601 (CA) at 607–610.
[14] *Pritchard* (note 13).
[15] *Pritchard* (note 13).
[16] The Constitution of the Republic of Namibia Act 1 of 1990.
[17] *RH v DE* (note 6) at para 27.
[18] *RH v DE* (note 6).
[19] L McMillian 'Adultery as tort' (2012) 90(6) *North Carolina Law Review* 1988, http://scholarship.law.unc.edu/cgi/viewcontent.cgi?article=456 6&context=nclr, accessed 21 August 2023.
[20] *RH v DE* (note 6) at para 27.

Afrocentric perspective. In this regard, one would argue that Namibian and South African superior courts have actually failed to develop the common law through comparative-law tools and therefore merely transplanted foreign law into their jurisdictions and interpreted it as reflecting the ideals of their people.

Many years ago, the court in *Green v Fitzgerald*,[21] held that adultery was no longer a criminal offence in our law, because it had become obsolete owing to its disuse. In *Rosenbaum v Margolis*, Blackwell J stated:

> the criminal sanction for adultery having disappeared, the only remedy left to an injured husband is an action for divorce against his wife, with the claims ancillary thereto, and for damages against the adulterer. In so far as the latter may be regarded as a deterrent and in the public interest, I can see no good reason why it should not ensure equally in favour of the wife. There is something, in my opinion, to be said for the view that an action for damages against an adulterous third party is out of harmony with modern concepts of marriage and should be abolished. But as long as the action remains, it should remain in favour of both sexes alike.[22]

It should be stressed that, although the action was viewed as disadvantaging women, this is no longer the case because equality legislation has been enacted to protect the rights of women.[23] The rights of women are also included in international agreements.[24] The other academic authors who argue that the claim should be abolished hold the view that the action is outdated and archaic and that it has lost its place in the context of modern society.[25]

In Namibia, the courts have made it clear that public policy and the legal convictions of the community are informed by our constitutional values and norms. Therefore, the courts have stressed further that an examination of the origin of the action and its development reveals that it is fundamentally inconsistent with our constitutional values of equality in marriage, human dignity and privacy. Accordingly, such an examination also demonstrates that the action has lost its social and moral substratum, too, and is no longer sustainable in our law. It can, however, be argued that this reasoning was premised mainly on the South African

[21] *Green v Fitzgerald* 1914 AD 88.

[22] *Rosenbaum v Margolis* 1944 WLD 147 at 158.

[23] See the Constitution of the Republic of Namibia Act 1 of 1990 and The Married Persons Equality Act 1 of 1996.

[24] For example, the United Nations Convention on the Elimination of All Forms of Discrimination against Women.

[25] J Church '*Consortium Omnis Vitae*' (1979) 42 *THRHR* 380–381; DSP Cronjé & J Heaton *South African Family Law* 2 ed (LexisNexis, 2004); HR Hahlo *South African Law of Husband & Wife*, supplement to 4 ed (Juta & Co, 1980) 31; Carnelley (note 11).

judgments (copy and paste) which are largely Eurocentric and that the courts failed to a larger extent to use comparative-law tools effectively and were likely to have reached incorrect conclusions.

In South Africa alike, the apex courts both referred to the changing societal attitude towards adultery in South Africa and elsewhere.[26] Other common-law jurisdictions have followed suit in abolishing the action, including Ireland, Barbados, Jamaica, and Trinidad and Tobago.[27] The courts have also pointed out that an action of this nature does not exist in France, the Netherlands, Germany or Austria. In its comparative survey, the Constitutional Court of South Africa at the time noted that the action was still operative in a number of African jurisdictions, including Zimbabwe, Botswana and Namibia, although it had been abolished in the Seychelles. Despite the prevailing Afrocentric approaches, though, the courts have opted to copy and paste Eurocentric views and approaches.

20.3 NAMIBIA

In 2016, the Supreme Court of Namibia declared that Namibians who commit adultery with married individuals are no longer at risk of being prosecuted for damages by disgruntled parties to the marriages they interfered with as third parties. The Supreme Court case of *James Sibongo v Lister Lutombi Chaka & Another*[28] was delivered on 19 August 2016. The High Court case of *Van Straten v Bekker*[29] was subsequently delivered on 25 August 2016. The Supreme Court concluded that the award of damages in an action for adultery against a third party was no longer sustainable in our law. The High Court also stressed that the action has lost its lustre in the modern day and there are winds of change which are currently blowing in some jurisdictions, such as South Africa. A judgment of the Constitutional Court in South Africa, upholding a judgment of the Supreme Court of Appeal of that country, held that no damages should henceforth be recoverable from a third party for adultery.[30]

In *Van Straten v Bekker*, Smuts J ruled that third-party claims for adultery had to be abolished as they were based on outdated Namibian morals and values that considered wives to be the property of their husbands, in a case in which a husband was seeking N$100 000 in adultery damages from a man who allegedly slept with

[26] *RH v DE* (note 6) at paras 27–28, *DE v RH* 2015 (5) SA 83 (CC) at paras 23–44.
[27] *DE v RH* (note 26).
[28] Case No SA 77/2014.
[29] *RH v DE* (note 6).
[30] *RH v DE* (note 6).

his wife.[31] As alluded to earlier, Smuts J pointed out that an examination of the origin of the action (demanding compensation for adultery) and its development reveals that it is fundamentally inconsistent with our constitutional values of equality in marriage, human dignity and privacy. That examination also demonstrates that the action has also lost its social and moral sub-stratum and is therefore no longer sustainable.[32]

The court added that grounds for adultery compensation claims were founded on an outdated English legal proceeding known as 'criminal conversation', which was abolished by the English courts in 1970. Furthermore, adultery allegations were based on the 'antiquated concept' that a husband had property rights over his wife, which may be viewed as treating women as simple 'service-providers' for their male counterparts. Therefore, several other countries that had inherited the English adultery law had long since abolished it– South Africa, New Zealand, Australia, Scotland and Canada being among them, the court reasoned. Whereas the Namibian courts superficially transplanted the law on adultery, it is also difficult to point out the comparative strategy or methodologies which were used in the case law.

In *Van Straten v Bekker* the judge stated further that while the right to marry and start a family is a fundamental value entrenched in the Namibian Constitution, any legal action based on adultery could not protect any marriages because it did not strengthen weak marriages or breathe life into those that were collapsing.[33] He went on to point out that, in the vast majority of cases, infidelity was the aftermath of unhappy marriages rather than the cause of their dissolution. The decision by the judge is based on the understanding that, while the major engine for law reform lies with the Legislature,[34] the courts are nonetheless obliged on occasion to develop the common law in an incremental way. These occasions are dictated, first, by the Constitution, which imposes a duty on the courts to develop the common law so as to promote the spirit, purport and objectives of the Bill of Rights. Second, they should be driven by the acceptance that the courts can and should adapt the common law to reflect the changing social, moral and economic fabric of society and that we cannot perpetuate legal rules that have lost their social sub-stratum.[35]

However, what was not fully interrogated by the learned Smuts J is the issue of the legal convictions of society regardless of the changing times. The law must reflect

[31] *RH v DE* (note 6).

[32] *RH v DE* (note 6).

[33] *Van Straten v Bekker* (note 6).

[34] As was also pointed out in *Sibonga v Chaka & Another* (SA 77/2014) [2016] NASC 16 (19 August 2016).

[35] See, eg, *Du Plessis & Others* (note 8) at para 61; *Carmichele v Minister of Safety & Security &Another* (Centre for Applied Legal Studies Intervening) 2001 (4) SA 938 (CC) (2002 (1) SACR 79; 2001 (10) BCLR 995; [2001] ZACC 22) at para 36.

the society for which it is passed. The *boni mores* of society or the legal convictions of the community, which in effect constitute expressions of considerations of legal and public policy, are of particular significance in determining wrongfulness. And wrongfulness is an essential element of delictual liability in Namibian law, under the *lex Aquilia* and the *actio iniuriarum*.

Is there compelling empirical data that informed Smuts J's finding in this matter? This question has not been fully resolved. Instead, reference was made to the matter of *Le Roux v Dey (Freedom of Expression Institute and Restorative Justice Centre as Amici Curiae)*,[36] where the *boni mores* principle was formulated in this manner:

> In the more recent past our courts have come to recognise, however, that in the context of the law of delict: (a) the criterion of wrongfulness ultimately depends on a judicial determination of whether – assuming all the other elements of delictual liability to be present – it would be reasonable to impose liability on a defendant for the damages flowing from specific conduct; and (b) that the judicial determination of that reasonableness would in turn depend on considerations of public and legal policy in accordance with constitutional norms.

The above, according to Smuts J, means that, especially in determining whether conduct should be regarded as wrongful –that is, whether delictual liability should follow – courts are more sensitive to the dynamic and changing nature of the norms of our society. In justifying this position, the court made reference to the decision taken by the Canadian Supreme Court in the case of *R v Salituro*,[37] in which Lacobucci J held:

> Judges can and should adapt the common law to reflect the changing social, moral and economic fabric of the country. Judges should not be quick to perpetuate rules whose social foundation has long since disappeared. Nonetheless there are significant constraints on the power of the Judiciary to change the law … In a constitutional democracy such as ours it is the Legislature and not the courts which has the major responsibility for law reform … The Judiciary should confine itself to those incremental changes

[36] 2011 (3) SA 274 (CC) (2011 (6) BCLR 577; [2011] ZACC 4) at para 122. See also *F v Minister of Safety & Security &Others* 2012 (1) SA 536 (CC) (2012 (3) BCLR 244; [2011] ZACC 37) at paras 117–124; *Roux v Hattingh* 2012 (6) SA 428 (SCA) at para 33.

[37] (1992) 8 CRR (2nd) 173, also [1991] 3 SCR 654.

> which are necessary to keep the common law in step with the dynamic and evolving fabric of our society.[38]

The development of the common law can raise complex questions. It must be questioned as to what the judges in the matter relied upon to justify the supposed 'changing mores of our society the delictual action based on adultery'. Such decisions raise the uncomfortable discourse of Westernisation and/or acculturation using the law as an instrument. Public policy and the legal convictions of the community are relevant and significant in determining the element of wrongfulness, a prerequisite of delictual liability. There is no compelling evidence to substantiate the judges' findings apart from their reliance on foreign law. This is a key problem of this decision and the comparative approach, as outlined in our arguments in this chapter.

20.4 SOUTH AFRICA

The South African Constitutional Court had the opportunity to decide on third-party claims on adultery much earlier than the Supreme Court of Namibia has done. In the famous case of *DE v RH*,[39] the question of infidelity and the remedies available to an injured spouse were raised before the Constitutional Court in 2015, in front of some of South Africa's most learned legal minds, as both a constitutional and a public-interest matter. It therefore fulfilled the requirements which vest the Constitutional Court with the power to hear such a case. The court began by stating that the issues at hand were whether, in the legal context, when a spouse commits adultery:

1. Does the non-adulterous spouse have a right of action in delict against the third party for injury or insult to self-esteem (*contumelia*);
2. Does the non-adulterous spouse have a right of action in delict against the third party for loss of comfort and society (consortium); and
3. If so, is there justification for the non-adulterous spouse?

There was no doubt that delictual acts were part of South Africa's legislation, until the Supreme Court of Appeal's ruling in the same case, which led to the case being brought before the Constitutional Court. In the High Court of Pretoria, the

[38] Quoted with approval by Kentridge AJ in the South African Constitutional Court in *Du Plessis & Others* (note 8) at para 61 and in *Carmichele* (note 35) at para 36.

[39] *DE v RH* (note 7).

Applicant (Mr DE) had successfully sued Mr RH for damages arising from Mr RH's adultery with Mr DE's former wife, Ms H. Mr DE filed a claim for loss of consortium and *contumelia* under the *action iniuriarum*. The Supreme Court of Appeal then asked, *mero motu* (ie, on its own initiative), whether the claim should be kept in South Africa's law at all. According to the court, the Applicant did not have a claim for loss of consortium based on the facts, but he did have a claim for *contumelia* based on the law at the time. The Supreme Court of Appeal, in contrast, stated that, based on existing *boni mores* in South African society, it was time for the claim to be dropped from our legal system.

The court discussed the claim's history, the evolution of foreign law and analogies, and also our evolving culture and its values. The claim had become obsolete, according to the court, and could no longer be upheld. The court was evolving the common law and expunging an ancient action that, in the court's judgement, had become obsolete, in conformity with its authority.

The applicant's argument before the Constitutional Court focused on three constitutional issues: (1) the Supreme Court of Appeal's failure to develop the common law in accordance with the Constitution; (2) the right to dignity; and (3) the constitutional importance placed on marriage and the family by s 15(3) of the South African Constitution.[40]

The Constitutional Court held that the most essential question to be answered was whether the claim could continue to exist and that this question could be answered by assessing whether adultery fits the criterion of wrongfulness for liability to attach today within society's existing mores. The court addressed the fact that the claim was based on patriarchal traditions that considered a female spouse as chattels (property) and that the action might be taken by a male spouse in the case of another man who had deprived him of his chattels in the form of his wife.

This is also obvious from the fact that the claim is only against the third party and not against the wife, who is only the property that is the subject of the claim rather than another subject.

In *Rosenbaum v Margolis*[41] the claim was made open to spouses to overcome the discriminatory aspect of the claim, which was later confirmed in *Foulds v Smith*.[42]

[40] Section 15(3) of South Africa's Constitution provides as follows: *(a)* This section does not prevent legislation recognising – (i) Marriages concluded under any tradition, or a system of religious, personal or family law; or (ii) Systems of personal and family law under any tradition, or adhered to by persons professing a particular religion. *(b)* Recognition in terms of paragraph *(a)* must be consistent with this section and the other provisions of the Constitution.

[41] *Rosenbaum* (note 22).

[42] 1950 (1) SA 1 (AD).

The court cited Kentridge AJ's statement in *Du Plessis & Others v De Klerk & Others*,[43] in which the learned judge noted that judges

> can and should adapt the common law to reflect the changing social, moral and economic fabric of the country. Judges should not be quick to perpetuate rules whose social foundation has long since disappeared.

The court went on to discuss the ways in which societal norms regarding adultery are changing and also how attitudes towards children born of adulterous marriages are changing. These children are accorded all of the rights that any child born to married parents is entitled to. This is an illustration of a 'softening' of the attitude towards infidelity. In addition, the court mentioned that the penal offence of adultery is being abrogated by disuse. The court also considered academic papers on the subject, all of which, with the exception of a few, adopted the same position on the claim's continued existence: it is outmoded.

The applicant claimed that the delict was available to protect marriage as a sacred institution in its previous form. In response, the court emphasised the recent liberalisation of divorce laws, which now allow spouses to divorce based on an 'irretrievable breakdown of marriage' rather than on the particular circumstances that had to be present in the past to end a marriage. The court went on to declare unequivocally that it was not saying that marriage as an institution should not be safeguarded, citing *Dawood & Others v Minister of Home Affairs & Others*,[44] among other cases.

Many other jurisdictions, particularly those founded on English civil law, where the majority of countries had moved to abolish a claim like this, were examined in depth by the court. Some governments kept track of both the claim and the criminal offence, but these are few and far between. In view of specific statements declared by the Constitutional Court itself, the applicant claimed that all of the preceding was for naught. The Constitutional Court stated in *Dawood* as follows:[45]

> Marriage and the family are social institutions of vital importance. Entering into and sustaining a marriage is a matter of intense private significance to the parties to that marriage for they make a promise to one another to establish and maintain an intimate relationship for the rest of their lives which they acknowledge obliges them to support one another, to live together and to be faithful to one another. Such relationships are of profound significance to the individuals concerned. But such relationships have more than personal

---

[43] *Du Plessis & Others* (note 8).
[44] [2000] ZACC 8.
[45] *Dawood & Others* (note 44).

> significance, at least in part because human beings are social beings whose humanity is expressed through their relationships with others. Entering into marriage therefore is to enter into a relationship that has public significance as well. The institutions of marriage and family are important social institutions that provide for the security, support and companionship of members of our society and bear an important role in the rearing of children … The importance of the family unit for society is recognised in the international human rights instruments referred to above when they state that the family is the 'natural' and 'fundamental' unit of our society.

The petitioner used these forceful remarks in support of his argument that the claim should be part of our legislation. The court then explained the meaning of its decision, stating that it dealt with laws governing the immigration of spouses of South African citizens, in addition to the case of *Minister of Home Affairs & Others v Fourie & Others; Lesbian and Gay Equality Project & Others v Minister of Home Affairs & Others*,[46] which dealt with the law prohibiting foreigners from marrying South African citizens. The court determined that there was a fundamental difference between laws prohibiting the pleasure of marriage, such as those prohibiting homosexual marriage, and those that spouses tried to use to 'hold up' a marriage that was collapsing for non-legal reasons. The court quoted Carnelly's 'One Hundred Years of Adultery – Reassessment Required' as follows: 'Love and respect are the foundations of a solid marriage and not legal rules.'

Finally, the court stated that it was up to the spouses to maintain control over their relationship because they were the ones who had taken solemn vows and had sworn to remain faithful. In addition, the court weighed the rights of the adulterous spouse and the third party to privacy, dignity and freedom of person and association against the rights of the non-adulterous spouse to dignity. It also considered the multifaceted nature of human relationships, where any number of acts and omissions could lead to the disintegration of a marriage relationship, which ultimately resulted in the divorce. The court ruled that judging marital fidelity in terms of money seems to be a mistake in today's world.

In his concurring judgment (signed by Cameron J), Chief Justice Mogoeng stated:

> I agree with these views. The law does and can only create a regulatory framework for the conclusion of marriage and the enforcement of obligations that flow from it. It can also help ensure that barriers to family life are removed. The rest is in the hands of the parties to the marriage.

[46] [2005] ZACC 19.

> Barring exceptions, they decide freely to get married and it is within their ability to protect their marriage from disintegrating.[47]

As a result, the court determined that bringing a claim against a third party for a spouse's adultery is outmoded and inconsistent with modern societal values. Such a claim is therefore no longer a part of the South African legal system. While this ruling was legally valid, the results of the 'softening' approach to infidelity across all genders is concerning to people who cherish family values; moreover, it is impossible to anticipate how far the courts will go in their effort to reduce the importance of marital commitment.

20.5 ZIMBABWE

The law in Zimbabwe is akin to the law that currently obtains in the jurisdiction as discussed above.[48] In this regard, there has been some degree of consternation from some feminists, who incline to the view that some judges appear to adopt a lackadaisical approach to adultery cases, considering the fact that it affects Zimbabwean women more than men. In this regard, they take the view that the law has treated the issue of adultery with less seriousness than it deserves.[49]

Soon after the South African Supreme Court of Appeal passed judgment in *RH v DE*, Justice Hlekani Mwayera of the High Court of Zimbabwe handed down judgment in the case of *Njodzi v Matione*[50] in January 2016. In this matter, the court refused to follow the South African example and declare the action of damages for adultery unconstitutional. The central question was whether in the Zimbabwean context these foreign decisions were applicable? In other words, one has to consider whether the reasoning adopted in South Africa, Seychelles, Canada and New Zealand is possible and applicable in the light of the normative framework and social context of the Zimbabwean Constitution.[51] From the case law it is settled in that jurisdiction that, in arriving at damages for adultery, the following factors have to be considered:

- The social and economic status of the plaintiff and the defendant.
- The character of the spouse involved.
- Whether or not the defendant has shown contrition.

---

[47] *Lesbian and Gay Equality Project & Others* (note 46) at paras 70–71.
[48] *Takadiini v Maimba* 1996 (1) ZLR 737.
[49] S Chirawu 'Till death do us part: Marriage, HIV/Aids and the law in Zimbabwe' (2006) 13 *Cardozo JL & Gender* 29.
[50] (HC 11253/14) [2016] ZWHHC 37 (14 January 2016).
[51] *Njodzi* (note 50).

- The need for deterrent measures against the adulterer.
- The level of award in similar cases.[52]

The court went on to note that, of course, the circumstances of each case must be subjected to scrutiny as the court makes its decision. The reason behind adultery damages is the protection of the sanctity of the institution of marriage.[53] Furthermore, in *Katsimbe v Buyanga*,[54] Robinson J affirmed the purpose of adultery damages as the protection of the institution of marriage when he remarked as follows:

> Before addressing myself to the quantum of damages to be awarded to the plaintiff, I wish to say that, in my view, where a third party is shown to have intruded sexually upon a marriage and to have contributed to the breach of duty of marital fidelity which each spouse owes the other by committing adultery with one spouse, the courts, in the absence of mitigating circumstances, should be seen, in their award of damages, to come down hard on the adulterer or adulteress as opposed to treating him or her with kid gloves for a variety of 'expedient' reasons.

Precedents in the Zimbabwean jurisdiction reveal that adultery damages are underpinned by the need to preserve the sanctity of marriage. The Matrimonial Causes Act provides sanctions in the case of divorce and the distribution or apportionment of property. Divorce is granted in circumstances where it has been shown that the marriage has broken down irretrievably. Adultery is still a recognised ground of divorce and, for this reason, it is still part of Zimbabwean law.[55] Therefore, clearly, to all intents and purposes, the Legislature as it currently stands condemns adultery in Zimbabwe.[56]

While there is substance and wisdom in the stance of the Zimbabwean position, it is also interesting to analyse the reasoning and to witness how the Zimbabwean court distances itself from the South African and Namibian positions on adultery law. From a comparative perspective, it is interesting to observe how South Africa transplanted foreign decisions and Namibia in turn further transplanted the same position on adultery law, whereas Zimbabwe refused to adopt that position. Interestingly, in all these judgments there is a comparative element or survey whose methodologies can actually be challenged and questioned. The traditional

---

[52] *Njodzi* (note 50) at 5; see also *Khumalo v Mandishona* 1996 (1) ZLR 434; *Nyakudya v Washaya* 2000 (1) ZLR 65 (C); *Chenesai Rateiwa v Tsistsi Venge* HB 152/11.

[53] *Njodzi* (note 50).

[54] 1999 (1) ZLR 256 H at 258–259.

[55] *Njodzi* (note 50) at 5.

[56] *Njodzi* (note 50).

Western-oriented approach to studying comparative law and understanding traditional-law systems has often been used with little or no benefits accruing to African indigenes.[57] Another synopsis of other jurisdictions is outlined below.

20.6 NIGERIA

In Nigeria, the law still takes a very strict view on adultery. The legal system there is pluralist in nature and consists of English, customary and Islamic laws, all of which regard adultery as a matrimonial wrong and a ground for divorce.[58] The Nigerian Matrimonial Causes Act of 1970 deals with damages in respect of adultery.[59] A party may, in a divorce petition based on adultery, join the other party as a respondent and claim damages for the adultery.[60] Damages are not, however, awarded if the adultery has been condoned, whether subsequently revived or not or if a decree of divorce based on the adultery is not granted, or the adultery was committed more than three years before the date of the petition.[61]

In assessing the damages, some factors to be taken into account were set out in the Nigerian case of *Mohammed v Mohammed*.[62] They include the actual value of the adulterous spouse to the petitioner, that is, both pecuniary and consortium; the injury to the claimant's feelings and the blows to their honour; the co-respondent's means and conduct; the conduct of the spouse themself, especially the adulterous spouse whose harshness or cruelty might have undermined the non-adulterous spouse, and the co-respondent's knowledge that the adulterous party is married.

In *Adeyinka v Ohuruogu*,[63] the Supreme Court of Nigeria stated that the damages were intended to compensate for loss of consortium and outrage to honour and family caused by the adultery and not to punish the adulterer.

20.7 BOTSWANA

In Botswana, customary courts are arranged in a hierarchy, from lower courts of record located in select villages to higher courts of appeal, culminating in the

[57] EJ Eberle 'The method and role of comparative law' (2009) 8(3) *Washington University Global Study Law Review* 451–486.
[58] As discussed in *Van Straten* (note 6) at paras 29–30.
[59] Section 31.
[60] Section 32.
[61] Section 31(2) and (3).
[62] (1952) 14 WACA 199.
[63] (1966) 1 All NLR 210 at 212–213.

customary court of appeal for the whole tribe based at the tribal capital. Appeals can be made to either of the two national customary courts of appeal – one of which is in the north and the other in the south of the country.[64] From there, appeals go to the High Court. The customary court of appeal is located in Serowe, the tribal capital. Village courts of record are more formal than ward hearings, where many family disputes are initially heard and often settled.[65] Throughout the tribal court system, hearings are free and held without lawyers. The court system in Botswana is at present robust, there being hundreds of courts of record in which thousands of cases are heard every year.[66]

Adultery as a legal offence in Botswana has undergone radical changes in recent years, both in statutory and in customary courts.[67] According to Werbner and Werbner:[68]

> Adultery judgments in customary courts in Botswana reflect changing everyday practices and normative understandings both with regard to marriage and broader ideas of gender equality. These changed perceptions parallel a worldwide shift in the legal understanding of adultery from being a crime to a civil offense and then, more recently, a non-offense.

Social change movements and judicial reforms responsive to both regional and international gender and judicial activism have arguably influenced recent judgments in the Botswana High Court regarding adultery.[69] Although the country's customary courts continue to recognise adultery as an offence known as *breaking the yard*, they, too, follow customary law as 'living law'; that is, they are responsive to considerations of equity and quotidian practices that parallel wider ideologically critical movements and also historical processes of judicial innovation and legal reform elsewhere.[70]

20.8 UNITED STATES

According to Glass,[71] the United States is experiencing a crisis of unfaithfulness. In this regard, she noted that some courts had defined adultery as not involving moral

---

[64] C Fombad 'Customary courts and traditional justice in Botswana' (2004) 15(1) *Stellenbosch Law Review* 166–92;

[65] Ibid.

[66] Ibid.

[67] P Werbner & R Werbner 'Adultery redefined: Changing decisions of equity in customary law as "Living Law"' (2020) 43 *Botswana PoLAR* 136–152.

[68] Ibid.

[69] Werbner & Werbner (note 67).

[70] Ibid.

[71] SP Glass & JC Staheli *Not Just Friends: Rebuilding Trust and Recovering Your Sanity after Infidelity* (2004) 329-330, https://www.barnesandnoble.com/w/not-just-friends-shirley-glass/1112397906?-type=Audiobook, accessed 21 August 2023.

turpitude and therefore not inherently prejudicial. Social science surveys depict that at least 20 to 50 per cent of US adults admit to committing adultery, whereas some studies place the adultery rate at 70 per cent.[72]

The US Supreme Court has held that the state has an interest in protecting the institution of marriage while at the same time bearing the duty to uphold freedom of association as a fundamental right protected by the US Constitution. As a result, from the 1980s, most states in the United States had derecognised adultery-based torts such as alienation of affection and criminal conversation.[73] There is, apparently, an emerging awareness that liberty gives substantial protection to adult persons in deciding how to conduct their private lives in matters pertaining to sex. Issues that informed this approach have included the need to emphasise personal choice, to keep the courts out of the bedroom, to decriminalise sex acts and to remove the use of the law to legislate morality.[74] That notwithstanding, US law still recognises the adultery-based tort of 'intentional infliction of emotional distress' as any intentional, reckless or negligent conduct of a person that is outrageous or exceeds all bounds of tolerance or decency and causes another person severe emotional distress.[75]

20.9 INDONESIA

In December 2022, Indonesia's parliament unanimously voted to ban sex outside of marriage. Once in force, the bans will affect both foreign visitors and citizens. The bans are part of an overhaul of the country's criminal code that has been in the works for years. The new code also expands an existing blasphemy law and retains a five-year prison term for deviations from the central tenets of Indonesia's six recognised religions: Islam, Protestantism, Catholicism, Hinduism, Buddhism and Confucianism.[76] The code still needs the approval of the president and the government says it will not be fully implemented as yet.[77]

The amended criminal code stipulates that sex outside marriage is punishable by a year in jail and cohabitation by six months, but adultery charges must be based on

[72] Ibid.

[73] NA Patel 'The state's perpetual protection of adultery: Examining *Koes-Tler v Pollard* and Wisconsin's faded adultery torts' (2003) 1013 *Wisconsin Law Review* 2.

[74] As discussed in *Van Straten* (note 6) at para 33.

[75] *Van Straten* (note 6).

[76] Associated Press *Indonesia Criminalises Adultery, But the Law may Take up to Three Years to Take Effect* (nd), https://www.npr.org/2022/12/06/1140889660/indonesia-criminalizes-adultery-but-the-law-may-take-up-to-3-years-to-take-effect, accessed 21 August 2023.

[77] Ibid.

police reports lodged by a spouse, parents or children.[78] A parliamentary taskforce finalised the Bill in November 2022 and law-makers unanimously approved it in December 2022. Others praised the amendments as a historic step. It is not easy to break away from the colonial living legacy, even though Indonesia no longer wants to use colonial products. Finalising the process demonstrates that even 76 years after the Dutch Criminal Code was adopted as the Indonesian Criminal Code, it is never too late to produce laws on your own[79] – a reflection of the level of civilisation of a nation.

20.10 AFRICAN UBUNTU AND LIVING CUSTOMARY LAW AS CORNERSTONES OF COMPARATIVE LAW IN AFRICA

In Africa, adultery has for a long time been regarded as a social evil and a blatant aberration from the morals of humanity. The legal consequences of committing adultery have varied according to place, community values, the historical era and the prevailing ideology.[80] In African communities, adultery has for a long time also been viewed critically and treated as a serious issue, as it has been treated as a criminal offence in some and a civil wrong in others. The approach to adultery has been largely informed by religious and cultural notions of the inviolability of marriage. The civil action of *contumelia* is therefore touted to be geared to protect marriages and family values through the awarding of damages against a paramour who is adjudged to have violated and desecrated marriage and the marital bed.[81]

Generally, the union of a marriage under customary law is viewed as sacred and holds a significant role in the advancement of the society, because such communities place marriage on a pedestal. When two parties jointly engage in an act of adultery, customarily they are perceived as having desecrated the holy union that is marriage. As a result, there are avenues for action to be taken among some communities, which may also lead to a punishment being imposed on the wrongdoers.[82] Adultery is therefore classified as a wrong and may be brought before

---

[78] Ibid.

[79] Ibid.

[80] M Carnelley *Laws on Adultery: Comparing the Historical Development of South African Common Law Principles with those in English Law*. (2013), http://www.scielo.org.za/pdf/funda/v19n2/01.pdf.

[81] As discussed in the *Van Straten v Bekker* case (note 6) at paras 24–25.

[82] See MO Hinz & NE Namwoonde (ed) *Customary Law Ascertained, 1, The Customary Law of the Owambo, Kavango and Caprivi Communities* (Namibia Scientific Society, 2010); MO Hinz & A Gairiseb (ed) *Customary Law Ascertained, 2: The Customary Law of the Bakgalagari, Batswana ba Namibia and Damara Communities of Namibia* (UNAM Press, 2013); MO Hinz & A Gairiseb (ed) *Customary Law Ascertained, 3: The Customary Law of the Nama, Ovaherero, Ovambanderu, and San Communities of Namibia* (UNAM Press, 2016); JU Kavari 'Estates and systems of inheritance

a community court to be resolved as a dispute. There is common consensus that the act of adultery is a violation of the innocent spouse's personality rights and the payment of compensation is seen as 'wiping the tears'.[83] African indigenous justice systems and customary laws reflect the values enshrined over time by the ancestors.[84]

The word 'ubuntu' is derived from a Nguni (isiZulu) aphorism: *Umuntu Ngumuntu Ngabantu*, which can be translated as 'a person is a person because of or through others'.[85] Ubuntu can be described as the capacity in an African culture to express compassion, dignity, humanity, reciprocity and mutuality in the interest of building and maintaining communities with justice and mutual caring.[86] The ubuntu philosophy represents an African conception of the human being and their relationship with the community that embodies the ethics which define Africans and their social behaviours.[87] In Africa, sociocultural underpinnings are rigorously applied and the African ubuntu philosophies and lore are omnipresent throughout the continent, necessitating its incorporation and application in our legal systems. The courts' reasonings in some judgments on the law on adultery is far from being in touch with the spirit, lore and values of ubuntu and African living customary laws. Marriage is regarded sacred in African societies, therefore the spirit of ubuntu and recognition under customary laws resonates well with the institution of marriage in the African context.

There is accordingly a comparatively advanced understanding of ubuntu which can be attributed to its extensive application, deconstruction and endorsement in African socio-cultural life, in the academic literature and in leading judicial pronouncements drawn from African comparative perspectives.[88] The

among Ovahimba and Ovaherero in Kaokoland' in *The Meanings of Inheritance: Perspectives on Namibian Inheritance Practices* (Legal Assistance Centre, 2005), http://www.lac.org.na/projects/grap/Pdf/meaninheri.pdf, accessed 21 August 2023.

[83] MO Hinz *Traditional Governance and African Customary Law: Comparative Observations from a Namibian Perspective* (2007), http://www.kas.de/upload/auslandshomepages/namibia/Human Rights/hinz.pdf, accessed 21 August 2023.

[84] C Mapaure 'Reinvigorating African values for SADC' (2011) 1 *SADC Law Journal* 152; P Ongyango *African Customary Law: An Introduction* (African Books Collective, 2013).

[85] See D Tutu *God has a Dream: A Vision of Hope for Our Future* (Rider, 2004).

[86] D Tutu *No Future without Forgiveness* (Rider, 1999).

[87] L Mbingi & J Maree *Ubuntu: The Spirit of African Transformation Management* (Knowledge Resources, 2005).

[88] See N Ndeunyema *Re-invigorating Ubuntu through Water: A Human Right to Water under the Namibian Constitution* (Pretoria University Law Press, 2021); C Rautenbach 'Exploring the contribution of ubuntu in constitutional adjudication: Towards indigenization of constitutionalism in South Africa?' in C Fombad (ed) *Constitutional Adjudication in Africa* (Oxford University Press, 2017) 293.

Makwanyane[89] decision of the South African Constitutional Court pioneered the judicial explication of ubuntu as a legal concept. Mahomed J's *obiter* in *Makwanyane* articulates the ethos of ubuntu as follows:[90]

> Ubuntu expresses the ethos of an instinctive capacity for and enjoyment of love towards our fellow men and women; the joy and the fulfilment involved in recognizing their innate humanity; the reciprocity this generates in interaction within the collective community; the richness of the creative emotions which it engenders and the moral energies which it releases both in the givers and the society which they serve and are served by.

In a case of succession under customary law, the Lesotho High Court in *Mokoena v Mokoena*[91] determined as follows:

> The widow has a customary right to expect her husband's relatives to protect her and the property that her husband left her with … It is contrary to Basotho culture, good conscience and a sense of what is right in the African sense – that applicant should be attempting to deprive the widow of her house and arable lands (*masimo*). It is not *botho* or ubuntu to dispossess a widow.

Similarly, in Uganda, the Constitutional Court in *Solvatori Abuki & Another v Attorney General*[92] (a case concerning the constitutionality of the Witchcraft Act in Uganda) stated:

> Of course, the concept of 'ubuntu', the idea that being human entails humaneness to other people, is not confined to South Africa or any particular ethnic group in Uganda. It is the whole mark of civilized societies … It will be recalled that the word 'ubuntu', though linguistically peculiar to only certain groups, is a concept embraced by all the communities of Uganda.

In addition, African society is characterised by images or a vision of life where everything is linked: life and the supernatural, human behaviours and natural

---

[89] *S v Makwanyane & Another* 1995 (3) SA 391 (CC).
[90] *S v Makwanyane & Another* (note 89) at para 263.
[91] *Mokoena v Mokoena* [2007] LSHC 14.
[92] *Solvatori Abuki & Another v Attorney General* [1997] UGCC 10.

phenomena, law, power and that which is sacred.[93] The application of rules is traditionally not directly intended to punish the guilty but to restore the accord within a group and consolidate harmony and solidarity or cohesion. Most of the laws copied from the Western model do not adapt to the African legal culture because those patterns do not share the same values of the people where they have been transplanted. The comparison of legal systems in Africa – especially in sub-Saharan Africa, which are more similar in historical, social, economic and cultural circumstances – is of more practical value in solving the continent's legal problems.[94] The comparativist, the historian, the anthropologist and the linguist can conduct an effective comparative analysis of traditional systems of law in Africa to discover the common core of the African legal cultures that would help the African legislators and courts to take into account the African specificities when they create new laws.

Therefore, Africa's rich history and the application of comparative law should not be an academic luxury but a necessity for integrating and managing its unique legal systems.[95] Since African legal systems have been founded on imposed law, legislators and courts continue to use foreign legal values, concepts, models and rules unfavourably. Mancuso warns that the abandonment of the community-centred approach in favour of a model based on individualism and the centralisation of law has created a problem: that of adaptation and effectiveness for this transplanted and imposed law.[96] African law is a unique legal family of the world, having a legal structure with specific peculiarities and differences from the legal traditions in the rest of the world.[97] The interaction among the different legal orders present in the African legal systems and the kind of 'mixity' that is the outcome of such interaction is something unique that we find only in Africa.[98] Therefore, an African legal model presents unique features and characteristics with elements of pure African reality and a communitarian approach that takes into account a larger number of interests beyond the individualist Western formulations and doctrines.

Finally, it is crucial to comprehend the impact of colonialism on comparative legal studies in Africa.[99] The historical method (a survey of the history of the different laws to be compared); the method of reviewing customary or natural law;

---

[93] S Mancuso 'Comparative law in the African context' in S Mancuso & CM Fombad (eds) *Comparative Law in Africa: Methodologies and Concepts* (Juta & Co, 2015) 26.

[94] Mancusa (note 93) 29.

[95] CN Okeke 'African law in comparative law: Does comparativism have worth?' (2011) 16(1) *Roger Williams University Law Review* 1.

[96] Mancuso (note 93) 29; see KV Mbambi 'Les droits originellement africains dans les recents mouvements de codification: Le cas des pays d'Afrique francophone subsaharienne' (2005) 46(1–2) *Les Cahiers de Droit* 315.

[97] Mancuso (note 93) 32.

[98] Ibid.

[99] Okeke (note 95) 42.

the law and cultural method or approach (ascribes uniqueness to every culture, differences in legal systems, law as an expression of culture or the cultural context of law); the critical approach (a movement to strip comparative law of its Eurocentric cloak), and to a certain extent the functional method or approach can be applied in crafting unique and significant methodological approaches to comparative legal studies in Africa.[100] As to the topic at hand, we must also be mindful that

> [f]oreign law may be so divorced from its transplanted environment that it is meaningless to the local populace. Laws when they are borrowed need to be interpreted and modified to fit the local circumstance.[101]

20.11 CONCLUSION

This chapter is a comparative overview of various jurisdictions regarding developments in the law on adultery. Even though the emphasis was more on Namibia, South Africa and Zimbabwe, the work also provides a synopsis of the positions in other jurisdictions such as Nigeria, Botswana, the United States and Indonesia. The choice of jurisdictions was mainly necessitated by their similarities and differences and the somewhat interesting socio-legal developments in the law on adultery in southern Africa and elsewhere.

The chapter has advanced a strong case for African countries to rethink their reliance on comparative law and the integration of ubuntu and living customary law vis-à-vis the contemporary developments on adultery law. Comparative law has largely been employed as a tool for advancing social engineering in pursuit of Western imperialist agendas.[102] In the process, African countries have lost their identities and value systems by employing foreign legal systems to regulate their societies. It is therefore imperative that reliance on comparative law be reviewed in African law schools,[103] in legal practice, in courts and in any other relevant legal

---

[100] For a discussion of the methodological approaches to comparative legal studies in Africa see Okeke (note 95) 43–48.

[101] T Waelde & J Gunderson 'Legislation reform in transition economies' (1994) 43(2) *International and Comparative Law Quarterly* 369–370; KH Michael 'Comparative legal studies in Africa: A methodological way' in S Mancuso & CM Fombad (eds) *Comparative Law in Africa: Methodologies and Concepts* (Juta & Co, 2015) 58–59.

[102] TV Warikandwa & SK Amoo 'African Law in comparative law: A case of undermining African jurisprudence and promoting a new world order agenda?' in A Nhemachena, TV Warikandwa & SK Amoo *Social and Legal Theory in the Age of Decoloniality (Re-)Envisioning Pan-African Jurisprudence in the 21st Century* (Langaa Research & Publishing Common Initiative Group, 2018).

[103] See CM Fombad 'Africanisation of legal education programmes: The need for comparative legal studies' in S Mancuso & CM Fombad (eds) *Comparative Law in Africa: Methodologies and Concepts* (Juta & Co, 2015).

institutions.[104] Law reforms must not be driven by Western legal reforms, fashions and traditions, but should rather integrate and apply the ubuntu philosophy and values and living customary laws and lore as cornerstones of African jurisprudence. In the South African and similarly the Namibian judgments discussed above, it is evident that comparative law was employed as a tool for advancing social engineering in disregard of the African context, spirit, values and religious and cultural norms. Are there compelling empirical data for the judges' findings in these matters? Indeed, there is no evidence to substantiate the judges' findings apart from their reliance on foreign law. The courts, in the interests of justice and society, should develop the common law but that should not amount to usurping the Legislature's function of making law.

The judgments in Namibia and South Africa illustrate a softening of the attitude towards infidelity. However, the reason behind awarding damages for adultery is the protection of the sanctity of marriage and the family as institutions. There is nothing unconstitutional when one considers the purpose of adultery damages. Marriage is a human institution which is regulated by law and protected by the Constitution, which in turn creates genuine rights. Adultery is regarded as a sin in most Christian and African communities. Whereas Namibia and South Africa are influenced by Western jurisdictions, the courts in Nigeria and Zimbabwe, in contrast, espouse an African vantage point (ubuntu) in their judgments and they have accordingly developed a criterion for awarding damages in an action for adultery.

REFERENCES

Associated Press *Indonesia Criminalizes Adultery, But the Law may Take up to Three Years to Take Effect* (nd), https://www.npr.org/2022/12/06/1140889660/indonesia-criminalizes-adultery-but-the-law-may-take-up-to-3-years-to-take-effect, accessed 21 August 2023.

Carnelley, M 'One hundred years of adultery–reassessment required?' in SV Hoctor& M Kidd (eds) *Stella Iuris Celebrating 100 Years of Teaching Law in Pietermaritzburg* (Juta & Co, 2010).

Carnelley, M *Laws on Adultery: Comparing the Historical Development of South African Common Law Principles with Those in English Law* (2013), http://www.scielo.org.za/pdf/funda/v19n2/01.pdf, accessed 21 August 2023.

Chirawu, S 'Till death do us part: Marriage, HIV/Aids and the law in Zimbabwe' (2006) 13 *Cardozo Journal of Law & Gender* 29.

Church, J '*Consortium omnis vitae*' (1979) 42 *THRHR* 380–381.

[104] Warikandwa & Amoo (note 102).

Cronjé, DSP & Heaton, J *South African Family Law* 2 ed (LexisNexis, 2004).

Eberle, EJ 'The method and role of comparative law' (2009) 8(3) *Washington University Global Study Law Review* 451–486.

Fombad, C 'Customary courts and traditional justice in Botswana' (2004) 15(1) *Stellenbosch Law Review* 166–192.

Fombad, CM 'Africanisation of legal education programmes: The need for comparative legal studies' in S Mancuso & CM Fombad (eds) *Comparative Law in Africa: Methodologies and Concepts* (Juta & Co, 2015).

Glass, SP & Staheli, JC *Not Just Friends: Rebuilding Trust and Recovering Your Sanity after Infidelity* (2004), https://www.barnesandnoble.com/w/not-just-friends-shirley-glass/1112397906?type=Audiobook, accessed 21 August 2023.

Hahlo, HR *South African Law of Husband & Wife*, supplement to the 4 ed (Juta & Co, 1980).

Hinz, MO *Traditional Governance and African Customary Law: Comparative Observations from a Namibian Perspective* (2007), http://www.kas.de/upload/auslandshomepages/namibia/HumanRights/hinz.pdf, accessed 21 August 2023.

Hinz, MO & Gairiseb, A (ed) *Customary Law Ascertained, 2. The Customary Law of the Bakgalagari, Batswana ba Namibia and Damara Communities of Namibia* (UNAM Press, 2013).

Hinz, MO & Gairiseb, A (ed) *Customary Law Ascertained,* 3. *The Customary Law of the Nama, Ovaherero, Ovambanderu, and San Communities of Namibia* (UNAM Press, 2016).

Hinz, MO & Namwoonde, NE (ed) *Customary Law Ascertained, 1. The Customary Law of the Owambo, Kavango and Caprivi Communities* (Namibia Scientific Society, 2010).

Kavari, JU 'Estates and systems of inheritance among Ovahimba and Ovaherero in Kaokoland' *The Meanings of Inheritance: Perspectives on Namibian Inheritance Practices* (Legal Assistance Centre, 2005), http://www.lac.org.na/projects/grap/Pdf/meaninheri.pdf, accessed 21 August 2023.

Libebe, EL 'Analysis of the Namibian Superior Courts' judgements on the action for adultery against a third party: The implications on African customary laws and jurisprudence' in A Nhemachena, TV Warikandwa & SK Amoo (eds) *Social and Legal Theory in the Age of Decoloniality (Re-)envisioning Pan-African Jurisprudence in the 21st Century* (Langaa Research & Publishing CIG, 2018).

Mancuso, S 'Comparative law in the African context' in S Mancuso & CM Fombad (eds) *Comparative Law in Africa: Methodologies and Concepts* (Juta & Co, 2015).

Mapaure, C 'Reinvigorating African values for SADC' (2011) 1 *SADC Law Journal* 152.

Mbambi, KV 'Les droits originellement africains dans les recents mouvements de codification: le cas des pays d'Afrique francophone subsaharienne' (2005) 46(1–2) *Les Cahiers de Droit* 315.

Mbingi, L & Maree, J *Ubuntu: The Spirit of African Transformation Management* (Knowledge Resources, 2005).

McMillian, L 'Adultery as tort' (2012) 90(6) *North Carolina Law Review* 1988, http://scholarship.law.unc.edu/cgi/viewcontent.cgi?article=4566&context=nclr, accessed 21 August 2023.

Michael, KH 'Comparative legal studies in Africa: A methodological way' in S Mancuso & CM Fombad (eds) *Comparative Law in Africa: Methodologies and Concepts* (Juta & Co, 2015).

Ndeunyema, N *Re-invigorating Ubuntu Through Water: A Human Right to Water under the Namibian Constitution* (Pretoria University Law Press, 2021).

Okeke, CN 'African law in comparative law: Does comparativismhave worth?' (2011) 16(1) *Roger Williams University Law Review* 1.

Okeke, CN 'Methodological approaches to comparative legal studies in Africa' in S Mancuso & CM Fombad (eds) *Comparative Law in Africa: Methodologies and Concepts* (Juta & Co, 2015).

Ongyango, P *African Customary Law: An Introduction* (African Books Collective, 2013).

Patel, NA 'The state's perpetual protection of adultery: Examining *Koes-Tler v Pollard* and Wisconsin's faded adultery torts' (2003) 1013 *Wisconsin Law Review* 2.

Rautenbach, C 'Exploring the contribution of ubuntu in constitutional adjudication: Towards indigenization of constitutionalism in South Africa?' in C Fombad (ed) *Constitutional Adjudication in Africa* (Oxford University Press, 2017).

The Remnant Study Bible. King James Version (Remnant Publications Inc, 2010).

Tutu, D *No Future without Forgiveness* (Rider, 1999).

Tutu, D *God has a Dream: A Vision of Hope for Our Future* (Rider, 2004).

Waelde, T & Gunderson, J 'Legislation reform in transition economies' (1994) 43(2) *International and Comparative Law Quarterly* 369–370.

Warikandwa, TV & Amoo, SK 'African law in comparative law: A case of undermining African jurisprudence and promoting a new world order agenda?' in A Nhemachena, TV Warikandwa & SK Amoo (eds) *Social and Legal Theory in the Age of Decoloniality (Re-)Envisioning Pan-African Jurisprudence in the 21st Century* (Langaa Research & Publishing Common Initiative Group, 2018).

Warikandwa, TV & Libebe, EL 'Namibia superior courts' findings on adultery claims: A case of undermining African jurisprudence?' in TV Warikandwa & J Baloro (eds) *Namibia's Supreme Court at 30 Years – A Review of the Superior Court's Role in the Development of Namibia's Jurisprudence in the Post-Independence Era* (Konrad Adenauer Foundation/Supreme Court of Namibia/University of Namibia, 2021).

Werbner, P & Werbner, R 'Adultery redefined: Changing decisions of equity in customary law as "Living Law"' (2020) 43 *Botswana PoLAR* 136–152.

CASES

Carmichele v Ministry of Safety & Security & Another (Centre for Applied Legal Studies Intervening) 2001 (4) 938 (CC)

Chenesai Rateiwa v Tsistsi Venge HB 152/11

DE v RH (CCT 182/14) [2015] ZACC 18

DE v RH 2015 (5) SA 83 (CC)

Du Plessis & Others v De Klerk &Another [1996] ZACC 10; 1996 (3) SA 850 (CC)
F v Minister of Safety & Security & Others 2012 (1) SA 536 (CC) (2012 (3) BCLR 244; [2011] ZACC 37)
Foulds v Smith 1950 (1) SA 1 (AD)
Green v Fitzgerald 1914 AD 88
Katsumbe v Buyanga 1991 (2) ZLR 256
Khumalo v Mandishona 1996 (1) ZLR 434
Mangole v Rapuleng 1990 BLR 450 (HC)
Mapuranga v Mungate 1997 (1) ZLR 64
Mokoena v Mokoena [2007] LSHC 14
Njodzi v Matione (HC 11253/14) [2016] ZWHHC 37 (14 January 2016)
Nyakudya v Washaya 2000 (1) ZLR 65 (C)
Pritchard v Pritchard and Sims [1966] 3 All ER 601(CA)
RH v DE (Case No 594/2013) [2014] ZA SCA 133
Rosenbaum v Margolis 1944 WLD 147
Roux v Hattingh 2012 (6) SA 428 (SCA)
S v Makwanyane & Another 1995 (3) SA 391 (CC)
Sibonga v Chaka & Another (SA 77/2014) [2016] NASC 16 (19 August 2016)
Solvatori Abuki & Another v Attorney-General [1997] UGCC 10
Takadiini v Maimba 1996 (1) ZLR 737
Timothy Chinyadza v Melton Phiri HH 76–2009
Van Straten v Bekker (I 6056-2014) [2016] NAHCMD 243 (25 August 2016)

LEGISLATION

Constitution of the Republic of Namibia Act 1 of 1990
Married Persons EqualityAct 1 of 1996
Matrimonial Causes Act of 1970
United Nations Convention on the Elimination of All Forms of discrimination against Women, 18 December 1979

21

Secessionism or self-determination vs territorial sovereignty: a comparative analysis of legal arguments for secessionist movements in Namibia, Canada and Spain

Christian Harris

21.1 INTRODUCTION

One of the most controversial topics in international law is the right to self-determination. The extent to which international law recognises this right in practice has long elicited contentious disputations in this field. Proponents of self-determination have used the notion of remedial secession as a pillar of their argument; opponents of self-determination, the more so African states, have embraced the international-law concept of *uti possidetis* to assert their right to territorial sovereignty. Although it is acknowledged that there are dozens of political entities in the secessionist movement that are seeking independence from a mother state, for the purposes of chapter special emphasis will be placed on separatist movements in Namibia, Canada and Spain.

The secessionist movements in the Third World countries have manifested themselves in a variety of ways. In Namibia, a secessionist movement calling itself the Caprivi Liberation Army attacked government installations at Katima Mulilo, the capital of the then Caprivi Strip (now renamed Zambezi region). Several people, mostly members of the security forces, lost their lives. The rebellion was eventually crushed with brute force. In the aftermath, suspected rebel soldiers, leaders and perceived supporters of the movement were detained and tried for treason. The Caprivi treason trial became Namibia's longest trial since independence. After 16 years, several of the accused were convicted and sentenced to long prison sentences. Others were acquitted and are seeking compensation from the state for malicious prosecution. While the Caprivi secessionists decided to take up arms to overthrow Namibian rule from the Caprivi Strip, separatist movements in Canada and Spain did so using political and/or legal means.

In Canada, the first fully fledged secessionist movement emerged in Nova Scotia shortly after confederation in response to economic grievances, but it was quickly defeated.[1] No other serious separatist force appeared in an English-speaking province for another century. In Quebec, the Manifesto of the Patriotes in the Rebellions of 1837 had included a declaration that the province seceded from Canada.[2] However, decades later, the issue of independence for Quebec once again came to the fore. This chapter therefore explores the various arguments for and against the right to self-determination in relation to both the Caprivi and the Quebec questions.

Whereas the right to self-determination is an internationally recognised concept, controversy surrounds the same status vis-à-vis to secessionism. Although the right to self-determination and secessionism are different concepts, they are nevertheless related. Heraclides,[3] states that the main bulwark against secession is the principle of self-determination, adding that the principle of self-determination gained more prominence in the late 1950s and 1960s.[4] Interestingly, there is a school of thought which argues that self-determination does not always equate to the right to secession.

To determine whether a secessionist entity meets the requirements for statehood, it is imperative to understand the various theories. The first theory in this regard is the declaratory theory of secession. According to this theory, a state exists if it possesses a permanent population, a defined territory, a government and the capacity to enter into relations with other states; if a state fulfils these criteria, then it exists regardless of recognition.[5] In contrast, the constitutive theory of secession places more emphasis on the recognition of statehood rather than on statehood alone.[6] Finally, whereas the declaratory theory asserts that the existence of a state is independent of recognition, the constitutive theory stresses that for a state to exist, it must receive formal recognition

---

[1] R Foot 'Separatism in Canada' *The Canadian Encyclopedia* (Hurtig Publishers, 2006) 1, https://www.thecanadianencyclopedia.ca/en/article/separatism, accessed 21 August 2023.

[2] Ibid.

[3] A Heraclides *The Self-determination of Minorities in International Politics* (BPCC Wheatons Ltd, 1991) 21.

[4] Ibid.

[5] AE Eckert 'Constructing states: The role of the international community in the creation of new states' (2002) 13 *Journal of Public and International Affairs* 19–39.

[6] Eckert (note 5) 24.

specifically and also possess the capacity to enter into relations with other states – which many unrecognised states have the ability to do.[7]

21.2 RELATIONSHIP BETWEEN SECESSIONISM AND THE RIGHT TO SELF-DETERMINATION UNDER INTERNATIONAL LAW

In its external dimension, political self-determination is implemented either through the formation of an independent state or through integration into or association with an independent state.[8] Secession is a means by which external self-determination may be achieved.[9] Dugard and Raič add that secession may be defined as the separation of part of the territory of a state carried out by the resident population with the aim of creating a new independent state or acceding to another existing state.[10] The right to secession is not clearly spelt out under international law, though: international law is mostly neutral on the issue of secession.[11] The closest recognition of the right to secession is found in the UN Charter. Whereas international law embraces the right to self-determination for all people, and while this right can effectively translate into remedial secession, international law positively allows for this outcome only in the case of decolonisation and in some cases occupation.[12]

The notion of self-determination is quite complex and multifaceted.[13] To explain this, a claim may border on the desire for external self-determination, that is, the establishment of a sovereign and independent state, the free association with or integration into an independent state or the emergence into any other political status freely determined by a people. Alternatively, it could be a desire for internal self-determination, that is, the pursuit of a people's political, economic and social development within the framework of an existing state. In this regard, questions of federalism, devolution and autonomy could also arise.[14]

---

[7] Ibid.

[8] J Dugard & D Raič 'The role of recognition in the law and practice of secession' in MG Kohen *Secession: International Law Perspectives* (Cambridge University Press, 2006) 101–102.

[9] Ibid.

[10] Dugard & Raič (note 8) 103; see also C Haverland 'Secession' in *Encyclopedia of Public International Law 10* (Elsevier Science Publishers, 1987) 384.

[11] M Sterio *Self-determination and Secession under International Law: The New Framework* (Law Faculty Articles and Essays, 2015) 847.

[12] Sterio (note 11) 29.

[13] VP Nanda 'Secessionism and self-determination under international law' (2001) 29 *Denver Journal of International Law & Policy* 305.

[14] Ibid.

The UN Charter itself provides for the right to self-determination: Arts 1(2) and 55 have for decades been cited as the cornerstones of claims for the right to self-determination. Article 1(2) states:

> To develop friendly relations among the nations, based on the respect for the principle of equal rights and self-determination of peoples, and to take other appropriate measures to strengthen universal peace.

Article 55 provides as follows:

> With a view to the creation of conditions of stability and well-being necessary for peaceful and friendly relations among the nations, based on respect for the principle of equal rights and the self-determination of peoples, the United Nations shall promote higher standards of living, full employment, and conditions of economic, social progress and development, solutions of international, economic, social, health, and related problems, and international, cultural, educational co-operation, and universal respect for the observance of human rights and fundamental freedoms for all, without distinction of race, sex, language, or religion.

Scholars have reiterated that the first international legal case to be heard regarding self-determination was the *Aaland Islands* case of 1920.[15] In this instance, this group of islands brought their case to the Council of the League of Nations to enquire whether the citizens of Aaland could assert their self-determination and return from Finland to the Kingdom of Sweden.[16] The council held that '[p]ositive international law does not recognise the right of national groups, as such, to separate themselves from the State of which they form a part by the simple expression of a wish'.[17]

In the SWA/Namibia case, the ICJ held that the right to self-determination had become applicable to non-self-governing territories, rendering South Africa's presence in Namibia illegal under international law.[18] Two of the nine core international human rights instruments – the International Covenant on Civil and Political Rights (ICCPR) and the International Covenant on Economic, Social and

[15] *Aaland Islands* (1920) LNOJ Spec Supp No 3.

[16] International Court of Justice 'Legal consequences for states of the continued presence of South Africa in Namibia (South West Africa) notwithstanding Security Council Resolution 276' (1971) *ICJ Reports* 16; see also M Abel *Is There a Right to Secessionism under International Law?* (2020) 1, https://www.e-ir.info/2020/05/18/is-there-a-right-to-secession-in-international-law/, accessed 21 August 2023.

[17] Ibid.

[18] Ibid.

Cultural Rights (ICESCR) in Art 1 – acknowledge the right to self-determination.[19] Article 1 of the ICCPR and ICESCR stipulates as follows:

Article 1

1. All peoples have the right of self-determination. By virtue of that right they freely determine their political status and freely pursue their economic, social and cultural development.
2. All peoples may, for their own ends, freely dispose of their natural wealth and resources without prejudice to any obligations arising out of international economic co-operation, based upon the principle of mutual benefit, and international law. In no case may a people be deprived of its own means of subsistence.
3. The States Parties to the present Covenant, including those having responsibility for the administration of Non-Self-Governing and Trust Territories, shall promote the realization of the right of self-determination, and shall respect that right, in conformity with the provisions of the Charter of the United Nations.

21.3 CONCEPT OF SOVEREIGN SELF-DETERMINATION

According to Wheatley, there is a distinction between acts of separation and acts of secession.[20] In this regard, Wheatley posits that separation is a process by which a new sovereign and independent political unit is created with the consent of the existing 'parent' state.[21] Secession refers to the situation where a new state is established and recognised without the consent of the 'parent' state. The international legal status of a state remains unaffected by the separation or secession of part of its territory.[22]

At present there are a number of active secessionist movements across the world, from Kashmir and Catalonia to Kurdistan, to mention only three. However, very few have managed to create a nation successfully. Since the Second World War there have been only four: Bangladesh from Pakistan in 1971, Eritrea from Ethiopia in 1993, Timor-Leste from Indonesia in 2002 and South Sudan from Sudan in 2011.[23]

---

[19] See Art 1 of the ICCPR and also of the ICESCR.

[20] S Wheatley *Democracy, Minorities and International Law. Cambridge Studies in International Law* (Cambridge University Press, 2005) 85–86.

[21] Ibid; see also J Crawford *The Creation of States in International Law* (Oxford University Press, 2007) 214.

[22] J Crawford 'State practice and international law in relation to secession' (1998) 69 *British Yearbook of International Law* 85–86.

[23] C Stein 'Successful secessionist movements and the uncertainty of post-secession quality of life' BA (Hons) in Political Science and Psychology Thesis (Oregon State University Honors College,

In addition, the principle of self-determination has repeatedly been set aside since the 20th and the beginning of the 21st century. Cases that stand out are (1) India's annexation of the Portuguese enclaves within the territory of Goa, Damao and Din in 1961; (2) the annexation of West Irian by Indonesia in 1969; (3) the occupation and subsequent annexation of East Timor by Indonesia in 1975.[24] In the 21st century, the United Kingdom's reluctance to relinquish control over the Chagos Islands to Mauritius and Russia's invasion of its neighbour, Ukraine, are yet other examples of the complete disregard of the right to self-determination.

21.4 SUBJECTS OF THE RIGHT TO SELF-DETERMINATION

According to Crawford,[25] the notion of a right presupposes the identification of a subject. However, Fitzmaurice is not in total agreement with this position. He posits that 'it is in fact ridiculous because the people cannot decide until somebody decides who are the people'.

21.4.1 What is meant by 'people'?

The definition of what constitutes a people remains ambiguous under international law. As asserted by Anaya,[26] in all areas of the globe, segments of humanity are clinging to bonds of race, language, religion, kinship and custom, and are projecting those bonds into the political future. Anaya posits further that in all too many instances, recent events remind us, the interactive patterns of ethnic and national groupings are oppressed by creatures of human organisation grounded in the modern system of states.[27] According to Vezbergaite,[28] a people has a right to determine its 'self' by deciding what form of self-determination it will choose. However, he also cautions that international law does not provide any clear criteria about how to define 'a people'. In contrast, Murswiek links a people to a territory. He states:

> A people as a group which can be a holder of the right to self-determination exists only if it lives in a distinct territory, where it constitutes the majority

2016) 1, file:///C:/Users/Tumisang%20Harris/Downloads/SteinChloeE2016%20(1).pdf, accessed 21 August 2023.

[24] A Cassese *Self-determination of Peoples: A Legal Reappraisal* (Antony Rowe Ltd, 1995) 190–191.

[25] Crawford (note 22) 115.

[26] J Anaya 'The capacity of international law to advance ethnic or nationality rights claims' in W Kymlicka *The Rights of Minority Cultures* (Oxford University Press, 1990) 321.

[27] Ibid.

[28] I Vezbergaite 'Remedial secession as an exercise of the right to self-determination of peoples' LLM Thesis (Central University of Europe, 2011) 17, file:///C:/Users/Tumisang%20Harris/Downloads/vezbergaite_ieva.pdf, accessed 21 August 2023.

and where it is able to speak its own language, develop its own culture, cultivate its traditions, or practice a particular religion.

Irrespective of the confusion regarding the definition of 'a people', Crawford[29] asserts that there are nevertheless still references to peoples in some important international documents that have been blessed by government assent. The Preamble to the United Nations Charter begins by asserting that 'we the peoples are determined to eliminate the scourge of war'.[30] Moreover, Art 1(1) of the two principal Human Rights Covenants[31] states: 'All peoples have the right of self-determination.'[32]

However, Higgins is of the view that 'peoples' in all relevant instruments is to be understood in the sense of all the peoples of a given territory and therefore minorities do not have a right of self-determination.[33] Higgins asserts further that the right to self-determination 'allows choices as to political and economic systems within the existing boundaries of the state', but these choices are to be made by the entire population of a state.[34]

21.5 ARGUMENTS FOR SECESSION

Proponents of secession often rely on the concept of remedial secession as a strong legal argument for self-determination. International law recognises that all peoples have the right of self-determination, which may be seen to provide a basis for secession as a remedy.[35]

21.5.1 Remedial secession

The right to remedial secession has been used as a cornerstone for pro-separatist movements across the world. Remedial secession endorses the possibility of secession in situations where peoples are oppressed by their parent states and/or not

[29] R Falk 'The rights of peoples (in particular indigenous peoples)' in J Crawford (ed) *The Rights of Peoples* (Clarendon Press, 1998) 25.

[30] Ibid.

[31] ICCPR and ICESCR (note 20).

[32] Ibid.

[33] R Higgins *Problems and Process – International Law and How We Use It* (Oxford University Press, 1995) 123–124.

[34] Ibid.

[35] P Findi & SM Basir 'Legality of secessionism under international law' 2020 *International Journal of Psychological Rehabilitation* 1.

adequately represented in the political structures of the parent states.[36] It is argued that this right can be exercised with justification only where a people are faced with colonial rule or foreign occupation. Other than these two situations, there seems to be no explicit right of secession for entities aspiring to independence.[37] In its 1975 *Western Sahara* Advisory Opinion, the International Court of Justice (ICJ) described the essential component of self-determination as 'the freely-expressed will of the people'.[38]

On this score, Schachter[39] formulated standards for determining a people's entitlement to independence. These are:

1. The claimant community should have an identity distinct from the rest of the country and inhabit a region that largely supports separation in the given circumstances.
2. The community has been subjected to a pattern of systematic political or economic discrimination.
3. The central regime has rejected reasonable proposals for autonomy and minority rights of the claimant community.

In terms of the Helsinki Final Act 'all people always have the right, in full freedom, when and as they wish, to determine their internal and external political status', but that this should be exercised with regard to the territorial integrity of states.[40] Scholars have therefore argued that where a state fails to provide 'government representing the whole people belonging to a territory without distinction as to race, creed or colour', as required under international law, it cannot invoke the principle of territorial integrity to limit peoples' right to self-determination. According to Abel, this therefore suggests that where a territorial group within a state is denied meaningful access to self-determination, it can assert a right to self-determination externally, through secession from that state.[41]

---

[36] J Vidmar 'Remedial secession in international law, theory and (lack of) practice' (2020) 6(1) *St Antony's International Review* 37–56.

[37] M Sterio *The Right to Self-determination under International Law: 'Selfistans', Secession and Great Powers* (Routledge, 2013).

[38] A Small 'An unintended legacy: Kwame Nkrumah and the domestication of national self-determination in Africa' (2017) 17(1) *African Human Rights Law Journal* 68–88.

[39] O Schachter 'Sovereignty – then and now' in R Macdonald (ed) *Essays in Honour of Wang Tieya*, (Martinus Nijhoff, 1993) 684.

[40] Organisation for Security and Co-Operation in Europe, Helsinki Final Act (signed 1 August 1975), Principle VIII.

[41] Abel (note 17) 4.

21.6 ARGUMENTS AGAINST SECESSIONISM

The national law of many states, especially their constitutions, prohibits most forms of secession.[42] The constitutional affirmation of a country's territorial sovereignty is one example of the way secessionist ideas are suppressed in many countries. Therefore, requiring citizens to commit to the territorial integrity of a country can mean that anyone who advocates secession might be violating the constitution.[43] In the *Katanganese* case, the African Commission on Human and Peoples Rights held that it had an obligation to uphold the territorial integrity and sovereignty of all member states of the OAU and those states party to the African Charter.[44]

State practice, particularly in Africa, has shown a general tendency towards the protection of territorial integrity at the cost of post-independence expression of the right to self-determination.[45] In post-colonial Africa, struggles continue to be waged under the banner of self-determination and these have been thwarted with reference to the right of a state to its territorial integrity.[46] What constitutes territorial integrity was stated by the court in the Island of Palmas case:[47]

> Territorial sovereignty is, in general, a situation recognized and delimited in space, either by so-called natural frontiers as recognized by international law or by outward signs of delimitation that are undisputed, or else by legal engagements entered into between interested neighbours, such as frontier conventions or by acts of recognition of states within fixed boundaries.

According to Ginsburg,[48] secession debates occur against two background rules of international law. First, states have rights to territorial integrity and cannot be dismembered. Second, peoples – including national minorities – have the right to self-determination. This does not mean that there is a right to secession under international law (outside the context of decolonisation from European powers)

---

[42] S Dion *Secession and the Virtues of Clarity* (Macdonald-Laurier Institute of Public Policy, 2011) 11–12.

[43] T Ginsburg *Secession, Constitution Brief* (2018) 1–6, https://www.idea.int/sites/default/files/publications/constitution-brief-secession.pdf, accessed 21 August 2023.

[44] *Katanganese Peoples Congress v Zaire, African Commission on Human and Peoples Rights*, Comm No 75/92 (1995).

[45] D Mnyongani 'Between a rock and a hard place: The right to self-determination versus *uti possidetis* in Africa' (2008) XLI *Comparative and International Law Journal of Southern Africa* 464.

[46] Ibid.

[47] Island of Palmas case (or Miangas), *United States v Netherlands Award* (1928) II RIAA 829, ICGJ 392 (PCA 1928), 4 April 1928, Permanent Court of Arbitration [PCA]. The PCA was approached to decide whether the Island of Palmas was part of the Netherlands or United States territory.

[48] Mnyongani (note 45) 464.

but that secession is one way in which states can meet their obligation to provide self-determination to subnational groups.[49]

Several scholars have posited that the United Nations resolutions on self-determination vis-à-vis secessionism are not binding on Member States. According to Matsumoto,[50] the UN General Assembly is not entitled to impose responsibility on an administering state, specifically in respect of a non-self-governing territory, to transfer part of its territory to the people or populations. In addition, Schwed[51] declares that '[t]here is a general consensus that resolutions of the General Assembly were never meant to be international law by virtue of their mere passage', and he concludes that '[t]he wording of the Charter never grants the General Assembly legislative powers; instead it consistently limits it to an exhortatory capacity'.

Furthermore, scholars such as Johnson[52] are of the opinion that

> [a]lthough under the Declaration on Friendly Relations all Member States are recommended to assume responsibilities to promote self-determination and to support the UN in implementing the principle of self-determination, no legal rights are accorded to the people or populations of a non-self-governing territory. The rights and duties are addressed only to the Member States and expected to be implemented in the friendly relations among the neighbouring States.

21.6.1 *Uti possidetis*

Opponents of secessionism often rely on the doctrine of *uti possidetis* to discourage separatism. The *uti possidetis* doctrine has been explicitly endorsed by most African states. As implicitly posited by Dugard,

> realising that the redrawing of the map of Africa along ethnic lines would destroy the stability of the continent, post-independence African leaders and the Organisation of African Unity invoked the principle of territorial integrity.[53]

The principle of *uti possidetis* seems to have been invoked and applied first in Spanish America, inasmuch as this was the continent which first witnessed the phenomenon

---

[49] Mnyongani (note 45) 464.

[50] S Matsumoto *Separatism in Africa – a Fundamental Problem: Policy Brief* (2019) 5, https://www.policycenter.ma/sites/default/files/PB%20-%2043-19%20%28Matsumoto%29%20%281%29.pdf, accessed 21 August 2023.

[51] A Schwed 'Territorial claims as a limitation to the right of self-determination in the context of the Falklands Islands dispute' (1982) 6 *Fordham International Law Journal* 45.

[52] CD Johnson 'Toward self-determination – a reappraisal of friendly relations' (1973) 13 *Georgia Journal of International and Comparative Law* 148.

[53] J Dugard 'Secession: Is the case of Yugoslavia a precedent for Africa?' (1993) 5 *African Journal of International and Comparative Law* 163, 165.

of decolonisation involving the formation of a number of sovereign states on territory formerly belonging to a single metropolitan state.[54] According to Shaw, *uti possidetis juris* is today widely acknowledged as the doctrine of customary international law that has proven to be central to determining territorial sovereignty in the era of decolonisation.[55] However, it is not clear whether this practice turned into a customary rule of international law endowed with a regional scope or remained a simple practice devoid of any binding force – or crystallised instead into a general principle of law, as was held by the two Latin American judges of the ICJ (Armand-Ugon and Moreno Quintana) in the *Sovereignty over certain Frontier Land* case.[56] In the light of the *Frontier Land* case, Cassese posits that since this practice developed and was upheld at a time when self-determination had not yet reached the status of a legal principle in the international community, for our purposes the specific question of the legal status of the practice is largely immaterial.[57]

Several cases have been heard since *Katanga* that have buttressed the principle of *uti possidetis* in Africa. For example, the border dispute between Libya and France was decided in 1994 by the ICJ on account of a colonial-era treaty between Libya and France from 1955. This was even though the 1955 treaty was no longer in force.[58]

The ICJ decision in the *Kasikili/Sedudu Island* case of 1999, which involved Botswana and Namibia, also relied on the principle of *uti possidetis*. In this case, the court held that while Namibia had historically occupied the island, a treaty between two colonial powers (Germany and England) from 1890 was of greater value in establishing the boundary between the two nations.[59]

21.7 REQUIREMENTS FOR THE CREATION OF A STATE

According to Shaw,[60] citing Art 1 of the Montevideo Convention on the Rights and Duties of States, the widely accepted criteria of statehood in international law are as follows:

(a) A permanent population;
(b) A defined territory;

---

[54] A Bell & E Kontorovich 'Palestine, *uti possidetis juris* and the borders of Israel' (2016) 67(58) *Arizona Law Review* 636.

[55] MN Shaw 'The heritage of states: The principle of *uti possidetis* today' (1996) *67 British Year Book of International Law* 75–115.

[56] ICJ, Reports 1959, 240; Cassese (note 24) 248 and Crawford (note 22) 178.

[57] M Behiels (2022). *Quebec Province, Canada* (Britannica.com, 2022) 1, https://www.britannica.com/place/Quebec-province, accessed 21 August 2023; see also Cassese (note 24).

[58] *Territorial Dispute (Libyan Arah Jamuhiriya/Chad)* (Judgment) (1994) ICJ Reports.

[59] *Kasikili/Sedudu Island (Botswana/Namibia)* (Judgment) (1999) ICJ Reports.

[60] M Shaw *International Law* 5 ed (Cambridge University Press, 2003) 178.

(c) Government;
(d) Capacity to enter into relations with other states.

This section deals with the requirements for the creation of a state. Reference made to practical examples of attempts to create states in selected parts of the world: in particular, the Quebec and Caprivi cases, among others. The section starts with a discussion on Quebec, a province in Canada.

21.7.1 Quebec

Quebec is a province of Canada – one of ten, to be precise. It is also one of two national territories which comprise the federal parliamentary State of Canada.[61] Quebec has an estimated population of eight million people.[62] At 80 per cent, it is the largest French-speaking province in Canada. Settled by the French in 1608, Quebec was conquered by British troops in 1759; by the Treaty of Paris of 1763, which formally ended the Seven Years War in Europe, sovereignty over Quebec was transferred from France to Great Britain. Eventually, when the British North America Act creating the State of Canada was concluded in 1867, Quebec became part of the federal state.[63]

The historical relationship between English-speaking and French-speaking Canadians was characterised by violence and mistrust until the 20th century.[64] It was not until the rebellious mindset of the Quiet Revolution and, more specifically, the reactions of the 1965 findings of the Laurendeau-Dunton Commission on Bilingualism – particularly concerning the extent of bilingualism in the federal administration – that French-speaking Quebeckers began to clamour for the right to live as French-speakers in the various spheres of their society.[65] In 1976 the radical Parti Quebecois in the Quebec province set in motion a process for an independence referendum. The first referendum in this regard was held in 1980 but ended in defeat for the separatists.

In 1995, after a tripartite agreement between the Parti Quebecois, the Bloc Quebecois, and the Action Democratique du Quebec, another referendum was held to determine Quebec's sovereignty. As with the 1980 referendum, this resulted

[61] Cassese (note 24) 248.
[62] Behiels (note 57).
[63] Cassese (note 24) 248.
[64] B Smith *Quebec Referendums* (2013) 1, https://www.files.ethz.ch/isn/167605/RP13-47.pdf, accessed 21 August 2023.
[65] C Harris 'Linguistic rights in Africa: A critical analysis of the survivability of Namibia's indigenous languages. LLD Dissertation (University of Namibia, 2021) 53, file:///C:/Users/charris/Downloads/Doctor%20of%20Philosophy.%20April%202021-final%20draft-Thursday.pdf, accessed 21 August 2023.

in defeat for the separatists. However, unlike the 1980 referendum, the 'no' vote was a narrow victory over the 'yes' vote.[66]

(a) Do the Quebecois have a legal right to self-determination?

The question whether the Quebecois have the right to secession vis-à-vis self-determination is twofold. Proponents of Quebec's independence often refer to principles of international law to argue their case. The UN Charter and the Universal Declaration of Human Rights, the Vienna Declaration of 1993, the Helsinki Final Act are among international legal instruments often cited by proponents of Quebec independence.[67]

However, opponents of Quebec independence argue that international law does not grant autonomous regions or states within a federal government system the right to determine their international status freely, regardless of whether they represent ethnic and cultural groups distinctly different from the rest of the population.[68]

Although self-determination has also been used in conjunction with the principle of territorial integrity so as to protect the territorial framework of the colonial period in the decolonisation process and to prevent a rule permitting secession from independent states from arising, the Canadian Supreme Court had a different opinion in this regard:[69] it noted in the Quebec case that

> international law expects that the right to self-determination will be exercised by peoples within the framework of existing sovereign states and consistently with the maintenance of the territorial integrity of those states.[70]

In assessing the legality of any unilateral secession by Quebec in terms of Canadian constitutional law, the court stressed the relevance of 'four fundamental and organizing principles of the Constitution'.[71] These are federalism, democracy, constitutionalism and the rule of law, and respect for minorities.[72] In the words of the court:

> These defining principles function in symbiosis. No single principle can be defined in isolation from the others, nor does any one principle trump or exclude the operation of any other.[73]

[66] P Dumberry 'Lessons learned from the Quebec secession referendum before the Supreme Court of Canada' in MG Kohen (ed) *Secession: International Law Perspectives* (Cambridge University Press, 2006) 418–420.
[67] RM Hanna 'Right to self-determination in re secession of Quebec' (1999) 23 *Maryland Journal of International Law* 1–35.
[68] Cassese (note 24) 251.
[69] Shaw (note 60) 231.
[70] (1998) 161 DLR (4th) 385 at 436; 115 ILR 536.
[71] Paragraph 32.
[72] P Radan 'Constitutional law and secession: The case of Quebec' (1998) *Macquarie University Law Review* 69–85, http://classic.austlii.edu.au/au/journals/MacarthurLawRw/1998/4.pdf, accessed 21 August 2023.
[73] Ibid.

These principles dictate that, under Canadian constitutional law, secession requires a negotiated amendment to the Canadian Constitution.[74] The court ruled:

> [T]he secession of Quebec from Canada cannot be accomplished by the National Assembly, the legislature or government of Quebec unilaterally, that is to say without principled negotiations, and be considered a lawful act. Any attempt to effect the secession of a province from Canada must be undertaken pursuant to the Constitution of Canada, or else violate the Canadian legal order.[75]

21.7.2 Caprivi/Zambezi

The Caprivi strip, now Zambezi region, is a part of Namibia with a unique history and geography. According to the 2011 census, the region had an estimated population of slightly less than 100 000. However, this number does not include 'Caprivians' residing in other parts of the country.

The name 'Caprivi' derives from Leo von Caprivi, who succeeded Otto von Bismarck as Chancellor of Germany in 1890,[76] whereas the name 'Zambezi' derives from the river separating Namibia and Zambia. Caprivi strip/Zambezi region is the name of the panhandle (narrow strip of land) protruding from the northeast corner of Namibia and in the direction of Botswana and Zambia.[77] It is one of the 13 political regions of Namibia. Von Caprivi obtained the strip from Great Britain as part of a general settlement (1890) between the two countries.[78] It gave the former German colony of South West Africa (now Namibia) access to the Zambezi.[79] For political reasons, the Caprivi strip was renamed Zambezi.[80]

The people of the Zambezi region are customarily divided into two main political groups: the Masubiya and the Mafwe. The Masubiya are both ethnically and linguistically a homogenous Bantu-speaking group of people, living mainly in the eastern part of the region.[81] The Mafwe, on the other hand, comprise almost all the non-Masubiya people of the Zambezi region.[82]

---

[74] Ibid.

[75] Ibid.

[76] F Maho *Few People, Many Tongues: The Languages of Namibia* (Gamsberg Macmillan, 1998) 45.

[77] B Kangumu 'Contestations over Caprivi identities: From precolonial times to the present' PhD Thesis (University of Cape Town, 2008) 14.

[78] See the Anglo-German Treaty [Heligoland-Zanzibar Treaty] (1 July 1890).

[79] Ibid.

[80] I Shinovene 'Caprivi is no more' *The Namibian* 9 August 2013.

[81] Maho (note 76) 45.

[82] Historically, Mafwes consisted of Mafwe-Mashi, Mbalangwe, Totela, Yeyis and Hambukushus. Today the Mayeyis have broken away and formed their own traditional authority.

(a) Secessionist insurrection

In the early hours of 2 August 1999, a group of Namibians calling themselves the Caprivi Liberation Army launched a surprise attack on government installations at Katima Mulilo in the then Caprivi region. The insurrection was immediately and brutally crushed. In it, about ten people lost their lives. In the aftermath, hundreds of suspects were detained by security forces and others were alleged to have been tortured.[83] As a result of the attacks, a state of emergency was declared by the then President Sam Nujoma, who vowed to crush the rebellion.[84] True to his word, the Namibian Defence Force managed to suppress the rebellion in its entirety. However, proponents of Caprivi/Zambezi independence have since resorted to activism to advance their agenda. An obscure Caprivi activist movement calling itself the Caprivi Concerned Group (CCG) and the banned pro-secessionist party known as the United Democratic Party (UDP) appear to be the only entities continuing with the 'struggle' for Caprivi independence. Interestingly, these groups often claim not have a secessionist agenda; instead, they claim to be advocating the release of so-called 'political prisoners' being held in Namibian prisons. These 'political prisoners' are those Namibians who were tried and convicted of treason by the state after the failed secessionist attacks at Katima Mulilo.[85]

The reason for the insurrection remains obscure to this day. In neighbouring Zambia a secessionist movement led by the Lozi ethnic group exists; it wants to declare the western part of that country an independent state.[86] Some analysts are of the opinion that Caprivi secessionists may be aiming at incorporating the region within a revived Barotseland. According to the secessionist leader, Mishake Muyongo, the Caprivi has been deliberately marginalised by the ruling SWAPO[87] party, which has instead invested in its northern Ovamboland stronghold – the most populated area of the country.[88] The government is also accused of having dabbled in the ethnic politics of the region, weakening Mafwe influence in the eastern Caprivi. In weakening the Mafwe, Muyongo alleged that the government had instigated the Mayeyis and Mafwe of the Kongola area to break away from the main Mafwe Traditional Authority at Linyanti.[89]

---

[83] T Amupadhi 'Govt admits abuses' *The Namibian*, 12 August 1999.

[84] T Amupadhi 'President vows to crush rebels' *The Namibian*, 9 August 1999.

[85] Caprivi Concerned Group *Do Caprivians Constitute a Nation?*, https://www.capriviconcernedgroup.com/do-caprivians-constitute-a-nation/, accessed 21 August 2023.

[86] BBC 'Barotseland kingdom seeks to leave Zambia' *BBC News*, 29 March 2012, https://www.bbc.com/news/world-africa-17546620, accessed 21 August 2023.

[87] South West Africa People's Organisation.

[88] 'The Caprivi secessionist crises' *The New Humanitarian*, 9 August 1999, https://www.thenewhumanitarian.org/report/8468/namibia-caprivi-secessionist-crisis, accessed 21 August 2023.

[89] B Kangumu & GN Likando 'Mission education in the eastern Caprivi Strip during the colonial times, ca1920s–ca1964' (2015) 4(1) *Journal for Studies in Humanities and Social Sciences* 205–215.

(b) Legal and political arguments of Caprivi secessionists

Like elsewhere in the world, the Caprivi secessionist movement employs international-law principles in advancing their separatist agenda. They argue that the UN and African Charters explicitly guarantee that all peoples have the right to self-determination and to determine their political status. Namibia has ratified these instruments or treaties. There are several ICJ opinions which support the right to self-determination.[90] They argue further that Art 20(1) of the African (Banjul) Charter states that 'colonized or oppressed peoples shall have the right to free themselves from the bonds of domination by resorting to any means recognized by the international community'.[91]

In addition to international-law remedies, Caprivi secessionists are calling for a referendum on the Caprivi issue. As implicitly stated by the leader of the CCG, Edwin Samati:

> Since the formation of the CCG in 2012, it has not engaged in any illegal activities, but has done everything in terms of the law. We are not calling to secede Zambezi, but rather we are exercising our democratic right and in a peaceful manner to call for a referendum where the inhabitants can also exercise their rights to choose whether they want to be part or not of Namibia. Hence, if there are those who harbour plans to secede, we instead giving them a chance to join a dialogue and not run in the bush with guns.[92]

The statement by Samati is confusing and incoherent. He claims that his group does not want to secede Zambezi from Namibia, yet he is calling in the same sentence for a referendum for Caprivians to decide on whether they should be part of Namibia or not. One does not need to be an international-law expert to deduce that the CCG's ultimate goal is to secede the Zambezi from Namibia.

The Caprivi secessionists also argue that since they are a 'minority' being persecuted by the majority ethnic group – the Owambos in this instance – they are of the opinion that international-law principles on independence favour them. In addition to this grievance, the secessionists argue that the government in the capital Windhoek has over the years reduced the size of the Caprivi/Zambezi region by 'donating' land to Botswana and the neighbouring Kavango region.[93] They argue that this is yet another example of the Namibian government's persecution of their people.

---

[90] Caprivi Concerned Group (note 85).
[91] Ibid.
[92] O Simasiku '"Caprivi" group says no threat to peace' *Windhoek Observer*, 10 June 2022.
[93] Ibid.

(c) Counter-arguments from the Namibian government

The Namibian government has steadfastly rebuffed the secessionist attempt as a rebellion which has no legal basis. In fact, state prosecutors in the marathon Caprivi treason trial relied continually on Art 1 of the Namibian Constitution, which prohibits any form of secessionism. Article 1 states:

> (1) *The Republic of Namibia is hereby established as a sovereign, secular, democratic and unitary State founded upon the principles of democracy, the rule of law and justice for all.*
> (2) All power shall vest in the people of Namibia who shall exercise their sovereignty through the democratic institutions of the State. [Emphasis added]

(d) Does Caprivi/Zambezi meet the criteria for statehood?

All in all, the Namibian government appears to have fully endorsed the international-law principle of *uti possidetis* to effectively suppress any agitation for secessionism. In non-colonial situations, secession may take place only with the approval of the parent state. Such approval may be given by the constitution of the parent state or in some other form, either prior to the declaration of independence or following an initial unilateral declaration.[94] In this case, Caprivi/Zambezi is not under Namibian colonialism. Ironically, the secessionist leader, Mishake Muyongo, actively participated in the constituent assembly that drafted the Namibian Constitution prior to 1990. Article 1 of the same Constitution to which Muyongo appended his signature declares Namibia as a 'unitary state'. As it stands, there are no legal provisions that allow for any part of Namibia to secede from the parent country.

One of the requirements for secession is that the claimant community should have an identity distinct from the rest of the country and inhabit a region that largely supports separation in the given circumstances. Although Caprivi secessionists argue that they are linguistically and culturally different from other Namibians, this argument lacks substance. Like elsewhere in Africa, Namibia is a multi-ethnic country made up of different tribes who for the most part are linguistically, historically and even politically different from one another. The same argument for secession could be used by the Rehoboth Basters, who are of mixed race and constitute a distinct minority ethnic group. The indigenous San ethnic group, who are racially and culturally different from the numerically superior Bantu groups, can also claim the same right of self-determination as the Caprivi secessionists.

The second requirement is that the community has been subjected to a pattern of systematic political or economic discrimination. Although the Zambezi region

---

[94] D Raič *Statehood and the Law of Self-Determination* (Kluwer Law International, 2002) 314–315.

is poor, it is not the poorest in Namibia. Of the estimated 568 418 poor people in Namibia, 21% are found in the Kavango region whereas Ohangwena and Oshikoto account for 15% and 14% of the poor respectively. Subsistence farming employs 58.3% of the population in Kavango and 53.3% and 44.3% in Ohangwena and Oshikoto respectively.[95] Therefore, the argument by secessionists that the Zambezi region is deliberately being marginalised may not be true if the official statistics are to be believed. The government has invested heavily in the infrastructure of the region, as succinctly stated by Amupanda et al.[96]

In the domain of infrastructure, the Zambezi region has benefited in two key respects: first, the opening of the Trans-Caprivi Highway in 1999 and, second, the completion of the Sesheke Bridge over the Zambezi River in 2004. Both of these developments have benefited the people of the region and made their access to the rest of Namibia and to Zambia much easier. The Walvis Bay–Ndola–Lubumbashi Development Road (previously the Trans-Caprivi Corridor and until 2004 the Trans-Caprivi Highway) opened in 1999 and runs from Rundu in the Eastern Kavango along the former Caprivi strip (now Zambezi region) as the B8 road to Katima Mulilo on the banks of the Zambezi River, which forms the border between Namibia and Zambia. The Katima Mulilo Bridge spans the river to the Zambian town of Sesheke, from where the recently upgraded paved road runs to Livingstone, joining the main north–south highway to Lusaka.

The third and last requirement is that the central regime has rejected the reasonable proposals for autonomy and minority rights of the claimant community. This requirement is difficult for the Namibian government to fulfil as the Constitution, which is the supreme law of the land, prohibits all forms of secessionism, federalism and the like. The proposal for autonomy has been advanced by local academics, though. According to Amupanda et al,[97] in concrete terms, the Namibian government should grant amnesty to all the persons, including Mishake Muyongo, who were involved in the 1999 uprising. Based on the notion of reasonableness, the protracted trial should be concluded as a matter of urgency. Furthermore, the policy of decentralisation should be embellished and implemented to allow for meaningful autonomy in the region. The regional governor ought to be directly elected by the voters of the region.[98]

---

[95] United Nations Development Programme *Poverty and Deprivation in Namibia Report*, https://www.undp.org/sites/g/files/zskgke326/files/migration/na/undp_na_povred_npcreport-sum_2015.pdf, accessed 21 August 2023.

[96] JS Amupanda, A du Pisani & RA Tyitende 'Namibia's 1999 Caprivi conflict and the consequences of a peace building deficit – a first consideration' 2020 *Journal of Namibian Studies* 7–37.

[97] Ibid.

[98] Amupanda, Du Pisani & Tyitende (note 96) 31.

The call for the government to grant some form of autonomy for the Zambezi is highly likely going to be resisted by the state, though. The government's strong anti-secessionist stance may be justified to prevent a pandora's box from opening. Besides the Caprivi secessionists' troubles, other potential separatist movements exist in the country. Some in the Rehoboth Baster community of central Namibia have in the past agitated for some form of self-determination as opposed to independence from or within Namibia.[99]

In addition to the secessionist challenges in the Zambezi, there are opposition parties that have openly called for Namibia to become a federal state. Like the Caprivi secessionists, the late Herero Paramount Chief Kuaima Riruako was an advocate of Namibia's becoming a federal state, citing the state-sponsored marginalisation of minority ethnic groups in the country. Riruako stated:

> We are not calling for secessionism or tribal violence ... we just want a federal system to give minority groups an equal opportunity to participate in the way they are ruled. The current unitary Namibian state had failed over the last 13 years of independence because it only benefits the 'majority tribe' which controls all State resources. For one to get a job in the public sector, the person must first be Oshiwambo speaking and second a SWAPO member. People's ranks in the army, police and the public service also depend on the two criteria.[100]

21.8 CONCLUSION

The ongoing disputation over the right to self-determination versus the corresponding right of states to embrace the notion of sovereignty and territorial integrity will continue to inspire debates among academics, policy-makers, jurists and politicians for many years to come. The irony in this debate is that public international law recognises both the rights of states to affirm the notion of territorial sovereignty and the need to accord some recognition to regions or parts of a state to secede on account of remedial secession.

However, judging from the available literature, one can deduce that most scholars are of the opinion that self-determination does not necessarily equate to independence. Opponents of Quebec's independence argue that secession is

[99] C Wren '*Rehoboth Journal*; fearful Namibian tribe raises flag of freedom' *New York Times*, 4 April 1990, https://www.nytimes.com/1990/04/04/world/rehoboth-journal-fearful-namibian-tribe-raises-flag-of-freedom.html, accessed 21 August 2023.

[100] P Kuteeue 'Herero chief wants a federal system' *The Namibian*, 15 August 2013.

recognised as a possibility, not a right.[101] A provincial government has no right to appoint itself as the government of an independent state. It cannot legally secede unilaterally without first securing a negotiated agreement with the Canadian state. But it does not have that right, under either international law or domestic law. The Supreme Court of Canada confirmed, in its 1998 opinion, that for the secession of a province from Canada to be considered, in legal terms, must require an amendment to the Constitution, which perforce requires negotiation [para 84] within the existing constitutional framework [para 149].

Of the two main types of self-determination – internal and external – the former appears to be the more favoured by some states. The Canadian government, in its efforts to undermine Quebec's secessionist movement, opted for internal self-determination. The Province of Quebec is now regarded as a 'nation' within Canada with its own law, culture and French as the sole official language.

In contrast, the Namibian government's approach to the Caprivi/Zambezi issue has largely been based on Art 1 of the Namibian Constitution, which declares the country to be a unitary and democratic state. The doctrine of *uti possidetis* has also been embraced by the government in relation to the Caprivi issue. Therefore, it can be concluded that the Namibian government's attitude to the Caprivi issue is rooted in both domestic and international considerations.

The quest for Caprivi secessionism is also hampered by the fact that there is no evidence that it has the support of the so-called Caprivians. Although a survey of the attitudes of Caprivians towards independence has never been conducted, it is widely accepted that the majority favours remaining part of Namibia. Some observers augment this assertion by pointing to the fact that the ruling SWAPO party enjoys widespread support in the region, including in areas from where the majority of secessionist ringleaders hail.

REFERENCES

Abel, M *Is There a Right to Secessionism under International Law?* (2020), https://www.e-ir.info/2020/05/18/is-there-a-right-to-secession-in-international-law/, accessed 21 August 2023.

Amupadhi, T 'President vows to crush rebels' *The Namibian*, 9 August 1999.

Amupadhi, T 'Govt admits abuses' *The Namibian*, 12 August 1999.

Amupanda, JS, Du Pisani, A & Tyitende, RA 'Namibia's 1999 Caprivi conflict and the consequences of a peacebuilding deficit – a first consideration' 2020 *Journal of Namibian Studies* 7–37.

[101] S Dion *Secession and Democracy: A Canadian Perspective* (Realinstitutevolcano.org, 2013) 3, https://media.realinstitutoelcano.org/wp-content/uploads/2013/04/stephane-dion-secession-democracy-canada.pdf, accessed 21 August 2023.

Anaya, J 'The capacity of international law to advance ethnic or nationality rights claims' in W Kymlicka *The Rights of Minority Cultures* (Oxford University Press, 1990).

BBC 'Barotseland kingdom seeks to leave Zambia' *BBC News*, 29 March 2012, https://www.bbc.com/news/world-africa-17546620, accessed 21 August 2023.

Behiels, M *Quebec Province, Canada* (2022), https://www.britannica.com/place/Quebec-province, accessed 21 August 2023.

Bell, A & Kontorovich, E 'Palestine, *uti possidetis juris* and the borders of Israel' (2016) 58 *Arizona Law Review* 636.

Cassese, A *Self-determination of Peoples: A Legal Reappraisal* (Antony Rowe Ltd, 1995).

Crawford, J 'State practice and international law in relation to secession' (1998) 69 *British Yearbook of International Law* 85–86.

Crawford, J *The Creation of States in International Law* (Oxford University Press, 2007).

Dion, S *Secession and the Virtues of Clarity* (Macdonald-Laurier Institute of Public Policy, 2011).

Dion, S *Secession and Democracy: A Canadian Perspective* (realinstitutevolcano.org, 2013), https://media.realinstitutoelcano.org/wp-content/uploads/2013/04/stephane-dion-secession-democracy-canada.pdf, accessed 21 August 2023.

Caprivi Concerned Group *Do Caprivians Constitute a Nation?*, https://www.caprivi-concernedgroup.com/do-caprivians-constitute-a-nation/, accessed 21 August 2023.

Dugard, J 'Secession: Is the case of Yugoslavia a precedent for Africa?' (1993) 5 *African Journal of International and Comparative Law* 163, 165.

Dugard, J & Raič, D 'The role of recognition in the law and practice of secession' in MG Kohen (ed) *Secession: International Law Perspectives* (Cambridge University Press, 2006).

Dumberry, P 'Lessons learned from the Quebec Secession Referendum before the Supreme Court of Canada' in MG Kohen (ed) *Secession: International Law Perspectives* (Cambridge University Press, 2006).

Eckert, AE 'Constructing states: The role of the international community in the creation of new states' (2002) 13 *Journal of Public and International Affairs* 19–39.

Falk, R 'The rights of peoples (in particular indigenous peoples)' in J Crawford (ed) *The Rights of Peoples* (Clarendon Press, 1998).

Findi, P & Basir, SM 'Legality of secessionism under international law' 2020 *International Journal of Psychological Rehabilitation.*

Foot, R 'Separatism in Canada' *The Canadian Encyclopaedia* (2006), https://www.thecanadianencyclopedia.ca/en/article/separatism, accessed 21 August 2023.

Ginsburg, T 'Secession' *Constitution Brief*, 2018, https://www.idea.int/sites/default/files/publications/constitution-brief-secession.pdf, accessed 21 August 2023.

Hanna, RM 'Right to self-determination in re secession of Quebec' (1999) 23 *Maryland Journal of International Law* 1–35.

Harris, C. (2021). 'Linguistic rights in Africa: A critical analysis of the survivability of Namibia's indigenous languages LLD Dissertation (University of Namibia, 2021), file:///C:/Users/charris/Downloads/Doctor%20of%20Philosophy.%20April%202021-final%20draft-Thursday.pdf, accessed 21 August 2023.

Haverland, C 'Secession' in *Encyclopaedia of Public International Law* (Elsevier Science Publishers, 1989).

Heraclides, A *The Self-determination of Minorities in International Politics* (BPCC Wheatons Ltd, 1991).

Higgins, R *Problems and Process – International Law and How We Use It* (Oxford University Press, 1995).

International Court of Justice 'Legal consequences for states of the continued presence of South Africa in Namibia (South West Africa) notwithstanding Security Council Resolution 276' 1971 *ICJ Reports* 16.

Johnson, CD 'Toward self-determination – a reappraisal of friendly relations' (1973) 13 *Georgia Journal of International and Comparative Law* 148.

Kangumu, B 'Contestations over Caprivi identities: From precolonial times to the present' PhD Thesis (University of Cape Town, 2008).

Kangumu, B & Likando, GN 'Mission education in the eastern Caprivi Strip during the colonial times, ca1920s–ca1964' (2015) 4(1) *Journal for Studies in Humanities and Social Sciences* 205–215.

Kuteeue, P 'Herero chief wants a federal system' *The Namibian*. 15 August 2013.

Maho, F *Few People, Many Tongues: The Languages of Namibia* (Gamsberg Macmillan, 1998).

Matsumoto, S *Separatism in Africa – a Fundamental Problem: Policy Brief* (policycentre.ma, 2019), https://www.policycenter.ma/sites/default/files/PB%20-%2043-19%20%28Matsumoto%29%20%281%29.pdf, accessed 21 August 2023.

Mnyongani, FD 'Between a rock and a hard place: The right to self-determination versus *uti possidetis* in Africa' (2008) XLI *Comparative and International Law Journal of Southern Africa* 464.

Nanda, VP 'Secessionism and self-determination under international law' (2001) 29 *Denver Journal of International Law & Policy* 305.

The New Humanitarian 'The Caprivi secessionist crises' *The New Humanitarian*, 9 August 1999, https://www.thenewhumanitarian.org/report/8468/namibia-caprivi-secessionist-crisis, accessed 21 August 2023.

Radan, P 'Constitutional law and secession: The case of Quebec' 1998 *Macquarie University Law Review* 69–85, http://classic.austlii.edu.au/au/journals/MacarthurLawRw/1998/4.pdf, accessed 21 August 2023.

Raič, D. *Statehood and the Law of Self-determination* (Kluwer Law International, 2002).

Schachter, O 'Sovereignty – then and now' in R Macdonald (ed) *Essays in Honour of Wang Tieya* (Martinus Nijhoff, 1993).

Schwed, A 'Territorial claims as a limitation to the right of self-determination in the context of the Falklands Islands dispute' (1982) 6 *Fordham International Law Journal* 45.

Shaw, M *International Law* 5 ed (Cambridge University Press, 2003).

Shaw, MN 'The heritage of states: The principle of *uti possidetis* today' (1996) 67 *British Year Book of International Law* 75–115.

Shinovene, I 'Caprivi is no more' *The Namibian*, 9 August 2023.

Simasiku, O '"Caprivi" group says no threat to peace' *Windhoek Observer*, 10 June 2022.

Small, A 'An unintended legacy: Kwame Nkrumah and the domestication of national self-determination in Africa' (2017) 17(1) *African Human Rights Law Journal* 68–88.
Smith, B *Quebec Referendums* (2013) 1, https://www.files.ethz.ch/isn/167605/RP13-47.pdf, accessed 21 August 2023.
Stein, C 'Successful secessionist movements and the uncertainty of post-secession quality of life' BSc (Hons) in Political Science and Psychology Thesis (Oregon State University Honors College, 2016), file:///C:/Users/Tumisang%20Harris/Downloads/SteinChloeE2016%20(1).pdf, accessed 21 August 2023.
Sterio, M *The Right to Self-determination under International Law: 'Selfistans', Secession and Great Powers* (Routledge, 2013).
Sterio, M *Self-determination and Secession under International Law: The New Framework* (Law Faculty Articles and Essays, 2015).
United Nations Development Programme *Poverty and Deprivation in Namibia Report*, https://www.undp.org/sites/g/files/zskgke326/files/migration/na/undp_na_povred_npcreportsum_2015.pdf, accessed 21 August 2023.
Vezbergaite, I 'Remedial Secession as an exercise of the right to self-determination of peoples' LLM Thesis (Central University of Europe, 2011), file:///C:/Users/Tumisang%20Harris/Downloads/vezbergaite_ieva.pdf. accessed 21 August 2023.
Vidmar, J 'Remedial secession in international law, theory and (lack of) practice' (2010) 6(1) *St Antony's International Review* 37–56.
Wheatley, S *Democracy, Minorities and International Law. Cambridge Studies in International Law* (Cambridge University Press, 2005).
Wren, C '*Rehoboth Journal*; fearful Namibian tribe raises flag of freedom' *New York Times*, 4 April 1990, https://www.nytimes.com/1990/04/04/world/rehoboth-journal-fearful-namibian-tribe-raises-flag-of-freedom.html, accessed 21 August 2023.

CASES

Aaland Islands (1920) LNOJ Spec Supp No 3
International Court of Justice (ICJ) Western Sahara Advisory Opinion, 1975
Island of Palmas case (or Miangas), United States v Netherlands, Award, (1928) II RIAA 829, ICGJ 392 (PCA 1928), 4 April 1928
Kasikili/Sedudu Island (Botswana/Namibia) (Judgment) (1999) ICJ Reports
Katanganese Peoples Congress v Zaire, African Commission on Human and Peoples Rights, Comm No 75/92 (1995)
Sovereignty over certain Frontier Land case ICJ Reports 1959
Territorial Dispute (Libyan Arah Jamuhiriya/Chad) (Judgment) (1994) ICJ Reports

LEGISLATION

African (Banjul) Charter OAU Doc CAB/LEG/67/3 rev 5, 21 ILM58 (1982)
Helsinki Final Act, 14 ILM 1292, 1 August 1975

International Covenant on Civil and Political Rights (ICCPR) General Assembly Resolution 2200A (XXI), 16 December 1966
International Covenant on Economic, Social and Cultural Rights (ICESCR) Treaty Series, vol 999, 16 December 1966
Montevideo Convention on the Rights and Duties of States 26 December 1933
Organisation for Security and Co-Operation in Europe, Helsinki Final Act (signed 1 August 1975), Principle VIII
UN Charter 26 June 1945
Universal Declaration of Human Rights of 10 December 1948
Vienna Declaration of 1993

22

Locus standi in Namibia: a serious impediment to social justice

John Nakuta

22.1 INTRODUCTION

Namibia is said to be one of the most unequal societies in the world: the country is burdened with the triple challenges of poverty, unemployment and inequality. The scourge of housing poverty in the form of informal housing has, in particular, reached alarming proportions in the country. This begs the question: Could a bona fide public-spirited member of the general public wishing to challenge the abhorrent living conditions of informal settlements institute legal proceedings to challenge the inadequacies of government actions and/or omissions in this regard? Such a person, in all probability, would be characterised as an interfering busybody. A group of women residing under such abhorrent conditions wishing to institute a legal challenge to demand better service would most likely suffer the same fate.

Neither of these potential litigants has the necessary *locus standi* to institute such legal proceedings. That, needless to say, is in accordance with the Namibian legal position governing *locus standi*. The situation would be totally different if these hypothetical cases were to be instituted in, say, India, Kenya, South Africa or Zimbabwe. This is so because these jurisdictions reformed and liberalised the traditional common-law rules on *locus standi* with which their legal systems were previously hackled. Namibia lags behind in this respect. This chapter strongly advocates change in this area of the law as a way of facilitating, attaining and advancing social justice for the underprivileged.

The focus here is on *locus standi*, also known as standing, as a procedural justiciability of a claim. The question of *locus standi* is separate from the substance of a case. It is therefore a matter to be decided *in limine* before the merits of a case are considered. Namibia's current law on standing is governed by the common law.

These rules are particularly restrictive and exclusionary in nature. This chapter does not seek to regurgitate the doctrinal meaning of *locus standi*; neither does it attempt to give a chronicle account of the evolution of the common-law rules of *locus standi* in the country. Instead, it engages in a comparative exercise to show how the traditional rules of *locus standi* have been reformed and liberalised in comparative jurisdictions – specifically, countries which share a similar colonial legal heritage with Namibia. The ultimate objective is to flag the deficiencies in the common-law rules of *locus standi* in promoting and attaining social justice in the country. The point is made that the rules on standing in their current form perpetuate inequality and injustice. In this context, the deficiencies of the current rules on standing are illustrated using the example of the right of residents of informal settlements to adequate housing in Namibia.

The chapter showcases the way the traditional rules of *locus standi* have been liberalised in other comparable jurisdictions: Kenya, South Africa and Zimbabwe. Whereas reforms in these jurisdictions have been aided and facilitated through constitutional provisions, the example of India is also presented, because the judiciary in that state led the charge of liberalising the rules of *locus standi* by their own volition to advance social justice to the underprivileged. It is recommended that the Namibian superior courts should follow the example of their Indian counterparts in this regard.

This comparative analysis admittedly only scratches the surface; however, the issues covered here should serve as the basis for the arguments put forward to liberalise the rules of *locus standi* in Namibia. This is considered imperative to advancing the cause of justice in the public-law arena and to strengthening the rule of law.[1]

22.2 SETTING THE SCENE

In her 2018 annual thematic report, the former UN Special Rapporteur on adequate housing, Leilani Farha, stated that

> the scope and severity of the living conditions in informal settlements make this one of the most pervasive violations of human rights globally.[2]

Namibia is no exception: the housing situation there has been characterised as 'distressing'.[3] The housing challenge cuts across all classes of society but is more

[1] M Ershadul & M Ehteshamul 'Liberalization of the traditional rule of *locus standi* in the United Kingdom and Malaysia: A comparative study' (2012) 39 *Journal of Malaysian and Comparative Law* 27.

[2] United Nations General Assembly *The Right to Housing for Residents of Informal Settlements* UN Doc A/73/310/Rev.1 (2018) 2.

[3] JB Nakuta 'The right to adequate housing in Namibia: A right not vindicated' (2021) 1 *Namibian Journal of Social Justice, Namibia's Housing Crisis in Perspective* 23.

pronounced among the urban poor, specifically those relegated to living in informal settlements and squalor.[4] The living conditions in these informal settlements, to echo Farha, can at best be described as shocking, deplorable and intolerable.[5] The most recent national statistics reveal that close to 40 per cent of urban households throughout the country reside in informal settlements.[6] The living conditions in these informal settlements violate, without fail, each of the justiciable elements of the right to adequate housing as guaranteed under international human rights law. These are security of tenure; availability of services, materials, facilities and infrastructure; affordability; habitability; accessibility; adequate location, and cultural adequacy.[7]

The 2018 thematic annual report of the former Special Rapporteur on adequate housing makes it abundantly clear that all aspects of the right to adequate housing accrue equally to the residents of informal settlements. The very title of the report, 'The Right to Housing for Residents of Informal Settlements', buttresses this point. The scope and severity of the living conditions in informal settlements in the country make these residential areas one of the most pervasive violations of the human rights of dignity, security, health and life.[8]

Indeed, a recent study on the state of housing informality in Namibia depicts a compelling picture of non-compliance with the government's unassailable obligation to respect, protect and fulfil the right to adequate housing of residents of informal settlements in the country. The study portrays sorry tales of non-recognition, deprivation, deterioration and endemic housing poverty in addition to a serious accountability gap in the housing sector.[9] The right to adequate housing of residents of informal settlements is undoubtedly one of the most blatantly violated rights in the country. Curiously, to date, no claim to vindicate the right to adequate housing for these residents has been instituted before the courts. This begs the question: Why not? Phrased differently: What, if any, are the access to justice challenges for residents of informal settlements in Namibia wishing to challenge the government's omissions in this regard? This article asserts that the current rules governing *locus standi* in the Namibian legal order are among the chief impediments to social justice litigation in the current legal order in Namibia.

---

[4] United Nations General Assembly (note 2) 1.

[5] Ibid.

[6] Namibia Statistics Agency *Namibia Inter-censal Demographic Survey 2016 Report* (NSA, 2017) 101.

[7] See General Comment No 3 of the United Nations Committee on Economic, Social and Cultural Rights, para 8*(a)*–*(g)*; see also African Commission on Human and Peoples' Rights *Principles and Guidelines on the Implementation of Economic, Social and Cultural Rights in the African Charter on Human and Peoples' Rights* (ACHPR, 2010) paras 77–79.

[8] United Nations General Assembly (note 2) 1.

[9] JB Nakuta 'A human rights analysis of housing informality in Namibia: Challenges, ambitions, and misses' Unpublished PhD thesis (Maastricht University Faculty of Law, 2023) 254.

However, before delving into a discussion on *locus standi*, it is important first to discuss briefly the central role of the right to an effective remedy as guaranteed under international human rights law.

22.3 RIGHT TO AN EFFECTIVE REMEDY

The Latin maxim *ubi jus, ibi remedium* – meaning 'where there is a right, there is a remedy' – postulates that where law has established a right there should be a corresponding remedy for its breach. In other words, remedies correlate with rights. The right to a remedy for human rights violations is accordingly guaranteed in a number of international and regional human rights instruments. These include Art 8 of the Universal Declaration of Human Rights, Art 2 of the International Covenant on Civil and Political Rights, Art 6 of the International Convention on the Elimination of All Forms of Racial Discrimination, Art 14 of the Convention against Torture and other Cruel, Inhuman or Degrading Treatment or Punishment and Art 39 of the Convention on the Rights of the Child.[10]

The African Charter does not explicitly provide for the right to an effective remedy. However, other African human rights instruments provide for an effective remedy as a free-standing right. For instance, the Protocol to the African Charter on Human and Peoples' Rights (ACHPR) on the Rights of Women in Africa (the Maputo Protocol) requires states party to provide for appropriate remedies to 'any woman whose rights or freedoms as guaranteed in the Protocol have been violated'.[11] The African Commission, though, through its ever-evolving human rights jurisprudence, has filled the gap in the African Charter in respect of the right to an effective remedy. Two sets of principles and guidelines issued by the African Commission are relevant to this theme. For instance, the Principles and Guidelines on the Right to a Fair Trial and Legal Assistance in Africa affirm that everyone has the right to an effective remedy by competent national tribunals for acts violating the rights granted by the constitution, law or the Charter.[12] The Principles and Guidelines on the Implementation of Economic, Social and Cultural Rights

[10] See United Nations General Assembly in its Resolution 60/147 *Basic Principles and Guidelines on the Right to a Remedy and Reparation for Victims of Gross Violations of International Human Rights Law and Serious Violations of International Humanitarian Law* UN Doc A/RES/60/147, https://www.ohchr.org/EN/ProfessionalInterest/Pages/RemedyAndReparation.aspx, accessed 21 August 2023.

[11] See Art 25 of the Protocol to the African Charter on Human and Peoples' Rights on the Rights of Women in Africa (the Maputo Protocol).

[12] African Commission on Human and Peoples' Rights *Principles and Guidelines on the Right to a Fair Trial and Legal Assistance in Africa*, African Union Doc DOC/OS (XXX) (2010) 247, Principle C, para (a).

(ESC rights) in the ACHPR similarly affirm the right to an effective remedy for violations of ESC rights by expressly providing for 'effective domestic remedies'. To this end, it specifically directs that the violation of ESC rights protected under the ACHPR entitles affected individuals and peoples to effective remedies and redress under domestic law.[13] Furthermore, in the celebrated *SERAC* case, the African Commission held that the state's obligation to respect housing rights requires it to guarantee access to legal remedies where infringements have occurred.[14]

The Special Rapporteurs on adequate housing have emphasised the right to an effective remedy in the context of the urban poor and informal settlements. In her 2013 report on urban tenure security, the former Special Rapporteur, Raquel Rolnik, called on states to ensure that the urban poor in their jurisdictions have access to effective remedies through judicial and administrative mechanisms.[15] For her part, Leilani Farha stressed that residents of informal settlements should have avenues through which they are able to claim and enforce their right to adequate housing.[16] To this end, she called for informal justice processes to be established to adjudicate over land and housing issues as a way of mitigating prohibitive legal costs.[17]

The content of the right to an effective remedy has gradually been interpreted and developed by the respective international and regional human rights bodies. For instance, in its General Comment 9 the Committee on ESC rights stated as a general principle of international law that 'appropriate means of redress, or remedies, must be available to any aggrieved individual or group, and appropriate means of ensuring governmental accountability must be put in place'. The African Commission has listed three elements of a remedy that pass muster in terms of the Charter: availability, effectiveness and sufficiency. In this regard, the Commission in *Jawara v The Gambia* held:

> A remedy is considered available if the petitioner can pursue it without impediment, it is deemed effective if it offers a prospect of success, and it is found sufficient if it is capable of redressing the complaint.[18]

---

[13] African Commission on Human and Peoples' Rights *Principles and Guidelines on the Implementation of Economic, Social and Cultural Rights in the African Charter on Human and Peoples' Rights* (ACHPR, 2010) para 21.

[14] *The Social and Economic Rights Action Center and the Center for Economic and Social Rights v Nigeria*, Communication 155/96 (30th Ordinary Session, October 2001) para 61.

[15] United Nations General Assembly/Raquel Rolnik *Annual Report of the Special Rapporteur on Adequate Housing as a Component of the Right to an Adequate Standard of Living, and the Right to Non-discrimination in this Context* UN Doc A/67/286 (2012) para 80.

[16] United Nations General Assembly/Leilani Farha *Annual Report: Main Focus: The Right to Housing for Residents of Informal Settlements* UN Doc A/73/310/Rev.1 (2018) para 88.

[17] Ibid.

[18] *Sir Dawda K Jawara v The Gambia*, Communication 147/95 (27th Ordinary Session, 11 May 2000) at para 61.

The right to an effective remedy is guaranteed in Arts 18 and 25(2) of the Namibian Constitution. These provisions enable aggrieved persons to challenge impugned administrative actions and violations of and/or threats to human rights respectively. The judicial interpretation of 'aggrieved persons' as referenced in these articles has to date been interpreted along the lines of the common-law criteria of *locus standi*.

22.4 CONCEPTUAL UNDERSTANDING OF *LOCUS STANDI*

The Latin term *locus standi*, the expression which is used in Namibian courts, has been defined in various ways: it is used interchangeably with terms such as 'standing' and 'title to sue'.[19] *Locus standi*, as rightly noted by Ershadul and Ehteshamul, is in essence the right of an individual or a group of individuals as the applicant, plaintiff or appellant to institute legal proceedings in a court of law for the adjudication of a matter.[20] Therefore, at the core of *locus standi* lies the question whether

> the litigant[s] is/[are] entitled to have the court decide the merits of the dispute or of particular issues.[21]

Phrased differently, it goes about

> whether the litigant[s] should be permitted to enter the court portals to bring an action for decision.[22]

The standing enquiry, as noted by Nichol, accordingly focuses on the party (or parties) who brings the matter before a court and not on the issue(s) to be adjudicated.[23] Okeke invokes the metaphor of a tubular sieve used to sift the chaffs from grains to bring the issue of *locus standi* into better focus. *Locus standi*, in his analogy, acts as a sieve that is used to sift the chaffs from grains in legal matters,[24] where the chaffs refer to frivolous petitions or litigation.[25] The grains, on the other hand, refer to those petitions or that litigation in which the litigant maintains a

---

[19] M Danung & J Ileka 'The concept of *locus standi*: A dogmatic impediment to justice or a flexible tool of convenience?' (2022) 4(1) *International Journal of Comparative Law and Legal Philosophy* 54.

[20] Ershadul & Ehteshamul (note 1) 23.

[21] *Warth v Seldin* 422 US 490 (1975) at 498.

[22] Ershadul & Ehteshamul (note 1) 23.

[23] GR Nichol Jr 'Rethinking standing' (1984) 72 *California Law Review* 85.

[24] GN Okeke 'Re-examining the role of *locus standi* in the Nigerian legal jurisprudence' (2013) 6(3) *Journal of Politics and Law* 209.

[25] Ibid.

substantial interest to the extent that refusing to hear them would be a case of defeating the ends of justice.[26]

The traditional restrictive common-law rules of *locus standi*, a relic of Namibia's colonial legal heritage, were developed to protect a narrow set of private-law rights.[27] Over time, courts all over the world have begun to relax the insensitivity and rigidity of the common-law rules of *locus standi*. For instance, in the United Kingdom, as chronicled by Ershadul and Ehteshamul, such a change of attitude was observable in the so-called *Blackburn's* case(s).[28] The perception of *locus standi* has similarly undergone transformation in former British colonies such as India, Kenya, South Africa and Zimbabwe. Such a judicial change of attitude is aptly captured in the Indian case of *Dr George Mampilly v State of Kerala*.[29] The statement of the High Court in Kerala is worth quoting verbatim in this instance, given its pertinence in crystallising the dynamic nature of the law. The Honourable High Court of Kerala observed:

> Courts have now acknowledged that where there has been violation of constitutional or legal rights of persons who, by reason of their socially or economically disadvantaged position, are unable to approach the court for judicial redress, a member of the public could move the court for enforcement of such rights of such persons.[30]

Therefore, the court reasoned:

> Members of the public are [accordingly] enabled, in appropriate cases to come forward to protect the rights of person or persons belonging to a determinate class who, by reason of poverty, helplessness or disability or socially or economically disadvantaged position, are unable to approach the court for relief. This principle has been extended to cases where no specific regal injury is caused to a person or to a determinate class or group of persons by the act or omission of State or public authority and injury is caused only to public interest.[31]

---

[26] Ibid.

[27] Z Hinson & D Hubbard *Locus Standi: Standing to Bring a Legal Action. Access to Justice in Namibia. Proposals for improving Public Access to Courts* (Legal Assistance Centre, 2014) iii.

[28] Ershadul & Ehteshamul (note 1) 26; see also *Blackburn v Attorney General* [1971] EWCA Civ J0510-2.

[29] 1984 KLT SN 17 (Case No 29).

[30] *Dr George Mampilly* (note 29).

[31] *Dr George Mampilly* (note 29).

Importantly, the court added:

> Where there is a public wrong of public injury by an act or omission by the State or a public authority which is contrary to the Constitution or to any law, any member of the public having sufficient interest can maintain an action to or redress such public wrong or public, injury.[32]

It bears stressing, though, that those who come forward to stand in the proverbial gap for others are expected to act in good faith, not for personal gain or private profit or out of political motivation or any other oblique consideration.[33] That, arguably, now stretches the curious reader's imagination to wonder to what extent the perception of *locus standi* has undergone transformation and/or liberalisation in Namibia over the years.

22.5 *LOCUS STANDI* IN NAMIBIA

The Namibian Constitution deals with *locus standi*, or standing, in Arts 18 and 25. Article 18 endows 'persons aggrieved' by the acts and decisions of administrative bodies and/or administrative officials with the right to seek redress in a competent court of law or tribunal. Article 25(2) of the Constitution, for its part, covers 'aggrieved persons' alleging that their fundamental right or freedom guaranteed in the Constitution has been infringed or threatened, giving them a right to claim redress. The phrase 'persons aggrieved' or 'aggrieved persons' is not defined in the Constitution and has accordingly proven contentious, the exact meaning of the phrase having remained largely ambivalent. This raises the question: Who really is entitled to approach a court for redress? Our superior courts have dealt with this question on an ad hoc basis, with respect, in a rather unsatisfactory manner. This is largely because Namibian courts interpret standing under Arts 18 and 25(2) with strict reference to the Roman-Dutch common law's 'direct and substantial interest' requirement. For instance, in *Kerry McNamara Architects Inc & Others*,[34] Strydom and Mtambanengwe JJ, for the High Court, held that the inclusion and use of the words 'aggrieved persons' in Art 18 to claim redress for unlawful, unfair, and unreasonable administrative action was

> not intended to widen the ambit to also include persons who would otherwise not have had standing to bring proceedings [under the common law].[35]

---

[32] *Dr George Mampilly* (note 29).

[33] *Ashok Kumar Pandey v State of West Bengal* (2004) 3 SCC 349.

[34] *Kerry McNamara Architects Inc & Others v Minister of Works, Transport and Communication & Others* 2000 NR 1 (HC).

[35] *Kerry McNamara Architects Inc & Others* (note 34) 11.

The traditional common-law rules of standing are particularly narrow, restrictive and limiting of rights. They require the applicant to demonstrate a direct and substantial interest in the subject-matter and outcome of an application. The courts have expressed the fear that permitting an applicant to sue when they lack common-law standing would open the floodgates of litigation. The 'floodgates' argument essentially proffers the view that courts would be engulfed by a torrent of frivolous or vexatious litigation against the state.[36] Liberalising standing, in the words of Justice Parker, may lead to 'any busybody, meddling and misguided crusader approaching the Court when he or she knows he or she has no *locus standi*'.[37] The 'floodgates' argument has in the meantime been discarded in other comparable jurisdictions. For example, Pickering J, in the matter of *Wildlife Society of Southern Africa & Others v Minister of Environmental Affairs and Tourism of the Republic of South Africa & Others*, held the following regarding the 'floodgates' argument:

> it may sometimes be necessary to open the floodgates in order to irrigate the arid ground below them. I am not persuaded by the argument that to afford *locus standi* to a body such as [the] first applicant in circumstances such as these would be to open the floodgates to a torrent of frivolous or vexatious litigation against the State by cranks or busybodies. Neither am I persuaded, given the exorbitant costs of Supreme Court litigation, that should the law be so adapted cranks and busybodies would indeed flood the courts with vexatious or frivolous applications against the State. Should they be tempted to do so, I have no doubt that an appropriate order of costs would soon inhibit their litigious ardour.[38]

Some judicial decisions, admittedly, appear to run in the direction of a more liberal approach to standing. For instance, in *Uffindell*, the High Court held that, in giving effect to its

> constitutional duty under Article 5 to respect and uphold the fundamental rights and freedoms enshrined in Chapter 3 of the Constitution, [it] must also interpret Article 25 in a broad, liberal and purposive way .... [39]

---

[36] *Ngxuza & Others v Permanent-Secretary, Department of Welfare, Eastern Cape & Another* 2001 (2) SA 609 (E) at headnotes.

[37] *Nguvava v Ovambanderu Tribal Authority & Others*, A 312/2010 [2010] NAHC 182 (4 November 2011) (unreported) at para 9.

[38] 1996 (3) SA 1095 (Tk) at para 1106E.

[39] *Uffindell t/a Aloe Hunting Safaris v Government of Namibia & Others* 2009 (2) NR 670 (HC) at para 15.

Again, in its *Trustco* ruling, the Supreme Court strongly emphasised this point:

> In a constitutional State, citizens are entitled to exercise their rights and they are entitled to approach courts, where there is uncertainty as to the law, to determine their rights. The rules of standing should not ordinarily operate to prevent citizens from obtaining legal clarity as to their legal entitlements.[40]

These pronouncements, as progressive as they are, were concerned only with the exigencies of the respective cases they dealt with and not with the proverbial elephant in the room. Even though the courts were prepared to liberalise the standing in these two cases, they refrained from developing the Roman-Dutch common-law standing in tandem with the Constitution. In fact, this type of judicial conservatism was once again displayed in two recent cases where the aggrieved parties intended to institute a class action and public-interest suits respectively. These should be juxtaposed with the jurisprudence of comparative jurisdictions such as South Africa, Kenya and Zimbabwe. These countries introduced far-reaching changes to their common law of standing. In this regard, the changes in the arena of class action and public interest standing are of particular interest in this debate.

22.5.1 Class action in Namibia

Class action is also known as representative action in other jurisdictions. The essence of a class action, as clarified by Loots, is that one person may bring an action in the interests of a class of persons all having the same cause of action.[41] The most important feature of a class action is that other members of the class, although not formally and individually joined, benefit from and are bound by the outcome of the litigation unless they invoke prescribed procedures to opt out of it.[42] In other words, the judgment binds all and the benefits of a court's ruling accrue to all.[43] Class actions allow for litigation for small claims on a mass scale.[44] They allow

[40] *Trustco Ltd t/a Legal Shield Namibia & Another v Deeds Registries Regulation Board & Others* 2011 (2) NR 726 (SC) at para 18.

[41] C Loots 'Standing, ripeness and mootness' in S Woolman & M Bishop (eds) *Constitutional Law of South Africa* 2 ed (Juta & Co, 2018) 7.

[42] *Permanent Secretary Department of Welfare, Eastern Cape Provincial Government & Another v Ngxuza & Others* (493/2000) [2001] ZASCA 85 (31 August 2001) at para 7.

[43] *Permanent Secretary Department of Welfare, Eastern Cape Provincial Government & Another* (note 42).

[44] J Weiner *Class Action Law Suits in South Africa* (Helen Suzman Foundation, 2018), https://hsf.org.za/publications/hsf-briefs/class-action-law-suits-in-south-africa, accessed 21 August 2023.

for claimants to band together and for evidence that is in common to be pooled to make a strong case.[45]

In the *Tsumib case*,[46] the Namibian Supreme Court affirmed that a class action is not recognised in Namibian law.[47] To provide context, in *Tsumib*, eight members of the Hai||om San community sought permission from the High Court to bring a future representative or class action on behalf of all Hai||om people in Namibia to institute six distinct claims.[48] The claims centred on their ancestral home, the Etosha National Park, from which the Hai||om people were forcibly evicted in 1954 without compensation by the then South African colonial regime.[49] The application essentially requested the court to relax the rules on standing – specifically, to allow them to represent not only themselves but also the Hai||om people in general, because of the clear interest they had in determining the rights they sought to assert on behalf of the Hai||om people and the Hai||om minority group.[50] The main argument of both the government and the Hai||om Traditional Authority, in contrast, was that the Traditional Authorities Act 25 of 2000 strips the Hai||om people of their ability to enforce their rights independently, allowing only the Traditional Authority to represent the Hai||om community in legal matters.[51] The High Court dismissed the application for leave to represent the Hai||om people.[52] The court reasoned that the applicants had not exhausted the internal remedies provided for by the Traditional Authorities Act 25 of 2000 to assert their rights. Nor had they challenged the constitutionality of the provisions of the Act that they perceived to be an obstacle in the way of their asserting their rights. It concluded further that it is not legally permissible for the applicants to approach the court for leave because, should such relief be granted, the court would be aiding the applicants in circumventing the provisions of the Act.[53] On appeal, the Supreme Court similarly

---

[45] Ibid.

[46] *Tsumib v Government of the Republic of Namibia* (SA 53-2019) [2022] NASC (16 March 2022).

[47] *Tsumib* (note 46) at para 74.

[48] *Tsumib v Government of the Republic of Namibia* (A 206/2015) [2019] NAHCMD 312 (28 August 2019) at para 14.

[49] U Dieckmann 'The impact of nature conservation on the San: A case study of Etosha National Park' in T Hohmann (ed) *San and the State: Contesting Land, Development, Identity and Representation* (Rüdiger Köppe Verlag, 2003) 50.

[50] *Jan Tsumib & Others* v *Government of the Republic of Namibia & Others*, Case No A206/2015: Founding Affidavit; Heads of Argument; Transcripts of Court Proceedings, 26–29 November 2018 at para 73.

[51] Legal Assistance Centre 'The Etosha case: Who can bring ancestral land rights claims?' (2022) 79 *Pro Bono* 3, https://www.lac.org.na/news/probono/ProBono_79-ETOSHA_CASE.pdf, accessed 21 August 2023.

[52] *Tsumib* (note 46) at para 67(1).

[53] *Tsumib* (note 48) at para 61.

dismissed the application, albeit on different grounds. The Supreme Court held that the common law already has mechanisms in place to overcome the unavailability of a class action. One such way is by establishing a voluntary association.[54] The suggestion that the Hai||om people should form a voluntary association in pursuit of redress for their ancestral land presents its own complexities, though. The merits and demerits of such a voluntary association are beyond the scope and purpose of this article, though.

It is important to note that comparative jurisdictions such as South Africa, Kenya and Zimbabwe have since entrenched class action in their respective constitutions. These constitutions, in strikingly identical language, create the express entitlement that 'anyone' asserting a right in their respective Bill of Rights could litigate

> as a member of, or in the interest of, a group or class of persons ….[55]

A class action suit was instituted in the case of *Ngxuza & Others v Permanent-Secretary, Department of Welfare, Eastern Cape & Another.*[56] This was reportedly the first class action instituted in South Africa.[57] The case concerned the plight of a large number of Eastern Cape disability grantees who alleged that their disability grants had been unlawfully and unfairly cancelled by the welfare authorities. On their behalf, three pensioners aiming to secure the reinstatement *en masse* of their cancelled pensions instituted a class action suit. Froneman J found that the three pensioners had standing to challenge the impugned administrative action on behalf of their class.[58] He also found that the cancellation of the disability grants without affording the beneficiaries a hearing was an infringement of their constitutional right to just administrative action as guaranteed by s 33 of the South African Constitution.[59]

Article 22(2)*(b)* of the 2010 Kenya Constitution, in similar fashion, allows persons acting on behalf of others to institute court proceedings. In tandem with this constitutional allowance, the High Court at Malindi in the case of *Bahola Mkalindi Rhigho v Michael Seth Kaseme & 2 Others* remarked that the interests of a particular community over ancestral land may be either collectively or individually

[54] *Tsumib* (note 46) at para 77.

[55] See s 38*(c)* of the 1996 Constitution of South Africa; Art 22(2)*(b)* of the 2010 Kenya Constitution; Art 85(1)*(c)* of the 2013 Zimbabwe Constitution.

[56] *Ngxuza & Others* (note 36).

[57] J Handmaker 'Introduction to special issue: Class action litigation in South Africa' (2021) 37(1) *South African Journal on Human Rights* 2.

[58] *Ngxuza & Others* (note 36) 629–631.

[59] *Ngxuza & Others* (note 36) 625–631.

pursued.[60] Also, the court held, it does not matter that a particular member of the community is not directly affected.[61]

Article 85(1)*(c)* of the 2013 Constitution of Zimbabwe similarly allows persons acting on behalf of others to institute court proceedings. Towards this end, the Zimbabwean legislature enacted the Class Action Act (Chapter 8:17) to give effect to this constitutional injunction.

22.5.2 Public interesting standing (*actio popularis*) in Namibia

In the *NamRights* case,[62] a human rights organisation brought an application to challenge the Olufuko cultural practice. Olufuko is a girls' initiation ritual practised by the Aawambo people in northern Namibia. The Olufuko ritual has both strong support and strong opposition.[63] The supporters see the practice as upholding the Ovambo tradition and culture, whereas the opposition see it as a harmful cultural practice that should not be followed in contemporary Namibia.[64] NamRights falls in the latter group. In this context, it sought an order from the High Court to prevent the revival of 'Olufuko'. NamRights claimed that, as a human rights organisation, it has standing to bring the application in the public interest, specifically on behalf of the teenage girls who are subjected to this cultural practice. However, Parker J for the High Court did not agree. He viewed NamRights and its representative, Mr Ya-Nangolo, as a meddlesome busybody or bystander who has no standing. In fact, the court reiterated the legal position that under the current rules of standing 'a private individual can only sue in his/her own behalf and not on behalf of the public'. In other words, that the law as it stands does not recognise *actio popularis*. The court accordingly dismissed the application with costs.[65]

The *NamRights* judgment, for the purposes of comparative law, is in stark contrast to that of *Loveness Mudzuru and Ruvimbo Tsopodzi* v *Minister of Justice, Legal & Parliamentary Affairs NO & Others*[66] handed down by the Constitutional Court of Zimbabwe in 2016. This case dealt with the issue of child marriages. Two young women aged 19 and 18 years approached the court to challenge the practice of child marriages on the ground that it infringes the fundamental rights of girl children

[60] [2012] eKLR at para 39.
[61] *Bahola Mkalindi Rhigho* (note 60).
[62] *Namrights Inc v Government of Namibia & Others* 2020 (1) NR 36 (HC).
[63] Kuoppala, S 'Reviving tradition at the Olufuko Festival 2016 – girls' initiation ritual in contemporary Namibia' Master's thesis in Study of Religions (Helsingfors Universitet Faculty of Theology, 2018) 4.
[64] Ibid.
[65] *NamRights Inc* (note 62) at paras 21–31.
[66] Judgment No CCZ 12/2015 Const, Application No 79/14.

who are subjected to early marriages. It is important to point out that the litigants were not victims of early child marriages themselves. This notwithstanding, the Constitutional Court remarked that the interests of the girl children subjected to early marriages raised by the litigants is a matter of public interest.[67] They cannot be said to have acted in bad faith or out of extraneous motives. Neither can they be seen as meddlesome busybodies seeking a day in court and/or making cheap personal publicity. Far from it. The two young women, in the view of the court, were driven by the laudable motive of seeking to vindicate the rule of law and the supremacy of the 2013 Constitution of Zimbabwe.[68] This was found sufficient to afford them standing as provided for in s 85(1)*(d)* of the 2013 Constitution of Zimbabwe.[69] The court, importantly, stressed that the public interest standing provision in the Constitution of Zimbabwe was introduced for the purpose of

> providing expansive access to justice to wider interests in society, particularly the vulnerable groups in society, the infringement of whose rights would have remained unredressed under the narrow traditional conception of standing.[70]

The constitutional changes introduced in respect of *locus standi* in the three surveyed jurisdictions ushered in opportunities for opening up access to justice and making it more accessible to ordinary people. The absence of similar ground-breaking constitutional and/or legislative provisions is arguably the chief reason why the Namibian Judiciary is still trapped in the conservative grip of the common-law rules of standing. It appears that Namibia's superior courts lack the courage and the will to develop the archaic and strict rules of standing to espouse the spirit, purport or objects of the Namibian Constitution.[71] The Namibian Judiciary is arguably not ready to take the requisite bold step to break new ground in respect of standing.[72] In stark contrast, a survey of the Indian jurisprudence reveals that the actions of the Indian Judiciary, faced with the very same constitutional hurdle, tell a totally different tale. The Indian Supreme Court is celebrated for having liberated itself from the traditional ways of thinking and making innovative use of its judicial

---

[67] *Loveness Mudzuru and Ruvimbo Tsopodzi* (note 66) 23–25.

[68] *Loveness Mudzuru and Ruvimbo Tsopodzi* (note 66) 23.

[69] *Loveness Mudzuru and Ruvimbo Tsopodzi* (note 66).

[70] *Loveness Mudzuru and Ruvimbo Tsopodzi* (note 66) 17.

[71] JB Nakuta 'Ancestral land claims: Why bygones can't be bygones' in W Odendaal & W Werner (eds) *'Neither Here nor There': Indigeneity, Marginalisation and Land Rights in Post-independence Namibia* (Legal Assistance Centre, 2020) 159.

[72] Ibid.

power by developing a variety of avenues for making access to justice a reality.[73] Effecting radical changes and alterations made in the requirements of *locus standi* was part of such judicial overhaul.[74] Namibia can learn from India in this regard.

22.6 CALL FOR THE LIBERALISATION OF THE COMMON-LAW RULES OF STANDING IN NAMIBIA

The requirements of *locus standi* as alluded to above are one of the most serious stumbling blocks to the advancement of social justice in Namibia. The traditional doctrine of *locus standi* is of ancient vintage and insists on direct injury. In other words, the aggrieved party alone has a right to bring an action. This, needless to say, provides a convenient escape route to those who wish to bypass the real issues on the merits by reliance on peripheral and procedural shortcomings.[75] Many a time a person or a class of persons who by reason of their poverty or disability or socially or economically disadvantaged position would be those who cannot approach the court for relief are denied this avenue to redress injustices.[76] This reality, in the words of Bhagwati J, caused

> judges in India … [to ask] themselves the question: Can judges really escape addressing themselves to substantial questions of social justice? Can they … simply follow the legal text when they are aware that their actions will perpetuate inequality and injustice? Can they restrict their inquiry into law and life within the narrow confines of a narrowly defined rule of law?[77]

The answer to these questions was found to be a resounding no. The Supreme Court of India variously held that public interest is be promoted by a spacious construction of *locus standi.* In this regard, the words of Bhagwati J warrant verbatim quotation:

> if no one can have standing to maintain an action for judicial redress in respect of a public wrong or public injury, not only will the cause of legality suffer but the people not having any judicial remedy to redress such public wrong or public injury may turn to the street and in that process, the rule of

[73] M Chaudhary *Changing Contours of* Locus Standi *in Indian Constitutional Jurisprudence* (2010), https://www.ukca.in/2010/07/10/changing-contours-of-locus-standi-in-indian-constitutional-jurisprudence-2/, accessed 21 August 2023.

[74] Ibid.

[75] Ibid.

[76] Ibid.

[77] Ibid.

> law will be seriously impaired. It is absolutely essential that the rule of law must wean the people away from the lawless street and win them for the court of law.[78]

This kind of judicial thinking was followed in many other Indian judgments. For example, when the Bombay pavement dwellers were threatened with eviction by the Bombay Municipality, the court extended standing to one Olga Tellis.[79] The petitioner was a public-spirited journalist and not personally affected by the eviction proceedings. This, however, did not deter the court from hearing the complaint. The court was primarily concerned with the serious issue before it, namely, that the people who were affected by virtue of their social standing were unable to approach the court for relief.[80] Again, in the matter of *Sunil Batra v Delhi Administration*[81] a three-judge Bench held that

> technicalities and legal niceties are no impediment to the court entertaining even an informal communication as a proceeding for *habeas corpus* if the basic facts are found.[82]

This statement was made in reference to a letter written by two prison inmates about the plight of the other inmates being treated as a writ petition.[83] It is suggested that, when interpreting the Constitution, Namibian courts should, like their Indian counterparts, take into account the fact that 'procedural prescriptions are handmaids, not mistresses of justice'.[84] It must surely matter that a great number of litigants, including those who do not come to the court, are not sophisticated litigants but the rural poor, the urban lay and the weaker societal segments for whom the law will be an added terror.[85] This is the context against which the call for the breaking of ranks with the conservative common-law rules of standing must be viewed. Furthermore, the Namibian Superior Courts are also similarly reminded of the ground-breaking *Mabo v Queensland* ruling of the Australian High Court which rejected the racist and repugnant *terra nullius* doctrine. This court held:

> If it were permissible in past centuries to keep the common law in step with international law, it is imperative in today's world that the common law

[78] Chaudhary (note 73) at para 20.
[79] *Olga Tellis v Bombay Municipal Corporation* 1985 (3) SCC 545.
[80] *Olga Tellis* (note 79).
[81] (1978) 4 SCC 409 at para 409.
[82] *Sunil Batra* (note 81).
[83] *Sunil Batra* (note 81).
[84] *Mumbai Kamgar Sabha, Bombay,* AIR 1976 SC 1455.
[85] *Mumbai Kamgar Sabha, Bombay* (note 84).

> should neither be, nor be seen to be frozen in [old age principles and rules that perpetuate inequality and limit access to justice].[86]

There can be no doubt that continued adherence to the right-limiting nature of the Roman-Dutch common-law principle on standing perpetuates inequality and limits access to justice. There is no cogent reason, to paraphrase Froneman J, for a restrictive interpretation of the 'aggrieved persons' provisions of the Constitution because of the narrow content given to standing under the common law.[87] The Namibian Law Reform and Development Commission (LRDC) seems to agree with this contention: in 2014, it investigated possible changes to the laws relating to standing and produced what they call the Standing in Civil Actions Bill. The Bill essentially seeks to expand the definition and scope of standing in civil actions. For instance, it suggests various forms of standing: organisational, representative, public interest and standing in constitutional matters. The LRDC rightly expressed the view that the current rigid standing requirements have a disproportionate effect on low-income, poorly educated or otherwise marginalised groups.[88] They prevent such persons from accessing the courts.[89] Regrettably, the Bill has been gathering dust for the past nine years despite its importance to expanding access to justice.

The urgent introduction of a flexible and generous approach to the rules of *locus standi*, as propagated by the LRDC, is necessary to promote access to courts and to facilitate access to justice for the poor. The Indian Judiciary has led the charge in this regard. Importantly, the relaxation of the rules of standing in India has been achieved without the aid of constitutional amendments and/or legislative reform but through sheer commitment to social justice. The judicial tendency in Namibia to interpret the phrase 'aggrieved persons' in the Constitution in a narrow and restricted manner akin to standing under the common law is archaic, outdated and long past its sell-by date. More specifically, it perpetuates inequality and injustice. The unsatisfactory lack of progress made in overcoming the scourge of informal housing in the country, as highlighted at the beginning of this article, arguably affirms this.

International human rights law directs that where a significant number of individuals are deprived of basic shelter and housing, a state in whose jurisdiction such deprivation occurs is prima facie failing to discharge its obligations under

[86] *Mabo v Queensland* (No 2) (1992) 175 CLR 1 at para 41.
[87] In *Ngxuza & Others* (note 36) 619.
[88] Republic of Namibia Law Reform and Development Commission *Locus Standi* Discussion Paper No 27 (LRDC, 2014) para 5.1.2.
[89] Ibid.

the International Covenant on Economic, Social and Cultural Rights (ICESCR).[90] Namibia is a state party to the ICESCR. By parity of reasoning, it follows that the scourge of housing informality suggests prima facie non-compliance with the state's obligations of conduct and obligations of result.[91] It is puzzling, therefore, why the glaring lack of progress and urgency in resolving the crisis of informal housing in the country remain unchallenged. In fact, the UN Committee on Economic, Social and Cultural Rights Committee expressed its concern at the notable absence of jurisprudence invoking the ESC rights violations in Namibia.[92] Adherence to the restrictive, exclusionary and narrow rules of *locus standi*, in my view, is a prime contributing factor to this. For instance, women – the group most disproportionately affected by the inadequate sanitation situation in informal settlements – are currently precluded from banding together as per the *Tsumib* mantra to challenge the gross human rights violations they are collectively subjected to in these settings. Similarly, an aggrieved member of the public is currently not able to challenge the egregious inaction and lack of urgency in dealing with the serious informal housing problem in the country. Indeed, the 'direct and substantial interest' tag of the common-law standing, as rightfully observed by Hinson and Hubbard, directly and indirectly creates a rule-of-law problem. The 'direct and substantial interest' tag immunises and insulates prima facie unlawful or unconstitutional conduct from judicial scrutiny.[93] Surely a select group of residents of informal settlements as a class of persons, or a bona fide public-spirited member of the general public (even though not personally affected) wishing to challenge the abhorrent living conditions of informal settlements, cannot be considered as being mere interfering busybodies.

22.7 CONCLUSION

The procedural requirement of *locus standi* to approach a court of law to have a complaint adjudicated is not unique to Namibia. The need for such a requirement is fully acknowledged and appreciated. To avoid any doubt, this article has therefore not argued for the doing away of that requirement. It has, however, called for its reform and liberalisation in order to achieve the kind of social justice that Namibian

---

[90] United Nations Committee on Economic, Social and Cultural Rights *General Comment No 3: The Nature of States Parties' Obligations (Art 2, para 1, of the Covenant)* UN Doc E/1991/23 (1990) para 10.

[91] United Nations Committee on Economic, Social and Cultural Rights (note 90) para 1.

[92] United Nations Committee on Economic, Social and Cultural Rights 'Concluding observations on the initial report of Namibia' UN Doc E/C.12/NAM/CO/1 (2016) para 6.

[93] Hinson & Hubbard (note 27) iii.

society yearns for. The traditional common-law rules of standing relied upon by the courts are a serious impediment to achieving this. Admittedly, changes in respect of *locus standi* would be best achieved through constitutional and/or law reform, as was effected in the constitutions of the comparative jurisdictions surveyed for this chapter. However, the Namibian superior courts are implored to invoke their inherent judicial powers, as has been the case in India, to reform and liberalise the archaic, outdated and rights-limiting traditional common-law rules on standing.

REFERENCES

African Commission on Human and Peoples' Rights *Principles and Guidelines on the Implementation of Economic, Social and Cultural Rights in the African Charter on Human and Peoples' Rights* (ACHPR, 2010).

African Commission on Human and Peoples' Rights *Principles and Guidelines on the Right to a Fair Trial and Legal Assistance in Africa*, African Union Doc DOC/OS (XXX) (2010).

Chaudhary, M *Changing Contours of* Locus Standi *in Indian Constitutional Jurisprudence* (2010), https://www.ukca.in/2010/07/10/changing-contours-of-locus-standi-in-indian-constitutional-jurisprudence-2/, accessed 21 August 2023.

Danung, M & Ileka, J 'The concept of *locus standi*: A dogmatic impediment to justice or a flexible tool of convenience?' (2022) 4(1) *International Journal of Comparative Law and Legal Philosophy* 54.

Dieckmann, U 'The impact of nature conservation on the San: A case study of Etosha National Park' in T Hohmann (ed) *San and the State: Contesting Land, Development, Identity and Representation* (Rüdiger Köppe Verlag, 2003).

Ershadul, M & Ehteshamul, M 'Liberalization of the traditional rule of *locus standi* in the United Kingdom and Malaysia: A comparative study' (2012) 39 *Journal of Malaysian and Comparative Law* 27.

Handmaker, J 'Introduction to special issue: Class action litigation in South Africa' (2021) 37(1) *South African Journal on Human Rights* 2.

Hinson, Z & Hubbard, D *Locus Standi: Standing to bring a Legal Action. Access to Justice in Namibia. Proposals for improving Public Access to Courts* (Legal Assistance Centre, 2014).

Kuoppala, S 'Reviving tradition at the Olufuko Festival 2016 – girls' initiation ritual in contemporary Namibia' Master's thesis in Study of Religions (Helsingfors Universitet Faculty of Theology, 2018).

Legal Assistance Centre 'The Etosha case: Who can bring ancestral land rights claims?' (2022) 79 *Pro Bobo* 3, https://www.lac.org.na/news/probono/ProBono_79-ETOSHA_CASE.pdf, accessed 21 August 2023.

Loots, C 'Standing, ripeness and mootness' in S Woolman & M Bishop (eds) *Constitutional Law of South Africa* 2 ed (Juta & Co, 2018).

Nakuta, JB 'A human rights analysis of housing informality in Namibia: Challenges, Ambitions, and Misses' Unpublished PhD thesis (Maastricht University Faculty of Law, 2014).

Nakuta, JB 'Ancestral land claims: Why bygones can't be bygones' in W Odendaal & W Werner (eds) *'Neither Here nor There': Indigeneity, Marginalisation and Land Rights in Post-independence Namibia* (Legal Assistance Centre, 2020).

Nakuta, JB 'The right to adequate housing in Namibia: A right not vindicated' (2021) 1 *Namibian Journal of Social Justice, Namibia's Housing Crisis in Perspective* 23.

Namibia Statistics Agency *Namibia Inter-censal Demographic Survey 2016 Report* (NSA, 2017).

Nichol, GR Jr 'Rethinking standing' (1984) 72 *California Law Review* 85.

Okeke, GN 'Re-examining the role of *locus standi* in the Nigerian legal jurisprudence' (2013) 6(3) *Journal of Politics and Law* 209.

Republic of Namibia Law Reform and Development Commission *Locus Standi Discussion Paper No 27* (LRDC, 2014).

United Nations Committee on Economic, Social and Cultural Rights *General Comment No 3: The Nature of States Parties' Obligations (Art 2, para 1, of the Covenant)* UN Doc E/1991/23 (1990).

United Nations Committee on Economic, Social and Cultural Rights 'Concluding observations on the initial report of Namibia', UN Doc E/C.12/NAM/CO/1 (2016).

United Nations General Assembly Resolution 60/147 *Basic Principles and Guidelines on the Right to a Remedy and Reparation for Victims of Gross Violations of International Human Rights Law and Serious Violations of International Humanitarian Law* UN Doc A/RES/60/147, https://www.ohchr.org/EN/ProfessionalInterest/Pages/RemedyAndReparation.aspx, accessed 21 August 2023.

United Nations General Assembly/Raquel Rolink *Annual Report of the Special Rapporteur on Adequate Housing as a Component of the Right to an Adequate Standard of Living, and the Right to Non-discrimination in this Context* UN Doc A/67/286 (2012).

United Nations General Assembly 'The right to housing for residents of informal settlements', UN Doc A/73/310/Rev.1 (2018).

United Nations General Assembly/Leilani Farha *Annual Report: Main Focus: The Right to Housing for Residents of Informal Settlements* UN Doc A/73/310/Rev.1 (2018).

Weiner, J *Class Action Law Suits in South Africa* (Helen Suzman Foundation, 2018), https://hsf.org.za/publications/hsf-briefs/class-action-law-suits-in-south-africa, accessed 21 August 2023.

CASES

Ashok Kumar Pandey v State of West Bengal (2004) 3 SCC 349

Bahola Mkalindi Rhigho v Michael Seth Kaseme & 2 Others [2012] eKLR

Blackburn v Attorney General [1971] EWCA Civ J0510-2.

Dr George Mampilly v State of Kerala 1984 KLT SN 17 (Case No 29)

Jan Tsumib & Others v Government of the Republic of Namibia & Others, Case No A206/2015: Founding Affidavit; Heads of Argument; Transcripts of Court Proceedings, 26–29 November 2018
Kerry McNamara Architects Inc & Others v Minister of Works, Transport and Communication & Others 2000 NR 1 (HC)
Loveness Mudzuru and Ruvimbo Tsopodzi v Minister of Justice, Legal & Parliamentary Affairs NO & Others Judgment No CCZ 12/2015 Const, Application No 79/14.
Mabo v Queensland (No 2) (1992) 175 CLR 1
Mumbai Kamgar Sabha, Bombay, AIR 1976 SC 1455
Namrights Inc v Government of Namibia & Others 2020 (1) NR 36 (HC)
Nguvava v Ovambanderu Tribal Authority & Others, A 312/2010 [2010] NAHC 182 (4 November 2011) (unreported)
Ngxuza & Others v Permanent-Secretary, Department of Welfare, Eastern Cape & Another 2001 (2) SA 609 (E)
Olga Tellis v Bombay Municipal Corporation 1985 (3) SCC 545
Permanent Secretary Department of Welfare, Eastern Cape Provincial Government & Another v Ngxuza & Others (493/2000) [2001] ZASCA 85 (31 August 2001)
Sir Dawda K Jawara v The Gambia, Communication 147/95 (27th Ordinary Session, 11 May 2000)
The Social and Economic Rights Action Center and the Center for Economic and Social Rights v Nigeria, Communication 155/96 (30th Ordinary Session, October 2001)
Trustco Ltd t/a Legal Shield Namibia & Another v Deeds Registries Regulation Board & Others 2011 (2) NR 726 (SC)
Tsumib v Government of the Republic of Namibia (A 206/2015) [2019] NAHCMD 312 (28 August 2019)
Tsumib v Government of the Republic of Namibia (SA 53-2019) [2022] NASC (16 March 2022)
Uffindell t/a Aloe Hunting Safaris v Government of Namibia & Others 2009 (2) NR 670 (HC)
Warth v Seldin 422 US 490 (1975)
Wildlife Society of Southern Africa & Others v Minister of Environmental Affairs and Tourism of the Republic of South Africa & Others 1996 (3) SA 1095 (Tk)

LEGISLATION

Constitution of the Republic of South Africa, 1996
Kenya Constitution, 2010
Namibia Constitution, 2014
Protocol to the African Charter on Human and Peoples' Rights on the Rights of Women in Africa (the Maputo Protocol)
Zimbabwe Constitution, 2013

About the Editors

Emeritus Professor Samuel Kwesi Amoo
Professor Amoo was appointed a member of the academic staff of the Faculty of Law (today the School of Law) of the University of Namibia in August 1995 and retired in December 2018. He was involved in both undergraduate and graduate tuition and performed various administrative responsibilities, including serving as Dean of the Faculty of Law and Acting Director of the Justice Training Centre. He also performed quasi-judicial functions in his capacity as chairperson and member of the panels of various boards, councils and disciplinary hearings. He is an admitted legal practitioner and an accredited mediator of the High Court of Namibia. He has written extensively on the Namibian legal system.

Dr Tapiwa Victor Warikandwa
Dr Warikandwa is an Adjunct Professor at the University of Venda in South Africa, as well as a senior lecturer in the Department of Law at the University of Botswana. He previously served as a senior lecturer and Head of Department for Private Law in the School of Law at the University of Namibia. He studied for his Bachelor of Laws, master's and doctoral degrees at the University of Fort Hare, South Africa, and specialises in a variety of fields, such as comparative law, international trade law, mining law, jurisprudence and labour law. Prior to coming to Namibia, he worked as a legal officer and later a legal advisor in the Ministry of Public Services, Labour and Social Welfare in Zimbabwe. He is an established author and editor of several publications and is currently the lead legal researcher for Namibia on the Global One Ocean Hub Project.

Dr Kennedy Kariseb
Dr Kariseb is a senior lecturer in the School of Law of the University of Namibia. He holds a master's (*cum laude*) and a doctorate in law from the University of Pretoria, South Africa. His areas of expertise are in international human rights law (with a particular focus on Africa), public international law and comparative law. As an academic, he is involved in both undergraduate and graduate tuition and supervision, and has assumed various administrative responsibilities, including previously serving as Head of Department for Public Law at the School of Law of the University of Namibia. Outside the university community, he serves on several boards and adjudicatory panels, including the Magistrates Commission of Namibia, the National Heritage Council and the Appeal Board of the Media Ombudsman.

About the Authors

Christian Harris is a lecturer in the Department of Public Law and Jurisprudence at the University of Namibia. He previously served as a Development Planner and Legal Officer in the Ministry of Gender Equality and Child Welfare and the Ministry of Justice, respectively, prior to his appointment as a lecturer. He graduated from the University of Namibia with a BJuris, an LLB, an LLM and a PhD in Law, in addition to obtaining an Advanced Diploma in Management from Stadio Multiversity, previously the Southern Business School.

Clever Mapaure studied Law at the University of Namibia, was awarded a BJuris in 2007 and in 2008 graduated *cum laude* with the Specialised Certificate in Customary Law. In 2009 he graduated *cum laude* with his LLB degree and was awarded the Vice-Chancellor's Medal as the university's Best Undergraduate Student. In 2010 he was awarded an LLM *cum laude* and in 2020 obtained his PhD in Law at the same institution. He is a renowned scholar with a key interest in customary, environmental and comparative law.

Dennis Uatuuapi Zaire is a Senior Programme Manager at the Konrad Adenauer Foundation. He currently holds the following academic degrees: an LLM in International Business Law, University of Hull, an LLM in International Trade Law, University of Nottingham Trent, and an LLB (Honours) from the University of Hull. Dennis has written and published on various topics regarding law, politics and general issues of interest to society in Namibia. He has co-edited a publication on Namibia's foreign relations. He is also currently a doctoral candidate in law at the University of Namibia School of Law.

Eugene Lizazi Libebe is a former magistrate who now lectures in the department of Public Law and Jurisprudence at the School of Law of the University of Namibia. He holds a BJuris and an LLB (University of Namibia), and an LLM in International law (University of Cape Town). His areas of interest and publications include public international law, natural resources law, economic law, environmental law and policy, African jurisprudence, decolonisation, law of evidence, family law, statutory interpretation, legislative drafting, sociology, philosophy and criminal law.

George Mousourakis is a Professor of Law and a leading scholar in comparative law. He teaches in the School of Law and the Graduate School of Humanities and

Social Sciences at Hiroshima University, Japan. He is currently a member of various academic and professional bodies and is regularly invited to participate in national and international scholarly conferences and workshops.

John Nakuta is a social justice scholar affiliated to the University of Namibia. He teaches human rights law and administrative justice. He holds advanced qualifications in law and education: a PhD (University of Maastricht), an LLM (University of Utrecht), an LLB (University of South Africa), a Higher Education Diploma (University of Namibia) and an Education Diploma (Perseverance College of Education). He has served the University of Namibia in various managerial positions, including directing the now-defunct Human Rights and Documentation Centre from 2010 to 2015. His socio-legal research interests are concerned with justice, human rights, the rule of law and governance.

Kenneth Ferdie Mundia joined the University of Namibia in January 2011. He has an LLD degree from the University of Pretoria. Before moving to the University of Namibia, he held various positions in the Ministry of Justice between 2005 and 2010. His research interests are the philosophy of law, legal theory, legal interpretation, jurisprudence, comparative law, transformative constitutionalism and land reform. His research interests are informed by continental Africa's traditions of philosophy, legal theory, jurisprudence and legal hermeneutics. He served as head of department in both the Department of Commercial Law and Public Law and Jurisprudence in the then Faculty of Law. He is currently the Director of the Justice Training Centre at the University of Namibia.

Manfred O Hinz studied law and philosophy at the University of Mainz, from which he graduated in 1960. After studying Sociology, Anthropology, and African and Oriental Languages at that university, he was appointed a full professor at the University of Bremen in 1971. He joined the Faculty of Law of the University of Namibia at its inception and was Deputy Dean and Dean of the Faculty for several years. He returned to Germany in 2010 and has since held the title Emeritus Professor in the Department of Public and Procedural Law of the School of Law of the University of Namibia. At the University of Bremen he works as the Director of the Centre for African and Migration Studies. In 2014 he was appointed Adjunct Professor in Law and African Studies at the Jacobs University in Bremen.

Masake Pilisano holds LLD and LLM degrees from Stellenbosch University, a Master's in Policing Practice (Southern Business School) and LLB and BJuris degrees from the University of Namibia. He is an Associate Professor, Deputy Head of Department and former Acting Head of Department of Social Sciences in the Faculty of Human Sciences, Namibia University of Science and Technology.

He has been admitted to the list of Professional Investigators (Counsel Support Section) of the International Criminal Court. In addition, Masake has also served in various capacities in the Namibian Police Force, including as a unit commander, subdivision head and staff officer to the Commissioner of the Criminal Investigation Directorate.

Ndatega Victoria Asheela-Shikalepo is the Associate Dean in the School of Law at the University of Namibia. She is the School's first female Associate Dean and the youngest in the history of Law deans at the University of Namibia, having joined the then Faculty of Law nine years ago. She holds the following qualifications: LLD and LLM degrees, both from the University of Pretoria, and both LLB and BJuris degrees from the University of Namibia. She is also an admitted legal practitioner of the High Court of Namibia and serves on the Council of the Law Society of Namibia Council and on the Board for Legal Education.

Petrus T Damaseb is currently the Deputy Chief Justice and Judge-President of the Republic of Namibia. In this position, he serves as an *ex officio* member of the Supreme Court and deputises for the Chief Justice in the performance of his functions as head of the Judiciary. He also serves as an *ex officio* member of the Judicial Service Commission of Namibia. His academic journey began in 1981 at the United Nations Institute for Namibia (UNIN) in Lusaka, Zambia, where he pursued professional and academic studies and obtained a Diploma in Development Studies and Management with a bias towards law. In 1984, he qualified as a magistrate from Zambia's National Institute of Public Administration (in association with UNIN), after which he obtained a United Nations scholarship to read law at the University of Warwick, obtaining an LLB (Honours) degree in 1988.

Rebekka Haimbili graduated from the University of Namibia with an LLB (Honours) degree and also earned an LLM from the university. Her studies focused on Namibia's land issue, particularly land reform. She is a High Court of Namibia Admitted Legal Practitioner with expertise in corporate advisory, aviation law, public law, criminal defence and civil litigation. The following legal disciplines interest her: commercial law, banking law, public law, and compliance. Rebeka worked as a research assistant on two study guides for the University of Namibia: Comparative Law and Jurisprudence. At present, she works in the Office of the Judiciary as a Senior Legal Officer and Judges' Assistant.

The late Professor Walter Joseph Kamba was the founding Dean of the then Faculty of Law of the University of Namibia. Prior to his role at the University of Namibia, he served the Faculty of Law at the University of Dundee as a lecturer and spent more than 11 years there as an academic, eventually even serving as the Dean of Faculty. Upon his return to his native Zimbabwe in 1980, Professor Kamba was appointed Vice-Chancellor of the University of Zimbabwe, formerly the University of Rhodesia. In addition to his academic career, he was a renowned scholar, orator and influential figure in higher education in Africa. In 1982, in recognition of his outstanding contributions, the University of Dundee awarded him an honorary doctorate.

Index

A
academic studies 45–9
academic teaching 382
actio de in rem verso 294
action iniuriarum 561
Administration of Justice Proclamation 21 of 1919 238
administration of law 167, 171–3
adultery law 576, 580
Africa, comparative law in 305–10
Africa Continental Free Trade Agreement (AfCFTA) 312, 315, 370
African academics 331, 332
African Charter on Human and Peoples' Rights (ACHPR) 504–5, 532, 536–8, 612
African Christianity 219–21
African Commission 538, 542, 612
African communities 217, 399, 576
African comparative law 323
African context 130, 221
African Continental Free Trade Area (AfCFTA) agreement 2, 4
African customary laws 6, 30, 316, 396, 397, 400, 401, 402, 412
African Diaspora 217
African dispute resolution system 404
African human rights 218–19
African indigenous justice systems 400
African indigenous law 359, 404
Africanism 355, 411
African judicial systems 305
African jurisprudence 27, 140, 209, 216, 581
African laws 133, 216, 303, 305, 308, 311, 360, 412
African law schools 306, 373
African legality 140, 154, 159, 161
African legal systems 325, 373, 405, 579
African legal theories 210
African legislators 308
African *lingua franca* 350
African living customary laws 577
Africanness 222–3
African philosophy 316, 355
African philosophy of law 216
African political systems 424, 425
African socialism 140, 142, 151, 152–8, 158–64
African socialists 154, 158
African society 141, 304, 401, 410, 561, 577, 578
African traditional law 222, 223
African ubuntu 576–80
African ubuntu philosophies 577
African Union (AU) 2, 186, 195, 312
African Union Commission (AUC) 187
agricultural land 480, 489, 499–500
Agricultural (Commercial) Land Reform Act 6 of 1995 479, 492
Americanisation of legal systems 17
analytical positivism 216
analytical systems 426
anarchist utopianism 165
ancient Greece 78–80
Ancient Rome 80–3
Ante-Projects of 1987 280
anthropological jurisprudence 419
applicable international human rights treaties and conventions 532–3
Argentinean Civil Codes 293, 295

Argentinean law 279, 290
arguments against secessionism 593–5
Aristotelian logical inference 87
artificial intelligence (AI) 4, 13
Asian legal philosophies 29, 337
Asian studies 418
Askov case 541
assessment of reasonableness 552–3
Asset Movement and Financial Services CC (AMFS) 253
Associated Traditional Knowledge Act 408
Athenian democracy 165

B
bail systems 507–8, 525
Barotse law 426
Bill of Rights 455, 521
Bohannan–Gluckman debate 420
Botswana 573–4
Brazilian enrichment law 283–95
Brazilian enrichment liability 293
Brazilian provision 293
British colonial rule 155
British parliamentarianism 388
Bruni v Kahunda 258–9

C
Canada 464–5, 604
Canadian Supreme Court 566, 597
canon law 86, 110–11
capitalism 157, 340, 351
Caprivi Concerned Group (CCG) 599
Caprivi secessionists 600, 601, 604
Caprivi strip 585, 586, 598–603
Chinese socialist law 144–5
Chisimba case 557
Christian community 110
Christian Humanism 219
Christianity 113, 146, 147, 396
Christian socialism 145–8
civilian systems based on Roman law 259–63
civil law 9–11, 104, 106, 114, 143, 278
The Civil War in France (1871) 149
class action in Namibia 618–21
coatas voluntas 289
Code civil des Français (Code civil) of 1804 10
Código Civil y Commercial de la Nación (CCCN) 279, 281
Cold War 12, 20, 26, 139
colonialism 337, 340, 341, 397–400
colonialists 316, 422
colonial laws 351–5
colonial structural formations as manifestation of coloniality 355–7
comments on Article 1, 534–5
comments on Article 2, 535–6
commission of inquiry into claims of ancestral land rights and restitution 439–41
common core among nation-states 198–201
common-law model 9–11, 143, 245, 406
Community Courts Act of 2003 407, 438, 439
comparability 71–2
comparative jurisprudence 368, 419, 445–7
comparative law 1, 4, 17–19, 23–4, 101, 182, 195, 211, 234–7, 239, 304, 305, 313, 314, 328–31, 343–8, 368, 379–80
comparative-law-based learning in Namibia and Africa 384–6
comparative-law tool, customary law as 403–5
comparative legal studies 306, 309
comparative teaching of law 72–3
comparative technique 23
comparativism 134
A Comparison between Moisac and Roman Laws 83
comparison process 71–2
conceptual understanding of *locus standi* 614–16

condictio indebiti 252, 253, 254, 255
Consciencism 223–5, 226
consequences of expropriation 490–6
Constitutional Amendment Act 17, 488
constitutional bail concept 512
constitutionalism 455, 456
constitutional law 169–71
contemporary challenges to customary-law application 409–11
Continental Europe 185, 263–5
contract law 251
contumelia 576
convergence 20–2, 132, 322
Council of State 246, 247
Council of Traditional Leaders Act of 1997 408, 430
counter-arguments from Namibian government 601
court decisions 420
Court of Justice of the European Union 247
court system in Namibia 229
Covenant rights 535
creating African law 132–4
criminal conversation 562, 565
criminal law 40, 399
Criminal Procedure Act 438, 516, 519, 524
cross-cultural comparison 65, 69–70
cross-pollination 150
cultural adequacy 611
cultural analysis 369
cultural approach 321
customary law 30, 396, 399, 402, 407

D

decolonial comparative research, methodological challenges to 358–62
decolonial comparative theory 354
decoloniality 357–8
decolonial theory 339–43, 353
decolonising African legal education 317
Decretum Gratiani 86
Decretum or *Concordia discordantium canonum* 86
democracy 158–64
democratic socialism 148–50
determination of compensation 493–6
Dewey's pedagogical theory 383
distinction between horizontal and vertical application 456–7
divide-and-conquer strategy 356
Doctrine of Drittwirkung 468
doctrine of eminent domain 474, 476–90
domestic law (*ius civile*) 81, 235
domestic law of Rome 81
domestic legal system 6
domestic Roman law (*ius civile*) 82
Draft Common Frame of Reference (DCFR) 251, 265–7
dramatis personae 253
Drittwirkung 468, 470
droit idéalrelatif 42
Dutch Civil Code (Nederlands Burgelijk Wetboek (BW)) 288
Dutch Criminal Code 576

E

East African Community (EAC) 325
Eberle's approach 125
e-commerce 29, 367
economic analysis method 131, 320–1
Economic, Social and Cultural Rights (ESC rights) 612–13
EdictumTheoderici 84
effect of colonialism on comparative-law studies in Africa 316–17
efficient problem-solving 326–7
eligibility for bail 522–3
eminent domain 477
English law 63, 70, 354, 410
enrichment claim 256–7
enrichments 263
the Environmental Management Act 211
epistemological parameters 184
eponymous legal traditions 116

eponymous models 103
ethical jurisprudence 153
ethnophilosophical assessment 224
Eupraxophers 221
Eurocentric jurisdictions 562
Eurocentric laws 403
Eurocentric norms 354
European Civil Code 251, 265
European Court of Human Rights (ECHR) 247, 541
European Enlightenment 420
European languages 427
European legal families 346
European Union (EU) 129, 197
expropriation 474, 475

F
family law 40, 169
Federal Constitutional Court (FCC) 468, 469
female genital circumcision (FGC) 328
feudal nobility 88
First International Congress of Comparative Law 42
first model or approach 508–19
flavour of blackness 222–3
folk systems 426, 427, 428
French Civil Code 54, 288
French codification 283
French or German Civil Code system 27
functional approach to comparative legal studies 318–19
functional method 130–1, 360–2
functions of comparative law 43–60, 374–9

G
German Basic Law 235
German Civil Code 10
Germany 467–9
Ghana 483–4, 512–15
globalisation 4, 181, 357–8, 372, 389
globalising world 381–3
global justice system 182
Global North knowledge 181, 209
Gluckman–Bohannan debate 425, 427, 432
Glück-Windscheid schools 264
Gorbachev administration 143
Government Resettlement Policy 482
Gresham's law in economics 43
Grosfoguel postulates 341
grouping of legal systems 102–4

H
Hanse Law School (Germany/Netherlands) 387
harmonisation 56, 131, 196–8, 200
harmonisation of laws 55–8, 325–6, 380, 434–9
hegemonic globalisation 17
Helsinki Final Act 592
High Court 230–1
Hindu law 110–13
historical development 106–7
historical method 130, 317–18
homicide laws of Attica 78
horizontal approach 457
Horvath's typology 341
humanism 219–21, 226
Human Rights Committee 534, 535

I
identification phase 65, 124
Immigration Control Act 7 of 1993 189, 190
imperial European laws 400
imperial German government 421
inarticulate major premise 215
income tax law 168
Indian Constitution 476
Indicial Civil Codes 279
indigenous justice systems 412
individualism 357, 579
Indonesia 575–6
integrating several African legal frameworks 314–15

International Court of Justice (ICJ) 58, 199, 247, 311, 380, 592
International Covenant on Civil and Political Rights (ICCPR) 504, 505–7, 531–2, 533–6, 588
International Covenant on Economic, Social and Cultural Rights (ICESCR) 588–9, 626
International Criminal Court (ICC) 327, 387
international criminal law 5
international economic law 371
international human rights conventions and standards 538–42
international human rights jurisprudence 535
international human rights law 625
internationalisation 20–2
internationalisation of laws 181, 182–90
internationalisation of legal systems 201–5
international law 58, 191–5, 368, 380, 474, 477, 585
International Monetary Fund (IMF) 173, 357
international understanding 59–60
interpretation 381, 445–7
intra-cultural comparison 65, 69–70
Islamic law 57, 110, 115–16, 385
ius commune 198, 206
ius naturale 198

J
Jewish law 110, 113–15
Jewish legal system 114
Jewish religion 111
judaism 113
judicial activism 215
judicial cross-fertilisation 182
judicial cross-fertilisation in Namibia 237–9
judicial process 379–80
jurisdiction 437–9
jurisdictions with historical ties to English law 244–5
jurisprudence of the right to fair trial under municipal law 542–51
jurisprudential outlook 66–7
jurisprudential theories 212

L
Lancaster House Constitution 486
law and cultural approach 132, 321
law of nations (*ius gentium*) 81
law of the Tiv of Nigeria 425
law on adultery 559
law on third-party claims for adultery 561–4
law reforms 50–3, 581
laws of civilised nations 372
learning outcomes 382–3
legal anthropology 418, 420–30, 425
legal comparatism in classical antiquity 78–83
legal comparativism 304, 305, 315
legal comparitism in middle ages 83–7
legal context in micro-comparison 70–1
legal cross-fertilisation 236
legal education 374–8, 381–3
Legal Education Act in 1962 323
legal education, modification of 323
legal harmonisation 319
legal institutions 108–9
legal pluralism 235, 352, 441–5
legal positivism 153
legal reforms 128, 323–5, 378–9
legal scholars 5, 13
legal systems 60, 109, 123, 182–90, 338
legal systems classification 105
legal thinking 107–8
legal transplant manifests as coloniality 348–58
legal transplants 19–20, 337, 343–8, 344, 352, 357–8
legal unification 310
legislation 50–3

legislature 503, 509
Legrand's approach 346
Legrand's stance 347
Lepaulle 46
living customary law 576–80
locus standi 533, 609, 610, 616–23
loss of enrichment 259
Louis XIV 20
Luo customary law 70
Lusophone jurisdictions 245
Luth case 468–9

M
Maastricht University (Netherlands) 387
macro-comparison 60, 120, 121
macro–micro dichotomy 121
magistrate's courts 229, 231–2
maintaining peace and security 532–3
Marbury v Madison Secretary of State 240
marriage 203
Marxist–Leninist ideology 107
Marxist–Leninist philosophy 139, 142
Max-Planck Institutes 52
Mbeki (African Renaissance) 218
meaning of comparative law 40–3
micro-comparison 60, 63, 120, 121
monster-statement 417–20
Montesquieu, Baron de la Brède et de 94–8
Moore's notion of semi-autonomous social fields 429

N
Namibia 328–31, 458–61, 478–83, 515–19, 556, 564–7, 609
Namibia Law Reform and Development Commission 211
Namibian Agricultural (Commercial) Land Reform Act 6 of 1995 495
Namibian cases 252–9
Namibian Constitution 330, 476, 478, 554, 555, 565
Namibian Constitution's Art 144, 328
Namibian courts 202, 211, 233
Namibian customary-law ascertainment project 30, 420, 430–3
Namibian Judiciary 493
Namibian law 182, 252, 254, 255–6, 566
Namibian legal system 181, 210–16, 251
Namibian model 516, 524
Namibia's judicial review mechanism 240–4
National Development Plan 1 (NDP1) 482
national level, unifying or harmonising 57–8
natural law 80, 319–20
negotiorum gestio 284, 285–6
negritude 222–3
neo-colonialism 340
New American Movement (NAM) 150
Newton's laws of gravitation 42
Nguni (isiZulu) aphorism 577
Nigeria 573
Nigerian laws 312
nine tribes (*neun Stammesgesellschaften*) 428
19th century 185
the 1948 International Declaration of Human Rights 329
Nkrumah (Nkrumaism and Consciencism) 218
non-convergence approach 132, 322
non-governmental organisations (NGOs) 194, 195, 538
non-hegemonic legal transplant 345
non-interference 185
non-national laws 387
non-religious societies 370
non-State entities 194
non-traditional mechanisms 195
non-Western governments 322
non-Western indigenous customary law 62
non-Western religious law 385
Northern Rhodesia Order in Council of 1924 484

Northern Rhodesia Public Lands Acquisition Ordinance of 1929 485
numerical comparative law 13–14
Nyerere (Ujamaa) 218

O

Odendaal Commission 432
Organisation of African Unity (OAU) 185, 186, 312
Organisation pour l'Harmonisation en Afrique du Droit des Affaires (OHADA) 310, 325

P

'*paiement de l'indu*' (*condictio indebiti*) 288
pan-African associations of law 323
pan African jurisprudence 562
pan-African Parliament 197
Paris Commune 149
1900 Paris International Congress 44
penal laws 503, 504
pioneers of comparative law during renaissance and enlightenment eras 87–98
place-based learning approach 372
Platonic natural law 79
police power 476
polis 80
political anthropology 418
political self-determination 587
post-colonial laws 339
Post-Glossators 86
post-*Martin Kpebu* approaches 525
postmodern comparative jurisprudence 30
postmodern comparative law 3, 14–15
postmodernism 15
Pothier, Robert-Joseph 91–2
Pothier school 264, 288
Pound's jural postulates 215
power of eminent domain 476
practical socialism 167
praetor peregrinus 81
praetor urbanus 82
pre-colonial period 410
pre-Justinianic Roman law 85
Prevention of Illegal Eviction from and Unlawful Occupation of Land Act 19, 214
primitive forms of socio-political organisation 421
principle of African liberty 223–5
problem-solving approach 71, 326
process of comparison 64–71
protection of individual rights 490–3
Protocol to ACHPR 536–8, 612
public interesting standing in Namibia 621–3
public international law 371, 496
public law 18, 196
public policy 561, 567

Q

Quebec's law 389, 596–8, 604
questioning hybridisation 349–51

R

radical cultural relativism 347
recognition of African customary law 397–400
recommendations 522–4
regional level, unifying or harmonising 56–7
relevance of African customary law 400–3
relevance of jurisprudence in comparative legal processes 210–16
religious legal systems 109–16
remedial secession 591–2
Roman-Dutch common law 328, 625
Roman-Dutch law 237, 341, 344, 351, 354, 371, 372, 410, 426, 562
Roman law 9, 10, 106
Romano–Germanic civil law 107, 140
Roman *Orbis terrarum* 82
Royal Dutch Shell 326

rule-based comparative legal analysis 13
Rule of Law 162
Russian Revolution 152

S
School of Natural Law 90, 91
school of the Glossators 85
scientific method 42, 43
scientific socialism 151
secessionist insurrection 599
Second World War 39, 50, 153, 185, 378
selected jurisdictions, application by 458–69
self-determination 32, 585, 586
semi-autonomous social field 429
Senghor (Negritude) 218
Sharialaw 385
shift from transnational to global law 22–3
sic utere tuo ut alienam non laedas 199
sine causa 264, 284, 286
social and economic consequences of expropriation 496
social context 67–70
Social Gospel movement 148
socialism and law 164–9
socialist communities 166
socialist law 108, 139, 143–4
socialist system 170, 172
socialist systems of law 62–3
socio-legal comparative law 15–16
South Africa 465–7, 484, 519–22, 567–71
South Africa Muslim marriages 326
South African bail jurisprudence 520
South African Supreme Court and Constitutional Court decisions 205
southern African countries 491, 496
Southern African Development Community (SADC) region 197, 211
Southern African Development Community Tribunal (SADC Tribunal) 489, 490
sovereign self-determination 589–90
sovereignty 183, 190
Soviet law 70, 139
Soviet Union 139, 140
Special Rapporteurs 613
Spirit of the Laws (*de l'spirit des lois*) 94
stare decisis in Namibia 232–3
state sovereignty 476–90
state sovereignty and development 474
Stoic philosophy 80
structural–functional anthropology 424
subjects of right to self-determination 590–1
submissions 522–4
sub-Saharan Africa 185, 379, 400
substantive considerations 540–1
Supreme Court 189, 230, 233, 239

T
Tanganyika Order in Council of 1920 399
teaching comparative law 72, 73, 386–9
Theophrastus' approach 78
third model or approach 519–22
Tilburg University (Netherlands) 387
Traditional Authorities Act 430, 432
traditional comparative law 3, 7–9, 22
traditional leadership 434–7
Trans-Caprivi Highway in 1999 602
trans governmentalism 23
translations 427
transnational legal influences 345
Treasury Authorizer 254
Treasury Back Office 254
Treasury Department of the Bank 253
Treasury Inputter 254
Treasury Verifier 254
tribal violence 603
Tswana law 438
21st-century legal education and practice 310–13

U
ubuntu 218–19, 226
ubuntuism 218–19

ujamaa (Swahili for 'familyhood') 157
undue payment 286–90, 290–2
unequivocal acceptance 357
unification 55–8, 131, 200, 319, 380
unification of laws 196–8
Union Miniere du Haut-Katanga 151
United Nations (UN) 185, 195
United States 52, 461–3, 574–5
universal declaration of human rights 504
Universal Declaration of Human Rights 612
unjust enrichment in Continental Europe 259–67
unjust enrichment in England 267–78
unjust enrichment in English law 267
unjust enrichment in Namibia 258
unjustified enrichment in Argentina 279–83
unjustified enrichment in South American jurisdictions 279–95
uti possidetis 594–5
utopian socialism 150–2

V
Vedas 112
vertical approach 457
Vico, Giovanni Battista 92–4
violation of rights under international conventions and treaties bodies 540–1

W
wage labour–capital relationship 168
Western concept of law 6
Western law 353, 386
Western legal systems 304, 343
Western model 579
Western rule-of-law principle 388
world's legal systems classification 11–12

Z
Zambezi region 356, 598–603
Zambia 484–6, 510–12, 556
Zambian Constitution 539, 553
Zambian humanism 220, 221
Zambian Human Rights Commission 542
Zambian law-enforcement agencies 557
Zambian model 509, 525
Zimbabwe 486–90, 571–3

www.ingramcontent.com/pod-product-compliance
Lightning Source LLC
LaVergne TN
LVHW060010210926
848481LV00013B/3684
9789994557233